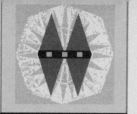

Adolescent
Life Experiences

THIRD EDITION

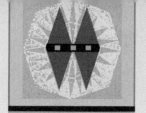

Adolescent Life Experiences

THIRD EDITION

Gerald R. Adams
University of Guelph

Thomas P. Gullotta
Child and Family Agency/Eastern Connecticut State University

Carol Markstrom-Adams
West Virginia University

Brooks/Cole Publishing Company
Pacific Grove, California

 I(T)P ™ The trademark ITP is used under license.

Brooks/Cole Publishing Company
A Division of Wadsworth, Inc.
© 1994 by Wadsworth, Inc., Belmont, California 94002. All rights reserved. No part of this book
may be reproduced, stored in a retrieval system, or transcribed, in any form or by any means—electronic, mechanical, photocoying, recording, or otherwise—without the prior written permission of
the publisher, Brooks/Cole Publishing Company, Pacific Grove, California 93950, a division of
Wadsworth, Inc.

Printed in the United States of America
10   9   8   7   6   5   4   3   2   1

Library of Congress Cataloging-in-Publication Data

Adams, Gerald R.
      Adolescent life experiences / Gerald R. Adams, Thomas P. Gullotta, Carol Markstrom-Adams.
   — 3rd ed.
            p. cm.
      Includes bibliographical references and index.
      ISBN 0-534-16236-3
      1. Adolescence.   2. Adolescent psychology—United States.
   I. Gullotta, Thomas.   II. Markstrom-Adams, Carol.
   III. Title.
   HQ796.A246   1994
   305.23'5—dc20   93-14517
                                                                                 CIP

Sponsoring Editor: Vicki Knight
Editorial Assistant: Lauri Banks-Ataide
Production: PC&F, Inc.
Production Services Manager: Joan Marsh
Permissions Editor: Mary Kay Hancharick
Cover Design: Katherine Minerva
Cover Photo: Ed Young Photography
Photo Researcher: PC&F, Inc.
Indexer: PC&F, Inc.
Typesetting: PC&F, Inc.
Cover Printing: Color Dot
Printing and Binding: R. R. Donnelley & Sons, Crawfordsville

To the memory of Hershel Thornburg and John Hill—former presidents of the Society for Research on Adolescence. Their example will be long remembered and admired.

ABOUT THE AUTHORS

Gerald R. Adams, is a professor of Family Relations and Human Development at the University of Guelph. He holds graduate degrees in child psychology, school psychology, human development, and family studies. He is the senior series editor for *Advances in Adolescent Development* and is a consulting/associate editor of such journals as *Journal of Primary Prevention, Journal of Early Adolescence, Social Psychology Quarterly, Journal of Adolescence,* and others. His research focuses on personality and social development, family relationships and socialization processes, and social problems during adolescence. Gerald has served as a consultant for the National Science Foundation, National Institute of Mental Health, National Institute of Health, Boy Scouts of America, and Social Science and Humanities Research Council of Canada. He is co-author of *Physical Attractiveness: A Cultural Imperative* (1978), *Understanding Research Methods* (1989), and with Tom Gullotta and Sharon Alexander, *Today's Marriages and Families: A Wellness Approach* (1986).

Thomas P. Gullotta is the chief executive officer of one of the nation's oldest children's service agencies, the Child and Family Agency of Southeastern Connecticut. A nationally recognized expert in the fields of primary prevention and adolescence, he holds an academic appointment at Eastern Connecticut State University in both the psychology and education departments. He is the founding editor of *The Journal of Primary Prevention,* serves as a general series book editor for *Advances in Adolescent Development,* and is the senior book series editor for *Issues in Children's and Families' Lives.* He currently serves on the editorial boards of the *Journal of Early Adolescence, Adolescence,* and chairs the Gimbel National Child and Family Scholar Awards Program. A consultant for the Center for Substance Abuse Prevention and other federal agencies, his practice and academic interests are in the development of primary preventive interventions to enable the healthy development of youth living in their families in their communities.

Carol Markstrom-Adams received her Ph.D. in developmental psychology at Utah State University and is currently in the Division of Family Resources at West Virginia University. One of her primary research interests is identity development among ethnic and religious minority adolescents. In particular, she has interests in processes underlying identity formation, the role of contextual factors in identity formation, and identity intervention. In addition, Dr. Markstrom-Adams is interested in Erik Erikson's ego virtues, and has recently devised a measure of these constructs. In a third line of research, Dr. Markstrom-Adams has been utilizing a combination of qualitative and quantitative techniques to investigate contextual and developmental factors operative in adolescents' attitudes toward interfaith dating. Her publications have appeared in such periodicals as *Family Relations, Developmental Psychology, Child Development, Sex Roles,* and *Journal of Adolescence,* among others.

PREFACE

The third edition of *Adolescent Life Experiences* marks twelve years of collaborative scholarship on this text and in other professional activities. As authors we are committed to a broad interdisciplinary examination of the field of adolescence. We have aimed to inform, educate, and entertain in each of the three editions. Our major goal has been to write a comprehensive text that inspires young people and their parents to make a difference in their own and each other's lives.

In prior editions there were two authors. Gerald Adams's background and interests are in human development and developmental social psychology, and Thomas Gullotta has concentrated on social history and clinical social work. Both have shared interest in primary prevention and issues of social intervention. In continuing our commitment to an interdisciplinary perspective, Dr. Carol Markstrom-Adams joins us to expand our perspective on ethnic and minority issues. Collectively, our expertise of research, teaching, and clinical practice now bridges psychology, sociology, family relations, social work, and primary prevention/social intervention. We hope this interdisciplinary emphasis provides a strong and broad perspective for analyzing research on adolescence.

Adolescent Life Experiences, Third Edition, contains many new features. In addition to broadening the interdisciplinary nature of our writing team, we have continued to search out and cite research from a multitude of disciplines, including medicine, psychiatry, psychology, sociology, social work, nursing, education, ethnic studies, history, political science, and anthropology. Recognizing the growing interdependence between the United States and Canada, we have added more material on youth in Canada (and beyond). This expansion reflects our commitment to the study of adolescence from a contextualist and international perspective. Finally, we have added information from more than 350 new research studies to the references for this text.

The third edition of *Adolescent Life Experiences* offers several new features. The text is written with a developmental contextualist perspective. The adaptive, facilitative, and pluralistic nature of individual development is recognized in each chapter. Particular attention is given to five groups: American Indian, African American, Mexican American, Asian American, and White Americans. Perspectives and findings from North America (including the United States and Canada) and beyond broaden the contextualist perspectives of this new edition.

New material is offered in each chapter to update and expand coverage. The text has been broadened in consideration of both normative development and social problems during adolescence. Exciting new material on identity, self-esteem, physical development, family dynamics, schools and peers, eating disorders, gangs, runaways, and suicide and depression can be found in the third edition.

Finally, the book has been reorganized to make the boxes, figures, tables, and pictures highlight important issues within each chapter. We trust that readers will continue to find useful the concluding sections summarizing the major points of each chapter, the broad authoritative findings summarized throughout the text, and authors' attempts to integrate a wide range of findings from the allied social science disciplines focusing on the study of adolescence.

Each part of this book contains new information on issues associated with ethnic/social minority youths and their families. We are sensitive to the changing views of appropriate labels for varying reference groups, but find the research literature uses varying labels for the same group. Therefore, in keeping with the primary sources for this text, we have used a mix of labels as used in the published research journals. We do not want to offend anyone when we refer to a given group as either Black or African American or Hispanic, Latino, or Mexican American. We are merely attempting to reflect the variations that still exist in the published sources we used to prepare this text.

We hope you find this edition readable, suitably organized, and comprehensive in its content and quality. *Adolescent Life Experiences,* Third Edition, is well suited for instructors and students who want in-depth, authoritative coverage from an interdisciplinary viewpoint. Prior editions have been used successfully in departments of education, psychology, sociology, child development, family studies, human development, social work, home economics, and nursing programs. This textbook demonstrates that by integrating findings from these various disciplines we gain a much fuller understanding of adolescence. We believe that to understand adolescence one must take an interdisciplinary perspective.

ACKNOWLEDGMENTS

Many people provided assistance and understanding during the writing of *Adolescent Life Experiences,* Third Edition. We are especially thankful to our spouses for their encouragement and support. Sometimes our own children have found us absent due to the demands of time associated with writing. We hope we haven't been too absent for their well-being.

We are in particular debt to C. Deborah Laughton and Charles (Terry) Hendrix, former editors at Brooks/Cole, for giving us a chance to write the first edition of this textbook. Both Deborah and Terry have been supportive editors and over the years have become personal friends to both of us.

We thank our chief editor, Victoria Knight, for her support. Other important people in the Brooks/Cole family that have been helpful include Joan Marsh and Laurie Banks-Ataide among others. Likewise we're grateful to the staff of PC&F, Inc. especially Louise Gelinas and Elaine Gibson.

Likewise, we have profited from several thoughtful reviews by colleagues who are teaching at various universities throughout North America. We appreciate constructive criticism by Martin Ford, Stanford University; Eagan Hunter, St. Edward University; Dale Johnson, University of Houston; Marvin R. Koller, Kent State University; Jill Kreutzer, Colorado State University; Jean Hill Macht, Montgomery County Community College; Judy Rohr, Tennessee Technical University; Neal Rudberg, San Diego Miramar College; Thomas S. Parish,

Kansas State University; William Penrod, Middle Tennessee State University; Gwendolyn T. Sorell, Texas Technical University; Marc Baranowski, University of Maine; Mark Durm, Athens State College; Mary S. Link, Miami University; and Rhonda Richardson, Kent State University.

We have taken their important reviews seriously. Thanks to our reviewers' and colleagues' sharing of their insights, suggestions, and recommendations, we believe that this version is a substantive improvement over the second edition.

Finally, we continue to appreciate our own cooperative professional association and personal friendship and loyalty. This third edition has left the two original authors' relationship as strong as ever. We are excited about making this team a threesome; our friendship and collegial association now include another colleague. What more of a thrill might any professional activity bring than being able to combine informing students wishing to understand the nature of adolescence with the friendship of colleagues who enjoy working together?

Gerald R. Adams
Thomas P. Gullotta
Carol Markstrom-Adams

BRIEF CONTENTS

CONTENTS

CHAPTER 2   Understanding Adolescent Behavior and Development   28

PART TWO   Influences on Adolescent Development   59

CHAPTER 3   Adolescent Family Relations   60

CHAPTER 4

Peers   92

CHAPTER 5

Education   122

CHAPTER 7   Intellectual and Cognitive Development   186

CHAPTER 8   Personality Development in Adolescence   220

CHAPTER 11   Gender Differences and Sex-Role Development   292

CHAPTER 12   Adolescent Sexual Behavior and Development 316

PART FOUR   Dealing with Issues of Concern: Intervention and
Prevention   343

CHAPTER 13   Helping Adolescents: Intervention and
Prevention   344

CHAPTER 14   Problems of Adolescent Sexuality   366

CHAPTER 15   Drugs   406

CHAPTER 16 Crime and Delinquency 452

CHAPTER 17   Eating Disorders   486

PART ONE

Demographic Characteristics and Theories of Adolescence

Chapter 1
Adolescents Today: Problems and Prospects

Chapter 2
Understanding Adolescent Behavior and Development

Adolescents Today:
Problems and Prospects

- Why Study Adolescence?

- What Is Adolescence?

- A Statistical Snapshot of U.S. Youth

- A Snapshot of Canadian Youth

- A Life Stage with Heightened Risk

- Organization of This Textbook

When thinking of adolescence, we remember exciting but awkward years full of challenges, transitions, hope, promise, and frustration. We recall special events: getting our driver's license, acting in a school play, going steady, finding a new best friend, going to the prom, or helping to win a state basketball tournament. Less positive recollections also emerge: having good friends killed in car accidents, getting in trouble with the law, fighting at school, losing a parent to death, being caught drinking or smoking, or getting fired from a part-time job for being late. We suspect that you can add many positive and negative recollections that influence your own evaluation of adolescence as a **life stage.**

Our former students have shared their recollections of adolescence and revealed the themes of this life stage in vivid detail. Many portray adolescent life with a sense of unevenness as a period of growth, fluctuation, and transition. They recall a time of excitement, action, change, and uncertainty. They remember some of these events with a smile and others with remorse or even sorrow. The majority of youths, however, view adolescence as an easy time, a period of fun filled with friends, new adventures, success in school, and support by parents. Indeed, one might conclude from such descriptions that they experienced adolescence as a smooth, calm, and successful period. These two general themes are but a few of the many self-perceived realities of adolescent life. There may be as many themes and stories as there are people who have experienced adolescence.

Although most people perceive a personal uniqueness in their adolescent experiences, in reality adolescents share many themes with their contemporaries and with those before and after. Many of the basic developmental patterns of growth are and will continue to be similar from one generation to the next. We must all crawl before we walk, think simply before we think complexly, and so on. This isn't to deny individual differences. Indeed, tremendous variations in behavior and development do exist. Rather, many youths share similar individual characteristics but may not know or live near others who are like them.

In this text we introduce you to several typical themes of adolescent life. We examine the developmental trends in physical, psychological, and social growth. We also discuss the variations, or individual differences, that might stem from gender, race, socioeconomic status, and other factors. However, our major focus is on common themes for all adolescents.

We believe strongly in the important role that social context plays in influencing adolescent behavior and development. At times our zealous interest in helping other people perceive and understand the tremendous influences of the social environment on human behavior will carry us into the examination of history, culture, and the many societal "isms" that impede productive growth—for example, sexism, racism, and dogmatism. But we maintain that only when you examine individual behavior and development in the broader context of social, physical, and cultural realities will you understand them deeply. We believe that such probing analysis will bring you closer to self-understanding. In addition, if you aspire to become an educator, counselor, youth worker, or similar professional, it will give you a better understanding of the complexity of adolescent life and the demands this complexity places on prevention and intervention efforts.

Throughout the text we draw heavily of the fields of developmental psychology, psychiatry, sociology, anthropology, education, social work, and family studies (among other allied social sciences) to provide a relatively broad and comprehensive analysis of adolescence. Indeed, we believe that an understanding of the complexity of adolescence requires an integration of multiple perspectives. No single discipline has a monopoly on the facts about adolescent behavior or development.

Why Study Adolescence?

We are often asked: "Why study adolescents? Aren't they just a by-product of their childhood?" Our answer is straightforward. In the not-too-distant past, at the height of the influence of psychoanalysis, it was reasoned that infant and early childhood experiences, psychological growth, and social influences were the central factors affecting lifelong development. Many scholars assumed uncritically that early development provided the single most important foundation for success and maturity. In the past 30 years, however, life-span developmental psychologists have documented that growth and development are a continuous process. Each stage in life contributes to the remaining stages. Certain unique contributions within every stage can result in positive *and* negative behavioral or developmental outcomes.

Participants at professional conferences commonly say that the failure to have a successful life experience in infancy or early childhood will result in relatively *permanent* psychological or social damage. It is true that the successful completion of important life-stage tasks (for example, attachment in infancy) will help provide a more solid foundation and promise for the next stage (autonomy behaviors in early childhood; for example, read Gjerde, Block, & Block, 1991, regarding the effects of the family during the preschool years on adolescent symptoms of depression). But such completion (1) doesn't ensure successful future development and (2) doesn't mean that the previous failure can't be corrected. Indeed, most psychological or social phenomena that result in negative developmental outcomes can be ameliorated or positively resolved. The problem, however, is that the longer the problem exists, the greater the resources and effort needed to correct it, and society sometimes isn't willing to pay the price.

Why, then, study adolescence? First, it is the way station between the dependency of childhood and the independence of adulthood. It provides a period for gradual change, experimentation, and preparation for what is to come. Second, it has its own themes that are shared by most adolescents yet are unique to the life stage: first preparations for a career, leaving home, a spurt in growth, and so forth. Each of these developmental and behavioral themes is worthy of our analysis and understanding. It may, indeed, be important to identify the positive and negative developments of adolescence to ensure effective socialization and provide a positive foundation for a successful transition to adulthood.

Finally, we need to study adolescence to understand individual differences in behavior, development, or experiences that underpin social problems such as teenage pregnancy, juvenile and adult crime, or eating disorders. Indeed, what might at a glance appear to be a unique adolescent life experience for a select few may in the fullest truth be more typical than atypical. For example, with more that 60% of American youths sexually active by age 17 and with their rate of contraceptive use low, it is actually surprising that teenage pregnancy isn't more common. Moreover, recognizing that more than 80% of 17-year-olds have illegally drunk beer, wine, or other alcoholic beverages, we must question whether drinking should be viewed as a social problem unique to a subclass of youths. Most high school youths admit they have broken a law, committed a misdemeanor, or engaged in some form of delinquent act. The only difference between them and those who go to prison may be that they didn't get caught, were given a break by the legal system, or had parents who covered for them. The importance, then, is to find what contributes to adolescent health and social problems and to use this information to guide social and educational policy, prevention programs, and social intervention.

What Is Adolescence?

Before we examine the general characteristics of contemporary adolescents, we should ask about the nature of adolescence. How can we define adolescence as a specific life stage?

Through analysis of historical documents it can easily be demonstrated that the definition of adolescence changes as society evolves. Many definitions can be found. Indeed, the nature of adolescence itself varies with different scholars' descriptions. For example, little formal agreements exists about the actual beginning and ending of adolescence. Rather, each discipline studying adolescence appears to have its own perspective. Some years ago one of us investigated a variety of sources to discover commonalities and differences regarding the start and end of adolescence. We theorized that every life-stage entity, such as adolescence, would have a clear beginning and end. We found, however, considerable differences among disciplinary perspectives.

A Physiological Definition

A **physiological definition of adolescence** has often been proposed (see Douvan & Gold, 1966; H. Jones, 1949). In such a definition, adolescence begins when the reproductive organs and **secondary sex characteristics** (body hair, breasts) begin to change in late childhood; the end of adolescence is associated with the full maturation of the reproductive system. Given that testicle growth is predictive of pubic hair and skeletal changes in boys, it is reasonable to assume that the beginning and end of adolescence are related to sexual development. Similarly, consistent production of fertile eggs and regularity of the menstrual cycle signal the end of adolescence for girls (Douvan & Gold, 1966).

As suggested in most physiological definitions, however, it is difficult to determine if adolescence actually begins with hormonal changes that occur at least two years before major body changes are visible or begins when secondary sex characteristics emerge. Likewise, fertility is an unclear and unseen element for determining the end of adolescence. Can fertile youths sometimes be so immature socially that it is best not to recognize them as young adults?

A snapshot of
adolescence;
a mosaic of youths.

A Cognitive Definition

Others have suggested a reasoning-based, **cognitive definition of adolescence**. Acquisition of the ability to reason enables a person to use symbols, abstractions, and complex problem-solving strategies in thinking. From this perspective, as children come to develop thinking processes that are independent of concrete and observable objects in the immediate environment to include abstract thoughts and metacognition (thinking about thinking), they are thought to be qualitatively different and thus emerging into adolescence. Although this approach is logical (and potentially defendable) and has been supported by many specialists in adolescence (for example, Ausubel & Ausubel, 1966; Elkind, 1967), measuring when the cognitive transition in adolescence begins is very difficult. Our experience with youths suggests that this process is gradual. At what point in the transition, then, would we recognize the child as an adolescent? Further, if one is to be considered an adolescent, is abstract thinking necessary in understanding both ideas *and* social relationships? Likewise, what is the end of adolescence? Is it the ability to use abstract thinking and logical reasoning in *all* physical and social realms of life? If so, are adults who do not use abstract and logical thinking processes to be considered adolescents? Given that close to one-third of the adult population in the United States is unable to engage in abstract thinking, is a large minority of adults still in childhood? Since cognitive development doesn't occur all at once but happens gradually in a complex manner, a cognitive definition of adolescence may best be seen as limited in its ability to set out precisely the beginning and ending of adolescence.

A Sociological Definition

The **sociological definition of adolescence** uses very different standards for the beginning and ending of adolescence. Mixing its criteria, it defines the onset of puberty (or sexual maturity) as the start of adolescence while using social criteria to determine its end. For example, Hans Sebald (1968) has argued that adolescence ends when young people have established a coping style consistent with the demands of their social world and when society recognizes their entry into adulthood. Sometimes this entry is through a formal rite of passage, an event with considerable societal support and ceremony. LaVoie (1973) has argued, however, that coping abilities and societal recognition may not occur at the same time. The adolescent may attain one without the other. An illustration would be marriage during the teenage years. Is a married 17-year-old girl an adult, or is she an adolescent who has prematurely moved into an adult role while remaining an adolescent?

The sociological approach creates certain ambiguities, too. In particular, the end of adolescence and the beginning of adulthood may be difficult to define in a specific manner because of differences in societal standards. Even though a boy may be able to enter the armed forces at 18 or even younger, he may not be able to drink, to be married without parental permission, or even to vote. Thus, multiple steps may be required before an adolescent is appropriately defined as an adult.

Chronological and Eclectic Definitions

Some authors have avoided the problem of former definitions by using a simple **chronological definition** (C. E. Ramsey, 1967) or an **eclectic definition of adolescence** incorporating indexes from a variety of perspectives (McCandless, 1970). Once again, however, both strategies create certain problems in definition. The chronological definition of the second decade of life as adolescence is too simple. It has little flexibility and may create false assumptions about the beginning and end of this period. A prepubescent 10-year-old may not be best viewed as an adolescent, while a 22-year-old who is living at home, going to school, and fully dependent on parents for financial support may best be considered a late adolescent.

The eclectic approach, which argues that multiple perspectives or dimensions should be combined, creates problems of measurement and inconsistency. If one uses physiological, sociological, and psychological indexes, does a person have to measure up to all three to be considered as entering or leaving adolescence?

At this point you might say: "I'm confused! Which is it?" And, perhaps, "So what?" You have a right to be confused—so are the specialists. The definition you select can be justified; but no matter which one you use, there can be problems. In particular, the definition you use can have tremendous implications for social policy. If you argue for a given definition with its specific criteria for the beginning and end of adolescence, you are setting the stage for inclusion and exclusion of certain youths for legislated education, services, and available resources. For example, in many medical insurance policies dependent children are covered after age 18 only if they continue their education. Otherwise, they are considered independent and given adult status.

We don't have a conclusive answer to the many problems surrounding a definition of adolescence. However, we side with those who view adolescence as a social or political invention. In this perspective, adolescence and its definition are thought to change with changing economic, political, or technological conditions. In current American society, the definition seems to coincide with the various phases of education required or provided for adolescents. Early adolescence is thought to be that time spent in middle school or junior high school. Middle adolescence is the high school years. Late adolescence is that period provided for college, technical school training, apprenticeships, or entry-level military service. And to this we add youth (or young adulthood). The period of youth is, for a select few, an extended period of education for professional degrees, during which they remain economically dependent on the family or other institutions to provide partial financial support to complete highly technical training.

A "Learner's Permit" Definition

Returning to our primary concern, we believe adolescence should be viewed as a period of transition, a period that differs in length for each individual. We agree with Franklin Zimring (1982) in his analysis of the legal world of adolescence. Adolescence is best viewed as a growing-up process that includes making decisions and making mistakes. However, the context is such that the mistakes will ideally result in minor negative outcomes, ones that the person can recover from relatively easily without long-lasting negative consequences. Adolescence is thus a gradual phasing into adulthood, in which the youth is given increasing responsibilities with each new grant of freedom. Zimring calls this view a *learner's-permit theory* of adolescence: "The adolescent must be protected from the full burden of adult responsibilities, but pushed along by degrees toward the moral and legal accountability that we consider appropriate to adulthood" (1982, p. 96). Thus, adolescence is a period of experimentation, of practice in making decisions, of making mistakes and discovering one's errors, and of gradually assuming new freedoms while building toward adult responsibilities.

In legal parlance it is common to talk about the **age of majority.** In simple terms this means a period when one's freedoms and responsibilities are equivalent to adults'. In the phasing process of a learner's-permit theory of adolescence, several forms of age of majority might be appropriate. At 16 years of age, for example, we may say to adolescents that, assuming they have proven their competence to drive (through a driver's test), they have reached the driving age of majority. They are free to be licensed and drive wherever they wish but are also expected to obey all driving laws and to assume responsibility for their actions on the road. Another age of majority may be 17 or 18, when youths decide whether to continue their formal schooling. At 20 or 21, youths arrive at a societally prescribed drinking age of majority. They can drink alcohol within legal restrictions, can become intoxicated if they desire, but are held responsible for their actions while drunk.

In the learner's-permit theory, adolescence emerges when the young person is given freedoms not afforded a child. In junior high schools, for example, students can commonly select a small portion of their curriculum, have initial opportunities to take part in school government, and have expanding choices of extracurricular activities. This process broadens with each new educational phase in high school, college, or vocational training. However, each new phase

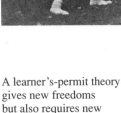

A learner's-permit theory gives new freedoms but also requires new responsibilities.

of freedom brings increasing responsibilities. Adolescence ends when a youth has acquired the age of majority for legal, economic, work, school, and moral responsibilities. Thus, each youth ends adolescence at a different point in life. Some terminate adolescence during the late teens by leaving home, entering work, getting married, assuming parenthood, and so forth. Other youths remain in adolescence (or youth, if you will) well into their late 20s to complete a formal education. Indeed, prolonging adolescence may be the best choice in a technological society to ensure ample education before entering adulthood. Such youths may be better prepared to face the economic, social, moral, and personal demands of a complex society.

A Statistical Snapshot of U.S. Youth

Given our belief that adolescent behavior and development must be viewed in the physical, social, and environmental contexts of life, we think that the nature of each birth cohort has substantial influences on adolescents in that cohort. The size and nature of each cohort and the opportunities that its members experience are determined by social, historical, and economic events. In turn, cohort characteristics influence the political and economic factors that determine available resources. Recognizing this notion, private and federal agencies or foundations have formed several commissions to provide a portrait of North American youth. Of particular use is a document entitled *Youth and America's Future,* which was supported by the W. T. Grant Foundation. We draw from this report (Wetzel, 1987) to give you a general overview of the population characteristics, family life, income, education, employment, health, and criminal activity of American adolescents.

Population

In earlier years the world of adolescents was an expanding population. Resources were provided to educate this growing population, and a healthy economy gave promise to everyone who wanted to work. The picture is considerably different today. The total number of youths is shrinking; one might even agree with the foundation's report that this decrease is dramatic (Wetzel, 1987). As Figure 1–1 demonstrates, in the two decades between 1980 and the year 2000, the number of adolescents between the ages of 15 and 24 will decrease. Indeed, between 1980 and 1995, there will be a decline from 43 million youths to 34 million youths. However, the overall percentage in the total population is projected to remain around 14+% of the population between 1990 and 2050. See Table 1–1.

This reduction will have both benefits and costs. Foremost, we believe that society can ill afford to throw away or lose a shrinking (albeit stable) and necessary commodity. Adolescence will be treated as an increasingly scarce and precious resource that must be assisted to grow, mature, and become productive for the sake of the total population. The face of the U.S. work force will be substantially altered by a reduced number of available youths. Greater competition will be found among companies wanting workers. The military, which thrives on young people for its forces, will compete more rigorously with schools and colleges that will have fewer students and more openings. Indeed youths seeking education beyond high school will profit from available scholarship, training, and fellowship opportunities. Youth employment in such outlets as fast-food chains will change dramatically. Indeed, we can already see in fast-food commercials promotions for employing the elderly alongside high school students in hamburger shops. We can also see that reduced crime rates are likely with fewer youths in our population, that schools will be closed down for lack of enrollment, and that consumer markets for the adolescent will decline or change with declining adolescent populations.

Figure 1–1 Population figures for U.S. youth, age 15–24. (From *American Youth: A Statistical Snapshot,* by J. R. Wetzel. Copyright © 1987 by The William T. Grant Foundation Commission on Youth and America's Future. Reprinted by permission.)

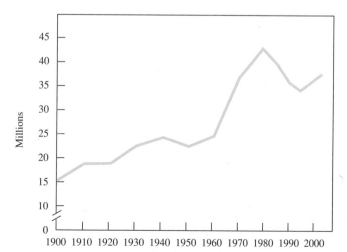

Youths 15–24 years old, in millions	
1900	14.951
1910	18.212
1920	18.821
1930	22.487
1940	24.033
1950	22.260
1960	24.576
1970	36.496
1980	42.743
1985	39.794
1990	35.548
1995	34.110
2000	36.088

Table 1–1   Aging Gracefully

Percent Distribution of the Population by Age: 1990 to 2050 (Middle series. Consistent with 1990 census)									
	1990	*1995*	*2000*	*2005*	*2010*	*2020*	*2030*	*2040*	*2050*
Total	100.0	100.0	100.0	100.0	100.0	100.0	100.0	100.00	100.0
Under 5	7.6	7.4	6.9	6.6	6.6	6.6	6.4	6.4	6.4
5 to 13	12.8	13.1	13.1	12.5	11.9	11.8	11.7	11.5	11.6
14 to 17	5.3	5.6	5.7	5.9	5.7	5.2	5.3	5.3	5.2
18 to 24	10.8	9.5	9.5	9.8	10.1	9.2	9.1	9.2	9.0
25 to 34	17.3	15.5	13.6	12.7	12.9	13.3	12.4	12.4	12.5
35 to 44	15.1	16.2	16.3	14.8	13.0	12.3	12.9	12.1	12.2
45 to 64	18.6	19.9	22.2	24.9	26.5	24.9	22.1	22.5	22.5
65 & over	12.5	12.8	12.7	12.7	13.3	16.6	20.2	20.7	20.6
85 & over	1.2	1.4	1.6	1.7	1.9	2.0	2.4	3.6	4.6
100 & over	0.0	0.0	0.0	0.0	0.1	0.1	0.1	0.2	0.3

Source: Census and You, January 1993, 28(1), 2.

Regarding population changes, it is important to recognize the major impact of immigration to America that has occurred since 1970. Clearly, there is an ever-increasing diversity in the adolescent population because of this influx. Since 1970 the United States has gained 1.35 million youths between 15 and 24 years of age. Most of them have come from Central America, Mexico, and Asia. This changing face of the population base brings with it problems of assimilation into U.S. culture, problems associated with language, and an expanding minority with considerable cultural, educational, occupational, family, and mental-health needs that may not be fully understood by the primarily White social and human service providers and educators (McShane & Adams, 1988).

As Figure 1–2 shows, the U.S. Bureau of the Census projects a leveling off in the number of Black youths in the coming years, with a relatively sharp increase in Hispanic youths. A projected decline of White youths is anticipated until around the year 2000, with a stable population projected thereafter. Because the census bureau lumps data on American Indians and Asian/Pacific Islanders, it is difficult to project for these minorities. However, we can anticipate some increase for both populations (Wetzel, 1987).

We can speculate that several challenges will face the United States in the future. First, the special educational and mental-health needs of a growing, pluralistic society seem evident. Increased strife between minorities competing for living space is possible; in particular, Black/Hispanic confrontations are likely. Our knowledge base of Black adolescents is poor, and for Hispanic and Asian youths it is even less established. We shall particularly need to understand better the development and behavior of minority youths by the 21st century.

Family Life

Youths are delaying marriage, a trend we suspect will enhance marriage, because the partners will be more mature and will make a better mate selection. For example, the median age at first marriage increased more than two years between 1975 and 1985. (Along with this trend is increased entry by women into postsecondary

Although high numbers of youths provide a national labor pool, it also costs a society in educational expenditures.

education.) However, 11% of all 15- to 24-year-olds are married. The divorce rate is very high for this early-marriage group. According to Wetzel (1987), in March 1985 for every 1000 women in this age range who had married, 95 were already divorced and 74 were separated. This statistic reflected an increase from 29 divorced and 36 separated per 1000 married observed in the 1960s.

Of those youths who remain single, many choose to live in their parents' home. Six of every ten men and nearly five of ten women remain living with their parents beyond high school. Thus, in 1986, 22.5 million 15- to 24-year-olds were living in families with at least one older person, usually a parent or relative. Moreover, 6.3 million of these—approximately 28%—were living in a single-parent home. Clearly, youths are remaining economic dependents of adults for longer periods.

By remaining at home, adolescents may not experience certain important independence experiences that increase their ability to become adults. Further, those who are in single parent homes may not receive a full socialization into family living during an important period of life. Indeed, many homes may be full of conflict from divorce, separation, and financial difficulties involving alimony, child support, and so forth. We know very little about the effects of late adolescents' experiences in such families on their emerging preparation for marriage and their own family life.

In general, for all ages, ethnic groups, and household incomes, there has been a decline in fertility since the early 1950s. Teenage birthrates fell from 86 per 1000 in 1952 to 52 per 1000 youths in 1983, a dramatic drop of approximately 40% during this period. However, in 1983 more than half of the total births by teenagers were out of wedlock, with financially disadvantaged women three to four times more likely to become pregnant, regardless of race.

Despite this decline in fertility rate, a relatively large number of teenage pregnancies (more than 1,000,000 in 1988) still occur. The financially disadvantaged are at considerable risk for an out-of-wedlock birth. Given that minority

Figure 1–2 Projections of U.S. youth population, age 15–24. (From *American Youth: A Statistical Snapshot,* by J. R. Wetzel. Copyright © 1987 by The William T. Grant Foundation Commission on Youth and America's Future. Reprinted by permission.)

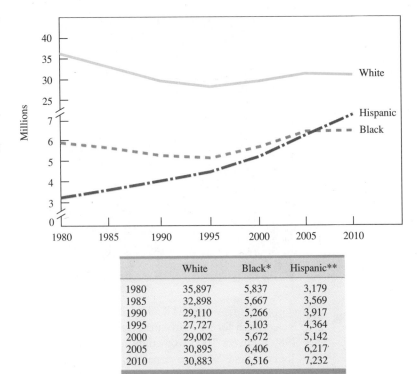

	White	Black*	Hispanic**
1980	35,897	5,837	3,179
1985	32,898	5,667	3,569
1990	29,110	5,266	3,917
1995	27,727	5,103	4,364
2000	29,002	5,672	5,142
2005	30,895	6,406	6,217·
2010	30,883	6,516	7,232

* These figures are from the middle series of projections by the U.S. Bureau of the Census.
** Hispanics can be of any race and, therefore, constitute part of the white and black figures. These figures come from the high series of projection because the middle series for Hispanics assumed no undocumented immigration and a net arrival of only 5,000 Puerto Ricans on an annual basis. Both assumptions are demonstrably conservative.

status and financial deprivation are still linked to some degree in the United States, minority women are at greatest risk for an out-of-wedlock pregnancy.

Income

Despite the delay in marriage, about 1 of every 12 families is headed by a person younger than 25. Given the recent difficult economic times, it probably comes as no surprise that 1 of every 5 families with a youth as head of the family earns an annual income of less than $5000. Indeed, youth-headed families have incomes 46% less than that of the average American family. Once again, there are considerable racial differences in family income. As Figure 1–3 shows, considerably more Black and Hispanic youths between the ages of 16 and 21 live in conditions of financial poverty than do Whites.

In 1985 approximately 1 million youth-headed families were classified as living in poverty. These families included 1.2 million children, most of whom were below the age of 6 years. Sixty percent of these families were headed by a young mother caring for her child(ren) without assistance by a father. Such young mothers typically are less educated than their peers, are less likely to be enrolled in school, are likely to have children with learning disabilities, are likely to have children who have confrontations with the juvenile justice system, and are likely to be unemployed as often as they are employed.

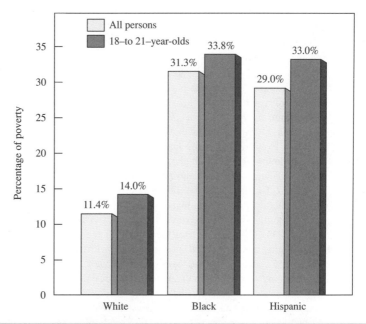

Figure 1–3 Poverty rates of U.S. 16- to 21-year-olds, 1985. (From *American Youth: A Statistical Snapshot,* by J. R. Wetzel. Copyright © 1987 by The William T. Grant Foundation Commission on Youth and America's Future. Reprinted by permission.)

	Total persons			In poverty			Poverty rate		
	White	Black	Hispanic	White	Black	Hispanic	White	Black	Hispanic
All ages	200,918	28,485	18,075	22,860	8,926	5,236	11.4%	31.3%	29.0%
18 to 21	18,225	3,182	2,075	2,557	1,076	686	14.0	33.8	33.0

Note: Numbers in thousands

Whereas the majority of White teenagers live in middle-class families, a significant proportion (approximately 12%) are likely to face financial deprivation. Minority youths are three to four times as likely to have to contend with poverty during their adolescent years. If one becomes a young mother, regardless of race, the probability of poverty is high. If the youth as head of a household is Black or Hispanic, the probability is even higher. In sum, the income level for youths under 25 is less than optimal. No wonder an increasing number of youths are remaining at home longer, delaying marriage, and showing declines in fertility. The U.S. economic support base appears to be eroding for working youth, requiring more education, more family dependence, and less early opportunity for independence. (See Box 1–1 for a global perspective).

Education and Work

During adolescence, completion of schooling is necessary if one is to acquire the skills and knowledge for successful employment. Comparative statistics on educational attainment reveal a gain over four decades for American youths. As Figure 1–4 demonstrates, the gains are evident for high school and college graduates and for Blacks, most minorities, and Whites. Wetzel (1987) indicates that Hispanics, however, remain considerably below Whites and Blacks in educational attainment.

Box 1–1   Global Status of Youth: Implications for National Development

Richard and Margaret Braungart (1989) have used a data set of 123 countries and have calculated a youth-to-adult ratio. Their findings reveal that most nations have high numbers of youth, relative to adults. For example, the youth ratio for Australia was .52, United States .54, and Canada .60. At the lowest end are well-established countries like Sweden (.34), Japan (.37), and the United Kingdom (.39). At the highest end are countries such as Honduras (1.00), Malaysia (1.01), and Zimbabwe (1.16). In the cases of ratios greater than 1.0 there are actually fewer adults than children. These findings indicate that the world system is stratified by age. Further, 83 of 123 nation-states have high to very high youth ratios, indicating that most nations have large numbers of youth to contend with—North American countries being somewhere in the middle.

The authors have also addressed the issue of whether youth ratios are correlated with national development. Using factors such as gross national product, unemployment rate, educational expenditures, and other economic, political, social, and educational factors, they computed correlations with the youth ratio. Many negative correlations were observed. That is,

high youth ratios were associated with lower educational expenditures, school enrollment, urbanization, and economic development.

Clearly, the sheer numbers of adolescents in many countries puts a major strain on the ability of a country to provide adequate health, well-being, and educational literacy. As Braungart and Braungart (1989) conclude, "These research findings support the proposition that the age composition of a society and its level of national development have a significant impact on the **global status of youth**" (p. 125).

Once again, an optimistic view would be to see a large youth population as a promising work force—one with energy, promise, and opportunity. A pessimistic view would see it as a detriment. With adequate resources, countries with high youth ratios will no doubt become future leading economic nations. Without resources the future probably looks dismal. A similar analysis could be completed for minority groups within a given country to determine how age stratification is associated with national development for ethnic groups.

There is, nonetheless, some disconcerting evidence regarding schooling. Hispanics are close to being twice as likely to drop out of high school as Blacks, while Blacks are only 2% to 3% more likely to drop out than Whites. But for all groups the strongest predictor of dropping out of school is poverty. As Figure 1–5 reveals, poor families are more likely than affluent families to have adolescents who drop out. The very families that need their youths in school, to make important educational gains to ensure employability, are those that have the highest dropout rate.

Although employability is determined by many factors, a sluggish economy has in some parts of the country created considerable competition for jobs at the bottom of career ladders. Further, because of inflation, today's adolescents generally enter the labor market relatively early and combine their schooling with work. To illustrate, 11.5 million youths were in the U.S. labor force in 1960. By 1980 this number had increased to 25.4 million, a rise of over 120% in labor-force participation. Most of these youths were both working and going to school. For example, Wetzel (1987) reports data indicating that 92.5% of all 16- and 17-year-olds in 1986 were students, with 41% of them employed part or full time.

Because many students, of financial necessity, must combine work and school, unemployment creates a special problem for students in need. Unemployment is higher for the 15- to 24-year-olds than for persons aged 25 or older. This is a persistent trend dating back to the early 1950s. Also, unemployment is a greater problem for Blacks and Hispanics than it is for Whites. This

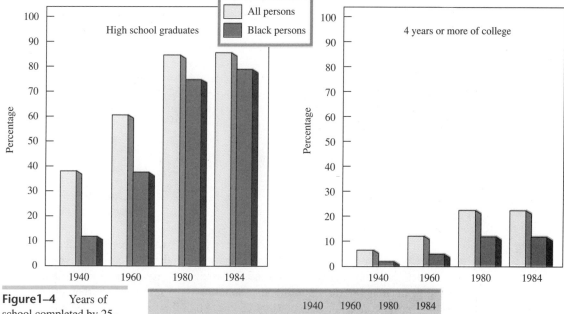

Figure1–4   Years of school completed by 25- to 29-year-olds. (From *American Youth: A Statistical Snapshot,* by J. R. Wetzel. Copyright © 1987 by The William T. Grant Foundation Commission on Youth and America's Future. Reprinted by permission.)

	1940	1960	1980	1984
All persons (25 – 29)				
Completed high school	38.1	60.7	84.5	85.9
4 years or more of college	5.9	11.1	22.1	21.9
Blacks				
Completed high school	11.6	37.7	75.2	78.8
4 years or more of college	1.6	4.8	11.4	11.6

factor may account, in part, for why minority adolescents obtain less education than Whites: resources may not be as readily available, even for a determined teenager. Further, as Figure 1–6 reveals, failure to graduate accentuates the unemployment problem for all youths, but particularly for Blacks.

Health

Certainly today's youths enjoy better health than their parents' or grandparents' generation. Likewise, life expectancy is increasing with each new generation. Whites and Hispanics have approximately the same life expectancy, but Blacks lag. Men are gradually catching up with women in their expected longevity. Each new generation experiences better health care, nutrition, medication, immunization, and public health (quality sewers, water, sanitation), thereby having a better chance for a healthy and productive life.

Crimes of Violence

Crime is no small part of an adolescent life experience. According to Wetzel (1987), one of five teenagers and one of six 20- to 24-year-olds were victimized in 1984. Perhaps crimes of violence are the most disturbing. One of every 33 Americans older than 11 years of age experiences in a single year an assault,

Figure 1–5 Persons aged 20–21 not enrolled in school in March 1986 and not high school graduates, by race and poverty status. (From *American Youth: A Statistical Snapshot,* by J. R. Wetzel. Copyright © 1987 by The William T. Grant Foundation Commission on Youth and America's Future. Reprinted by permission.)

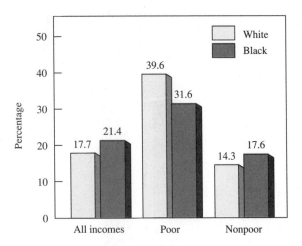

robbery, or rape. Just about one of five youths experiences a violent crime annually. In 1984 alone, 2.3 million youths were victimized; one-third were physically injured, and many required medical treatment. Youths in inner cities experience much higher rates of crime that do those in the suburbs. Suburban youths experience more crime than do rural youths. All of this crime is likely to reduce youths' ability to take advantage of educational and employment opportunities that would enhance their lives and provide better preparation for adulthood.

Gangs also appear on an increase. One news release indicated that Los Angeles had more than 600 gangs with 70,000 members who caused 387 deaths in 1987 alone. Likewise, Chicago had 100 gangs with 10,000 members, and New York City had 50 gangs with 5000 members. Further, many gangs are now establishing branches in neighboring communities. Ronald Stephens, executive director of the National School Safety Center, told us that drug abuse, truancy, and violence and intimidation are the primary behaviors of gangs. Further, weapons formerly

Figure 1–6
Unemployment rates among high school graduates and dropouts, by race, October 1986. (From *American Youth: A Statistical Snapshot,* by J. R. Wetzel. Copyright © 1987 by The William T. Grant Foundation Commission on Youth and America's Future. Reprinted by permission.)

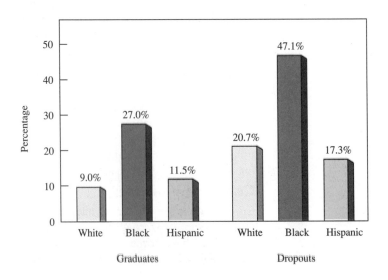

used by gangs—fists, chains, knives—are now being replaced by shotguns, automatic weapons, and explosives. The outlook for gang members isn't very promising. Stephens indicated that 80% of the 8800 incarcerated youths in California were gang members. Likewise, the safety of other adolescents and youths who are not members but share the same neighborhoods is clearly compromised.

A Snapshot of Canadian Youth

Growing up in Canada is both similar to and different from growing up in the United States. To illustrate, we examine some distinctions regarding age, living arrangements, education, work activity, and income. Further, similar selective indicators shall be examined for Canadian youths. A document titled *Canada's Youth* by Statistics Canada (Ross, 1989) provides the basis for this discussion. The conclusions drawn from these reports are based on a careful use of census and other data.

Age and Marital Status

From 1981 to 1986 Canada's population increased from 24.3 to 25.3 million—substantially fewer people live in Canada than in the United States even though the land mass is comparable. Although the total population grew, the 15- to 24-year-olds decreased from 4.7 to 4.2 million. Proportionately, the youth population declined from 19.1% to 16.5% over the five-year period.

Accompanying this population decline is an increase in delayed marriage. In 1981, 71.4% of males and 50.7% of females in the age range of 20 to 24 years were single. In 1986, these proportions increased to 78.9% and 60.0% respectively. The increase in the number of single youths coincides with other changes in living arrangements, educational pursuits, and work activities.

Living Arrangements

Figure 1–7 depicts the proportion of adolescents and youths living at home. Not only are young people postponing marriage, but they are also living with parents longer. Male youths living at home outnumber female youths. Further, more young women than men leave their parental home to marry or cohabitate. The

Many Canadian adolescents remain at home during late adolescence and young adulthood. Canadian youths may be less likely to live on their own before starting their own family.

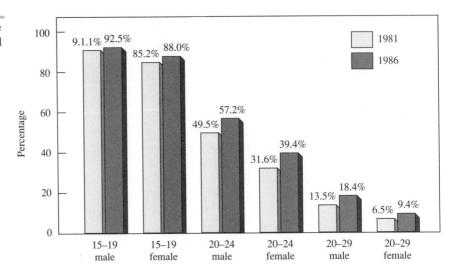

Figure 1–7 Percentage of youth living in parental home by age and sex, Canada, 1981 and 1986. (*Source:* 1981 and 1986 Census of Canada, *Statistics Canada, 1986.*)

evidence suggests Canadian youths are very committed to a family life. For most youths, the impetus to live in a family is seen either in remaining home or starting a family of their own. We suspect this emphasis on family living puts certain extra stress and strains on relationships for Canadian families. This may be a meaningful and important difference between Canadian and U.S. life experiences.

Education

Many changes have occurred in educational experiences during the last three decades. The number of youths attending high school increased from 64% in 1981 to 73% in 1986. A longer perspective reveals that in 1951 only one in two were attending school full time. In 1986, this proportion has increased to approximately three of four. Most recent data indicate that over half of the youths graduating from high school have received at least some postsecondary education. Further, school attendance is about equal for males and females. Women dominate the educational majors in commerce, business administration, arts, humanities, health, education, recreation, and counseling, and males dominate in engineering, mathematics, and applied sciences. Therefore, even though the proportion of youths in the total population is declining, the educational level is increasing. This means Canada has a smaller number of youths, but their increasing education level means the country has a more skilled and educationally prepared work force. However, with the exception of business interests for females, educational career choices appear sex-role delineated, with women selecting nurturing vocations and men opting for analytic and scientific jobs.

Work Activities

Work patterns are changing in Canada. For high school adolescents, the percentage of youths working full time has decreased from 46% in 1980 to 35% in 1985. However, part-time employment has increased from 54% to 65%. In that the proportion of youths who stay at home with parents and have gone for more school has increased over this period, the increase in part-time work is due to the former conditions.

The type of employment is gradually changing for adolescents. In 1981, youths were most represented in trade and finance, insurance, and real estate. By 1986, they were mostly employed in trade and community, business and personal services. The technical and demanding job employment of the early 1980's is giving way to jobs with less immediate advancement opportunities (as in the United States).

The employment picture for adolescents is not complete without an appreciation of youth unemployment. As the Canadian economy has slumped, unemployment rates have increased. The unemployment rate in 1981 was 14% and had increased to 17% in 1986. At the same time, adult unemployment rose from 5.5% to 8.6% between 1981 and 1986, and by the early 1990s had risen again to approximately 11%. Clearly, staying in school longer to acquire more education and technical skills is increasingly important for youths to avoid problems of unemployment.

Income

In 1985, the average income for teenagers was $3,337 and was one-third that of youths 20 to 24 years of age. For both teenagers and youths, the average income of males ($8,719) was larger by 26.3% to that of females ($6,901). The context of household residency must be considered in understanding the implications of these income figures.

Of all youths, 42% of the teenagers and 26% of the youths between the ages of 20 and 24 years were living with parents whose family income generally ranged between $25,000 and $60,000. Clearly, additional youth income enriched an already comfortable financial situation. However, for youths living alone, three of five persons had to live on an income of less than $10,000. Further, youths living alone as a parent (1.3%) averaged less than $7,229 annual income. By anyone's standard, these youths are living alone or with their child(ren) in a state of poverty.

Summary

This brief overview provides a general portrait of the characteristics of contemporary North American adolescents. These findings may make pessimists feel we are in a sorry state. However, for the more optimistic, balancing the desirable and undesirable facts provides a sense of promise, direction for needed programs, issues for future legislation, and necessary social change. We believe the best perspective notes the trends honestly, recognizing that at any point in history certain trends show promise for youths' future while others point to evident problems.

A Life Stage with Heightened Risk

As we indicated, many health or social problems are now so prevalent that it is difficult to describe them as special or atypical issues. For example, Johnston, O'Malley, and Bachman (1988) report that in 1975, 85% of high school students reported illegal use of alcohol during the previous 12 months; in 1987 the figure was 86%. Further, 40% in 1975 and 36% in 1987 reported using marijuana or hashish during the year. This use occurred even though in both 1975 and 1987 students overwhelmingly perceived both substances as harmful to their health. Older adolescents were higher users than younger ones (Johnston et al., 1987).

Although there is an evident downward trend in the use of certain drugs (for example, cocaine), other drugs are increasingly used (for example, inhalants). Clearly, adolescents remain at risk for drug use that can damage their health or social well-being.

Adolescents are thought to be, by nature, high risk-takers (Irwin, 1987). The media portray them as frequently living on the edge. They appear to experiment and engage in dangerous and foolish activities. In recent years researchers have concluded that early adolescents (middle school or junior high age in particular) are at the greatest risk for negative social and psychological consequences. The evidence clearly indicates that the transition through adolescence is filled with many risks.

Using national data provided by the U.S. Bureau of Statistics on the incidents of accidental, homicidal, and suicidal deaths in 1979 and 1984, Adams, Bennion, & Openshaw (1990) examined these years for differences in age, gender, and ethnic group to compare groups for risk implication. They carefully controlled for size of living birth cohorts to ensure appropriate comparisons between 1979 and 1984, a practice that is far too uncommon. The findings confirm Irwin's assumptions and reveal some frightening results.

On the positive side, we found a decline in deaths between 1979 and 1984 for the full age range between 1 and 24 years: 23,560 accidental, 6864 homicidal, and 5398 suicidal deaths occurred in 1979—more than 36,000 youths died violent deaths—whereas in 1984, 17,972 accidental, 5588 homicidal, and 5258 suicidal deaths occurred—approximately 28,000 violent deaths. This is a decline of 24%, 19%, and 3% in accidental, homicidal, and suicidal deaths respectively. Although the trends are promising, however, the United States is still losing the equivalent of a medium-sized town population each year from needless and violent deaths. Clearly, this loss supports the notion that adolescents are at risk as a life-stage group. However, the downward trends raise hope. (See also Box 1–2).

There are relatively consistent gender differences. Fewer females died violent deaths at every age in both 1979 and 1984. Accidental deaths declined 25% for males and 19% for females. Homicides declined 22% for males but only 7% for females. Suicides declined only 1% for males, with an 11% decline for females.

Racial differences between 1979 and 1984 revealed decreases in traffic deaths of 12% for Blacks, 25% for Whites, and 17% for other minority youths. Homicidal deaths decreased 7% for Blacks and 20% for Whites. However, a 6% *increase* was observed among the remaining minority youths. Finally, a substantial 19% decrease in suicidal deaths for Blacks was observed, with a 2% *increase* for the remaining minority youths.

In an analysis of major importance to our concerns about whether early, middle, or late adolescence is the riskiest substage, we compared groupings of those aged 1 to 4, 5 to 9, 10 to 14, 15 to 19, and 20 to 24 for their incidence of death due to homicide, motor vehicle accidents, and suicide. Figures 1–8 to 1–13 depict gender, race, and age differences for suicide, homicide, and traffic accidents. The numbers on the vertical axis represent the number of cases per 100,000 living youths. Whereas gender and race differences can be found at any given age comparison (for example, between males and females in the age category 15 to 19 for suicidal deaths), a similar age trend is found for all forms of death. The 10- to 14-year-olds are approximately

Box 1–2   Adolescent Social Behavior and Death: Risk Taking and Risk Avoidance

Charles Irwin (1987) correctly notes that the majority of causes of death during adolescence are behavioral (for example, auto accidents, suicide, carrying a weapon) and that we need to document the social behaviors that can result in adolescent death. Along with colleagues he maintains that the following key concepts are central to understanding survival during adolescence:

1. Positive or healthy adolescent development is fostered by a supportive environment during early adolescence that is followed by gradual or graded steps toward autonomy.

2. Exploratory **risk-taking behaviors** include both constructive and destructive exploration. Constructive risk taking may be necessary for positive developmental outcomes, and destructive risk taking may create undesirable health risks.

3. Adolescence is not inherently unstable, turbulent, conflictful, or associated with negative outcomes. Understanding patterns of positive major biological and psychosocial changes during adolescence that provide new abilities, skills, or potentials facilitates our understanding of how positive growth supports health-promoting behaviors.

4. Healthy or positive development is encouraged through a socialization process of supportive engagement between adolescents or youths and adults or peers in the social context of family,

school, work, or community.

5. The characterization of what is considered normal or abnormal development must be viewed in the demographic, socioeconomic, psychological, biological, sociological and historical/cultural contexts in which adolescents live.

These various principles are basic to our text. Further, we believe with Irwin that as we look at any life stage from an "at-risk" perspective, we should always think of two sides of people's behavior: risk taking and its outcomes (suicide, homicide, reckless driving) and risk avoidance (rejecting peer pressure, selecting study over drinking). Although risk-taking exploratory behaviors are central to experiential learning during adolescence, the more maturity, coping skills, and interpersonal resources youths possess through healthy development, the lesser the risk in many of these behaviors. Such youths are better able to see dangers, selectively engage in risk taking, recognize possible outcomes, and avoid circumstances with unhealthy conclusions.

This text examines the constraining and supportive factors in institutions such as the family, school, and peer group. Then it analyzes biological, social, and psychological changes that improve an adolescent's functioning. The last chapters present material regarding risk-taking behaviors and unhealthy behavioral and developmental outcomes.

at the same risk as other childhood age groupings. However, the 15- to 19-year-olds double in risk of death, with the 20- to 24-year-olds almost doubling the risk again.

These data clearly show that high school and post-high school adolescents are more likely to confront risk than are younger youths. Findings such as these have led us to focus primarily on the analysis of middle and late adolescence in this book. However, we do recognize special important concerns regarding early adolescence when we discuss central themes.

Organization of This Textbook

This text begins with an overview of the demographic characteristics of contemporary adolescents, including some projections for the near future. We have identified the general living, schooling, and working conditions of North American youths and have examined some positive and negative implications. We have also presented evidence (the most drastic or dramatic—that is, death) to support our argument that adolescence is unique in its riskiness. And we have shown that

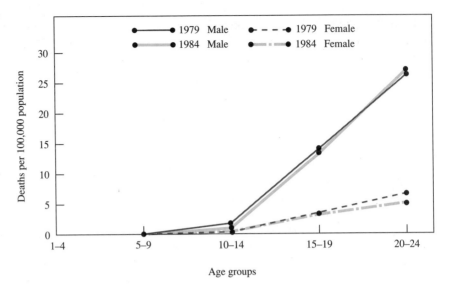

Figure 1–8   Death by suicide, by gender and age group, 1979 and 1984. (G. R. Adams, L. D. Bennion, D. K. Openshaw & C. R. Bingham. Windows of vulnerability: Identifying critical age, gender, and racial differences predictive of risk for violent deaths in childhood and adolescence. *Journal of Primary Prevention,* 1990, 10(3), 223–240.)

middle and late adolescence are greater risk periods than early adolescence. Beginning with this foundation, we have used the following conceptualization to organize the four parts of the book:

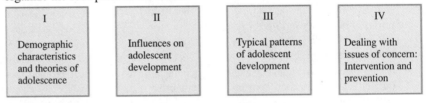

I	II	III	IV
Demographic characteristics and theories of adolescence	Influences on adolescent development	Typical patterns of adolescent development	Dealing with issues of concern: Intervention and prevention

Our demographic portrait sketches the broad context of adolescent life. In the next chapter, we present theories that provide an understanding of how scholars analyze

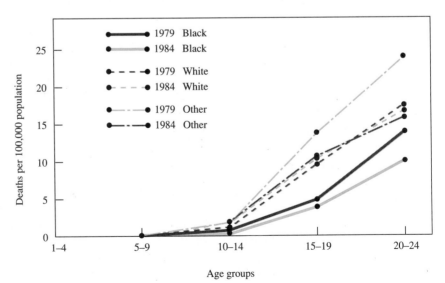

Figure 1–9   Death by suicide, by race and age group, 1979 and 1984. (G. R. Adams, L. D. Bennion, D. K. Openshaw & C. R. Bingham. Windows of vulnerability: Identifying critical age, gender, and racial differences predictive of risk for violent deaths in childhood and adolescence. *Journal of Primary Prevention,* 1990, 10(3), 223–240.)

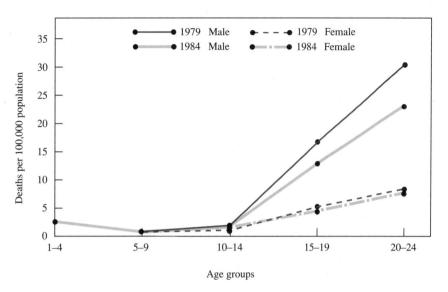

Figure 1–10   Death by homicide, by sex and age group, 1979 and 1984. (G. R. Adams, L. D. Bennion, D. K. Openshaw & C. R. Bingham. Windows of vulnerability: Identifying critical age, gender, and racial differences predictive of risk for violent deaths in childhood and adolescence. *Journal of Primary Prevention*, 1990, 10(3), 223–240.)

adolescent behavior and understand adolescent development. Then in Part Two, chapters on the family, school, and peers build a framework for appreciating the physical, social, and psychological context of adolescent development. This appreciation is carried into Part Three, where we discuss general psychological, social, and physical development. Where possible, each chapter analyzes the contribution of social context to adolescent development, identifying enhancing and constraining factors. Finally in Part Four, building on this understanding of social context and adolescent behavior and development, we examine many of the social and health problems associated with adolescence. We do so within a historical framework and summarize trends, theories, and consequences. In each of these chapters we also show how prevention and intervention have either been used or can be used in helping adolescents.

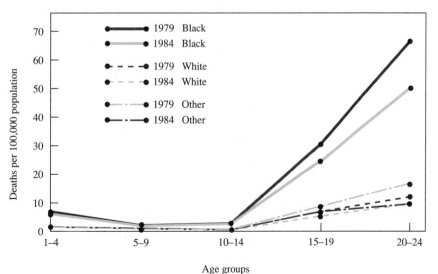

Figure 1–11   Death by homicide, by race and age group, 1979 and 1984. (G. R. Adams, L. D. Bennion, D. K. Openshaw & C. R. Bingham. Windows of vulnerability: Identifying critical age, gender, and racial differences predictive of risk for violent deaths in childhood and adolescence. *Journal of Primary Prevention*, 1990, 10(3), 223–240.)

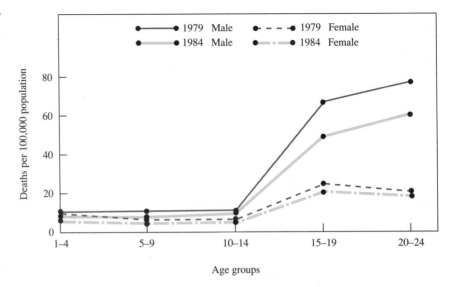

Figure 1–12 Death by motor vehicle accident, by sex and age group, 1979 and 1984. **(**G. R. Adams, L. D. Bennion, D. K. Openshaw & C. R. Bingham. Windows of vulnerability: Identifying critical age, gender, and racial differences predictive of risk for violent deaths in childhood and adolescence. *Journal of Primary Prevention,* 1990, 10(3), 223–240.)

Throughout this text we look at the hard and sometimes cold facts about adolescent behavior. This book is for instructors and students who want to analyze adolescence comprehensively. Some of the material is demanding; complex behaviors and developmental principles are, at times, difficult to grasp. However, a little extra effort will provide you with a fuller understanding and bring a great sense of accomplishment as well.

This edition includes additional information on ethnic adolescent behavior and development. Both the United States and Canada have large existing ethnic groups. Not only do these groups have reasonably high fertility, but both countries also have continuing waves of new immigrants. As one ethnic demographer has concluded:

Canada's current position in the international migration system is similar to that of Australia and the United States, and it is for this reason that all their countries show

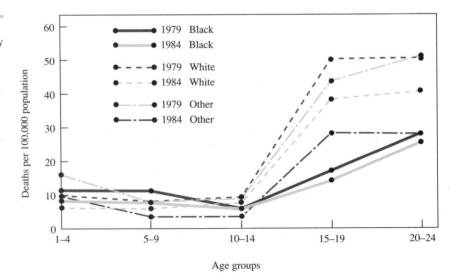

Figure 1–13 Death by motor vehicle accident, by race and age group, 1979 and 1984. **(**G. R. Adams, L. D. Bennion, D. K. Openshaw & C. R. Bingham. Windows of vulnerability: Identifying critical age, gender, and racial differences predictive of risk for violent deaths in childhood and adolescence. *Journal of Primary Prevention,* 1990, 10(3), 223–240.)

some major parallel trends in immigrant origin. All these countries were settled through massive immigration, hence they have multi-ethnic populations and a relative openness . . . to ethnically diverse immigration from the Third World. All three still see themselves as nations in the building phase, hence are open to sizeable immigration . . . Gradually a bridgehead of "pioneer" immigrants from the Third World has built up in all three countries and now exerts internal pressure for the admission of ethnic kin (Simmons, 1990, p. 147–148).

Therefore, both countries have and continue to be assisted in person power by wave after wave of invited (or previously enslaved) cohorts of various ethnic groups. Each group has provided new energy to the work force—much of it at the lower-paying jobs. Each has added a new dimension to the cultural and social mosaic of North America. With ethnic diversity has come the need to understand group variations in behavior and development. Therefore, each chapter in this edition includes a section on subcultural and/or minority groups, their family, or community and what they bring to adolescent development in the form of social-contextual influences. However, even though this text emphasizes multicultural awareness, we don't pretend to cover all that is known or needs to be known about ethnic factors. We do hope this feature of the text will encourage readers to pay increasing attention to multicultural issues in the remainder of their education experience.

Major Points to Remember

1. There are many definitions of adolescence. Each describes the processes that begin and end this life-cycle period. The most common definitions have been physiological, cognitive, sociological, and chronological. Many scholars propose an eclectic perspective.
2. We believe that adolescence is a political or social invention. Therefore, we agree with Zimring's learner's-permit theory of adolescence. This theory proposes a phasing of freedoms as youths reach an age of majority, with new responsibilities added for each new freedom.
3. A statistical snapshot of contemporary adolescence suggests:
   a. shrinking youth population until the end of this century
   b. an increasing diversity in minority youth
   c. longer delays before marriage, greater experience with divorce, and longer periods of living with parents, because of economic dependence
   d. relatively high teenage pregnancy rates, with many young mothers becoming single heads of households
   e. youth-headed families remaining close to the poverty level, with minority youths three to four times as likely to deal with financial deprivation
   f. a need for more education if youths are to be successful, with increasing numbers of students completing high school and college
   g. poverty remaining as the strongest predictor of dropping out of school
   h. better health and longer life expectancy, but with considerable problems remaining: alcohol and drug use, AIDS, crime, and so on
4. Adolescence is viewed as a life stage with heightened risk. Evidence suggests that middle and late adolescents are particularly vulnerable.

CHAPTER

2

Understanding Adolescent Behavior and Development

- Some Features of Theory

- Theories of Adolescent Behavior and Development

Some scholars portray adolescents as turbulent, uneven, moody, and defensive. Others view them as victims, puppets of larger political systems or stranded in school because the work force cannot provide adequate employment. Many popular writers present adolescence in stereotypical terms. Indeed, far too many myths have been perpetrated about adolescence. Portrayals of a strife-ridden period of crisis; a wide generation gap between adolescents and their parents; a drug-ridden, free-loving, sexually based youth culture; and other equally overstated or false accounts have dominated the public's view of adolescence. As Adelson (1986) has suggested, we have been swayed by the news media's views of adolescence and have come to accept far too many myths as truth.

But how, then, should we look at adolescence? How do we come to understand adolescents and avoid the pitfalls of stereotypes? We believe that the best way is through the use of widely accepted theories about adolescence, hypotheses derived from such theories, empirical tests of these hypotheses, and modification of the original theories based on the facts. This chapter helps you build an understanding of theoretical frameworks that are commonly used to explain adolescent behavior and development.

In this chapter we review several theoretical perspectives useful in understanding adolescent behavior. We examine the basic focus of each perspective and illustrate it with one or two theorists. Further, in a series of boxes we make tentative generalizations derived from the perspective. We urge you to make your own generalizations and to compare the generalizations derived from the various perspectives summarized in this chapter.

Some Features of Theory

Theory construction is the process of arriving at meaningful propositions about social behavior through the use of reasoning. For a theory to be useful, it must offer a concise conceptual understanding of a particular behavior and specify its key elements. The theory must also clearly delineate the factors (for example, physiological, psychological, or social) that are proposed as causing the behavior to emerge or change. Finally, the theory must be stated in such a way that it is testable. This last requirement is called **operationalization.** It is essential that both researchers testing the theory and those applying it understand how to define and measure its key variables.

All theories contain two types of elements. The **independent variable** is the element thought to cause some change in behavior or, put another way, to produce a behavioral outcome. The **dependent variable** is the element thought to change as a result of the independent variable. If a new educational program has been found to improve social skills, then the program is the independent variable, and the improved social skills are the dependent variable. When referring to the operationalization of a theory, researchers are referring to the conceptualization and measurement of the independent and dependent variables.

Theories of Adolescent Behavior and Development

From the *biosocial* perspective adolescent behavior is primarily attributed to biological change. Major contributors include G. S. Hall (1916) and Barker (1953).

From an *interpersonal-relations* perspective adolescence is examined as a personal attraction and exchange process (Berscheid & Walster, 1974; Levinger, 1974; Levinger & Snoek, 1972). *Sociological* and *anthropological* theories emphasize the influence of social environments and institutions on adolescent behavior (Benedict, 1938; K. Davis, 1940). The *psychological* or *psychosocial* theories of adolescence typically stress human experience instead of genetics, studying such factors as perception, stress, or emotional disturbance (Erikson, 1950, 1954; Havighurst, 1972). Two final theoretical perspectives are the *social-cognitive* orientation of such scholars as Bandura (1977), McCandless (1970), and Selman (1976a, 1976b), which focuses on how the process of learning affects adolescent life experiences, and the *psychoanalytic* orientation of Freud and his followers, which emphasizes the intrapsychic mechanisms of personality.

The Biosocial Perspective

The biosocial perspective has the longest tradition among theories of adolescence. Given that adolescence is associated with physical growth and maturational and biochemical changes, many theorists have suggested that social behavior in adolescence is predicted by a physical process. Since it is difficult to argue that social behavior causes physical growth, hormonal secretions, or biochemical changes, most theorists have argued that certain biological processes are causal mechanisms that generate social behavioral changes in adolescence. We illustrate this perspective through the early writing of G. Stanley Hall and Roger Barker.

As the first president of the American Psychological Association, G. Stanley Hall is also the father of adolescent psychology.

G. Stanley Hall

A psychologist and an educator, Hall (1904) believed that through an evolutionary mechanism adolescents could acquire certain traits as they underwent critical life experiences. He maintained that these traits could be transmitted to one's progeny at the time of conception. Thus, if adolescents are exposed to the right kind of environmental conditions, their acquisition and transmittal of positive traits improve humanity itself.

In what is called a psychological theory of **recapitulation,** Hall believed that each individual in his or her course of development retraces the history of humanity. Therefore, each person, beginning in childhood, lives through a period of animal-like primitiveness and a later period of savagery and ultimately enters a stage of maturity that reflects a more civilized nature. This view is the source of the expression **"Ontogeny** recapitulates **phylogeny."**

Hall thought that childhood was dominated by instinct and adolescence by a susceptibility to environmental influences (Grinder, 1967). According to one summary of Hall's theory:

> Thus, at adolescence the progression of recapitulating instincts gave way to the primacy of cultural influences. Hall believed firmly that if human civilization was to be advanced, effective change could be induced only by supplying the appropriate educational experiences for the generation of adolescents; childhood was too early, and adulthood was too late, (Adams, Higgins-Trenk, & Svoboda, 1975, p. 24)

This view that it is possible to improve humanity gave working with and educating adolescents a new and important social meaning.

Hall left another influential legacy. The concept of *Storm and Stress* was central to his beliefs. He portrayed adolescence as a period of both upheaval, suffering, passion, and rebellion against adult authority and physical, intellectual, and social change. It was not this viewpoint but the scientific community's criticism of his overemphasis on the inheritance of acquired personality traits that brought his influence on the study and education of adolescents to an end.

Roger Barker

Although a variety of contemporary psychologists are interested in the psychological and behavioral implications of physiological attributes for development, few have concentrated on adolescence. Roger Barker, however, has focused on adolescent development (1953). In contrast to Hall's emphasis on genetic mechanisms, Barker has used a strong social-psychological orientation. Since adolescence is a period of rapid physical growth and improvements in coordination, he has maintained that adolescence is a transition period between childhood and adulthood. Further, during adolescence different parts of the body grow at different rates, so that the individual is advanced according to some developmental indexes but behind on others. These asynchronous conditions remind us that the individual is no longer a child but not yet an adult.

Recognizing that we live in an age-graded culture that separates individuals into social groups according to age, Barker has proposed that children are separated into their own social group, from which specific forms of behavior are expected and accepted. One major determinant of movement from the childhood group into the adult social group is the degree to which the individual has acquired a mature physique. Therefore, children who mature earlier than others are thought to be assimilated into adult social roles at an earlier age. But during adolescence every individual is at least briefly in a stage of asynchronous development. For example, a youth may have a child's voice but an adult's physique. Because of this ambiguity in physical change, the adolescent is left in a marginal situation. No longer a child and not yet an adult, the adolescent is thought to behave in ways that are guided by behavioral expectations for both childhood and adulthood. Thus, body image and the manner in which it is interpreted by society may contribute to adolescent behavior. (See Box 2–1.)

Summary

Many social science theorists have addressed the relationship between physical development and social behavior. Hall argued that social experiences during adolescence led to the internalization of traits that were inherited by the next generation. No direct proof has been found for this position, but the biosocial perspective continues in other forms. For example, Barker has argued that physical development has an important impact on the movement from childhood to adult social groups. Rather than stating that physical development is associated with the acquisition of traits that are transmitted to one's progeny, he has argued that one's physique determines one's social experience. During adolescence physical development is sometimes asynchronous, and this state of development creates a period in which the youth is neither child nor adult. Because of this marginal social status,

---

Box 2–1   Generalizations from a Biosocial Perspective

In the form of if/then statements we suggest two generalizations from the biosocial perspective to demonstrate the potential practical utility of theories.

1. Differential rates of physical growth between peers will result in different levels of acceptance by adults for adultlike behavior. For example, a tall and more muscular boy may be allowed more independence by parents and teachers than a shorter, less physically developed peer.
2. Changes in physical stature (and the associated changes in hormones and biochemical processes)

will be associated with other social-behavioral and psychological changes. For example, more fully developed and menstruating girls will be more interested in boys, dating, and sexuality issues than nonmenstruating peers.

Can you think of other possible biosocial generalizations? As you read the chapters on physical and sexual development, check to see if you can find support for our generalizations and your own.

---

the adolescent behaves in both childlike and adultlike ways. This process accounts for the perceived turbulence and vacillation of so-called adolescent behavior.

The Interpersonal Relations Perspective

The interpersonal-relations perspective is a modern social-psychological alternative to the biosocial perspective of days past. Social psychologists interested in the interpersonal behaviors of adolescence have proposed a variety of theories to describe the emergence of pairing, heterosexual interests, or intimacy behavior. Nearly everyone knows that adolescence is a period when interest in the opposite sex heightens. In the interpersonal-relations perspective there are two general types of theories to account for this phenomenon. Some theorists draw on aspects of social or physical attractiveness as mechanisms that draw one person to another. This theory typically does not detail how or why the attraction process emerges but, rather, describes how it unfolds. In the other view, psychological and physiological processes are proposed to account for the emergence of a "social sensitivity" and interest in the opposite sex. It explains emotional states and changes in psychological functioning in the context of peer relations and interest in the opposite sex. Both types of theories, however, are modern alternatives to those proposed by Hall and other biosocial theorists. We briefly discuss the theories of George Levinger and of Ellen Berscheid and Elaine Walster (Hatfield) to illustrate these two theories.

George Levinger

As adolescents begin to recognize their interest in the opposite sex, the two sexes increase their contacts, usually in groups. These group contacts are the mechanism by which adolescents identify potential choices in the dating marketplace. In examining and interacting with the group, the adolescent begins to feel certain attractions toward particular members of the group. The attractions, or positive attitudes toward another, are associated with pleasant sensations that provide the foundation for an intimate personal relationship.

George Levinger and a colleague (Levinger, 1974; Levinger & Snoek, 1972) have proposed a stage theory of **pair relatedness** to describe the unfolding of the intimate relationships that emerge during late adolescence. Figure 2–1 portrays

Figure 2–1 Levels of pair relatedness. (From "A Three-Level Approach to Attraction: Toward An Understanding of Pair Relatedness," by G. Levinger. In T. Huston (Ed.), *Foundations of Interpersonal Attraction.* Copyright © 1974 by Academic Press. Reprinted by permission.)

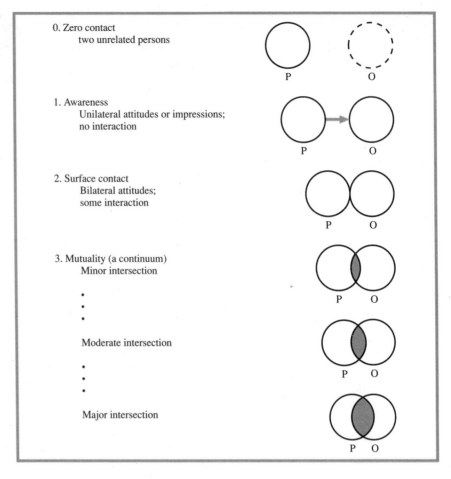

this process in schematic form. (*P* refers to "person" and *O* to "other.") Initially, adolescents meet in neutral settings or in social groups. Before this time they have had no formal contact, so they are shown as independent individuals in the figure. When they are attracted to each other, three levels of relatedness emerge as the relationship moves toward increased intimacy.

In the first of the three stages, the two adolescents become *unilaterally aware* of each other. This unilateral awareness consists of limited information and impressions about the other and is based entirely on physical characteristics (looks, race, and so on). As the figure depicts, there is perceptual evaluation but no real interaction at this stage. When, usually within the adolescent group, reciprocal contacts occur between the two individuals, they are entering the second stage, called *surface contact.* Surface contact may come in the form of transitory meetings, such as in a cafeteria line, at a party, or at a bus stop, or it may appear in the form of a segmental role relation. In this type of relation, there is communication, but it offers little to the other. For example, one adolescent may buy a soda from the other at the high school concession stand, but their exchange is very formal and defined by the roles of purchaser and vendor. They may remark about the weather or ask each other how they did on a recent exam, but the interaction is brief and only marginally informative. However, due to attraction toward each other, they may enter the third stage and move toward a more intimate relationship. *Mutuality,* or interdependence, implies that as the relationship becomes more intimate, the two gradually share more knowledge and feelings and invest more of themselves in each other. As shown in the figure, mutuality progresses on a continuum from minor to major involvement. Levinger believes that this stage of pair relatedness is at first characterized by such behaviors as mutual gazing, touching, and helping and gradually evolves into sharing, disclosing, and reciprocal liking and loving with mutual commitments for the future (see Box 2–2).

Ellen Berscheid and Elaine Hatfield

As mutuality between teenagers heightens, romantic attraction compels them toward thoughts of love. This attraction may lead to strong emotional feelings that are best described as passionate love. Many theorists believe that feelings of love are maintained by the rewarding nature of the relationship. Perhaps passionate love also maintains some of its strength through the fantasies that are associated with the loved one. However, during adolescence, fantasies about rewarding events with one's partner may create a heightened sense of love that is not borne out in actual experience. As many psychiatrists would recognize, fantasies (or wish fulfillments) are poor substitutes for actual reinforcing behavior, so that many early experiences with love are intense but fleeting.

Usually, when we think of love among adolescents, we think of intense emotional feelings. As an aid to understanding the mechanisms behind them, Berscheid and Hatfield (1974) have summarized a "two-component theory of passionate love." Drawing on Schachter's earlier work (1964) on emotional experiences, they have proposed that physiological arousal can be cognitively labeled as love, thereby defining it as a passionate feeling. As long as one experiences an arousal state that is judged as being associated with another person, this arousal state can be interpreted as love. Once the arousal state disappears, the feeling of love is thought to diminish quickly.

Professors Berscheid (left) and Hatfield (right) are exemplary scholars interested in social relations in adolescence.

Box 2–2   Sex Differences in Romantic Love and Self-Disclosure

There has been considerable discussion about whether females need to feel in love before they can establish a prolonged relationship. Males, on the other hand, are thought not to need this precondition of love. One study (G. R. Adams & Shea, 1981) explored the possibility of sex differences in the relationship between romantic love and self-disclosure. A total of 343 youths responded to both a self-disclosure and a romantic-love scale at the beginning and the end of a six-week dating period. Scores on the two measures were used to predict later behavior. Clear sex differences were found: for females, romantic affect was a necessary precondition for self-disclosure, while for males, self-disclosure was a precondition for romantic affiliation. Although this study did not explore the relation between love and sexual intercourse, these data suggest that female adolescents who perceive themselves as being in love may be more inclined than those who do not feel in love to engage in sexual relations.

According to Berscheid and Hatfield, several conditions can create an arousal state that may enhance sensations of romantic passion. Unpleasant emotional experiences, such as a frightening event, a perceived rejection, or sexual frustration, can create arousal states just as can pleasant experiences, such as need satisfaction or excitement and pleasure. It may be that the more ambiguity or uncertainty exists about the cause of the arousal state, the greater the likelihood during dating that the physiological excitement will be labeled as passionate love.

Summary

Adolescence is a period of major changes in social relations. Interest in the opposite sex emerges, and new experiences of love evolve. Many people think these early romantic experiences provide the foundation for later, more mature relationships. Principles of social psychology such as mutuality or arousal states can help us understand the mystery of young love. (See Box 2–3 for further information.)

The Sociocultural Perspective

The sociocultural perspective on adolescence focuses not on physical growth or hormonal mechanisms but on general cultural factors that influence social behavior. The influence of such things as norms for behavior, mores, cultural expectations, social or cultural rituals, group pressures, or technological influences is the key to understanding adolescent behavior. Sociologists and cultural anthropologists describe behavior and development from this perspective.

One of the authors can remember in his undergraduate training in sociology and anthropology the excitement he felt when hearing lectures on comparing preindustrial and postindustrial cultures and learning how each cultural type differed in its expectations about acceptable adolescent behavior. Comparisons of tribal customs, rites of passage, and expectations by adults in the community differed with the society's level of development, its economic or work base, its technology, and the cultural heritage of the family, tribe, or society. It quickly became apparent to him that understanding any form of human behavior required an appreciation of the cultural or social

---

Box 2–3   Generalizations from an Interpersonal-Relations Perspective

Two proposed generalizations from the interpersonal-relations perspective include:

1. Interpersonal attraction between a male and female adolescent can lead to mutuality if the adolescents are given an opportunity to spend time together, talk, or enjoy themselves in a group setting.

2. Further, if during this interaction they have shared an emotional experience, they may label this experience as a form of love. This form of love is known as passion or puppy love and is likely to be very intense but short lived.

What might be other practical generalizations from this perspective?

---

context, the historical events surrounding the adolescent's life, and the social forces operating in a given context.

Three early scholars from this sociocultural perspective who have profoundly influenced our understanding of adolescent behavior are Kingsley Davis, Ruth Benedict, and Margaret Mead.

Kingsley Davis

Kingsley Davis's (1940) treatise on the sociology of parent/youth conflict is a classic illustration of a grand theory from a sociologist's perspective. The foundation of his argument is that because modern society changes very rapidly, each new generation is reared in a social milieu different from that of the previous generation. Since each generation's experience of a "differential cultural content" guides its actions, parents find it difficult to guide the new generation, and clashes are inevitable. According to Davis,

> since the parent is supposed to socialize the child, he tends to apply the erstwhile but now inappropriate content [of his own day]. He makes this mistake, and cannot remedy it, because, due to the logic of personality growth, his basic orientation was formed by the experiences of his own childhood. He cannot "modernize" his point of view, because he is the product of those experiences. . . . To change the basic conceptions by which he has learned to judge the rightness and reality of all specific situations would be to render subsequent experience meaningless, to make an empty caricature of what had been his life. (P. 525)

Davis states that conflict is also inevitable for other reasons. As youths are arriving at the peak of their physiological prowess and have a superabundance of energy, their parents are beginning to lose their physiological capacities and to conserve the energy they have left. Davis argues that the social system limits competition between generations to avoid competitive feelings of jealousy but in the process diminishes a wide variety of opportunities for youth. The result is heightened frustration in many of the young and ensuing conflict with their parents.

Another important source of conflict is that youths dream of utopian ideals, while parents have become pragmatists through experience and the usual conservatism that comes with age. This natural dichotomy provides the ground for conflicting communication. The generations, in search of their own form of truth, are unable to speak with each other because of their different perspectives on life. Youths cry for change; their parents call for patience and contend that time will change the youths' perspective.

But parents are charged with the duties of "parental authority." They are expected to guide their young, offer them advice, and help them find direction. However, since the two generations have been molded by different cultural and social milieus, parental authority seems less meaningful, and conflict easily arises.

A last major source of conflict is that many parents find it hard to let the adolescent go, to allow a smooth emancipation from the family. In our society there are few institutionalized steps to guide this ticklish process, so that the ambiguity of the situation creates conditions for conflict over the relinquishment of authority. In addition, our society offers an immense range of spiritual, moral, occupational, and social choices, and in their concern for the well-being of their offspring, many parents try to provide direction during this time, when it is often neither desired nor, generationally speaking, appropriate.

Ruth Benedict

From a similar perspective, anthropologist Ruth Benedict (1938) has addressed the major problems of rearing youth to fill adult positions in society. Recognizing that every society should offer cultural conditioning for future social roles, she has examined continuities and discontinuities in preparing individuals for social roles across the life cycle. She wrote that

> all cultures must deal in one way or another with the cycle of growth from infancy to adulthood. Nature has posed the situation dramatically: on the one hand, the newborn baby, physiologically vulnerable, unable to fend for itself, or to participate on its own initiative in the life of the group, and, on the other, the adult man or woman. Every man who rounds out his human potentialities must have been a son first and a father later and the two roles are physiologically in great contrast; he must first have been dependent upon others for his very existence and later he must provide such security for others. This discontinuity in the life cycle is a fact of nature and is inescapable (p. 161).

Professor Benedict provided sound anthropological information on adolescent behavior. Her pioneering efforts are still meaningful today.

Thus, the natural pathway of the cycle of growth brings with it changes in social roles, each role developing out of earlier role experience. However, the manner in which society conditions youths for adult responsibilities appears to vary considerably from culture to culture. In our culture people must make major adjustments in assuming new roles, so that the potential for periods of conflict is high. For example, in many cultures the children are given work assignments and taught to be responsible individuals early in life, but in our society adolescents are given little opportunity to experience meaningful work until they are thrust into adult social roles. This discontinuity in cultural conditioning is also found in social expectations about submissiveness. Children are expected to submit to parental authority, but as youths they are expected to become more dominant as they approach adulthood. However, it is in the realm of sexuality that adolescents experience the greatest discontinuity in preparation for adulthood. During adolescence sexual urges are to be denied, but during adulthood they are (within the bounds of social convention) to be expressed. As children we are conditioned to view sexuality as dangerous and wicked, and for many adults this lesson is hard to unlearn, creating major adjustment problems in marital relationships.

Because our culture is age-graded, we demand different social behavior from different age groups. However, there is little continuity in preparing children and adolescents for adult social roles. Therefore, late adolescence, in Benedict's discontinuity perspective, is believed to be associated with conflict, strife, and major social adjustments. (For another anthropological perspective see Box 2–4.)

Margaret Mead

Not all cultures are filled with stressful experiences for adolescents, according to Mead's (1928a, 1928b) studies of primitive societies. In some societies adolescents are readily and easily initiated into adulthood. Young girls, when sexually mature and capable of reproduction, and young boys sexually mature and able to work or hunt, are encouraged to marry and start their own households. No obvious forms of storm or stress are observed during the transition from adolescence into adulthood. Thus, notions of storm and stress during adolescence are thought by Mead to be a cultural invention, not a biological necessity. Lambert, Rothschild, Altland, and Green (1978) summarize Mead's contribution to the study of adolescence as follows:

> In her cross-cultural research of that period, as well as that of later years . . . [she] indicates that there are two possible means of avoiding the storm and stress of adolescence: (1) through a continuity of one's role in life, evolving with the gradual granting by society of status, privilege, and responsibility to its young people and (2) through specific rites, usually at the time of puberty, by which the new status of the young person is recognized. (P. 9)

Accordingly, Mead's work points to the importance of *rites of passage* and societal recognition of the acquisition of a new social status. These events point to the individual's progression from one life transition to another. Sebald (1984) suggests that celebrations, in the form of rites of passage, serve three primary functions. First, the initiate is *informed* of the new rights and new obligations. Second, the tribe, community, or society is altered through public *announcement*

Margaret Mead's scholarship serves as an exemplary of the sociological and anthropological perspectives. Her work is considered by many as legendary!

Box 2–4   An Anthropological Examination of the Nature of Adolescence

Alice Schlegel and Herbert Barry, in *Adolescence: An Anthropological Inquiry,* (1991), have examined 186 preindustrial societies using an ethnographic methodology. From this sample, these social scientists have looked for commonalities and differences between societies. They identify several universal generic features of adolescence:

1. Adolescence as a social stage is found in 173 societies for boys and 175 for girls.

2. Public initiation or ritual activity is observed in 68% of societies for boys and 79% for girls. Ceremonies are usually public events—more often for boys than girls.

3. The end of adolescence for boys is usually between two and four years after puberty and generally two years for girls.

4. Adolescents spend most of their waking hours with adults of the same sex. Fathers and mothers are the most important adults. However, fewer boys than girls remain in close relations with same-sex adults. Therefore, peer groups assume greater salience for boys than girls.

5. Conflict is more often greater between fathers and sons than between mothers and sons or between daughters and either parent.

6. Evidence suggests that for most races and cultures, the passage into adolescence is less traumatic for girls and supported by intimate social contact with same-sex kin. The transition for boys is less smooth and is generally accompanied with a dramatic decoupling from the family.

These and other findings might explain the dramatic risk (described in Chapter 1) of violent death for teenage boys. In the process of growing up boys may have to find their social place in peer groups that are not closely monitored and supervised by male adults. In turn, young males compete for social status in their peer groups where risk-taking behaviors may achieve higher social status. However, it may also place adolescent boys at greater risk of death. For social groups where the male role model is predominantly portrayed as either weak or socially deviant (drug user, pimp, chronically unemployed, drunkard, etc.), risk-taking behavior in the peer group may be accentuated.

that societal reactions or actions must now change to be consistent with the initiate's new status. Finally, these ceremonies function to elicit the *emotional response* of loyalty, fidelity and commitment, through public displays of societal approval for the new role.

Summary

Both the sociological and the anthropological perspectives have frequently focused on conflict between parents and adolescents. Davis has concentrated on the impact of rapid social change on parent/youth conflict, whereas Benedict has addressed the implications of discontinuity between childhood and adolescence and between adolescence and adulthood for conflict and adjustment. In contrast, Mead has addressed issues of continuity, the granting of status, privilege and responsibility, and the role of rites of passage. It should be evident that these perspectives highlight technological advancement, intergenerational issues, and cultural conditioning as key elements in the study of adolescence. (See also Box 2–5.)

The Psychosocial Perspective

The psychosocial perspective on adolescence examines the relationship between the psychological adjustment of growing up and the social conditions that foster or impede it. Typically, stress and crisis are presented as central psychological

---

Box 2–5   **Generalizations from a Sociocultural Perspective**

Two potentially useful generalizations from the socio-cultural perspective are:

1. Generational differences between parents and their adolescent children may create conflict if they emerge during a social or historical period when the parents reflect a conservative value system and the adolescents reflect a more liberal one.

2. Generational differences are most likely to be manifested in strife and verbal conflict between parent and child over behavior by the child with peers that is not permitted in the family.

Can you suggest additional generalizations from the sociocultural perspective?

---

processes in growth. Stages of development and turning points are usually noted. Resolutions in growth can be positive or negative, and the resolution at one turning point has implications for later such resolutions. In contrast to the sociocultural perspective, which recognizes the potential uniqueness of each culture, most psychosocial theories urge for universal stages (or turning points), with uniqueness in context considered to be of only secondary importance. Although sociocultural influences are recognized, the focus is on similarities between social groups or cultures rather than differences.

Erik Erikson

Erik Erikson has provided a description of adolescence that recognized historical, social, cultural, and familial influences on adolescent development.

Erik H. Erikson is perhaps the most noted theoretician to have addressed adolescent development from a psychosocial perspective. He views adolescence not as a period of personality consolidation but as an important stage of life that functions as a transition between important issues in the life course. In particular, he has expanded the social setting of the classic parent/child relationship to include a larger cultural and social influence. His intriguing investigation of the individual's struggles in life does not negate the unconscious influences of instincts but rather emphasizes the developmental opportunities, defeats, and triumphs of normal living. According to Erikson (1950), the personality (or ego) has the duty to synthesize past and present experiences in integrating inner life (instincts) with social influences (social planning).

Erikson examines central problems people of the same age and sociocultural background face over their life span. Although the concept of developmental crisis is universal, each specific crisis is mastered according to the individual's cultural circumstances. But the mastery of each crisis is only one of many dilemmas that are faced in the continuous process of social living. According to Erikson (1954), with the personal resolution of each new life crisis, the ego incorporates a new quality into the ego identity (global personality). Therefore, a healthy personality is acquired through the resolution of a series of life crises (dilemmas). With each new resolution there is a corresponding personal recognition of a meaningful accomplishment and a growing sense of personal achievement.

Erikson has delineated eight major dilemmas that are universally experienced over the life course. (See Table 2–1.) Each dilemma has a positive (desirable) pole, which represents social maturity, opposed by a negative (undesirable) pole, which represents the fixated characteristic of that developmental crisis.

Table 2–1   Erikson's eight major dilemmas and their approximate life stages

Crisis point	Stage in life
Basic trust versus mistrust	Infancy
Autonomy versus shame and doubt	Early childhood
Initiative versus guilt	Childhood
Industry versus inferiority	Early adolescence
Identity versus role confusion	Adolescence
Intimacy versus isolation	Youth
Generativity versus stagnation	Adulthood
Integrity versus despair	Old age

Source: Erikson, E. H. (1950). *Childhood and Society,* New York: Norton.

In the first normative crisis the infant must confront the dilemma of establishing either a sense of *basic trust* in the social and physical environment or a sense of *mistrust.* A sense of trust emerges through the social care and comfort provided by the primary care giver. The neonate, totally helpless and vulnerable, elicits in the mother a need to support, protect, and attend to the infant. With this support as a foundation, accompanied by minimal experiences with uncertainty, the infant acquires a sense of basic trust. Once this feeling of trust is established, it generalizes to new experiences. However, should the infant experience poor care giving, a sense of mistrust develops, leading to apprehension or fearfulness in novel situations.

In the second normative crisis the child confronts a dilemma that results in either a sense of *autonomy* or feelings of *shame and doubt.* As children mature, they demonstrate a need to explore and venture out from a previously defined and secure psychological space. Reaching out, through such acts as walking and climbing, brings them to thresholds of new and important experiences of self-extension. Children use their parents as a base of exploration and call on them to provide reinforcement and guidance for such exploratory behavior. Appropriate support for gradual extension aids their sense of autonomy and prevents the development of shame and doubt.

The adventurous conquest of space and a growing sense of independence drive children into new and complex social spheres. Therein lies the rudimentary foundation for a resolution of the third normative crisis, *initiative* versus *guilt.* A growing sense of initiative challenges children to master new learning tasks. This challenge, when met successfully, creates a feeling of self-responsibility, establishing a meaning and purpose for their existence. Thus, they begin to initiate activities that test their capacities and present and future roles, while trying to get others involved in these activities. Guilt is thought to accrue with the initiation of acts of aggressive manipulation that exceed the limits of their capabilities. Therefore, the conflict of this stage is between the searching for a sense of initiative and the passive (guilt-ridden) acceptance of having attempted activities beyond one's psychological limits.

The fourth normative crisis revolves around the development of a sense of *industry* or the internalization of a sense of *inferiority.* Turning increasing attention to individual striving toward competence, mastery, and achievement, early adolescents begin to recognize the importance of becoming a worker or provider. They gradually come to sense that they must *do* or *accomplish* something to gain recognition, to become a productive individual. Both in and outside the home, children increasingly receive both organized and informal instruction as they mature. Through instructional activities they come to understand the cultural and technological ethos of society. Should they fail to experience achievements that are supported by an adult role model who promotes positive identification, they are inclined to develop a sense of inadequacy or inferiority. This sense of inadequacy can easily lead to despair and to self-restricted behavior.

Although the development of industry is an important behavioral outcome in early adolescence, the resolution of a sense of *identity* versus *role confusion* is the hallmark of adolescence proper. The major question demanding an answer in this fifth normative crisis is "What can I be?" Therefore, the emphasis is on becoming what one aspires to become. To address this question, the ego has the difficult task of integrating the adolescent's past and future. Previous and present identification are synthesized into a meaningful sense of identity. Although the parents remain major agents of social support, the influence of the peer group increases. Play, a necessary ego function, is mostly replaced by social experimentation in which the adolescent tests different roles in varying situations to acquire feedback, which aids in the development of interpersonal attitudes and roles.

Even though identity is the focal point of the adolescent experience, all the previous normative crises have contributed to identity development. First, a healthy and vital personality requires a sense of trust in oneself and others. Without a sense of trust, infants are incapable of reaching any meaningful self-realization. Thus, a feeling of estrangement occurs as they withdraw into themselves.

A feeling of independence is also necessary for establishing a self-directed life-style. Toddlers must be encouraged to extend themselves, to obtain a will to be themselves. To accomplish this task, they must have faith (a sense of trust) in themselves and others. With maturation, new experiences and roles within an expanding social radius provide the support for emerging feelings of purpose and ambition. As this sense of direction emerges, we are inclined to describe youths as relaxed, vital, and more themselves. Educational experiences allow them to channel energies into learning technological skills, which aid in developing feelings of pride and enjoyment in accomplishment. These influential factors combine to form the structure of a psychosocial identity. The basic virtues that distinguish a sense of identity from a state of role confusion are devotion and fidelity to specific and personally meaningful roles and groups in society.

Erikson views the adolescent life experience as a state of **moratorium,** as a period in which adolescents are expected to prepare themselves for the future and provide an answer to the question "Who am I?" He warns of the dangers of being unable to fulfill this commitment. Should adolescents fail to develop a sense of identity, they remain lost without direction, like ships tossed in the winds of time. Perhaps an even greater danger is the development of negative identity. If adolescents question their own potential or their individual places in society, they may establish a negative identity. Unable to specify a social niche, they may identify with delinquent or criminal elements, thus locking themselves into an identity that continuously confronts society. This confrontation may lead them to wear an "identity mask" that they will be unable to remove even if they want to.

As adolescents are propelled into the career world, they begin to establish intimate relationships with the intention of future marriage. There is, at this point, a growing need for partnership and affiliation. Only now can the ego maintain enough strength that it can sustain commitment to, and sacrifice for, another person. According to Erikson, the search for intimacy is founded in mutual sharing and trust. The accomplishment of a sense of *intimacy* results in a fusion of two identities in the form of sexual union and close friendship. The negative counterpart of intimacy is a sense of *isolation*. Avoidance of intimacy is characterized as self-absorption. Due to a fear of losing themselves in the identity of another, some individuals are incapable of a strong intimate relationship. This negative resolution is represented in such actions as prejudice, overcompetitiveness, and combative attitudes and behavior.

Fulfillment of intimacy requires a sense of shared identity (Maier, 1965), a feeling of solidarity reflected in compatibility and sharing. Indeed, Freud used the phrase *Lieben und Arbeiten* (love and work) to characterize the fully mature person (1947, 1948). By this he meant that a fully functioning and mature person must have a sense of occupational identity but also be capable of a productive career that does not interfere with the ability to love and be loved. To arrive at this state, adolescents or youths must have trust in their environment, view themselves as autonomous, industrious, competent, and self-directed, and be capable of sharing their lives with another.

Crisis resolutions during childhood and adolescence or youth also influence a late normative crisis. Erikson theorizes that positive resolution of such crises as the development of initiative, identity, and intimacy provides the foundation for a fulfilling social and working life. Indeed, a positive identity is thought to precipitate the next crisis, *generativity* versus *stagnation*. Once the individual has a self-defined identity, the need for intimacy is thought to emerge naturally.

The last normative crisis is the development of a sense of *integrity* versus a sense of *despair*. Successful resolution of this crisis leads to feelings of accomplishment and fulfillment during the late adult years. Unsuccessful resolution leads to feelings of despair, of incompleteness, and of an unfulfilled life.

Other Theorists

Robert Havighurst has developed a psychosocial model similar to Erikson's theory. In his *Developmental tasks and education* (1951), Havighurst has proposed that at different periods in life the individual is called on to master age-specific tasks. Accomplishment of developmental tasks associated with maturational change, schooling, work, religious experience, and so on is a prerequisite for self-fulfillment and happiness.

Another psychosocial perspective on human behavior used to investigate adolescent populations is **situationism** or *interactionism* (Bowers, 1973; Ekehammar, 1974; Lerner, 1976, 1978, 1979). This perspective assumes that certain personality traits are productive in certain situations but not in others. Lerner states that behavioral change involves the dynamic interaction of multiple sources of influence on human behavior and development. These sources include such

Professor Lerner is a contemporary psychologist recognizing the social context of adolescent behavior.

factors as biological, psychological, historical, and sociocultural influences that occur in many situations and environments. Thus, certain psychological or biological attributes may create productive consequences depending on the situation.

Lerner, Lerner, and Tubman (1989) describe two different versions of biological influences. One version suggests that genetic determination has a direct effect on individual development. In this model, genetic factors are thought to determine the association between organismic growth and change and other psychological characteristics:

> For example, Freud believes that the physiological changes of puberty alters not only a person's drive level, but his or her ego defenses, object relations, attitudes, and values; simply, an inevitable and universal developmental disturbance—involving physiology, personality, and social behavior—is caused directly by the biological changes of puberty. (Pp. 15–16)

A competing perspective focuses instead on mediation and interactional, or developmental contextual themes. This viewpoint argues that characteristics of the person influence, and in turn are influenced by, the social context—a multidirectional relation among biological, psychological, and social factors. To illustrate, Lerner, Jovanovic, Delaney, Hess, and Von Eye (1988) have examined the direct and indirect effects of physical attractiveness on grade performance in school. In this study, physical attractiveness of the adolescent was slightly associated with grades. However, teachers rated attractive children as more competent and, in turn, teachers' ratings of scholastic competence were highly correlated with grades earned. Further, adolescents perceived themselves as competent when teachers held high ratings of their scholastic competence, and again, in turn, self-perceived competence predicted high grades. The direct and indirect effects are depicted in Figure 2–2. This illustration underlines the importance of studying the direct and indirect effects within a developmental contextual model.

Figure 2–2 Direct and indirect effects of physical attractiveness and competency on grade point average. (Adapted from "Organismic and Contexual Bases of Development in Adolescence: A Developmental Contextual View." In G. R. Adams, R. Montemayor and T. P. Gullotta, *Advances in Adolescent Development,* Vol. I, 1989. Copyright © 1989 by Sage Publications. Reprinted by permission.)

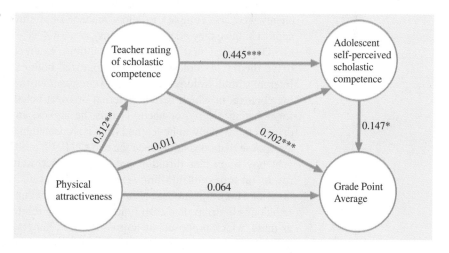

In this text, we present many findings that are direct influences. However, the majority are further examples of the indirect effects among biological, psychological, and social influences. (See Box 2–6 for several generalizations from the psychosocial perspective.)

Summary

In Erikson's psychosocial perspective, adolescence and youth are associated with the development of industry, identity, and intimacy. Although the family establishes the basic foundation for positive development, the broader social and cultural environment also influences development. Erikson argues that in the course of our lives we experience several important dilemmas that can be resolved in either a positive or a negative fashion. Positive resolution is necessary to ensure a fully functioning, capable, and mature individual. Learning that one is competent and capable of industry, locating oneself in the social world, and developing intimate involvement with another are some of the essential ingredients in a successful adolescence, youth, and adulthood.

The Social-Cognitive Perspective

Early in the development of theories of child and adolescent behavior, considerable attention was given to the importance of reinforcement and punishment in building and maintaining positive behaviors. In this early view, adolescents were viewed as being analogous to machines, merely reacting to physical and social stimuli. A common term for this model was **behavioral, or mechanistic, theory.** Through its application to children, involving the imitation of modeled behavior, a social-learning perspective emerged. **Role models** are thought to provide visible behavior for examination by children. When they emulate role-modeled behavior, children are either reinforced by society for engaging in similar behavior or, through an *identification* with the model, are vicariously self-rewarded for being like the person identified with. Although this perspective is useful for understanding some behaviors, psychologists working with adolescents found that clients were too complex to allow reliance on a simply reactive social-learning approach; thus, they adapted the theory.

One of the first theoretical evolutions emerged in McCandless's (1970) **drive theory** of adolescence. He recognized both external and internal stimuli. Internal stimuli, referred to as *drive states,* can ensure learning through reinforcing contexts in which certain external or overt behaviors provide a mechanism for reducing a drive or need. That is, he argues, any response that "reduces a drive is more likely to be learned (that is, repeated in similar circumstances) than a response that does not reduce the drive" (1970, p. 9). For example, if an adolescent boy finds that flirtation produces counterflirtation from girls and that it results (at times) in fulfilling sexual needs, his satisfaction reinforces the likelihood of future flirtatiousness in heterosexual encounters. Further, increases and reductions in drive states can function as strong reinforcements. Arguments such as these, which proposed such drive states as hunger, search for comfort, avoidance of pain, or sexual satisfaction as motivational factors, were the early beginnings of a social-cognitive perspective.

Box 2–6   Generalizations from a Psychosocial Perspective

A psychosocial perspective on adolescent behavior might include the following illustrative generalizations:

1. Positive resolutions of crises and stress during infancy and childhood will provide a solid foundation for positive resolution at major adolescent turning points.
2. Universal psychosocial crisis points can be found among cultures, demonstrating the commonality of humankind.

3. Family, community, peers, church, ethnic group, and other factors in the social environment are important to positive development. All forms of development are promoted by a social group or institution that demonstrates to the adolescent that he or she is noticed, is important, and makes a difference to the group.

Can you identify other possible generalizations from this perspective regarding child and adolescent behavior?

Whereas the early drive theory of adolescence recognized emotional states (drives) as mediating internal factors necessary to understanding human behavior, in the course of time a blending of theory regarding cognitive and social development resulted in the general field of social cognition. The cognitive sciences focus on thinking, reasoning, and information processing. The social-development sciences focus on feelings, motives, abilities, purposes, beliefs, competencies, and personality structure. Blending the two, one gets a perspective on how adolescents reason about themselves and others and how the mediational factors of thoughts, feelings, motives, desires, and intentions influence competencies in behavior and development toward maturity. We briefly review the ideas of two notable theorists who have contributed significantly to this emerging social-cognition perspective, Albert Bandura and Robert Selman. We review the work of the late Jean Piaget and Lawrence Kohlberg which is related to Bandura's and Selman's theories, in Chapter 7, on cognitive development.

Albert Bandura

Albert Bandura provides a comprehensive social-learning theory of adolescence.

Bandura (1977) has provided a comprehensive social-learning theory applicable to the study of behavioral change in adolescence. He proposed that improving people's sense of **self-efficacy** can result in a mastery of behavioral tasks. Thus, the cognitive process of *efficacy expectation* actually increases the likelihood that the desired behavioral outcome will occur.

The social mechanisms that facilitate the expectations of personal mastery include four major sources of influence. First, accomplishment or improvement of skills is conducive to behavioral change when an adolescent is exposed to performance opportunities, observes how others successfully perform the desirable behavior, or is provided with self-instruction experiences.

Second, vicarious experience, in which the adolescent has the opportunity to view live or symbolic models, provides an important source of information that enhances expectations of self-efficacy. Similarly, verbal persuasion, which includes suggestion, exhortation, and interpretation, facilitates efficacy expectations. Finally, stressful or taxing situations elicit emotional arousal, which can develop personal competency. Fear-provoking thoughts about perceived ineptitude can create states of high anxiety that may be diminished by seeing how others cope in similar situations, thereby removing dysfunctional fears.

Observational learning has powerful effects on children's and adolescents' acquisition of both social and antisocial behavior. In a classic statement of observational learning, Bandura (1969) delineated three primary effects of exposure to modeled behavior. (1) An adolescent can, when functioning as an observer, acquire new response patterns. (2) Observation of a model's behavior may strengthen *or* weaken inhibitory responses; that is, by watching the actions of another, an adolescent may confirm his or her intent not to act in a given way or may engage in a behavior that was previously inhibited or denied. (3) Viewing another's behavior may serve as the impetus to engage in the same action. Thus, **modeling** can produce novel responses by providing cues on new behavior, inhibit or disinhibit existing behavioral patterns, or facilitate previously learned behaviors.

In accordance with these three possibilities, the social interaction of adolescents in peer groups can stimulate new response patterns through observational learning. For example, one can observe certain stereotyped behaviors, such as similar verbal expressions or dancing style, in almost any adolescent peer group. Through watching one another, the peer group provides a setting for imitation learning of a variety of behaviors. Peer modeling influences can also inhibit or disinhibit behavioral patterns that have been relatively fixed in the structured home setting. However, new observational experiences can have either inhibiting or disinhibiting effects on morals, values, or social actions. It is possible that adolescent boys and girls who have been taught that sexual liberties are morally wrong outside marriage may relinquish this constraint following observation of promiscuous behavior among peers.

Robert Selman

Whereas Bandura's theoretical framework focuses on self-efficacy and expectations, Robert Selman (1976a, 1976b, 1980) examined the role of social **perspective taking** as it influences an adolescent's behavior. Further, he assumed that role-taking abilities mature in five stages of development. Each stage is assumed to be associated with its own unique form of role taking and corresponding social behavior.

Selman portrays the child at the first level (*Stage 0*) as egocentric and undifferentiated. This stage is thought to be most commonly between 3 and 7 years of age. Children at this stage can correctly recognize subjective states or emotions in themselves and others, but they frequently assume mistakenly that what is true for themselves is likewise true and of equal importance for others. With maturity they come to differentiate the subjective perspective-taking process (*Stage 1*). In this next stage they begin to realize that the perspective of others can be similar to or different from their own. Generally, this realization emerges sometime between the fifth and ninth year of life. With further maturity considerable advancement is observed in *Stage 2* (ages 6 to approximately 12), when children develop the cognitive capacity to contemplate their thoughts and feelings from another person's perspective. For example, when they harm another child, given the chance, they can now put themselves into another person's shoes and see how that person

Robert Selman has recognized the role of social perspective taking in the development of adolescents.

might view them unfavorably as an aggressor or bully. During early adolescence *Stage 3* (ages 9 to 15) youths begin to develop a mutual or reciprocal form of perspective taking. They start thinking about the way they themselves think, the way another person might be thinking about them, and so on. During the latter part of this stage, they can even assume a third-party view, putting themselves in the shoes of a disassociated person who might look at the perspectives shared by themselves and others. This third-party mutuality clearly broadens perspective-taking abilities and increased objectivity. At Selman's highest level, *Stage 4,* the individual moves to a deeper analysis, and a broader societal perspective emerges.

The implications of increasing complexity in perspective taking center on a movement from egocentrism to perspectivism. At the lower levels of development, behaviors are bound by a selfish focus on understanding oneself in regard to others. At the higher levels, understanding of self is based on the perspective of others. Greater capacity to learn through interaction with others is possible. Thus, greater consideration of the perspectives of others can be found in the behavior, intentions, and interactions of adolescents in social contexts. The self is no longer egocentric but is, rather, part of a mutual and reciprocal social system.

Summary

The social-cognitive perspective began with a strong focus on role modeling and the implications of (1) vicarious reinforcement through identification and (2) society's rewards for emulating role models. It evolved into including the mediating effects of drives or cognitive processes. Drive theory stresses the effects of increasing or decreasing drives as causal factors in learning. Self-efficacy theory focuses on the influence of expectations in producing behavior. More recent theory examines the association between the perspectives of self and others and identifies maturational stages to predict behavioral outcomes. (See Box 2–7 for generalizations from a social-cognitive perspective.)

The Psychoanalytic Perspective

Psychoanalytic theory has assumed an eminent position in the study of adolescence. This perspective was introduced to U.S. audiences in the early 1900s, when Sigmund Freud addressed the faculty at Clark University under the auspices of G. Stanley Hall, who, as we have noted, was one of the major figures to popularize the study of adolescence. Since that time, psychoanalytic theory has permeated North American philosophy, psychology, education, and literature.

Sigmund and Anna Freud

Psychoanalytic theory consists of the recognition of two powerful forces in direct opposition—inherent instinctual needs and the need to live in a social group (Maddi, 1968). According to this perspective, humans are individualistic (agency) and selfish, but still in need of social living (communion). Hence, Sigmund Freud thought, people are in constant conflict. On the one hand, they want to maximize their instinctual gratification; on the other, they must learn to do so in socially sanctioned ways to avoid punishment as social beings.

Box 2–7 Generalizations from a Social-Cognitive Perspective

Two practical generalizations from a social-cognitive perspective might be:

1. The degree to which you believe you can master or influence the world is associated with successful past experiences in getting things done. Behavioral techniques that include reinforcement for a job well done, rehearsal and encouragement, and observation of others' success are excellent tools to be used in changing adolescents' behavior. Indeed, helping youths develop an expectation that they can be suc-

cessful is one way of changing their behavior without ever directly reinforcing it.

2. Individual differences in perspective-taking ability can influence social behavior. Less mature, more self-centered youths will learn less from observations of others. Low role-taking skills will result in less ability to analyze one's performance from the perspective of others. Therefore, behavior can be improved by improving perspective-taking ability, which, in turn, increases the likelihood of useful self-criticism, self-analysis, and self-instruction.

Therefore, during childhood a personality mechanism evolves that is referred to as the *ego*. The ego is the executive of personality; it distributes and governs the involvement of psychic activities in the internal and external world. The ego's activities are involved with perceptions, discrimination, recognition, and experience relevant to the satisfaction of instinctual demands. The ego has the ability to test reality—that is, to manipulate actions in the external world to determine whether they are effective in reaching a goal. The ego's major function is to attempt to satisfy the demands of the *id* (instincts) from the external world while observing the dictates of the third component of personality, the *superego*.

The superego is the judge of all behavior. It is our internalized moral code. It develops through differentiation of part of the ego's function into an internal social-control structure. Through experience with their parents, children are

Sigmund and Anna Freud—father and daughter—have greatly influenced interpretation of behavior through psychoanalytic theory.

thought to assimilate what they perceive to be the parental standard of good and bad. Therefore, through the process of internalization they develop an inner authority that aids in controlling behavior. Technically, the superego consists of two main systems (C. S. Hall, 1954). The *ego-ideal* comprises children's perceptions of their parents' view of what is right and moral and wrong and immoral. These standards are internalized when parents model behavior and reward acceptable and desirable actions. The *conscience,* which is the antithesis of the ego-ideal, punishes behavior that is unacceptable by eliciting feelings of inferiority and guilt. Through socialization experiences with the parents, including punishment, disapproval, and reasoning, children gradually internalize rules and come to punish themselves for transgressions by experiencing guilt.

Through a gradual developmental process the structure of the child's personality differentiates the diffuse psychic energy of the instincts, or id. Due to the inability of the id to function in the external world, and in service of the id, the ego acquires limited energy from the instincts and ultimately comes to restructure some of that energy into the superego. This process is thought to provide the energy necessary to check the urges of the id and keep its selfishness in balance with the needs of society.

These developments lead to occasions when the child or adolescent experiences either a feeling of being overwhelmed with stimulation or a feeling of being threatened by anticipation of impending pain. These experiences initiate feelings of anxiety, which are expressed by the ego. According to Freud (1926), feelings of anxiety are experienced in three primary ways. *Reality anxiety* is the realistic fear of something dangerous in the external world. *Neurotic anxiety* is the fear that the instincts will gain control and cause the individual to engage in a punishable act. *Moral anxiety* is a perceived experience of threat from the conscience; that is, the individual feels conscience ridden. If the ego cannot cope with anxiety and feels overwhelmed, the personality will resort to primitive means of coping. The methods of coping with anxiety are referred to as *defense mechanisms.* Defense mechanisms can be thought of as means by which the personality deals with painful experiences, internal conflicts, personal inadequacies, and the associated anxiety.

During childhood a variety of infantile sexual impulses (instincts) evolve that heighten the defensive interchange between the ego and the id. During the so-called *oral stage,* the sexual instinct is satisfied through autoerotic stimulation of the mouth. The infant is assumed to have fantasies of "swallowing up" the mother, making her part of itself. This fantasy behavior is thought to be the precursor of a psychological process called *identification.* Through accepting and rejecting what is edible and inedible, the child learns defense mechanisms associated with introjection and denial.

During the toddler years there is thought to be a marked shift in the anatomical location of the sexual instinct from the mouth to the anus. As children experience both pleasurable and unpleasurable stimulation from the voiding and withholding of feces, they come to experience inevitable frustration or conflict with the parents during toilet training. Freud assumed that in this *anal stage* they enjoy the stimulation of expulsion, and he referred to it as an anal-sadistic expulsive period. He assumed that children might sadistically retain their feces as a hostile reaction toward their parents or eliminate as a sign of giving/loving. The primary defense mechanism emerging during this stage is *denial*. While during the oral stage children are thought to fantasize denial, during the anal stage they act out denial mechanisms.

In the next stage of life, there is a shift in sexual sensitivity to the genitalia. Using the classical legend of Oedipus, Freud maintained that in all children there emerges a hidden desire to possess the opposite-sexed parent. The boy desires his mother and wishes to remove his father, whose presence is a barrier to that possibility; the girl desires her father and wishes to have a child by him through displacement of her mother. It is perhaps the resolution of this *phallic stage* of life that is central to the psychoanalytic model when applied to the study of adolescence.

Originally, both boys and girls view their mother as the primary love object while feeling resentment toward their father, who is a rival for the mother's affection. The boy's desires are thought to bring him into strong conflict with his father. The child fears retaliation by the father in the form of physical damage to his genitals. Therefore, the boy represses his incestuous thoughts about his mother and his hostility toward his father because he fears for his well-being. This fear is referred to as *castration anxiety*. Thus, castration anxiety, together with subtle rejections by the mother, creates repression tendencies in the male child. Incestuous feelings for the mother are replaced by tender affection and concern, and through identification with his father the child vicariously satisfies some of his sexual desire for his mother.

For the female, resolution of the *Oedipus complex* (sometimes referred to as the *Electra complex*) is different. The female child must resolve her original instinctual urges for her mother and replace them with a new love object, the father. According to Freud, this occurs when the girl discovers that the obvious male genitalia are absent. Blaming her mother (unconsciously) for the fantasized castration, the girl displaces her love to the father, who still possesses the "valued" sex organ. *Penis envy*, therefore, compels the daughter toward identification, in a sexual way, with males. In essence, the female feels that she has lost something that the male is afraid to lose (C. S. Hall & Lindzey, 1967) and thrusts herself into sexual identification with a male through penis envy. Freud argued, however, that at the close of this stage the repression of the Oedipal fantasy is strong for males but is always weak for females. Therefore, as adolescents, females are thought to be more quickly threatened by fears of homosexual images, which might bring them back to an Oedipal stage.

Freud also thought that during late childhood and early adolescence there emerged a more tranquil period. During this so-called *latency* period the ego is thought to be freed from the earlier conflict between sexual instincts and social norms. Therefore, the latency period is a time when the child can consolidate gains in ego and superego development. Psychosexual activities dissipate, allowing new interests, activities, and achievements to develop. During this period most children extend themselves into social activities in the neighborhood, peer group, school, and community organizations. The early adolescent is thought to be capable of partial sublimation of instincts through socially acceptable channels. For example, aggressive urges can be comfortably channeled into competitive sports; sexual drives can be channeled into creative arts, music or drama. Adolescence, however, brings new and forceful implications in coping with sexual instincts.

Anna Freud (1958), Sigmund's daughter, refers to this period of life as one of internal disharmony. She maintains that with the onset of adolescence the intrapsychic equilibrium between instinctual demands and ego mechanisms is temporarily disrupted, resulting in a period of storm and stress. New and strong genital urges emerge during pubescence. The ego consolidation of the youth in latency is threatened by a new genital orientation that can also revive the pregenital urges that have been controlled through an ego defense called *repression*. Repression is a defense mechanism guarding against instinctual forces through hiding from one's consciousness certain unrecognized fantasies, wishes, or thoughts. The anxiety accompanying pregenital urges and Oedipal strivings renews the use of old defense mechanisms. Engaged in combat, the demanding id is constantly confronting the ego, therein creating the image of the adolescent as continuously undergoing vacillations in ego functioning. Overly sensitive to other's every word and action, the adolescent is thought to be coping with the establishment of defense mechanisms, which are viewed as legitimate and normal attempts at restoring intrapsychic peace.

According to Anna Freud, several major problems and appropriate defense mechanisms are characteristic of the period of adolescence. First, the ego attempts to displace the conflict associated with the reemergence of an Oedipal relationship with the parent. She argues that in a defensive attempt to mitigate the anxiety associated with the regressive urge to return to this early attachment to the parent, the adolescent withdraws love from the parent and extends feelings of love toward a parent substitute (*displacement*). This process often leads the adolescent to treat the parent with a callous indifference while expending much time and energy on the parent substitute. We have heard more than one parent say, in reaction, "If I hear one more word about this Mr. Jones, I'm going to explode!"

Another solution to this same problem is a defensive *reversal of affect*. When adolescents react with just the opposite affect experienced with the parent during childhood, they are responding with a defense mechanism called *reaction formation*. This negative reaction toward the displacement of love from a parent to a significant other does not diminish the regressive urges characteristic of adolescence. Rather, it further heightens the anxiety accompanying this urge and increases defensive behaviors of denial, uncooperativeness, and hostility. Still other adolescents resolve this same issue by withdrawing into themselves. Unfortunately, doing so merely inflates the ego process. The resolution gives rise to increased narcissism (self-love) and the corresponding fantasies of omnipotence (all-powerfulness). Sometimes this overattachment to the self can lead to increased attentions to body sensations and feelings of *hypochondriasis* (perceived body illness).

The last reaction to pregenital urges associated with infantile sexual instincts focuses on the pathological defense mechanism known as *regression*. Through regressive behavior the adolescent returns to earlier coping mechanisms where the internalization of the *primary identification figure* (parent) is capable of reducing anxiety. The adolescent incorporates and acts out the perceived qualities of the parent that soothed the early infantile sexual needs.

Anna Freud argues that another major problem associated with adolescents occurs when the ego fails to defend against the regressive urge to return to infantile sexual impulses. Should the ego, when driven by overwhelming id demands, lose control and fail to discriminate between vital and purely pleasurable sensations, psychotic reactions emerge. Often the adolescent, in a paralyzing attempt to maintain a feeling of control, will turn to *ascetic* psychological functions. Due to the inability to maintain a balance between ego and id functions, the adolescent will deny himself or herself experiential sensations of pleasure and joy, feelings of hostility and sexual pleasure, and even food, water, or sleep. Yet another psychological outcome of this same dilemma is described by Anna Freud as the *uncompromising adolescent.* Instead of resolving the breakdown between the id demands and the ego functions through ascetic behavior, the adolescent refuses to blend and integrate opposites—that is, to develop ego mechanisms that diminish id tension. Rather, the mind is kept separate from the feelings of the body, and reality never intermingles with fantasy. It would appear that this reaction happens in very impulsive or righteous youths who are either overindulging in id sensations or guarding against them through rigid adherence to moral behavior.

The early work of Sigmund and Anna Freud is recognized to this day. Their efforts remain a famous example of a theory that has attempted to explain both normal adolescent development and the deviance and pathology that can emerge when a weak personality has been formulated during childhood. Although it has been argued that much of the psychoanalytic perspective is empirically unsupportable (Maddi, 1968), it is still much used in clinical approaches to adolescent problems.

Peter Blos

With a richness provided by extensive psychoanalytic training and experience in working with disturbed youth, Peter Blos (1962) has offered the most influential, in-depth, contemporary discussion of the substages of adolescent development. Blos partitions adolescent development into four segments: preadolescence, early adolescence, adolescence proper, and late adolescence. As Sigmund Freud did, Blos views the period of latency as providing the necessary consolidation of ego functions to extend activities beyond the family. This maturation of ego functioning decidedly prepares the child for handling the increased instinctual-drive levels encountered at puberty, while *sublimation* capacities developed during the latency period enable the child to channel incremental instinctual energy into socially approved psychosocial activities.

Reflecting much of what Sigmund and Anna Freud maintained, Blos proposes that the preadolescent period marks an apparent turnabout in instinctual control. Physical maturation related to the onset of pubescence leads to increases in instinctual sexual drives, and control markedly diminishes. Ego functioning defensively regresses to pregenital and infantile levels, and early displacement of aggressive and sexual drives to family figures is temporarily lost. Almost any fantasy, thought, or movement is potentially erotic. Youths become easily distracted and quickly stimulated, and they maintain high erotic sensitivity. A sweep of an arm across the preadolescent's shoulder can stimulate an erotic fantasy or lead to an instant penile erection. This supersensitivity to erotic stimulation, coupled with disintegrating ego controls, occasionally makes it difficult to teach or even reach the preadolescent.

As one would expect, instinctual gratification can bring the preadolescent into conflict with superego directives and codes. This normal conflict increases the experience of anxiety, which the ego attempts to control through such defensive solutions as repression, reaction formation, and displacement. To circumvent the superego/id conflict, the ego develops a new mechanism that Blos argues is characteristic of the preadolescent period. To avoid the discomfort of anxiety associated with a highly erotic body, the ego learns to *socialize* guilt experiences. The preadolescent will develop a way to project guilt feelings on group members, individuals, or abstract collectives. In this manner the preadolescent can reduce anxiety by minimizing psychic responsibility through projection of shared guilt feelings.

The central conflict of the preadolescent period revolves around the establishment of a genital orientation. Increasing sexual drives are accompanied by resurgent feelings about pregenital fantasies associated with early maternal relationships. Responding to this regressive pull toward infantile (Oedipal) relationships, the male preadolescent is thought to enter the "chum" stage of exclusive affiliation with male groups. Similarly, strong regressive urges pull the preadolescent female toward her mother. In reaction to the "homosexual" threat to femininity, the female thrusts herself into heterosexuality to ward off pregenital instinctual drives.

Early adolescence can be viewed as an exciting period of interpersonal blossoming. As the incestuous urges are once again repressed, there is a release of formerly unavailable sexual energy for forming new love attachments. However, through this releasing process the superego is temporarily weakened. With the diminished effects of the superego codes that govern conduct, the young adolescent may experience problems in self-control. To restore a sense of internal order, the adolescent may desperately search for a new attachment to escape the confusion, loneliness, and isolation that result from the diminishing emphasis on the incestuous love attachment to the parent.

It is not surprising that in dealing with this confusion the adolescent turns to "the friend." Blos contends that friendship established at this stage of life is not the same as the preadolescent "companion-in-adventure" or "secret-sharing" partnership. Rather, this new interest in a friend is a narcissistic desire to admire and love another person who possesses some quality that the child can vicariously attain through friendship. However, differential sex effects surround the consummation of friendship. The boy appears relatively sure of his masculinity, but the girl intensely questions her sexual orientation, and sexual ambiguity plagues her thoughts. In our earlier overview of the Oedipus complex, we note that the female does not repress the phallic conflict as firmly as the male. Therefore, the bisexual tendency of this period represents an intermediate stage between phallic fantasies and heterosexual genital orientation for girls. The girl, still unsure of her sexual orientation, oscillates between masculinity and femininity and may overcompensate for or deny the existence of any feminine characteristics.

This gradual turn to heterosexuality marks the advent of what Blos calls adolescence proper. In some ways, adolescence proper is the most confusing period of adolescence. As narcissistic, primitive self-gratification is slowly replaced by attachments to significant others, the ego attempts to deal with the integration of these new attachments with an accompanying instinctual-drive reduction. In the process of testing these new alternatives, the ego appears to alternate between active and passive functions. This alternation results in behaviors commonly called *adolescent*. The adolescent may fluctuate between sensitivity and coarseness, gregariousness and solitude, optimism and pessimism, idealism and materialism, or indulgence and asceticism.

A dominant theme exists during adolescence proper. As early Oedipal fantasies are repressed, freeing new energy for heterosexual attachments, a brief state of *mourning* occurs due to the experienced state of emptiness and isolation that follows the renunciation of the Oedipal striving. Also, the adolescent, now experiencing a new awareness of needing to belong, feels for the first time a sense of tenderness and a feeling of sentimentality. But this tender affect can develop only after the adolescent has relinquished narcissistic drives and shifts sexual energy to heterosexual involvements.

According to Blos, late adolescence maintains a strong similarity to the latency period and is to be considered a time of psychic consolidation. During this period the adolescent assumes primary genital striving in a relatively irreversible direction. The adolescent's *character formation* consolidates, and personality characteristics stabilize to form a constancy of ego choices and preferences.

Summary

The psychoanalytic tradition in the study of adolescence has been strong and influential. Its focus has led to considerable study of intrapsychic development during childhood and adolescence. Unfortunately, this perspective leads one to conclude that personality growth ends during adolescence, so that adult behavior is predictable. Adult-development research has shown that adolescence is but one of many transition stages in the life course. Nonetheless, students of adolescent development who fail to appreciate the details of psychoanalytic theory would have a large gap in their training for work within the field of adolescent psychology or development. (See Box 2–8.)

The emerging perspective of developmental contextualism.   Recent calls for prioritization of research objectives on adolescent development (for example, Zaslow & Takanishi, 1993), a multitude of editorial statements (in such periodicals as *Journal of Adolescence, Journal of Adolescent Research, Journal of Early Adolescence, Journal of Youth and Adolescence, Journal of Research on Adolescence, Journal of Adolescent Health, Youth & Society*), and annual review series (*Advances in Adolescent Development*) are recognizing the need to

Box 2–8   Generalizations from a Psychoanalytic Perspective

We suggest the following two generalizations:

1. Adolescents struggle with inherent needs that often conflict with the demands of society. Their psychological functioning and the resulting behavior reflect how they are coping with these internal needs and with external social forces. When the two are incompatible, stressful behaviors are common. When the two are compatible, the adolescent is generally less anxious, more adaptable, and more even in mood and behavior.

2. The character and behavior of an adolescent reflect inner resolution of emotional turmoil. The broader the failure to resolve early childhood stages in psychosocial or psychosexual development, the greater the likelihood of wider and deeper emotional problems during adolescence and young adulthood.

Can you develop other generalizations? How might you practically apply these and all former generalizations to working with normal adolescents? disturbed adolescents? early, middle, or late adolescents?

---

examine the developing adolescent within a broader bio/psycho/socio/historical context. Even though it is described by several labels, we believe this emerging perspective is best called developmental contextualism. The complexity of this perspective demands an interdisciplinary research agenda, and thus this text takes an interdisciplinary or cross-disciplinary approach to adolescence.

One discussion of the emerging paradigm and its multiple complexities has been presented by Jessor (1993). His research, which is part of an extensive research network in the United States, considers the transformation of adolescent development from preadolescence through adolescence and into young adulthood in the larger context of the social, economic, political, and cultural environment. This perspective views adolescent behavior and development in the interacting contexts of family, school, and peers as part of the larger social structure. To understand adolescent behavior comprehensively, Jessor argues we must recognize and understand the risk and protective factors of at least five types of variables: biology/genetics, social environment, perceived environment, personality, and behavior.

Biology/genetic risk factors may include family history of mental illness, alcoholism, or genetic-determined disease. Protective factors may include high family intelligence, rate of maturation, or physical body features. *Social environment* risk factors may include poverty or racial inequality, with protective factors coming from high quality schooling or cohesive family relationships. *Perceived environment* risk factors include such things as modeling of social deviance with protective factors reflected in high controls against deviance. *Personality* characteristics that may create risk could include low self-efficacy or low expectation for success with protective functions coming from values on achievement or intolerance of deviance. *Behavior* enhancing risk include problem behaviors (for example, drinking, failure to study, drugs) with protective factors including conventional behavior (for example, church attendance, involvement in school).

In the remainder of this text we consider many contextual factors—including ethnicity, poverty, and gender—and discuss both risk and protective functions in each of these five domains. In particular, regarding ethnic/minority issues we identify many protective features of the family and community that facilitate positive growth and development for minority youths.

Major Points to Remember

This chapter demonstrates the complexity of understanding adolescent behavior and development. Many theoretical perspectives describe and explain the nature of adolescence. We grouped these perspectives loosely as follows:

1. *Biosocial perspectives* typically focus on the interaction between the adolescent's physical growth and development and the social behavior that surrounds such development. G. Stanly Hall and Roger Barker are two theorists writing from a biosocial perspective.
2. *Interpersonal-relations perspectives* are modern derivations of the biosocial perspective. The focal point of interest, however, is adolescents' emerging interests in heterosexual and social relationships. The social psychologists George Levinger, Ellen Bersheid, and Elaine Hatfield are representatives of this perspective.
3. The *sociocultural perspective* is supported by sociologists and anthropologists. Focal points of concern include cultural norms, mores, expectations, and rituals. Frequently, comparisons are made between cultures or subcultures to demonstrate differences and similarities between adolescents from different social groups. Kingsley Davis, Margaret Mead and Ruth Benedict were early representatives of this classic line of theorizing.
4. The *psychosocial perspective* examines the interface between psychological adjustment and social context. It focuses on issues of crisis and stress in the resolution of turning points in development. In contrast to the sociocultural perspective, which commonly looks at cultural relativity or the uniqueness of cultural influences, the psychosocial perspective more commonly looks for universal similarities among cultures. Erik Erikson is the most noted theorist espousing this perspective.
5. The relatively newer theorizing from the *social-cognitive perspective* is less comprehensive than many other theories. Instead, it focuses on the interface between cognitive and social processes and how they can be used to understand adolescent behavior. This perspective has been proposed by a number of loosely related theorists, each of whom identifies important inner psychological states or stages and related social processes. Contemporary theorists include Albert Bandura and Robert Selman.
6. Finally, the *psychoanalytic perspective* focuses on psychosexual and emotional stages of growth and the corresponding emergence of defense mechanisms and other intrapsychic behavior. This perspective is best recognized in the writings of Sigmund Freud, Anna Freud, and Peter Blos.

PART TWO

Influences on Adolescent Development

3

Adolescent Family Relations

Most young people are blessed with warm, understanding, nurturing mothers and fathers. Looking back now at our adolescent years, we find it hard to understand why we were so reluctant for our friends to see us with our families. We wonder why we (outfitted in ragged, twice-patched jeans) felt self-conscious when we were caught by our friends in family activities. It is surprising that our families managed, most of the time, to display such superhuman patience.

Despite gloom-and-doom writings suggesting the demise of the family in the United States, most U.S. families report satisfaction with family life and family members (National Commission on Children, 1991). We believe that the family is "here to stay" to steal a phrase from Mary Jo Bane (1976). Although the form may change, the basic functions the family performs will continue indefinitely. Research evidence suggests that these functions can be carried out by widely varying family structures and that there is no single ideal family form in contemporary society (Gullotta, Adams, & Alexander, 1986).

In the first part of this chapter, we identify those family functions that enhance adolescent development and psychosocial well-being. Later we examine how social scientists have typologized the ways in which families facilitate or retard the behavioral growth of adolescents. To do adequate justice to this topic would require an entire book. Therefore, we urge you to view this chapter as you would an impressionist painting that conveys the mood, richness, and feeling of the subject matter but not the fine, intricate detail that a Renaissance painting would.

Age Differences and Family Interaction

If one is to believe Hollywood scriptwriters, the age of adolescence is marked by a high degree of intrafamilial conflict. These disputes are aggravated by age differences such that the so-called generation gap might best be described as the generation Grand Canyon. But, other than in television soaps and teenage-rebellion movies, there is little empirical evidence to support a belief that a major generation gap exists between parents and young people (Lerner, 1993). For example, two recent studies examining family life found young people to be generally satisfied with the quality of family life and in strong agreement with their parents on a number of issues. The first study by the National Commission on Children (1991) surveyed 1700 households with children between the ages of 10 and 17. When asked who cares about them, 94% of the youth felt their mother cared for them; 82% felt their father cared for them; 43% felt their grandparents cared for them; 33% felt a teacher cared for them; and 15% felt a minister, priest, or rabbi cared for them. To the question, Do you have an "excellent" relationship with your children?, 78% of intact families with "happy" marriages said yes. Fifty-four percent of intact families with "unhappy" marriages said yes. Stepfamilies in "happy" marriages said yes 54% of the time. This decreased to 33% if the remarriage was "unhappy." Sixty-four percent of the one-parent households responded yes.

In the second study the overwhelming majority of high school seniors in 1990 indicated agreement with their parents on topics such as what to do with your life (71%), how to dress (62%), the value of an education (86%), roles for women (71%), racial issues (64%), and religion (69%). In this study the greatest disagreement occurred with the topics of how to spend money (59% disagreed), dating behaviors (53% disagreed), and, interestingly, politics (52% disagreed). Of particular interest is the fact that these reported agreement/disagreement levels have remained virtually unchanged since 1975 (Institute for Social Research, 1992). This study and others like it (Jacobsen, Berry, & Olsen, 1975) tend to confirm the notion that family values and beliefs are carried over from childhood into adolescence and adulthood. Or, as one bit of folk wisdom goes, "You grow up to be what your parents are."

Other evidence further confirms this last point. In a telephone study, 31 male and 33 female tenth-graders were questioned on three random occasions to determine the level of conflict between parent and child. Of 192 contacts, 68 were marked by parent/child conflict (Montemayor, 1981). Although one argument occurred every three days, this level of disagreement does not by any standards paint a picture of high intrafamilial conflict.

Understandably, as the quality of family life deteriorates the conflict between adolescents and their parents increases (Whittaker & Bry, 1991). Interestingly, most disagreement between adolescents and their parents are not resolved. Studies suggest that fewer than 20% reach a compromise or negotiated settlement. The most common approach to not solving a problem is to let the issue fade away. Problem solving decreases as adolescents grow older and if they are males (Smetana, Yau, & Hanson, 1991).

Finally, Montemayor and Hanson (1985) questioned the commonly held belief that arguments between adolescents and their parents most often involve independence issues. Their study of 64 young people and their families suggests that it is interpersonal issues rather than independence issues that cause disagreements.

Now that we have cast aside the old notion that parents and their adolescent offspring are constantly at each other's throats, let us look at the evidence on their frequency of interaction. Urie Bronfenbrenner (1970, 1974) has long argued that parents are increasingly spending less time with their offspring, thus permitting other forces to come to bear in influencing children's development. In particular, Bronfenbrenner argues that the peer group has come to replace the family as a prime influence in adolescence.

For example, one group of researchers reported that part-time work decreased the time adolescents spent with their families but had no effect on the time spent with peers (Greenberger, Steinberg, Vaux, & McAuliffe, 1980). In another study, observational data drawn from parks, fast-food outlets, schools, and the like showed that adolescents spent most of their time with friends, not parents. There were, however, some interesting gender variations. For instance, from age 13 to age 16, sons interacted with parents more than daughters did. Between the ages of 16 and 19, daughters outdistanced sons in time spent with parents (Montemayor & Van Komen, 1980). We can conclude from this last study that both sexes are highly peer oriented (a finding supported by other researchers—for example, Berndt, 1979; Young & Ferguson, 1979) and that males and females at different times in adolescence are influenced to a different extent by their parents.

Data from the National Commission on Children (1991) further underscore these observations. Eighty-one percent of the parents interviewed did not feel they spent enough time with their children. When queried about their involvement with their 14 to 17 year old children, 34% had played a game with their adolescent in the past week; 75% had spoken with the adolescent's teacher in the last year; 64% had attended a PTA meeting; 43% had helped with homework; 49% had gone on a class trip; and 40% were involved with a youth group. Compared to other age groups, youth over the age of 14 received less time from their parents than did younger youth. When young people were asked with what frequency did their parents miss important events 58% of mothers and 43% of fathers almost never missed an event.

Given that young men and young women interact differently with their parents, what is the nature of that interaction? Youniss and Smoller (1985) observed that the adolescents in their study, while pursuing independence from their family, nevertheless sought the family's continued emotional support and guidance. Another particularly interesting finding involved adolescents' views of their parents. It appeared that parents played very well-designed roles. Fathers were viewed routinely as the enforcer of family and societal values. Mothers were seen as supportive and as using reason rather than discipline. Although fathers were described by young people in this study as trying to be helpful, they were perceived, especially by daughters, as distant and impersonal. This confirms the finding that adolescents more often seek advice from their mothers than their fathers (Greene & Grimsley, 1990).

Some Basic Family Functions

Our understanding of young people and the research literature leads us to believe that the generation gap is no more than a hairline crack. Certainly, there is disagreement but not rampant conflict between young and old. Unquestionably, the peer group is a very powerful influence, but one should not quickly dismiss the influence of home life on the adolescent. Adolescents may not want their families on stage as they parade with their peers, but most want and need their parents in the wings to support their first attempts at adult roles.

Although the frequency of interaction with parents may be relatively low during adolescence proper, we believe that parental influence remains high. Indeed, the early theoretical work of Ausubel and Sullivan (1970) suggests that the parents, in their benevolent love for their offspring, actually encourage movement away from over involvement and toward a peer orientation. In the early years of a child's life, an infantile ego or personality structure leads to dependence. This dependency on parental approval creates a highly manageable and obedient child, but one who is overly identified with the parent. However, as the child is allowed to experience other sources of gratification (such as peers), the child comes to recognize that the parent is incapable of being all things at all times. Thus, peer interaction allows the youth to develop a sense of volitional independence. In this way the power of the peer group to provide other sources of information and gratification reduces the exclusive association of power with parental figures.

An approach for understanding adolescent development and behavior in respect to context is offered in systems theory of the family. Sources of analysis in family systems theory include *boundaries, elements,* and the *relationships* between the units. Family members are regarded as interrelated elements that have enduring relationships with one another. Boundaries have external and internal aspects and serve to distinguish various types of relationships (Leigh, 1986). For example, an external boundary is demarcated according to who is part of a particular family and who is not (Lamanna & Riedmann, 1991). For example, the house a family lives in is a physical illustration of an external boundary. An internal boundary defines subgroups and coalitions within the family. For example, it is not uncommon for siblings to form coalitions and for parents to hold a boundary between their generation and the children's. Hierarchies are implicit in boundaries with the parents' generation (especially with two-parent families) holding the most power (Leigh, 1986). Boundaries define and demarcate the parameters of the family, clarify role expectations and role performance, and contribute to the stability of relationships between family members.

Given the interconnectedness of family members, family members in the system are highly susceptible to causality and the associated effects. That is, when one family member experiences an event, all family members are affected, even if the event occurred outside of the family boundary. For example, in the case of an adolescent who is performing poorly in school, the family is likely informed of these problems. Parents are likely to monitor the adolescent's school performance. As the adolescent's and parents' behaviors adapt to this situation, siblings are indirectly affected. Minimally, siblings observe changes in the relationship between their parents and the adolescent, and the siblings' behavior might change because of these observations. Even with the inevitability of change due to the cause-and-effect dynamics of social relationships, families are oriented toward equilibrium and will, through feedback, regulate themselves and maintain stability and balance (Lamanna & Riedmann, 1991).

A good illustration of systems theory of the family is David Olson's circumplex model. According to scores on continuums of cohesion and adaptability, families can be classified into one of 16 potential family systems. Cohesion and adaptability, along with communication are regarded as three basic functions that the family provides before, during, and after adolescence that are never fully replaced by the peer group or any other social structure over the course of a lifetime (Olson, Russell, & Sprenkle, 1980). First, the family provides a sense of *cohesion.* This cohesion, or emotional bonding, creates the conditions for identification with a basic primary group and enhances emotional, intellectual, and physical closeness. Second, the family provides a model of *adaptability;* that is, it illustrates through its basic functioning how a power structure can change, how role relationships can develop, and how relationship rules can be formed. Adolescents who experience rigid (low-adaptability) family types are likely to internalize a rigid interaction style. On the other hand, too much adaptability may create a chaotic style. Thus, a reasonable balance seems appropriate for this function. A similar conclusion might be drawn on cohesion. Too much cohesion is likely to enmesh the adolescent in his or her family, while not enough creates a sense of disengagement or lack of caring by family members. Finally, the family

---

Box 3–1   The Mexican-American Family: A New Perspective

The majority culture in the United States for over half a century has portrayed the Mexican-American family to be authoritarian, male dominated, inarticulate, anti-intellectual, and violent (Carroll, 1980). This same stereotype has portrayed the Mexican-American adolescent as a school failure and as a substance-abusing, gang-involved youth (Mirandé, 1977).

In recent years this view has been called into question as Mexican-American researchers have examined their own culture's behavior. In Leigh and Peterson's (1986) outstanding work on adolescents and families,

Mirandé (1986) writes that instead of seeing poor school behavior, this new group of revisionist scholars finds Mexican-American students placing cooperation among young people above the competition between students that most schools stress. Rather than seeing a flawed family structure, the revisionists observe a structure that has survived the incredible destructive forces of prejudice and discrimination. Consider these assertions, and discuss the pressures that minority adolescents face when living in a majority culture.

---

provides a network of *communication* experiences through which the individual learns the arts of speech, interaction, listening, and negotiation. (See Box 3–1.)

We can think of no other social group that allows the adolescent to experience and experiment with feelings, interaction styles, or communication skills so freely. Adolescents with too much or too little experience in each of the three basic family functions are likely to be placed at risk in their intellectual or social development. When these at-risk youths seek assistance, the helper must try to build what the family has not accomplished. The basic assumption behind our argument is that a middle ground exists on emotional identification with the family, adaptability, and communication needs. Too much may be as damaging for adolescent development as too little. We can examine this argument further by reviewing a classic line of research that has focused on at least two of the three basic family functions.

Parental Discipline Styles

In an early review of the consequence of different parenting styles for children's development, Wesley Becker (1964) summarizes a "gross anatomy" of parental behavior. Using a model from the earlier work of Earl Schaefer (1959), Becker conceptualizes the behavioral correlates of two basic functions of the family. Elements of cohesion are defined in terms of a love/hostility continuum, while adaptability is reflected on a control/autonomy continuum. As outlined in Figure 3–1 the four extreme types of parental behavior, in relation to one another, result in specific styles of discipline. A warm but controlling parent who restricts the behavior of the child will be either overprotective or indulgent in parenting style. Conversely, a cold or unemotional parent who controls the child through restrictive

Figure 3–1 A conceptual relationship between dimensions of cohesion and adaptability in parenting styles.

	Warm and loving	Hostile and cold
Controlling and restrictive	Overprotective or indulgent	Dictatorial and antagonistic
Permissive and understanding	Democratic and cooperative	Indifferent and detached

Parenting styles can range from overindulgence, to cooperative, through controlling and dictatorial, to indifferent and detached.

parenting will be dictatorial and antagonistic. Should a parent be undemanding and permissive with the child but highly nurturing, the parenting style will be democratic and cooperative. Finally, if a parent is cold or hostile and also permissive, the parenting style will be one of indifference and detachment from the child.

Becker (1964) concludes that specific behavioral and personality traits are likely to be developed from these four parenting styles. He reports research data suggesting that in a warm and controlling family environment a child is likely to become a polite, neat, dependent adolescent. In contrast, in a hostile but controlling environment a child is likely to become withdrawn, neurotic, and quarrelsome. A warm and permissive family environment is thought to create an active, highly social person who is independent. A hostile and permissive environment is associated with a noncompliant and highly aggressive adolescent.

The implications of the basic functions of the family should be evident from this research. Cohesion and adaptability mechanisms provide interpersonal structure to the family and communicate several basic messages that are internalized by the adolescent and manifested in behavior and personality. Let us now examine some additional examples of how the family can either facilitate or retard positive development for adolescents. Then we shall briefly examine some of the implications of this research for intervention with adolescents.

Some Examples of Family Influences

The influence of the family on adolescent development and behavior has been studied by sociologists, psychologists, educators, psychiatrists, nurses, developmentalists, and other social-science professionals. The effects on adolescents of family identification, family structure, parenting styles, maternal and paternal personality characteristics, and a host of other family-related variables have been explored. Some examples of such research are included here to provide an introduction to the massive body of research data important for working with adolescents.

Closeness to the Family and Parental Identification

Family sociologists have repeatedly documented that while adolescents and their parents may not maintain a straightforward, one-to-one agreement on social issues, there is a strong agreement on degree of closeness of family members (for example, see Jessop, 1981). Adolescents and parents alike view themselves as being very close to their family members. Indeed, crosscultural research comparing adolescents' perceptions of the family indicate that while in other societies (such as Israel) youths view society as a direct extension of the family, American youths view the family as an institution unto itself (T. Becker, 1976). Indeed, American youths view the family as the only institution of society deserving of absolute trust, loyalty, and obligation. There can be no doubt that an important aspect of life for adolescents is identification with the family.

Although much of the early research on parental identification focused on a sex-role hypothesis that adolescents would primarily identify with the parent who provided the more appropriate sex-role model, Gerald McDonald (1977, 1980) has demonstrated that regardless of the sex of the adolescent or parent, parental identification is more closely associated with the perceived degree of power held by the mother or father. In other words, the parent who is perceived to have more control of resources in that family will have more influence over the offspring's behavior through imitation or modeling processes. This finding clearly suggests that our understanding of family influences on adolescent behavior hinges, in part, on our understanding of which parent in the family is seen by the adolescent as having more social power.

Parental Influences on Personality Development

In our earlier review of Becker's (1964) work, we demonstrated that parental discipline styles can have a reasonably strong influence on the social and behavioral development of children and adolescents. The importance of paternal and maternal support for personality development needs to be underscored. For example, parental support has been found to be one of the strongest familiar predictors of the development of the belief that an individual has direct and significant control over his or her own destiny (internal locus of control) (Scheck, Emerick, & El-Assal, 1973). Similarly, the ability to understand another's perspective during adolescence is associated with being reared in a home where the parents share support and affection (G. R. Adams, Jones, Schvaneveldt, & Jenson, 1982). Thus, the family function of cohesion and bonding sets the foundation for positive personality and social-behavior development in adolescents.

Earlier in this text we explored the meaning of identity and developmental trends in identity formation. As one might suspect, the family has meaningful effects on identity development, too. For example, according to a study on the effects of autocratic, democratic, and permissive parental styles on identity formation, in an autocratic home adolescents cannot express their own views, nor are they allowed to take initiative in self-regulation. In contrast, a democratic home encourages participation in finding solutions to family issues, although the ultimate decision are still made by the parents. In a permissive home the adolescent has nearly an equal say in decision making. In this study only a father's democratic style had a positive influence on identity-achievement formation for male and female adolescents (Enright, Lapsley, Drivas, & Fehr, 1980). Interestingly, little attention has been given until recently to the influence that fathers have on their children, but this study and others like it clearly show that the father's parenting style strongly influences identity formation. Further, these studies suggest that a warm and loving father who is interested in hearing the perspective of his offspring, but maintains the right to make final decisions, facilitates identity formation (G. R. Adams, Dyk, & Benmon, 1987).

Several investigations have demonstrated an important relationship between parenting style and adolescent ego development. Adolescents with high ego development have been found to come from families described as more flexible (adaptability), trusting (cohesion), and closer than the families of adolescents with lower ego development. As one might expect, the families of adolescents with higher ego development are also more supportive of greater autonomy and individual responsibility (L. G. Bell & Ericksen, 1976). Finally, higher ego functioning by parents is associated with their giving more interpersonal support to their children (Peterson & Hey, 1976).

Parenting and Antinormative Adolescent Behaviors

In a succinctly worded article, Diana Baumrind (1978) states that one of the major functions of the family is to encourage a sense of social competence in offspring. By *social competence.* Baumrind means an adolescent's ability to delay gratification without the absolute denial of sensual pleasure, taking the perspective of another without denying self-realization, and obeying reasonable laws while confronting injustice or unreasonableness in a law or statute. Failure to develop a sense of social competence is a major determinant of adolescent alienation. Thus, it is the very basic functioning of the family that lays the foundation for such *antinormative* behavioral consequences for adolescents.

Baumrind's (1978) research suggests that an authoritarian discipline style combining supportive parenting with rational and firm control that recognizes children's individual interests is most conducive to shaping social competence. In contrast, and authoritarian parenting style that treats children as subordinates and fails to encourage them to express their own opinions may be least conducive to social-competence development. Several investigations exploring antinormative behaviors during adolescence support Baumrinds's conclusion. Overcontrol and restrictive interactions between parent and child have been associated with suicide (Kerfoot, 1980), drug abuse (Gantman, 1978), and male aggression (Bandura, 1960). Collectively, these studies show that families can provide a foundation for normative social development or set the stage for antinormative behavioral patterns in both male and female adolescents.

Families and Minority Adolescents

Social Support Among Ethnic and Racial Minority Families

McGowan and Kohn (1990) define social support as emotional, informational, material, and/or instrumental help that is provided to others to assist with daily living and to buffer environmental and personal stress. Many minority groups place a strong emphasis on the role of the **extended family** as a source of social support for children and adolescents. In many cases, parenting is nor regarded as the sole task of mothers and fathers; rather, parental responsibilities are distributed throughout the kin (family) network. In many minority households there are a number of parental figures to whom adolescents can appeal for emotional and physical support and guidance. Enhanced feelings of security and belongingness are likely outcomes when adolescents are reared in expansive, broadly shared parenting systems.

The social support networks of many North American ethnic and racial minority groups are characterized by such shared parenting responsibilities. In some American Indian tribes the extended parental network is evidenced through the extension of the label "mother" to one's mothers' sisters. The term "father" is broadened to include one's fathers' brothers (Burgess, 1980). In general, American Indian children are considered important extensions of the family, and their needs are integrated into the whole of family life (Burgess, 1980). Many American Indian tribes exhibit a collective interdependence that is illustrated in the Lakota Sioux term *tiospaye*. In the *tiospaye,* individual needs and responsibilities are issues of the extended family. For example, LaFromboise and Low (1989) note that when problems are experienced by American Indian adolescents, the community and extended kin network strive to restore the adolescent's connections within the group.

Taylor (1986) has also found a variety of factors among African-American families indicative of social support—for example, frequent family contact with extended family members, proximity of relatives, and a high degree of family affection. In Taylor's investigation (1986), in contrast to individuals in older age groups, adolescents and young adults, 18 to 25 years of age, reported receiving the most support from family members. Furthermore, never-married family members reported receiving the most support in contrast to family members in other marital-status categories.

Additional evidence of support can be found among African-American families. For example, Berg-Cross, Kidd, and Carr (1990) have found among mothers, fathers, and their 14- to 16-year-old adolescents, that with higher stress levels, disclosures and cohesion between family members increased. It is unknown if this phenomenon is found across other ethnic families.

It also is important to note that when families are isolated from their ethnic communities, support diminishes. Huang and Ying (1989) indicate that in traditional Chinese culture, the extended family is the primary family unit. Strong emphasis is placed on adoption of expected family roles with corresponding meeting of obligations and responsibilities. With migration to North America, many family relationships are disrupted. Some families have sought to reconstruct their extended kin network, while others have attempted to disentangle from traditional roles and responsibilities. Thus, for more Westernized Asian families, social support is diminished.

Social support is of particular importance when intervening with troubled minority youth. For example, Gibbs (1990) notes that extended families and fictive (socially adopted) kin among Black families can be a resource in working with troubled youth. Oyemade and Washington (1990) summarize findings that juvenile delinquents are significantly less involved with their extended families than with other groups. Chavey and Roney (1990), in citing from the work of Buriel, note that "integration with indigenous Mexican culture promotes good mental health behavior" (Chavey & Roney, 1990, p. 74). Rodriguez and Zayas (1990) regard the solidarity of Hispanic families as a means of preventing adolescent antisocial behavior. In particular, values of obedience and respect toward parents and the risk of bringing shame and dishonor to the family may inhibit delinquent activities among some Hispanic adolescents. In the prevention of substance abuse among American Indian adolescents, Edwards and Egbert-Edwards (1990) argue for coordinated community involvement that involves tribal leaders and elders. We conclude from such observations that any prevention or treatment program should involve as many family members as possible (including clan members).

Socialization of Collectivist and Communal Ideals

Another aspect of the strong social support networks found in many ethnic minority families is that often minority adolescents are socialized more along the lines of collectivist as opposed to individualist values. Rotheram and Phinney (1986) note that the dimension of group versus individual orientation is one of the most widely investigated behavioral dimensions in minority studies. In particular, Japanese, Hawaiian, and Mexican cultures are examples of groups that emphasize affiliation, cooperation, and interpersonal relationships. North American and many Western European cultures are more representative of the individualistic orientation.

In general, evidence exists that traditional values of Asian-American (especially Japanese and Chinese) cultures value a group orientation. Nagata (1989) states that traditional Japanese values for in-group unity, group consensus, and the discouragement of individuality have contributed to characteristics of present-day Japanese-American families. Feldman and Quatman (1988) found that Asian American parents' expectations concerning when their adolescents will engage in more autonomous behavior occurs later than Euro-American parents' expectations.

Evidence for socialization toward collectivism is evident among African-American families as well. Socialization of minority children toward greater collectivism, as opposed to individualism, is reflected in disciplinary styles. Portes, Dunham, and Williams (1986) have found that Black mothers' disciplinary practices among young adolescents are more strict than those used by White mothers. These investigators argue that experience in a society that has been historically oppressive and prejudice toward this minority group results in Black families' placing greater emphasis on behaving correctly, particularly in public. It also could be argued, however, that more strict disciplinary styles are a by-product of socialization that stresses connectedness to others. Thus, the importance of learning proper social behavior may be given greater emphasis.

Dornbusch, Ritter, Herbert, Leiderman, Robers, and Fraleigh (1987) investigated parenting styles as reported by White, Asian, Black, and Hispanic adolescents. In contrast to While families, both male and female adolescents of the three minority groups were higher on an index of authoritarianism. On the authoritative index, Asian, Black, and Hispanic females reported their families lower, in contrast to white females. Male Asians and Hispanics reported their families as less authoritative than did White and Black adolescents. The Asian, Black, and Hispanic females reported their families as less authoritarian than did the White females. In contrast, male Asians and Hispanics reported their families as less authoritarian than did White and Black adolescents. Asian and Hispanic males scored the highest and Black males the lowest on permissiveness in parenting styles. For females, Hispanics scored the highest and Blacks the lowest on permissiveness. These findings support the notion that, for some minority groups, more firm parenting styles are evident and perhaps are more conducive to socialization toward collectivism.

Differences among ethnic groups with respect to family interaction patterns are likely, in part, the by-products of socialization. For example, Hsu, Tseng, Ashton, McDermott, and Char (1985) explored family interactions in Japanese-American and Caucasian families with adolescent children. They note that the two groups differed regarding aspects of individual autonomy. For example, the Japanese were more reluctant to express individual thoughts and feelings. Furthermore, the Japanese also were found to be less willing to accept responsibility for their own thoughts, feelings, and actions, and were more invasive in their interactions. In individual communication, family members frequently speak for one another. These findings may be reflective of the Japanese culture's value to maintain harmonious interpersonal relationships.

What may further enhance some ethnic groups' high sense of collectivism are specific features that set a particular group apart from other groups. For example, among other traits, a strong sense of family, adherence to Mexican-Catholic ideology, and the use of Spanish demarcate Mexican-Americans from other groups (Buriel, 1986). Indeed, Diaz-Guerrero (1986) summarizes the research literature on socialization of Mexican-American children and adolescents and concludes that, in contrast to Anglo-Americans, Mexican-Americans are more family centered and more cooperative in interpersonal activities.

In general, more strict and authoritarian parenting styles of some minority families may be reflective of a desire to socialize children toward the adoption of proper communal roles. Socialization toward group values and interpersonal behavior may mean that the Anglo-American value of training independence may not be as central for minority families. Instead, socialization may be more focused on one's group and taking on the proper roles and behavior of that group.

Components of Culturally Specific Socialization

Consistent with the experience of all family contexts, ethnic and racial minority parents have the tasks of socializing their offspring for interaction in the broader societal context and of preparing their children to adopt responsible, socially approved roles in society. Superimposed on these normative criteria of socialization is an additional challenge to teach minority children and adolescents the necessary skills for coping with their minority status in society. Two components of culturally specific socialization are (1) to teach children and adolescents about their cultural heritage and to impart a sense of pride in one's group, and (2) to sensitize children and adolescents to the realities of ethnic and racial prejudice and discrimination and show them how to manage this.

More specifically, Miller and Miller (1990, p. 170) note that the socialization tasks of African-American parents encompass four issues:

1. To "negate dominant cultural messages which undermine self-esteem and efficacy"
2. To "validate uniqueness"
3. To "teach strategies for emotional and physical survival in the face of racism"
4. To "foster the development of coping mechanisms for dealing with legal and de facto discriminatory experiences"

Spencer (1985) notes, in relation to Black adolescents, that they face certain risks if they have not been socialized to understand and take pride in their culture before moving into the broader societal context. For example, the failure of Black parents to develop ethnic consciousness in their children may result in "race dissonance" illustrated by Black children's preference for White culture (Spencer, 1987).

Unfortunately, there is little evidence that culturally specific socialization occurs in families. In fact, some minority parents may minimize the need to teach about specific ethnic and racial issues. For example, Spencer (1987) reports that Black parents typically are not teaching their children about Black history and civil rights. Black adolescents confirmed these statements and reported that the school provided most of the instruction in African-American culture. Black parents report a belief that the 1960s took care of many inequities in the system and that it is sufficient to teach generic societal values only. Thus, many Black parents "transcend race" in respect to socialization (Spencer, 1985).

Providing culturally specific socialization is further complicated in the case of adolescents whose parents are of two different racial groups. For example, Miller and Miller (1990) discuss the issue of mothering the biracial child of Black-White unions. They argue that neither the mother nor the father of the biracial child can fully identify and empathize with their offspring's unique minority status. Yet, parents do bear the responsibility of preparing their child for a bicultural minority role in society. In the case of Black-White biracial children, their experiences are likely to be similar to those of African-American children. Therefore, it is important that socialization should incorporate issues of African-American culture. Nonetheless, the individual should be allowed to integrate components of both racial/ethnic backgrounds into a single identity. Furthermore, biracial children and adolescents should be prepared for the potential that they may never find complete acceptance in either the African-American or White communities, although we hope the day might come when race is not a characteristic that determines acceptance into any mainstream social group.

Problems in providing culturally specific socialization to adolescents can be more fully appreciated by realizing that parents also must fight against deleterious cultural forces for the preservation of their own sense of cultural identity. For example, many American Indian parents of current and recent generations experienced unnatural childrearing experiences of their own by attending boarding schools for much of their childhood and adolescence. From the boarding school experiences and related attempts to assimilate American Indians, many tradition-al parenting practices have been lost or destroyed. Furthermore, the introduction of White cultural values competes with traditional American Indian parenting practices. More recently, however, many American Indian tribes are making con-scious efforts to rekindle traditional cultural practices, including parenting prac-tices. The continuation of such efforts, with the strong participation of tribal elders, may help present-day adolescents acquire traditional parenting skills they can use in turn when raising their offspring.

Implications of Basic Family Functions for Intervention with Families

A democratic, warm, interacting, and partially restricting family structure may be best for positive adolescent development (Kandel, 1990). Such a family style provides moderate cohesion, is highly flexible and adaptive, and encourages social interaction and communication between parents and adolescents. More often than not, adolescents who find themselves being confronted by the law, having school problems, or engaging in antinormative behaviors come from fam-ilies that provide very little of the three basic functions outlined in this chapter. Providing an intervention service to youths in a nonfamilial context and return-ing them to a poorly functioning and unsupportive family environment are not conducive to positive results. Therefore, we strongly urge future interventionists to be highly sensitive to building social-intervention programs that recognize the family as a major influence on adolescent behavior. We are hopeful that in so doing, future interventionists will build a diagnostic component into their pro-grams that examines the strengths and weaknesses of the adolescent's family-support system and will attempt to remedy weaknesses. In particular, we urge that such remedial attempts emphasize programs that center on the three basic family functions of cohesion, adaptiveness, and communication. Although there are other important variables, these three are central to the positive functioning of a family. In the remainder of this chapter, we examine some of the issues fac-ing adolescents living in new family forms. (See Box 3–2.)

Family Changes

Life was so much simpler in the old days. There were Mom, Dad, the dog, a cat, and two, three, or maybe four children. The grandparents lived in the same town, and the family's ancestors were buried there. Mom stayed at home. Dad always said that's where a woman belongs. She sewed, cleaned, cooked, and cared for the children before settling back in the evening to read *Life*'s feature story about Clark Gable's latest movie. Divorces were unheard of among the good people, and it was only the widowed who remarried. If this portrait of the good old days were true—and it is not—this chapter might have expressed concern over the changes that are shaping the American family today. Women have left the kitchen for the workplace and are beginning to achieve long-deserved job equity

---

Box 3–2   Preserving Families

It was a late fall afternoon. Fog hugged the ground. Skies were overcast, and a damp chill cut through Sharon's clothing. A twelve-year-old junior high school student, she hurried home from a friend's house. She had promised her mother and stepfather that she would be home for lunch. Nearing her own home, she heard the radio blaring from the kitchen and knew instinctively that her mother and stepfather had been drinking. She dreaded their behavior when they were intoxicated. Rude suggestive remarks and boisterous laughter about her sexual development had become commonplace. On this particular afternoon, in the presence of her mother and with her participation, Sharon was forcibly disrobed and made to perform several sexual acts on her stepfather. Sharon eventually fled the house and reported the assault to friends whose parents contacted the police.

Two years later the court trial against her mother and stepfather was concluded. Sharon's stepfather was sentenced to seven years for his sexual assault. Her mother was given probation with orders to continue in an outpatient drug treatment program. She was further ordered to work with the intervening agency in an attempt to reunite her with Sharon, now 14, and in frequent trouble in the community.

This renunciation effort is part of a recent nationwide movement called intensive family preservation. The three most common forms of this clinical intervention are efforts to maintain the family unit or at least part of that unit after a young person had been determined to be at imminent risk of removal by state protective service authorities, efforts to reunify a family that has been separated for abuse, neglect, or for reasons of imprisonment, and efforts to stabilize a family unit and improve their level of functioning after renunciation has occurred. The development of intensive family preservation services is an admission that even severely dysfunctional families are often times less damaging to young people than institutional care or independent living. This admission has resulted in the significant investment of resources by several states to assist family members in developing the necessary skills to more successfully live together. (See Blau, Whewell, Gullotta and Bloom, 1994, for a description of one such program.)

In Sharon's situation a foster home, outpatient counseling, and self-help services had not comforted the hurt she had so wrongly endured. In the past year she had become increasingly defiant and sexually active. This is a pattern of behavior not unusual for young people victimized by family members. The judge in this court case, recognizing this all-to-familiar pattern, took the unusual action of attempting to reunite child with her repentant mother. The reunification effort brought a master's level mental health clinician into the family's home for up to 20 hours a week. This clinician is supported by other professional staff such that the family has access to help in their home 24 hours a day 365 days a year, if necessary.

Fourteen months have passed since the reunification effort began. They have been trying months. Sharon has left home overnight on several occasions. Living together for mother and daughter remains tense, and tears of anger and hurt flow freely. Yet, unlike so many other young people with similar stories, Sharon has not disappeared to the street and a short life of addiction. Sharon has not been bounced from one foster home to another. Sharon does not find herself in a correctional school or living independently at state expense in some cheap motel. Some may argue with these seemingly modest achievements. For those individuals, we suggest a walk along the streets of New Orleans, Los Angeles, Toronto, New York, or a dozen other cities at 2:30 A.M. and observe the Sharons of this world living in misery.

in the marketplace. Marriages made today stand an almost equal chance of being broken tomorrow. Remarriages bringing young people from their family of birth together in new families are increasingly commonplace. To make clear the effects of these changes on the adolescent, we need to examine the past and then look at studies that address those effects, beginning with the myth that families in the past were geographically stable.

Mothers in the Work Force

When one considers that the early farms were self-sufficient units, the issue of women in the work force as a recent family change becomes essentially a question of semantics. On the farm, woman tended the family garden, cared for livestock, nursed children, prepared foodstuffs for winter storage, made clothing, turned lye and ash into soap, and performed hundreds of other tasks. The woman was doctor, teacher, soldier, lover, and mother (Vanek, 1980). As the agrarian economy turned industrial and the home was no longer the center of production, the woman's role changed from producer to carer for children and home while males traveled to work in the factories. Certain industries were female dominated, but the women in these positions were generally single rather than married (Bane, 1976)

Interestingly, in at least some ethnic groups women carried on home industries. For example, in the 1920s in Buffalo, New York, although ethnic family customs kept southern Italian women out of the factories, these women still contributed to the financial solvency of the family. They took in boarders and operated any number of small industries from their homes, ranging from making artificial flowers to baking to sewing. With male employment often temporary and erratic, these women's earnings were an important contribution to the family's ability to care for itself (McLaughlin, 1973).

Even with these cottage industries, the official percentage of married women in the work force was 4% in 1890 and less than 15% in 1940. With the advent of World War II, the number of working married women climbed, and it reached nearly 30% in 1956, 42% in 1974, 59% in 1980, and well in excess of 70% in the 1990s. With that growth has evolved a new understanding of a mother's employment in relationship to her children and husband (Bane, 1976; Glueck & Glueck, 1957)

The early social-scientific literature on mothers in the work force portrayed the children as victims. According to Bossard (1954), working mothers are physically exhausted and thus neglect the supervision and training of their children. As a result, the children feel lonely and neglected and tend to take advantage of the lack of maternal control to behave in an antisocial manner.

Bossard and other early researchers recognized that in many families the mother had to work for economic reasons. Nevertheless, the early research in this area reflected a decidedly dim view of maternal employment. For instance, Glueck and Glueck (1957) reported that on some measures, such as the degree of a child's emotional disturbance and the use of the mother's leisure time, no significant differences were found between mothers who worked full time and nonworking mothers. On other measures, though, such as the mother's supervision of children and husband/wife marital satisfaction, the working mother was a poorer supervisor with a less satisfying marriage than her nonemployed counterpart. The Gluecks' severest criticism was reserved for the mother who worked part time: she "flits erratically from job to job—probably because she finds relief thereby from the burden of homemaking and the rearing of children" (p. 346). They observed that this particular type of working mother seemed to contribute the most to the conditions that spawn delinquency:

> We are confronted with mothers who for intellectual or temperamental reasons cannot or will not adequately fulfill the role of motherhood. This . . . suggests the need

of individualization in determining how to improve the situation in the home of working mothers. An overall government policy of financial grants to mothers is not enough and may even be disadvantageous in some cases where it is not true economic need but rather the desire for the latest gadgets to "keep up with the Joneses" that may be the propulsive motive. (Pp. 349–350)

As the number of women in the labor force continued to grow in the 1960s and as additional data were collected, a decidedly different perspective emerged on the effects of working mothers on their adolescents. According to a report published in the early 1960s, neither the daughters of nonworking mothers nor the daughters of mothers who work full time are as emotionally and socially developed as girls whose mothers work part time. These girls were also found to be mature and to have good peer and family relationships: "They show an unusual independence of thought and values generally rare among girls. . . . These psychological features of the girls developed, we suggest, from a modeling process in which the girls identify with and draw their ideals from their own active and autonomous mothers" (Douvan, 1963, pp. 149, 160). More than three decades later these remarks must bring a smile to a generation raised during the feminist movement.

Studies collecting data on such variables as achievement, childrearing practices, adolescent personality adjustment, and adolescents' attitudes toward working mothers showed no clear trends for the next few years. But by 1973 a review of the literature concluded that while there were differences of opinion overall, "there is no clear evidence for disturbance or maladjustment among children of working mothers" (Wallston, 1973, p. 91).

Several more recent studies amplify this view. Collectively, they observe advantages in social and emotional growth result for young girls whose mothers work. Boys neither benefit from nor are harmed socially or emotionally by their mothers' working. These studies find that work is generally a satisfying experience for mothers, that adolescents do not experience high stress resulting from such work situations, and that the family system is adaptable (Armistead, Wierson, & Forehand, 1990; Bird & Kemerait, 1990; Gottfried & Gottfried, 1988; Hillman & Sawilowsky, 1991; Paulson, Koman, & Hill, 1990; Orthner, 1990). And although mother's employment may only equal 25% to 33% of father's income, it is responsible for keeping many families out of poverty, creating savings, and purchasing the family home (Hanson & Ooms, 1991).

Data from the National Commission on Children (1991) suggest that even though working mothers may feel uneasy about how much time they spend with their children their children do not share these same feelings. When asked if they have "the right amount of time" with their family 66% of not employed women said yes; 60% of women working less than 34 hours per week said yes; 29% of women working between 35 and 40 hours per week said yeas; and 22% of women working more than 41 hours per week said yes. Interestingly, their children, regardless of mother's working situation, felt that time and attention received was adequate for at least 80% of the sample. Overall, it appears it is not the quantity but the quality of time spent with the child that affects the mother/child relationship (Marotz-Baden et al., 1979).

More and more mothers are assuming demanding professions while some fathers are staying home to raise children.

Fathers in the Home

If the world were to end today and the only records of our civilization that survived for future study by archaeologists were the family television shows of the 1950s, what a unique picture they would offer of American home life. Whether the archaeologists examined *Ozzie and Harriet, Leave It to Beaver, The Donna Reed Show,* or our favorite, *Father Knows Best,* they would observe fathers at home and involved with their families. They would see that in times of crisis the father's Solomon-like mind settled not only the mother's frayed nerves but also the turmoil involving their adolescent children. How confused these archaeologists would be if uncovered a university library, for no amount of searching in the literature on the father's role in the family would turn up anything to support what they saw and heard on film.

To their surprise, in reading Glueck and Glueck (1957) they would find that fathers with working wives were either overly strict disciplinarians with their children or were inconsistent and too lenient with them. They would further learn that the mother's, not the father's, role in the family was crucial. In fact, the Gluecks suggested that the mother's employment contributed to the father's parenting difficulties: "To the extent that a mother's absence from home in gainful employment engenders a father's inadequate discipline of the children, the working mother must be charged with contributing, albeit indirectly, to the delinquency of her children" (pp. 347–348).

Frankly, until recently fathers have not had a role in the caring for and nurturing of their children in the eyes of society. The father's responsibility to the family was to provide the food on the table, the clothes on the family members' backs, and the roof over their heads. All other responsibilities (save perhaps mowing the lawn) fell to the wife. This primitive division of labor could be defended when the father was in the fields and the mother was filling several roles in the home; but as mothers have found themselves in the work force in unprecedented numbers, this division of labor no longer makes sense.

Pleck (1979) offers three different views on a role system that finds husbands spending 1.6 hours a day on housework and child care while their employed wives spend 4.8 hours a day. The first, the "traditional perspective," suggests that the father's role is financial support, not housework or parenting. The second, the "exploitation perspective," contends that men use housekeeping and parenting responsibilities against women to keep them in servitude. The third, the "changing-roles perspective," suggests that an evolutionary process is occurring. "Reflecting a transitional problem of adjustment" (p. 485), women's roles have changed much faster than have men's roles.

More than a decade has passed since Pleck published his observations. Have fathers changed their childrearing behavior? Results are not encouraging. For example, in one study fathers spent only an average of 21 minutes per week with their children and most of this time was spent with sons (Crouter & Crowley, 1990). The quality of the marriage appears to have an effect on time involvement. As the quality of the marriage deteriorates so, too, does time with children (Harris & Morgan, 1991). Somewhat more encouragingly, in one other study of 91 Canadian families, fathers were found to be more accepting of their adolescent children as family time increased (Almeida & Galambos, 1991).

From the National Commission on children (1991), we can draw two inferences. First, 82% of the youth sampled felt that their father really cared for them. Second, 43% reported their fathers almost never missed an important event in their lives. Nevertheless, it appears that even though 72% of women between the ages of 25 and 54 are in the labor force significant role changes have not occurred. Child care has been purchased or sought from relatives. Household cleaning chores continue to be performed by mother or outside help. The preparation of meals if not performed by mother is accomplished by visits to fast food restaurants. These expenses sap 46% of her wage earnings (Hanson & Ooms, 1991).

Collectively, these findings present less than encouraging evidence as to father's involvement in family life. And yet, a gradual change may be under way, a change that might be discerned if longitudinal data were available. Thus, researchers will study with great interest family leave data that will be generated in the coming years. With the 1993 passage of the *Family and Medical Leave Act,* workers in firms with fifty or more employees may request up to 12 weeks of unpaid leave a year for purposes such as the birth of a child, adoption, and the care of a sick family member (Landers, 1993). Once analyzed, will this data demonstrate greater involvement of fathers in the family? Some answers to this questions should be available by the end of this decade.

Divorce

The entry of women into the work force . . . has its own effects on divorce rates. A positive by-product of women's economic independence is that a woman who can earn a decent living herself does not have to remain in an impossible marriage because of money alone. . . . Moreover, wives' employment subtly alters relationships of power and submission within marriage. A wife's new independence can strengthen the husband-wife relationship, but increased equality also can produce new stresses or cause old stresses and resentments to surface. Women who are less submissive by and large will put up with less and expect more. One consequence may be the realization that a marriage has not lived up to the high hopes of husband or wife and a decision to end it, particularly when cultural attitudes toward divorce make it far less socially shameful than it once was. (Keniston, 1977, pp. 21–22)

Although this passage indicates that divorce has freed both men and women from the shackles of marriages that do not work, the question of the feelings of the "by-products"—the children—is another matter. This problem has been the subject of numerous research articles and books in the past decade, but of these, very few have focused on the adolescent. Before we look at what is available, it might be helpful to look at the history of this behavior and its growth in the United States.

Historical Background

Before the advent of Christianity, the dissolution of a marriage was a civil affair. The changes in the 20th century that have made divorce easier are really nothing more than a return (for very different reasons) to practices that existed until the sixth century (Alvarez, 1981).

In Rome, for instance, marriage was a civil contract that could be dissolved by having either spouse declare a bill of divorce in the presence of seven adult Roman citizens (Kitchin, 1912). Enlightened as the Romans may have been, equality between the sexes was not one of their strong points, and while women could divorce for 12 reasons, men could divorce for 15, including a wife's "going to dine with men other than her relations without the knowledge of or against the wish of her husband and frequenting the circus, theater, or amphitheater after being forbidden by her husband" (p. 109).

It was Christianity, Kitchin (1912) contends, that redefined the nature of marriage in society. From a civil arrangement between two individuals (most often established by parents), marriage became a spiritual affair. The married state came to represent, in the eyes of church leaders, more than the uniting of two moral beings: it was "a model in miniature of the eternal marriage of the church with Christ" (Alvarez, 1981, p. 111). Did such a redefinition end divorces? The answer is no. Other solutions were devised by the populace like desertion and bigamy. Thankfully, with the passage of liberalized divorce laws in the 1960s, these solutions no longer need to be exercised.

Demographics

To gain an appreciation for the rise in divorces, it is useful to look at the past. Official records report a divorce rate in 1880 of 1 divorce for every 21 marriages in the United States, rising in 1916 to 1 for every 9 marriages. At the end of World War II (1946) the divorce rate skyrocketed to 1 divorce per 3.7 marriages. By 1950 it had declined slightly to 1 per 4 marriages, and it remained at about that level for several years. However, in the late 1950s rates again began to rise. In 1968, for example, 1 divorce occurred for every 3.5 marriages; by 1970 this had increased to 1 divorce for every 3 marriages. As we entered the 1990s, for nearly every 2 marriages 1 divorce occurred (U.S. Census Bureau, 1992a). For the year 1990, this meant that an estimated 1,175,000 divorces were granted in the United States (U.S. Census Bureau, 1992a).

The Census Bureau reported that for 1988 the median duration of marriages in the United States was 7.1 years. At the time of divorce, the women's median age was 32.6, her former husband's 35.1 (U.S. Census Bureau, 1992b). In 1988, 1,044,000 children (nearly one child/divorce—0.89%) were involved in divorce proceedings in the United States. Work by Rankin and Maneker (1985) suggests the presence of children affects marital stability. In their sample parents with children over the age of two appeared to be discouraged from dissolving their marriages.

Box 3–3   Effects of Parents' Divorce on Late Adolescents

Although the clinical and research literature is rich in observations regarding the impact of divorce on children and young adolescents, little attention has been paid to the effect of parental divorce on people in their late teens and early 20s. What effect parental divorce has on this age group was addressed by a group of researchers at Pennsylvania State University (Cooney, Smyer, Hagestad, & Klock, 1986). From their sample of 39 male and female college students between the ages of 18 and 23, the authors reported:

- Students felt angry, vulnerable, and under enormous stress at the time they learned of their parents' decision to divorce. Most students also reported a lack of peer-group support. In nearly every case this lack was related to the student's recent transition to college.

- Students observed changes in their relationships with their parents. For women in this sample the relationship with their mother intensified at the expense of the relationship with their father.
- Students expressed conflicting loyalties to their parents. For many, this conflict was most acutely felt during the holidays.
- Students worried over their parents' future and their own future role in their parents' lives.

Considering the findings of this study, it would appear that the parental decision to divorce is painful and that all young people, regardless of age and circumstance, face the task of handling it.

If divorce rates remain at present levels, estimates are that 38% of White children born in 1980 will be members of single-parent households for some period of time before age 16. For Black youth, the chances of experiencing a single-parent household are significantly greater. By age 16, 75% of Black youth will be members of such families (Bumpass, 1984). Moreover, the number of two-parent households continued to decline from 40% of all households in 1970 to 31% in 1980 to 26% in 1990 (U.S. Census Bureau, 1991b).

Effects of Divorce on Young People

In one of the earliest studies of the reactions of adolescents to their parents' divorce, Reinhard (1977) found surprisingly few negative feelings. The majority of the sample, even though unhappy with the divorce, did not view their parents' decision as senseless or immature but as the correct action. Adolescents in this study saw themselves as assuming more responsibility in the family as a result of the divorce but did not view this responsibility negatively, nor did they express anger or a sense of loss of love. They also did not try to conceal the divorce from peers. Significantly, peers seemed to respond in an accepting fashion, and social relationships were enhanced as a result. Finally, these young people did not report any antisocial behavior, leading one generally to conclude that the divorce of their parents was not a particularly earth-shaking experience. (See Box 3–3.)

With a few notable exceptions, these general findings reappear in the current literature. Even the exceptions that exist suggesting, for example, that academic self-concept suffers (Smith, 1990) or that female delinquency may be related to broken homes cannot establish causality, for there are confounding variables (like parental emotional illness and alcoholism) that make it extremely difficult to attribute a sample's acting-out behavior to single-parent homes (Offord, Abrams, Allen, & Poushinsky, 1979).

These methodological problems are most noticeable with the most famous of all clinical longitudinal studies on divorce and its impact on young people. The study, the latest by Wallerstein (Wallerstein, 1989; Wallerstein & Blakeslee, 1989), suggests that adolescents are a high risk for emotional distress following a family divorce. This distress may become apparent years after the event occurred. Wallerstein describes it as a "sleeper" effect in which the young adult finds it difficult to commit to an intimate relationship. Or young people, seemingly role diffused, appear unable to establish life goals for themselves (Wallerstein, 1989; Wallerstein & Blakeslee, 1989). And yet as Hetherington and Furstenberg (1989) appropriately caution, the Wallerstein clinical sample had a large number of families which had been dysfunctional for years before the divorce occurred. Inability to control for these sample effects may have skewed her findings toward higher levels of dysfunctional behavior in their offspring.

For instance, studies with fewer of these sampling problems on a variety of measure such as locus of control and ego identity (S. M. Crossman, Shea, & Adams, 1980) and androgynous sex-role orientation (Kurdek & Siesky, 1980a) have found young people not to differ significantly from their peers in intact homes. In fact, these young men in one study had higher ego-identity scores than peers from intact homes (Grossman et al., 1980).

Adjusting to Parental Divorce

What facilitates a young person's healthy adjustment to divorce? Wallerstein (1983) believes that young people must resolve six tasks in order to get on with their own lives in a healthy fashion. The first task is to "acknowledge the marital rupture." Ideally, after an initial regression, young people will come to grips with this fact by the end of the first year. The second task is to "disengage from parental conflict" and to resolve for themselves that they cannot save their parents or replace a divorced spouse (Sessa & Steinberg, 1991).

The next task is "resolution of loss." In a divorce all young people feel hurt and rejected, some more than others. Parish (1981) has reported that young people carry into college feelings that divorce is a stigma. Moderating this sense of loss is the ability to share this loss (Kurdek & Siesky, 1980b; Luepnitz, 1979). The ability to reach out to friends for social support is important in accepting a divorce. Equally important is the way the parents approach the divorce. Warm, loving relationships maintained by *both* parents with their offspring after a divorce facilitate adjustment (Emery, 1982; Kurdek, 1981), but continued parental battles and anger, increase adolescent stress and dysfunctional behavior (Forehand, McCombs, Long, Brody, & Fauber, 1988).

The fourth task is "resolution of anger and self-blame." Wallerstein (1983) believes that young people do not accept the concept of no-fault divorce. They hold one or both parents or themselves responsible. Their anger, until resolved, may be expressed internally in withdrawal or depression or externally in acting-out behavior in the family, at school, or in the larger community. The fifth task involves "accepting the permanence of the divorce," giving up dreams that the divorced couple will reunite. The last task to be accomplished is "achieving realistic hope regarding relationships." Young people need to come, in the end, to believe they *they* are capable of establishing meaningful relationships and not be obsessed with fears over their ability to love and care for another.

When young people do not succeed in handling these tasks, intrapersonal or interpersonal difficulties are sure to arise. Thus, studies reporting that academic self-concept suffers (Smith, 1990), that drug use is higher (Fleweling & Bauman, 1990; Needle, Su, & Doherty, 1990) that sexual experiences are earlier (Flewelling & Bauman, 1990), and that an increased risk for delinquency exists (Offord, Abrams, Allen, & Poushinsky, 1979) should not be surprising. Nor should it be surprising that many of these same studies describe lonely, needy, and vulnerable young people who fear disappointment in love, express lower life-attainment expectations, and feel powerless (DeVall, Stoneman, & Brody, 1986; Parish, 1987; Wallerstein, 1985, 1987, 1989).

Is it possible to cope and adapt after a parent's divorce? There is good evidence to support Nelson's (1982, p. 57) comment that "children's social maladjustment following divorce is a temporary rather than an enduring reaction." Kurdek, Blisk, and Siesky (1981) found, for instance, that four years after the parents' divorce their sample of upper-middle-class young people evidenced little self-blame or hope for parental reconciliation. These young people, the authors wrote, had a high level of interpersonal reasoning and an internal locus of control and were older than children cited in other studies who were less able to cope. Furthermore, because the divorce has not occurred recently, the authors believe, these young people were able to place this event in perspective.

One recent study suggests that parental divorce does have a moderately negative impact on the adult well-being of young people. Its authors speculate that the combination of lower single-parent income and reduced contact with father contribute to young adult reports of depression, lower life satisfaction, lower educational attainment, lower job satisfaction, and poorer physical health (Amato & Keith, 1991). The role of the biological father in divorced families is not clear. Some studies identify him as playing an important role (Asmussen & Larson, 1991) while other find his presence less important than his continued adequate financial support (Furstenberg, Allison, & Morgan, 1987). In this last regard, the Census Bureau (1991c3) reports that four months after a father leaves a household income for that household drops 37%.

A series of studies supports the father's emotional value in the family by showing that young people from divorced families have lower levels of self-esteem than do young people from nondivorced homes (Parish & Taylor, 1979; E. Young & Parish, 1977). Moreover, young people from divorced households evaluate their families more negatively than do children and adolescents from intact families. These negative expressions, it seems, are modified to at least some degree if a remarriage occurs (Parish & Dostal, 1980).

In interpreting the results of these studies, we would agree with others that divorce does not always leave serious psychological scares on young people (Cherlin, Furstenberg, Chase-Lansdale, Kiernan, Robins, Morrison, & Teitler, 1991; Santrock, 1987). Although it is true that 40% of young people living in the United States will live sometime in a divorce household and even though it is also true that these households experience considerable pain, it is also true that in many instances this emotional suffering was present long before a divorce occurred (Cherlin et al., 1991; Long, Forehand, Fauber, & Brody, 1987). It is not divorce per se that is solely responsible for this hurt. Divorce is the culmination rather than the instigation of pain for many of these young people. Further, in our own work we have found that although the divorce procedure itself is extremely stressful for adolescents, long-term disability seldom occurs. Finally, the reports of more marital dissatisfaction by adult children of divorced parents may result from a more realistic and honest appraisal of the marriage contract. The higher levels of separation or divorce in this group may represent fewer inhibitions about ending an unsuccessful marriage, which in its unhappiness and conflict may do more psychological damage to children than a divorce.

Implications

There is no question that adolescents experience considerable stress in their parents' divorce process, but this stress does not have to create lasting emotional damage. In the studies we have reviewed, those young people who were able to muster the necessary emotional supports around them to make it through the upheavals in the family's life escaped the problems of others unable to do so.

The role of the community should be to extend that necessary emotional support. The support can be as informal as lending an ear in a friendly way, or it can be the formation of self-help groups through community mental-health centers or churches. For those young people who want counseling, the counseling should focus on helping them establish an identity separate from their families'. Family therapy (with both parents present) should focus on avoiding the use of the children as chess pieces in the divorce process. The parents should be helped to:

- Work on resolving their conflicts, or at least not inflict them on the children
- Work on developing or maintaining a caring, supportive relationship with their children
- Develop or take advantage of whatever social support systems are available (McCall & Stocking, 1980. p. 12)

School personnel can help young people realize that they are not responsible for the divorce and that they cannot heal the break. The staff can also help them realize "that parents divorce each other, not their children" (L. D. Rubin & Price, 1979, p. 555); that the feelings of loneliness and anxiety accompanying a divorce are not permanent; that single-parent families can be emotionally nurturing; and that young people cannot expect happiness but must work at having a satisfying life (Rubin & Price, 1979). These efforts will not eliminate the hurt, but they can provide the incentive to seek the emotional supports necessary to cope with it.

Remarriage

The remarried family, called by such names as *reconstituted* or *blended,* sounds at times more like a beverage than a family group. And this really only begins the problems; items in these families may be his, hers, theirs, his ex's, her ex's, his children's, her children's, his parents', her parents', their parents', and so on. In this last section we examine whether widespread remarriage is of recent vintage and what, if any, effects it has on adolescents when "his" children are added to "her" children, resulting in "their" children.

Historical Background

Paul Landis once remarked that if one in six divorced persons remarried, "it is clear that sequential polygamy is more common in our society than polygamy in some societies of polygamous cultural norms" (1950, p. 628). His remark indicates not only society's difficulty in adhering to its ideal of monogamy but also its reluctance to accept remarriage as a regular event in the life cycle of the present-day family.

Remarriage was not uncommon in the colonial era. There is also evidence to suggest that as many as one in eight individuals remarried in the early 1700s. Almost all of these new marriages occurred after the death of a spouse. As remarriage rates indicate, the thought of remarriage after a divorce was not even entertained until well into this century. For example, in 1910, among all women between the ages of 15 and 44, 6% remarried. This percentage grew to 9% by 1940 and to 13% by 1950. In this decade perhaps 25% of all women will have entered into a second marriage by midlife (Furstenberg, 1980). The trend is unmistakable; the question is what effects remarriage has on the 7 million young people living now with a stepparent (U.S. Census Bureau, 1990).

The Effects of Remarriage on Young People

Over the years that it takes most people to marry, to acquire a house, a dog, and a car, and to have children, they have time to adapt to change. Yet consider the newly remarried family with children. In some ways it is analogous to a frozen TV dinner. Preparation time is minimal—just marry and combine. The potential for things going haywire in this instant family is high, and many reports support the conclusions of a study by Bowerman and Irish (1962):

> Homes involving steprelations proved more likely to have stress, ambivalence, and low cohesiveness than did normal homes. . . . Stepmothers have more difficult roles than do stepfathers. . . . Stepdaughters generally manifested more extreme reactions toward their parents than did stepsons. The presence of stepparents in the home [tended to diminish children's] level of adjustment. (p. 121)

And yet our understanding of remarried life is not as bleak as that depicted in the above passage. Many stresses must be handled and readjustments made, but stepparents and stepchildren can succeed if the new family resolves four some-what amorphous issues.

Entry of a New Stepparent

The first issue is the entry of a new stepparent into a family. Several writers have discussed the difficulty many stepparents have in entering a family in which the position of mother or father has been "frozen"—filled by the child(ren) (Goldstein, 1974; Messinger & Walker, 1981; Visher & Visher, 1983; Whiteside, 1982). These authors believe "freezing" happens because the single parent turns to the children between marriages for emotional support, love, and even guidance. Reordering this structure is a delicate and often painful process, during which offspring feel rejected by their natural parent.

Role Ambiguity in Stepparenthood

Roles and boundaries are unclear in newly formed stepfamilies. Some authors have gone so far as to say that "organizational disturbance in stepfamilies is inevitable" (Fast & Cain, 1966, p. 485); others have commented that stepfamilies are "forever scrambling to maintain some semblance of equilibrium" (Visher & Visher, 1978, p. 255). This search for order is the second issue that new families must resolve. It occurs partly because society has not been able to respond quickly enough to the new variations found within stepfamilies. As Prosen and Farmer (1982) observe, *stepparent* originally meant a new individual in a household who replace a dead parent, not a living one. In replacing a living parent, a stepparent becomes an "added" parent. Furthermore, the replaced parent rarely disappears (Goldstein, 1974). Thus, the new stepparent not only is initially frozen out of a role but also has the additional burden of wondering what that role should be (Kent, 1980; Nelson & Nelson, 1980; Ransom, Schlesinger, & Derdeyn, 1979; Whiteside, 1982). Many authors counsel that time, understanding, and tolerance will resolve this issue. A stepparent's role is not ascribed but achieved, and that role can vary from family to family (Messinger & Walker, 1981; Visher & Visher, 1983; K. N. Walker & Messinger, 1979).

Reaction of Offspring to the Remarriage

The ability to thaw a family's structure to permit a stepparent to play a role is advanced or retarded by the immediate and long-term reactions of offspring to the remarriage. Young people in a remarriage face some difficult new life circumstances. Not only have they been separated from one natural parent, but they have obtained a surrogate parent, possibly new half-brothers and half-sisters, and other assorted kinfolk. The potential for conflict is certainly present.

Accordingly, it is not surprising that some studies show that remarriage has negative effects on young people. More mental-health problems are reported for young people in remarried homes than from those in homes broken by death or divorce, although all three groups show more dysfunction than children in intact families (Garbarino, Sebas, & Schellenbach, 1984; Langner & Michael, 1963; Rosenberg, 1965). Some suggest that a young person's poor adjustment to remarriage may result from wishes that the biological parents would remarry, guilt over imagining that the child caused the divorce, or failure to resolve the loss (Prosen & Farmer, 1982). Some authors believe that a child's age is not important in determining a stepparent's success in parenting (Palermo, 1980). Other disagree, suggesting that as young people grow older, it becomes more difficult for stepparents to assume a parenting role (Kompara, 1980).

Finally, some studies find that young people in remarried households with stepfathers commit more delinquent acts (Haney & Gold, 1977). Kalter (1977) underscores this point by adding that, for girls, higher levels of drug use and sexual activity are associated with having a stepfather. Kalter offers the possible explanation that much of this acting-out behavior is due to a "lack of incest barrier between stepfather and daughter" (p. 47). Goldstein (1974) suggests that much of the hostility between adolescent girls and stepfathers may be an attempt to "protect the participants from their sexual impulses" (p. 438). In contrast, others see these problems as emerging from the difficulty daughters may have in accepting their mothers as sexually active beings (Visher & Visher, 1983).

Unquestionably, there is a lowered incest barrier (Fast & Cain, 1966; Schulman, 1972). These feelings are complicated by the stepfamily's struggle for cohesiveness at the same time the adolescent is trying to resolve Oedipal issues and to separate from the family. One author suggests that the resolution of this situation rests, to a great extent, with the natural mother's ability to "maintain the incest taboo" (that is, to ensure that the relationship does not acquire incestuous overtones). If she is successful in establishing the taboo, she relieves her daughter and husband of the need to maintain a mask of "pseudo-hostility" (Goldstein, 1974).

But not all the writings about young people living in stepfamilies are filled with warnings. Several studies have found few serious problems for young people living in stepfamilies. According to one study, for instance, "The impact of divorce, father loss, and solo parenting [on evaluations of self and parent] tends to be modified when the remaining parent . . . remarries" (Parish & Dostal, 1980, p. 350). The direction of this change depends on which parent remarries. For fathers, the evaluations of both self and the father improve; for mothers, the situation is the reverse. However, the difference for mothers is not significant (Parish & Dostal, 1980). In other work with a sample of 98 female college students who had lost a father to death or divorce, those whose mothers had remarried felt more secure and evaluated themselves more positively than the others (Young & Parish, 1977). Burchinal (1964) compared five family types—unbroken, single-parent (mother head of household), remarried (mother/stepfather), remarried (father/stepmother), and remarried (both parents)—for differences in personality characteristics and social relationships. He found no differences in personality characteristics (proneness to disease, nervousness, anxiety, mood changes, envy, withdrawal) of the adolescents in these five family types and no particular differences in social relationships, school/community activities, academic average, popularity, or attitudes toward school. These findings led Burchinal to conclude:

> It is true that some children will suffer extreme trauma because of divorce or separation and consequent withdrawal of one parent, and for some, their development will be affected deleteriously. However, even in these cases, it is difficult to assess whether the difficulty occurs because of divorce or whether it reflects the conflict preceding the divorce and separation. Nevertheless . . . there is no question that . . . family dissolution and, for some families, reconstitution, was not the overwhelming influential factor in the children's lives that many thought it to be. . . . Acceptance of this conclusion required the revision of widely held beliefs about the detrimental effect of divorce upon children. (p. 54)

Burchinal's view that remarriage can be a positive or negative experience for offspring, depending on conditions not directly related to the marriage, is shared by K. L. Wilson, Zurcher, McAdams, and Curtis (1975). To see whether differences exist between young people in unbroken homes and young people with stepfathers, these researchers examined 106 social and psychological factors from two large national surveys. Their findings supported Burchinal's. They further questioned the accuracy of such stereotypes as the "evil stepfather" and the idea that having a stepfather is emotionally damaging. They suggested that remarriages (with a stepfather) are not inferior to natural-parent families.

Finally, one group of researchers reported that "the social behavior of children is not necessarily less competent in stepfamilies than in intact families" (Santrock, Warshak, Lindbergh, & Meadows, 1982, p. 480). These researchers set up a laboratory situation in which equal numbers of boys and girls, 6 to 11 years of age, in remarried, divorced, and intact families were observed interacting with their parents. These children and the (step)parents were asked first to plan a weekend activity together and then to discuss "the main problems of the family" (p. 475). These exercises were videotaped and then analyzed for content. The researchers found that boys in stepfather families showed more competent social behavior than boys in intact families. However, girls in stepfather families displayed more anxiety than girls in intact families. No differences were observed between divorced and intact families. Interestingly, and importantly, the authors noted that differences between stepfamilies and intact families were compounded by the marital conflict present in those families. In this sample, boys from intact families and girls from stepfather families had more marital conflict in their homes than their counterparts. This report of personal functioning tied to family environment echoes Nye's (1957) observation that young people's behaviors are affected less by the form of their family than by the degree of happiness found there. We would like to emphasize this last point. There is nothing sacred about any family form. Young people wither just as quickly in unhappy and unnourishing nuclear families as in unhappy and unnourishing divorced or remarried families. We will admit that young people prosper more readily in a nuclear family untouched by severe marital turmoil. However, it is not the single-parent or remarried family structure that impedes maturation. Rather, it is the turmoil found in the original nuclear family that contributes to developmental delays—delays that can be reversed in a new family form.

Parenting Issues

The final issue that the stepfamily must resolve is parenting. Children's fairy tales are filled with stories of the cruelty that stepparents (stepmothers in particular) show to their stepchildren. For example, who among us has not felt anger toward Hansel and Gretel's, Snow White's, or Cinderella's wicked stepmother? Stepfathers have escaped this stigmatization, although it has been suggested that the giant in "Jack and the Beanstalk" symbolizes a stepfather (Visher & Visher, 1978).

One reason stepmothers have fared so poorly in the research literature is that they are so intimately connected to children. Stepparenting is no easy task, particularly when the children are adolescents. One group of scholars have found that young people's adjustment to stepfamily life is related to the degree of consistency and parental agreement that exists in the new family (Fine, Donnelly, & Voydanoff, 1991). Not surprisingly, researchers have found that adolescents have the greatest difficulty in accepting discipline from a stepparent (Lutz, 1983). Because stepmothers are more likely than stepfathers to have close contact with the children in the new family, a stepmother faces more disciplinary issues, and problems inevitably arise involving her authority to discipline her husband's children. Most authors agree that a stepparent should not try to step into the role of natural parent too quickly. Many advise stepparents that it may be better in the beginning to attempt friendships with their new stepchildren rather than parent relationships (Kompara, 1980).

According to Kompara (1980), permitting a young person the time to mourn enables the stepparent to move from friend, perhaps, to parent with a smaller chance of rejection. Settling parenting issues in such a way that the parents are

---

Box 3–4   Tips on Preparing to Live in Step

This selection illustrates well one of the educational tools of prevention—namely, anticipatory guidance. The following advice is intended to help parents deal with the pressures that confront almost everyone with children who remarries:

- Plan ahead! Some chapters of Parents Without Partners conduct "Education for Remarriage" workshops. Contact your local chapter or write to Parents Without Partners, 7910 Woodmont Ave., Washington, D.C. 20014.
- Examine your motives and those of your future spouse for marrying. Get to know him or her as well as possible under all sorts of circumstances. Consider the possible impact of contrasting lifestyles.
- Discuss the modifications that will be required in bringing two families together. Look for similarities and differences in your ideas about childrearing.
- Explore with your children the changes remarriage will bring—new living arrangements, new family relationships, effect on their relationship with their noncustodial parent.
- Give your children ample opportunity to get to know your future spouse well. Consider your children's feelings, but don't let them make your decision about remarriage.
- Discuss the disposition of family finances with your future spouse. An open and honest review of financial assets and responsibilities may reduce unrealistic expectations and resulting misunderstandings.
- Understand that there are bound to be periods of doubt, frustration, and resentment.

- Let your relationship with stepchildren develop gradually. Don't expect too much to soon—from the children or from yourself. Children need time to adjust, accept, and belong. So do parents.
- Don't try to replace a lost parent; be an additional parent. Children need time to mourn the parent lost through divorce or death.
- Expect to deal with confusing feelings—your own, your spouse's, and the children's. Anxiety about new roles and relationships may heighten competition among family members for love and attention; loyalties may be questioned. Your children may need to understand that their relationship with you is valued but different from your relationship with your spouse and that one cannot replace the other. You love and need them both, but in different ways.
- Recognize that you may be compared with the absent parent. Be prepared to be tested, manipulated, and challenged in your new role. Decide, with your mate, what is best for your children and stand by it.
- Understand that stepparents need support from natural parents on childrearing issues. Rearing children is tough; rearing someone else's is tougher.
- Acknowledge periods of cooperation among stepsiblings. Try to treat your stepchildren and your own with equal fairness. Communicate! Don't pretend that everything is fine when it isn't. Acknowledge problems immediately and deal with them openly.
- Admit that you need help if you need it. Don't let the situation get out of hand. Everyone needs help sometimes. Join an organization for stepfamilies; seek counseling.

Source: National Institute of Mental Health, *Yours, Mine and Ours: Tips for Stepparents* (DHHS Publication No. ADM 78–676). Washington, D.C.: U.S. Government Printing Office, 1978, pp. 3–4.

cooperating with each other in a *consistent* fashion reduces the chance that stepmothers (or stepfathers) will be viewed as witches (or evil giants) and will increase the probability that the French term for stepmother, *belle-mère* ("beautiful mother"), will be applied (Schulman, 1972).

The book *Yours, Mine, and Ours* (see Box 3–4) notes the possibility of joint custody of the children. In the last fifteen years, divorcing spouses have been increasingly successful through the judicial process in making childrearing a continued shared responsibility. Although the effects of joint custody are still unclear on the emotional health of children, we can observe that the road to joint custody is strewn with potential pitfalls but may be worth the trip for some.

Joint-custody arrangements can work if both parents try to make it successful. Studies indicate that a successful joint-custody arrangement is likely to involve parents who have a strong ideological commitment to the concept and an equally strong devotion to their children. Furthermore, they believe in each other as parents, can tolerate differences in each other, and can keep their own former marital problems out of the way (Ahrons, 1981; Steinman, 1981). Surprising as it may seem, fathers can be "quite capable and successful in their ability to be the primary parent of their children" (H. J. Friedman, 1980, p. 1179).

These positive reports, however, do not mean that joint custody or visitation rights always work. As Wallerstein's studies over the years have shown, years after the divorce half of the females and nearly one-third of the males continued to display anger and hatred toward their former spouse, leading 60% of the children in this study to feel rejected (Wallerstein, 1989). As an earlier study has shown these situations are strife ridden:

> Although the majority of parents tried to honor the children's visiting time, 20% of the women saw no use in the father's visits and actively tried to sabotage each meeting. This fighting between parents reached pathological, even bizarre, intensity; one refined mother, for example, smeared dog feces on the face of her husband when he arrived to see his children. (Wallerstein & Kelly, 1980a, pp. 1536–1537)

Even families who try to behave in a civilized fashion after the divorce may not escape problems. Futterman (1980) has found numerous examples in his clinical caseload of "friendly, cooperative, mutually agreed-upon divorce settlements" (p. 526) in which the children have not worked through the process and experience difficulties at home and in school. Messinger and Walker (1981) caution that "to deny the pain of separation is the creation of a repressive atmosphere that includes denial of the children's sense of loss" (p. 431). They urge that young people be given an opportunity to share their feelings with their natural and new parents.

In our experience, problems in the relationship between the parent who has custody and the one who does not are often the hardest on young people. The divorce process is extremely painful in many families, and young people are sometime used as pawns in the separation battle. Few of the wounds incurred by the spouses in the divorce struggle are ever healed, and many couples continue the struggle for years after the divorce. The young person in this situation continues to be used by each parent until the youth learns to manipulate and use them. Our experience suggests that some of these parental-relationship problems can be reduced only if the natural parents agree not to pull the children into the divorce process in attempts to get even with the other partner.

Families do not fit one mold. Family problems, too, cannot be neatly pigeonholed. Remember that each family functions as a system whose health is determined by it members. When working with families, attempt to view the world through their eyes not your own. Try to find not dysfunctions but strengths in families, and work to rehabilitate them by using those strengths rather than by taking the families apart and reconstructing them from the ruins.

Major Points to Remember

1. The generation gap is more a figment of imagination than reality. Peers do have a great deal of influence on their fellows during adolescence, but that does not mean that parents or schools have none.
2. The family serves certain basic functions. It provides cohesion, or emotional bonding; a model of adaptability; and a network of communication experience.
3. All parenting styles differ, but research on families has identified four main types. These are warm and loving, hostile and cold, controlling and restrictive, and permissive and undemanding. It is highly unlikely that one would find many pure examples of one parenting type. Many families show degrees of each style.
4. The family exercises strong influence, even in adolescence, on such factors as personality development and social competence.
5. As we move closer to the 21st century, we come to appreciate the variety of experiences and the multitude of family forms existing today. These include but are not limited to the nuclear family, the single-parent family, and the blended family.
6. Were this 1950, the very thought of mothers in the work force would be condemned. As the percentage of working mothers has grown beyond 30% in 1956 to over 70% in the 1990s, society has learned to accept the idea and to be aware of the benefits and occasional problems that accompany this family style.
7. The involvement of fathers in family life fall short of mother's involvement.
8. When discussing divorce, we have been increasingly inclined to comment that three things in life are now certain: death, taxes, and divorce. The divorce rate is rapidly approaching the level in which one in two marriages ends up in court.
9. Research suggests that while the process is difficult, painful, and emotionally bruising, young people can, with love and help, make it through their parents' divorce.
10. It has been estimated that 80% of divorced individuals remarry. As a result, instant families consisting of children from one or both former marriages are growing more commonplace. Remarriage offers more than its share of challenges to adolescents, who must learn to balance emotional ties to more than one set of parents.
11. This balancing process can be made easier by the divorced parents' working together to raise their children.
12. The most important part of working with families is to build on strengths. Because there are so many family styles, the goal of intervention is to help the family find the style that is most comfortable for that particular family. So long as that style does not harm family members or other families, it should be considered functional for that family.

4 Peers

- Peer Groups

- Developmental Changes in Influence and Involvement

- Ethnic and Racial Minority Adolescents and Peer Relations

- Adolescents, Peer Groups, and Their Use of Leisure Time

- Adolescents and Work

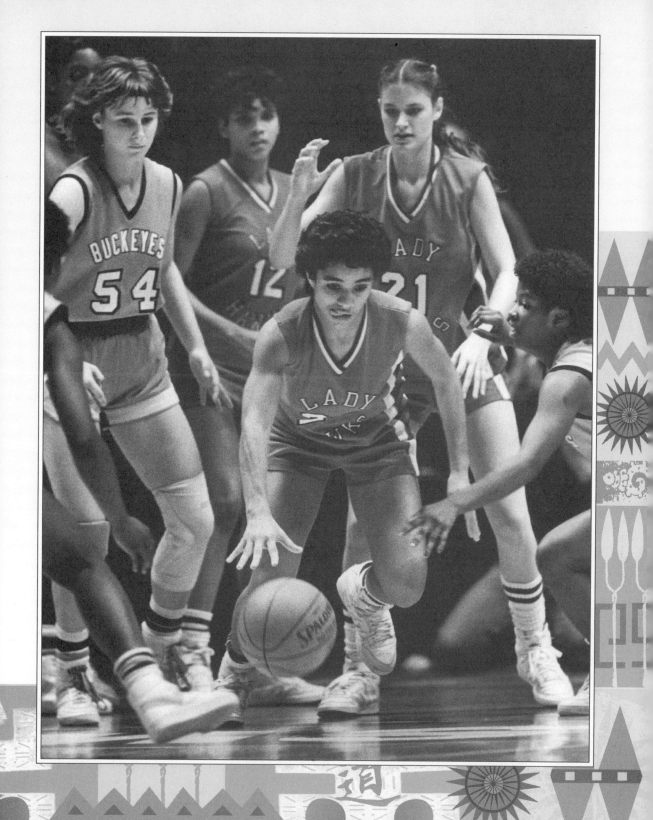

efore the late 1800s, children and adolescents remained at home working side by side with their parents, so that they constantly lived under the direct or indirect control of an adult. With greater migration to the cities and with more parents working away from home, however, children have increasingly come to be on their own. Decreasing adult supervision, increasing autonomy, and an educational system built on the "peer culture" (J. S. Coleman, 1961) may have provided the foundation for contemporary concern about peer-group influences. Indeed, the concern is so great today that television commercials occasionally include such statements as "Parents, do you know where your children are?" (And sometimes it's "Children, do you know where you parents are?")

Current concerns about parental supervision or peer influences may be warranted. Since adolescence is a period of heightened self-consciousness, and for many, a period of increased need to be like others, it is not uncommon for an adolescent to get into trouble because of the need to belong. In this chapter we look at peer groups and examine their influence on adolescent behavior. We also take up the adolescent's use of leisure time to watch television, listen to music, play video games, and participate in sports. Finally we examine adolescents at work.

Peer Groups

Group Formation

Writers have advanced a number of theories about why early adolescents turn to peer groups. Blos (1962) argues that the forming of adolescent friendships is associated with changing aspects of psychological drives that are associated with narcissism and emerging phallic conflicts. Erikson (1968), from his life-crisis perspective, points out that friends offer constructive feedback and information on self-definitions and perceived commitments. Social-cognition theorists, such as McCandless (1970), are inclined to see peer groups as important because of their reinforcing nature. Still other scholars have viewed peer-group formation from either an intergenerational-conflict perspective (K. Davis, 1940) or a discontinuity perspective (Benedict, 1938).

Regardless of why peer groups emerge, it is clear that in at least early adolescence young people prefer to be in the company of groups of other young people (B. B. Brown, Eicher, & Petrie, 1986; Montemayor & Hanson, 1985; Montemayor & Van Komen, 1985; Reisman, 1985). For example, a two-year study of 335 early adolescents from grades six to eight found that as these young people grew older, groups formed, telephone usage increased, and, by the eighth grade, dating began. Nearly half the males and females in this study acknowledged having "made out" by the eighth grade (Crockett, Losoff, & Petersen, 1984). Beyond the obvious attractions of peers to adolescents who have discovered their sexuality, there are other reasons for peer relations. One is the mutual support and guidance that the peer group offers adolescents in contrast to the adolescents' perceived view of their parents as authoritarian (Hunter, 1985; Moran & Eckenrode, 1991). Collectively, these data indicate that both quantitatively and qualitatively the socialization experience of adolescents is focused on peer interaction.

Some Determinants of Friendship

Since adolescents spend considerable time with peers, it is important to know how they choose their close friends. Many laboratory studies have shown that similarity of interests, values, and opinions is a major determinant of interpersonal attraction in general (Whitbeck, Simons, Conger, & Lorenz, 1989). Extensive research by Kandel (1981b) indicates that the most common characteristics of adolescent friends are similar age and same sex and race. Other social variables contribute to friendship formation but are much less influential. Kandel's research also suggests that involvement and behavior in school—specifically, educational expectations, grades, frequency of cutting classes, number of days absent, and time spent doing homework—are similar for close friends. Finally, Kandel (1973) and others (Whitbeck, Simons, Conger, & Lorenz, 1989) have found that engaging in delinquent activities such as the use of illicit drugs, particularly marijuana, plays an extraordinary role in the choice of friends. Adolescents who smoke marijuana or tobacco, drink beer, wine, or hard liquor, or use psychedelic drugs are more likely than not to have friends who do the same, lending some credence to the old statement "You can tell a lot about people by the friends they keep."

Friendship Formation and Peer Behavior

Surprisingly little is known about the processes underlying friendship formation. As Kandel (1981b) has noted, the similarity between friends could be due to either (1) assortative pairing, in which friends are selected on the basis of similarity, or (2) a socialization process in which friends influence each other. Through an examination of stable and changing friendships over the course of a year, Kandel was able to document that both processes occur. She has also reported that marijuana use, educational aspirations, political attitudes, and reported participation in minor forms of delinquency are of particular importance in the assortative and socialization processes. Thus, we must conclude that the sharing of certain characteristics contributes to friendship formation, while a socialization process appears to enhance the friendship over time.

Although adolescents are peer centered, their interactions with their peers may be egocentric. In a naturalistic-observation study of group discussions by male adolescents (B. M. Newman, 1976), most of the subjects' comments reflected joking, exaggeration, elaborations on truth, or perceived invulnerability. However, when these adolescents were interacting with an adult leader, many of their comments showed discouragement. Indicating discontent with the adult world, boys remarked that adult leaders were unable to take them seriously. Interactions with peers far exceeded those with adults (79% versus 21%). East (1989) has further elaborated on this point in a study of several hundred early adolescents who were asked to identify socially supportive adults. These young people identified social support (affection, nurturance, and instrumental help) coming most from their mothers, significantly less from their fathers, and "uniformly" withheld by their teachers.

The Emergence of Groups

Understanding why groups emerge during adolescence requires us to recognize the psychosocial nature of adolescence. The world of the adolescent is youth oriented. We have already seen that adolescents spend most of their time interacting with other adolescents. Adults working in schools, in churches, and with youth groups both passively and actively encourage this interaction. For example, one study observed that the secondary-level teachers overwhelmingly used lectures to communicate information. This study reported that less than 1% of instructional time "required some kind of open response involving reasoning or perhaps an opinion from students" (Goodlad, 1984, p. 299). Indeed, it has been observed that teachers passively accept students' membership in almost any peer group without making formal attempts to modify friendship patterns (P. R. Newman & Newman, 1976). On the other hand, teachers actively solicit youths with specific characteristics for membership in certain school-related groups. Have you ever thought about the common characteristics of adolescents who are office helpers, hall monitors, teachers' assistants, and so forth? Contrast these characteristics with those of adolescents assigned the role of class stooge or resident J. D. (juvenile delinquent).

Thus, social contexts encourage group identity rather than social alienation. This social process can be viewed in terms of psychosocial conflict (P. R. Newman & Newman, 1976). Adolescents are pressured by individual and social needs to identify with a social group or experience a pervasive sense of alienation and personal isolation. If an adolescent chooses to identify exclusively with the family, there is always the potential for self-perceived perennial childhood; if let unattached to a social group, the adolescent is probably going to experience difficulty in reducing the tension associated with isolation and loneliness. Thus, group formation is a natural consequence of a social structure that establishes interpersonal pressures to identify with at least one peer group. (See Box 4–1 for social processes that influence peer group formation.) In the next section we explore some of the contemporary peer groups that adolescents join.

Interpersonal Influence

It is clear that adolescents influence one another, and social-cognition theory provides a useful framework for understanding the mechanism behind this influence. As Kandel (1981b) has indicated, interpersonal influence can emerge from (1) imitation, in which one person observes the behavior of another and emulates it, or (2) social reinforcement, in which a person is rewarded for adopting the behaviors or values of another. Kandel's data suggest that both processes occur. However, imitation of both peers and parents appears to be more influential than social reinforcement by either of them, particularly in the case of marijuana use.

One fundamental question that parents often ask is whether older peers overly influence younger adolescents. This concern has particular importance in that our contemporary school system places younger adolescents with older youths. Furthermore, due to economic or building pressures, school districts are increasingly inclined to place younger and younger students in schools with older peers. One research report (Blyth, Hill, & Smyth, 1981) indicates that younger students

Box 4–1   The Social Psychology of In-Groups and Out-Groups

Similarity in race, same sex, and similarity in age, are the three most common characteristics of adolescent friendships (Kandel, 1981b). One way to examine the underlying dynamics of race and ethnicity in peer relations is through the social psychological theory of in-group and out-group relations. When an individual is born into a group or affiliates with a group as a child, adolescent, or adult, he or she is a member of an in-group. Similarity is a factor that strengthens in-group connections. Out-groups are those groups of which the individual is not a member.

There are many positive aspects of in-group membership. According to social identity theory, a sense of self stems from membership in and affiliation with various social groups (Hinkle & Brown, 1990). Members of in-groups typically develop positive feelings of belongingness, cohesion, and group pride. On the other hand, the tendency may be for in-groups to feel group superiority and to express prejudice toward out-groups. Discrimination is also a common practice between in-groups and out-groups.

In reality, people may be members of a variety of in-groups based on such factors as race and ethnicity, gender, religion, interests and hobbies, athletic activities, educational level, and so on. The more groups of which a person is a member, the greater the potential for contact with out-group members. Thus, it would seem that one way to minimize prejudice and discrimination among adolescents is to provide multiple opportunities for interaction and cooperation between out-groups. However, in order to be effective, certain favorable conditions are necessary for in-group and out-group contact. Brigham (1986) summarizes five key points:

1. *Participants have equal status with one another.* Brigham (1986) notes, however, that equal status has not characterized interracial contact in the United States.

One implication of this point for promoting contact between adolescents of various ethnic and racial backgrounds is to strive for equivalence in socioeconomic status. Thus, tension that results from differences in income and social class is inconsequential.

2. *Competition increases group hostilities, thus, intergroup contact should include opportunities for mutual interdependence and cooperation.* The introduction of common goals is an effective way to enhance interdependence between groups that formerly have been in conflict.

High schools might introduce common goals that require cooperation of students from a variety of ethnic and racial groups. Athletic teams are a good illustration of how in-group and out-group members can be brought together and share common goals.

3. *Personal relationships and the development of friendships should be encouraged by social norms and authorities.* In-group adolescents can be taught that many of their needs and interests are shared with out-group adolescents, and vice versa. Emphasizing communality, as opposed to differences, provides the basis for building friendship.

4. *Characteristics of group members do not reinforce negative stereotypes of the groups.* Emphasize the many attributes of individuals that are contrary to common stereotypes. In doing this, schools should make sure that they are providing equal opportunities for all students to express their talents and strengths. Furthermore, recognize individual efforts.

5. *Encourage generalization of changed attitudes to new people and situations.* Once adolescents have been exposed to the misleading nature of stereotypes with respect to one out-group, have them explore misconceptions they may hold about other out-groups.

---

may experience detrimental consequences in schools with older students. When ninth-graders were moved into a high school containing ninth and tenth grades, they were found to show more worry about their school environment, increased drug use, and increased concern about victimization. Similar, but less obvious, effects were noted when seventh-graders and eighth-graders were educated in the same building with ninth-graders. More recently, a study by Gifford and Dean (1990) found that ninth-grade students in junior high school settings were more involved in extracurricular school activities than their counterparts in senior high

Friendships play an important role in adolescence.

school settings. In addition, these young people also had better attitudes toward school and higher grades than ninth-graders in 9–12 school settings. To ease the transition from one school setting to another, one group has designed an effective program that increased parent-child tutorial involvement, heightened teacher awareness and used peer mentors (Jason, Kurasaki, & Neuson, 1993). Preventive interventions of this nature that sensitize school officials and that educate, support, and guide the new student hold future promise for reducing the stress of school change.

Clearly, older peers can have a potent influence on an adolescent's perception and behavior. However, we still do not know what school or peer-group structure is best suited for positive growth during adolescence. For just as a senior can intimidate a freshman as we have read so too can a freshman heckle a seventh- or eighth-grader.

Developmental Changes in Influence and Involvement

Scholarly and popular writings on adolescent development are full of statements about the growing importance of peers during adolescence. In particular, much attention has been given to the proposed importance of peer groups in the gradual movement toward individual autonomy. According to one summary,

> The youngster uses the support and example of his contemporaries in making the transition from parental control to personal autonomy. Peer opinion weighs heavily with the adolescent, so much so that the youngster often seems little more than a prisoner of peer norms. . . . He looks to his peers for support and guidance. In rejecting one source of authority, the parent, he substitutes another, the peers. (Douvan & Adelson, 1966, p. 198)

From Parental Influence to Peer Influence

A number of studies have documented the effect on adolescent behavior of the change from parental to peer influence (Sebald, 1989; Utech & Hoving, 1969; J. W. Young & Ferguson, 1979). For example, one investigation assumed that different reference groups would be consulted for advice on different issues. In this study young people were asked to indicate to whom they would be most likely to turn for advice on a variety of issues (Sebald, 1989). For advice on education, career, or monetary subjects, adolescents sought advice from parents. On subjects such as dress, dating, drinking, and other social activities peer influence predominated. This less than all-powerful influence of peer groups on all behavior has been demonstrated by others (Berndt, Miller, & Park, 1989). Their study found that on matters of attitudes toward school and behavior in school settings that parents were reported to be more influential than peers.

Another study of 272 12- to 15-year-old English girls provided cross-cultural support for these findings. On moral issues, parents' perceived values dominated. In contrast, on issues such as grooming and social activity, peer values dominated

Struggles can occur because of the conflicting influences of parents and peers.

(Nile, 1981). These data appear consistent with J. C. Coleman's (1978) focal theory of adolescent development. According to this theory, differing themes associated with parental and peer influence on adolescent behavior are likely to occur at different ages. Coleman provides evidence suggesting that fear of rejection by peers, which seems to reach its peak at about age 15 or 16, influences deference to peer opinions.

Although the developmental change from parental to peer influence is well documented, much less is known about the factors that contribute to it or about its impact on parent/adolescent relationships. Sullivan and Sullivan (1980) have argued that adolescent development tasks include the paradoxical one of increasing independence while maintaining an affectionate and supportive relationship with parents. Parents and adolescents themselves may differ in their readiness for increased autonomy, and some degree of conflict over attempts at increased independence is inevitable (J. C. Coleman, 1978). The initial departure from home may be the major gauge of the effects of independence on parent/adolescent relationships. Sullivan and Sullivan compare male adolescents who lived at home and commuted to college with others who boarded at the school on several measures of independence and parent/child communication. Not only were boarders inclined to see themselves as more independent, but they reported higher levels of satisfaction with their parents than did commuting adolescents. Boarders also reported increasingly higher levels of affection for and communication with their parents on departing for college. Perhaps by expressing independence outside the home, adolescents both enhance their importance to their parents and reduce the direct conflict associated with striving for independence. Commuters, on the other hand, see their parents every day and are inclined to demonstrate their independence in ways that continue to lead to direct conflict. Of course, in this situation parents are consequently likely to experience confrontations over parental versus peer views on social behavior, so that the peer-pressure effect is enhanced. Other evidence suggest that the difference in conflict level for female adolescent boarders and commuters may be even sharper. Because females may be more readily swayed through their affiliate tendencies by peer-group behavior (Curtis, 1975), female adolescents who live at home and commute to college may challenge their parents more than do males over conflicts in social or moral judgments.

Parental relationships with adolescents may actually be an extremely important factor in understanding the effects of peers on adolescent behavior. We have often heard parents say that their adolescents never listen, that they don't care about the family, or that they won't stay home. On the other side, we have heard these same adolescents complain that their family life is unsupportive and lacking in warmth and understanding. Therefore, it is possible that adolescents are pushed as much as pulled toward increasing peer-group involvement. In a study comparing adolescents having a low-quality or high-quality relationship with adults on reported dependence on or autonomy from peer groups (Iacovetta, 1975), adolescents who reported a high-quality relationship had many fewer peer-oriented contacts, reported less dependence on peers, and claimed more overall autonomy. The results of another investigation (T. E. Smith, 1976) also suggest that parental attributes are stronger predictors of peer-group involvement than peer characteristics. Thus, degree of peer-group involvement may be more closely associated with degree of parental supportiveness than with the lure of peer groups themselves. Since, on the average, with increasing age adolescents become more peer oriented in their social behavior, we might suspect that parents either consciously or unconsciously encourage this orientation even though some conflict is likely to occur because of it.

One must conclude that (1) parents and peers can have independent effects on an adolescent's behavior and that (2) parents and peers can somehow have a combined effect. Kandel's data on adolescent use of marijuana (Kandel, 1973, 1974; Kandel, Kessler, & Margulies, 1978) illustrate these two processes. For example, she has shown that when an adolescent is exposed to conflicting peer and parental role models, the adolescent is more likely to respond to peer pressure. However, the highest rate of adolescent marijuana use occurs when peers use marijuana and the parents use other, legal drugs.

From Same-Sex Involvement to Opposite-Sex Involvement

Adolescence is not only a period of increasing influence by peers but also a period of change in peer involvement from unisexual to heterosexual. Peer relations, when examined from a group-formation perspective, emerge in *cliques* and *crowds*. A crowd is a large group of adolescents who affiliate with one another through the identification of a common leader or idol. Membership in a crowd does not ensure a close relationship among all the members; rather, a crowd is a collection of smaller groups referred to as cliques. A clique is composed of several adolescents who are very close friends. In contrast to membership in a crowd, belonging to a clique entails maintaining a close relationship with all the other members. The initiation and development of peer groups is a gradual social process involving both cliques and crowds.

A classic field-observation study by Dexter Dunphy (1963) in Australia offers important insight into this process, which is shown in Figure 4–1. In early adolescence (Stage 1), boys and girls initially maintain small, same-sex cliques. These same-sex cliques soon begin to interact. Gradually the leaders and higher-status group members form additional cliques based on heterosexual relations. Next, the newly formed heterosexual cliques come to replace the same-sex cliques. Furthermore, these heterosexual cliques associate with one another in a larger crowd during group functions and social activities. In late adolescence the crowd begins to disintegrate into small cliques or couples. The crowd loses its utility as couples begin to bond and make longer-range commitments.

Ethnic and Racial Minority Adolescents and Peer Relations

Social Interaction Between Groups

The discussion in Box 4–1 centers on processes of intergroup interaction identified through research in social psychology. However, variations in ethnic and racial minority adolescents' affiliations with peers also can be examined in terms of reference-group orientation. Reference-group orientation is defined as "labels, values,

Figure 4-1 The development of heterosexual cliques, crowds, and couples. Individual sets without an arrow are non-interacting. Sets with arrows are interacting groups. Overlapping sets are interacting between included figures only.

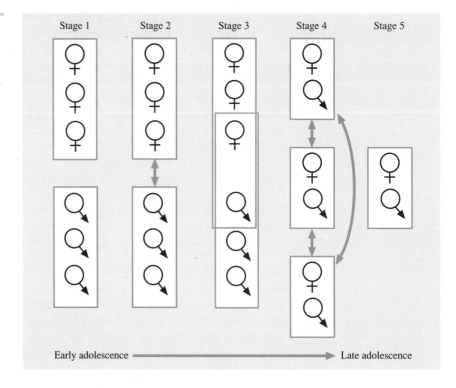

attitudes, preferences, and behaviors specific to particular ethnic groups" (Rotheram-Borus, 1990, p. 1075). This perspective assumes that the individual selects the ethnic group against whose standard the self is compared. Three categories of reference-group labels identified by Rotheram-Borus (1990) are *bicultural, mainstream,* and *strongly ethnically identified. Mainstream* ethnic minorities label themselves according to the values of the broader society. In contrast, *strongly ethnically identified* individuals adopt a label and values consistent with the norms of their ethnic minority group. *Bicultural* individuals are able to adopt reference-group labels indicative of both their ethnic minority group as well as the broader societal culture.

Rotheram-Borus (1990) has examined reference-group orientations and social interaction across groups (cross-ethnic contacts) among Asian, Black, Puerto Rican, and White adolescents attending a racially balanced high school. As might be expected, 66% of the Whites self-identified in the mainstream culture. Forty-three percent of Blacks, 47% of Puerto Ricans, 46% of Asians, and 17% of the Whites identified themselves as bicultural. Smaller percentages of the minority individuals self-identified as mainstream or strongly ethnically identified.

Adolescents who self-identified as bicultural or mainstream were significantly more likely than the strongly ethnically identified group to engage in cross-ethnic contacts. Indeed, cross-ethnic group contacts were found to be quite frequent. Forty percent of students reported five or more contacts per week with cross-ethnic peers. Activities of the cross-ethnic peers included studying, getting together, attending cross-ethnic parties, and going to church. In comparison to the other three groups, the Asian students had significantly fewer cross-ethnic contact.

Reference-group theory and research indicates that accepting bicultural values enhances (for some minority youths) social involvement in our increasingly diverse society in North America. Some people might argue that a strong ethnic identity is best for social adjustment and minority group interests. Others might think reference-group theory suggests that greater interpersonal involvement and crossgroup understanding resulting from a bicultural orientation is a desireable consequence. We return to the issue of ethnic and racial minorities and peer relations within the school context in Chapter 5.

Collectivist and Communal Ideals in Peer Relations Among Minorities

In Chapter 3, we note that many ethnic and racial minority groups are oriented to communal or affiliative family relations as opposed to socialization toward individualism. A unique field observation study by Hutchison (1987) supports these assertions through an examination of the leisure behavior of Blacks, Hispanics, and Whites in public parks in the Chicago area. This rich data set is comprised of 3,072 observations of 18,000 groups engaged in more than 300 commonplace, exotic, and defiant activities. The average size of groups was largest for Hispanics (5.7 persons), followed by Blacks (3.8 persons), and smallest for Whites (2.5 persons). The majority of Whites (51.7%) were engaged in activities as individuals, and 27.1% were involved with peers. In contrast, 38.7% of Blacks and a much lower number of Hispanics (9.6%) were engaged in individual activities. Approximately the same percentage of Blacks also engaged in activities with peer groups (37.9%). Peer group activity among Hispanics was less (20.8%) than mixed group activities (29.8%). Mixed groups were comprised of people of different ages and multiple family groups. In addition to multiple family group activities, nuclear family activities also were higher among Hispanics (14.5%) in contrast to Blacks (4.4%) and Whites (6.1%).

With respect to sex composition of groups, male groups dominated among Whites (51.8%) and Blacks (55%). The majority of Hispanic groups also were comprised of males (34.2%) or were predominantly male (18.6%). Young adult groups were most typical among Whites (34.4%) and Blacks (26.1%), in comparison to other age groupings from childhood to elderly ages. Mixed age groups were highest among Hispanics (47.8%).

The findings of Hutchison (1987) support the notion that not only are individualistic values (expressed in the form of individual/group behavior) more commonly perpetuated among White culture, but they are also reflected in the high degree of individually oriented behavior of Whites in nonhousehold, public settings of parks. Hispanics show the greatest adherence to communal values: they had the largest size groups, the highest number of group activities, and the lowest number of individual activities. Furthermore, an orientation toward more familial or multifamilial involvement is more common among Hispanics than is peer group activity. In contrast, although Blacks also show a greater tendency toward affiliation than do Whites, Black groups are more likely to be a peer group than a mixed or family group.

Peer Social Support Among Minorities

Consistent with a communal orientation, the strong social support networks characteristic of many ethnic and racial minority groups also was noted in Chapter 3. Social support is not only a phenomenon of the extended family, but it is also evident in close social support networks of friends and peers.

Coates (1987) notes the importance of social support as a buffer against stress and as a facilitator of competence in adolescence. Social support is particularly important for Black adolescents because it may aid in the achievement of important goals that are otherwise hindered through social inequality. A similar problem exists for other racial minorities who are victims of prejudice and discrimination. However, strong interpersonal bonds among Black adolescents means that strong pressure to adhere to peer group norms is present, and sometimes, unfortunately, that pressure may be toward antisocial and self-destructive behaviors (Gibbs, 1989). Resistance to joining a peer group and resistance to engaging in antisocial activities may result in social isolation and ridicule for some minority adolescents.

Research suggests that not only are Black females' social support networks different from those of males, but also female networks may be of a more intimate nature. Gibbs (1989) summarizes literature on interpersonal relations among Black youth and notes strong same-sex peer groups. Black female peer groups, in particular, serve as a social support network in communities characterized by many single-parent families and few community resources.

Findings by Coates (1987), in particular, suggest different social realities for Black female adolescents as compared to their male counterparts. Black female adolescents estimate a greater number of persons known overall than do Black males. However, females have less frequent contacts with their social networks than do males. Males not only have more frequent contact, but also report meeting with members of their network in a greater variety of settings. Females report that they meet members of their social network in more intimate settings than do males. Furthermore, a higher proportion of females than males report having small friendship groups (less than five persons), and more males than females report their friendship groups consist of more than ten people.

The apparent realities of social support from peers for minority adolescents is twofold. On the positive side minority youths live in a strongly connected social world that can be filled with broad social support from friends and peers. Although the degree of connection may vary between girls and boys, this broad connection may provide a wide network of concern and caring. However, if this network is defiant, norm-breaking, or delinquent, the influence may be socially or psychologically detrimental.

Adolescents, Peer Groups, and Their Use of Leisure Time

Frankly, we are not sure whether society influences adolescent tastes, adolescents influence adolescent tastes, or adolescents influence society's tastes. We do suspect that the interactions are complex and revolve around archetypal themes of individuality and independence. We have selected several of the most interesting and explore them in the remainder of this chapter. (See Table 4–1.)

Table 4–1   Daily leisure activities of high school seniors, by type of activity and sex: 1976 to 1990

Activity and sex	Percent participating in activity each day								
	1976	1980	1984	1985	1986	1987	1988	1989	1990
Watch television	71	72	73	72	74	71	73	71	72
Males	71	72	76	74	77	74	74	77	74
Females	71	73	69	69	71	69	71	66	70
Read books, magazines, or newspapers	59	59	53	51	50	48	46	47	47
Males	58	59	52	50	50	49	47	48	50
Females	62	59	54	52	51	48	46	46	46
Get together with friends	52	51	48	47	49	47	50	51	49
Males	55	55	51	52	52	49	54	56	52
Females	48	47	43	43	46	45	48	46	45
Participate in sports and exercise	44	47	44	43	44	44	44	44	46
Males	52	57	54	53	54	55	57	55	56
Females	36	38	33	34	36	34	31	33	34
Spend at least one hour of leisure time alone	40	42	44	42	42	43	42	42	41
Males	39	40	42	40	40	44	41	44	40
Females	41	44	45	45	43	44	42	41	42
Work around house, yard, or car	41	40	41	35	34	33	32	29	28
Males	33	30	35	28	27	27	25	24	22
Females	49	49	47	42	41	38	37	34	35
Ride around in a car for fun	—	33	34	35	36	36	37	36	34
Males	—	38	40	39	41	40	41	42	36
Females	—	28	27	31	31	32	33	31	32
Play a musical instrument or sing	28	29	30	29	27	28	27	27	28
Males	22	25	24	24	22	24	23	23	26
Females	35	34	37	35	32	32	31	30	31
Do art or craft work	12	13	12	11	14	14	13	13	15
Males	10	12	14	12	14	15	12	13	15
Females	13	14	10	10	13	13	12	13	14
Do creative writing	6	5	6	6	7	6	6	6	7
Males	4	4	6	4	6	6	6	5	6
Females	6	6	6	7	7	7	6	7	8

—Data not available.

Source: U.S. House of Representatives, Select Committee on Children, Youth, and Families, *U.S. Children and Their Families: Current Conditions and Recent Trends,* 1987, page 120.

Televison: "Hey, Kids, What Time Is It?"*

In two exhaustive reviews of the literature on the effects of television on youth, Leibert and Sprafkin (1988) and Murray (1980) provide information gathered from three decades of research in the area. The picture that emerges from their efforts is disturbing because of the tremendous impact on our attitudes and behavior that we have permitted television to have.

Television viewing begins as early as the first year of life. Most children begin watching television before they are walking, talking, and playing with other children. It is estimated that U.S. and Canadian youth consume 18,000 hours of television during their adolescent years (Carruth, Goldberg, & Skinner, 1991). Few of us can probably remember a time when a television set was not in our homes. But for those few who can, the arrival of a set meant that as preadolescents we spent less time reading, listening to the radio, visiting friends, or going to the movies. We used television for emotional release, to engage in fantasy, and to be informed (of how many cereal-box tops it took to acquire some terribly essential communicator code ring). We used television to have something to talk about with our friends and to compare ourselves against some idealized version of youth appearing in shows like *Lassie, Rin Tin Tin, The Cosby Show,* or *Family Ties*.

Television and Adolescence

The effect of television on the academic performance of young people is in most cases damaging. Researchers report that, as a general rule, as viewing time increases, grades decrease. Young people of lower socioeconomic status appear to watch television more than do those of higher status. Also Blacks spend more time with television and radio than Whites (Brown, Childers, Bauman, & Koch, 1990.) An additional finding is that as intelligence decreases, viewing time increases. Adolescents with high self-esteem watch less television than those young people who think poorly of themselves (Gerbner, Gross, Morgan, & Signorielli, 1984; Leibert & Sprafkin, 1988; Murray, 1980; Tucker, 1986). Crosscultural studies show that television viewing by a majority of 13-year-old students in many nations exceeds three hours a day. (See Box 4–2.) In the United States 73% of 13-year-olds watch more than three hours of television daily. Viewing time for the youth in the United States has been rising. In the 1960s 17% of young people watched three hours of television a day; this figure increased to 29% in the 1970s and to 73% in 1988 (Lawrence, Tasker, Daly, Orhiel, & Wozniak, 1986; U.S. Department of Education, 1989). It should be noted that television watching peaks during early adolescence and declines sharply thereafter. The preadolescent and the early adolescent appear to use television as a companion. As adolescents grow older, they seek out places to meet and socialize with other young people.

Television as Reality

The overwhelming weight of evidence indicates that television strongly shapes adolescents' attitudes toward people, places, and things. If they see it on television, they tend to believe it. If you accept this statement, for a moment, as truth

---

*"Hey, kids, what time is it?" was the opening line on one of our childhood television favorites, *The Howdy Doody Show*.

Box 4–2 Watching the Tube: A Cross-cultural Perspective

The following are the percentage of 13-year-old students, by amount of time per day spent watching television in 5 countries and in the Canadian provinces of Ontario and Quebec for the year 1988.

Country or Province	0–2 hrs	3–4 hrs	5 hrs or more
		(% of students)	
United States	27	42	31
United Kingdom	28	45	27
Ireland	45	41	14
Spain	46	41	13
Korea	49	44	7
Ontario (English)	35	43	22
Quebec (French)	49	40	11

Why do you think viewing habits are so similar in so many countries? What may account for Korea's and Quebec's lower viewing times? Are we becoming a world of one visual image?

(U.S. Department of Education, 1989)

(you can't believe everything you read), then you can view television as a means for shaping public opinion and behavior. For example, consider the clothing that young people wear. Studies suggest that as adolescents increase in age, peer influence in their choice of clothing increases (Eicher, Baizerman, & Michelman, 1991; Koester & May, 1985; Littrell, Damhorst, & Littrell, 1990). Studies also report that adolescents are drawn to designer labels (Lennon, 1986). Where did this awareness of designer labels originate? How do fashions move from relative obscurity to popularity? The answer, of course, can be found on the commercial breaks between music videos.

Television's critics might be more forgiving if it were not for other issues, such as the sexual exploitation of women that routinely fills the airwaves (Nystrom, 1983) or the televised encouragement of violence. Literally scores of reports have documented the damaging effects of watching excessive televised violence (for example, Bandura, 1965; Berkowitz, 1962, 1964; Goranson, 1975; Murray, 1980). (See Box 4–3.) Finally, some evidence suggests that lack of access to parents due either to maternal employment or parental absence is associated with increased viewing time by adolescents (Brown et al., 1990). Thus, absence of effective monitoring of viewing time by parents or substitution of alternative activities may be a primary factor in understanding likely negative influences.

Music

Any parent will tell you that musical taste emerges during adolescence. It has been estimated that young people listen to more than 10,500 hours of music during their adolescent years—a figure roughly equivalent to 12 years of schooling

Box 4–3   Television, Violence, and Young People

"The report of the Surgeon General's committee states that there was a high level of violence on television in the 1960s. Although in the 1970s there was considerable controversy over definitions and measurement of violence, the amount of violence has not decreased (approximately eight violent incidents per hour). Violence on television seems to be cyclical, up a little one year, down a little the next, but the percentage of programs containing violence has remained essentially the same over the past decade. . . .

"What is the effect of all this violence? After ten more years of research, the consensus among most of the research community is that violence on television does lead to aggressive behavior by children and teenagers who watch the programs. This conclusion is based on laboratory experiments and on field studies. Not all children become aggressive, of course, but the correlations between violence and aggression are positive. In magnitude, television violence is as strongly correlated with aggressive behavior as any other behavioral variable that has been measured. The research question has moved from asking whether or not there is an effect to seeking explanations for the effect.

"According to observational learning theory, when children observe television characters who behave violently, they learn to be violent or aggressive themselves. Observational learning from television has been demonstrated many times under strict laboratory conditions, and there is now research on when and how it occurs in real life. Television is also said to mold children's attitudes which later may be translated into behavior. Children who watch a lot of violence on television may come to accept violence as normal behavior."

Source: National Institute of Mental Health, Television and Behavior: Ten Years of Scientific Progress and Implications for the Eighties (DHHS Publication No. ADM 82–1195). Washington, D.C.: U.S. Government Printing Office, 1982, p. 6.

(Brown & Hendee, 1989). Indeed, a strong argument can be made that rock music provides the very foundation of what adolescence is all about. It may provide the peer-cultural expectations of adolescent behaviors in such matters as love, activism, values, parent relations, leisure, and schooling.

Music offers its young listener the chance to be conformingly "with it" in the pop 40 or to be nonconformingly cool in the counterculture, whether it's rap, heavy metal, punk rock, or good old rock and roll. Interestingly, the influence of music and the message it carries to young people has not been intensively studied by the academic community. According to an investigation of the relationship between time spent listening to music and academic behavior by adolescents in grades seven to nine (Burke & Grinder, 1966), the more time spent listening to youth-culture music, the lower the grade-point average, the less time spent in studying, and the lower the academic aspiration. it is unclear from this investigation whether time spent listening to music actually lowers academic standards or whether poor students listen to more youth-culture music.

In what may be the only major study of its kind, LaVoie and Collins (1975) also attempted to assess the effects of music listening on adolescents' academic behavior. Adolescents in grades nine to twelve were asked to complete study units dealing with either literature, mathematics, physical science, or social science while listening to either rock, classic, or no music. Follow-up testing for retention of material clearly indicated that listening to rock music interfered with both immediate and longer-range recall of information. LaVoie and Collins argue that rock music has its own rewarding power, "since its informational value for the adolescent provides a source of identification with peers" (p. 64). Therefore, when intellectual activities must compete with rock music, the music, with its strong reward power, will provide a stronger reinforcing effect.

Recent studies have concluded that most youth did not understand the lyrics of the songs they heard (Greenfield et al., 1987; Thompson, 1993; Wanamaker & Reznikoff, 1989). As might be imagined, comprehension of the words to a song increased as young people grew older.* These researchers also found that music videos did not stimulate the imaginations of young people.

The marriage of video to music more than a decade ago has significantly changed the relationship of youth to music. One indicator of this relationship is the estimate that 43% of all adolescents in the United States view MTV at least once a week (Thompson, 1993). Mental images once formed to rhythm, beat, and perceived lyrics are now created by video mixer and special effects. Research has found that those images more often than not are violent or sexually suggestive. The majority of concept videos studied portrayed women in stereotyped fashion as weak and sexually provocative (Brown & Hendee, 1989; Sun & Lull, 1986; Vincent, Davis, & Bronszkowski, 1987).

The influence these video images have on adolescents is uncertain. Do songs and videos like Madonna's *Papa Don't Preach* encourage adolescent pregnancies by glorifying the romantic relationship? Certainly, Madonna's impressive physical appearance in that video does not fit either her dancing outfit or our understanding of the bulging waistline that accompanies a pregnancy. Similarly, do Prince's video antics encourage youth to increase public displays of hanging tongues or masturbation? For that matter, has Michael Jackson's video behavior increased the sale of crotch supports, "Quell," or nonbinding underwear? Scholars continue to debate whether these performers and countless other have encouraged poor behavior or provided healthy outlets for fantasy and aggressive feelings.

Finally, in work with delinquent and hospital populations, scholars (Gold, 1987; King, 1988; Shatin, 1981) have found that music could encourage behavior that was counterproductive to the therapeutic process. Music, particularly heavy metal, that glorifies sadistic, violent, or drug-using behavior can work to the detriment of such patients.

To some extent, these same observations can be made about the young person on the street wearing a radio like a hearing aid or the one glued to the television set watching a surrealistic music video. It is, to a degree, a travel back in time to our youth to observe vacant-eyed, rocking, moaning teens going through some ancient, mystic ritual of adoration of a rock idol. This sort of behavior has appeared with each new generation of young people and will probably continue into the future.

---

*Readers who can remember the song *Louie Louie* by the Kingsmen should recall the controversy when it appeared. The concern was that the lyrics described an act of fornication. No one could be sure of this, of course, because no one could understand the lyrics. Given this situation, today's college youth should know that their parents rushed out to buy millions of copies of this 45-rpm recording and hid away in their bedrooms to play it at $33\frac{1}{3}$ rpm in a futile attempt to understand it. Recently, the Kingsmen revealed that the lyrics were not obscene but that the recording equipment was so bad that no one would have been able to tell anyway. Incidentally, the lyrics by Richard Berry tell the story of a sailor pining to a bartender about his girlfriend (Rockwell, 1990).

Implications

The influence of both television and music on young people is unmistakable. Both have significantly enlarged adolescents' knowledge of the world, in one sense creating a global village, but they have also restricted it by monopolizing young people's attention. At their best these media inform, entertain, and enrich. At their worst, they encourage racism, sexism, and violence. The answer to curbing these abuses rests, in our minds, not in increased legislation but in parental action. Parents need to become aware of the music young people listen to and the programs they watch. We do not encourage adults to censor but to become actively involved in discussing the messages these media impart to young people. To do so, of course, takes time, time with young people, and that is something we very strongly encourage.

Video Games

Before we begin this section we feel the need to remind the older returning student with adolescents at home that video games are not new to this generation of youth. The first ones appeared in the early 1970s and enjoyed initial financial success until the latter part of that decade only to reemerge in the mid 1980s. The lineage of the video game can be traced back to that of the pinball machine, which occupied the leisure time of previous generations of youth dressed in turned-up blue jeans, white socks, and penny loafers in the bowling alleys and soda shops that today are malls. This seemingly reassuring news provides little comfort to many parents, however, who worry about the influence these games may have on today's youth (Garver, 1990). Indeed, given that one cable network has a contest

Electronic technology continues to change the leisure time of contemporary adolescents.

show with a video game theme, that magazines are bought to outwit computer foes, and that none other than PBS airs *Where in the World is Carmen SanDiego?* (a popular computer program, now game show), maybe they have a point.

It is estimated that 90% of adolescents in the United States and Canada play video games. The typical video-game player has been described in studies as young, male, and bright. The game is seen as an electronic friend, suggesting that some of these youth may have difficulty creating friendships. Interestingly, players are not perceived as being in trouble with authorities more than non-players. The stronger interest males have in video games has been explained by the fact that most games involve violent or aggressive acts like escaping from danger, pursuing some evil creature, or waging warfare. We believe the powerful reinforcing element found in video games can be explained by the interactive capabilities. Regardless of one's size, strength, age, or agility a youth can pit himself or herself against another human player or the machine with color, 3D action, and stereo sound thrown in for good measure. Further, unlike friends who can tire of an activity, these games can continue so long as the batteries or power pack operate. Given the hostile nature of most of these games, it is not surprising to find studies showing increased levels of aggressive feelings in young people following a game. Whether these games are helpful in letting off steam or in encouraging hostile behavior remains uncertain (Cooper & Mackie, 1986; Griffiths, 1991; Schutte, Malouff, Post-Gorden & Rodasta, 1988).

Sports

Involving 20 million youth between the ages of 6 and 15 and costing an estimated $17 billion a year, the sheer popularity of athletic activity among family members suggests it to be a positive outlet for young people (Danish, Petitpas, & Hale, 1990). Reviews of the literature support the view that most educators, parents, doctors, and young people view sports in a positive light (Simon, 1979). For example, Simon reports that parents feel that athletics is an essential part of their children's development. School personnel, less glowingly but nevertheless strongly, support athletics though they voice concern that parents are a primary problem with athletics (Maresh, 1992; Yaffe, 1982). Many school personnel see parents as unruly spectators and poor coaches and as overdesirous of having their children win.

The attitudes of physicians toward athletic competition are determined, Simon (1979) found, by the nature of the sport involved. Physicians' approval diminishes rapidly as the violent nature of the sport increases. Thus, while baseball and swimming are widely approved of, 85% of all physicians surveyed disapprove of tackle football as too damaging to the body to be encouraged as a school sport. Finally, young people overwhelmingly find sports rewarding in social areas as well as in motor-skills development. Simon concluded:

> Positive attitudes were expressed by all intimately involved in children's sports with overwhelming support given by parents and children. Favorable attitudes were also expressed by educators and physicians, though they were slightly more cautious in their accolades of children's sports programs. . . . For once the attitudes and behaviors of the American public seem to mesh—something must be right about kids' sports! (P. 189)

But not all views of sports are as laudatory as Simon's. Sage (1978), for instance, understands sports not as good, clean fun but as a contributor to the formation of a bureaucratic personality. Sabo and Runfola (1980) describe sports activities as "the most crucial socializing forces in the development of the superman syndrome in American society" (p. ix). They blame the "association between [sports], violence, and masculinity" for encouraging "the prevalence of rape and wife-beating, the rising tide of sado-masochistic sexual images in men's magazines, and the eroticized violence against women in television and cinema productions" (p. xiii). The authors conclude the preface to their thought-provoking book *Jock: Sports and the Male Identity* with a quote from Marie Hart (1971) that despite women's entry into the field of athletic activity, "American society cuts the penis off the male who enters dance and places it on the woman who participates in competitive athletics" (p. xiv). Clearly, here are two rather different views of sports and their role in society. In this section we examine each argument more closely with an eye toward gauging the impact this leisure-time activity has on the social and emotional development of the adolescent.

Proponents

Summarizing the findings of authors and researchers who support competitive sports, Dowell (1970) reports that the benefits of such sports are found in four broadly defined areas: physical development, emotional development, social development, and miscellaneous benefits. Some of the benefits of competitive sports in the physical area are the development of motor ability and body strength. In the emotional domain, advocates argue, sports teach self-control and are an outlet for nervous energy. Within the social domain, Dowell finds evidence from various sources to suggest that sports teach citizenship, encourage social acceptance of the athlete by his or her peers, and contribute to later educational and financial success. In the fourth, miscellaneous category, sports advocates state that athletics reduce delinquency, encourage fitness, increase sportsmanship, and are a better use of leisure time than watching television, for instance.

Examining the specifics of some of these claims, Otto and Alwin (1977) found that team-sports participation is a major entry card into the social elite of a school. Their study of 340 young people in Michigan high schools in the late 1950s showed that athletes in school had higher education aspirations, higher job aspirations, higher IQs, and higher grades than their nonathletic classmates. Interestingly, 15 years later, in a follow-up on these young people, the authors found that these earlier levels of aspiration had been translated into reality. Attempting to explain why high school team sports seem to have such a positive effect on later life, Otto and Alwin suggest that three factors are important. They argue that sports teach interpersonal skills, label participants as successful individuals, and establish important social contacts. All of these factors, needless to say, are important in order to be successful in society.

The findings of Otto and Alwin (1977) support the earlier work of several researchers. Skubic (1956) and Seymour (1956) found, for instance, that team sports improve social adjustment and social competency. Orlick (1972) reported that young people who engage in team sports are more social, dominant, aggressive, enthusiastic, confident, vigorous, and tough-minded than young people who do not. Finally, J. S. Coleman (1961), Iso-Aloha and Hatfield (1986), Rehberg (1969), and Spady (1971) also confirmed that a significant positive relationship exists between high school team sports and educational aspirations and attainment. But not all the literature on team sports is laudatory, as we have already noted. In the next section the critics of team sports argue their case.

Opponents

"If competitive sports builds character, it a character fit for a criminal" (G. B. Leonard, 1971, p. 77). "To play this game you must have fire in you, and there is nothing that stokes fire like hate" (Vince Lombardi, football coach, cited in Freischlag & Schmidke, 1979, p. 183). If these quotes suggest an overemphasis on winning, and encouragement of violence, and a stance that the end justifies the means regardless of sportsmanship, then you already have a good idea of the arguments against competitive sports. McEwin (1981) found research literature both praising sports and damning it. Many critics contended that the body of the young athlete was overtaxed. This demand to perform too often results in permanent damage to the adolescent's body (such as to knee ligaments) that will rule out sports activity later in life. Disturbingly, the number of sports-related injuries is climbing for young people under the age of 15. More than 6 million youngsters are injured each year in sports activities (McEwin, 1981). Is the nature of sports for young people, critics ask, to emphasize winning, so that some less skilled team members never play and so that an adolescent becomes consumingly specialized in only 1, 2, or at best 3 of the more than 50 sports in existence?

Rowley (1987) questions whether a negative stigma is attached to females who participate in sports activities. His studies challenge findings that peer cooperation and social relationships improve. Rather, he notes an increase in antisocial behavior and aggressive acts. And although athletes may express higher educational aspirations, his work cannot establish an actual relationship between that aspiration and higher academic results.

Ogilvie and Tutko (1971) state that sports do not build character. Their study of young athletes suggests that "most athletes indicate low interest in receiving support and concern from others, low need to take care of others, and low need for affiliation" (p. 61). Achieving success in the high school sports arena is a "ruthless" process that is not conductive to developing warmth, understanding, and concern for their fellows, the authors contend.

Burchard (1979) and Freischlag and Schmidke (1979) contend that sports are a legal war in which "athletes are encouraged to nail, crush, crucify, and stick opponents. Blitzes, bombs, sacks, and kills are recorded in team statistics" (Freishchlag & Schmidke, 1979, p. 184). This idea that one's opponent is the enemy and that the coach is a general leading his troops conjures up images of war, of the Christians and the lions, of the Roman arena and the gladiators. It should be noted that this image is further encouraged by the television networks, which open these gladiatorial battles with adrenaline-stimulating music and cutaway film footage of the athletes donning their gear.

Beisser (1980) suggests that the reason for elevating sports to such a lofty position of importance not only for youths but also for all of society can be traced to a changing culture in which the male has lost his role. He states that equality of the sexes in the workplace and the changing nature of industry, with robotics displacing workers, have essentially emasculated the American male. Sports, then, is a way to recapture former glory, a way to reenact rituals from a former time. In these rituals the players retain superhero status while young women on the sidelines dressed in cutesy little outfits play out stereotypical roles as virginal worshipers (that is, cheerleaders) (Hich, 1980). Fasteau (1980) supports this view with his observation that male athletes are most respected when they are understood to be dominant, self-controlled, and insensitive.

Examining the role that violence plays in sports, Freischlag and Schmidke (1979) argue that alienation and social rootlessness interact to result in violence in sports both on the field and among the spectators. J. Robinson and Godbey (1978) and Parkhouse (1979) find that the coach's attitude, perhaps his preoccupation with winning, may affect the kind of play that occurs: "'I'd give anything—my house, my bank account, anything but my wife and family—to get an undefeated season. . . . [Another coach comments] 'I'd lie, cheat, and steal' [to win]" (p. 39).

J. McCarthy (1978) identifies four primary factors contributing to violence. The first, "me-mania," reflects the individual's desire for attention and that individual's regard for others. The second concerns the "media's attention to violence." This attention, McCarthy argues, promotes and inflames school rivalries far beyond their original level. Third, the coach must assume some responsibility. When high school football coaches incite teams by biting off the heads of live frogs (no kidding—live frogs) to get out there and win, then they are encouraging violent play. Finally, the rules of certain sports are written in such a way as to permit a violent level of play.

These issues concern females as well as males, critics contend. Although at one time society may have considered the "weaker sex" unfit for the rigors of outdoor life (expressed in the following 1912 quote), that sort of woman is now a nearly extinct species:

> Other things being equal, the man who has had the most experience in outdoor sports should be the best aviator. By the same token women should be barred. . . . Women have not the background of games of strength and skill that most men have. Their powers of correlation are correspondingly limited and their ability to cope with sudden emergency is inadequate. (*Outing* editorial, 1912, cited in M. Hart, 1971)

Since the federal government's long-overdue Title IX regulation ordered schools to provide equal opportunity for women to participate in sports, women have demonstrated their sports abilities. The issue that we address in the conclusion of this section is whether sports for both females and males need be this way.

Implications

The evidence is strong that athletic activity exerts an extremely powerful and potential positive influence on young people's lives. The proponents of sports assume that the current socialization process is unquestionably positive. The critics of team sports are not as convinced. These critics are not against sports per se

---

Box 4–4   The Cost of Winning

The need to win regardless of the cost is no better illustrated than by the common practice of wrestlers to cut their weight or, to use the vernacular, "suck down." The principle behind the act is to shed enough pounds to allow a wrestler to compete in a lower weight class. Experience suggests that the athlete who can manage the weight loss and compete in the lower weight class will win. The following comments by two young men who engage in this behavior with the knowledge of their parents and coaches illustrate critics' charges that many in society have lost sight of the purpose of athletic activity.

My preseason weight is a bit over 130 pounds, but I wrestle at 118 pounds. I want to wrestle at 114 pounds, because I know I could win all the time because I'd fight smaller kids. . . . I'd lose the weight and then gain it all back and then have to lose it all over again. One time I had trouble making the weight. I took a laxative and got real sick. I thought I would die.

I normally weigh 158 pounds but wanted to wrestle at 132 pounds. I had problems though, because I wouldn't do it right. I'd go up and down with my weight. I'd starve for a day, make weight, wrestle—a few times I though I'd throw up right on the mat—and come home and pig out, you know, eat everything in sight. I knew it wasn't good for me, but it's part of wrestling.

"It's part of wrestling"—but does it need to be?

---

but against what they see sports as having become. Curing society's ills through violent conflict between two teams is not the answer, these individuals suggest.

Supporting their position is the largest survey of student attitudes toward athletic activity yet undertaken (Hartley, 1990). Ten thousand youth ovewhelmingly indicated that they participated in sports activities for fun, not competition. Lack of enjoyment was the primary reason given for why young people left sports. These youth also saw the development of skills as more useful than winning and were motivated to participate for more reasons than simply win/loss statistics. For them, issues of health, peer acceptance, and adult approval mattered.

If we give serious consideration to these critics' arguments, what changes could be encouraged in sports? First, coaches and parents have a major responsibility for deemphasizing winning and emphasizing skill development. One outstanding example of this approach is ACT (Athletes Coaching Teens). This program uses sport activities as the means to encourage high-risk, inner-city adolescents to reduce dysfunctional behaviors. The program emphasizes goal setting and problem solving. It strives for sport to achieve, as Danish has so eloquently phrased it, an activity where one need not continue "to have to prove oneself, it can be a place where one begins to know oneself. When knowing becomes as important as proving, sport becomes an essential vehicle for developing personal competence" (Danish et al., 1990, p. 190).

Second, sports activity should be encouraged not in one or two areas but in several, and it should be integrated with other leisure activities, particularly the arts. Exposing young people to the intricacies and physical demands of dance, for instance, would serve to broaden young people's experience beyond these small social groups. Finally, society needs to value, recognize, and emphasize other ways in which young people can achieve feelings of self-worth. (See Box 4–4.)

One example of such a program that has achieved success in this area is in operation in Connecticut. Called Creative Experiences, the program uses the arts to develop physical, social, and emotional skills while giving young people an opportunity to experience feelings of recognition, self-worth, and importance. The program is intergenerational in that it encourages adults to participate in its activities for young people and is built on the philosophy that all members are equal (A. Smith, Goodwin, Gullotta, & Gullotta, 1979).

Another example of a competency enhancement program is ROPE (Rite of Passage Experience). Founded on the belief that young people are not provided with clear pathways into adolescence and later early adulthood, ROPE integrates group "Outward Bound" type challenge activities with peer and adult involvement in exercises that create a deeper awareness and respect for self and others. Like Creative Experiences, the program believes that young people succeed when they give to others. Thus, a community improvement project is an integral part of the ROPE graduation exercise (Blumenkrantz & Gavazzi, 1993).

These programs are two of many new experiments occurring around the United States and Canada that emphasize the promotion of social competency in youths. The application of these principles to sports and other leisure-time activities could foster the type of social-emotional growth that critics feel is lacking in sports activities today.

Adolescents and Work

The history of unemployment for adolescents mirrors that of the U.S. economy. When economic times are good, generally speaking, employment opportunities are available. When the economy is in recession, unemployment figures for youth rise. (See Table 4–2.) The phrase "generally speaking" is used because Black adolescents are significantly more likely to be unemployed than are Whites. The 1989 unemployment rate for White male youth 16- to 19-years-old was 16%; it was 32% for Blacks. This pattern continued into early adulthood. Unemployment rates for 1989 for White 20- to 24-year-olds was 9% and for Blacks, 18%. Hispanic youth ages 16 to 19 historically have fared better with unemployment rates at least 10% lower than Blacks. For young adults ages 20 to 24, Hispanic unemployment rates were only slightly higher than White young adult unemployment rates. Unemployment rates for women observed similar racial/ethnic patterns.

Today as in the past, chronic youth unemployment affects only a small percentage of U.S. teenagers. Estimated to be about 10% of the total, these unemployed youths are most often city dwellers who belong to ethnic or racial minorities (Eberly, 1991; Rodriquez, 1980; W. T. Grant Foundation, 1988). Among this group, those most likely to remain unemployed are youths who have dropped out of school (Eberly, 1991; Congressional Budget Office, 1980; Hamilton, 1982; R. C. Rist, 1982; W. T. Grant Foundation, 1988).

Family background, too, seems to exercise some influence over an adolescent's success in finding a job. Those with the greatest success are from middle-class,

Table 4–2   Unemployment rates of 16- to 24-year-olds, by sex, race/ethnicity, and age: 1950 to 1989

Sex and year	All races		White[1]		Black[1]		Hispanic[2]	
	16 to 19 years old	20 to 24 years old	16 to 19 years old	20 to 24 years old	16 to 19 years old	20 to 24 years old	16 to 19 years old	20 to 24 years old
Men								
1950	12.7	8.1	—	—	—	—	—	—
1955	11.6	7.7	11.3	7.0	13.4[3]	12.4[3]	—	—
1960	15.3	8.9	14.0	8.3	24.0[3]	13.1[3]	—	—
1965	14.1	6.4	12.9	5.9	23.3[3]	9.3[3]	—	—
1970	15.0	8.4	13.7	7.8	25.0[3]	12.6[3]	—	—
1975	20.1	14.3	18.3	13.1	38.1	24.7	27.6	16.3
1980	18.3	12.5	16.2	11.1	37.5	23.7	21.6	12.3
1981	20.1	13.2	17.9	11.6	40.7	26.4	24.3	14.2
1982	24.4	16.4	21.7	14.3	48.9	31.5	31.2	18.3
1983	23.3	15.9	20.2	13.8	48.8	31.4	28.7	17.1
1984	19.6	11.9	16.8	9.8	42.7	26.6	25.3	12.7
1985	19.5	11.4	16.5	9.7	41.0	23.5	24.7	13.0
1986	19.0	11.0	16.3	9.2	39.3	23.5	24.5	13.0
1987	17.8	9.9	15.5	8.4	34.4	20.3	22.2	10.2
1988	16.0	8.9	13.9	7.4	32.7	19.4	22.7	9.2
1989	15.9	8.8	13.7	7.5	31.9	17.9	20.2	9.7
Women								
1950	11.4	6.9	—	—	—	—	—	—
1955	10.2	6.1	9.1	5.1	19.2[3]	13.0[3]	—	—
1960	13.9	8.3	12.7	7.2	24.8[3]	15.3[3]	—	—
1965	15.7	7.3	14.0	6.3	31.7[3]	13.7[3]	—	—
1970	15.6	7.9	13.4	6.9	34.5[3]	15.0[3]	—	—
1975	19.7	12.7	17.4	11.2	41.0	24.3	27.9	17.2
1980	17.2	10.4	14.8	8.5	39.8	23.5	23.4	11.9
1981	19.0	11.2	16.6	9.1	42.2	26.4	23.5	13.6
1982	21.9	13.2	19.0	10.9	47.1	29.6	28.2	17.0
1983	21.3	12.9	18.3	10.3	48.2	31.8	27.9	16.4
1984	18.0	10.9	15.2	8.8	42.6	25.6	22.8	12.3
1985	17.6	10.7	14.8	8.5	39.2	25.6	23.8	12.1
1986	17.6	10.3	14.9	8.1	39.2	24.7	25.1	12.9
1987	15.9	9.4	13.4	7.4	34.9	23.3	22.4	11.4
1988	14.4	8.5	12.3	6.7	32.0	19.8	21.0	10.7
1989	14.0	8.3	11.5	6.8	33.0	18.1	18.2	12.2

—Data not available.

[1]Includes Hispanics.

[2]Hispanics may be of any race.

[3]Includes black and other races.

NOTE: The unemployment rate is the proportion of those in the labor force who are not working and are seeking employment.

Source: U.S. Department of Labor, Bureau of Labor Satistics, *Employment and Earnings* (January issues); and Labor Force Statistics derived from the *Current Population Survey: A Data Book,* vol. 1, Bulletin 2096.

The cost of unemployment on adolescents may be more damaging to society than just a bunch of youths loitering on streets.

well-educated families. Those with the least success are lower-class and poorly educated. The influence of the family is not direct but, rather, indirect in that education is ultimately related to occupation and thus to income:

> For both blacks and whites, family background has a strong effect on the amount of education young people receive; this in turn has considerable impact on the types of jobs they get. For white young men parental occupation is as important as the young man's I.Q. in predicting educational attainment. For blacks, although parental occupation is not so strong a factor, the size of the family is. Black young men from very large families receive less education, and education in turn affects wages. (S. M. Hill, Shaw, & Sproat, 1980, p. 2)

How the relationship between poverty and unemployment is translated into social costs is examined next.

The Social Costs of Unemployment

Employment is necessary for survival. In fact, many researchers would suggest that it is necessary for one's positive mental health. Adolescent unemployment has been linked to lower levels of self-esteem, higher degrees of emotional stress, and family unrest (Furnham, 1985; Patton & Nolles, 1991). Without a job or some other legitimate means of support, people have no way to acquire food, clothing, and shelter and must make a decision about how to obtain money in other ways. The unemployed adolescent is at particular risk for becoming engaged in illegal activities for money (Swinton, 1980). Prostitution, drug dealing, robbery, and other forms of unsanctioned or illegal behavior almost always have just one purpose: obtaining money.

This consequence of unemployment is clearly shown in Harvey Brenner's (1980) analysis of the social costs of youth unemployment. He writes that the ratio of youth unemployment to the total unemployment rate is (statistically) significantly related to motor-vehicle fatalities, mental-hospital admissions, and narcotics-law violations and to nearly all major crimes, including criminal homicide, rape, assault, robbery, auto theft, and prostitution. With each additional percentage-point rise in youth unemployment, Brenner estimates, there is a corresponding rise in arrests for those crimes.

According to Bowman (1990) chronic joblessness is a major challenge for African American youths in the United States. Discouragement about finding a job is very severe and continues into adulthood. Discouragement and self-blame can increase maladaptive responses. However, Bowman indicates that many Black youths diminish maladaptiveness by relying on strong kinship bonds, religion, and ethnic coping orientations (specific ethnic behaviors that facilitate coping). In particular, Black cultural resources appear to nurture a general sense of personal efficacy. Self-empowerment, together with family and kin encouragement of cultural pride and school success, helps some Black youths beat the odds of unemployment and associated discouragement.

The Value of Employment

From the Great Depression until recently, research suggested that work enhances adolescent development. Work, according to the Kettering Foundation report on youth employment, teaches responsibility and instills discipline in the adolescent (F. Brown, 1980). It creates a sense of social identification with society. It uses the adolescent's time and energy in a productive capacity, for which the adolescent receives financial compensation. Employment in U.S. society is essential for feeling meaningful, having self-respect, and being able to express oneself.

Thus, it is with interest that scholars have looked at reports suggesting that these aforementioned ennobling aspects of work during adolescence may no longer apply. Greenberger, Steinberg, and their associates contend that whereas in the past work and responsibility were related, this relationship no longer exists for the vast majority of American youths. Rather, large numbers of youths are employed in positions requiring no independent decision making (Greenberger & Steinberg, 1981, 1986). For example, consider the grocery checkout clerk. With the optical scanner and the computerization of inventory, the counter clerk's skills, never terribly complicated to begin with, have been reduced to passing a universal product code bar over a scanner beam.

These authors suggest that the belief that work exposes adolescents to positive adult role models is no longer true. Indeed, their studies suggest that while the time spent with family and other adults decreases, time spent with peers does not change (Greenberger & Steinberg, 1981; Greenberger, Steinberg, Vaux & McAuliffe, 1980). Finally, they suggest that the employment opportunities available to young people are boring, repetitive, and dull. Rather than encouraging an interest in work, they produce apathy (Greenberger & Steinberg, 1986). Consider, for example, fast-food clerks who push a button that dispenses a predetermined amount of soda into a cup. Think about their other job functions. Is there any aspect of their automated activity that varies? Is there any variation on the theme? These authors would answer no.

Somewhat moderating this dismal view is a study that reports young people perceiving benefits from working under certain circumstances. In contrast to jobs that require little intellectual stimulation, the authors find that when job skills are related to a young person's future career aspirations, benefits result. They also report a powerful relationship between job stress and students' mental health status with emotional health declining as stress increases (Mortimer, Finch, Shanahan, & Ryu, 1992) However, although this study provides some hope, the intriguing unanswered question is, How many opportunities of this type are available to young people or, for that matter, adults?

Implications

As we examine the issue of work in adolescence, we are torn between two persuasive arguments. The first notes the importance of employment; the second notes the dehumanizing aspects of that work for adolescents. Nevertheless, in our opinion, employment and job experience are important. The failure to gain work experience during adolescence appears to adversely affect people in later life.

We could call for a new commitment to education. There is clearly a powerful relationship between education achievement and ultimate job attainment, and that approach should not be discounted. But the problem of unemployment really weights most unfairly on only one segment of society. No minor adjustment in educational funding, student work attitudes, or the like will alter the fact that discrimination is a factor in youth unemployment. Until we come to grips with this issue, unemployment will continue to exacerbate the problems that confront many young people.

Major Points to Remember

1. Peer groups influence adolescents' preparation for adult roles as well as the youth culture itself.
2. These groups constitute a highly reinforcing setting for specific adolescent behaviors.
3. Peer groups do not replace parental influence, but they do supplement it.
4. A generational consciousness, or identification with one's youthful reference group, is an important influence on values and behaviors.

5. Television has a tremendous impact on young people. Research has shown that it can affect academic performance, shape attitudes, and influence behavior. Music and video games have a similarly powerful effect for good or evil.

6. Proponents believe that sports encourage physical health, promote body development, and strengthen emotional and social development.

7. Opponents believe that sports in their most excessive and violent forms harm physical health, encourage violence, and diminish concern for others.

8. Unemployment is one of the most pressing problems for minority youth.

9. Chronic unemployment affects only a small minority of teenagers in our society. The chances for unemployment increase when an adolescent has a poor education and few financial resources and is a member of a minority ethnic or racial group.

10. Crime and mental illness are significantly related to unemployment. As unemployment rises, homicide and other crimes, motor-vehicle fatalities, and admissions to mental hospitals rise as well.

CHAPTER

5 Education

- The Development of the U.S. School System

- The Social Fabric of the School

- School Contexts and Ethnic and Racial Minorities

- School and Family Influences on Learning

- Education, Careers, and the Future

- Truancy, Dropping Out, and School Violence

- Some Alternatives to the Present Educational System

It has been said that if you added together all of the money spent on all of the schools in the United States, it would far surpass the budget of any single group of industries. For the year 1991 that funding amounted to $372 billion for elementary, secondary, and postsecondary education (U.S. Census Bureau, 1992c). Certainly, the growth of education in the country over the past 100 years suggests a strong commitment to the belief that knowledge is the key to success. Given the tools to work with, any number of immigrant or native-born youngsters who applied themselves could reasonably expect to get their fair share of the pie. Thus, through the years, parents have dressed their children, equipped them with lunch pails, pencils, and rulers, and sent them off to school to learn. But to learn what?

Three fundamental beliefs shaped the educational destiny of the United States (Ihle, 1981, discussing the work of Cremin, 1980). The first was a commitment to the interconnectedness of schooling and religion. Children should be taught virtuous behavior; and how better to do that than teaching religious beliefs? The second was that a free people must have the skills to govern themselves. These basic skills encompassed the three Rs and instruction in morality and patriotism. The third belief can best be described as the attitude that practical knowledge is as useful as book learning, and perhaps more so. Thus, opportunities for self-instruction through libraries, museums, fairs, and the like were made readily available to ordinary people.

Actually, education was made fully available only to White men. It was not available to minorities or to women. The education of women, for example, involved domestic instruction in managing the home and in providing "moral guardianship" for the family. (See Box 5–1.) Similarly, Blacks were deprived of educational opportunities or, if instructed, were taught the need for obedience.

The school is a miniature social system in which people learn to function in society. Students spend 12 years encountering authority figures (in the form of teachers), rules, other students, and peer pressure. As they progress through the educational maze from elementary to junior high to high school, they will be expected to assume the responsibilities of becoming independent, contributing members of society. In this chapter we explore how this huge educational industry came to be developed. We examine the social structure of the adolescent's life in school and the influence of family background in acquiring an education, as well as the problems of truancy, dropping out, and school violence. Finally, we look at the success of some suggested alternatives to the traditional high school.

The Development of the U.S. School System

According to *The Student and the Schoolmate,* circa 1858, "As a general rule, the more schoolhouses there are, the fewer prisons there will be." There are two views of the history of U.S. education, and they are radically different. According to the first, the passing of education laws to eradicate ignorance as early as 1642 in the Massachusetts Bay Colony was indicative of the colonists' "sense of mission . . . that they would need not only educated leaders and clergy, but an educated populace as well" (Hechinger & Hechinger, 1975, p. 17). Historians subscribing to this view believe that education emerged as a positive force promoting those aspects of the new republic considered to be most attractive. Education encouraged self-sufficiency and promoted social and economic mobility.

Box 5–1   A Woman's Place

The revisionist historians argue that education was used not to stimulate social change and mobility but to maintain class, racial, and ethnic distinctions. Textbooks of the 18th and 19th centuries provide one means of investigating this charge. The following is a short "moral" lesson that 19th-century instructors used in class to improve the elocution of their students. Does it support the argument of the revisionist historians?

A WORLD OF TROUBLE

Characters—Thomas Basswood, a mechanic; Susan Basswood, his wife; Uncle John, one who gives good advice.

Scene I.—A room. Susan sewing.

Susan. O, dear me! I believe no woman ever had half so much to do as I have. It is drudge, drudge, drudge, from morning till night. This is a world of trouble.

Enter Thomas Basswood.

Thomas. Well, Susan, how are all the children?

Susan. They are all well, You don't ask how I am. You never think what a slavish life I lead.

Thomas. Slavish life?

Susan. I have to drudge like a slave from morning till night. No sooner is one thing done than another must be begun. I wonder how I have stood it as I have.

Thomas. It is just the same with me, Susan. I have to work all day. But I do not regard that as a hardship.

Susan. You never regard anything as a hardship. Your work is different from mine. This is a world of trouble. (*Sighs.*)

Thomas. Nonsense! This is a very good world, Susan. The people in it make it bad.

Susan. That means me, I suppose.

Thomas. Come, come, Susan; don't grumble all the time.

Susan. Who is grumbling? I cannot speak a word lately without being accused of grumbling.

Thomas. Because, my dear, you seldom utter a sentence which does not contain a complaint. If you would be a little more cheerful, things would go much better with you.

Susan. How can a body be cheerful with as many troubles as I have?

Thomas. Your troubles are very few and very insignificant. They exist in your own imagination.

Susan.. Just what you always say.

Thomas. I must say one word more, Susan. I am heartily disgusted with this continued fault-finding. My home has become a very gloomy and disagreeable place lately.

Susan. I suppose I make it so.

Thomas. You do, Susan. I have not seen a smile on your face, nor heard a pleasant word from your lips, for a year. It is enough to wear a man out. I can't stand it.

Susan. (*Cries.*) You have no sympathy for me in my trials and troubles.

Thomas. You don't have any trials and troubles. It is all nonsense! You have a good house, well furnished; plenty to eat, drink, and wear. You have to keep busy; so do I. So do your father and mother. Your little crosses are not worthy to be called trials and troubles. I haven't come into the house for six months without being told that this is a world of trouble, and being compelled to listen to a long list of grievances, which are too trivial to be mentioned.

Susan. I am a monster. I suppose. (*Cries.*) (*Exeunt.*)

[*Lapse of One Year*]

Scene II.—Susan, seated at a table.

Susan. O, dear me! This is a world of trouble, and every year brings some new trial. My husband, who used to be a steady and industrious man, has taken to drinking, and he hardly ever comes home sober now. O, dear! This is a real trouble.

Box 5–1   A Woman's Place (continued)

Enter Thomas, slightly intoxicated.

Thomas. Well, wife, is supper ready?

Susan. Not yet, Thomas.

Thomas. What's the reason it isn't ready? I'm in a hurry. There's to be a turkey raffle at the tavern tonight, and I'm going.

Susan. Don't go, Thomas.

Thomas. Yes, I will.

Susan. You never stay home evenings now. Do stay with me this evening.

Thomas. No, I won't.

Susan. It didn't use to be so. You never stay at home now.

Thomas. I don't mean to. Do you think (*staggers*) I'd stay here and hear you grumble and growl all the evening? I won't d'zo it.

Susan. O, Thomas! You are—(*Pause.*)

Thomas. Well, what am I?

Susan. O, dear me!

Thomas. What am I?

Susan. You are—

Thomas. I'm drunk. Why don't you say it right out? I'm drunk. (*Staggers.*) I used to be a respectable man. I ain't now.

Susan. Why do you drink?

Thomas. Because you grumble—that's why I drink—why I get drunk. Supper ain't ready, you say. I'll go without supper then.

Susan. Stay at home tonight.

Thomas. I won't d'zo it. (*Staggers off.*)

Susan. A drunkard's wife! Alas, that I should come to this! (*Weeps.*) I shall die, I know I shall.

Enter Uncle John.

Uncle J. Ah, Susan, in tears?

Susan. O, Uncle John! My husband has just left me—and he is intoxicated. He never says at home now.

Uncle J. You don't wonder at that—do you? How often have I told you that your complainings would bring about some great calamity? It has come, I fear. You have made his home a place of misery, and he flies from it to the tavern.

Susan. I, Uncle John?

Uncle J. Yes, you, Susan. (*She reflects.*)

Susan. May Heaven forgive me! You are right. But what can be done?

Uncle J. Perhaps nothing. It may be too late. But, Susan, promise not to grumble any more, and I will talk with Thomas. He is a good-hearted man, and I think will reform if you will do so.

Susan. I will—O, how gladly!

Uncle J. Wives should never grumble. It makes home so unpleasant that husbands prefer the tavern. (*Exeunt.*)

(Source: *The Student and Schoolmate,* Scientific Pursuits, circa 1858, pp. 200–207.)

The heroes of this movement were men like Horace Mann (the father of the public-school movement) who saw that "education . . . is the great equalizer of the conditions of men—the balance wheel of the social machinery" (Hechinger & Hechinger, 1975, p. 59). Together with Henry Barnard (the first U.S. commissioner of education), Mann is portrayed as struggling against attempts by the church to dominate education, advocating local taxation to support common schools, and establishing teacher training and libraries.

Listing the accomplishments of the school movement, the early historians saw education as promoting social progress. Schools were credited with taking children out of the sweatshops and the fields. Schools were said to encourage class mobility and equality of opportunity. Reason was triumphing over the forces of ignorance (Cubberley, 1934; Monroe, 1940).

A second view of education, emerging from the writings of Katz (1973, 1975), Nasaw (1979), Kett (1977), and others, is not as laudatory. Interest in education is not viewed as a way to encourage egalitarianism but as a way to exercise continued control over a rapidly growing number of "foreign" immigrants. In response to a fear of losing control, Nasaw argues, the privileged classes sought to indoctrinate the new arrivals with a healthy does of republican thinking.* The wealthy, he reports, funded a number of social experiments through such organizations as the Society for the Prevention of Poverty to remedy the growing "problems" occurring with the influx of new immigrants—particularly the Irish Catholics—into the cities.

One such noble experiment was the introduction of the Lancaster system of education. Named after its creator, Joseph Lancaster, a Scottish Presbyterian with a devotion "to humiliation as a technique of discipline" (Kett, 1977, p. 47), the Lancaster system used a special classroom-seating plan and student assistants to instruct large numbers of pupils in a single classroom. Nasaw (1979) describes the system as "more appropriate to a feudal kingdom than to a New World Republic" (p. 23). The instructor sat like an overseer above the pupils while the student assistants roamed throughout the classroom enforcing order and discipline. Punishment for such crimes as talking, being out of one's chair, or being dirty or truant did not involve the birch switch so common in the one-room schoolhouse. Instead, punishment involved stooping for hours in a corner of the room, serving as a footstool, walking backward around the classroom with one's head in an ox's yoke, or (although Kett doubts that it was ever used in the United States) being suspended from the ceiling in a cage.

The method of instruction in Lancaster's school was a strict form of rote learning called dictation. The instructor would communicate the words or other information to be learned to the head student assistant, who in turn would communicate this information to each group of students. The students would then be expected to record this information on their slates. The slates would then be inspected by the assistants. Once corrections and punishments were dispensed, the process would begin again.

---

*For a further description of the social forces at work here, see Chapter 16.

Barbaric as this system may appear, it received resounding praise from its wealthy financial backers. Here was a system that encouraged order and discipline among the young hoodlums roaming the streets of the new cities. Moreover, here was a system that was "both economical and effective [using the same principles of] labor saving machinery [that had been] pioneered in the production of factory goods" (Nasaw, 1979, p. 21). Nevertheless, this system of privately financed education would slowly die out as the movement for common schools gained momentum.

The movement to create publicly supported common schools was fueled by several factors. One of these, the influx of immigrants, seems to have been the most important influence in winning the taxation battles that had spelled defeat for the common school before 1850. The revisionist historians argue that these new waves of Irish Catholics overwhelmed the capacity of the private sector to accommodate their "Americanization." Faced with wandering youths who appeared to be without proper supervision and moral direction, first the more industrialized states, and later the agricultural states, passed taxation laws to support local public education.

The movement of young people into these institutions was encouraged from 1851 onward by compulsory-education laws. First enacted in Boston and then spreading to other cities and then to entire states, these laws served several purposes. Not only did they provide enforcement powers to move the "ruffians" off the streets, through the schools, and into reformatories, but they enabled a struggling economy to create more employment opportunities for adults at the expense of young people. Young people's participation in society was gradually being redefined from provider to consumer, from worker to learner (Katz, 1975; Kett, 1977).

Which of these two perspectives is accurate? To accept the revisionist view of U.S. education is to accept education without a future or hope for reform (Ravitch, 1977). If all reform movements in education have been attempts to sort out individuals, to categorize and stigmatize others, and to continue the status quo, what faith can one invest in the leaders of new movements to change the educational system? On the other hand, the evidence that the revisionists have gathered in defense of their argument cannot be easily swept aside. The comments of American leaders in education show a concern for promoting education not only as a worthwhile endeavor but also as a means of social control:

> No one at all familiar with the deficient household arrangements and deranged machinery of domestic life, of the extreme poor and ignorant . . . can doubt that it is better for children to be removed as early and as long as possible from such scenes and such examples and placed in an infant or primary school. (Barnard, 1851, cited in Katz, 1975, p. 10)

We suspect that both views are partly accurate depictions of the development of the U.S. educational system. The privileged classes supported the educational movement partly because the Industrial Revolution demanded a new breed of worker—one who would surrender "republican" defiance for compliance to work rules and work hours. The qualities prized in 1837 in the description that follows of a young lad were not the qualities that encouraged productivity:

> "Johnny, my dear, come here," says his mama.
> "I won't," cries Johnny.

"You must, my love, you are all wet, and you'll catch cold."

"I won't," replies Johnny.

"Come, my sweet, and I've something for you."

"I won't."

"Oh! Mr. ——, do, pray, Johnny, come in."

"Come in, Johnny," says the father.

"I won't."

"I tell you, come in directly, sir—do you hear?"

"I won't," replies the urchin, taking to his heels.

"A sturdy republican, sir," says his father to me smiling at the boy's resolute disobedience. (R. Bremner, 1970, p. 344)

Yet the idea that education offers a promise of success was embraced by the masses. Clearly, there were individuals who had used their schooling opportunities to rise above their station and succeed. This belief was also shared by the privileged classes as they sought with the common people to deny education to certain elements of society.

The Social Fabric of the School

Why go to school? For decades the reason given by parents to their children has been "So you'll learn to read and write and get a good job." The understanding of the parents in this communication is that education translates at some point into an opportunity for a better life. But as with most things, the agendas of students, parents, and schools do not always mesh. James S. Coleman (1961), E. E. Snyder (1969), and John Goodlad (1984) observe, for instance, that the social structures of schools most often emphasize values other than education. The status systems of some high schools place considerable value on athletics for males and social success for females. In addition to the *content* of what qualities or characteristics acquire status among peers, two status-system attributes influence peer recognition. One of these is the *ascriptiveness* of the system. Coleman finds evidence that, depending on the school, high status may be awarded because of who a person is rather than what that person does. It appears, for instance, that schools with a student body that is predominantly upper middle class tend to place a higher value on the socioeconomic indicators of success than do schools without a large number of wealthy students. Finally, how content and ascriptiveness interact affects the *range* of attributes that will be rewarded with status by the student body. In some schools, sports like football and basketball completely dominate the status system. In other schools, combinations of these factors work to dictate who receives recognition.

As one example of how this process works, indulge one of the authors of this text as he remembers that social status in his high school was dominated by a combination of variables. In content, sports were relatively unimportant. The small size of the school prohibited a football team, and soccer, the sport played at the school, had not yet achieved a U.S. following. Furthermore, winning seasons at this small, private preparatory school were rather unusual. Scholarship was recognized. Savoir-faire with the opposite sex was recognized. This was an all-male school. Perhaps, though, the most important characteristic was the car one drove.

We shall push aside the Freudian interpretation that deprived of a coeducational experience, we advertised our sexual prowess through our cars. At any rate, we religiously spent lunch hours staring under the hoods of vehicles. Not a single one of us knew a thing about caring for a car, but stare we did. In an era of gasoline at 28.9¢ a gallon and songs like *Little Deuce Coupe, 409,* and *Little GTO,* the lowly "beetle" was scorned, and the " 'vette" was elevated to goddess stature. As can be imagined, the ascriptiveness of the system was directly related to socioeconomic status. The range of recognition on the scale of peer status found the semiathletic type who had good grades, an attractive girlfriend, a fast car, and money a school social leader. Depending on how much a student deviated form this ideal pattern, his membership in the controlling elite diminished to nonexistence.

As Coleman (1961) observes, because adolescents are deprived of the power to "dispense material rewards," the social statuses that adolescents confer on their peers "show the patterns of rewards and punishments dispensed by the adolescent society" (p. 314). In inner-city schools gang membership may be the primary element in achieving social recognition. In other schools different combinations may influence status. Interestingly, status issues strongly affect student motivations for attending school. Once the student voices the two most often heard reasons for attending high school ("earn more money" and "get a better job"), a fascinating assortment of other reasons emerges for attending high school—and, for that matter, college. In our discussions with students over the years, the following statements frequently surfaced: I go to school to party; to find somebody to marry; because I don't know what I want to do; to be with my friends; and, rarely, because I enjoy learning.

The social fabric we have described thus far is the one created by the students. There is a second social fabric that intertwines with that of the adolescent: the social structure of the school.

The school is expected by society to impart knowledge and encourage good citizenship, "ethical character," sound bodies, proper use of leisure time, and skills sufficient to acquire employment (Faunce & Munshaw, 1964; Hawby, 1990). The means to achieve these goals has been the comprehensive high school. In a rejection of specialized schools that would channel students into specific careers, the comprehensive high school evolved to encompass the educational needs of both the vocationally oriented and the college-bound youth. This multipurpose institution can be considered a uniquely American institution in which students from all types of backgrounds come together and experience different kinds of learning, including not only academic courses but extracurricular activities as well (Conant, 1967).

The system is not without its critics, who contend that it is no more humane or democratic than Lancaster's academic factories. They observe that in adolescence, when young people most need adult relationships for guidance, support, and understanding, we strip them of that support (Gullotta, 1983). They are moved from elementary school, in which contact with teachers is high, to an assembly-line system in which they receive 45-minute or 50-minute doses of knowledge from specialists. Gregory and Smith (1987) contend that the large comprehensive high school is a basically flawed institution whose very size

---

Box 5–2   Cross-Race Contact in Schools

An interesting application of Dunphy's (1960) notions of adolescent groups to race relations was performed by Zisman and Wilson (1992). In this combined qualitative and quantitative study, the tight-knit and close-knit natures of cross-race interactions were explored according to observations of eighth- and ninth-grade students in a school cafeteria. There was an approximately equal balance of White and Black students in the school, with smaller numbers of Hispanics, Asians, and other minority groups.

Beginning with a fundamental awareness that students return to the same tables day after day to eat their lunches, the existence of three types of eating arrangements are identified. *Cliques* are tight-knit groups that tend to be small and introverted. Clique members always eat together with little visiting of other groups.

Loose-knit groups are quite fluid and characterized by a fair degree of table-hoppers. Although these groups tend to be large, they do have a stable core of members. *Collectives* represent the third type of eating arrangement. Collectives eat in close proximity to one another, but with little emotional and verbal contact with one another.

Forty-one percent of eighth-grade and 63% of ninth-grade groups were racially integrated. The loose knit groups were characterized by greater racial integration than were the cliques or collectives. It was concluded that the table-hopping behavior of loose-knit group members provided more opportunities for cross-race contact. Furthermore, since less intimacy was required in the loose-knit groups, there may have been greater willingness to engage in cross-racial interactions.

---

breeds dehumanization. Underscoring this point are Sizer (1983), who observes that the U.S. high school system is essentially unchanged from 1880, and Goodlad (1984), who points out that total direct teacher/pupil interaction in a typical high school amounts to a measly seven minutes a day. According to some critics, the school breeds frustration (Cottle, 1971; Silberman, 1970). Others have reported findings strongly suggesting that young people are channeled into failure by forces other than their lack of ability (Cicourel & Kitsuse, 1963; Rosenthan & Jacobson, 1968).

School Contexts and Ethnic and Racial Minorities

Integration and Social Relations

In Chapter 4 we discuss social interaction between peers of different ethnic and racial backgrounds. We continue that discussion in the framework of intergroup friendships in the school context. An examination of desegregation in the classroom provides information on what occurs in relationship formation when adolescents from different racial and ethnic groups are educated conjointly.

Desegregation has been established in order to provide equal opportunities in education for minority students. A second but less frequently stated purpose of desegregation is to promote positive crossracial relations (Hallinan & Smith, 1985). An indicator of the latter can be observed in the degree and quality of interactions between racially mixed groups of adolescents. (See also Box 5–2.) Not all schools are alike; thus, school characteristics may foster or inhibit goals of the integration process (Miller, 1990). No matter how difficult it may be to identify important school characteristics, it is critical to define the *structure* of the classroom as a contextual factor that is influential in friendship formation.

There are two different hypotheses that can be applied to cross-racial friendships in the desegregated school context. According to the opportunity hypothesis, the group that is smaller in number in a classroom has more possibilities for cross-race contacts than the group that is larger in number. Furthermore, as the number of members of one group increases in a classroom, opportunities for interaction with these group members also increases. Since contact is required for friendship development, it is argued that the minority group will have a larger proportion of cross-race friendships (Hallinan & Smith, 1985). In the second hypothesis, it is argued that cross-race contacts in the classroom are influenced by student's adherence to issues of social status. Specifically, because the lower-status (minority) group is a recipient of prejudice, they are at-risk for the development of lower self-esteem. Continued prejudice is experienced with subsequent loss of self-esteem by the minority group. Lower-status members turn to one another for social support and reject interaction with the dominant group. Thus, cross-racial friendships are inhibited.

A variety of investigations have been conducted on varying themes of these two hypotheses using the sociometric technique. This technique typically asks students to identify their best friends in the classroom. In one such study, Hallinan and Smith (1985) find more support for the opportunity hypothesis among Black and White older children and young adolescents in interracial classrooms. Specifically, they report that the probability of cross-race friendships increases for both Blacks and Whites as the proportion of the other-race peers increases and the proportion of same-race peers decreases. Being in either a Black or White minority does not diminish friendliness of minority students. It also is reported that interracially balanced classrooms maximize cross-race friendships for both Blacks and Whites.

DuBois and Hirsch (1990) also examined friendship patterns in a junior high school in which approximately one-fourth of the students were Black. The proportion of White and Black students in this school were reflective of the community census proportions and not derived through desegregation procedures. Most of the Black and White students report having an other-race school friend (over 80%). This figure falls when students are asked if they have an other-race school friend with whom they were close. Twenty-three percent of Whites and 47% of Blacks indicate that they see a close other-race school friend outside of the school context. Thus, in mixed-race school settings, having a friend of another race is quite common, but cross-race friendship patterns diminish outside of the school context. Black students are more likely to maintain ties with their close other-race friend outside of the school context. This finding correlates with the opportunity hypothesis.

Given that Blacks are smaller in number in the school context they had more opportunities for contact with White students. Since Blacks in this study have less accessibility to same-race peers, they indicate an adaptive response through greater willingness to engage in cross-race friendships.

Although there appears to be evidence for the opportunity hypothesis, it also is important to explore the response of the majority White students to the friendliness of the minority Black students. Clark and Ayers (1988) address this topic

Adolescents may go to elite, moderately affluent, or poor schools. Understanding school influences requires the recognition of different economic conditions.

in a study of seventh- and eighth-grade Black students who were attending a predominantly White school. Using a sociometric strategy, researchers asked students to rank their three best friends. Reciprocated friends are those students who also are selected as a best friend by one of their best-friend choices. Nonreciprocated friends are those in which mutual selection does not occur. The authors find that the Black students are significantly more likely to be in the unreciprocated group (40%) than are the White students (14%). They conclude that in desegregated classrooms, particularly when there is a smaller number of minority students, Blacks may have more difficulties than Whites in forming reciprocated friendships. Predominantly White schools are good for White students' friendship formation, but not so for Black students in those schools.

Clearly minority students must find adaptive strategies to cope in the minority classroom context. Evidence has been reviewed that supports greater friendliness of Black students when they are in such a context. In addition, Miller (1989) found that Black high school students who were bused to affluent suburban schools exhibit four patterns of adaptation. These patterns are specifically linked to social interaction styles. Some Black students adapt to predominantly White high schools through being a model student. These students earn high grades, have plans for college, and generally represent characteristics of being good students. Although they seem to assimilate into the White school environment and form friendships with White students, their Black peers feel hostile toward their seemingly White-oriented behavior.

A second pattern of Black students' adaptation is through the pursuance of interracial friendships. This group represents involvement in school activities, popularity, and opportunities for interaction with the opposite sex. A third adaptation pattern was found in students who also are highly involved in school activities and well integrated in the school context, but do not date. They also are highly concerned with unfair school rules and vocalize their perceptions of unfair treatment toward Blacks. The fourth adaptational pattern used by Black students is characterized by a philosophical agreement with the aims of desegregation. These students do not become directly involved in school activities. The findings of Miller (1989) demonstrate varying patterns of adaptability to minority school contexts.

It is important not only to consider the classroom structure as a contextual variable in cross-race friendship formation, but also to examine factors of social class and community wealth. In studying the same sample (Miller, 1989), Miller (1990) reports that inequality in income produced negative interracial interaction. In fact, it is argued that the greater the income discrepancy, the less welcome are minority students. Miller (1990) concludes that in order to have positive experiences in desegregation the following factors should be met: (1) equivalent social class indicators between the groups (minority students should not be bused to suburbs that are highly affluent); (2) schools should have increased minority enrollment (in Miller's study 2.6% to 8.5% of the student body were Black minority students); (3) more minority staff are needed in desegregated schools; and (4) specific programs to meet the needs of minority students are necessary.

Academic Achievement Among Minority Adolescents

A topic of great concern among educators is lowered academic achievement of some minority groups. The *cultural difference approach* and the *cultural discontinuity approach* are two major theoretical perspectives that attempt to explain the school performance of minority students. The cultural difference approach is regarded as micro-ethnographic (Trueba, 1988). The notion is that differences in communication style, motivation style, cognitive style, classroom social organization and social relations, interaction style, and literacy and writing between Anglo and minority cultures contribute to school failure among minority children (Ogbu, 1987). Minority students are typically taught in a learning environment that is embedded in Anglo cultural values. Discrepancies between the student's orientation and the expectation that he or she conform to the Anglo mode of education result in a less than desirable educational experience for the minority student. Thus, a common outcome is lowered academic achievement.

In contrast, the cultural discontinuity approach is macro-ethnographic in nature. Ogbu (1987) identifies three types of minority groups in U.S. society. The history of each group's interaction with the broader U.S. society influences their academic achievement. *Autonomous minorities* are known as minority groups primarily in a numerical sense. Such groups (for example, Jewish) have cultural frames of reference that encourage academic success. Hence, they tend not to be characterized by problems in reading and writing. *Immigrant minorities* are groups that have moved to the United States voluntarily. Similar to autonomous minorities, they do not exhibit lingering problems in school failure. Some Asian groups are illustrative of immigrant minorities.

In contrast to autonomous and immigrant minorities, *castelike or involuntary minorities* were brought into the U.S. system through slavery, conquest, or colonization (for example, Blacks and American Indians). These groups exhibit the most difficulties in school achievement and success.

Both the cultural difference approach and the cultural discontinuity approach can enhance sensitivity to issues of academic achievement among minorities. In examining the micro-ethnographic context of the school environment, the cultural difference approach heightens sensitivity to the role of culture in the learning process (Trueba, 1988). The cultural discontinuity approach is useful in accounting for intergroup variability in achievement (that is , why some minority groups tend to do well in school and others do not). Given this theoretical summary, the following discussion focuses on what factors have been associated with academic achievement and success among minorities.

Factors That Contribute to Academic Achievement Among Minorities

Asians are representative of immigrant minority groups that exhibit high academic achievement. For example, Schneider and Lee (1990) have identified several factors as being associated with high academic achievement among East Asian immigrants: (1) expectations of parents, teachers, and peers for high academic success; (2) parental efforts to direct children's out-of-school time toward academic tasks; and (3) factors associated with Asian culture that are rewarded in the school environment (that is, quiet, industrious, disciplined, and orderly natures).

In contrast to Asians, poor academic achievement is associated with other groups that fall into Ogbu's (1987) characterization of castelike minorities. Nonetheless, factors associated with academic success among castelike minorities can be identified. In reviewing findings reported in the literature, the following factors are suggested as promoting academic achievement among Blacks: (1) impressing on Black youth the many linkages between school performance and employment, as well as sensitizing schools and parents to the positive influence parents can have on their offsprings' academic orientation (DeSantis, Ketterlinus, & Youniss, 1990); (2) maintaining high academic standards, providing information on college enrollment, teachers exhibiting commitment to providing additional help and tutoring, and having positive role models (Kaufman & Rosenbaum, 1992); and (3) instilling educational and achievement values (Ford, 1992).

Academic success among Hispanics has been associated with a college-prep training based in effective communication skills (Abi-Nader, 1990). Cardoza (1991) found that educational aspirations, role models, and choosing to delay marriage and childrearing were predictive of college attendance among Hispanic females. It also has been found that consistent systematic support from families is associated with staying in school among Hispanics (Delgado-Gaitan, 1988).

A study by de Baca, Rinaldi, Billig, and Kinnison (1991) is a good example of applying principles of the cultural difference approach to the school context. A rural school serving elementary and middle-school American Indian students established a schoolwide effort that resulted in lower student absenteeism, higher achievement, increased self-esteem among students, reduction in referrals to special education, and greater parental and community involvement. Efforts taken by this school included, among other activities, reduction of class sizes, establishment of learning centers, provision of tutors and an after-school tutoring program, establishment of a computer lab, implementation of incentive programs, and integration of the students' cultural heritage into the educational context. The programs implemented in this particular school demonstrate cultural sensitivity to the educational needs of American Indian students.

School and Family Influences on Learning

As we have noted, the school system is not without critics charging it with creating an environment of failure, not an environment of success. The source of much of this disillusionment can be traced to a study commissioned by Congress in passing the Civil Rights Act of 1964:

> Sec. 402. The Commission [of Education] shall conduct a survey and make a report to the President and Congress, within two years of the enactment of this title, concerning the lack of availability of equal educational opportunities for individuals by reason of race, color, religion, or national origin in public educational institutions at all levels in the United States, its territories and possessions, and the District of Columbia. (Mosteller & Moynihan, 1972, p. 4)

The intent of Section 402 was to document for all time the gross inequality of educational opportunities that existed between minorities and Whites, between those trapped in poverty and the middle class. Everyone, including Coleman, the principal investigator in the study, assumed that "the study will show the difference in the quality of schools that the average Negro child and the average White child are exposed to. You know yourself that the difference is going to be striking" (cited in Mosteller & Moynihan, 1972, p. 8).

The study that resulted was one of the largest social-science research projects ever undertaken. It involved nearly 4000 schools, more than 60,000 teachers, and 570,000 students. Miraculously, it was delivered within its two-year deadline. In 1966 Congress was able to look at a study that has been described by some as a breath of fresh air in a locker room of myths and by others as the most damaging indictment of public education ever produced.

EOEO: A Landmark Report

This study generated both passionate anger and passionate praise. Essentially, the report, *Equality of Educational Opportunity (EOEO)*, offered five major findings. First, and not unexpectedly, the Untied States was found to be a segregated society. Of the White students in the nation, 80% attended schools that were 90% to 100% White. Next, and as expected, minorities were found to be learning less than Whites, and the poor, less than the middle and upper classes. The third finding, which also received much attention, was that minority students with feelings of control over their environment (an internal locus of control) and a positive self-concept performed at a higher academic level than White students. Up to this point *EOEO* had confirmed the suspicions of its creators: schools were segregated, the poor and minorities were learning less than Whites, and those Horatio

Algers capable of pulling themselves up by their own fortitude in a "White man's" society succeeded. What was not expected where the next two findings. School facilities (that is, books, the number of teachers, teacher training and experience, the school's physical plant and its equipment) were not found to be unequal. Furthermore, the variable that contributed most to a young person's learning was family background (education, socioeconomic status, ethnic group).

What is so disturbing about these last two findings is that, according to the report, spending programs to improve schools, to train teachers, and to purchase additional equipment will not improve a student's learning. The country and the educational world, which had been expecting a call for launching a Marshall Plan of school reconstruction, were rocked by these findings. Reanalysis of the data by others found errors in *EOEO*, but these errors only diminished the importance of variables outside the family (Mosteller & Moynihan, 1972).

In the years that followed *EOEO*, additional arguments were introduced to account for the disparity in achievement levels between the poor and the middle class. One of these reaffirms the importance of family background by noting that if unlimited funds were spent on equalizing high school facilities, the equalization would reduce the standard deviation of achievement scores among seniors by no more than 1% (Jencks et al., 1972). Jencks and his associates contend that if the United States is truly committed to achieving equality of opportunity, emphasis should be shifted from the education front to correcting social, racial, and economic inequalities. They state that such an effort, if successful, could eliminate as much as 20% of the difference between Blacks and Whites on achievement tests.

The general ineffectiveness of the high school for redressing social inequality is reexpressed by Jencks and Brown (1975) in a study contending that characteristics typically associated with "good" comprehensive high schools have little consistent effect in raising students' achievement scores. They find that at least for Whites, "more money, more graduate courses for teachers, smaller classes, socioeconomic, desegregation, and other traditional remedies" (p. 320) are not likely to decrease the disparities between successful and unsuccessful students.

The image of education fared no better with the publication of Rosenthal and Jacobson's book *Pygmalion in the Classroom* (1968). Investigating the impact of teacher expectations on grades, the authors devised an ingenious experiment in which they selected by chance students to be academically successful. They informed these student's teachers that these pupils had received high scores on Rosenthal's "late bloomers' test" (in actuality a commonly used IQ test). With no other intervention in the system, these students one year later were reported by their teachers to have "blossomed." Rosenthal and Jacobson argue that teacher expectations can contribute strongly to a student's failure. Clearly, this report did not sit well with the embattled educational community, and with the failure of more than a score of attempts to replicate the findings of the study, a sinister mood emerged among educators, with some suggesting that Rosenthal and Jacobson's work be rejected.

The negative influence of teacher expectations on students' academic behavior was confirmed, however, with the publication of R. Rist's (1970) paper. Rist followed a group of elementary school students from kindergarten into the third grade as they underwent a process of labeling and stigmatization. He found that social position (that is, similarity to the teacher's socioeconomic status) had a greater influence on learning than any other variable. Kindergarten teachers, Rist observed, spend the greatest amount of instructional time with and give more positive reinforcement to children most like themselves. As the socioeconomic gap widens between the student and the teacher, the more likely it is that the student will be ignored. Rist found that this type of treatment influences children to misbehave and that the misbehavior confirms the labels attached to them and stigmatizes them from that time forward.

In the meantime, ignoring the policy implications of *EOEO,* a well-meaning Congress and Johnson administration had embarked on a series of compensatory-education programs, of which Head Start is probably the best known. Based on the work of M. Deutsch, I. Katz, and Jensen (1968) and others, these programs attempted to provide an educationally enriched environment for minority youngsters. However, as reports of failure emerged (some of which, as with Head Start, were incorrect), attention shifted to a question of genetics instead of to the policy implications of *EOEO.*

The trigger for this shift was a carefully constructed academic paper by Arthur Jensen published in the *Harvard Educational Review* in 1969. Beginning his argument with the long-known fact that Blacks score about one standard deviation (15 points) below Whites, Jensen stated that genetics might contribute to the lower IQ scores of Blacks as a group.

The reaction of the academic community was swift and negative. J. S. Kagan (1969) found Jensen's work to be filled with "major fallacies" involving such points as his "inappropriate generalization from within-family IQ differences to an argument that separate racial gene pools are necessarily different" (p. 274). Kagan pointed out that Jensen had ignored evidence of the strong impact that environmental influences have on intelligence and noted that compensatory-education programs had not been evaluated enough to allow one to categorically dismiss their potential impact on raising IQ scores.

Some researchers (for example, Bodmer & Cavalli-Sforza, 1970) argue that in a nation inherently unequal because of years of racism and oppression, it is impossible to compare blacks and Whites fairly. Others find strong evidence to support an argument that environmental influences contribute strongly to IQ scores. For example, in a study of Black children adopted by White parents, Blacks adopted by upper-middle-class White families had higher mean IQ and achievement scores than White students in their schools (Scarr & Weinberg, 1976).

Thomas Sowell (1981), a Black economist with the Hoover Institute, offers yet another possible explanation for this IQ gap. He states:

> History shows there is nothing unique about the Black IQ level. . . . Group IQ averages at or below 85 have been common in history and currently. In the 1920's . . . numerous studies showed these kinds of IQ averages for such American ethnic groups as the Italians, Greeks, Poles, Hispanics, Slovaks, and Portuguese. A more recent study shows Mexican-Americans with lower average IQ's than Blacks in the 1940's, 1950's and 1960's, and Puerto Ricans with lower average IQ's than Blacks in the 1970's. (P. 753)

The people Sowell (1981, 1986) is talking about were recent immigrants. We suggest that these individuals then and Blacks, Puerto Ricans, and other minority groups now have an important element in common. The element is poverty. And poverty for unborn children is particularly cruel. Poor prenatal nutrition increases by 25% a baby's chances of falling at least 250 grams below the normal 1400 grams in brain weight by age 6 (Hodgkinson, 1979). The true significance of this point is that brain growth is essentially completed by that age. We and others (Hodgkinson, 1989) suggest that rather than genetic factors, it is the environmental condition of poverty that accounts for the difference in IQ scores.

One of the by-products of the controversy starting with the publication of *EOEO* is a beginning understanding of the differences in U.S. society. The idea of the melting pot is being replaced by a recognition of the pluralistic nature of society. IQ achievement tests are recognized as being culturally biased. Language differences are recognized, and in many parts of the country bilingual programs have been started. The work emerging from the publication of *EOEO* also indicates that the school is not all-powerful.

Both Illich (1970) and J. Holt (1976) believe that we should discontinue our long tradition of making schools seem like prisons in which children are confined by virtue of their age. These authors propose establishing an educational environment in which education is not compulsory, in which violence against students is not condoned, and in which the teacher/student relationship is redefined. Holt explains his impassioned view of the present educational system:

> School is [a] compulsory-treatment institution. Society has decided that one group of people, teachers, shall do all sorts of things to another group of people, the students, whether they want it or not, until the teachers think the students measure up. . . . Such people like to say that no one should have the right to choose to be illiterate—a right I have any time I travel to a foreign country. A global schoolhouse would be a world . . . in which one group of people would subject the rest of us to various sorts of tests, and if we did not measure up . . . require us to submit to various kinds of treatments, i.e., education, therapy, etc., until we did. A worse nightmare is hard to imagine. (P. 111)

Finally, we come to a recognition that the family is the major influence on young people and their ultimate success in society. Not only do socioeconomic factors influence grades but so do parental disciplinary and decision-making styles. Harsh discipline negatively affects academic performance, while joint parent-youth decision making appears to improve school performance (Dornbusch, Ritter, Mont-Reynaud, & Chen, 1990; Wentzel, Feldman, & Weinbeger, 1991). Furthermore, if the family is the victim of racism and oppression, it will not be able to provide its children with the same life chances that an advantaged family can. The policy implications of this view remain untouched as issues too sensitive to deal with, for ultimately the problem becomes that

> if less-advantaged children are to have equal education opportunity, an equivalent school budget is not enough; enough must be spent to provide an equivalence of environment as well. Or, if equivalence of environment is too rigorous a requirement, then it may not be unreasonable to insist on home and communal environments that do not negate the effects of the school expenditures. (Broudy, 1972, p. 106)

Twenty Years Later: A Nation at Risk

Approximately 20 years after the publication of *EOEO* a new series of educational reports appeared. Focusing less on differences between the classes and races, there studies looked at the growing inability of the U.S. secondary school system to educate its students. The most ambitious of these reports was a multi-million-dollar, eight-year study of that system by Goodlad (1984).

Analyzing voluminous data from over 27,000 interviews and classroom observations, Goodlad concluded that the educational system was in need of a drastic overhaul. Specifically, schools need to be made smaller. The sprawling comprehensive high school is an impersonal, dehumanizing institution. Next, a core curriculum needs to be developed that will provide all students with a common frame of reference to prepare them to be participating members of society. Third, the common practice of tracking students into high-, average- and low-ability classes is destructive and should be abolished. Goodlad's observations reaffirm the works of Rosenthal and Jacobsen (1968) and R. Rist (1970). Finally, with regard to secondary education, a career track for teachers other than one leading into administration needs to be developed to keep bright instructors in the classroom.

Sizer (1983) sounds a similar theme. His work examining secondary schools concludes that they have remained essentially unchanged since the 1880s. Yet although the institutions have remained unchanged, their goals have grown exponentially. The result, he finds, is that after 12,000 hours of inhabiting school buildings young people are only marginally literate and are unprepared to accept their responsibilities in the wider world.

Underscoring these points, Powell's (1985) study of high school students suggests that the average student is lost in the modern high school. Using the analogy of the shopping mall, Powell reports that many students wander aimlessly for four years up and down the corridors of education. Not unhappy with their educational program but intellectually unchallenged for most of the time, they blunder into the English store or the social science store to sample a course here or taste a subject there. Others report that 20% of the nation's youth have serious reading problems (Marquand, 1985) and that one 17-year-old in eight is illiterate (U.S. Department of Labor, 1987).

Finally, almost two decades after changing our understanding of the factors that primarily account for academic achievement, James S. Coleman and his associates (1982, 1987) added their insight to this issue. After comparing public and private schools, this research team concluded that private schools did a better job of educating young people than did public schools. The private-school climate, they found, is more orderly, the enrollment in academic courses is higher, and performance expectations are greater than in public schools.

And Then There Was Project 2000

At a meeting in Charlottesville, Virginia, in 1989 President Bush and the nation's governors, including Bill Clinton, governor of Arkansas, agreed to several national goals for U.S. education that, if reached, would improve student achievement by the end of this decade. In this section we look at four of these goals, asking the question how the United States might achieve them by the year 2000.

President Clinton as well as past president Bush and past Prime Minister Mulroney recognize the growing educational needs in North America. The future requires much sacrifice and resources to ensure a bright future for adolescents as they become adults.

Goal 1. By the year 2000, all children in the United States will start school ready to learn.

This first goal is eloquent in its simplicity. But how do you prepare children for school? Is the question the readiness of children for education or parents for parenthood? (See Chapter 13 on adolescent parenthood.) Is the question one of access to health care, adequate nutrition, clothing, and housing? Or, is the question one of access to quality early child care? The authors would agree all children should be ready for education. And yet, even though the effectiveness of the early childhood program Head Start has been established, it remains that 80% of the children eligible for Head Start are not enrolled for lack of adequate funding (Kagan, 1990). Regarding housing, there are an estimated 8 million low-income individuals seeking affordable housing. And yet, the low-income housing supply has been estimated at 4 million housing units (Hodgkinson, 1989). Of the estimated 37 million people in the United States without health insurance, 12 million are children. (See Box 5–3.) Twenty-five percent of the pregnant women in the United States receive no medical care during the first trimester of their pregnancy (Hodgkinson, 1989). If this first goal is to be achieved then these issues will need to be addressed now if children are to ready for school for the year 2000.

Goal 2. By the year 2000, U.S. students will leave grades four, eight, and twelve having demonstrated competency in challenging subject matter, including English, mathematics, science, history, and geography; and every school in the United States will ensure that all students learn to use their minds well, so that they may be prepared for responsible citizenship, further learning, and productive employment in our economy.

Young people spend roughly 9% of their childhood years in school (Bracey, 1991). Many scholars would suggest that they spend much of that time in unchallenging classroom situations learning rote skills (Darling-Hammond,

Box 5–3   School-Based Health and Social Services Centers

There were days that Marvin just ached all over. His joints would swell, and his energy level was nowhere. "Man, I'm 16 years old. I'm not supposed to feel this way. I need me some Geritol or something," he'd joke to his friends. At the urging of his father, Marvin visited one of the school-based health centers that the second author of this book directs. Enrolled by his parents for services at the center, Marvin saw a nurse practitioner, and after blood work on Marvin was completed and reviewed, antibiotic treatment for an acute case of Lyme disease was started. Marvin responded quickly to treatment, becoming in his junior and senior years a regular customer for sports physicals, throat cultures, and tragically, after the violent death of an older brother, counseling services.

What is a school based health center? It is a place in or near a school where a parent gives written permission to allow a young person to go to receive primary physical or mental health services confidentially. Staffed by physicians, nurse practitioners, and school workers, the center can provide routine services for a variety of common ailments, including sexually transmitted diseases. Centers work closely with parents, school officials, and the youth's pediatrician (should there be one) providing services that promote healthy life-styles, and they discourage the development of harmful behaviors like smoking and eating disorders.

In recent years, concern has been expressed over school-based health centers' prescribing or dispensing contraceptives. Interestingly, only 14% of the estimated 400 school-based health centers nationwide presently distribute or prescribe contraceptives. Data for Child and Family Agency's six years of operation indicate that the majority of service requests are for counseling assistance for problems with depression, interpersonal relationships, and substance misuse. Principal physical health care issues include upper respiratory problems, minor sports injuries, physicals, and attending to chronic health care problems. Eighty percent of secondary school students are enrolled in centers the Child and Family Agency operates. Fifty-five percent of these youth have no other source of medical care. Many are not poor enough for Medicaid and therefore have no medical insurance.

Gullotta and Letarte (1994) believe that school-based health services will become commonplace before this decade is over. They provide ready access to quality care to a population of youth that are medically underserved. School based health centers, he believes, are the start of a transformation that will see schools join in cooperative ventures with other agencies to serve the "whole" needs of children and adults in communities.

Source: T. P. Gullotta & L. Letarte (1994). The changing paradigm of community health: The role of school-based health centers. *Adolescence,* in press.

1990). To better understand the progress that needs to be made in this area, it would be useful to examine the National Assessment of Educational Progress Tests (NAEP), which are administered each year to a representative sample of young people ages 9, 13, and 17 across the United States. Proficiency is scored on a 0 to 500 scale. A score in the 150 range represents "rudimentary" reading ability; in the 200 range "basic" proficiency readers. "Intermediate" readers in the 250 range can search for specific information and make generalizations, while "adept" readers in the 300 range can find, understand, and explain complicated information like that found in an editorial of the *Wall Street Journal* or *The New York Times* (U.S. Census Bureau, 1991; U.S. Select Committee on Children and Their Families, 1989).

On the 1988 NAEP, nearly all 13-year-olds (99.8%) could read at the rudimentary level, meaning they could carry out simple, discrete tasks. Of those, 95.1% also could read at the basic level, meaning they could understand specific information. Fifty-eight percent of the sample could read at the intermediate level. That is they could read an eighth grade textbook. Roughly 11% scored at the adept level.

As Table 5–1 demonstrates, the mean scores for young people have not changed dramatically from 1977 to 1988. The single exception to this observation is found with 17-year-old Black youth, who have improved their average scores by 31 points over that period of time. Still, not a single group average broke the 300 range enabling them to understand complex information (U.S. Census Bureau, 1991, p. 155).

To improve these scores some people including former President Bush, have endorsed the concept of choice (vouchers) leading to a free market in what otherwise might be described as a monopoly. Others have called for a national curriculum. Still others call for increased federal funding.

Goal 3. By the year 2000, U.S. students will be the first in the world in mathematics and science achievement.

For more than a decade students in the United States have not compared well against their counterparts in other nations. For example, in science the United States ranks 15th out of 17 developed nations (Kirst, 1991). Again, to have a perspective on this issue we use the NAEP proficiency scores for science and mathematics. As Table 5–1 illustrates, little movement in science has occurred over the last decade. U.S. youth score at age 17 at roughly the "adept" level. Scores for males exceed that of females. White 17-year-old students exceed Black and Hispanic students by more than 30 points. Scores in mathematics, although higher, reflect the same trends. No discernible improvement over the last decade can be observed, with previously noted gender, racial, and ethnic differences increasing somewhat (U.S. Census Bureau, 1991; see Table 5–1).

Several explanations have been offered for these less than stellar performances. One explanations is that research design controls partly explain the poor performance. The problem is, or so it has been suggested, that the United States does not restrict students from taking the exam. Perhaps with a more discriminating pool of exam takers achievement scores would improve (Rotberg, 1990). A second argument offered is that gender differences in these scores are not the result of genetic differences but rather the result of biased tests and gender tracking against women (Wellesley College Center for Research on Women, 1992). We are not sure that we would subscribe to sample tailoring to improve the United States science and mathematics scores. Rather, it appears to us that science, mathematics, and reading need to be more fully integrated into a curriculum free of bias and free of steering to improve the achievement levels of all, not just some, youth. (See Box 5–4.)

Goal 4. By the year 2000, every person in the United States will be literate and will possess the skills necessary to compete in a global economy and to exercise the rights and responsibilities of citizenship.

Presently, about 40% of the U.S. public cannot find information in a newspaper article and 30% cannot write a simple letter to explain to a company that an error

Table 5–1   Test Scores–High School Graduates. Proficiency Test Scores for Selected Subjects, by Characteristic: 1977 to 1988
(Based on The National Assessment of Educational Progress Tests which are administered to a representative sample of students in public and private schools. Test scores can range from 0 to 500. For details, see source)

TEST AND YEAR	Total	SEX		RACE			Less than high school	High school	PARENTAL EDUCATION		
		Male	Female	White¹	Black¹	His-panic			More than high school		
									Total	Some college	College grad-uate
READING											
9-year-olds:											
1979–1980	215	210	220	221	189	190	194	213	226	(NA)	(NA)
1983–1984	211	206	214	218	186	187	195	209	223	(NA)	(NA)
1987–1988	212	206	216	218	189	194	193	211	220	(NA)	(NA)
13-year-olds:											
1979–1980	259	254	263	264	232	237	239	254	271	(NA)	(NA)
1983–1984	257	253	262	263	236	240	240	253	268	(NA)	(NA)
1987–1988	258	252	263	261	243	240	247	253	265	(NA)	(NA)
17-year-olds:											
1979–1980	286	282	290	293	243	261	262	277	299	(NA)	(NA)
1983–1984	286	284	294	296	264	268	269	281	301	(NA)	(NA)
1987–1988	290	286	294	295	274	271	267	282	300	(NA)	(NA)
MATHEMATICS											
9-year-olds:											
1977–1978	219	217	220	224	192	203	200	219	(NA)	230	231
1981–1982	219	217	221	224	195	204	199	218	(NA)	225	229
1985–1986	222	222	222	227	202	205	201	218	(NA)	229	231
13-year-olds:											
1977–1978	264	264	265	272	230	238	245	263	(NA)	273	264
1981–1982	269	269	268	274	240	252	251	263	(NA)	275	282
1985–1986	269	270	268	274	249	254	252	263	(NA)	274	280
17-year-olds:											
1977–1978	300	304	297	306	268	276	280	294	(NA)	305	317
1981–1982	299	302	296	304	272	277	279	293	(NA)	304	312
1985–1986	302	305	299	306	279	283	279	293	(NA)	305	314
SCIENCE											
9-year-olds:											
1976–1977	220	222	218	230	192	175	199	223	(NA)	237	232
1981–1982	221	221	221	229	189	187	196	218	(NA)	229	231
1985–1986	224	227	221	232	199	196	204	220	(NA)	236	235
13-year-olds:											
1976–1977	247	251	244	256	206	213	224	245	(NA)	260	267
1981–1982	250	256	245	257	217	228	225	243	(NA)	259	264
1985–1986	251	256	247	259	222	226	229	245	(NA)	258	264
17-year-olds:											
1976–1977	290	297	282	296	262	240	265	284	(NA)	296	309
1981–1982	283	292	275	293	249	235	259	275	(NA)	290	300
1985–1986	289	295	282	296	259	253	258	277	(NA)	295	304

NA Not available   ¹Non-Hispanic.

Source: U.S. National Center for Education Statistics, *Digest of Education Statistics,* 1990, and U.S. Census Bureau (1991). *Statistical abstract of the United States* 111th ed., Washington, D.C. p. 155.

Box 5–4   Science and Adolescent Women

For many years data have supported findings that adolescent females do not perform as well as males on tests that determine science and mathematical ability (Benbow & Stanley, 1980, 1983; Kramer, 1991; Steinkamp & Maehr, 1984). On Scholastic Aptitude Tests (SATs), for example, males have outscored females by roughly 50 points for the past two decades. In 1989 male average SAT scores were 500 compared to female scores of 454. On other measures like the American College Tests and the NAEP similar differences have been observed (U.S. Census Bureau, 1991). Collectively these examinations provide evidence that males score about one-half a standard deviation higher than do females.

Several arguments have been offered to explain these continuing differences. Camill Benbow and Julian Stanley (1980, p. 1264) suspect these differences result from "superior male mathematical ability, which may in turn be related to greater male ability in spatial tasks." Others believe that gender steering is occurring (Steinkamp & Maehr, 1984). That is, to be a scientist is to be masculine, and adolescent women should not be masculine. This argument has been further extended to imply that being successful in school is unfeminine. Several authors and groups like the American Association of University Women have decried this situation and called for an end to suspected tracking practices that steer women away from these courses and higher enrollment in high school math and science classes (Pallas & Alexander, 1983; Benz, Pfeiffer, & Newman, 1981; Wellesley College Center for Research on Women, 1992).

What do you think? Did your experiences in high school confirm the steering hypothesis? Are the sexes different in their ability?

had occurred in a billing statement (Mikulecky, 1990). In part, this may explain why most popular magazines are written at a fourth-grade reading level with story lengths that rarely exceed a few hundred words. It may also explain the growing tendency to read headline or "sound bite" news. That is, keep it simple for the stupid—KISS.

If we sidestep the issue of how we choose to define the term *literate,* than there is some encouraging data that suggest that most—but certainly not all—people in the United States are striving to improve their knowledge. For instance, compared to 1984, when 74% of the adult population had their high school degree or its equivalency, the percentage had increased to 78% by 1987 (U.S. Census Bureau, 1991b). GED exams, which are taken after a course of study by individuals who have not completed a standard high school program, continue to rise. More than 750,000 GED exams were taken in 1990, up nearly 100,000 over the previous year (Hayes, 1991). Adult educational services are more available and from more sources than ever before. For example, U.S. business provides nearly 18 million courses to more than 15 million employees each year. Even though we believe the goal of literacy for everyone is unattainable, for many improvement is under way.

And Now: Project 2000+

For the past twelve years the federal government has envisioned its role in education as limited. With the election of Bill Clinton as president, will that policy change? Will Project 2000, an effort crafted with President Clinton's involvement, take a different direction?

In an October 1992 *Phi Delta Kappan* article published just before the election, Bill Clinton presented the following positions on education. First, there should be a "meaningful national exam system" that would identify children in need of help and provide the educational assistance needed to remediate their learning difficulty. Next, he proposed to create a "level playing field" to enable all young people to be ready to enter school and benefit from their educational experience. Efforts in this area included not only full funding for Head Start but also a statement that every young person deserved to attend a school without fear of bodily harm. Third, to reduce the school failure rate, Clinton would expand training and scholarship opportunities through a "national apprenticeship program" modeled after European programs for non-college bound youth. His efforts in this area would increase the number and quality of skilled craftspeople. Finally, candidate Clinton vowed to develop the means by which young people seeking higher education could fulfill that ambition (Clinton, 1992). Early into his term, President Clinton has taken several tentative steps on each of these matters, from proposing increased funding for Head Start to a national youth service movement. His success on these and other issues will be determined by Congress and the electorate.

Summary

The cynical reader might say, "So what? More than 30 years ago we were provided with information that could have brought about change, but it was ignored. Here were are three decades later. Why the concern now?"

For the cynical the issue is essentially demographic. As the U.S. birthrate declines to historic lows, the value of each child increases proportionately. Beginning with this decade, the overwhelming majority of all new employment positions will require education beyond high school. The number of young people in the work force between the ages of 16 and 24 will drop from 30% in 1985 to 16% in the year 2000. It is projected that 20% of the labor force will be minorities (Darling-Hammond, 1990; U.S. Dept. of Labor, 1987; Wattenberg, 1987). In short, by the close of this decade employment opportunities for youth will exceed the available number of young people. When one reconsiders the illiteracy rate and the fact that minority-youth unemployment remains astronomical, the reason for concern becomes apparent.

For the less cynical, these studies and goal statements are merely a continuation of the concern expressed for all children. The interest that society has in those children is clearly represented in the $372 billion people in the United States spent to educate their young people in 1991. Perhaps these calls for action will be heeded this time. If not, the problems will not disappear. Other individuals, in other years, will raise similar issues until the situation is finally corrected.

It would have been nice to end this section on a less decidedly sour note. (See Box 5–5.) In the first edition of this book we were able to remark positively that together, the educational system and the family had achieved positive changes. For example, the number of young people enrolled in high school grew from 6.7% in 1889 to 15.4% in 1909, 73.3% in 1930, and 90% in 1958. This figures still remains in excess of 90% (U.S. Census Bureau, 1991). Sadly, the

Box 5–5   **A Cross-Cultural Perspective: Education in Japan**

The spectacular success of the Japanese people in trade and scientific developments has led to a growing world influence. In the United States many critics perceiving Americans doing business as usual have argued U.S. institutions to imitate the Japanese. Nowhere is this call greater than in education. Critics of American education point out the typical Japanese high school graduate has an educational level comparable to that of an American college graduate. An impressive 94% of Japanese students graduate from high school. Finally, on international science and mathematics tests Japanese low scorers outperform American high scores.

Observers note that in contrast to the U.S. system's 180-day school year, the Japanese have 240 days, including a half-day of school on Saturdays. Course work is more difficult. Homework is mandatory. *Shiken jiqoko* (examination hells) are used to select only the best and brightest Japanese students for intensive advanced academic preparation. Many students attend after-hours schools. And in the ultimate contrast to American students, Japanese young people clean their own schools and serve their own lunches (Shimahara, 1985; M. White, 1987; Sato & McLaughlin, 1992).

As pleasant or frightening as these observations may sound, playing with the structure of the school system alone will not improve the U.S. educational system. As Shimahara and White point out, education is central to the Japanese culture. Few Japanese mothers are employed outside of the home. Rather, they are "employed" in preparing their children for education. Furthermore, the Japanese society is very homogeneous. Minorities constitute only 3% of the population. The divorce rate is one-third that of the United States, and only 5% of the population lives in single-parent families. Education involves more than schools. It involves families.

number of young people completing high school has not been so high. Graduation rates in 1986 for 18- to 24-year-olds were 60% for American Indians, 59.1% for Hispanics, 76.4% for Blacks, and 83.1% for Whites (Quality Education for Minorities Project, 1990). More serious still, an estimated 55% of White high school graduates, 80% of Hispanic high school students, and 84% of Black high school graduates, did not possess enough academic skills to enter college (Sheldon, 1987). And even if they had the skills, increases in college tuitions and cuts in federal loan programs for students prevent many talented minority youths from attending college. For example, in 1977, 50% of Black high school graduates enrolled in college. By 1982 this figure had declined to 36% (Bracey, 1986). Finally, although the United States is one of the richest nations in the world, it had the dubious distinction of ranking only 49th in literacy (Larrick, 1987).

Positive Effects of Schooling

Despite the evidence just put before you, there are data indicating that schools do impart knowledge. For example, a study of 18,000 adults showed that knowledge increases as level of education increases (Hyman, Wright, & Reed, 1975). Moreover, while wage discrimination against women and Blacks still exists, the earning gap narrows as education increases (Hispanic Policy Development Project, 1987; Hodgkinson, 1979; U.S. Bureau of the Census, 1987). Finally, think back for a moment to your own educational experience, If you are typical, you have fond memories of school. Most students want school to be a friendly and relaxed place. And certainly Powell (1985) reports a "deep satisfaction" among most students

Figure 5–1   Earnings and Education

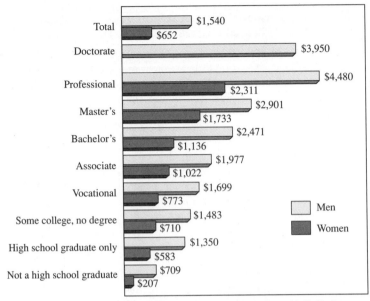

Total	$1,540 / $652
Doctorate	$3,950
Professional	$4,480 / $2,311
Master's	$2,901 / $1,733
Bachelor's	$2,471 / $1,136
Associate	$1,977 / $1,022
Vocational	$1,699 / $773
Some college, no degree	$1,483 / $710
High school graduate only	$1,350 / $583
Not a high school graduate	$709 / $207

☐ Men ■ Women

Note: There were not enough women with Ph.D. degrees in the survey to list their mean monthly earnings.

Source: U.S. Census Bureau (1991). Does Education really pay off? *Census and you, 26,* p. 8.

with their educational setting. Indeed, as Erik Erikson (1968) has written so eloquently, for many of us a teacher has made all the difference in the world.

Even though we are unclear in our own minds who deserves credit, it is clear that as people in the United States grow older they return to school and this time they graduate. It may be the disappointment of low salaries, increased maturity that accompanies age, or a desire for knowledge (See Figure 5–1.) Regardless of the reasons, 30% of the present college population is over 25 years of age with 12% over the age of 34 (U.S. Census Bureau, 1991c). Among Blacks 35 to 44 years of age, their lifetime high school completion rate has increased from 63% in 1980 to 80% in 1990, and their college completion rate has increased from 8% to 15% for the same years (U.S. Census Bureau, 1991d). In 1970, 4.5% of the total Hispanic population had completed four or more years of college. This had doubled to 10% in 1989 (U.S. Census Bureau, 1991). Over the past fifty years, the percentage of all individuals between the ages of 25 to 29 not completing high school declined from 61.9% in 1940 to 14.5% in 1989 (U.S. Census Bureau, 1991). Furthermore, although science and mathematics scores are cause for concern, U.S. scholars still are responsible for more than a third of the world's publications in clinical medicine, biomedical research, biology, earth/space sciences, and mathematics. In areas such as chemistry and physics, they are responsible for more than 25% of the published scientific papers (Rotberg, 1990).

Clearly, there is room for improvement in how the United States educates its youth, in particular, those young people who are not White males. Nevertheless, it would be unfair to ignore the interest people in the United States have in improving their educational abilities.

Education, Careers, and the Future

Myth has it that life used to be predictable. You were born in one community, grew up in one house, were educated in one school, married one person, worked in one job, and returned back to that house to eventually die at home. Look around you and the inaccuracy of that myth is readily apparent. What concerns us in this section is the issue of career education and its role in today's society.

U.S. society has always experienced change. The difference between the recent past and the present is the rate of change. Needless to say, since World War II the rate of change has accelerated. This rapid change makes it extremely difficult to predict the future. For example, Thomas Gullotta remembers in 1973 purchasing his first calculator. "Miracles of technology," he thought, "a calculator with a square-root key for only $73." Today, as he walks through the enclosed suburban malls that did not exist when he was a youth, he could buy a computer for that amount of money. Consider another example. In the mid-1960s the American automobile industry was unrivaled. Car production was at historic highs. If a young person decided in 1965 to embark on a career as a spot welder for American Motors, his or her guidance counselor would have probably thought the decision was a wise one. Who would ever have thought that less than 25 years later spot welders would have been replaced by robots and that American Motors would have been bought and sold twice?

Thus, the traditional notion that career education introduced young people into established, lifelong occupational structures is no longer valid. Indeed, it has even been demonstrated that high school grades, class rank, and aptitude have no relationship to employment status (Bracey, 1992). Consequently, a new understanding of the role of career education is slowly emerging. It is based on the following beliefs: First, throughout life, change will be the only constant. Next, during an individual's work life, he or she will probably have several jobs, very possibly in different employment fields. Last, successful career education programs need to expand young people's understanding of the multitude of options available to them.

Does career education alone influence the decisions that young people make regarding their ever-changing career path? Obviously, the answer is no. Several other significant forces exist:

1. Individual factors such as intelligence, work attitude, and ambition
2. Family factors such as income, religion, race, and parental attitudes about the importance of education
3. General societal factors such as current attitudes about gender roles, public aid for education, and levels of racism
4. Chance

The first three factors are self-explanatory, but the fourth deserves a brief explanation. It may be that despite all of the best intentions of educators and parents, young people begin their careers as much by chance as any other factor. A part-time college job may provide experience that leads to full-time employment after graduation. A friend of the family may know the personnel officer of a corporation. Or, perhaps, Mom owns 51% of the corporation. The point is that chance rather than a deliberate planning effort may be the most important factor. To illustrate, the actress Annette Funicello, of Mickey Mouse Clubhouse and beach-blanket-film fame, shares the story that Walt Disney by chance observed her performing in a dance recital. This accidental encounter provided her with the opportunity to establish a very successful career as an entertainer.

Even if we are correct that chance is a significant factor, we do not mean that you should give up all career planning. Graduating from high school and joining that intellectual elite minority of American citizens who have graduated from college is, on average, a wise investment.* Data suggest that high school graduates earn half again as much as nongraduates and that college graduates earnings are twice as large as nongraduates'.

Truancy, Dropping Out, and School Violence

For some young people formal education is a source of unhappiness, and for a variety of reasons they either avoid attending school whenever they can or leave before graduating. Others behave destructively at school, damaging property and threatening or attacking people.

Truancy

Like running away, playing hooky is a national pastime. Neither behavior is particularly accepted—idleness has long been popularly thought to breed trouble—but until recently neither has been investigated by the scientific community.

There are essentially two kinds of explanation for truancy. The first can be described as a psychological explanation. According to this view, the influence of the school on truancy is less important than personal and family variables. J. H. Kahn and Nursten (1962), for instance, sketch a picture of truancy involving three types of young people—those with character disorders, those with psychoneurotic problems, and those with psychotic conditions.

Most of the psychological research in this area focuses on the need of the mother to retard her adolescent's attempts to gain independence and shows that she must be helped to relax her grip on the young person's life and let the adolescent go. This point of view is illustrated by Sperling (1967) and C. Goldberg (1977), who suggest that truancy is the result of an excessively close mother/child relationship in which ambivalence over separation issues creates Oedipal conflict. They suggest that the return of the young person to school as soon as possible and family treatment are both needed to deal with truancy. According to Nielson and Gerber (1979), the problems of truants are often serious and longstanding. They found that truants were depressed and angry, with many committing delinquent acts. If the truant has older brothers and sister, they, too, are often truants. The families of these young people experience many problems, with divorce, unemployment, illness, and alcoholism not uncommon (Sommer & Nagel, 1991). Although these young people see the value of school,

---

*It is estimated that nearly 21% of the U.S. population has graduated from college (U.S. Census Bureau, 1991)

few, if any, have a positive relationship with the school staff. The open hostility that these adolescents feel for the staff serves to fuel a cycle of increased truancy.

Not everyone agrees that truancy is the by-product of a struggle between parent and child. Some researchers, relying heavily on their observations of the social structure of the school, suggest that the system may work against some young people. For instance, Albert Cohen (1955) argues that the school is essentially a middle-class structure that frustrates lower-class individuals by denying them recognition. This frustration motivates young people to stay away from school and seek other means of recognition.

In view of our earlier discussion of the work of Rosenthal and Jacobson (1968) and Rist (1970), Cohen's argument is compelling. Deprived of the opportunity to feel worthwhile, to be valued, and to achieve status, the frustrated young person turns away from education in many instances. As the frustration grows, the probability of that young person's completing high school diminishes.

Dropping Out

In large U.S. cities in any given year, roughly 40% of the young people enrolled in high school will drop out. Nationwide, although the figure is 15 percentage points lower, it is still a disturbingly high 4.3 million students a year (Hahn, 1987; Strother, 1986). The consequences of this decision for young people are considerable. The dropout has roughly a one in three chance of finding employment. If successful in the job search, those jobs pay the 18- to 24-year-old an average yearly salary of $6,000 (Hayes, 1992).

Several reviews of the literature have identified the factors that predict which young people are most likely to leave school (Beck & Muia, 1980; Hahn, 1987; Howard & Anderson, 1978; Strother, 1986; Gage, 1990). Many dropouts come from poor families. The home life for many is strained. They have a history of truancy and trouble with school authorities. Their parents are likely not to have completed high school. Felice (1981) maintains that for many Black students, dropping out is a rejection of the school's racist and discriminatory behavior. The influence of culture is unmistakable, according to Howard and Anderson (1978). Echoing Cohen's (1955) observation that the school is essentially a middle-class institution, they assert:

> Whereas the middle class emphasis is on order and discipline, the lower class emphasis is on avoidance of trouble or involvement with authorities, development of physical prowess, skill in duping others, the search for excitement and a desire for independence from external controls. Thus, while socialization in middle class families prepares youths to compete successfully in school, lower class children are not prepared to conform to the academic and informal requirements of school. The lower class child, not prepared to be studious, obedient, and docile, comes into conflict with the middle class teacher. His language, poor social adjustment and "cult of immediacy" impair his chance of success. (P. 225)

Other writers contend that peer influence also serves to accelerate the decision to leave school earlier (see, for example, Elliot, Voss, & Wendling, 1966; Parsons, 1959). Those at greatest risk are young people whose friends are no longer in school. Still other scholars observe that criminal behavior and dropping out of school are related (Thornberry, Moore, & Christenson, 1985) and that dropouts are poorly motivated students (Richardson & Cerlach, 1980).

We propose two strategies for breaking the truancy/dropout pattern. The first is based on Cohen's (1955) argument that the school denies the truant and the dropout recognition. Providing recognition to more students is clearly in order. Schools need to broaden their curricula to include such ideas as expanded work/study options, credit-for-experience programs, and alternative-learning centers to provide young people with an increased chance at recognition.

The basis for the second strategy is *EOEO*. If truancy and dropping out are essentially problems of the poor, then change will not occur until we address the fundamental inequalities of poor housing, inadequate medical care, and poor nutrition that exist in our society. These same inequalities help to fuel the anger and hatred that provoke violence in schools and turn many of them into armed camps.

Finally, we need to recognize that education on the timetable the United States has established may not be appropriate for all learners. Some young people will need more time to mature, to discover the need for education, to want to learn. Concepts like national youth service, which would enable youth to wander out of that psychosocial moratorium less hurriedly, are to be encouraged (Eberly, 1991; Woodring, 1989).

School Violence

In reading reports of school life in colonial times (before Lancaster introduced his school), one cannot help feeling that those quaint, one-room, stove-warmed buildings had more in common with *Blackboard Jungle* than with *Little House on the Prairie*. Kett (1977) reports that it was not uncommon for an unpopular teacher to be seized in his classroom by the older, stronger boys, taken outside, and thrashed. Teacher turnover was, needless to say, high. Because the teacher was usually a traveling instructor who lodged in the homes of village people, the community more frequently sided with their children in disputes or instances of violence than with the teacher. Times have not changed much; newspaper accounts of assaults, robbery, and other forms of violence in our schools today are common.

Reacting to reports of increased school violence, Congress in 1974 called for a report determining the extent of "illegal and disruptive" activities in schools. This study, which became known as the Safe School Study, involved more than 4000 schools initially. Nearly 650 schools had on-site visits, and 10 schools reporting a history of problems were studied intensively.

The study reported that acts of violence against individuals and property rose steadily throughout the 1960s and into the 1970s but appeared to have leveled off. This study was the first to report that adolescents were at greater risk of violent injury in schools than anywhere else (Violent Schools, 1979).

A decade and a half later more than 400,000 students were victims of violent crime during a six-month period in 1988 and 1989. More than one third of these incidents involved early adolescents (12- to 15-year-olds) inside or on school property. Early adolescents were more than twice as likely as older adolescents (16- to 19-year-olds) to be victimized at school. A close examination

of the data found that 37% of violent crimes and 81% of thefts against early adolescents occurred at school, compared with 17% of the violent crimes and 39%
of thefts against older adolescents (Whitaker & Bastian, 1991).

Additional data from the National Crime Victimization Survey of 10,000
nationally representative youth between the ages of 12 and 19 found nearly a
quarter of Black inner-city students worried about being attacked when going to
and from school. Six percent of the sample reported avoiding some place in or
around school (mostly restrooms) because they feared harm. Sixteen percent
reported knowledge of either a threat or an attack against a teacher. Fifteen percent reported gangs at their school (Bastian & Taylor, 1991). In another study of
U.S. eighth graders, 10% stated they had been offered drugs for purchase
(Hafner, Ingels, Schneider, & Stevenson, 1990). The estimated costs of school
crime range from $50 million to $600 million a year, with the Safe School Study
(1979) estimating $200 million a year. (See Table 5–2.)

Although these are in actuality small percentages, the effects of these figures
on the educational and social climate of schools are unmistakable. First there are
the calls in the media and from local boards of education for security guards and
increased discipline. Student rights are assailed for contributing to the problem.
Accompanying the cry for increased discipline is a call for increased use of corporal punishment.

Twenty-eight states continue to have rules permitting school personnel to
use reasonable physical force against students. Arguments that corporal punishment is "cruel and unusual" have not moved the U.S. Supreme Court to reverse
the April 19, 1977, decision approving corporal punishment. In Ingraham v.
Wright, the Court in a 5-to-4 decision held that the protections of the Eighth
Amendment do not apply to young people except in the criminal-justice process.
The majority opinion of the Court was that as schools are not prisons but "open"
institutions, "the school child has little need for the protection of the Eighth
Amendment" (Flygare, 1978). However, many people including the U.S.
Advisory Board on Child Abuse and Neglect (1991) would dispute the Court's
contention that the school is an open institution. Hampton and Gullotta (1995)
contend that violence in any setting encourages violence in return: The assistant
principal of an Atlanta high school was critically wounded and paralyzed by a
gun-wielding fifteen-year-old boy. The enraged student shouted, "You are not
going to whip me anymore!" (Welsh, 1978, p. 341). Supporting Hampton and
Gullotta's contention are studies showing that mothers who use severe punishment have more aggressive children than mothers who do not (Sears, Maccoby,
& Levin, 1957) and that children rated by their peers as being physically aggressive in the classroom have parents who use corporal punishment more often than
other parents (Eron, Walder, & Lefkowitz, 1971).

The problem of school violence is not easily solved. Calls for increased discipline (Bauer, 1985) and stronger leadership by principals (Ianni & Reusslanni,
1980) skirt the real issue: violent schools are not positive places (Wayson, 1985).
Increased security guards, metal detectors, identification cards, fences, and
closed-circuit television are not the answer. Such approaches do not solve the
underlying feelings of anger and hatred found in some schools: they suppress

Table 5–2   Students reporting at least one victimization at school, by personal and family characteristics

Student characteristic	Total number of students	Percent of students reporting victimization at school		
		Total	Violent	Property
Sex				
Male	11,166,316	9	2	7
Female	10,387,776	9	2	8
Race				
White	17,306,626	9	2	7
Black	3,449,488	8	2	7
Other	797,978	10	2*	8
Hispanic origin				
Hispanic	2,026,968	7	3	5
Non-Hispanic	19,452,697	9	2	8
Not ascertained	74,428	3*	—	3*
Age				
12	3,220,891	9	2	7
13	3,318,714	10	2	8
14	3,264,574	11	2	9
15	3,214,109	9	3	7
16	3,275,002	9	2	7
17	3,273,628	8	1	7
18	1,755,825	5	1*	4
19	231,348	2*	—	2*
Number of times family moved in last 5 years				
None	18,905,538	8	2	7
Once	845,345	9	2	7
Twice	610,312	13	3*	11
3 or more	1,141,555	15	6	9
Not ascertained	51,343	5*	5*	—
Family Income				
Less than $7,500	2,041,418	8	2	6
$7,500–$9,999	791,086	4	1*	3
$10,000–$14,999	1,823,150	9	3	7
$15,000–$24,999	3,772,445	8	1	8
$25,000–$29,999	1,845,313	8	2	7
$30,000–$49,999	5,798,448	10	2	8
$50,000 and over	3,498,382	11	2	9
Not ascertained	1,983,849	7	3	5
Place of residence				
Central city	5,816,321	10	2	8
Suburbs	10,089,207	9	2	7
Nonmetropolitan area	5,648,564	8	1	7

Source: From L. D. Bastian & B. M. Taylor (1991), p. 1. *School Crime* (NCJ-131645) (Washington, D.C.: U.S. Justice Department, 1991), 1.

these feelings. In the last section of this chapter, we examine the success of some possible alternatives to the present educational system. Some of them may be useful in dealing with this problem.

Some Alternatives to the Present Educational System

This chapter concludes on a more optimistic note than its predecessors in earlier editions. Not that we believe education is on the verge of a renaissance—it is not—at least not yet. Rather, we hold hope for three reasons. First, experiments in educating children differently are under way. Next, taxpayers across the country are revolting over "business as usual." Finally, by the end of the first decade of the next century, demographics will reshape the relationship between schools and communities regardless of the efforts of people committed to the status quo.

Experiments Under Way

For several years educators have attempted to identify characteristics of effective school programs. In a report to Congress by the General Accounting Office (1989) five of these features were delineated:

1. Effective school programs have strong purposeful administrative and instructional leadership that creates community consensus on educational goals.
2. Programs focus instruction on basic and higher-order skills.
3. Schools are orderly and safe allowing students and teachers to focus their attention on learning.
4. The expectation is that children can learn.
5. Continuous evaluation enables appropriate modifications of individualized educational programs and system efforts.

Emerging from these roots, efforts are under way to change the American educational experience. Here are some examples:

In Tennessee the state legislature funded a four-year study to determine the effect of class size on achievement. Project STAR (Student/Teacher Achievement Ratio) analyzed three classroom configurations: classes with one teacher and 13 to 17 students, one teacher and 22 to 25 students, and one teacher and an aide to 22 to 25 students. After four years, the study found that students in smaller classes scored significantly higher on achievement and basic skill tests than students in other settings. Consistent with findings presented in this chapter, children from more economically privileged backgrounds always outperformed students eligible for the free lunch program (Pate-Bain, Achilles, Boyd-Zaharias, & McKenna, 1992). The point is to remember that family variables like socioeconomic status (SES) and relationship instability (divorce, death, or serious illness in the family) matter (Frymier, 1992)!

In Minnesota, Milwaukee, St. Louis, Missouri, Cambridge, Massachusetts, and elsewhere, pilot programs permit parents a choice in selecting schools for their children. Initial findings from these efforts are not particularly encouraging. For instance, in St. Louis when inner-city parents were provided an opportunity to send their children to suburban schools, few parents enrolled their children. In Milwaukee, 65% of parents who had enrolled their children in the program withdrew in the second year. Still, these efforts are significant in their attempt to break down the social stratification that permeates education systems across the United States (Bracey, 1993).

Because of housing prices and local zoning practices, the United States and its school districts are stratified by race and income levels. We reside, work, and educate our children in a segregated society. Some programs may help to erode the educational caste system that has developed. Again, it should not be expected that student achievement scores from low-income and middle-income families will achieve parity. They will not. Nevertheless, *EOEO* demonstrates that low income youth benefit academically from educational placements with young people of higher socioeconomic status.

Finally, the creation of the New American Schools Development Corporation (NASDC) and the initial funding of 11 projects are exciting developments. In many respects these programs are reminiscent of alternative education programs that briefly flourished three decades ago. For example, the Audrey Cohen College project intends to link the classroom with the "real world." Each semester, community projects will be interwoven with coursework to demonstrate to the student the interconnectedness of the world in which the student lives.

The ATLAS project brings together James Comer of Yale, Theodore Sizer of Brown, and Howard Gardner of Harvard to implement the visions of these educational reformers. Schools under this model will be community-focused centers for active learning. They will also draw heavily on the knowledge and direct involvement of mental health professionals. This health-focused effort contrasts with historic understandings that schools are places of cognitive, not affective learning.

Finally, we mention Expeditionary Learning. Using many of the successful concepts previously developed by Outward Bound, this project involves students in such community activities as developing recycling centers and child care facilities and taps the talents of visiting artists, scholars, and business people. Against this stimulating backdrop, academic courses will be made "relevant" for students (Mecklenburger, 1992; Sherry, 1992).

Collectively, these efforts are not breakthroughs in the development of new learning systems. Indeed, these experiments have been discussed for years. Why, then, are we excited?

First, a prolonged taxpayer revolt is in progress. That revolt shows no sign of waning. In fact, given the expected increase in the number of families without school-aged children, the traditional voting constituency of education budgets (parents with school-aged children) will continue to decline. Unsuccessful schools—that is, schools that are not educating its youth, not building relationships with the parents of those youth (their voting constituency on budgets) and not demonstrating its relevancy to the wider community— will surely fail financially. Because we believe that schools that fail young people and their families should either change or go out of business, the failure of an individual school is not troubling to us. For too long too many students have failed.

Finally, we believe demographics will significantly alter education in the United States in the next century. Population projections of adolescents age 14 to 17 show a slight percentage rise from 5.3% of the total population in 1990 to 5.9% in 2005. This growth then declines to roughly 5.2% of the population through the year 2050. Correspondingly, individuals 85 years and older by the year 2050 are expected to make up 4.6% of the population (U.S. Census Bureau, 1993a). For a nation that had at its birth a median age of 18, this six tenths of one percent difference is astonishing (G. R. Adams & Gullotta, 1983)!

We believe that schools as places of learning for *only* youth will cease to exist by the year 2010. Schools will be redefined as lifelong centers for community learning, or they will go out of business. These new centers will become places in which public, private, and not-for-profit agencies will concurrently offer services. We expect that senior citizens, toddlers, and parents will freely wander school corridors receiving services ranging from child to family medical care, stopping, by the way, to dine on improved school meals that will include breakfast and dinner. What excites us about this vision (made possible by declining numbers of students against the backdrop of infrastructure expenditures) is the opportunity to rekindle a sense of community around learning. Will it happen? Stay tuned. The next century is almost upon us.

Major Points to Remember

1. Three forces helped to shape U.S. education: the need for religious instruction, the need for basic skills, and a respect for self-instruction.
2. There are two views on the history of U.S. education. One sees the educational movement in a favorable light. The other is less kind.
3. There are two social structures in every school. Status within these two structures is assigned for rather different reasons. The school staff dispenses academic rewards, while the peer group dispenses social status within the group.
4. Why students go to school often differs considerably from why we think they do.
5. The comprehensive high school has been praised by some as a triumph of democracy. Others find that it provides only a mediocre education for those who are not college bound.
6. *EOEO,* better recognized by many as the Coleman Report, is considered to be one of the most important studies on education ever undertaken. Its findings radically changed our understanding of how the educational system affects learning.
7. Following the publication of *EOEO,* several explanations emerged for the school system's apparent failure to educate. These explanations include the

self-fulfilling prophecy, the finding that cognitive deficits can be caused by poor nutrition, and the controversial argument that genetics may be a factor in the learning rates of certain groups of people.

8. Educational, individual, family, and societal factors, as well as chance, influence the changing career decisions individuals will make across the life span.

9. Explanations for truancy include the idea that parents and their children are overinvolved with one another and the belief that some young people are deprived of an opportunity to achieve recognition in schools.

10. School violence dates back to the nation's beginning. Interestingly, for young people between the ages of 12 and 15, school may be more dangerous than the streets. The response to this situation has been to increase security precautions at schools.

11. For demographic and financial reasons, schools will change in the next century.

PART THREE

Typical Patterns of Adolescent Development

CHAPTER

6

Physical Development During Adolescence

A dolescence is a period of tremendous changes in the body. Hormonal fluxes, a growth spurt, changes in body image, problems in coordination, acne, new concerns about clothing, self-consciousness about body image, and other physical and psychological realities face all adolescents, to varying degrees. Some adolescents experience little or no trauma over their physical changes, and others find this aspect of growing up a difficult undertaking. Being very tall too early, for example, can create expectations among teachers, parents, and others that one is mature beyond one's years. In contrast, being short can leave one with poor odds in the peer competition in athletics and dating. It can be difficult—indeed, outright frustrating—when the average girl in your class is a full foot taller than you and you want to ask the prettiest, tallest girl to a dance. In contrast, if you've grown too quickly, lack of coordination and awkwardness can make you feel like a giraffe just learning to walk.

In this chapter we take a serious look at many aspects of adolescent physical development. These include the hormonal basis of development as well as the psychological and sociocultural implications of puberty. In the final section of this chapter we propose a conceptual framework, based on social cognition mechanisms, for integrating our understanding of how adolescents may change because of their physical growth and body image.

Physical and Biological Aspects of Puberty

The onset of puberty is not a single, sudden event but a complex, gradual process (Warren, 1983). In perhaps oversimplified terms, puberty is characterized by (1) a spurt in physical growth, (2) maturation of physiological mechanisms, and (3) the appearance of secondary sex characteristics (for example, pubic hair or breast development).

Generational Differences in the Onset of Puberty

Imagine a toddler displaying all the features of puberty—a three-year-old girl with fully developed breasts or a boy just slightly older with a deep male voice. That is what we will see by the year 2250, if the age at which puberty arrives keeps getting younger at its current pace. (A. C. Petersen, 1979a, p. 45)

There can be no argument that the young (at least girls) are experiencing puberty earlier. A. C. Petersen (1979a) has reviewed a variety of studies that document this trend. For example, in Norway during the 1840s the average age for first menstruation (menarche) was 17; today it is 13. In the United States, where children appear to mature up to a year earlier than children in European countries, the age declined from 14.2 to 12.5 between 1900 and the 1970s. Indeed, J. M. Tanner (1962, 1975), perhaps the world's most noted specialist on physical growth in adolescence, has reported findings suggesting that the age of menarche has declined an average of four months in each decade over the past century. Two centuries ago a pregnant 13-year-old was unimaginable. Today, it is possible, though very rare, for an 11-year-old to give birth.

It is only fair, however, to indicate that the conclusions drawn by Petersen, Tanner, and others may be slightly misleading. Evidence summarized by Bullough (1981) suggests that historical documents stating that the average age for menarche during the mid-1800s was 17 years are incorrect. In particular,

Tanner has been noted as using a single source of information to document this claim. According to Bullough, other available sources from this early period of history suggest an average age of 14 years. The generational change in menarche may thus be less pronounced than earlier indicated. However, the general notion that menarche now occurs at an earlier age is not challenged.

The Hormonal Basis of Puberty

The onset of puberty is basically regulated by *endocrine glands,* important organs that create body changes through the secretion of chemicals into the bloodstream or lymphatic system. Put simply, several endocrine glands produce secretions (known as *hormones*) that interact with cells to create physiological changes. Although the intracellular mechanisms that allow cells to respond to hormone secretions are not completely understood, their role in pubertal change is well documented. The relationships among the various endocrine glands also partially remain a medical mystery.

One of the endocrine glands, the *pituitary gland,* is frequently referred to as the master gland. Actually, the pituitary gland is under control of the *hypothalamus,* which is part of the upper brain system. Although the pituitary gland controls the general level of endocrine production, the hypothalamus "instructs" the pituitary gland on the optimum level of hormone secretion, so the pituitary gland is really the workhorse.

In that the hypothalamus can instruct the pituitary gland through neurohumoral secretions, it has a very large role in the onset of pubertal change. In turn, the pituitary gland secretes hormones known as *gonadotropins,* which activate the *testes* and *ovaries,* parts of the endocrine system called *gonads.* Also in turn, the gonads secrete their own hormones, which have major physiological effects on puberty. The secretion from the testes is known as *androgen,* and the secretion from the ovaries is known as *estrogen.*

The capacity of the hypothalamus, the pituitary gland, and the gonads in combination to trigger pubertal change appears to exist even before birth, but the capacity is not used due to an inhibitory effect of the hypothalamus until certain physical conditions are met (Higham, 1980). According to some authorities, when a critical weight is reached, certain metabolic rates cause the hypothalamus to disengage the inhibitory mechanism. Some evidence suggests that weight of 48 kilograms (105.6 pounds) is needed before menarche can occur (Frisch & Revelle, 1971). Other evidence suggests that menarche will not occur until total body weight includes approximately 17% fat (Frisch, 1983).

As the hypothalamus disengages its inhibitory mechanism, it becomes increasingly less sensitive to gonadal hormones. Hence, the amount of sex hormones secreted increases, and the child gradually moves toward physical and sexual maturity. Pubertal hormonal maturation occurs about a year before changes in the body and its sex organs are visible (Daniel, 1983; Higham, 1980). During this early period there is an increase in two gonadotropins, known as *FSH* (follicle-stimulating hormone) and *LH* (luteinizing hormone). Generally, both gonadotropins increase between the ages of 7 and 11 in girls and 8 and 12 in boys. By the completion of pubertal changes, the level of both FSH and LH in the blood will have increased by as much as 200% to 300%. In females, FSH stimulates the growth of the ovarian follicles (these contain maturing eggs), and LH induces ovulation. Both hormones interact to stimulate estrogen secretion from the ovaries. In males, FSH stimulates the growth of the tubules in the testes and affects spermatogenesis (production of sperm); LH stimulates the production of the androgenic hormone *testosterone*.

During prepubertal life there is a low secretion of gonadal steroids or gonadotropins. The hypothalamus and the pituitary gland are controlled by a negative feedback mechanism that keeps the production of sex-related hormones to a minimum. As the child grows, there is a decreasing sensitivity to negative feedback control with a gradual increase in LH and FSH levels. As the youth matures, the LH and FSH gonadotropins increasingly influence gonadal production of hormones, which, in turn, have effects on physical and sexual maturation.

Nutrition and Puberty

The biological basis for timing of the onset of physical growth during adolescence is receiving new and careful attention by the medical field (Rees & Trahms, 1989). We speculate that this attention is, in part, being stirred by the increasingly reported incidence of eating disorders (Frisch, 1983). Indeed, evidence from nutrition and physical-training studies is showing an important association between level of body fat, onset of puberty, and corresponding fertility. Frisch (1983) reports, for example, on a comparison of nonanorectic and anorectic female patients showing that a loss of body weight in the range of 10% to 15% of normal weight for height results in amenorrhea (disruption of the menstruation cycle). Further, weight gains that approximate normal body weight result in a restoration of the cycle. Likewise, she reports other studies indicating that obesity is also associated with amenorrhea. Therefore, too little or too much fat can have a negative effect on the onset and regularity of the menstrual cycle. It is speculated from the study of hormone production that fatty tissue may be a significant extra source of estrogen supplementing the gonads. Likewise, due to physical training and body-fat levels, the lean body mass associated with athletes or ballet dancers may result in either delayed menarche or irregular menstrual cycles.

Typically, the focus at the onset of puberty on reproductive ability centers on females. But issues of fertility present concerns for both sexes. What few studies exist suggest that undernutrition and body fat are central factors in the onset of puberty for males, too. Frisch (1983) reviews several studies indicating that undernutrition in men results in a loss of sexual libido, followed by a loss of prostate fluid and, finally, by a decrease in the motility and longevity of sperm. Indeed, sperm production ceases altogether when weight loss is approximately 25% of a male's normal body weight. Fortunately, regaining weight can result in the restoration of all functions in exactly the reverse order.

What function does body fat play for the male and female adolescent? For males it may provide the necessary caloric needs to maintain a fully functioning reproductive system. For females it may not only have a similar impact but also provide the necessary caloric needs for maintaining a fetus once impregnated. The only data on this issue are not fully conclusive, but they are suggestive (see Brooks-Gunn & Petersen, 1983).

Physical change is very apparent when one sees junior high, high school, and college students together at the same time.

Body Development

The most eye-catching physical changes during adolescence occur when boys grow taller than their mothers and girls begin to develop breasts and wider hips. Generally, girls are about 11-years-old when the pubertal growth spurt begins, and boys are about 13-years-old (Brooks-Gunn & Petersen, 1983). In both sexes the growth spurt is primarily associated with the lengthening of the trunk; the legs reach their peak growth before the trunk does, which accounts for the leggy look of young adolescents (A. C. Petersen & Taylor, 1980).

As muscle tissue grows during this spurt, fat accumulation decreases. Overall, boys develop not only larger muscles but also markedly different physical characteristics associated with musculature. For example, boys develop more strength in relation to muscle size, larger hearts, higher systolic blood pressure, and a higher capacity for carrying oxygen in the blood (Petersen & Taylor, 1980).

There is also a major change in the relative width of the shoulders and hips for both boys and girls. Before pubertal change their body builds are fairly similar. With the onset of pubescence, boys' shoulders grow more rapidly, while girls' hips widen. Thus, after puberty boys' shoulders are wider in proportion to their hips than girls' are (M. S. Faust, 1977). It is very common among adolescent peer groups for friendly, and sometimes not so friendly, nicknames to emerge that accentuate physical changes.

Although changes in height and breadth are important in adolescent development, society is more inclined to recognize the rapid maturation of the reproductive system during this period (D. D. Logan, Calder, & Cohen, 1980). The major stages in sexual maturation are (1) the initiation of puberty, which occurs approximately six months earlier in girls than in boys; (2) the development of secondary sex characteristics, which takes approximately four years; and (3) menarche, which occurs approximately two years after the onset of pubertal change

(Marshall & Tanner, 1969, 1970). Within each sex the timing of these changes may, of course, vary a great deal from one individual to the next. Growth differentials in the general stages of puberty also occur between the sexes. For example, pubic hair develops about two years later in males than in females. However, the lag between pubic-hair and breast development in females is much greater than the lag between pubic-hair and genital development in males. The reason probably is endocrinological differences between the sexes in hormonal production (A. C. Petersen & Taylor, 1980). Table 6–1 summarizes the developmental sequences for genitals, pubic hair, and breasts.

Tanner's work on adolescent growth has frequently been used as the major standard for assessing pubertal development. His recent photographic series (Tanner, 1975) has been used by Morris and Udry (1980) to develop a series of self-assessment scales for measuring pubertal change.

Psychological Aspects of Puberty

The psychological consequences of puberty are twofold. First, there are individual psychological reactions and the corresponding attitudes, fears, moods, and related emotions of boys and girls. Second, there are the psychosocial interactions with family and peers.

The Psychological Impact of Body Development

Maturational changes affect how young adolescents feel about themselves. In a comparative study of boys and girls in the sixth grade, A. C. Petersen (1979b) found that girls had a less positive body image than did boys of the same age or older girls. Sixth-grade girls had considerable difficulty in acknowledging any feelings about their changing bodies. Although individual satisfaction with body changes increases with age, it is generally clear that pubertal changes do create some degree of stress associated with body image.

Brooks-Gunn (1986) has reviewed what is known about the psychological significance of puberty for girls. She notes that, in general, menarche heralds increasing social maturity, perceived and real peer prestige, self-esteem, heightened self-awareness of one's body, and increased self-consciousness (see, for example, Garwood & Allen, 1979; Koff, Rierdan, & Jacobson, 1981; Koff, Rierdan, & Silverstone, 1978; R. G. Simmons, Blyth, & McKinney, 1983). Therefore, we can conclude that puberty is related to increased social maturity. However, menarche as the milestone of pubescence for girls is also associated with a mixture of positive and negative emotions. In one study of adolescent females, about 20% reported positive emotions about menarche, 20% reported negative emotions, 20% had mixed emotions, and the rest had neutral emotions (Ruble & Brooks-Gunn, 1982). Likewise, it would appear that early-maturing girls who are unprepared for menarche report more negative experiences and emotions than do on-time or prepared peers.

According to Rierdan and Koff (1991) menarche has long been theorized as being associated with ambivalence and depression. In a test of this assumption, they compared premenarcheal and postmenarcheal sixth-grade girls on a commonly used assessment of depression. Their results confirmed the assumption

Table 6–1   Stages in Sexual Maturation

| | Characteristic | | |
Stage	Male genital development	Male and female pubic hair development	Breast development
1	Testes, scrotum, and penis are about the same size and shape as in early childhood.	The vellus over the pubes is not further developed than over the abdominal wall, i.e., no pubic hair.	There is elevation of the nipple only.
2	Scrotum and testes are slightly enlarged. The skin of the scrotum is reddened and changed in texture. There is little or no enlargement of the penis at this stage.	There is sparse growth of long, slightly pigmented, tawny hair, straight or slightly curled, chiefly at the base of the penis or along the labia.	Breast bud stage. There is elevation of the breast and the nipple as a small mound. Areolar diameter is enlarged over that of Stage 1.
3	Penis is slightly enlarged, at first mainly in length. Testes and scrotum are further enlarged than in Stage 2.	The hair is considerably darker, coarser, and more curled. It spreads sparsely over the function of the pubes.	Breast and areola are both enlarged and elevated more than in Stage 2 but with no separation of their contours.
4	Penis is further enlarged, with growth on breadth and development of glans. Testes and scrotum are further enlarged than in Stage 3; scrotum skin is darker than in earlier stages.	Hair is now adult in type, but the area covered is still considerably smaller than in the adult. There is no spread to the medial surface of the thighs.	The areola and nipple form a secondary mound projecting above the contour of the breast.
5	Genitalia are adult in size and shape.	The hair is adult in quantity and type with distribution of the horizontal for classically "feminine" pattern. Spread is to the medial surface of the thighs but not up the linea alba or elsewhere above the base of the inverse triangle.	Mature stage. The nipple only projects, with the areola recessed to the general contour of the breast.

Source: From "The Biological Approach to Adolescence: Biological Change and Psychological Adaptation," by A. Petersen and B. Taylor. In J. Adelson (Eds.), *Handbook of Psychological Adaptation.* Copyright © 1980 by John Wiley & Sons. Reprinted by permission.

that very early menarche is associated with higher levels of depression. Further, they compared pre- and postmenarcheal sixth- and seventh-grade girls. For the seventh graders no differences were observed in depression. Hence, early menarche is associated with greater depression tendencies than is observed when the timing is normative and young adolescents are expecting the onset.

Other less commonly examined issues of puberty for girls are breast development and body-hair growth. Once again, Brooks-Gunn (1986) reports that early breast growth is associated with higher reported adjustment, more positive body image, and more positive peer relations. However, there are also negative experiences. Early-developing girls report considerable teasing about their breast growth, with most of it coming from mothers, fathers, and female peers. The most common psychological reactions by girls to teasing are embarrassment and anger. These findings suggest that even though early breast development may be associated with several positive psychological changes, reactions to teasing indicate that not all females view this development as a positive one.

The psychological meaning of body-hair growth appears to be unassociated with any major psychological pattern of development. It may be that hair growth is generally less associated with symbolic messages of sexual and reproductive meaning in our culture; therefore, it is not associated with any substantial psychological reactions by either adolescent females or their friends and family members.

A rare study on the psychological effects of height, weight, and muscle development (Blyth et al., 1980) has demonstrated that both positive and negative effects are relatively small but significant among adolescents of junior high school age. This investigation suggests that overweight adolescents experience the most negative effects. Overweight boys were found to be the least satisfied with their weight, to have the lowest self-esteem, to maintain the least stable self-image, and to be the most self-conscious about their appearance. Although being tall was associated with satisfaction with height, it had no other reported effect (although basketball and football coaches were probably quite interested in these boys). For seventh-grade boys, early pubertal development was found to be associated with weight and muscle development.

Tobin-Richards, Boxer, and Petersen (1983) have also found that body weight is associated with satisfaction. Underweight females were found to be the most satisfied, followed by those of average weight, with overweight females the least satisfied. For boys, average weight was most satisfying, with underweight and overweight boys less satisfied. These findings follow the general societal preference for extreme thinness in girls and an average but muscular body in boys.

These investigations suggest that important psychological changes emerge during and after the onset of pubertal change. During this period, girls are more distressed than boys, but afterward they are less concerned about their appearance. For girls at least, pubertal change may actually stimulate psychological integration and maturity. Rierdan and Koff (1980) compared premenarcheal and postmenarcheal girls on a variety of psychological measures and found, in keeping with an earlier study (Koff et al., 1978), that the postmenarcheal girls possessed greater awareness of sexual differentiation and clearer sexual identification.

The psychological impact of puberty can be attributed either to the social messages associated with body change and new, more adultlike status or to hormone-induced emotional changes. Surprisingly, little is actually known about how much these two factors account for psychological changes during adolescence. One exemplary study that helps us understand the potential effects of gonadotropins on behavior during adolescence has recently been completed (Susman et al., 1987). These investigators examined the correlation between hormone levels and self-reported anger, nervousness, sadness, and impulse control. Their initial findings suggest that hormones are related to sad affect and anxiety levels, while some evidence also suggests that hormones may be associated with delinquency and rebellious behaviors. However, the findings were observed for males and not females. These findings suggest that as future research of a similar nature is undertaken, we shall gradually come to understand how hormonal levels may be associated with, or even be predictive of, major psychological and behavioral changes during adolescence and, possibly, the onset of pubescence.

The Social Impact of Body Development

Until recently little has been known about how bodily development affects adolescents' relations with family members and peers and whether the potential changes are disruptive and conflictual or beneficial and integrative (see Box 6–1 for three frameworks). In a short-term longitudinal study L. D. Steinberg and Hill (1978) initiated an investigation of the implications of physical maturity for the relationship between adolescent boys and their parents. In the first data-collection period, in which the families were asked to play a decision-making game, these investigators found that midpubertal boys were more assertive and disruptive than prepubertal or late-pubertal boys and were less likely to explain themselves during a family discussion. Data from the second collection period (L. D. Steinberg, 1979) indicate that before the onset of puberty the families had low levels of conflict and well-defined dominance relationships. The boys readily deferred to their parents and had little influence on family decision making. With the onset of puberty, the boys became quite assertive with their mothers. The mothers responded with counterinterruptions or with less deference to their sons' interruptions.

In an apparent reaction to the conflict between son and mother, the father began to take a more assertive stance toward the son, with the outcome of less assertiveness by the son toward the mother. Tension decreased, and the family-interaction pattern again assumed a state of equilibrium. Indeed, Steinberg reports that the family-interaction patterns for late-puberty boys became similar to those for prepubertal boys. But one should not assume that the individual family members were the same as before. Each is likely to have learned a new lesson: the son is growing up and is to be recognized as an increasingly mature person.

Social status and ability to compete can vary with differences in physical maturity.

Box 6–1   Varying Models of the Association Between Pubertal Change and Parent-Adolescent Interactions

Roberta Paikoff and Jeanne Brooks-Gunn (1991), in a substantial review of published research, have concluded that increased conflict and reduced warmth in parent-adolescent relationships occur during puberty. While few complete longitudinal studies have assessed various models to explain this phenomenon, these adolescent psychologists suggest three possible models. These models have been graphically depicted as follows:

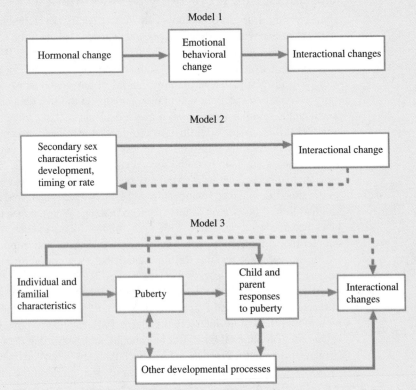

Source: Adapted from "Do Parent-child Relationships Change During Puberty?" by R. L. Paikoff and J. Brooks-Gunn, *Psychological Bulletin*, 1991, 110, 47–66. Copyright 1991 by the American Psychological Association. Adapted by permission.

In the first model, hormonal changes, in the form of concentration or fluctuation, heighten psychological arousal and emotional expression. In turn, parental responses may be negative or volatile. This implies an indirect effect from hormones on emotions and then on parent-adolescent interactions. However, a more direct effect might occur when increases in hormonal concentration may directly affect parent-adolescent relationships. (We lean more toward believing the indirect pathway in this model.) Illustrative research using this model includes studies by Udry (1988), and Paikoff, Brooks-Gunn, and Warren (1991). These investigations have examined the direct correlation between hormones and sexual behaviors or psychological states and/or the indirect association between hormones and behaviors and psychological states.

In the second model, pubertal changes in the form of early onset, duration or rate of change, or the creation of secondary sex characteristics, signal to both the adolescent and parent that the youth has become a reproductively

> ### Box 6–1   **Varying Models of the Association Between Pubertal Change and Parent-Adolescent Interactions** (*continued*)
>
> capable and more socially mature individual. Due to the shared meaning of this event the parent-adolescent relationship changes through heightened or new expectations that result in a reinterpretation of the adolescent's social status. (Much of the research by Larry Steinberg and John Hill in this chapter exemplifies this model.)
>
> In the third model, pubertal changes interact with individual/family characteristics and developmental changes or progression and mediate the effects of biological or physical characteristics on both child and parental responses to puberty and corresponding parent-adolescent interactions. Paikoff and Brooks-Gunn cite numerous studies that have partially addressed this complex model. For example, they indicate that research has demonstrated that girls experience an array of feelings about menarche. They appear hesitant to tell others. Many are ambivalent or self-conscious. These feelings could result in negative affect directed at mothers—particularly given that mothers are the most likely to know of the event. In some cases the event of puberty may create embarrassment or discomfort for parents (for example, possibly due to early onset), which in turn might influence parent-adolescent interactions. Regardless, parent-adolescent communications are likely to change due to the adolescent's increased psychological abilities over time, parents ability and comfort in accepting their daughters' increasing sexual nature, and perceptions and attributions about puberty and its meaning to family members. For further advanced reading we recommend a chapter by Downs (1990) on the social biological constructs of social competency.

A further, more recent study by L. Steinberg (1987b) has been directed at determining the potential distinctions between physical maturity and pubertal timing (reaching puberty early, on time, or late). Using a sample of more than 200 families with a first-born child between the ages of 10 and 15, he measured adolescent and parental reports of closeness and autonomy. As reported elsewhere (for example, J. Hill, Holmbeck, Marlow, Green, & Lynch, 1985a, 1985b), physical maturity was observed to be associated with increased emotional distance or conflict in the parent/child relationship. However, family conflict was associated with physical maturity for girls only, while early timing for boys was associated with conflict between them and their mother. Similar findings were *not* found between father and adolescent. Finally, Steinberg reports that late maturation appears to be accompanied only by increased behavioral autonomy by adolescents. Other direct assessments of interactive behaviors between parents and adolescents (for example, Hauser et al., 1985) reveal that substantial and important behavioral changes do occur as a function of the impact of pubertal timing.*

Hill and his colleagues (1985a, 1985b) have likewise examined the relationship between timing of puberty and adjustment in mother/adolescent communication. Using menarcheal status, these developmental psychologists have compared different levels of timing (early, on-time, late) in pubertal growth for seventh-grade girls on various social-behavioral measures. Like L. D. Steinberg and Hill (1978) they observed that disturbances in parent/child relationships emerged during the onset of menarche but about 12 months later returned to a level similar to that observed in the premenarcheal stage. As is frequently observed

---

*We recommend that interested students read the excellent research by Steinberg and his colleagues. In particular, we recommend Steinberg (1989) for an excellent treatise of physical maturation and parent-adolescent distance.

for boys and girls, the disruption was primarily within the mother/adolescent dyad. We attribute this finding to the fact that mothers still provide the most immediate and frequent child care for adolescents. Therefore, they are likely to be the primary target of sons and daughters striving for autonomy and social maturation.

An important investigation within the context of school suggests that the onset of puberty can play a significant role in early dating patterns. Simmons, Blyth, Van Cleave, and Bush (1979) studied the effects of school structure, onset of puberty, and dating experiences on self-esteem. Although the onset of puberty had little effect on girls' self-esteem in this study, early-maturing girls who had begun dating had very low self-esteem. Furthermore, if they attended a junior high school rather than a K through 8 school, their self-esteem was even lower. It appears that girls who begin to mature early and who face new social circumstances are likely to experience high levels of social/emotional stress. Additional evidence from Blyth, Simmons, and Zakin (1985) sheds further light on this conclusion. They found that earlier-maturing girls who were naturally heavier and stouter than their peers were considerably less satisfied with their body image. Therefore, although maturing early may give these girls a more adult appearance, in relation to their peers, they are heavier. Given the cultural ideal of thinness (M. S. Faust, 1983), these girls are likely to view their early growth in less than ideal ways.

Sociocultural Aspects of Puberty

The broader sociocultural impact of puberty can be seen in a wide variety of forms. We discuss four aspects. First, we look at how society helps boys and girls prepare for the event. Second, we examine the images of the body as portrayed by society. Third, we look briefly at sex-role issues. And finally, we explore some implications for sexuality.

Preparation for Bodily Change

Given that bodily changes in adolescence are universal, it might be expected that families, schools, or other social institutions would prepare young people for these changes. Surprisingly, little evidence can be found that any societal group pays more than lip service to such preparation. One might suspect, given the dramatic nature of the first menstruation, that particular attention is given to its impending occurrence. Moreover, because it is a "sign and symbol of womanhood" (Weideger, 1976) and a signal of fertility, one could expect the first menses to be treated as a sort of rite of passage. (A rite of passage is a ritualized recognition of a new status or role.) In that cross-cultural evidence suggests that women around the world view menarche as the primary signal of adult sexual status (see, for example, Laws & Schwartz, 1977; McCandless, 1970; Muensterberger, 1975), it is perhaps surprising that in contemporary North American society it is rarely written about (Delaney, Lupton, & Troth, 1976) or recognized by individuals outside the family (Laws & Schwartz, 1977; Seiden, 1976; Whisnant & Zegan, 1975). Although fifth-grade girls are commonly shown a film in school about menstruation, we suspect that the limited background of the teacher or school counselor in dealing with this development is unlikely to lead to a positive or truly informative learning experience.

In other cultures, however, even such limited formal preparation is rare. In a recent investigation of preparation for and reactions to first menses in several cultures (D. D. Logan, 1980), most information for premenarcheal girls came either from informal conversations with female friends or from mothers. In this study 68% of the respondents said that their mothers were their primary source of information. Individuals who were informed of the occurrence of menarche included mother (87%), sister (16%), female friend (13%), another female relative (12%), and teacher (4%). Like the teacher, the father was rarely informed (3%). One can suspect that the mother usually tells the father that their daughter "has become a woman," but the father is unlikely to be directly involved in heralding the event. The reactions of these individuals differed, ranging from advice on how to use a napkin (42%) to variations on "It's not much fun, but you'll get used to it" (13%) and "Be careful not to let others know" (2%). The most common reactions reported by girls themselves reflect fright and emotional upset (see, for example, Weideger, 1976; Whisnant & Zegan, 1975). On the other hand, it should be noted that many girls show no particular reaction one way or another. Likewise, Brooks-Gunn, Warren, Samelson, and Fox (1986) report evidence that disclosure associated with menarche is most likely to occur if close and reciprocal friendships exist.

The research literature on boys' preparation for body changes contains almost nothing on trends in preparation for nocturnal emissions or spontaneous erections, but what is available suggests that boys receive little or no preparation. For example, Shipman (1968) has reported a small study of 146 boys in which 90% indicated that they had received absolutely no formal information about nocturnal emissions. Furthermore, what little information they had acquired from their peers was inadequate. For those boys with the natural curiosity and initiative to find information, reading materials were the only answer, but we believe that it would be difficult for 14-year-olds with average reading ability to find and digest the materials. It would indeed be novel but possibly enlightening for parents or a church sex-education program to provide boys with information on the natural occurrence of nocturnal emissions, spontaneous erections, or tendencies to want to masturbate.

According to Shipman (1968), the reaction of many boys and girls to nocturnal emission or menstruation was a mixture of excitement, gratification, and fright. He does report an unusual case illustrating how joyful the experience can be when parents work together to ritualize a natural pubertal outcome. One girl reported:

> When I discovered it, I called my mother and she showed me what to do. Then she did something I'll never forget. She told me to come with her and went to the living room to tell my father. She just looked at me and then at him and said, "Well, your little girl is a young lady now." My dad gave me a hug and congratulated me, and I felt grown up and proud that I really was a lady at last. That was one of the most exciting days of my life. I was so excited and happy. (Pp. 6–7)

In summary, our society falls short in preparing adolescents for pubertal changes; preparation is usually left to happenstance. Without recognition or ritualization of major physical events, it is very difficult for adolescents to know when and how to change their behavior to accord with a more mature status.

Images of the Body

Standards of beauty, attractiveness, and appearance are portrayed through the media. These standards are reflections of a broader sociocultural ideal. Ideals are readily observed through an analysis of advertisements, commercials, billboard pictures, magazine covers, and related subtle but direct communications. G. R. Adams and Crossman (1978) made a synopsis of these sociocultural messages and summarized their observations in the following statement:

> Masculinity is judged by overall appearance and impression. The commercials on television will suggest the main attributes a man needs to be considered attractive and desirable. "The dry look" is important. "Reaching for the gusto" is absolutely essential. Using Right Guard and smelling of Brut, English Leather, Old Spice, Musk, or one of a half dozen other men's colognes is also necessary. And, depending upon his "type," he will drive a certain make and model of car, smoke a certain brand of tobacco, and above all, read Playboy magazine. He doesn't have to have a face like Paul Newman or Robert Redford or a physique like Adonis, though it won't hurt if he does. Primarily, he must be trim, rugged but not too rugged, manly, and have a nice smile.
>
> Femininity, on the other hand, is characterized by perfection in every detail. Unlike masculinity, femininity cannot be acquired merely by using the right deodorant and applying a number of external props. A woman must have hair with body and fullness that is marvelously highlighted. Each feature must be an equal contributor to her pretty face. She must have eternally young and blemish-free skin. Her figure must not only be trim but meet certain "idealized" standards to be considered beautiful. Her hands must be silky soft and not too large. Her nails must be long and perfectly trimmed. Her legs must be shapely, firm, preferably long, tanned in summer and devoid of any hair. (Pp. 21–22)

No wonder M. S. Faust (1983) has argued that thinness and perfection are the core of feminine beauty as portrayed by the advertising media. But do adolescents and adults actually internalize these sociocultural messages? There is evidence that early-adolescent females readily see facial attractiveness, body height, and body parts such as legs as central factors in the judgment of appearance (Tobin-Richards et al., 1983). Also, a survey of readers of *Psychology Today* indicates that women are most concerned about their facial and body appearance along with their weight; men are more concerned about the image of fitness (Cash, Winstead, & Janda, 1986). Clearly, certain idealized standards of facial beauty exist (Cunningham, 1986; C. F. Keating, 1985). Likewise, physical attractiveness functions as a mediator of the impact of pubertal change for girls (Zakin, Blyth, & Simmons, 1984).

Society also communicates to youngsters the importance of appropriate dress (Solomon, 1986). Adolescent's concerns and evaluations about their clothing can be seen through the findings of numerous research reports. Wearing of used clothing, for example, is viewed as highly negative and disconcerting to most adolescents (Hinton & Margerum, 1984). Security is associated with the number and quality of dresses and shoes in a female adolescent's wardrobe (Knees, 1983). This attitude appears most evident among Mexican-American youths. Brand names are extremely important, with designer jeans preferred (Lennon, 1986). Likewise, peer popularity and status are correlated with clothing conformity (L. L. Davis, 1984).

We can conclude from such findings that the sociocultural messages of thinness, attractiveness, and appropriate appearance are central factors in understanding the full importance of puberty and of physical attractiveness for adolescents. As a measure of that impact, a growing body of research literature indicates that extremes in physical appearance have a major influence on social relations, perceptions, personality development, social behavior, and life experiences in general (G. R. Adams, 1977a, 1977b, 1980). Beginning with initial interactions with strangers, we are all easily swayed in our assumptions about another's behavior and characteristics by physical appearance. Individuals who are judged to be attractive are generally thought of in positive terms. We suspect attractive individuals to be warm, friendly, successful, independent, and intelligent, while unattractive persons are viewed in unbecoming and undesirable terms.

The results of a number of studies suggest that the effects of physical appearance on social behavior do not stop with perceptions. (See Eagly, Ashmore, Makhijani, & Lorgo, 1991, for an extensive review of this research literature.) Rather, we are inclined to be more solicitous, helpful, and cooperative with attractive than with unattractive persons. According to the biblical forecast, the meek shall inherit the earth, but the research literature suggests that beautiful individuals will share in that inheritance.

Once again, it would be easy to suspect that the influence of physical appearance stops here—that while all this attention is nice, attractive individuals profit little beyond it. However, a series of investigations suggests that physical appearance can have both immediate and long-range consequences for the individual's social behavior and personality development. For example, attractive individuals, when contrasted with unattractive peers, have been shown to be better adjusted socially (R. M. Lerner & Lerner, 1977), to maintain higher perceptions of social effectiveness (Kleck, 1975), and to have more healthy personality attributes (G. R. Adams, 1977a). The social behavior of these individuals is also more effective. Facially attractive males and females appear to be more effective in resisting peer conformity pressures (G. R. Adams, 1977b) and to maintain a more resistant and assertive style in the face of undesirable social circumstances (Jackson & Huston, 1975) while also possessing a wide variety of interpersonal skills that enhance their effectiveness in influencing others (see, for example, Chaiken, 1979; Dion & Stein, 1978; W. Goldman & Lewis, 1977).

Thus, much of what we have reviewed in this chapter has great social significance. Those adolescents who progress through the various stages of physical development and come to be viewed as physically attractive are likely to have very positive personality and social development. However, for those youths who experience misfortune, the consequences are inclined to be the internalization of negative self-images, poor coping styles, and ineffective social skills. Perhaps by coming to understand how this pattern is inclined to occur, we can discover some of the implications for both prevention and intervention with adolescents who are viewed as unattractive in some way.

Elsewhere a review of the mechanisms that create both desirable and undesirable consequences for an adolescent's development has been provided in greater detail (G. R. Adams, 1981). Here we can only briefly discuss ways in which our society's pervasive emphasis on physical appearance is translated into consequences.

Two major mechanisms help us understand how physical appearance can actually lead to channeling human behavior and individual development. First when we come in contact with a person whose appearance is different from our expectation of normal appearance, there is an immediate tendency to become anxious. Due to this violation of normal social expectations, we react in ways that reduce our anxiety. We may stare at an unusually small or large person, or we may terminate our involvement as soon as possible. Over repeated experiences with such an individual, we may become less inclined to experience arousal and anxiety, but our initial reaction to novel and unexpected physical appearance is generally either staring or avoidance. Of course, staring makes the other person feel self-conscious, while abrupt departure makes the person feel unwanted.

The second mechanism is the internalization by both attractive and unattractive persons of social expectations of good and bad. One investigation (Snyder, Tanke, & Berscheid, 1977) provides some insight into how the internalization process may work. The researchers had male students conduct a telephone conversation with either an attractive or an unattractive female. Each female research subject was randomly placed in the unattractive or attractive condition. This process resulted in average physical appearance for the research subjects in both conditions. Further, the female subjects were unaware that the males had been told that they were to have a conversation with either a very attractive or a very unattractive female. The conversations were tape-recorded and scored on a variety of measures that assessed interpersonal effectiveness. In compliance with a self-fulfilling prophecy, those women in the attractive condition became very adept in their phone conversation, while the women in the unattractive condition became socially ineffective. Thus, this investigation indicates that when others view us as attractive, they may do subtle things that encourage us to become animated, confident, and adept in our social behavior. However, when we are viewed as unattractive, we are likely to be treated in ways that lead our behavior to become ineffective. To some degree, we are what others expect us to be.

Gender-Related Role Expectations

J. P. Hill and Lynch (1983) have argued that society encourages greater compliance with traditional views of femininity for girls as they enter pubescence. Although boys have previously been encouraged to identify with male things and girls to identify with female things, as girls physically become women, society intensifies its expectations of gender-related roles.

Hill and Lynch cite protective behaviors such as chaperoning, increased parental vigilance, and the lessening of permissiveness as evidence of an intensification of role expectations. Further, an analysis of a wide variety of studies supports this hypothesis. The evidence indicates that girls develop specialized interests related to academic achievement, become less self-assured, show heightened interest in interpersonal relationships, and are less self-confident but more self-conscious during early adolescence. Focusing on more expressive and feminine interests and behaviors, young adolescents may be increasingly channeled to recognize their role as bearers of children. Thus, the onset of puberty for girls may bring forth yet another sociocultural reality to deal with. Further, this reality may be difficult to handle if it is seen as interfering with the girl's own interests or aspirations.

Sociocultural Expectations Regarding Sexuality

Adolescents are bombarded on the screen, in books, and throughout the other media with images of their own bodies as sexual stimuli. And indeed, as we discuss in Chapters 12 and 14, on sexuality, adolescents do become sexually active as they chronologically and physically mature. Numerous studies show that sexual maturation and heterosexual involvement are natural facts of life (for example, see Westney, Jenkins, & Benjamin, 1983). However, we know little about how maturing boys and girls learn to cope effectively with their physical growth as it relates to their emerging sexuality. Nonetheless, it seems that adolescent boys and girls must deal pretty much on their own with their body image and attractiveness, the recognition of their changing body, the intensification of gender-related role expectations, and their emerging sexual maturity. Thus it should be no surprise that teenage pregnancy rates are high in North America, that most youths engage in sexual intercourse without using birth control, and that many adolescents express considerable confusion about their physical growth during adolescence and the impending implications for a sexually active or sexually inactive heterosexual or homosexual life-style. We discuss these issues further in subsequent chapters.

Bodily Variations and Growth Disorders

Although most adolescents experience normal somatic development, a variety of atypical patterns can occur. Some of these patterns are mere reflections of constitutional variations, while others reflect genetic or hormonal deficiencies. But regardless of the cause, atypical growth patterns have important psychological consequences. In this section we briefly explore some of the anomalies in body development and examine their consequences for adolescents.

Early and Late Onset of Puberty

At the extremes of normal somatic development are early and late onset of pubertal change for both boys and girls. As we mention in previous sections, bodily development promotes the organization of varying psychological states. Therefore, early onset of puberty leaves the adolescent with less time for organizing the psychological consequences of rapid hormonal change. Conversely, late onset creates a prolonged period of functioning without the hormonal changes. Furthermore, for both early and delayed onset, adolescents must reconcile the inner psychological organization of their bodily appearance with its social-stimulus value to their peers, family members, teachers, and community. The early-maturing boy or girl is thrust into an adultlike world, while the boyish or girlish image of the late maturer leaves the individual in prolonged childhood. As a result, the early-maturing youth is overaccepted in his or her recognition of movement toward adulthood, while the late-maturing youth is underaccepted.

A synopsis of the two major longitudinal studies of early and late maturers (Oakland Growth Study and Berkeley Guidance Study) suggests important differences in psychological adjustment. Early-maturing boys were reported as being viewed as more attractive to their peers and to adults (M. C. Jones, 1965; M. C. Jones & Bayley, 1950), as having greater self-confidence, and as behaving more maturely (Mussen & Jones, 1957). However, early maturers were also found to be more somber, less intellectually curious, and more submissive than were late maturers (Peskin, 1973). It appears that early-maturing boys may respond to pubertal onset with inhibition and rigidity. In contrast to boys, early-maturing girls tended to be seen as less attractive than are later-maturing girls. As Clausen (1975) has remarked, a physically mature adolescent female is likely to be treated as a sex object and to be thrust prematurely into relationships with the opposite sex. As we note previously, early maturation in girls can lead to lower self-esteem (Simmons et al., 1979). Fortunately, by the time early and late maturers reach middle adulthood, there may be little difference in their psychological profiles. However, during adolescence proper, the early-maturing male is likely to prosper, while the early-maturing female is likely to experience tension, anxiety, and a poor self-concept.

As Steinberg (1987a) has succinctly stated, it is important to distinguish between attaining the status of puberty and the timing of this acquisition. The investigations we have cited thus far were classic in their influence on the study of timing. These investigations have inspired expanding research into the importance of timing for adolescents' psychosocial well-being.

Early, or precocious, puberty, has been shown to be associated with several undesirable long-term consequences. Heino and his associates (1985) report that such precociousness for girls is associated with a higher sex drive, earlier psychosexual maturity, and more frequent masturbation. Others (for example, Dornbusch et al., 1981) have suggested that earlier dating and sexual activity may likewise accompany early maturation. Likewise, one group in Sweden (Magnusson, Stattin, & Allen, 1985) reports that early puberty in girls is associated with more acting out (playing truant, smoking, noncompliance with parents' prohibitions) than is found in late-maturing girls. These and other investigations suggest that early maturation may, at least for females, be associated with several unfortunate and undesirable behavior or adjustment problems (P. D. Duncan, Ritter, Dornbusch, Gross, & Carlsmith, 1985; A. C. Petersen & Crockett, 1985). At this time, from a life-span perspective, we are uncertain whether the undesirable consequences associated with early onset of puberty create behavioral conditions that remain unfavorable as these girls develop or whether by adulthood any distinctions associated with timing of maturation disappear. Likewise, much too little attention is being given to the study of the timing of maturation for boys. This failure is probably caused by a difficulty in determining the best criteria for assessing early maturation in boys: X-rays, body height and weight, and nocturnal emissions versus masturbation, for example.

Developmental Disorders

When the gonads become sexually mature and active before age 8 in girls or before age 9 in boys, pediatricians are inclined to diagnose *precocious puberty*. When this condition occurs, the pubertal process is generally complete within two years. These children, or early adolescents, are usually two to three years more advanced in height than their age mates. However, these youths do not grow any taller than about 5 feet (Higham, 1980), since the cartilage of the bones fuses at an early age. Thus, these youths are taller than their peers during early adolescence but are much shorter after their age mates catch up and surpass them in normal development.

These adolescents understandably have formidable adjustment problems. Generally, boys' athletic prowess is poor, and their strength is minimal. Their discrepant stature creates a childlike image during later adolescence, although in early adolescence these boys appeared much older. Girls develop a full figure very early and are likely to be teased by their peers. According to some experts (for example, Money & Walker, 1971), the embarrassment of these adolescents can be minimized by placing them in advanced academic and social situations. One should not assume, however, that precocious pubertal change means promiscuous sexual behavior. Erotic thoughts do emerge at an early age, but there is no evidence to suggest that accelerated sexual behavior results (Higham, 1980).

Pubertal delay is diagnosed when the testicles fail to enlarge by age 14 or the breasts fail to develop by age 13. *Hypogonadism* is a primary cause of pubertal delay. Hypogonadism can be due to either gonadal failure or genetic deficiencies. Generally, youths with this condition have poor self-concepts and experience feelings of shame, anxiety, and embarrassment. Hormone-replacement therapy can correct many of the problems associated with pubertal delay. Unfortunately, there is some evidence to suggest that later in life these young people often experience adjustment problems associated with social and sexual self-image (Money & Clopper, 1974).

Severe Constitutional Disorders

Two major disorders in physical development during adolescence are caused by chromosome damage. *Turner's syndrome* consists of a 45, XY chromosome pattern and results in a female body without ovaries. Due to the absence of ovaries, the body fails to produce enough estrogen to bring about appropriate maturation. Even though the girl is capable of menstruation, she is sterile. Furthermore, she is likely to be short. Hormone therapy can help, but adolescents with this disorder may be inclined to become withdrawn, isolated, and dependent on their parents. Such withdrawal tendencies are more likely to be due to social rather than biological factors, however.

Klinefelter's syndrome consists of a 47, XXY chromosome pattern and produces a male body with small genitalia. Usually such males are sterile, and their secondary sex characteristics are generally poorly developed, which hampers sex-role and self-concept development. These adolescents are prone to retardation, social inhibition, and neurotic behavior (Higham, 1980). Although counseling and sex education can help adolescents with either Turner's or Klinefelter's syndrome, both types of youths are likely to experience a great deal of psychosocial or psychosexual disturbance.

Atypical Patterns in Stature

Two disorders are associated with shortness in stature. The rather rare disorder known as congenital *hypothyroidism* is associated with hormonal deficiency that results in limited brain-cell development. A more frequent cause of shortness is *hypopituitarism*. As with almost any type of height-related problems with children and adolescents, hypopituitarism generally makes youths vulnerable to disturbance in psychosocial development (see, for example, Money, 1975; Notttelmann & Welsh, 1986; Rotnem, Genel, Hintx, & Cohen, 1977; Steinhausen, 1977). Such youths experience problems with self-identity, sense of self-worth, and social competence. The results of a variety of studies suggest that boys with disorders in statural growth during adolescence experience such problems as

> social isolation, a sense of physical and psychological powerlessness and vulnerability, a distorted and negative body image, confusion about child and adult roles, general social and emotional immaturity, a sense of social and personal ineffectiveness, decreased self-esteem, problems in inhibition and regulation of normal aggression and self-assertion, difficulties in romantic and sexual relationships, and signs of childhood depression. (Feinman, 1979, p. 2)

This is a formidable collection of psychological and social problems for any individual to face. Likewise, evidence now shows that even minor physical anomalies can have negative consequences that persist from childhood into adulthood (Paulhus & Martin, 1986).

The Central Problem in Atypical Body Development

The major problem with atypical developmental patterns comes with the perceived discrepancy between body image and expectations associated with the individual's chronological age (Feinman, 1979). When physical appearance does not match what is perceived to be the appropriate social age for the adolescent, members of the community are inclined to expect the youth to act at the level of behavior appropriate for their apparent physical age. Thus, precocious youths are expected to behave in a mature manner for their chronological age, while delayed youths are kept in a childlike state for an extended period. These discrepancies are difficult to change. Individual counseling, parent education, and instruction of teachers and other professionals who come in contact with these young people can help. But it is much more difficult to educate peers, with whom these youths must live and work. Therein lies the major challenge. Assisting adolescents with growth disorders must include assistance in learning how to cope with the world of peers.

The long-range problems associated with physical anomalies and atypical growth patterns can be seen in a variety of case histories. Box 6–2, which presents the case history of a boy who had several operations as an infant to correct physical problems, shows how problems with stature and other physical anomalies can affect the lives of young boys.

A Dialectical/Interactional Perspective

We have covered a wealth of complex material in this chapter. Is it possible to link this material in such a way as to guide future understanding of physical appearance and its influences on behavior and development (for example, G. R. Adams, 1977a; Berscheid & Walster, 1974; Goffman, 1963; R. M. Lerner, 1985)? Based on our interest in understanding the effects of physical appearance on human development (for example, G. R. Adams, 1977a; 1982; Adams & Crossman, 1978), we have come to formulate our own theoretical and conceptual

---

Box 6–2   When I Get My Age!

"On examination, L. R. was a short, pleasant-looking mid-adolescent male with an athletic physique. He weighed 54 kg (approximately 108 lbs.) and was 160 cm (approximately 64 in.) tall. His age was $14\frac{1}{2}$ years. His appearance was bright and alert, and verbal productions were complete and appropriately responsive. The appearance of fitness was further enhanced by an elastic bandage worn around his waist anchoring the collecting bag to a left lower quadrant stoma (the consequences of a surgical procedure some time earlier). There were several surgical scars on the lower abdomen as well. He had normal adult pubic hair and genitalia and he reported that he was capable of erection and ejaculation, but denied having had sexual intercourse or actively engaged in masturbatory activity.

"The patient was in a ninth grade college bound program obtaining average to above average grades. He planned on becoming a doctor and saw himself as more goal oriented than his peers. He perceived that his teachers and family had always treated him differently from his peers, and he was frequently admonished to be careful and not to over-exert himself or get hurt. Although limited to noncontact sports, he successfully challenged these restrictions by being physically aggressive and pushing himself to the limit in those activities which he was permitted.

"In terms of peer relations, he had a few friends but no close ones, and he had never dated. When he talked about social interactions, he used phrases such as 'a kid like me' or 'when I get my age.'"

Source: (From S. F. Cogan, R. D. Becker, and A. D. Hoffman, "Adolescent Males with Urogenital Anomalies." *Journal of Youth and Adolescence,* 1974, *4,* 359–373.)

---

perspective. This perspective is called dialectical/interactional. Simply put, *dialectical/interactional* implies an interactive struggle between dialectical opposites. For example, a desire to be childlike is in opposition to adult responsibility. Resolution of this dialectic is accomplished only by an interactive resolution.

This perspective and its components should become clearer as we progress. We recognize, however, that the following material is highly complex. Nonetheless, careful reading and analysis can provide a useful synthesis and theoretical base for understanding physical development and appearance and its implications for adolescent behavior.

Elsewhere we have reviewed the research on physical attractiveness, physical disability, and physical stigma (G. R. Adams & Davis, 1987). Our synopsis indicates that both the stereotype of physical attractiveness and the stigma associated with physical deviance function as attributes that elicit narrowly defined and reasonably uniform social impressions across different ages, races, and cultures. Further, perceptions of physical attributes have been observed to be associated with stereotypical and stigmatized social-interaction patterns between people. As people interact based on impressions associated with a given physical attribute, not only do they interact in very stereotypical ways, but they also come to mirror each other's underlying expectations and messages. To illustrate, if we expect an early-maturing male to be more dominant, more athletic, and more socially mature, we are likely to interact in ways that encourage such behavior. In turn, through internalizing our expectations, the early-maturing youth may come to manifest these behaviors without needing our expressed or verbalized expectations. As we write earlier in this chapter, this is the self-fulfilling prophecy of physical attractiveness.

In many of the earlier theoretical papers on similar topics (for example, Berscheid & Walster, 1974; Goffman, 1963) little recognition was given to the realization that when we discuss the effects of physical appearance, we need to remember that we are studying continually developing and changing people in a changing society (Riegel & Meacham, 1976). Yet the study of adolescence has at its core the central concern with change. For adolescence is not a final end point but, rather, one stage of change between childhood and adulthood.

Our primary assumption is that as a person matures, there are periods across the life course associated with lesser or greater *sensitivities* to the importance of physical appearance. And as Buss (1985) has speculated, an increased focus on appearance may be associated with sensitivities that heighten self-consciousness, which influences other emotional and cognitive states. Indeed, the work of Roberta Simmons, David Elkind, and others clearly shows that self-conscious-ness is heightened during adolescence, along with interest in body image. For example, Simmons and her colleagues (R. G. Simmons & Rosenberg, 1975; R. G. Simmons, Rosenberg, & Rosenberg, 1973) have demonstrated through a psy-chological evaluation process for adolescents that physical and psychological maturation are interrelated. Simmons, Rosenberg, and Rosenberg (1973) note that early adolescents are more concerned about their looks than are younger children. Furthermore, these researchers have shown that the less satisfied chil-dren are with their looks, the more self-conscious they become, the lower the level of self-esteem, and the less attractive they report themselves as being (R. G. Simmons & Rosenberg, 1975). A positive self-concept in adolescents has also been related to positive feelings about the body (R. M. Lerner, Orlos, & Knapp, 1976). Hence, outer appearance has been shown to be associated with inner psy-chological functions.

As to situational influences associated with sociocultural factors discussed in this chapter, it can be demonstrated that physical stereotypes or stigmas oper-ate in numerous social settings (G. R. Adams, 1982). For example, evidence is found to demonstrate that influences related to attractiveness operate in dating, educational and work settings, marriage, legal and professional experiences, and other social areas. We believe that sensitivities to the stigmatizing and stereotyp-ing influences of physical appearance exist throughout the life span and that the onset of puberty and its corresponding body changes is one such period of sensi-tivity. Indeed, we go so far as to say that puberty is a stigmatized status and that it marks to society at large that a girl is now a woman—physically mature, capa-ble of reproductive potential, and sexually appealing. For a boy, puberty is stig-matizing in that the new status is one of prowess, competitiveness, physical maturity, and the capability of defending himself without reliance on his family.

Many developmentally oriented social scientists are interested in the study of stages of development. For example, they might contrast pubescent and non-pubescent youth, both physical statuses fixed during adolescence. However, Riegel (1976) argues that we have erred in our general tendency to study two or more things as if they were in a static or stable balance:

> Without any debate it has been taken for granted that a state of balance, stability, and rest is more desirable than a state of upheaval, conflict, and change. Thus, we have

always aimed for a psychology of satisfaction but not of excitement. This preference has found expression in balance theory, equilibrium theory, steady state theory, and indirectly in the theory of cognitive dissonance. (P. 690)

But growth and development involve change and movement. And Riegel's dialecticism focuses on transitions, providing the right framework for studying sensitive periods and the physical transformations that might accompany pubescence and physical growth.

At the core of our dialectical theory are the following assumptions. First, for every perspective there is a counterperspective. For every good there is an evil. For every thesis (hypothesis) there is an antithesis (counterhypothesis). Second, for every inner, psychological factor that influences behavior there is an outer, social factor. For example, as one judges one's own physical appearance (inner evaluation), so are others judging one's appearance (outer evaluation). Third, when inner evaluations are consistent with those made by others, we have a state of *congruence*. However, when these two forms of evaluations are at odds, a state of disequilibrium and tension occurs, and there is *incongruence*. Fourth, a state of *synchrony* exists when there is congruence, and a state of readiness for *change* occurs when there is incongruence between inner and outer assessments. Fifth, dialecticism assumes that incongruence and a state of change are affiliated with tensions and disequilibriums that demand action and resolution. Thus, dissonance and conflict are the necessary conditions for change. Finally, in a dialectical framework, discordance is believed to be the key influence for movement from a state of satisfaction or complacency to one of excitement and transformational change. Once again, according to Riegel (1977):

Crises represent steps or constructive changes aiming toward better synchronization along the different planes of progression (or parallel and congruent evaluations between inner and outer assessments). Crises in the constructive sense are the "knots" that tie together structural changes on the biological, psychological, cultural, and physical levels; they are also opportunities for change, and provide meaning to change. (P. 125)

In a nutshell, this view means that life events or physical changes, which create tension between self-assessments and evaluations by others, can create the conditions for potential negative or positive growth, if some degree of discordance exists. However, it likewise suggests that when social experiences confirm personal assessments, conditions are not present for change but offer reinforcement for compliance with societal expectations and lead to stability in development.

How, then, can we use this framework to understand puberty and its psychosocial effects? Let us conclude this chapter with our dialectical/interactional framework as applied to physical growth and development during adolescence. We set out the basic steps that we believe occur during the social-cognitive and socialization processes associated with puberty.*

---

*For an expansion on this topic we refer interested readers to one of our recent publications (G. R. Adams, Day, Dyk, Frede, & Rogers, 1992). Likewise, a commentary by Lerner (1992) and reflections in the form of a rejoinder might be of further interest (G. R. Adams, Ryan, Corville-Smith, Normore, & Turner, 1992).

Box 6–3   Risks of Early Maturation: A Swedish Study

A longitudinal study in Sweden (Magnusson, Stattin, & Allen, 1986) points to several major risks of early sexual maturation:

1. Early maturation is associated with having older friends.
2. It is associated with going steady at very early ages (83% of the early maturers versus 53% of later-maturing youths).
3. Forty-five percent of the early maturers versus only 11% of the later-maturing youths had sexual intercourse by age 14.5 years.

4. Early maturation is associated with higher rates of drinking and smoking hashish.

These findings indicate that in Sweden, and possibly in other liberal countries, early maturation may create a condition that increases risk-taking behaviors. What social or physiological mechanisms might be operating to account for the greater risk faced by these early-maturing girls? What factors in the United States and Canada might we be concerned about that interact with early maturation to increase such risks?

---

1. Puberty is a recognizable physical attribute that is accompanied by a societal status associated with change. It can be assessed through an inner awareness and by outer social evaluations by peers, parents, and other adults. The assessments (either positive or negative) can be in congruence but need not be so.

2. Not only is physical status critical to assessment, but so are its timing and the corresponding comparisons that adolescents make with same-age peers. When early maturation occurs, the adolescent female is more likely than not, because of society's judgments of the importance of thinness, to view this occurrence negatively because she sees herself as larger and heavier than her peers. For boys, early maturation is more likely to be associated with positive self-perceptions, in that body size allows them to be compared to older male peers, a desirable condition.

3. Physical appearance acquires meaning through social interaction in which self-assessments are confronted by the evaluations of others. This confrontation comes in the form of open discussions about actual body and facial appearance, teasing, and the hidden or unspoken expectations of behaviors that accompany perceptions of reaching a given physical status. (See Box 6–3). Early-maturing youths are likely to receive subtle communications associated with greater maturity, recognized sexual appeal, physical prowess, and so forth. Later-maturing youths are likely to experience expectations more closely associated with younger youths.

4. When adolescents have different perceptions of themselves than do parents or peers, a tension occurs that stimulates them to resolve or diminish the stress through movement toward reconciliation. This reconciliation can be constructive, through open dialogue and compromise, or it can be destructive, through defensiveness, defiance, or related psychologically protective behaviors. A constructive resolution will result in progressive growth toward maturity as an adult. A destructive resolution will result in regressive behavior and emotional duress.

5. Psychological growth involves compromising, recognizing changes in status, assuming new and productive behaviors associated with one's new social status, and reorganizing one's self-perceptions. Regressive or undesirable outcomes are likely to be associated with extremes of social anxiety, self-consciousness,

other negative mood states, and noncompliant behaviors. Hence, when early adolescents view their new physical status as undesirable, they are likely to have lowered self-esteem; increased self-consciousness; generalized anxiety; overconcern about body image, thinness, or weight; and manifestations of psychopathology and defensiveness. When they view their early maturation positively, adolescents are likely to accept their new status based on changes in physical maturity, assume increasing responsibility for their actions, find assurance and develop confidence in their new roles, and strive for increasing maturity in behavior, actions, and self-perceptions.

Major Points to Remember

1. The average age for the onset of pubescence has lowered during the past century.
2. Understanding the basic endocrinological changes associated with the onset of puberty requires an understanding of how the hypothalamus, the pituitary gland, and the gonads work together.
3. Changes in body development are generally visible by the 13th birthday. They reach their peak spurt some two years earlier in girls than in boys.
4. Survey evidence suggests that adolescents are given little preparation for impending physical changes.
5. The psychological consequences of physical development may be more dramatic for those adolescents who begin maturing early, are obese, or start dating early.
6. Parents are likely to make major changes in the manner in which they interact with their adolescents during the onset of puberty.
7. Constitutional variations in the growth process create numerous social and person-adjustment problems for the atypical adolescent.
8. Normal and atypical patterns in physical growth during adolescence affect body image and can influence social relations and personality development.
9. Variations in physical development can have important consequences for adolescent social relations, including family and peer relationships.
10. To understand the full complexity of physical growth and development, one must appreciate the biological, psychological, and sociocultural aspects of individual development.
11. The importance of physical growth should be viewed in the context of the degree of physical maturity and the timing of onset of puberty. Both desirable and undesirable psychological and social realities can accompany physical maturity and early or late timing.
12. Conceptualizing the process of development associated with pubescence can include a dialectical/interactional perspective. This process includes a comparison between the evaluations of oneself and those of others. Congruence in evaluations is associated with stability, and incongruence encourages change. Thus, conflict between inner assessments and others' evaluations encourages transformations, transitions, and growth. Growth can be progressive or destructive.

CHAPTER

7

Intellectual and Cognitive Development

- The Meaning of Intelligence

- Psychometric Evidence on Intellectual Growth

- A Psychometric Profile of U.S. Youth

- The Cognitive-Development Perspective on Intellectual Growth

- Cognitive Development and Minority Issues

- Formal Operations and Egocentrism

- Intelligence and Social Information Processing

- Cognition, Personality, and Social Understanding

- Women's and Men's Ways of Knowing

A questioning mind and an active vocal apparatus are commonly described as two central attributes of adolescents. Indeed, a major distinction between children and adolescents is thought to lie in qualitative changes in the way they think. Teachers and parents readily see this difference in trying to satisfy the curiosity of an adolescent as opposed to that of a child. A simple, concrete illustration will frequently satisfy an inquisitive child. An inquisitive adolescent, in contrast, typically requires deeper explanations, more abstract analysis, and an absence of contradictions by the explainer. Indeed, it takes a truly talented individual to instruct a group of adolescents.

To appreciate fully the behavior of young people, it is crucial to understand how they come to comprehend the world around them. Thus, in this chapter we examine intelligence and its development during adolescence. We present several ways in which adolescent intellectual development is studied. We begin, however, with the meaning of intelligence.

The Meaning of Intelligence

Although social scientists have not agreed on a single definition of intelligence, it is generally thought to be the underlying potential to function successfully and comprehend the realities of the world around us. Intelligence is also commonly held to include (1) the ability to deal with and comprehend abstractions, (2) the ability to acquire new knowledge or learn from experience, and (3) the ability to solve perceptual, mental, or social problems in new or unfamiliar situations.

There have been a number of very specific theories of what is meant by the word *intelligence*. Early researchers such as Charles Spearman and H. H. Goddard proposed that it was a single-dimensional faculty, which came to be known as the *g* factor. At the other extreme is the perspective proposed by J. P. Guilford, in which intelligence consists of more than 120 abilities that are identified by varying components of cognitive operations, differing products, and specific contents. It is tempting to argue that the more complex model provided by Guilford is the correct one. However, to be totally honest, there is no clear evidence to support one theoretical perspective over the other. Rather, these perspectives might best be seen as differing viewpoints with practical implications, more than as fixed "truths" about the nature of intelligence. The more straightforward implication is that should you accept intelligence as a single, unidimensional construct, then global tests of intelligence will suffice for appropriate measurement devices. However, should you accept a multifaceted viewpoint, then highly complex, multidimensional measurement devices will be needed. Similarly, a unidimensional theory would predict at least modest correlations with all behaviors thought to be part of intelligence. However, a multidimensional theory would predict high correlations between abilities and behaviors that reflect those abilities and would predict low correlations with nonrelated behaviors.

Understanding intellectual gains during adolescence requires a recognition that four major research perspectives dominate the field of study (see Keating, 1990). The perspective that has been used in both the unidimensional and the multidimensional theories is the *psychometric* viewpoint. *Psychometric* refers to assessments of psychological aptitudes (potentials). Psychometrically based assessments include responding to informational questions, solving puzzles, examining geometric figures, defining words, and so on. If you have ever taken a group or individual intelligence test, it was psychometrically oriented.

The second important way to study intelligence is to look at the cognitive processes that change as young people mature. This perspective is known as the *cognitive-development* viewpoint.

A third way in which intelligence is now being studied is based on *information processing* and its basic components. Scholars are studying mental-processing speed and capacity, attention and memory, and other cognitive processes without giving their primary attention to stages of development.

Finally, we believe there is a growing interest in the interface between social relationships and roles and a child's or adolescent's *social cognition.* Therefore, another emerging way in which intelligence is studied focuses on what we call social intelligence.

We turn first to the psychometric perspective on intelligence.

Psychometric Evidence on Intellectual Growth

Of the four perspectives, psychometric evidence offers both the strongest and the weakest approach to understanding adolescent intellectual growth. Its strength lies in its strong emphasis on scientific rigor in test construction. Highly reliable and valid instrumentation has been developed to verify both differences among adolescents and changes in intellectual-growth patterns over time. Two of the more familiar tests that have emerged from this perspective are the *Stanford-Binet* tests and the *Wechsler Intelligence Scale for Children.* But the strength of this perspective is balanced by its weakness. Although it provides highly reliable and valid evidence about intellectual growth, the perspective has a notoriously weak theoretical background, making it difficult to integrate conclusions from the multitude of studies that continue to emerge from this line of research.

The Measurement of IQ

Ever wonder how to compute your intelligence? Although there are several ways in which the so-called *intelligence quotient,* or IQ, can be measured or calculated, the general formula is

IQ = Mental age/Chronological age $\times$ 100

Mental age refers to one's score on items measuring such things as knowledge, verbal ability, perceptual problem solving, comprehension, and so forth. Chronological age is a person's age in years. By the use of this formula, a person whose mental age and chronological age match would have an IQ of 100. Thus, a person who is of average intelligence—or functioning at his or her age level—is given an IQ of 100. Scores lower than 100 represent delayed or retarded IQ development. Scores higher than 100 represent above-average IQs. It should be noted that there is evidence that IQ is not a permanent or fixed phenomenon, as once suspected, and that the typical formula for measuring IQ is based on an age comparison, with each person compared against the average score for peers of the identical age.

Measures of IQ are often used to place adolescents in various educational groups. The classification scheme most frequently used to identify gifted children or children who need a special-education program was devised by David Wechsler (1955). As Table 7–1 indicates, approximately 18% of any random population sample would include youths at the high (120 plus) and low (70 or less) extremes of IQ development. The IQ of the remaining youths would range between 80 and 119. The table should be a useful reference in understanding commonly used labels for IQ ranges.

Developmental Patterns

Nancy Bayley (1970), a noted expert in the field of intellectual development, has provided an excellent overview of much of the available research on intellectual development from infancy through middle adulthood. Drawing from the Berkeley Growth Study (a longitudinal study), she concludes that the general pattern of intellectual growth suggests rapid gains in IQ during childhood, gradual deceleration during adolescence and young adulthood, and a leveling trend during middle adulthood. Thus, a theoretical growth curve for intelligence would approximate the one depicted in Figure 7–1. Bayley notes, however, that this theoretical curve provides only a gross overview of general intelligence growth. When IQ is divided into its varying components, a somewhat different pattern emerges.

Between the ages of 16 and 36, intellectual-growth patterns vary according to the type of intelligence measured. Using Wechsler's intelligence scales, which divide intelligence into two major components, verbal skills (for example, vocabulary) and performance/manipulation (for example, puzzle solving), Bayley (1970) notes that adolescence may be more closely associated with crucial developments in performance/manipulation than with development of verbal skills. From this work Bayley has been able to show that mental abilities develop along different pathways. It is equally clear from her work that intellectual growth during adolescence occurs on a variety of dimensions.

Similarly, McCall, Appelbaum, and Hogarty (1973) compared mean IQ scores over a 15-year age span and have confirmed a variety of patterns in intellectual growth before and during adolescence. From an examination of longitudinal data, these investigators found five common patterns of development. These patterns are shown graphically in Figure 7–2. Cluster 1 shows a relatively stable pattern in IQ

Table 7–1   IQ Ranges and Classification Labels

IQ range	Label	%
130 and above	Very superior	2.2
120–129	Superior	6.7
110–119	Bright normal	16.1
90–109	Average	50.0
80–89	Dull normal	16.1
70–79	Borderline	6.7
69 or below	Mental defective	2.2

Source: Wechsler, 1955.

Figure 7–1 A Theoretical Growth Curve for Intelligence.

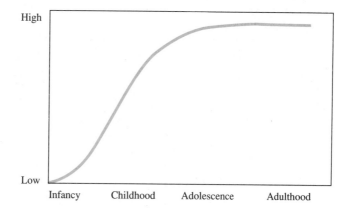

change and reflects the most common pattern. Clusters 2 and 3 decrease in childhood, but in adolescence Cluster 3 increases and Cluster 2 decreases. In contrast, Clusters 4 and 5 show sharp increases during childhood with corresponding decreases in IQ gains during adolescence. Thus, the relationship between IQ scores in childhood and adolescence is either (1) a pattern of stability, (2) an increase followed by a decrease, or (3) a decrease followed by an increase.

These investigators report that between the ages of 3 and 17 the average child's IQ score varied by 28.5 points, that one in every three children's scores increased by 30 points, and that one in seven children's scores increased by as much as 40 points. Not too surprisingly, high-IQ children were the most likely to show substantial increases in IQ scores, while low-IQ children were the least likely.

Finally, it is important to note that several sociocultural correlates of IQ gains were found in this study. Children and adolescents who increased in intelligence came from homes in which the parents encouraged intellectual capacities and reinforced engagement in intellectual tasks. Those whose intellectual performance declined or did not change most often came from low-income and culturally deprived families. Boys, in this study, tended to increase in intelligence

Figure 7–2 Changes in Mean IQ over Age for Five IQ Clusters. (From "Developmental Changes in Mental Performance," by R. B. McCall, M. J. Appelbaum, and P. S. Hogarty, *Monographs of the Society for Research in Child Development,* 1973, *38,* Whole Series No. 150. Reprinted by permission of The Society for Research in Child Development, Inc.)

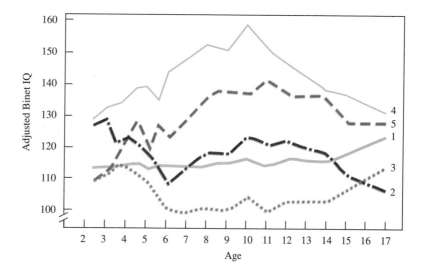

more than did girls; girls who were oriented toward traditionally masculine roles tended to increase in intelligence more than did girls oriented toward more traditionally feminine roles.

Similarly, several personality correlates seemed to be associated with increased IQ. For preschoolers, independent and competitive tendencies were most predictive of intellectual gains. For elementary school children, independence, competitiveness, initiative, and problem-solving orientations were correlates of progressive increases in IQ scores. For adolescents, a certain degree of interpersonal distance, coldness, and introversion related to important gains in IQ.

In summary, the results of these studies suggest that adolescence is associated with a variety of important changes in general intellectual development. For some young people, it is a period of rapid positive change. For others, it is a period of stability or decline in intellectual skills. Regardless of the pattern, for all adolescents, the developmental trend in intellectual change is associated with a host of factors other than mere inheritance of general intelligence. Internalization of personality characteristics or sex-role perspectives that focus on "attacking" or "analyzing" the world seems to increase intellectual ability. Coming from social or cultural groups that deemphasize intellectual pursuits may create the environmental conditions that lead to a decline in intellectual gains. Or having parents who fail to encourage engagement in intellectual tasks may have negative effects on IQ development. Thus, understanding intellectual growth is more complex than some might have us believe. Inheritance of a specific genetic potential is important, but a great many environmental conditions, interacting in very complex ways, are equally important in understanding patterns in intellectual growth during childhood and adolescence. Clearly, environmental influences can have substantial effects on intellectual growth.

Individual and Contextual Effects

Other studies have explored additional *personality, family, and schooling correlates* of intellectual development. One line of research has been directed at determining the personality traits of very bright adolescent boys who have either high verbal or high mathematic abilities. A comparison of verbally and mathematically gifted boys on several personality measures (Viernstein, McGinn, & Hogan, 1977) revealed that the verbally gifted youths were more independent, reflective, and mature. This finding suggests that different parent/child socialization experiences enhance the development of different personality characteristics and create different abilities in very bright adolescent boys. For example, in a study of gifted adults (Bloom, 1983) participants were asked what factors seem to have contributed to their development. They reported that special environmental support, excellent teaching, and consistent encouragement assisted them and contributed to their notable accomplishments.

Family configuration also contributes to intellectual growth. For example, birth order may affect IQ; later children have been found to have lower scores. Several theoretical models have been proposed to account for the effects of family configuration. Two prominent ones are the *economic/intellectual-environment* model and the *social/psychological* model. In the first model birth-order effects on intelligence are associated with family size and spacing between children. A

Adolescents vary in their cognitive ability, with each person having unique types and levels of ability.

larger family and closer spacing are thought to place greater demands on the economic resources of the family, weaken the intellectual environment, and thus influence intellectual development. However, the lower IQ development reported for later children is thought to be nullified by increased gaps between the births of siblings. Also according to this model, last-born children are handicapped due to their lack of experience in teaching younger children in the home (Zajonc, 1976; Zajonc & Markus, 1975).

The social/psychological model focuses on the interpersonal relationship between parents and children. This model proposes, like the first model, that older siblings will have higher IQs. The reasons, however, differ. According to this model, firstborns have greater demands placed on them, receive more attention from their parents, and internalize stronger achievement needs, all of which lead to intellectual gains.

Data from a test of the ability of these two models to predict the IQ scores of high school adolescents (Witt & Cunningham, 1980) support the usefulness of both. However, the social/psychological model may explain more total IQ-score development.

Correlates of IQ development in schooling experiences are less easy to identify than are family correlates. In a controversial study on school effects, Christopher Jencks and his colleagues (Jencks et al., 1972) at the Center for Educational Policy Research at Harvard University used research data from Census Bureau studies, Project Talent surveys, and the Equality of Educational Opportunity Survey data bank and drew several heatedly debated conclusions. First, elementary schooling is helpful for middle-class children but is crucial for lower-class children. Evidence from communities where schools were temporarily closed has demonstrated that lower-class youths are inclined to show substantial loss in IQ gains due to nonattendance. Other evidence suggests that gains in achievement are more likely to be lost during the summer months by lower-class than by middle-class children. At the secondary school level, adolescents have

Box 7–1   Massive IQ Gains in 14 Nations in a Single Generation!

Can you imagine going to the grocery store and reading on the front cover of a magazine like the *National Enquirer* the headline above? What's more, can you imagine finding a very similar title on a review article in one of the most prestigious journals of the American Psychological Association? Actually, it's not as unlikely as you might think. Indeed, James Flynn (1987) reports very interesting findings regarding intelligence gains in 14 countries, including Canada, New Zealand, the Netherlands, the United States, France, Norway, and Great Britain. Overall, Flynn was able to compare data from several nations, over many data sets, to find increases in IQ ranging from 5 to 25 points in a single generation. Many of these gains were traced to substantial environmental influences. Several other important findings were revealed that help us understand how IQ gains or losses can occur within a generation.

We can examine IQ increases either in the context of learning more information or in the context of displaying better problem-solving skills. To assess this distinction, we would need to compare the evidence for IQ gains from tests that use more general information (such as the Wechsler verbal IQ test) with that from tests that reduce reliance on culturally specific information (such as the Ravens) to assess intelligence. When Flynn made such a comparison, he found that IQ gains since 1950 were mostly reflective of increased problem-solving ability and not merely an increase in the body of information that one has. Thus, societies that encourage the development of problem-solving skills

and socialization experiences for their citizens enhance intellectual growth in substantial ways.

In the United States considerable concern has been raised about a decline in scores by high school students on the Scholastic Aptitude Test (SAT), which is commonly used as a college entrance examination. Flynn (1987) reports information that allows us to understand the discrepancies in several trends. From 1963 to 1981, comparisons on the Wechsler Adult Intelligence Scale tests (WAIS) revealed an overall IQ gain of 3.33 points. In comparison, the SAT verbal tests showed a decline equivalent to 4.32 IQ points. By examining what the tests measure, we discover that the WAIS is based on no more than elementary academic skills, whereas the SAT is based on advanced academic skills associated with problem solving and strong English courses. Therefore, while we have made gains in problem solving based on lower-level academic skills, we have had losses associated with the more advanced skills necessary for complex problem-solving. The ways to resolve this problem, we suggest, are a greater focus on developing advanced skills, requirements for more technical writing and development of communication skills, and more focus on abstract problem solving, as necessary to show SAT gains. To some, this means "back to basics." More accurately, it means back to advanced skill training in the basics, with less focus on general information and more on problem solving and learning how to learn.

shown to make more substantial cognitive gains when they are in school than when they are working, but even then, the gains in secondary school are well below those obtained in elementary school. (Also see Box 7–1 for IQ gains on an international level.)

Segregation has been billed as a major cause of lower IQ scores for minority children and adolescents. However, the research summarized by Jencks and his associates (1972) suggests that desegregation alone will not ensure improved IQ scores. Rather, the data suggest that desegregation must be associated with both better family economic conditions and better racial conditions if poor Black or White adolescents' intelligence scores are to improve.

In summary, there is ample evidence to support the notion that environmental conditions retard or enhance IQ development. However, much is yet to be learned about the specifics of such environmental effects and the ways in which they actually cause or enhance development.

A Psychometric Profile of U.S. Youth

An excellent illustration of the psychometric-based analysis of intelligence is reported by Bock and Moore (1986). Using the Armed Services Vocational Aptitude Battery (ASVAB) as a measure of intellectual potential, they tested 12,000 males and females from a national sample. The ASVAB consists of ten subtests that are independently timed and scored. Illustrative parallel items for each of the tests are provided by Bock and Moore to give some familiarity with the content for each subscale. (See Figure 7–3.) Most of the items are based on general knowledge and information, with some items in certain subscales focusing on elementary problem-solving skills (for example, Arithmetic Reasoning and Paragraph Comprehension).

Of particular interest is the comparison of the three largest sociocultural groups in the United States, Whites, Blacks, and Hispanics. In overview, considerable variations were observed across the three adolescent subgroups, with minority groups scoring, on the average, lower than the majority. When economic conditions were controlled for, however, relatively similar findings were observed for all three groups.

In analyzing their data, Bock and Moore dismiss any support for differences due to *genetic endowment*. Environmental effects appear to far outweigh heritability. Over the years, many have argued for a *linguistic* theory of group differences in IQ performance. That is, proficiency in middle-class English is proposed to account for differences between sociocultural or ethnic groups.

Figure 7–3 Illustrative Items from Eight Subtests of the Armed Services Vocational Aptitude Battery. (Higher scale numbers indicate greater difficulty.)
Source: R. D. Bock and E. G. Moore (1986). Advantage and disadvantage: A profile of American youth. Hillsdale, NJ: Lawrence Erlbaum, pp. 28–31. Copyright 1986 by Lawrence Erlbaum Associates.

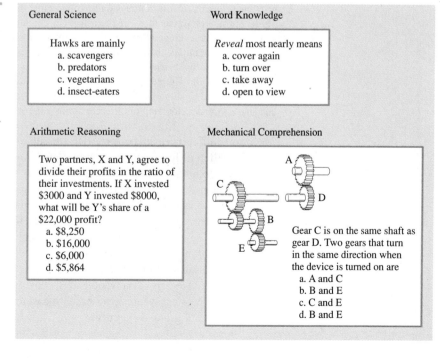

General Science

Hawks are mainly
 a. scavengers
 b. predators
 c. vegetarians
 d. insect-eaters

Word Knowledge

Reveal most nearly means
 a. cover again
 b. turn over
 c. take away
 d. open to view

Arithmetic Reasoning

Two partners, X and Y, agree to divide their profits in the ratio of their investments. If X invested $3000 and Y invested $8000, what will be Y's share of a $22,000 profit?
 a. $8,250
 b. $16,000
 c. $6,000
 d. $5,864

Mechanical Comprehension

Gear C is on the same shaft as gear D. Two gears that turn in the same direction when the device is turned on are
 a. A and C
 b. B and E
 c. C and E
 d. B and E

Some support can be found in the data of Bock and Moore for this hypothesis. There were differences between White and Hispanic groups on more language-based subtests, such as the Word Knowledge or Comprehension scales, but no differences were observed on subscales requiring minimal language proficiency, such as the Numerical Operations and Coding Speed tests. Even more important, any observed differences between sociocultural groups were so small that one wonders if they were actually meaningful. Further, there was actually little or no evidence for a language effect for Whites and Blacks. For Hispanics, the distinction may be that they are functioning in a bilingual language system, whereas Whites and Blacks are using English as their primary form of communication. Theories of *early deprivation* have also been commonly applied to explain sociocultural differences. The notion is that early cultural or educational disadvantage is common among minority groups and that early difference in scholastic performance for the disadvantaged will become more noticeable in adolescence. However, the scores in this investigation do not support this theory.

In contrast to these three widely used theoretical explanations, which found little support in their study, the investigators propose a *community-norm* theory to explain any observed differences. Their general argument is that schools are part of the local ecological, or community, system. They suggest that a school cannot set standards of attainment too far from those of the surrounding community. Therefore, the community standards will prevail. In an excellent statement on the implications of sociocultural differences, when observed, Bock and Moore assert that

> if we view individual behavior as largely an adaptation to the demands of a person's immediate social environment, we realize that children whose horizons are limited respond primarily to the norms of the community in which they play their part. These norms determine most of their speech, conduct, interests, aspirations, and motivations. The average effect of such determinants of behavior can be greatly different in communities that, for historical reasons, have been separated from the majority culture by barriers of communication and cultural interchange for many generations. In the United States the major sociocultural groups, and perhaps to a lesser extent the smaller ethnic communities, have existed under conditions that have encouraged the development of different norms. (1986, p. 94)

Therefore, differences in performance on subtests of the ASVAB can be explained by different local norms regarding performance. Sociocultural differences based on community norms can determine to what degree a youth interprets the meaning of directions such as "as fast as you can" in taking a test. Schools can make changes in local cultural standards and interpretation of instructions, responses associated with performance, and academic achievement. However, classroom teachers and their instructional influence can be seen as only one factor within a community-norm perspective. Students interested in further study of this issue are urged to read the monograph by Bock and Moore on a profile of the advantaged and disadvantaged in contemporary society. This report exemplifies the use of a psychometric-based measure of intelligence for understanding sociocultural group differences.

The Cognitive-Development Perspective on Intellectual Growth

Whereas the psychometric perspective emphasizes intellectual gains measured by numerical scores on IQ tests and the study of environmental conditions that accelerate or decelerate intellectual growth, the cognitive-development perspective emphasizes sequential changes in the manner in which people come to know and understand the world around them. One major strength of this perspective is its use of theoretical assumptions about how people develop new abilities to understand their physical and social world. This perspective draws on the world of objects and ideas (for example, ethics, religion, and so on) to test its assumptions within an environmentally valid setting. It has gained increased attention within the past 20 years, and until recently, it dominated the study of intellectual growth during childhood and adolescence.

According to the cognitive-development perspective, the study of intelligence is the study of *thinking*. The primary disciples of this perspective are Barbel Inhelder and Jean Piaget, whose *The Growth of Logical Thinking from Childhood to Adolescence* (1958) stimulated the extensive interest in the cognitive-development perspective. Besides the original, numerous interpretations or summaries of this important book are available (for example, Flavell, 1977; Furth, 1970; Wadsworth, 1971). For more extensive coverage of this perspective than we can provide here, we urge interested readers to consult these and other sources. We particularly recommend the classic *The Developmental Psychology of Jean Piaget,* by John Flavell (1963).

In overview, Inhelder and Piaget (1958) have proposed that cognition plays two essential roles. First, cognitions are organizing units that structure meaning and relations. Second, cognitions allow the individual to adapt to environmental change. The adaptation mechanisms include a balance between *assimilation* and *accommodation* processes. The assimilation of information involves the mental altering of information to conform to an existing cognitive structure. For example, an adolescent may attend a political meeting at which abortion issues are reviewed. The adolescent could use several aspects of the issues to support an existing perspective on abortion. The opposite adaptive process is that of accommodation. In this process, experience leads to modifications in existing structures and hence to a gain in knowledge or understanding. The accommodation process is the underlying mechanism for learning. According to Inhelder and Piaget, adaptation to one's environment involves an *equilibrium* (balance) between assimilation and accommodation. At times it is clearly adaptive to modify one's thoughts; at other times it is appropriate to seek out information that confirms an existing perspective. It is only when one system dominates the other that limited adaptiveness in cognitive growth and functioning occurs. Thus, assimilation, accommodation, and equilibrium are the basic mechanisms of cognitive development in Piaget's *stage* conception of development.

The cognitive-development perspective assumes that cognitions are transformed through an interaction between maturational or biological mechanisms and environmental experiences as the individual matures. It further assumes that a series of major sequential changes occurs in how one understands the world, and that at varying stages in childhood and adolescence different kinds of logical operations are available for processing information and understanding physical and social events. During childhood, thoughts (or cognitions) are limited by the mental apparatus available. For example, between the ages of 7 and 12 children focus on *concrete operations*. In particular, problems associated with seriation (the arrangement of a series of objects according to size) or classification of information can be successfully addressed at this time. Children in this age range understand that physical and social elements can be transformed into various shapes, sizes, ideas, and so on and that certain mental operations can be reversed. Reversibility implies the ability to trace a line of reasoning back to its starting point and may be one of the most important ingredients of intelligence. It emerges surprisingly late in childhood.

To understand the important cognitive developments in adolescence, it is useful to understand further the logical operations of cognition during childhood. As previously indicated, between the ages of 7 and 12 children learn seriation. Although younger children can see differences in the size of two objects and indicate which is, say, longer, it is not until the concrete operations of seriation emerge that the child is able to engage in the intellectual task of ordering more than two elements. The ability to seriate allows the child to recognize that $A<B$ and $B<C$, so that $A<C$. It is thought that seriation of length generally emerges before seriation of weight, with seriation of volume emerging just before adolescence.

Like seriation, classification emerges during the concrete-operations stage. Younger children have difficulty recognizing that two apples and two bananas equal four pieces of fruit. These children are unable to perform the logical operation of the addition of classes, while the concrete-operations child can do so. Indeed, the concrete-operations child soon comes to learn that there are multiple subclasses of a larger class. One of the authors has a fond childhood remembrance that when he first walked through a forest with his father, a tree was a tree. But through discussing with his father the various kinds of leaves and shapes and colors of trees, he soon began to recognize in simple terms that there were "pine-cone," "leaf," and "bushlike" subclassifications of trees. This discovery brought a totally new insight concerning the forest and enhanced communication with his father, who seemed to know everything there was to know about trees and forests.

The very strength of concrete logical operations is their limitation. A child at the concrete-operations stage finds it difficult to compete with older children. He or she is unable to solve problems involving hypothetical settings and has difficulty reasoning through completely verbal or highly complex information. Only with the emergence of the stage of *formal operations* is the child likely to engage successfully in such complex thought. While concrete thought is limited to solutions to tangible problems, the formal-operations stage enables the child (or adolescent) to engage in combinational thought, to solve verbal and hypothetical problems, and to understand proportionality. We briefly examine each of these abilities.

Not until the formal-operations stage does a child see that combinations of facts can be used to produce specific results. For example, if presented with five jars containing colorless liquids and told that combining three of the liquids will produce a specific color, a young child is likely to combine all five, whereas a slightly older (elementary-school age) child would generally proceed by combining pairs and probably stop after exploring paired combinations. Not until adolescence is a child likely to try all possible combinations and keep trying until the right combination turns up. Thus, combinatorial reasoning, or the ability to generate all possible combinations of a given set of elements, is one of the primary formal operations beginning during adolescence.

The isolation of the separate effects of several variables in a verbal task is equally difficult of the concrete-operations child. However, increased ability to combine and separate serialized information in verbal form is another important characteristic of formal operations. For example, until they reach 12 or 13 years of age, most children are unable to solve the following problem: "Edith is fairer than Susan; Edith is darker than Lilly; who is the darkest of the three?" (Wadsworth, 1971, p. 104)

The ability to recognize a hypothetical problem is a very important element of formal operations. It allows the child to search for a valid solution regardless of the initial hypothesis. If, for example, a logical argument began with "Suppose that snow is black," a child in the concrete-operations stage could not answer because snow is white. However, an older child or adolescent could overlook this information and focus on the logical conclusion by extracting the structure of the argument from its contents.

Understanding proportionality through multiplicative computation or reciprocity enables adolescents to generate solutions to highly complex problems. Even though very young children can use a balance beam or fulcrum, such as the seesaw at the playground, they have great difficulty in understanding the concept of proportionality and balance. Concrete-operations children can generally take a small weight and, through trial and error, place it closer to or farther from a fulcrum to balance a heavier weight on the other side. But they are unable to combine the information of weight and length to deal with proportions until after the formal-operations state has emerged.

Collectively, these new formal operations in the thinking process create the potential for important changes during adolescence. Dan P. Keating (1980) has summarized five major outcomes associated with the development of formal-operations logic during adolescence.

1. In contrast to childhood thinking, with its sensible here-and-now emphasis, adolescent thinking is associated with the world of *possibilities*. With an ever-increasing ability to use abstractions, the adolescent can distinguish both the real and the concrete from the abstract or the possible. Both the observable world and the world of possibility become interesting problems.

2. Through the ability to test *hypotheses*, scientific reasoning emerges. Hypothetical reasoning enables the adolescent to recognize the notion of falsification; that is, hypotheses can be generated and then eliminated as unsupportable, no matter how possible. Indeed, the adolescent spends time attempting to identify the impossible—a fascinating task in itself.

3. The adolescent can now think about the *future* by planning and exploring the possibilities of causation.

4. *Thinking about thoughts* (metacognition) is now possible. The adolescent becomes aware of cognitive activities and the mechanisms that make the cognitive process efficient or inefficient and spends time considering the internal cognitive regulation of how and what one thinks. Thus, introspection (or self-examination) becomes an integral part of ever day life.

5. Finally, the sophistication of formal operations opens the door to new topics—and an *expansion* of thought. Horizons broaden, not the least of which include religion, justice, morality, and identity.

The ability to appreciate the relationship between reality and possibility, combinatorial reasoning, and hypothetical deduction were originally proposed as structural aspects of thinking that emerge with formal reasoning on all tasks. However, intraindividual differences in ability to apply formal reasoning across several tasks have now been documented. Michael D. Berzonsky (1978) has therefore proposed a *branch* model for the establishment of formal operations. In this model, as Figure 7–4 shows, the application of formal operations is both content specific and based on esthetic and personal knowledge. Esthetic knowledge comes from experience with music, literature, or the arts; personal knowledge comes from interpersonal relations and concrete experiences. Furthermore, the ability to apply formal operations is not only relative to particular learning experiences but also specific to behavioral, symbolic, semantic, or figural content. Behavioral content involves nonverbal behaviors (for example, attitudes, motives, or intentions); symbolic content includes written symbols; semantic content involves ideas and meaning; and figural content involves visual representations of concrete objects.

The branch model suggests that the ability to use formal operations emerges more gradually than originally proposed by Piaget, for person experience with the varied aspects of life may determine the generality of application of formal operations. Thus, younger adolescents may be able to use formal operations in one academic subject but not in others. However, older adolescents, who have had more experience with schooling, personal relationships, and life in general, would be more likely to apply formal operations to increasingly wider areas of their lives.

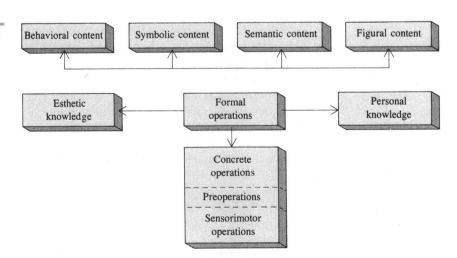

Figure 7–4 The Branch Model of Cognitive Development. (From "Formal Reasoning in Adolescence: An Alternative View," by M. D. Berzonsky, *Adolescence,* 1978, *13,* 279–290. Reprinted by permission of Libra Publishers, Inc.)

Research on Cognitive Development

An expansive body of research on cognitive development during adolescence has documented important developmental trends. Particular attention has been given to the emergence of formal operations and their relation to other psychological variables. We briefly highlight some of the published findings.

Developmental Trends

Inhelder and Piaget (1958) proposed that changes in logical operations are related to age. Cross-sectional age comparisons of children's and adolescents' performance on varying types of measurements provide strong support for the assumption that cognitive development is an age-related phenomenon (Bereiter, Hidi, & Dimitroff, 1979; Cometa & Eson, 1978; Douglass & Wong, 1977; Martorano, 1977). Research on changes in verbal reasoning (Bereiter et al., 1979), for example, has demonstrated that the ability to distinguish logically "certain" from "suggested" or "probable" conclusions in reasoning tasks gradually emerges between the ages of 7 and 12.

Other evidence clearly shows that not until a child has developed classification abilities in concrete operations can the child deal with the interpretation of metaphors. For example, in one study (Cometa & Eson, 1978), kindergartners and children in grades one, three, four, and eight took a battery of tests assessing stages of cognitive development while also interpreting a number of metaphors (for example, "When the wind blew, the leaves began to *dance*"; "John has always been *glued* to his mother"). Each response to the metaphors was evaluated as (1) anomalous (denying the possibility of metaphor), (2) syncretic (explaining only one part of a sentence), (3) repetitive (merely repeating), (4) concrete (giving a synonym for a term), or (5) adequate (responding in a manner acceptable by adult standards). Preoperational children were unable either to paraphrase or to explain the metaphors; most of their responses were syncretic or anomalous. However, there were major improvements with each new stage in cognitive development, particularly with the emergence of intersectional abilities, which allow the interconnection of two or more classification systems (this stage occurs between concrete and formal operations). The ability to reason out metaphors did not significantly improve further with the onset of formal operations.

Formal operations, which are thought to be the sine qua non (ideal function) of cognitive ability for adolescents, apparently begin to emerge between the ages of 12 and 15, but not always. In a study of the performance of girls in grades six, eight, ten, and twelve on formal-operations tasks (Martorano, 1977), not even the oldest group used formal operations in all the tasks. Thus, there appear to be varying stages in the use of formal operations. Other data suggest that formal operations may be used on physical tasks before being used in interpersonal contexts (Keating, 1980).

In a cross-cultural study examining adolescents from the United States, Austria, Italy and Germany, Karplus (1981) observed only 7% of eighth-graders responded to a test with formal operation reasoning. Indeed, Neimark (1982) suggests a majority of adolescents will not present formal operation thinking in solving scientific problems. These findings might be explained by possible limitations in social or educational experience.

Different socialization practices both in different ethnic groups and for boys and girls may account for other variations in the use of formal operations. In a comparison of Hong Kong Chinese and U.S. male and female adolescents on three dimensions of formal operations (Douglass & Wong, 1977), Chinese subjects responded with less advanced levels than U.S. subjects, while males performed better than females. Although older youths are more likely to develop formal operations than were younger adolescents, numerous social and cultural factors may influence differences in performance between groups of the same age but of different sex or ethnicity.

As we discuss earlier, two primary implications of the onset of formal operations are the development of the ability to use combinatorial thinking and formal hypothesis testing. According to a comparison of children in grades five through eight (Roberge, 1976), with increased age children develop the ability to use combinatorial reasoning, which enhances hypothetical deduction. Similarly, in a test of developmental trends in hypothesis-testing abilities (Moshman, 1979), seventh-graders, tenth-graders, and college students were compared on the cognitive capacities of (1) implication comprehension, or the ability to understand conditional relationships; (2) falsification strategy, which involves the search for falsification information to test a hypothesis; and (3) nonverification insight, which provides the realization that hypotheses are not conclusively verified by supporting data. As expected, younger subjects were less likely to have these capacities than were older subjects. Therefore, it is assumed that during adolescence, through the emergence of implication comprehension, falsification strategy, and nonverification insight, young people begin to develop formal operations of logical reasoning that enhance hypotheses-testing abilities. However, the data from this study clearly indicate that while these abilities begin to emerge during adolescence, they are by no means acquired by all youths even by the time they enter college (or perhaps graduate from college). Therefore, one cannot assume formal operations on age criteria alone.

Eliciting Formal Operations

It is important to recognize that several investigations suggest that the current state of research methodology may have led us to overestimate the age of onset of formal operations and to underestimate their frequency of occurrence (Danner & Day, 1977; Kuhn, Ho, & Adams, 1979; Stone & Day, 1978). Nonetheless, we can be fairly sure that formal operations begin during early adolescence, although under the right environmental conditions it may be possible for such logical reasoning to emerge during late childhood. Research has shown that exposure to problems requiring formal operations can enhance the ability to use such solutions (Kuhn & Angelev, 1976), but mere demonstrations appear to do little to advance formal-operations solutions. Rather, both exposure to and experience with problems are required before elementary schoolchildren can benefit. Whether young children can be stimulated actually to use formal operations is yet to be adequately determined.

The Relationship Between Formal Operations and IQ

From both the psychometric and the cognitive-development tradition in the study of intellectual development during adolescence, it would seem reasonable to suspect that IQ-test scores may predict the development of more advanced logical reasoning. Although psychometric theorists have paid extensive attention to defining individual differences in IQ scores among children, cognitive developmentalists have predominantly been concerned with the study of sequential stages and have ignored possible individual differences among children. Research evidence suggests that higher IQ scores are predictive of concrete operations for children aged 6 to 8 but that this relationship does not hold for older children (aged 10 to 12) and the development of formal operations (Kuhn, 1976a). However, in a comparison of bright and average early adolescents (D. P. Keating, 1975), bright adolescents were likely to be more advanced in formal-operations development. Thus, it would appear that students with higher IQ scores are more likely to be capable of using more complex reasoning strategies.

The Relationship Between Formal Operations and Moral Development

Cognitive development is associated with not only IQ score but also a variety of important social phenomena. For example, more advanced cognitive functioning is associated with higher levels of moral reasoning (Cauble, 1976). Indeed, complex moral thought may require combinatorial reasoning and hypothesis-testing skills. Thus, the effectiveness of moral-education programs may depend on their participants' stage of cognitive development. In a study on moral education (D. Faust & Arbuthnot, 1978), individuals who had not reached their full potential for moral reasoning given their current stage of cognitive functioning advanced, while individuals who had reached their full potential were unlikely to do so.

Cognitive Development, Self-Concept, and Social Behavior

Maturation in cognitive development not only produces new insights but also appears to have positive effects on self-concept and social behavior. For example, in an examination of the relation between cognitive development and the *ideal self* (a measure of self-concept and values), working-class and middle-class adolescents aged 12, 13, 15, and 16 were compared (Manaster, Saddler, & Wukasch, 1977). In all age categories, higher levels of cognitive development were associated with a more advanced ideal self. Research summarized elsewhere in this text has also demonstrated that a healthy self-concept appears to be a deterrent to delinquent behavior. Other research has demonstrated IQ differences between delinquent groups (Hecht & Jurkovic, 1978; Jurkovic & Prentice, 1977). Thus, cognitive development has effects reaching beyond the classroom.

Cognitive Development and Minority Issues

Among many theoretical attempts to explain possible differences in cognitive and intellectual differences between racial/ethnic groups, three explanations are summarized here—cultural deprivation/cultural difference, social class/sociocultural variation, and ethnoneurology/brain function theories. Each of these perspectives contain, in varying degrees and forms, an important contextual feature that is consistent with the general nature of this text. That is, we believe human development and its various forms and shapes (individual differences, patterns of development) are, in part, shaped by the social, economic, political, and cultural contexts in which human beings live. Furthermore, the various forms and shapes of human development, in turn, influence the nature of the social context in which people interact. Therefore, human behavior can be synchronous with an institutional context and result in productive social living. However, it can also be asynchronous, in which case the individual and his or her behavior is not productive in this discordant context. Refer to the discussion of interactionism in Chapter 2 on theories of adolescent development.

Cultural Deprivation/Cultural Difference Hypotheses

Lower academic performance of ethnic minority youths has been explained in terms of a cultural deprivation hypothesis. This perspective proposes that low-income and minority students perform poorly in school because of deficient socialization within a culture of poverty. Thus, low-income and minority youths are thought to live in a deficient social environment. Critics argued this perspective is overly focused on assimilation to mainstream White culture and ignores the integrity of minority ethnic cultural groups. Therefore, for many, the cultural deprivation perspective has been appropriately replaced by a cultural difference hypothesis. The cultural difference hypothesis counters that minority youths have rich alternative and highly adequate cultures, characterized by unique language, communication, cognitive, and motivational styles (Banks, 1988). Unfortunately, the cultural differences of such groups as African American or Mexican American households are not directly fostered by schools. Therefore, minorities are thought to be at a disadvantage in school performance and cognitive development.

For example, Cohen (1969) has identified an *analytic* and a *relational* learning style among U.S. children. In the analytic style the individual prefers to work independently, is competitive and task oriented, and is not highly responsive to the immediate social environment. The individual with a relational style is more sensitive to others, focused on common goals, and is cooperative in his or her work style. (These distinctions are similar, in many ways, to notions of individuality and connectedness as dimensions of identity formation, discussed later in Chapter 10.)

Anthropological research reveals that family and friendship groups that periodically perform shared or group functions socialize a relational learning style. More formal, hierarchical, or individualized task performance groups socialize an analytic style of learning. At least one review (Banks, 1988) of several studies suggest Mexican-American and African-American students are more likely to score highest on relational learning styles, with White Americans scoring highest on analytic styles. (Also, boys tend to be more analytic and girls more relational.) Therefore, minority cultures are thought to have a stronger "shared function" in their socialization styles. This is consistent with our earlier discussion of the role of family and its strong involvement as a support mechanism for minority youths in Chapter 3 on family relations.

Social Class Hypothesis

Other social scientists (particularly sociologists) have argued that the variation or diversity within ethnic groups is as great as that between groups. Even though any ethnic cultural group, such as Asian American, Mexican American, French Canadian, Inuit, and so on, shares certain general beliefs, attitudes, or values,

Improving schools alone will not raise the academic achievement of minority youths. We must also eliminate poverty and racism.

there are big differences within each group that may be accounted for, in part, by socioeconomic factors. For example, one author (Wilson, 1978) has argued that social class has a considerable influence on ethnic behavior. As Banks (1988) extrapolates from this work, this means that middle-class African-American and White-American children should manifest, on average, the same cognitive or learning styles, while middle-class and lower-class youths of the same ethnic group should differ due to socioeconomic factors.

Banks (1988) concludes in his review that social class accounts for considerable differences in a variety of indicators of cognitive and academic performance, but the effects of ethnicity persist beyond social class effects. Thus, support can be found for a cultural differences perspective. He argues this is true because minority groups who acquire middle-class status, still maintain contact with lower-class or mixed-class extended family members and friends. Hence, minorities will exhibit some similar behaviors regardless of social class. Another more narrowly focused account is offered by Slaughter (1988) on Black children and poverty. Collectively, these two accounts provide compelling evidence for the recognition of cultural differences as an important contextual factor in understanding adolescent behavior and development—particularly regarding intellectual and cognitive development.

Ethnoneurology/Brain Function Hypothesis

Schools have often assumed that all children arrive at its doors with the same general cognitive capacities. Teachers have generally used a White analytic learning style in teaching both majority and minority youths. However, an alternative viewpoint is that some students may be equipped with one way of thinking when another is being demanded by the school system.

TenHouten (1989) provides a further refinement of the cultural differences perspective by combining information on dual brain theory (cerebral lateralization) and ethnocultural perspectives. In simple terms the brain is divided into two hemispheres (halves or sides). The left hemisphere is thought to control language, verbal knowledge, and verbal usage. The right hemisphere, which also makes some contributions to language, is most important for spatial orientation and exploration, visual memory, and aesthetic comprehension and production. If the left hemisphere is damaged one can observe problems in reading, writing, arithmetic, and other academic-related skill problems. In contrast, if the right hemisphere is injured one might see problems with peer relationships, hand-eye coordination problems, problems with geometry, poor spatial orientation, and other personal relationship problems.

TenHouten (1989) hypothesizes that individual hemisphericity, or the tendency to rely on one hemisphere more than the other, is, in part, structured by sociocultural factors. In particular, he proposes that

> membership in a non-modern, archaic, aboriginal cultural—empathisizing spatial skills such as gathering, hunting, and route finding—could contribute to reliance on, and relatively high performance in RH-dependent (right hemisphere) gestalt-synthetic thought. Membership in a modern, industrial, and technological society—in which elaborated linguistic skills are inculcated by means of a mass educational system—could contribute to reliance on, and relatively high performance in, LH-dependent (left hemisphere) logical-analytic thought. (P. 155)

He goes on to review numerous studies to test his assumptions by comparing aboriginal and White Australian school-aged children and their parents. Through the use of many complex brain function tests for such things as performance hemisphericity, hemispheric activation, hemispheric preference, and lateral flexibility, he concludes that context-based sociocultural experiences together with different brain functions result in significant differences in cognitive styles between aboriginal and nonaboriginal children.

Findings such as these suggest that economic, political, and cultural factors can contribute to a cognitive orientation, or mode of thought, which results in children's tending toward a particular hemispheric brain orientation function-based learning style. Some people will be socialized in a culture that encourages the left hemispheric logical-analytic learning style. Others will be reared in a culture that encourages the use of right hemispheric gestalt-synthetic or relational learning styles. (Neither form of learning is superior, only different.) The former will learn best in an individualized learning environment that focuses on thinking, abstractions, and considering tasks independently. The latter will learn best in cooperative, role-modeled, observer environments that allow for hands-on manipulation and visual-spatial examination of learning tasks.

Summary

Environmental/contextual factors can be readily identified to account for differences between ethnic groups in cognitive performance and educational attainment. Sociocultural variations in cognitive and motivational styles have been documented. Ethnic differences may be due to cultural characteristics, and they may be influenced by social class or socioeconomic factors. Some evidence suggests that ethnoneurological differences that influenced cognitive learning styles may be determined, in part, by sociocultural factors that encourage one form of hemispheric learning over another. We suggest that educational outcomes may be determined, in large part, for minority children to the degree to which schools recognize natural and explainable differences in cognitive styles and structure their teaching styles to accommodate these differences, versus forcing children to assimilate and exclusively use a cognitive style of learning unsuited to their nature.

Formal Operations and Egocentrism

A Theory of Adolescent Egocentrism

Although the emergence of each new set of logical-reasoning operations during childhood and adolescence offers clearer differentiation of subject/object interactions, any emergent mental system has negative by-products in the form of various kinds of egocentrism. Egocentrism refers to the adolescent's belief that others are as interested in herself or himself as much as he or she is, and it is commonly accompanied by a sense of personal uniqueness and indestructibility. During childhood the individual is attuned to only concrete objects or experiences and so is perceptually bound to the immediate environment. Thus, childhood egocentrism consists of an inability to differentiate between mental constructions and perceptual information. For school-age children, the information rather than the mental process determines the product. Challenging this position leads them to change the data to fit their assumptions but does not lead to a changed position. Fortunately, through experiences in which children learn that there are data that conflict with their hypotheses, they learn the arbitrary nature of mental activities and constructions and gradually learn how to differentiate them from perceptual reality.

With the onset of formal operations, adolescents can conceptualize their own thoughts from those of other people. Adolescents can also construct contrary-to-fact propositions and reason about them. Recognizing the implications of these developments, David Elkind (1967) has proposed a corresponding theory of egocentrism. According to his account of how egocentrism emerges,

> Formal operational thought not only enables the adolescent to conceptualize his thought, it also permits him to conceptualize the thought of other people. It is this capacity to take account of other people's thought, however, which is the crux of adolescent egocentrism. This egocentrism emerges because, while the adolescent can now recognize the thoughts of others, he fails to differentiate between the objects toward which the thoughts of others are directed and those which are the focus of his own concern. (P. 1029)

In failing to make this differentiation, the adolescent falsely assumes that other people are as preoccupied with his or her thoughts and behavior as the adolescent is. Elkind (1967) has speculated from clinical observation that adolescent egocentrism is primarily manifested in preoccupation with and self-consciousness about physical appearance and interpersonal behavior. In particular, Elkind believes that young people are inclined to anticipate the reaction of others in social situations and to assume that others are as admiring or as critical of them as they are of themselves. Thus, adolescents construct what Elkind calls an *imaginary audience,* an illusion conceived by adolescents to be operative in all social settings. It is this imaginary audience that heightens self-consciousness.

Although adolescents fail to differentiate their concerns from those of others, they tend to overdifferentiate their own feelings. Because they see themselves as very important to the imaginary audience, they also come to regard themselves and their feelings as unique and special. No one else, according to adolescents, can know how intensely they feel. This feeling of uniqueness and intensity, which Elkind labels the *personal fable,* creates such thoughts as belief in one's own immortality, in unique and heretofore unheard-of personal relationships with God, or in the universal importance of personal relations and frustrations.

Fortunately, adolescent egocentrism gradually disappears. Through social and intellectual experiences, adolescents come to differentiate between self-preoccupations and the interests of others and to realize that other human beings are concerned about different (but sometimes related) thoughts, issues, and behaviors. Thus, adolescents are capable of gradually integrating the feelings of others into their own thoughts and feelings and recognizing their own limitations.

Research on Adolescent Egocentrism

Although Elkind's (1967) creative treatise on adolescent egocentrism has been well received, limited research has been conducted on this topic. However, two self-report techniques for measuring self-consciousness during adolescence have been developed that offer promise for the future. One technique (Enright, Shukla, & Lapsley, 1980) measures personal fable, imaginary audience, and self-focus; the other (Elkind & Bowen, 1979) focuses on two dimensions of the imaginary audience. Sample items from these two scales appear in Table 7–2. Data compiled in these and other studies (G. R. Adams & Jones, 1981b; Enright, Lapsley, & Shukla, 1979; Goossens, 1984) provide compelling evidence that adolescence is associated with a heightened sense of self-consciousness that diminishes during late adolescence and early adulthood.

There is considerable debate over whether cognitive development and the consolidation of formal operations are the crux of adolescent egocentrism (for example, Elkind, 1985; Lapsley, 1985; Lapsley & Murphy, 1985). Riley, Adams, and Nielsen (1984) found that formal-operational thought actually diminished self-consciousness, while Gray and Hudson (1984) and Goossens (1984) reported that imaginary-audience behavior was highest among concrete-operational youth. Riley and her colleagues suspect that social-interactional contexts are more likely than cognitive development to predict the level of self-consciousness of adolescents. Lapsley and Murphy (1985) suggest problems in interpersonal understanding as the major factors in the development of imaginary-audience and personal-fable behaviors.

Elkind (1967) has argued that experiences in social perspective taking and social interaction diminish adolescent egocentrism. Other researchers (Steinberg, Greenberger, Jacobi, & Garduque, 1981) argue that although schooling experiences and family discussions may contribute to this process, work experience may also be influential in diminishing adolescent egocentrism. Because the

Table 7–2   Items measuring personal fable, imaginary audience, and self-focus in adolescent egocentrism

Adolescent egocentrism/sociocentrism scale (Enright, Shukla, & Lapsley, 1980)	Imaginary-audience scale (Elkind & Bowen, 1979)

Personal fable
Coming to accept that no one will ever really understand me.
 	
Imaginary audience
When walking in late to a group meeting, trying not to distract everyone's attention.
 	
Self-focus
Thinking about my own feelings.
	Imaginary audience (abiding self)
	When someone watches me work . . .
	   I get very nervous.
	   I don't mind at all.
	   I get a little nervous.
	
	Imaginary audience (transient self)
	You are sitting in class and have discovered that your jeans have a small but noticeable split along the side seam. Your teacher has offered extra credit to anyone who can write the correct answer to a question on the blackboard. Would you
	• Go to the blackboard as though nothing had happened?
	• Go to the blackboard and try to hide the split?
	• Remain seated?

Source: R. D. Enright, D. G. Shukla, & D. K. Lapsley, "Adolescent Egocentrism-Sociocentrism and Self-Consciousness," *Journal of Youth and Adolescence,* 1980, *9,* pp. 101–116; and D. Elkind & R. Bowen, "Imaginary Audience Behavior in Children and Adolescents," *Developmental Psychology,* 1979, *15,* pp. 38–44.

workplace requires an adolescent to assume differing roles (for example, supervisor, follower, or co-worker) and provides an opportunity to interact with strangers and co-workers, work experience may enhance social understanding, particularly social sensitivity, social insight, and social communication. Social sensitivity is defined as the ability to read correctly others' feelings or thoughts—that is, empathy. Social insight includes the ability to comprehend the motivations and intentions behind behavior. Social communication includes referential communication (the ability to share information about one's own feelings) and social problem solving. Box 7–2 provides examples of these researchers' interview data that illustrate the positive effects of working on social understanding. For a more comprehensive discussion of research on adolescent egocentrism, we recommend a chapter on this topic by Daniel Lapsley (1990) published in *Advances in Adolescent Development* (volume 2).

Intelligence and Social Information Processing

In the evolution of how scholars look at intelligence, the individual is being seen as more active in the learning process (Sternberg & Powell, 1983). Early theories, while postulating a general *g* factor in intelligence, recognized higher mental abilities associated with attention, memory, and comprehension. But this initial research focused more on the content, or informational component, of intelligence. As new scholars addressed an old question, individuals such as David Wechsler began to recognize that intelligence consisted of multiple components. Wechsler (1958) identified two components, verbal and performance. The verbal component focused on such things as information, comprehension,

---

Box 7–2   Social Understanding in the Workplace

Social sensitivity

Interviewer: Why do you think [working] would help someone in life?

Supermarket bag boy: Well, . . . [kids] get used to being bossed around. You know, some people they don't know how to be bossed around. They can't take that, and you know, you learn to work with other people.

Social insight

Interviewer: Has work changed your feelings about people?

Fast-food worker: Yeah, . . . like respect their ways. You know people have other feelings about different things.

Social communication

Interviewer: How about learning to deal with people, do you think you've learned anything about that?

Supermarket checker: Some people are rude sometimes. I just ignore it and say "Thank you," and they walk away. . . . I just figure it's their problem. . . . They bought about $50 worth of groceries; that's what I'm here for; they pay my salary.

Source: L. Steinberg, E. Greenberg, M. Jacobi, & L. Garduque, "Early Work Experience: A Partial Antidote for Adolescent Egocentrism." *Journal of Youth and Adolescence,* 1981, *10,* pp. 148, 150, 151.

arithmetic, vocabulary, similarities, and digit span; the performance component focused on such things as picture completion, picture arrangement, coding, mazes, and other skills that have to do with visual and spatial representations. While other scholars elaborated on the complexity of intelligence (for example, Thurstone, Spearman, & Cattell), J. P. Guilford (1967) has provided the most complex model of intelligence. In his theory of the structure of intelligence, Guilford proposed no less than 120 mental abilities. This proposal is based on five operations, four contents, and six products ($5 \times 4 \times 6 = 120$ mental abilities).* In his theory, *operations* are cognitive processes such as awareness, discovery, integration, and differentiation. These operations include aspects of memory, the generation of many ideas (divergent production), arriving at a single most suitable conclusion or response (convergent production), and evaluation as a process. *Contents* of intelligence include visual or spatial representation and symbolic content such as that found in letters or words. The *products* of intelligence include such components of information as units, classes, relations, systems, transformations, and implications. A given person's form of intelligence may primarily center on select aspects of operations, content, and products. Indeed, the challenge to educators may be to actually find the form of intelligence that any given youth has and maximize it, while also helping develop other, less-well-developed forms.

Although early work recognized the content of information processing, the intermediate steps of Guilford's work on operations advanced an information-processing perspective. Gradually, the adolescent has come to be viewed as an active, information-seeking person who engages in complex thinking. Indeed, a new breed of researchers has moved toward including both information and the way in which it is processed to become useful knowledge. For example, Robert Sternberg (1977) has formulated the concept of *componential analysis.* Components appear

---

*Indeed, more recently Guilford has speculated that more than 150 mental abilities exist.

to be elementary processes by which people make internal representations of external objects or ideas and perform mental manipulations. Components are similar to Guilford's operations in some ways.

Sternberg recognizes five basic forms of information-processing components. *Meta components* are complex decision-making and problem-solving processes. *Performance* components are the actual internal manipulation processes. *Acquisition* components involve learning new information that can be stored in short-term memory or transferred to long-term memory. *Retention* components involve a librarylike mechanism with an organizational capacity to retrieve information. And *transfer* components are processes that generalize information from one task or problem to another. Each of these components is an essential mechanism in understanding intelligence.

Sternberg and Powell (1983) argue that from an information-processing view of intellectual development, there are several types of intellect. Processes need a knowledge base on which to operate; therefore, we can examine both the extent of knowledge acquired and the processes that work on specific knowledge bases. We can study memory capacity and why it increases, up to a point, with age. We can consider the strategies that people use in information-processing tasks. We can explore how internal representations of knowledge or information occur, how they are separated or integrated, and how they change. We can look at latencies in processing time and difficulties in processing information that delay understanding. And finally, we can examine the role of the integration of information-processing activities by ego mechanisms. Sternberg and Powell contend that the core of intelligence lies in the way a person allocates and adapts mental processes and resources to any given task.

Regarding adolescence, we know that control strategies involving metacomponents become more sophisticated between childhood and adolescence. More effective use of instructional rules and guidelines and more efficient performance of tasks emerge during adolescence. Information processing becomes broader with age: greater arrays of information are used, and there is more combinational thinking and better encoding of information. Adolescents have greater sophistication in comprehension than children because of their ability to look at connections. And they have greater flexibility in the use of strategies for gathering information. All of these developmental trends improve the problem-solving and decision-making abilities of adolescents. In Chapter 10 on identity development we describe how identity formation and development is influenced by social information processes.

Adolescent Decision Making

The importance of information processing can readily be seen in the decision-making activities of adolescence (Schvaneveldt & Adams, 1983). Given our recognition of the learner's-permit theory of adolescence and the role of freedom and responsibility, understanding decision making and how competence in this process grows provides us with important insights into adolescence. Indeed, Havighurst (1972) suggests that elements of decision making underpin all of the developmental tasks of adolescence; this is particularly true of educational and career choice, identity formation, and value selection.

Processes for decision making have been suggested by Janis and Mann (1977). In the *synthesis process,* the suggested ideal, adolescents examine a wide range of alternatives while evaluating the objectives to be accomplished. They consider negative and positive consequences for each alternative. When additional information is needed, they seek it out. They compare such information with previous facts and assimilate it into previously held views. They arrive at a decision and take action.

Tiedeman (1961) suggests seven "way stations" in adolescents' general decision making. First is *exploration,* in which information is gathered. Second is *crystallization,* where attractive and unattractive options are reviewed, and ideas are refined. Third, adolescents make a *choice,* followed by commitment, or allegiance. Fourth, they *clarify* they consequences of their commitment. Fifth, they put the decision into effect (*induction*). Sixth, a sense of selfhood and belief emerges (*reformation*). At this point youths become inflexibly rigid and adhere to the decision with great conviction. If they get opportunities to interact with older and more experienced people who react to their choices and commitments, such confrontations cause them to reflect on, reweigh, and possibly modify the earlier decision. This synthesis can result in *integration* and a more mature outcome.

Some decisions faced by adolescents are relatively minor, and their consequences are of little cost; others are monumental and have life-shaping consequences—for example, those involving marriage, parenthood, education, and career. Berdie and Hood (1965) have tried to assess what approach adolescents favor. They report that adolescents of high school age mostly use nonrational decision-making processes. However, few adolescents experience major decision-making opportunities, with perhaps the exception of contraceptive use if they are sexually active. For an excellent review of the role of decision making on adolescent development and education, we recommend *The Adolescent as Decision-Maker* (Worell & Danner, 1989).

Criteria for Decision-Making Competence

The ability to make wise decisions is a primary developmental task on the path to maturity. As Mann (1985) indicates, many cognitive processes are involved in decision making. These processes include searching for information, arriving at creative solutions, evaluating and judging, learning commitments, and remembering. These elements are roughly parallel to the component processes suggested by Sternberg (1977). From an information-processing or cognitive model, competence in making decisions stems from a logical approach to choices based on knowledge (information), a search for and consideration of viewpoints, and the process of turning choices into action.

Harmoni, Mann, and Power (1987) indicate that several criteria should be considered in assessing the competence of adolescents to engage in mature decision making. Are they prepared to select or make a choice based on information and voluntary action? Do they have a functioning level of metacognition that includes an understanding of personal, instrumental, and strategic knowledge? Do they have a capacity for creative decision making that involves the process of deriving novel ideas? Can they accept compromise when the ideal is not obtainable? For example, can they negotiate a mutually acceptable solution when a conflict of interest occurs between two or more individuals? Can they perceive the potential consequences of choices and actions? Do they seek out credible information? Are they willing to adhere to difficult choices in the form of commitment? And is there consistency and stability in their decisions over time?

Cognition, Personality, and Social Understanding

The Role of Cognition in Personality

It is useful to understand not only the nature of cognitive development and its implications for adolescent growth but also the role of cognition in general personality development and in adolescents' understanding of their social life. In traditional views of personality, cognition consists of stable and highly consistent dispositions, or traits. However, numerous social scientists have questioned the usefulness of this perspective for understanding personality. In particular, it has been argued that the trait approach ignores the meaning and implications of such related variables as age or sex, cognitive capacities, and the characteristics of the environment. Walter Mischel (1973) has argued that the term *trait* is merely a convenient label for a collection of inferred or observed behaviors. Although useful as a summary label for categorized behaviors, it does not explain how individuals organize such information. He proposes that certain cognitive mechanisms are used to construct mental systems (what Piaget calls schemata) to derive consistency from a complex array of behavioral information. Therefore, when we want to explain others' behavior, we call on these mental constructions to derive a sense of consistency. Furthermore, we use these mental constructions of traits to attribute cause to behavior. Although designating traits as causal factors may be highly questionable, Mischel and others (for example, Eiser, 1980) recognize traits as clearly serving the role of summary labels.

Mischel (1973) has indicated that his "cognitive social learning approach . . . shifts the unit of study from global traits inferred from behavioral signs to the individual's cognitive activities and behavior patterns, studied in relation to the specific conditions that evoke, maintain, and modify them" (p. 265). There are five basic cognition factors in this approach. The first factor is the operation on and transformation of information. Individual differences exist in *cognitive-construction competencies*. The branch model of formal-operations development has shown that formal operations can be applied to some but not all content matter at any given time. Thus, one youth may use formal operations in understanding mathematics but not in conducting interpersonal relations. Another may do just the reverse.

The second factor is the way in which a perceiver *encodes* and *selects* information to learn. To understand a youth's personality structure, it is essential to understand how he or she filters new information, selectively attends to specific pieces of information, and stores the information in short-term or long-term memory.

The relationship between these mental constructions and actual performance involves the third factor, the individual's *expectancies*. A well-established body of research has shown that in directing our behavior in the absence of new information or in a new social context, we draw on our expectancies of the outcome of the behavior. For example, if we have learned that cooperation is most likely to lead to positive reactions from others in certain situations, we are very likely to cooperate in similar situations if we want a similar outcome. Furthermore, the stronger the behavior-outcome expectancy, the greater the likelihood of resistance to change in behavior.

The fourth factor is the *subjective value of outcomes*. In situations in which two or more behaviors can emerge, the choice of behavior is likely to be partly determined by the perceived value of a specific outcome.

Finally, while external reinforcements or consequences of actions exert tremendous influence on behavior, it is also influenced by *self-imposed regulatory standards*. Each of us, through socialization, has adopted rules of conduct that are used to determine the appropriateness of an action, the sequencing of behavior, and the behavioral-termination process. According to Mischel (1973), only when we appreciate these five cognition variables and understand how they interact with varying stimulus-control or reinforcement contingencies in environmental settings will we come to understand the meaning of personality.

A brief case study will illustrate how this framework can be used to explain behavior and to direct therapy. Harry S. is a 16-year-old U.S. sex offender. In the past two years Harry has raped three teenage girls. He is now incarcerated and is undergoing therapy.

In therapy sessions it was disclosed that Harry's mental construction of females had been clouded by his deceased mother's actions. A prostitute for many years, she had frequently engaged in sexual relations in Harry's presence. Harry, who has a borderline IQ, has only a limited capacity to understand what he sees. His mental construction of human sexuality is based on his mother's sexual partners, who frequently beat or hit her during the course of the "trick." Too young to understand that the "John" was paying for sexual relations, Harry selectively encoded the violent aspects of the action. The behavior-outcome expectancy that Harry internalized was one of high reinforcement and no punishment for violent sexual action. Each "John" got what he wanted (sexual gratification) without experiencing punishment (legal action). Given the loneliness and despair of a young adolescent being reared in a poor foster-care arrangement, when Harry had a choice between involvement with a female and isolation, he was more interested in heterosexual contact. Furthermore, Harry had received little moral or ethical training and therefore had a very poorly developed self-regulatory system. Thus, as one might suspect, when with female acquaintances, Harry demanded sexual relations. If a female acquaintance resisted, he raped her. Nevertheless, Harry is a victim as well as a transgressor. His socialization, filtered through a limited cognitive capacity, taught him to expect and demand sexual relations in a heterosexual context.

Several intervention strategies are being used. Although Harry's intellectual abilities are limited, therapists are trying to change his mental construction of what sexuality means through modeling, role playing, and rehearsal of appropriate interpersonal behavior in a heterosexual context. Harry is also being taught more realistic behavior-outcome expectancies in a reality-therapy program in which he is rewarded for prosocial and punished for antisocial or destructive interpersonal behavior. Finally, he is receiving moral training on "right" and "wrong" behavior. As new cognition processes develop, Harry is being given, under guarded conditions, opportunity to use them in heterosexual situations.

A Cognitive-Processing Model of Sex Typing

One last illustration of the importance of cognitive processes for an understanding of personality appears warranted. A theoretical paper by Martin and Halverson (1981) has shown how gender stereotyping is actually a normal cognitive process that is based on an information-processing mechanism. These psychologists propose that the basic unit of cognition is the *schema*. Schemata (1) organize and direct attention to information, (2) regulate behavior, and (3) structure the interpretation of information. Martin and Halverson argue that one important type of cognition is the sex-related schemata. In particular, the own-sex schema directs the selection and categorization of sex-appropriate behavior. The own-sex schema structures experience by making schema-consistent information salient and schema-inconsistent information ignored or forgotten. Thus, the schema determines what is attended to, encoded, processed, or recalled. Finally, when the individual is placed in an ambiguous situation, the schemata deal with the ambiguity by providing missing information through existing knowledge already stored in the schematic mechanisms. Thus, sex typing may be based on normal cognitive processes associated with a sex-related schematic structure. Martin and Halverson's arguments are bolstered by the resilience of sex typing in children and adolescents in a society that has made substantial efforts to create more equalitarian sex roles.

The Role of Cognition in Social Understanding

Scholars are giving increasing consideration to the importance of cognition in social life. Robert Selman is one of the most visible researchers examining social cognition as applied to contemporary youth. Selman (1980) states, however, that it is inappropriate to merely transfer our understanding of classic cognitive development into the realm of social understanding. Rather, the development of social cognition in the form of conceptions, reasoning, or thought is distinct from, yet not unrelated to, nonsocial cognition.

To comprehend how adolescents understand social relationships, Selman proposes a theory looking at the structural development of social reasoning. His work focuses on *social perspective taking* and its developmental course. For Selman, social perspective taking includes understanding how people maintain related and coordinated views, not simply recognizing that two persons hold separate viewpoints. Further, he suggests that social perspective taking involves more than focusing from self to others in the Piagetian sense. Instead, he asserts that the social and psychological content is as important as the logical or operational thoughts that underpin it. Therefore, social perspective taking can be seen as a psychological infrastructure that provides a youth with a basic and important social-cognitive skill.

Selman (1980) reports a developmental pattern in social-perspective-taking skills. Further, the pattern has several steplike levels, which influence how a child understands his or her social or interpersonal relationships. At the first level (Level 0), which Selman calls undifferentiated and egocentric perspective taking, young children do not differentiate between the physical and psychological characteristics of other people. They also confuse intentional acts and feelings with unintentional ones. Although they may see differences in the actions of others, they cannot understand these differences. Children between the ages of 3 and 6 are most commonly in this level.

In Level 1 (differentiated and subjective perspective taking), which is common between the ages of 5 and 9, children advance in differentiating between physical and psychological characteristics of individuals. They come to better understand and differentiate intentional and unintentional behavior, and they develop an awareness of a unique, covert psychological life. Although some recognition of self and other emerges and an understanding of interpersonal causality begins to unfold, it is mostly one way. For example, a gift makes someone happy. However, giving a gift can make oneself happy, too. But to recognize this requires a reciprocity in perspective taking that children in early grade school seldom have.

Level 2, self-reflective and reciprocal perspective taking, is found in children between the ages of 7 and 12. Major advances that occur during this period include the ability to take a self-reflective view of the self. In learning how to reflect on the self, children also become highly conscious that other people may reflect on them, too. Now they can recognize that the visible self may not be a true reflection of the psychological self—that appearance can deceive. With a new emergence of more complex feeling and thinking states, children begin to truly put themselves into another persons's shoes.

Level 3, third-person and mutual perspective taking, normally emerges between the ages of 10 and 15. The most critical advance is found in the ability to take a true third-person perspective—that is, to step outside of the self as a system within self/other relationships and to assess and reflect on actions, intentions, and psychological characteristics of the self and others.

Level 4, in-depth and societal/symbolic perspective taking, commonly emerges after the age of 12 and may not be fully present until well into adulthood. At this stage, actions, thoughts, motives, or feelings are recognized to be psychologically determined, but they are not necessarily understood by the self through reflection. Thus, youths now recognize that they don't understand why they do certain things. With this new recognition comes an important corollary: they view their own personality and that of others as the total product of values, beliefs, traits, and attitudes, as a self-system that has its own complete and complex developmental history. In social relationships, multiple levels and layers of understanding now emerge through perspective taking. The Level 4 adolescent can think abstractly about many levels of self/other understanding and can see each level as having its own point of view.

The importance of this discussion is founded on the belief that developmental patterns must be recognized in all forms of cognitive or social-cognitive behavior. Aspects of maturation and differences in level of cognitive or social-cognitive functioning are central to understanding how adolescents think or understand within their own academic or social lives.

Women's and Men's Ways of Knowing

Adolescents commonly ask difficult questions. What is truth? How do I know what I know? Which viewpoint is the truth? Such questions focus on epistemological development and a person's way of knowing.

Two well-articulated theories have been proposed to understand the development of men's and women's ways of knowing. William Perry (1970) has published a book focusing on men: *Forms of Intellectual and Ethical Development in the College Years.* Further, Mary Field Belenky and associates have focused on women in their book *Women's Ways of Knowing:The Development of Self, Voice, and Minds* (Belenky, Clinchy, Goldberger & Tarule, 1986).

Perry's research indicates that male ways of knowing develop sequentially. Various stages (referred to as positions) provide coherent interpretive frameworks that individuals use to give meaning to their life experiences. The first and simplest position is called *basic dualism.* Students view life in simple dichotomies of right versus wrong, black versus white, and good versus bad. The individual looks to authorities to teach him right and wrong. With experience, however, the passive learner begins to see multiple perspectives, and dualism gives way to *multiplicity.* In this position the male becomes less dependent on authority and more personally, respecting the right to hold valid personal choices. When teachers then challenge the youth to provide evidence and support for personal choices, multiplicity gives way to *relativism subordination.* In this position individuals actively cultivate an evaluative approach to gaining knowledge. In time, many males make a full shift to *relativism,* where truth is viewed as relative to a person's unique perspective or framework and the context of each situation. In the process of acquiring relativism, knowledge becomes a construction,

Rootedness and connectedness are seen in women's relational and thinking styles already in early adolescence.

not merely a given. Furthermore, knowledge becomes contextually based and mutable, not fixed. Finally, Perry argues that relativism is a required ingredient in the construction of a personal identity. We describe process of identity formation more completely in Chapter 10.

Belenky and associates (1986) have documented similar categories in women's development of ways of knowing. Their work includes five major epistemological positions:

> **Silence** is a position in which women experience themselves as mindless and voiceless and subject to the whims of external authority; **received knowledge**, a perspective from which women conceive of themselves as capable of receiving, even reproducing, knowledge from the all-knowing external authorities but not capable of creating knowledge on their own; **subjective knowledge**, a perspective from which truth and knowledge are conceived of as personal, private, and subjectively known or intuited; **procedural knowledge**, a position in which women are invested in learning and applying objective procedures for obtaining and communicating knowledge; and **constructed knowledge**, a position in which women view all knowledge as contextual, experience themselves as creators of knowledge, and value both subjective and objective strategies for knowing. (P. 48)

In both the Perry and Belenky and associates perspectives, knowledge is acquired first through a passive learning style that with maturity evolves into an active learning style of social and personal construction. One basic difference is that men are likely to use separation and autonomy as their major psychological foundation for growth. Women are more likely to use a sense of connection and rootedness as underpinnings to growth in understanding and building knowledge. For a useful comparison between the two theoretical frameworks refer to Belenky and associates (1986).

Clearly male and female adolescents can evolve from a passive to active learning style. Males will use competition, autonomy, and separateness as the social process to acquire knowledge. Females will find ways of cooperating, connecting, and grounding as their primary social mechanisms for acquiring knowledge. We expand on this theme in Chapter 10 on identity development.

Major Points to Remember

1. A definition of intelligence includes the ability to understand both the physical and the social world.
2. In the psychometric assessment of intelligence, mental age and chronological age are compared on the performance of intellectual tasks. In the cognitive-development perspective, intelligence is assessed on the basis of whether specific cognitive abilities (such as seriation, verbal deduction, proportionality, and so forth) are used in the solution of a problem.
3. Data from both psychometric and cognitive-development studies confirm that important changes in intellectual ability occur during adolescence.
4. In general, intelligence is not totally fixed at birth (or inherited). Rather, certain factors in personality, family relations, and schooling can influence intellectual growth. However, the influence of each factor on IQ gain or loss appears to be limited.

5. Egocentrism is an important cognitive development during adolescence. However, social and work experiences are likely to decrease self-preoccupation.

6. Intelligence can be understood from an information-processing perspective. Operational strategies of processing can be examined to study how knowledge is gained and used.

7. Decision-making processes and actions can be considered as based on information processing. Competence in adolescent decision making is a complex, multifaceted process.

8. Social cognition and social perspective taking play a central role in personality development and the understanding of social relationships. Various stages in perspective taking can be observed, with the early stages being self-focused, the middle stages involving a self-reflective perspective, and advanced stages associated with multiple perspective-taking abilities.

9. Sequential developmental stages can be found for ways of knowing. For both men and women there is an evolution from being passive to active learners.

Personality Development in Adolescence

Although it is true that adolescence can be a tumultuous experience for some young people, for many more it is a relatively calm stage in life filled with gradual and continuous growth toward maturity. We are quick to recognize, however, that the word *maturity* is often used but seldom defined. When we refer to psychosocial maturity, therefore, we are talking about the general "character" of the person under consideration—about the total configuration of individual, interpersonal, and social-adequacy skills and the personality mechanisms that integrate them. Examples of individual adequacy include elements of self-initiative and self-control. Interpersonal adequacy includes communication skills. Social adequacy refers to the degree of openness, flexibility, and tolerance (see Greenberger, Josselson, Knerr, & Knerr, 1975). We propose that when parents or teachers refer to an adolescent as being immature, they are actually implying that he or she has weak social, individual, or interpersonal skills.

In this chapter we explore some of the general research findings on adolescent personality development that are important to an understanding of growth toward maturity and the corresponding formation of character. To begin, let us consider an interesting controversy: Does personality actually change during adolescence, or do we misperceive reality by comparing one generation with the next?

A Controversy over Adolescent Personality Change

Although adolescence is widely thought to be a period of either abrupt or gradual change in personality functions, some scholars propose that many of these supposed age changes in personality are actually reflections of differences among cohorts or of historical trends.

Scholars holding the first view cite longitudinal studies such as those described by Vaillant (1977). These studies have shown, for example, that neurotic defenses (such as reaction formation, intellectualization, displacement, or repression) heighten during adolescence but are replaced by more mature defenses (such as sublimation) during adulthood.

Defense mechanisms are psychological tactics that enable a person to handle unpleasant, anxiety-arousing emotions. Neurotic defenses are believed, in psychiatric circles, to be psychological mechanisms that block the expression of unconscious needs and anxiety. For example, a reaction formation is behavior that is just the opposite of a strong, unconscious emotional need. When an adolescent boy who loves his mother dearly and draws emotional support from her consistently responds to her attention with hostility and confrontation, he may be coping with unconscious emotional fears associated with lack of independence through a reaction formation.

Intellectualization, as an unhealthy defense mechanism, is a process of analyzing a problem from a purely intellectual perspective, while denying the affective or practical side of the issue. Therefore, when an adolescent is able to examine an issue only from an intellectual perspective at the exclusion of any emotional consideration, he or she is intellectualizing to avoid feelings of anxiety associated with emotional states that accompany the thoughts.

In contrast to intellectualization, displacement recognizes emotions but projects them toward something other than the real target. For example, we once worked with an adolescent who reported adamant hatred for his father's need to use a cane to walk. During the adolescent's early childhood, it was finally disclosed, he had been physically abused by his father. In return, a neurotic defense emerged in which the hatred of the father was displaced onto the cane to avoid the stress of recognizing hatred of a parent. In some cases the anxiety is so potentially overwhelming that an adolescent uses repression to prevent the emergence of an unconscious state of guilt or hatred. Repression involves suppression of feelings or thoughts into the unconscious part of the self. Fortunately, neurotic defenses are not used extensively in the course of normal development, and even a moderate level of usage steadily declines toward the end of adolescence (Vaillant, 1977).

In adulthood more mature coping mechanisms include sublimation, in which unconscious emotional states are directed toward socially acceptable endeavors. For example, hatred may be directed toward fair competition, or unconscious sexual needs may be fulfilled by giving of oneself through altruistic service or charity.

Research by Raymond Cattell (1979) has also provided compelling evidence for age trends in personality development during adolescence. His work shows that ego strength (or impulse control) is poor during early adolescence but gradually improves with age. Other personality factors, such as independence, the capacity to mobilize energy (direct one's efforts), and anxiety, also have been found to have an almost identical linear relationship with age; that is, with each age change there is a corresponding increase in the personality variable or characteristic.

An ongoing investigation referred to as the Toronto Adolescent Longitudinal Study provides further evidence for substantial age trends in adolescent personality development. Golombek and Marton (1992) have followed more than six hundred children through early, middle, and late adolescence. Overall they have observed that competence in personality function increased from early to middle adolescence, but remained stable between middle and late adolescence. Approximately 60% of the sample showed no obvious signs of personality disturbance, with approximately 24% manifesting consistent disturbed personality functioning. Regarding evidence of anxiety (distress, discomfort, tension), depression (prolonged sadness, gloominess, morbid thinking), and affection (tenderness toward others), several developmental trends were observed. These trends are depicted in Figure 8–1. Early and late adolescents (representing two major transition times) were the most anxious and most depressed. Early adolescents were the least affectionate, with middle and late adolescents the most tender. Regarding a wide array of behavioral problems that are connected to personality, Golombek and Marton (1992) report that early adolescence is associated with greater disturbance, with a general decline into middle and late adolescence. Some of their findings are reported in Figure 8–2. Clearly, these and other findings indicate that important age (or developmental) trends can be observed in adolescent personality development.

The unfortunate problem with this and other research demonstrating an age trend in personality change during adolescence is its basic methodological design. Cross-sectional or one-cohort longitudinal designs cannot be used to test whether the findings are reflections of true age changes or of cohort effects. To

Figure 8–1 Affect in early, middle, and late adolescence (*Source*: In S. C. Feinstein (ed.), Adolescent psychiatry: Developmental and clinical studies. Chicago: University of Chicago Press.)

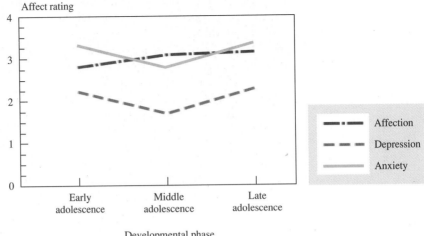

test this possibility, Nesselroade and Baltes (1974) assessed age cohorts between the ages of 13 and 18 over a two-year period. A total of 1800 male and female adolescents from 32 West Virginia public schools were included in the study. Although some age trends were observed, these investigators found that, as a whole, cohort differences reflecting historical and cultural movements accounted for most of the change in personality development. For example, on the whole, changes in conscience development, social/emotional anxiety, and achievement were really independent of age levels. These data suggest that when differing age cohorts (for example, 13-year-olds versus 14-year-olds) are followed over the course of their adolescence, major increases or decreases in personality variables might be found, but cohort differences in patterns of change are also likely to be evident.

This research means that not only will we find age changes in personality development during adolescence, but also each new age cohort is likely to be

Figure 8–2 Developmental changes in boys' behavior problems at home (*Source*: In S. C. Feinstein (ed.), Adolescent psychiatry: Developmental and clinical studies. Chicago: University of Chicago Press.)

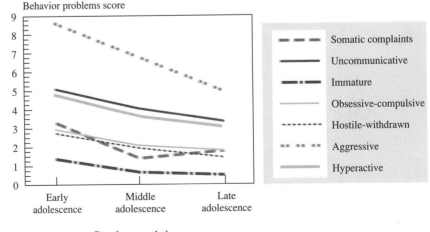

Box 8–1   Age Cohorts and Narcissism

The evidence provided by Nesselroade and Baltes (1974) indicates that there has been a gradual decrease in superego control. In other words, each new generation has had less control over natural impulses. In recent years an ever-increasing number of scholars have been discussing the growing narcissism (self-love) among adolescents. Some authors discuss the trend in terms of a "cosmetic" youth culture, while others write of the "spoiled" generation. A number of individuals see this trend reflected in the punk-rock movement. Others focus on drug usage, decreased academic performance, or student protest riots as evidence of increased impulsiveness and growing narcissism. What personal experiences have you had that support this notion of increased narcissism? What experiences refute this notion? Is it a correct reflection of societal change?

---

different from those preceding or following. (See Box 8–1.) Furthermore, the Nesselroade and Baltes data suggest that as adolescents we are as likely to develop certain personality characteristics that are similar to our age mates' as we are to follow some universal general pattern of development. Indeed, this conclusion means that each generation may be unique.

Character Formation During Adolescence

Although it is very likely that historical or cohort factors contribute to different patterns of growth in each new generation of adolescents, it is also true that major changes in personality do occur during adolescence. Clinical experience and psychoanalytically based research provide compelling evidence that the study of growth toward maturity can readily be viewed as the study of character formation. In stripping away the ambiguities surrounding the definition of character, we must conclude that the primary nature and functions of character are in its psychic structure and utility in regulating self-esteem and interpersonal behavioral styles (Blos, 1979). The study of character formation is important for working with young people because it helps in understanding how personality emerges and how feelings (positive and negative) about oneself are regulated. We begin our discussion of this psychological construct with some general definitions. Next we outline a theory of character formation and then examine some research.

Some General Definitions and Assumptions

In the literature on character formation, the ego is consistently examined in developmental terms. Thus, clinicians and scholars alike speak of ego development and ego stages. *Ego* refers to the *psychological mechanisms of the personality that provide an understanding of the world through the integration of information.* Furthermore, the ego is the storehouse of personality characteristics that eventually define character. Thus, character is the total configuration of personality characteristics and the processes by which these characteristics interact with the world. The ego is a psychological mechanism that operates to make the character possible.

Pride in one's personal heritage is an important aspect of character development.

Ego stages are thought to be potential fixation points, or plateaus, in development. Each stage is thought to reflect a particular character type with highly integrated cognitive and interpersonal styles of functioning. Finally, ego stages—or character types—are *motivational psychic structures that direct behavior, give meaning to experience,* and *filter information.* Thus, a given ego stage is believed to be predictive of a certain type of individual with highly specific behavioral tendencies. These behavioral tendencies are the direct consequence of how the personality processes information, assesses it, and assigns meaning to it. Although an individual can temporarily stop at a given stage, it is thought that the character of a given stage can be transformed by either psychological crisis from within or sociocultural conditions from without (Loevinger, 1976). Therefore, we prefer to use the term *plateau* rather than *fixation* in describing an individual's current stage or level of ego functioning.

One simple illustration of a common character type is the rigid personality. Certain individuals who have been reared in an authoritarian home are likely to develop a very rigid, moralistic personality in which everything is seen in simple right-versus-wrong terms. This personality type (character) leads the individual to ignore information that is inconsistent with his or her viewpoints at the expense of personal growth and change. In this case the character type can lead to undesirable consequences for higher levels of maturity.

The Adolescent Process of Character Formation

Although many scholars have stated that character formation undergoes changes during adolescence, surprisingly few have attempted to describe the major preconditions that stimulate such change. Piaget has proposed that major changes in cognitive abilities assist the adolescent in viewing the world in new and more sophisticated ways through the emergence of formal-operations logic. There is little doubt that structural changes in the manner in which adolescents perceive their world contribute very significantly to the process of character formation. When adolescents are capable of thinking about their own thoughts and are able to see the world around them in more abstract terms, ego processes allow more complex characters to form. But there are other processes of equal importance that contribute to the predictability of character formation during adolescence.

Drawing on his extensive psychotherapy with children and adolescents, Peter Blos (1976) has identified four essential preconditions for character formation during adolescence. The first is that the ego must loosen infantile object ties. Stimulated by pubertal change, adolescents gradually reorganize their identification with and commitments to parental figures to include other role models. This transformation permits a psychic restructuring that supports the establishment of new identification (for example, with friends) and the exploration of new independence.

The second precondition, which is perhaps the most difficult to understand, has to do with the implications of and necessity for trauma. Only though experience with traumatic conditions can an adolescent develop the special sensitivities to recognize and deal with the consequences of such dangerous occurrences as loss of emotional attachments, loss of self-control, or decline in self-esteem. Through experience with traumatic conditions, the ego comes to internalize a psychic mechanism that allows the residual trauma (emotional aftermath) to serve as an organizing force in the process of character formation. Thus, the potential trauma of negative psychosocial experiences can be converted into an adaptive function that allows the ego to cope with such situations and to gain from such experiences.

The third precondition is that a state of ego continuity must be maintained for appropriate, positive character formation to occur. In other words, before one can have a future, one must recognize the immediate past and develop a sense of heritage, of social identity, of where one comes from.

Finally, the fourth precondition is the resolution of bisexual orientation (yearning for relations with either sex). Sexual orientation must be resolved to diminish sexual ambiguity and provide a sense of committed sexual-identity formation.

In summary, the preconditions for and the organizing force behind the movement toward more mature character functioning include both cognitive and ego-mechanism changes. New logical-reasoning abilities and major changes in psychic structures allow the adolescent to surge ahead in personality functioning. But these new conditions may be merely the foundation for change. According to Blos (1979, 1985), the adolescent must experience occasional trauma, which sets the stage for a dialectic process of one force being countered by another. This dialectic process forces the adolescent to rethink his or her position. However, this rethinking must be accompanied by the security of a comfortable place in the family. Corresponding changes in ego stage or character formation are considered to be appropriate and normative occurrences during adolescence. No wonder that at some point we are likely to say to almost every adolescent we work with that he or she seems like a new or different person. Indeed, the adolescent has developed a new character through the change in ego mechanisms.

Ego Stages as Reflections of Character Types

Jane Loevinger's work on the specification and operationalization of six major character, or ego-stage, types is among the strongest and most useful in contemporary research literature. Although correlated with age, these ego stages are viewed as psychological constructs that are partially independent of age. Thus, young and old alike can be found in any given stage—plateaued, so to speak, at a particular level of ego development. Loevinger (1976) summarizes seven stages with three transitional phases (or half-stages). Each stage has its own character style.

The first stage, known as the *presocial,* or *symbiotic,* ego stage, is the lowest level of ego functioning. In this stage, individuals are capable of recognizing only their own needs and gratification and are oblivious to everything else. These individuals are in a symbiotic stage with their mothers and cannot distinguish between themselves and their mothers as unique and separate entities.

Once language and elementary reasoning have developed, individuals generally move into the second stage, the *impulsive* stage, which maintains a character style ruled by impulses. These individuals are preoccupied with satisfaction of physical needs and the expression of sexual and aggressive impulses. Such people are highly egocentric, fail to recognize rules, and view actions as good or bad only because they are punishable or rewardable.

In the *self-protective* stage, individuals recognize rules but obey them only if doing so is to their advantage. The self-protective character is deceptive, exploitative, and manipulative. A major transitional phase occurs between this stage and the next. At this point the individual is still manipulative yet obeys rules if doing so serves a purpose. (Usually rules are obeyed or manipulated solely on the basis of self-interest.)

In the fourth stage, a *conformist* character emerges with a strong emphasis on following rules. Disapproval of and shame after breaking rules dominate this character type. Individuals in this stage focus on the perceived importance of appearance, reputation, status, and material objects. Generally, the behavior of the conformist is stereotypically rigid in most ways. A transitional phase also occurs at the end of this stage. It is associated with the development of introspective abilities. In this phase a new self-awareness develops, self-criticism becomes possible, and recognition of psychological causation, or motives, grows.

The fifth stage, the *conscientious* character, is associated with the use of inner rules and the sensations of guilt that accompany social transgressions. The conscientious person is capable of recognizing feelings and motives that guide behavior and is consciously concerned with obligations, ideals, and internal standards of excellence. The transition from this stage is mediated by the third transitional phase, in which greater psychological complexity emerges and the individual realizes that social relations should be viewed as being on a continuum rather than as polar opposites.

The *autonomous* character, or the sixth stage, is associated with individuals who are concerned about inner conflicts and the balance between needs and ideals. These individuals are highly tolerant of differing views, are capable of seeing the complexity of life, emphasize individuality and autonomy, and are greatly concerned about self-fulfillment.

In the highest ego stage, the character style is one of *integrated wholeness*. People in this stage cherish individual differences rather than merely tolerating them. Although the last stage is thought to differ from the previous one, for most of us it is just as easy to view this stage as a subtle variation of the autonomous character. A more detailed summary of the major elements of the character style of each ego stage can be found in Table 8–1.

Illustrations of the interpersonal style of a preconformist (Stages 1, 2, and 3), a conformist (Stage 4), and a postconformist (Stages 5 and 6) adolescent should clarify ego-stage functioning. We were once asked to work with a family whose father had died. The mother began seeing other men a few months after her husband's death and married two years later. The stepfather and the mother's 14-year-old daughter battled constantly. Ultimately, the mother, stepfather, and daughter sought assistance. As part of a full psychological workup, all three were assessed on ego-stage functioning. The adults were postconformist, and the daughter was preconformist. Her preconformist interpersonal style was manipulative and exploitative. She would confront her stepfather as being unable to replace her father. She continually attempted to manipulate him through occasional docile compliance and subtle but pointed comments that he failed to do things as well as her deceased father. On almost a daily basis, she told her mother that she wished her dad were back and that it would be nice to have things the way they once were. In this illustration a young adolescent was placed too quickly into a new family arrangement, and her preconformist character could not deal with it. Ongoing counseling has helped her cope with the situation, and she is achieving meaningful gains in her ego-stage functioning and unfolding relationship with her stepfather.

One experience with a pregnant teenager in a family-relation program demonstrates how a conformist interpersonal style can lead to unexpected consequences for a family. The parents viewed their daughter as pleasant, easy to handle, rule abiding, and a good student. As most parents are, they were shocked by the news of the pregnancy. They said that their daughter was a good girl, knew the rules and values of the family, and had high standards. How, then, they wondered, did she find herself pregnant? The answer was vividly stated by the girl herself. In an informal conversation she disclosed that her relationship with her boyfriend was so important in assuring her a sense of belonging that making love

Table 8–1   Three Broad Stages of Ego Development

	Stage	Impulse control, "moral" style	Interpersonal style	Conscious preoccupations	Cognitive style
Pre-conformist	Presocial Symbiotic		Autism Symbiosis	Self versus nonself Self versus nonself	
	Impulsive	Impulsiveness, fear	Dependence, exploitiveness	Bodily feelings, especially sexual and aggressive	Stereotypes, conceptual confusion
	Self-protective	Fear of being caught, externalizing of blame, opportunism	Wariness, manipulation, exploitiveness	Self-protection, wishes, things, advantages, control	
	Transition from self-protective to conformist	Obedience and conformity to social norms; simple and absolute rules	Manipulation, obedience	Concrete aspects of traditional sex roles; physical causation as opposed to psychological causation	Conceptual simplicity, stereotypes
Conformist	Conformist	Conformity to external rules, shame, guilt for breaking rules	Helpfulness, superficial niceness	Appearance, social acceptability, banal feelings, behavior	Conceptual simplicity, stereotypes, clichés
Post-conformist	Transition from conformist to conscientious; self-consciousness	Dawning realization of standards, contingencies, self-criticism	Helpfulness, deepened interest in interpersonal relations	Consciousness of the self as separate from the group, recognition of psychological causation	Awareness of individual differences in attitudes, interests, and abilities, mentioned in global and broad terms
	Conscientious	Self-evaluated standards, self-criticism	Intensiveness, responsibility, mutual concern for communication	Differentiated feelings, motives for behavior, self-respect, achievements, traits, expression	Conceptual complexity, idea of patterning
	Transition from conscientious to autonomous	Individuality, coping with inner conflict	Cherishing of interpersonal relations	Communicating, expressing ideas and feelings, process and change	Toleration for paradox and contradiction
	Autonomous	Add*: Coping with conflicting inner needs	Add: Respect for autonomy	Vividly conveyed feeling, integration of physiological and psychological causation of behavior, development, role conception, self-fulfillment, self in social context	Increased conceptual complexity; complex patterns, toleration for ambiguity, broad scope, objectivity
	Integrated	Add: Reconciling inner conflicts, renunciation of unattainable goals	Add: Cherishing of individuality	Add: Identitiy	

Add means in addition to the description applying to the previous level.

Source: From "Ego Development and Interpersonal Style in Adolescence," by S. T. Hauser, *Journal of Youth and Adolescence,* 1978, 7, 333–352. Reprinted by permission of Plenum Publishing Corporation.

to someone she "loved" seemed both appropriate and necessary to ensure receiving love in return. Having now found herself pregnant, however, she lamented that she was experiencing intense shame and guilt for "letting her parents down."

Postconformist character may be seen during adolescence, but it is more likely to be observed in late adolescence—if at all. One unusual illustration was reported to us by a counselor working with runaways. A 17-year-old girl who had left home when she was 15 came to a runaway center for medical assistance for a bronchial infection. When interviewed about her reasons for running away, she said that people must cherish and respect their parents for their love and support but evaluate their own needs and find their own unique way. Thus, running away was justified as an autonomous act of free will and self-determination.

A series of eight small longitudinal studies (Redmore & Loevinger, 1979) illustrate that ego-stage functions advance from early to late adolescence. By the end of high school, however, the rate of change appears to level off. According to these studies, high intelligence is usually but not always associated with higher ego stage. There is some reason to suspect that lower socioeconomic status is predictive of lower ego-stage functioning, but because the data from these studies are confounded with race differences and limitations of sampling, this conclusion is only speculation. It does seem reasonable that due to limited opportunities, adolescents from lower socioeconomic backgrounds may not experience the environmental conditions necessary for higher ego-stage development. We suspect that given the right experiences, these adolescents would develop higher ego-stage functioning, too.

Unfortunately, national norms are not available on the proportion of early adolescents expected in each stage. However, work by Robert Holt (1980) provides national norms for late adolescents. As can be seen in Table 8–2, college students appear to have slightly higher ego-stage scores than do noncollege students, although the scores are not remarkably disparate.

Table 8–2   National Frequency Distributions of Levels of Ego Development

TPR Category	College (%) Male	Female	Noncollege (%) Male	Female	Total (%) Male	Female
Impulsive	4	2	2	3	3	2
Self-protective	3	3	15	7	10	6
Ritual/traditional	9	4	14	10	12	10
Conformist	12	10	26	26	21	20
Self-aware	41	39	34	41	37	40
Conscientious	22	31	9	10	13	16
Individualistic	8	9	1	3	3	4
Autonomous	—[a]	—[a]	0	—[a]	—[a]	1
Integrated	0	0	0	0	0	0
n	162	181	314	309	476	490

[a]Less than 1%.

Source: From "Loevinger's Measure of Ego Development: Reliability and National Norms for Male and Female Short Forms," by R. R. Holt, *Journal of Personality and Social Psychology,* 1980, *39,* 909–920. Copyright 1980 by the American Psychological Association. Reprinted by permission.

Beyond the age change and normative data, other investigators have found that the character styles of the ego stages are associated with predictable interpersonal styles. For example, Candee (1974) has shown that lower-stage adolescents tend to view politics in more concrete and emotional ways than do higher-stage youths, who see politics from a more complex perspective that includes the importance of justice and values. Similarly, Hauser (1979) found in a study of adolescent girls that postconformists had a more responsive and warm interpersonal style than did preconformists and conformists.

Consistent with expectations regarding the association of ego development, cognitive style, and impulse control (or moral functioning), as suggested in Table 8–1, it has been found that lower ego-stage functioning is associated with greater impulsivity, psychosis (Kishton, Starrett, & Lucas, 1984; Starrett, 1983), and hypochodriasis (S. N. Gold, 1980). Higher ego-stage development is predictive of fewer authoritarian attitudes (D. L. Browning, 1983), higher moral reasoning (Kitchener, King, Davison, Parker, &Wood, 1984), self-sufficiency (Deitch & Jones, 1983), more advanced identity development (Fitch & Adams, 1982), intellectual development (Alisio & Schilling, 1984), and higher self-esteem (Jacobson, Hauser, Powers, & Noam, 1984). Further, high ego development has been found to be negatively associated with psychopathological symptoms and behaviors (Noam et al., 1984). For example, higher ego development was predictive of lower levels of hyperactivity, aggressiveness, cruelty, and somatic complaints, among other symptoms (Noam et al., 1984).

A recent review of research on ego development has examined the probability of sex differences from early adolescence to adulthood. Drawing on 65 published research studies, Cohen (1991) concludes that female students, on the average, manifest higher ego development in early and middle adolescence (junior high and senior high school, respectively). However, by adulthood these differences disappear. Sex differences in ego development may be due to cognitive ability differences, differential rates in biological maturation between males and females, or different socialization experiences. Cohen indicates that relative evidence reveals no sex differences in cognitive ability on vocabulary and reading comprehension; therefore, the cognitive abilities hypothesis seems unlikely to account for sex differences in ego development. The hypothesis of differential rates in biological maturation is possible. However, in contrast to early-maturing boys, who experience a substantial positive outcome due to early maturation, early-maturing girls actually have more difficulties. Therefore, the biological maturation hypothesis remains at best tenable. The third hypothesis is the most likely of the three perspectives to explain the observed sex differences in ego development. In that girls tend to play in small groups that include opportunities for discussion and conversation, such play activity may encourage the growth of impulse control and interpersonal awareness that is associated with higher ego-stage development.

Findings such as those briefly summarized demonstrate that ego-stage assessments are useful in understanding character style and that character style is predictive of particular personality traits and interpersonal styles. Thus, understanding ego-stage development can enhance a person's corresponding understanding of adolescents' level of psychosocial maturity.

Family Contributions to Adolescents' Ego Development

Drawing on Stierlin's (1974) clinical analysis of disturbed families, Hauser and his associates have proposed that disturbed families suffer from impediments in communication that constrain verbal interactions and retard psychological growth in their children (Hauser et al., 1974). In contrast, healthy families are thought to engage in interactions that cognitively and affectively promote children's self-expression and psychological growth. In an observational study of family interactions with psychiatric and nonpatient high school students, healthy interactions were correlated with higher ego-stage development. In particular, problem solving and empathy in family interactions were enhancing, whereas devaluing and withholding behaviors were constraining (Hauser, 1991).

G. R. Adams and Jones (1981a), building on Parikh's (1980) findings that parents who encourage open discussion and use inductive reasoning in their disciplinary practices enhance ego development, further explored for enabling and constraining childrearing practices that are associated with high ego development among adolescents. This study found that maternal allowance of freedom and independence and paternal approval and praise fostered ego development, whereas paternal control and regulation constrained it. Findings by L. G. Bell and D. C. Bell (1982) indicate that flexibility and trust in family styles are growth enhancing for adolescents.

Cooper, Grotevant, and Condon (1983) suggest that an effective family includes an appropriate blend of individuality and connectedness. That is, families that allow self-expression within a relatively warm and supportive environment encourage individuality in their adolescents. Powers and her associates suggest that both cognitive and affective interactions either stimulate or interfere with psychological individuation or ego development (Power, Hauser, Schwartz, Noam, & Jacobson, 1983). Affective factors that are positive include support, mutuality, and nurturing behaviors. Stimulating cognitive factors include focusing on the problem or issue, constructive challenging of ideas, and mutual sharing of ideas and perspectives. Constraining affective factors are behaviors that are emotionally conflicting and inhibiting. Negative cognitive factors are associated with avoidance of the issue, denial or distortions in communication, or total rejection of the idea or issue. (For a special aspect of adolescent development see Box 8–2.)

In a major longitudinal study of ego development, Hauser, Powers, and Noam (1991) have documented several developmental patterns. Some adolescents were *profoundly arrested.* Others were *steady conformists,* fixated or plateaued at the conformist level. Three groups of progression were observed; *early progression,* movement from low stages to self-protective or conformist levels; *advanced progression,* movement from conformist to postconformist stages; *dramatic progression,* a transformation from a very low to one of advanced postconformist stages. Finally, a small number of youths manifested *accelerated development,* where they started at advanced postconformist stages and remained there over the course of the study.

Box 8–2   Grandparent/Adolescent Relations

Baranowski (1982) notes that studies of family interaction have focused primarily on relationships between two parents and an adolescent. However, grandparents can also function as important influences in a child's life. For example, Baranowski suggests that they may provide a sense of continuity between the past and the present and give the adolescent a stable psychological base from which to develop. Grandparents may also assist as arbitrators in conflicts between parents and the adolescent. Or the grandparent/adolescent relationship may provide the basis for attitudes toward aging and the elderly. Can you think of ways in which your grandparents influenced your development during adolescence? Were there enabling *and* constraining factors in these relationships? How did they differ from similar factors in your relationships with your parents?

Each of the six paths in ego development have particular family interaction styles. The profoundly arrested had less responsive family communication. Interactions were indifferent and unresponsive between the parent and teenager. These teenagers had impoverished connectedness between themselves and their parents.

Steady conformists were cooperative teenagers. However, they tended to be indifferent and withholding with their parents. Instead of being facilitative through accepting, explaining, and focusing behaviors, parents of steady conformists were observed to undermine the adolescent by devaluing the comments of their teenagers or by appearing indifferent or distracted. These adolescents were partially connected with some allowance for separateness—but they did not receive enough emotional and cognitive nutrients to make major progress in their ego development.

The three progressive groups in the Hauser and associates (1991) investigation had parents who ranged in their own ego development from conformist to autonomous ego stages. These parents were more engaging, offered more acceptance, gave more explanations, and facilitated focus in their interactions with their adolescents. In general, discussions included more empathic listening and problem-solving behaviors.

Finally, the accelerated development group was the most focused, active in discussions, and empathic in their communications. These families manifested a balance between individuality and connectedness that parallels similar families in the Cooper and associates (1983) research sample.

Collectively, these investigations indicate that progressive development requires parent-adolescent communication that includes acceptance and connectedness. However, there must be room for individuality, uniqueness, and separation from other's viewpoints.

Ego Development and Immigration: A Special Issue

Thousands of families with adolescents migrate to North America each year from Cuba, Haiti, Vietnam, Thailand, Mexico, and other countries. In general, identifying the factors that promote these adolescents' ego development and long-term adjustment to life in a new country has been neglected. A recent research report on a five-year longitudinal study of adolescents from 17 countries suggests three central facilitating factors (Arrendondo, 1984). Adolescents struggle with *belonging versus estrangement.* They must confront being from a minority; differing in dress, appearance, or physical characteristics; and facing racial and ethnic discrimination. For some of them, a sense of belonging comes with better education, citizenship, and political activity or membership in their immediate community. Reliance on their earlier *primary group's cultural values* likewise provides a base for new commitments by giving an anchor that ensures stability and guidance. They can make accommodations without rejecting their basic values. And third, *supportiveness of family relationships* and expectations of being successful increase their ability to find more complex or individual self-definitions, to avoid feeling marginal, and to realize their ambitions. As immigrating adolescents constructively face these three central issues, they are likely to manifest positive ego growth and complete the acculturation process within a new and adjusted life.

Moral Reasoning and Interpersonal Behavior

Part of character formation is the development of a value system built around a set of moral principles. Early theoretical and research efforts have provided three major perspectives on moral development. To ensure that we are clear about some fundamental terms used in discussing moral development, we first briefly define *morality, moral behavior,* and *moral character.* In a comprehensive review on moral conduct, Robert Hogan (1973) has made distinctions between each of these constructs. Morality is an external system of rules designed by society as general guidelines for social or interpersonal behavior. This societal code of conduct determines what is considered just and fair. Moral behavior, then, consists of actions in accordance with the rules. Moral character is not so much a person's actions, although they are important, as it is the motives, dispositions, or reasons behind them. Keep these distinctions in mind as you read the following discussion.

Three Theoretical Perspectives on Moral Development

The general tenets of the *cognitive-development perspective* most closely resemble elements of the theory of ego-stage development. In this perspective, children and adolescents are self-regulating individuals whose behavior is governed by conceptual rules. A norm of reciprocal respect between individuals guides social cooperation and moral conduct; moral behavior reflects the ways that individuals justify their actions; character is thought to be formed by internal judgmental principles. Thus, moral rules reflect the conviction that each person must maintain a sense of reciprocity between self and others. Furthermore, moral action stresses motive more than actual behavior.

In contrast, in the *learning-theory* perspective, commonly known as a stimulus/response or modeling orientation, the adolescent is a passive individual whose actions are determined by external forces. Morality as a system of social conduct is the inhibition (or behavioral repression) of forbidden or unsanctioned behaviors. Moral behavior consists of specific patterns that are acquired through the reinforcement of behavior or the observation of others' actions (modeling). Moral character, then, is based on the motive of acquiring positive reinforcement and avoiding punishment.

Finally, the *psychoanalytic perspective* delineates morality as a self-centered personality system that focuses on the inhibition of selfish instinctual drives. Checks and balances between instinctual drives and a social conscience are thought to define the primary boundaries of a sense of morality. Moral behavior, from this perspective, is studied through the examination of moral standards that are thought to originate with parental standards. Moral character is defined as conscience or internalized moral standards.

Each perspective has its own use. To understand, for example, the misconduct of a physically aggressive and violent adolescent boy, a therapist or teacher with a cognitive-development perspective would explore the youth's level of moral justification for his actions. A professional using a learning-theory orientation would look for the reinforcing elements in the acts of assault, attempt to identify role models that vicariously reinforce this misconduct, and specify the stimuli that trigger the aggressive behavior. Finally, a professional with a psychoanalytic perspective would concentrate on understanding parental relations, the regulation of guilt and conscience development, and the manner in which the youth succeeds or fails in controlling his impulses and desires.

Although all three perspectives are worthy of further attention, in the remainder of this section we focus on the cognitive-development perspective. We believe that in working with adolescents it is essential to understand how they gain moral knowledge and use moral rules to guide their behavior and justify their conduct (or misconduct).

Moral Stages and Rules of Conduct

The late Lawrence Kohlberg provided the single most comprehensive cognitive model on rules of conduct and how they define stages in moral development. He argues that rules of social conduct evolve through a series of stages. In the process of cognitive development, new cognitive abilities support the emergence of new rules of social conduct. These rules, or judgmental principles, are the essence of moral stages.

The late Lawrence Kohlberg made the study of moral reasoning a credible scientific undertaking.

Kohlberg (1969) proposed six universal stages of moral development. In Stage 1 individual judgments of justice are centered on obedience and punishment. At this stage the individual defers to others, either because they are thought to have superior talents or knowledge or because the individual wants to avoid potential trouble. In Stage 2 moral actions are based primarily on the satisfaction of one's own needs. In both Stage 1 and Stage 2, moral judgment is based on external, physical happenings rather than personal standards. Stage 3 has a highly conformist, or "good-person," orientation. Moral judgments are based on a need to please others and win their approval. Stage 4 is characterized by an almost blind respect for authority and a need to maintain the current social order. In both Stage 3 and Stage 4, moral rules and standards are built on maintaining the conventional order and performing proper and correct roles. Stage 5 is the recognition of reciprocity. Relationships and duties are defined in terms of contractual agreements between two or more individuals on acceptable standards of conduct. Finally, in Stage 6, rules of conduct focus on universal principles of mutual respect and trust.

Kohlberg (1969) supported this model of universal stages in moral development with age-trend data on boys aged 10, 13, and 16 in the United States, Taiwan, and Mexico. The general pattern was one of functioning at higher stages as age increased. Longitudinal studies by other researchers have also provided support for this sequence of moral stages (see, for example, Holstein, 1976; Kuhn, 1976b; Parikh, 1980; Rest, 1975).

Thus, adolescence is a period of moral development, as well as of ego development. As one matures, the principles of moral conduct become more complex. Lower levels of development are self-protective and oriented toward the external world. Middle levels are focused on following traditional roles and maintaining the existing social order. In the higher levels of moral judgment and psychosocial maturity, rules of conduct are based on reciprocity and on mutual agreements concerning correct social behavior.

A comparison of moral development and ego development is provided in Table 8–3. The table summarizes the comparative stages, with their general nature or function, and the similarities between the two perspectives. Clearly, the stages of development show substantial likenesses, with both reflecting

Table 8–3   Relations Between Stages of Moral Judgment and Stages of Ego Development

Moral stage	Ego stage	Common basis between perspectives
1. Obedience and punishment (deference to others' power or prestige, avoidance of trouble)	Impulsive (fear, dependence, impulsiveness)	Values based on external factors, bad acts, and self-focus
2. Naive egotism (focus on satisfaction of self)	Self-protective (expedience, exploitation, manipulation)	Values based on physical needs and protection, with limited recognition of intentionality
3. "Good-boy" morality (need for approval, attempt to please and help)	Conformist (conformity to rules, shame, guilt for breaking rules)	Values based on conformity to stereotypical images
4. Authority and maintenance of social order (respect for authority)	Conscientious (self-evaluation, responsibility, concern for communication)	Values based on obedience to good or right roles, following rules
5. Reciprocity, legalism (contractual agreements, avoidance of violation of will of others)	Autonomous (cherishing of interpersonal relations, respect for autonomy)	Values based on mutual sharing of standards
6. Universal moral principles (devotion to mutual respect and trust)	Integrated (individuality, reconciliation of inner conflicts, integrated self-identity)	Values based on mutual sharing, respect, and trust

changes from selfish and self-protective moral standards through conformism and maintenance of social order to very individualistic principles of morality. (For an alternative view see Gilligan, Ward, & Taylor, 1988).

Other data support the developmental nature of ego and moral development (for example, Gfellner, 1986a, 1986b) and their association. However, moral development may progress at a slower rate than does ego development. Further, Gfellner (1986a) reports that higher socioeconomic status may accelerate earlier and higher growth, particularly for girls. Kitchener and her associates present findings suggesting that females' higher scores are due to greater verbal ability (Kitchener et al., 1984).

However, we do not imply that one reaches maximum moral development during adolescence. Even though major and extensive growth does occur during adolescence, life-span research indicates that greater consistency and increasing philosophical reflectiveness occur as people mature and age (Pratt, Golding, & Hunter, 1983).

Moral Reasoning, Personality, and Behavior

There has been considerable debate over the association between moral judgment, personality, and social behavior. The research findings have been inconsistent. In one investigation, however, an association between moral judgment, political conservatism, and attitudes toward authority was found (Lapsley, Harwell, Olson, Flannery, & Quintana, 1984). Higher levels of moral judgment were associated with less political conservatism. Other studies support this finding (for example, Emler, Renwick, & Malone, 1983).

We are uncertain how moral reasoning is related to behavior (Locke, 1983). There may be causal influence at each stage. In young children or adolescents with lower levels of moral reasoning, for example, moral judgments may be affected by behavior. In teenagers or adults, however, moral reasoning may affect behavior by providing direction or ethical standards. Or moral reasoning may not directly affect behavior but instead determine the extent to which youths act on their moral judgments. It is well accepted that a developmental model explains changes in moral reasoning. But it remains uncertain how moral reasoning directly or indirectly influences behavior. (See Box 8–3 for one fascinating way in which moral judgment and sex-role behaviors may be related.)

Enhancing Moral Development

Kohlberg (1969) hypothesized that cognitive development and exposure to appropriate sociomoral experiences helped determine the rate of moral development. He advanced attainment of higher cognitive stages as one major underpinning for moral development. Likewise, he thought that personal experience involving moral responsibility, role taking, moral decision making, and interpersonal communication fostered higher levels of moral reasoning. A recent study by L. J. Walker (1986) indicates that cognitive development facilitates moral development but that higher education and experience in joint household decision making are the best predictors of moral maturity.

Box 8–3   Moral Judgment and Androgyny

In the discussion of sex-role development in Chapter 11 it is proposed that androgynous people are most interpersonally competent and socially adaptive because they identify with both aspects of masculine and feminine roles and behaviors. One might ask if higher moral reasoning is predictive of an androgynous sex role. Leahy and Eiter (1980) examined this associa-tion and found that postconformist (or postconvention-al) moral stages were predictive of more frequent androgynous self-images. Postconventional thinking appears to release people from gender-specific role behavior and free them to identify with universal quali-ties that allow for more adaptive behavior.

An analysis of 55 studies of educational intervention designed to stimulate moral judgment among junior and senior high school students, college students, and older adults provides strong evidence for the ability to improve moral judg-ments (Schlaefli, Rest, & Thomas, 1985). Programs using group discussion, enhancement of psychological development, and social studies and humanities courses have been offered as possible interventions. Group discussion of moral problems and psychological-development programs yield gains in moral judg-ment, with programs of 3 to 12 weeks optimal. Greater effects were found for the junior high school students, although positive stimulation in moral growth was observed for all ages.

One particular study is noteworthy in that it has focused on the effects of positive peer culture on the moral development of distressed youths in street gangs in Israel. Positive peer culture is defined as interactions with peers who engage in adult-accepted behavior. Sherer (1985) studied the effects of such group intervention on resistance to temptation, moral stage, and feelings after an offense, punishment, and confession. The results suggest that a positive, focused peer culture can be used effectively to stimulate advanced moral reasoning *and* moral action.

Family Contributions to Moral Development

It has been assumed for centuries that the family has a major influence on the adolescent's moral values. Research suggests that at least for young adolescent boys, there is a modest but significant relationship between their stage of moral development and their parents' (Haan, Langer, & Kohlberg, 1976). The results of other studies suggest that the mother's level of moral development influences the moral-stage functioning of adolescent boys. A comparison of the mothers of delinquent and nondelinquent boys (Hudgins & Prentice, 1973) revealed that the mothers of nondelinquents had higher levels of moral-stage reasoning. Further, nondelinquent boys scored higher than did delinquent boys on moral-reasoning abilities. Research on Indian and U.S. families (Parikh, 1980) indicates that hav-ing a parent whose moral-stage functioning is at least one stage higher assists moral development. Thus, modeling of more advanced moral-stage reasoning may advance development.

Parikh (1980) suggests that two additional factors contribute to the moral development of children and adolescents. Parents who encourage their children to engage in open democratic discussion of issues enhance their moral development, as do parents who model inductive-reasoning techniques in discipline. These findings are consistent with those reported by Cooper and her colleagues (1983) and by Adams and Jones (1981a).

Stages of Faith

Character development also includes attitudes and beliefs about spirituality. Most often religion is downplayed in texts on adolescent development. When discussions occur they are likely to focus on cults, the occult, or radical spirituality. In our discussion we briefly examine some general trends in religious attitudes and behaviors. Next, we present a developmental perspective to faith. Finally, we discuss some facilitative features and barriers to faith development.

Some Demographic Trends

A research team from the Search Institute in Minneapolis, Minnesota (Benson, Williams, & Johnson, 1987) summarizes the current state of knowledge on religion and presents new data on trends over the course of early and middle adolescence. Benson and associates conclude from Gallup Poll results that (a) 74% of 13-to 15-year-olds indicate religion is extremely important to them, (b) 95% of these same youths indicate a belief in a deity, and (c) 60% of their parents report their children receive some form of religious instruction, while (d) 83% indicate their children should receive a religious education.

In the Benson and colleagues (1987) investigation, the majority of early adolescents report religion is very important to them. However, girls placed more importance on religion than did boys. Furthermore, although boys saw religion as more restricting, young adolescents are likely, regardless of gender, to see the experience of religion as more liberating than restricting. Finally, most young adolescents see religion as having two dimensions. One dimension is vertical and focuses on the relationship between people and God. The communication is seen as being between people on earth with God in heaven. The other dimension is horizontal in nature. This factor involves communication between people and the importance of acts of love and justice.

Benson and associates draw the following conclusions by focusing on religious centrality, liberating religion, and horizontal religion:

1. The more central (important) religion is to the adolescent the more that youth will report:
   a. a positive attitude toward religion and the church
   b. higher self-esteem
   c. engaging in helpful behaviors toward others
   d. not engaging in the use of drugs or alcohol

2. The more liberating the view of religion, the more likely that:
   a. the youth will have a positive attitude about religion
   b. the teenager will have positive self-esteem
   c. the less likely the adolescent will be racially prejudiced
   d. the youth will be considerate and helpful to others
   e. the adolescent will refrain from antisocial behaviors and drug use
3. The more concern that adolescents have about horizontal communication (relationships of person to person):
   a. the greater the value placed on world peace
   b. the higher the concern for people

At the same time that Benson and associates document the important features of religion, it would seem that general attitudes about religious experience are declining. The fact may be that as children grow older, the less positive their attitudes become toward religion and religious education. For example, in one study that included a sample of 50 children in each of 8 consecutive years beginning with junior high and concluding with high school, Francis (1987) compared attitudes toward games, English, Math, History, School, Music, and Religion. Positive attitudes toward Games, English, School, Math, and History showed most declines and in some cases improvement. However, positive attitudes toward Religion showed an almost linear decline over the eight chronological ages that were sampled. Therefore, although Benson and associates show important positive features to religious involvement, Francis reports a general decline in positive attitudes toward religion during the junior and senior high school years. These contrary findings should both puzzle and concern contemporary religious leaders.

Basic Stages in Faith

What Kohlberg has done for understanding moral reasoning, James Fowler (1981) has done for stage of faith. After extensive observation, Fowler has defined several stages that occur in the development of faith.

In a prestage called *undifferentiated faith* the seeds of faith are sown by the facilitation of trust, courage, hope, and love. The degree to which an infant experiences abandonment or deprivation determines the foundation for later stage development. These assumptions (by Fowler) are consistent with Erikson's stages of psychosocial development, the major danger being that to overattend to a child enhances the possibilities of narcissism, while underattending results in a sense of isolation and failed mutuality.

The first stage is labeled *Intuitive-Projective*. It is an imitation process in which the child experiences and knows religion primarily through observations of the actions, moods, and stories of adults. This is the first stage of self-awareness. As one might expect, the child remains egocentric and fails to have a complete knowledge of the perspective of others. Nonetheless, with vivid imagination, the child strives to know the conditions of life and to understand the distinction between what is real and what only seems to be real. This process is facilitated by the emergence of concrete operational thinking.

In the second stage, known as *Mythic-Literal,* the child begins to internalize the stories and beliefs of religion. Beliefs are recognized as concrete rules. Symbols are seen as literal in meaning. Stories are the major way of understanding and valuing religion. As part of this stage, the child comes to understand the importance of reciprocal fairness, immanent justice, and the role of reciprocity.

Stage 3, *Synthetic-Conventional* faith, is associated with understanding beyond the family into spheres of school, work, media, and other social living contexts. This stage is commonly thought to be part of the adolescent life experience. The stage is highly "conformist," and the individual is not yet capable of developing an independent autonomous viewpoint. By this time the youth has a sense of value and meaning, but it is bolstered by external authority figures. Movement from this stage is facilitated by clashes or contradictions between authority figures. Growth can also occur due to self-reflection.

Stage 4, *Individuative-Reflective* faith, occurs when the individual must assume personal responsibility for his or her own commitments, life-styles, or beliefs. When the youth is forced to address unavoidable tension between the individual or group demands for critical self-assessment, faith becomes part of a self-identity. Through critical reflection on self-identity, the person is now able to hold a personal outlook or ideology. This stage may be the most central to the development of faith during middle and late adolescence, as we see in Chapter 10 on identity development.

In Stage 5, *Conjunctive* faith, which is usually obtained in adulthood, there is a more complete appreciation for symbols, myths, and rituals. A deeper sense of reality is possible. Likewise, Stage 6, *Universalizing,* brings with it the same complexity found in Loevinger's or Kolberg's final stages of development. Each of these stages is highly unlikely to be obtained as an adolescent and may even be rare for adults.

It seems, then, that as character develops during adolescence, it can be examined from ego-stage, moral-stage, or faith-stage perspectives. Collectively, development in each of these three life experience dimensions will come to be integrated into a general character type. Parks (1986) refers to this integration as the search for meaning, faith, and commitment. Part of such development involves specific character types and their interaction in social contexts. Box 8–4 illustrates how a religious character type in the form of religious ingroup versus outgroup experience can affect social life in certain community contexts.

Family Contribution to Faith Development

Fowler (1981) sees faith development in a sequential structure that parallels cognitive and moral stages. With increased facilitation in cognitive operations, corresponding increases in stages of faith are possible. With the emergence of concrete operations, movement through the early stages of faith is probable. When formal operations unfold, Synthetic-Conventional faith and more advanced stages of faith are possible. To this date, we are unaware of research exploring family influences on the development of Fowler's stages of faith.

Box 8–4   Religious Minority Versus Majority Contexts

Typically, when one thinks of minority group issues, race or cultural features are used as a distinction between people. However, Markstrom-Adams (1991) has examined the social implications of religious identity for social relationships using an ingroup versus outgroup comparison. In this investigation, Markstrom-Adams compared 47 non-Mormon youths with 36 Mormon adolescents. The non-Mormon group was conceptualized as an out-group because they were a religious minority in that community. The Mormon group was considered an ingroup because it constituted the majority of adolescents in the same community and surrounding area. From this qualitative investigation, several themes emerged. Mormon adolescents were reticent to engage in interfaith dating, were concerned about the beliefs, values, standards, and moral conduct of non-Mormons, and viewed dating as a precursor to marriage.

Markstrom-Adams (1991, p. 95) draws the following conclusions from her investigation:

1. "In communities characterized as having large religious majorities, religion becomes a major consideration in the selection of dating partners among adolescents."
2. "Whether a religious majority group will be more selective of dating partners depends on the nature of the majority group in the broader society. That is, if

the majority group is generally a minority group in the broader society, they may be prone to greater selectivity of dating partners."
3. "Individuals, who otherwise might be selective of their dating partners, may be less selective in a minority context due to the small number of potential dating partners of their religious faith. In such situations, potential dating partners may be regarded as acceptable for casual dating, but unacceptable for serious dating."
4. "When a particular religious community strongly endorses endogamy, dating among adolescents is more likely to be viewed as a precursor to marriage as opposed to the consideration of other functions of dating" (e.g., recreation, friendship).

We can see from such an investigation that religious faith is not only a way of thinking about religion and God, but also a psychological structure that serves a social mechanism function within the daily lives of adolescents. In this case, Markstrom-Adams shows how holding a particular faith within a given community can affect dating choices, opportunities, and values.

Have you had an experience that placed you in an outgroup context? How did it affect your behavior? Does this awareness of being in an outgroup make you more sensitive to prejudice? Discrimination?

Nonetheless, we maintain that the family is broadly recognized by society as an important factor in the transmission of values. Parental agreement on religious participation, religious supervision, and perceived support have been found to predict adolescent religious participation. However, Hoge, Petrillo, and Smith (1982) indicate the association between parents and teenage children's religious and social values may actually be less strong than one might anticipate. Although researchers will continue to debate this issue, we tend to believe that families are extremely important in the development of virtually every aspect of children's and adolescent's lives—including passing on values and the development of faith. (See Box 8–5 for an illustration of transmitting spiritual values among American Indians.)

For example, evidence indicates that parents who provide clear explanations and warmth and affection are better able to transmit positive values to their children (for example, see Eisikovits & Sagi, 1982). On the other hand, parents who engage in harsh and punitive behaviors are likely to deaden or dampen the value transmission between adolescent and parent (Matteson, 1975).

Box 8–5   American Indian Spirituality

In the broader U.S. society, religion is commonly interpreted according to Judeo-Christian traditions. However, it is important to recognize other forms of spirituality that are of great importance to some minority adolescents. In this section we recognize the many variations of American Indian spirituality that are based in traditions unique to the history and culture of North American Indian Tribes.

A feature common to many forms of American Indian spirituality is that provisions are made for the integration of children and adolescents into the broader spiritual community. Emphases on spiritual interconnections to others, to one's ancestors, and to the broader physical environment foster the development of a communal orientation that accentuates relatedness and social responsibility. Religion is not regarded as an independent component of existence; rather it is intertwined with all facets of life.

Not only are American Indian religious beliefs and practices incorporated into all aspects of existence, but religion also serves important functions at key transitional points across the life span (Gattuso, 1991). Specific rituals and rites of passage across the life span provide meaning, connection, and purpose to American Indians of all ages. In adolescence a critical rite of passage ceremony practiced in various forms by many American Indians tribes is puberty rites for girls at the time of first menstruation (Hultkrantz, 1980). These ceremonies are typically affairs of the extended family and the tribal community, and both young and old attend and participate. The puberty rite is a special celebration of the community that signifies the girl has become a woman. Perhaps the most well-known puberty rite is the Sunrise Ceremony practiced by the Apaches. During this ceremony the young woman is regarded as a representation of White Painted Woman, a Holy Woman of the Apaches (Gattuso, 1991). The young woman is thought to possess certain healing powers during the time of the ceremony. From participating in the rigors and demands of the four-day ceremony, the young woman acquires a greater sense of her own identity and purpose in connection with others in her community.

Non-Indian communities can learn much from such American Indian ceremonies as the Sunrise Ceremony, as well as American Indians' general integration of religion into all facets of life. At a time when adults are worried about the disinterest of adolescents in church and religion, something can be learned from how American Indian religions incorporate adolescents into the religious community through imparting meaning, purpose, and connection.

Major Points to Remember

1. A mature adolescent has individual, interpersonal, and social skills and competencies.
2. A general rule is that neuroticism declines and independence increases over the course of adolescence.
3. Character formation during adolescence helps to create the psychological structures of the adolescent. These ego structures are used in processing social information and assigning meaning to experience. Character formation occurs in stages, with potential plateaus.
4. Family communications that recognize self-expression and mutual sharing can facilitate adolescent's personality development, whereas controlling and inhibiting behaviors hinder development.
5. Adolescents' relationship with their grandparents may play an important role in promoting their personality growth. One possible way is through fostering fidelity and commitment to the past and providing a heritage on which to build for the future.

6. Moral development, as part of character formation, provides general rules for social and interpersonal behavior.

7. By facilitating cognitive development, we may be able to encourage growth in moral reasoning and behavior. In particular, group discussions, psychological development programs, and positive peer-culture experiences may be useful strategies.

8. A majority of adolescents and parents see religious training as important.

9. A focus on the centrality of religion, the liberation of religion, and person-to-person communication are associated with desirable individual and social outcomes for adolescents.

10. Stages of faith exist that are highly similar to ego and moral stages.

11. Parental behavior that involves clear explanations, expressed in an affectionate context, is likely to facilitate positive values transmission between parents and their children.

CHAPTER

9

Self-Concept and Self-Esteem

Much of adolescence is spent exploring psychological aspects of the self. Adolescents reflect often on their strengths, weaknesses, and fears and talk with others about these concerns. Strengths are reflected in confidence, self-certainty, and firm convictions. Weaknesses are observed in boisterous behaviors, withdrawal, or excessive self-centeredness.

The common unevenness in moods during adolescence may be a sign of this self-reflection. Long walks to "think," endless phone conversation with peers, and occasional confrontations with family members may merely be part of this self-analysis. All such behaviors are a natural part of development and are likely to reflect only temporary perturbations in relationships with others.

In this chapter we examine several lines of thinking regarding the self.

Theoretical Perspectives on Self-Development

The development of the self has its foundation in social development. As Damon (1983) remarks, however,

> Social development is a life process built upon a paradox (contradiction). The paradox is that at the same time we are *both* social and individual beings, connected with others in a multitude of ways, as well as ultimately alone in the world. This dual condition of connectedness and separateness begins at the moment of birth and remains with us all through life. (P. 1)

But what is thought of as a contradiction is in reality a complementary developmental association. *Connectedness* includes *integrating forces* that help to establish and maintain relations with others. *Separateness* evolves out of *individuation and differentiating forces*. We see connectedness to be an integrating force that encourages social identity. Separateness encourages personal (or ideological) identity. The two are complementary and needed forms of the self. It is difficult to conceive of people without considering the connection between their unique viewpoint and individual characteristics and their social roles and relationship with family, peers, and friends.

Recognizing that some scholars focus on individuality, connectedness, or both, we now examine three general theoretical frameworks that have been broadly used to explain self-development. The first is the pioneering perspective of William James, who divided the self into the *I* and the *me*. The second framework is social cognition, the examination of personal meaning in a social context. The third deals with the discrepancy in self-image between the real and the ideal self.

The Self and Self-Knowledge

Damon (1983) notes that one long-standing tradition in explaining the self is from the perspective of the individual's sense of self, or self-knowledge. Drawing on William James's pioneering distinction of the concepts of *me* and *I,* we can understand how self-knowledge is one fundamental form of social cognition. Likewise, we can see how the social and individual selves come to perform a complementary developmental function.

For James, the distinction between *me* and *I* was one of *self-as-known* versus *self as knower;* the *me* was what is to be known. The characteristics of this self-as-known included those of the *material* self (physical body, clothes), the *social* self (social behavior, reputation), and the *spiritual* or *psychological* self (beliefs, character). Such components of the self provided the substance for a response to questions such as "What are you like?" or "Who are you?"

The measurement of the self-as-known can be readily seen in the Offer Self-Image Questionnaire (Offer, Ostrov, & Howard, 1981). In this assessment adolescents are asked to respond to items measuring the degree to which various aspects of their psychological self (impulse control, emotional tone, body, and self-image), social self (social relationships, morals, vocational and educational goals), sexual self, familial self, and coping self (mastery of the external world, psychopathology, adjustment) reflect their own self-images. Individual scores are also compared with average scores derived from a large group to see if the person's self-as-known differs in social experience, clinical problems, or even cross-cultural comparisons (Olowu, 1983; Offer, Ostrov, Howard, & Atkinson, 1988; D. A. Rosenthal, Moore, & Taylor, 1983; S. M. Turner & Mo, 1984; Watanabe, 1985).

For example, Watanabe (1985) has assessed whether adolescents from military family backgrounds have a less advanced developmental self-image than comparable adolescents from nonmilitary families. This investigation revealed similar self-images for both groups, thus contradicting notions that the frequent moves and lack of stability of adolescents in military life are necessarily associated with poorer self-images and less knowledge about the self-as-known.

The self-as-knower, or the *I* in James's theory, is the "ego" in personality. The *I* organizes and interprets, construes, and creates the quality of personal experience. Thus, the *I* defines the meaningfulness of aspects of the *me*. Using the characteristics of the *me*, the self-as-knower provides interpretive power and inner understanding. The *I* selects aspects of the self that are important, provides the mechanism for uniqueness and individuality, and establishes a sense of personal identity based on a psychological equivalence of free will. In recent years, George Herbert Mead was a strong advocate of the *I* as the crucial aspect of self theory.

The concept of self-as-knower is illustrated in several contemporary theoretical perspectives. For example, Selman (1980) has identified three levels of developmental progression in understanding the self. In the youngest years of life no distinction is made between inner and outer life, and understanding is based on physical terms and what appears to be reality. In later childhood, children recognize differences between inner and outer states, and they begin to describe their "true self" in terms of more subjective inner states. But only in adolescence do youths become fully cognizant of their own self-awareness. The self-as-knower emerges in adolescence as an evolving entity that has gained increasing abilities to integrate the various disparate components of the *me* into an internally consistent self-conception (Damon, 1983).

This developmental progression of the self-as-knower is most clearly shown in a theoretical model outlined by Damon and Hart (1982). These developmentalists draw on the physical, active, social, and psychological aspects of the *I* and show how each is observable at different points in childhood and adolescence. They write that during infancy and early childhood bodily properties and material possessions are focal points for how individuals understand themselves. During middle childhood the self is defined in terms of capabilities viewed as relative to others. In early adolescence the focus of self-understanding is based on social-personality characteristics, while in late adolescence the focus is on belief systems, personal philosophy, and one's own thinking process. Only at the social- and psychological-self phases do adolescents come to recognize that the self can actively initiate and modify conscious experience and that both conscious and unconscious psychological processes are part of the makeup of an individual's self.

Social Cognition and Development of Self

One of the best-established lines of theorizing about the self is based on George Herbert Mead's (1934) philosophical thoughts on people's capacity to learn language and, through this process, learn to regard themselves from the perspective of others. This line of theory is commonly referred to as *symbolic interactionism*. According to Mead, speakers must learn to choose their words to communicate with meaning. Therefore, they must select words that are based first on the role of being a listener before speaking. Through a process of role or perspective taking, they consider the listener before speaking; thus, reality is provided by others through socially accepted meanings and perceptions of reality that are intertwined with their own perceptions and the anticipated reactions of others.

In Mead's symbolic interactionism, self-reflection is a social construction that involves reflecting on the self through the perspective of others. Like James's modern disciples, Mead has proposed several sequential stages in the evolution of self-reflection. Each stage provides a social-cognitive process that is typified by a social activity with a particular social-linguistic underpinning. These stages include a *play* stage characterized in the early years by a child's play at reciprocal roles. The *game* stage of childhood is marked by children's extensive involvement in organized activities based on rules. The structure of game behavior requires children to see the perspective of all those involved. An important implication is that they come to establish a sense of the *generalized other;* they move from seeing the self simply from an individual perspective to seeing the broader, organized perspective of the social group. The overall developmental task implied by symbolic-interaction theory is the goal of evolving a definite, organized self. Through play and game experiences children ultimately form a self-view that transcends the immediate perspective and includes others and their perspectives. (See Margolin, Blyth, & Carbone (1988) for an illustrative study from a symbolic interaction perspective.)

More contemporary examples of a social-cognitive perspective on self-development include the role-taking approach of Robert Selman (1980), the structural developmentalism of Beilin (1992), and other scholarly views on the orthogenetic developmental perspective (see Damon, 1983). Likewise, Leahy and Shirk (1985) summarize evidence to suggest that role-taking ability and peer interaction offer the necessary socialization processes that provide the foundation for thinking of the self in accepted ways based on consensual validation (mutual agreements), morals, and interpersonal perspectives.

In conclusion, the social-cognitive perspective blends the notions that (1) understanding of the self is associated with maturing cognitive structures and (2) such cognitive processes are based on self-reflection within a broader social context.

Real Self versus Ideal Self

Another perspective on self-development includes work on the real self versus the ideal self. It began with the seminal clinical-based theoretical work of Carl Rogers and his colleagues (for example, Rogers & Dymond, 1954) on the notion of *self-image disparity*. This disparity refers to the difference between an individual's assessment of self ("the real me") and the ideal self that the person aspires to be. Individual and social factors are thought to either enhance or interfere with a sense of positive self-regard. High congruence between what is and what is aspired for is an indication of positive self-regard and personal adjustment. High self-image disparity is thought to be predictive of poor social and personal adjustment and the use of denial and distortions as defense mechanisms to deal with the disparity.

An alternative view to this basically nondevelopmental perspective has been proposed by Achenbach and Zigler (1963). Drawing on a cognitive-developmental perspective, these scholars argue that increasing self-disparity is the natural outcome of normal growth and development to maturity. More specifically, they contend that as an individual matures, greater degrees of cognitive differentiation (higher levels of thinking) result in a greater likelihood of disparity. Furthermore, with increasing emotional maturity the person is thought to have a greater capacity to experience guilt as he or she comes to understand and incorporate more of the social demands, mores, and values of society. Therefore, psychological maturity should be reflected in a greater disparity between the broader ideal self-image and the reality of human faults and failures found in the real self. Thus, more cognitively advanced and also more emotionally mature people should experience greater self-image disparity than less developed individuals. But this disparity should not be seen as a sign of maladjustment.

An adolescent's sense of self may be represented in his or her clothing or dress.

More recently, Glick and Ziegler (1985) have analyzed these two competing theoretical views on self-image disparity. Comparisons of psychiatric and nonpsychiatric populations, groups with high and low social competency, neurotic and nonneurotic people, institutionalized and noninstitutionalized youths, and retarded and normal children have been analyzed. The data strongly indicate that (1) disparity in self-image is found more in older than in younger individuals, (2) self-image disparity is greater for more cognitively and socially mature individuals, (3) self-image disparity is not directly predictive of signs of maladjustment, and (4) self-image disparity is associated with greater self-demands and experience of guilt.

Conclusion

These three commonly used theoretical perspectives are but a few of the many approaches available for understanding adolescent self-concept. The notion of self-as-knower and self-as-known gives us insight into how the content and process of understanding the self, through distinctions regarding the *me* and *I,* are delineated. The social-cognitive perspective provides us with detail regarding cognitive development and the social context in which it occurs and helps us understand how the individual comes to conceptualize the self. Finally, the theory of self-image disparity helps us realize that distinctions between the real and the ideal self can be useful in understanding maladjustment. Indeed, we can speculate, in contrast to Rogers's earlier notions, that congruence between the real and the ideal self may be a reflection of less advanced and immature psychological self-development.

Let us turn next to the broader context of defining a healthy personality or self. It is from this next perspective that we can best appreciate what may be unhealthy or maladjusted from a self-development perspective. We shall draw on the long-established theoretical and research perspective of Morris Rosenberg and his colleagues (Rosenberg, 1979, 1985; Rosenberg & Kaplan, 1982).

Self-Concept and Psychological Well-Being

In all of the general theories of self-concept as applied to adolescent development, the general notion is that a higher or more advanced self-concept is associated with more positive psychological well-being. Psychological well-being is thought to include such diverse components as a sense of worth, confidence in oneself, perceived ability to perform well, self-efficacy, psychological comfort, and feeling good about one's self. If you are interested in extensive elaboration on this issue, you might turn to the *Social Psychology of the Self-Concept* (Rosenberg & Kaplan, 1982) or *Conceiving the Self* (Rosenberg, 1979) for further reading.

We can begin our analysis by asking what the central aspects of self-concept are and what evidence exists to support the assumption that a higher self-concept is associated with more positive psychological well-being. More recently, Rosenberg (1985) delineated the major characteristics of a good self-concept and, drawing on three large-scale studies of adolescents, has assessed the association between self-concept and psychological well-being. We briefly summarize his efforts and augment his conclusions with evidence from several smaller studies.

Rosenberg (1985) argues that a good self-concept includes a high self-esteem, feelings of "mattering," stability in self-concept, low vulnerability, a sense of personal control, low levels of public anxiety, and what he refers to as a "harmonious plane coordination." Drawing on the Youth in Transition Study, a sample of 2213 tenth-grade boys; the New York State Study, which includes 1678 boys and girls who were juniors and seniors in ten high schools; and the Baltimore City Study, involving 1155 students who were 12 years or older, Rosenberg assessed the degree to which each of the proposed aspects of a good self-concept is predictive of psychological well-being. We summarize many of the central conclusions about aspects of self-concept.

Self-Esteem

Self-esteem is recognized as a powerful motivational force. It is thought to be based on a human need to be valued or to hold a positive self-evaluation. It does *not* mean feelings of superiority, feelings of perfection, feelings of competence or efficacy. It refers, instead, to a sense of *self-acceptance,* a *personal liking* for one's self, and a form of proper *respect* for oneself.

Rosenberg reports data suggesting a moderate association between low self-esteem and dysphoric measures of psychological well-being. Dysphoria refers to hostility, embitterment, disenchantment, or other negative emotional states. Its opposite, euphoria, refers to positive emotional states and a sense of psychological comfort. In the three studies under consideration low self-esteem was observed to be associated with a greater likelihood of depression, lower reported happiness, more negative emotional states, greater anxiety, irritability, aggressiveness, impulsivity, and anomie (alienation). In contrast, high self-esteem was associated with a sense of command over one's life, willingness to take moderate risks, candidness, and feelings of life satisfaction. As Gecas (1982) reports, adolescents with high self-esteem are likely to be both happier and more effective human beings.

Savin-Williams and Demo (1983) suggest that adolescent self-esteem is not a single but a multifaceted phenomenon. They suggest that a *presented self* is that aspect of the person that is verbally and nonverbally revealed to others. The *experienced self* is the self as evaluated by the person. *Self-feelings* involve positive and negative emotions reported at any given moment. Examining a longitudinal data set, these human developmentalists conclude that the presented self is relatively stable during middle adolescence (ninth and tenth grades); that the experienced self is slightly less stable than the presented self; and that self-feelings are the least stable of the components of self-esteem. Nonetheless, even when self-esteem is subdivided into various types, it is a highly stable construct during adolescence.

However, numerous investigators report that the transition from elementary to junior high school is associated with changes in self-esteem (for example, Wigfield, Eccles, MacIver, Reuman, & Midgley, 1991) and that repeated school transitions are even more debilitating (Crocket, Petersen, Graber, Schulenberg, & Ebata, 1989). Likewise, adolescents may report differences in self-esteem due to community factors. For example, one investigation shows that adolescents' self-esteem is linked to parental education in rural communities (Sarigiani, Wilson, Petersen, & Vicary, 1990).

Because a variety of social conditions influence emotional states and feelings of self-worth, we might expect differences in sensations of self-esteem under different adolescent life conditions. For example, although some evidence (M. Rosenberg, 1965) suggests that coming from a less-valued social class or racial group is associated with lower self-esteem, comparisons of youths of different races but similar socioeconomic backgrounds have shown few differences in self-esteem (see, for example, Louden, 1980). Surprisingly, in various ethnic-group comparisons, girls appear to have lower levels of self-esteem than boys (Louden, 1980). Additional evidence (Offer, Ostrov, & Howard, 1977) suggests that boys have healthier self-perceptions than girls in four cultures (the United States, Israel, Ireland, and Australia). Although girls report having a more positive moral self-image, boys report healthier states of impulse control and sexual attitudes and behaviors. Given that impulse control and sexual behavior become central issues during the onset of pubescence, boys may maintain higher self-esteem because of their self-perceived ability to maintain control over sexual sensations.

It has been generally assumed by several theorists (for example, E. H. Erikson, 1968; S. Freud, 1969; B. McCandless, 1970) that the importance of self-concept and self-esteem is associated with the upheavals of the onset of pubescence and physiological changes in the reproductive system. Although there are some exceptions (for example, Dusek, 1978), several longitudinal studies have documented that self-concept and self-esteem change during adolescence. For example, in a comparison of the responses of boys and girls in grades 6 and 12 (Engel, 1959), self-esteem was generally stable, but boys became more personally oriented while girls became more socially oriented in their self-perceptions. A later study (R. G. Simmons, Rosenberg, & Rosenberg, 1973) found that early adolescents have poorer self-images and thus much lower self-esteem than older adolescents. Finally, in a longitudinal comparison of Black and White male and female adolescents (Gray-Little & Appelbaum, 1979), self-concept but not self-esteem was subject to developmental change. As in the previous study, as the subjects moved from childhood into early adolescence, there was a small but significant decline in positive self-concept.

These studies show that several sex-related differences can be expected in adolescents' self-esteem and that during early adolescence self-esteem is likely to decline for both boys and girls. For example, Roberts, Sarigiani, Petersen, and Newman (1990), in a longitudinal study, found self-image and achievement decline for girls but increase for boys from the sixth to seventh grade, with girls manifesting increases from seventh to eighth grade and boys showing stability. However, these declines in self-esteem are transitional factors that diminish in later adolescence and young adulthood. The declines are probably associated with the onset of puberty and major hormonal and physiological changes, although this conclusion is still speculative and needs further confirmation through longitudinal data. (For an interesting ethnographic study on the social construction of ability perceptions see Kramer, 1991.) High self-esteem has been found to be predictive of a multitude of important personality characteristics and social behaviors. For example, positive self-images are associated with positive mental-health indexes (Hauser, 1976), more mature intimacy skills, a sense of initiative, and acceptance of ethnic identity or heritage (Paul & Fischer, 1980).

Kahle, Kulka, and Klingel (1980) have argued that two theoretically plausible hypotheses might exist for predicting such relationships between self-esteem and interpersonal behaviors. From a *social-adaptation perspective,* it might be argued

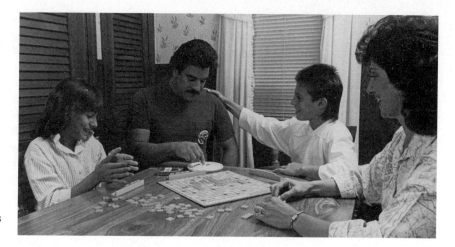

Positive social relationships within families encourages young people's self-esteem.

that self-esteem shapes the behaviors. However, from a *self-perception orientation,* it could be argued that the behaviors will determine self-esteem. Using a cross-lagged correlational technique, these investigators measured both self-esteem and interpersonal problems at two different times. Their data analysis demonstrated that low self-esteem was predictive of interpersonal problems, not that interpersonal problems created lower self-esteem. When working with adolescents, we must remember that just because a youth has a history of interpersonal problems he or she does not necessarily have a poor self-concept or lowered self-esteem. However, if that adolescent has a poor self-concept, it is very likely that he or she is or will be experiencing interpersonal problems. It would require an entire textbook to review all the determinants of self-esteem, but we briefly examine here some of the research on factors determining the level of self-esteem in children and adolescents. The very foundation of self-esteem appears to emerge in the family itself. Numerous studies have shown that high self-esteem among adolescents is associated with positive perceptions of and interactions with parents (see, for example, O'Donnell, 1976; Isberg, Hauser, Jacobson, Powers, Noam, Weiss-Perry, & Follansbee, 1989; Hoffman, Ushpiz, & Levyy-Shiff, 1988; Bartle, Anderson, & Sabatelli, 1989). Parental interest in the child's welfare also appears to be a primary factor in adolescent self-esteem. In a study of high school students (M. Rosenberg, 1963), lack of interest by their parents, measured by low interest in their friends, in report cards, and in engaging them in dinner conversations, was predictive of very low self-esteem.

Other data indicate that living in an environment in which the individual is associated with an outgroup or possesses some characteristic or trait that is devalued also diminishes self-esteem among adolescents (M. Rosenberg, 1975). An excellent illustration of this "dissonant context" principle can be found in a study comparing the self-esteem scores of Catholics, Protestants, and Jews who lived in neighborhoods that were predominantly of their own faith with the scores of those who did not (M. Rosenberg, 1962). The data indicate that living in a neighborhood not of one's own faith has a detrimental effect on self-esteem. Catholics living in Protestant neighborhoods had lower self-esteem than Catholics living in Catholic neighborhoods, and so forth.

Still other studies have demonstrated that school setting can have strong effects on self-esteem. Evidence indicates that the discontinuity of moving from the sixth grade to seventh grade in a new school has detrimental effects on self-esteem (Blyth, Simmons, & Bush, 1978). In contrast, girls who stayed in the same school from kindergarten through eighth grade show no detrimental effects. Other possibilities are that preadolescents who are not coping well in the elementary school (for example, are unpopular, have poor perceptions of their appearance) are inclined to do even less well in a new junior high school. Because they have to cope with a new environment, new friends, new teachers, and a new school program, these children are vulnerable to increasing damage to their self-esteem.

Although situational and schooling factors clearly may influence self-esteem in adolescents, another study suggests that the implications of academic success for self-esteem are carried over from adolescence into young adulthood. Bachman and O'Malley (1977) conducted a longitudinal investigation that identified some determinants of self-esteem as well as followed their effects on self-esteem into young adulthood. Using a complex statistical tool called path analysis, these investigators found that socioeconomic background had a strong effect on academic ability; that is, youths who came from higher socioeconomic groups had higher academic ability. This factor did not directly determine academic performance, but high academic ability and performance were both predictors of high self-esteem during high school. Thus, students who do well in school appear to have high self-esteem. High self-esteem during high school had two important effects on self-esteem in young adulthood. First, it was directly predictive of high self-esteem in adulthood. Second, it had a direct effect on further educational accomplishment and on occupational status, which in turn were predictive of self-esteem in adulthood. Thus, school-related and socioeconomic factors can contribute to self-esteem, and self-esteem during high school has an important effect on educational attainment and job success—and, consequently, self-esteem—during adulthood.

There are still other causes for individual differences in self-esteem among adolescents. A partial list includes the following:

1. Lesser ego development and more physical illness during adolescence are likely to be correlated with lower self-esteem (Jacobson, Hauser, Powers, & Noam, 1984).

2. Social talents or status values among peers consistent with traditional feminine gender-role stereotypes for girls are correlated with higher self-esteem (Hollinger & Fleming, 1985).

3. Androgynous and masculine characteristics, independent of social context, are correlated with higher self-esteem for boys and girls (Rust & McGraw, 1984; Ziegler, Dusek, & Carter, 1984).

4. Extreme or excessive pressure by parents on the adolescent to succeed in school are associated with lower self-esteem (Eskilson, Wiley, Muehlbauer, & Doder, 1986).

Indeed, some data suggest that students can lower their interest or commitment in academic performance when their own status is threatened, to defend against the loss of self-esteem (Faunce, 1984). Likewise, various studies suggest that adolescents who accept a deviant or negative identity and perceive that society in general also views that role as undesirable are likely to have low self-esteem (Chassin & Stager, 1984; Stager, Chassin, & Young, 1983). (See also Box 9–1.)

Many scholars who study the socialization of children and adolescents assume that parents have a broad influence on their offspring's self-esteem. While it would be impossible to review all of the studies on this issue, we can illustrate several recent findings of interest. First, we must indicate that our brief review does not include the substantial and complex issue of ethnic identity or heritage as a mediator of any conclusions that can be drawn. Studies such as that by B. Grossman, Wirt, and Davids (1985) show that ethnic identity and group differences based on such heritage can result in substantially different conclusions.

The quality of adolescents' relationships with both family *and* peers is associated with their self-esteem levels. Positive communication with both parents has a positive association with sons' and daughters' self-esteem (L. S. Walker & Greene, 1986). Further, but for girls only, positive peer relationships were also reported by Walker and Greene (1986) as predictive of higher self-esteem. Overall, while athletic ability and school performance can be predictive of reported self-esteem, Walker and Greene found that self-evaluation of popularity was the most important predictor of girls' overall self-esteem. Likewise, Litovsky and Dusek (1985) report that adolescents with high self-esteem perceive their parents as more accepting, as using less psychological control, and as being only moderately strict in enforcing rules. Indeed, other evidence suggests that family cohesion is positively correlated with adolescents' self-esteem and conflict is negatively correlated (Cheung & Lau, 1985). Indeed, these findings are of considerable interest when examined in the context of parental discord and family structure.

Long (1986) has examined the effects of divorce and other parental discord on the self-esteem of daughters. The separation of parents had no significant effect on their adolescent daughters' self-esteem. However, daughters living in an unhappy but intact household showed substantially lower self-esteem. Divorce had a lesser effect than living in an intact but unhappy home. Therefore, we might conclude from this and other studies that cohesion in the family, parental acceptance of the adolescent, and moderate restrictiveness by parents enhance self-esteem. Conflict and discord may decrease self-esteem through interpersonal stress, fear, continual uncertainty about confrontation, and negative emotional experiences in the household.

An important emerging line of research on the question of parental effects on adolescents' self-esteem is found in investigations of the predictive utility of one socialization theory versus another. For example, recent research has compared the predictive usefulness of symbolic interaction and social-learning theories for understanding adolescent self-esteem (Openshaw, Thomas, & Rollins, 1984). Symbolic-interaction theory posits that an adolescent's self-esteem is based on a parent's reflected appraisal of the youth's worth. Social-learning theory holds that self-esteem is based on the internalization of a parent's role-modeled level of self-esteem. Using self-report data from 184 families, these researchers found that a parent's reflected appraisal was stronger than role-modeled self-esteem in predicting the adolescent's self-esteem. However, the parent's self-evaluations also made an additional but less strong contribution to the prediction. Therefore, both theories provide some predictive usefulness in understanding adolescent self-esteem. Hence, Openshaw and his colleagues suggest that a theory integrating aspects of

---

Box 9–1 Effects of Puberty on Self-Esteem and Body Image

Roberta Simmons and Dale Blyth (1987) have summarized a major study of transition into adolescence. Because of pubertal changes in early adolescence, this substage has been thought by many to be a period of risk for psychological stress. Impaired self-esteem, increased self-consciousness, instability of self-image, and greater depression have been hypothesized. For girls, however, the timing of pubertal development was not found to predict such psychological risks. Likewise, developmental timing had only a few, very specific effects on boys' social-psychological reactions in early adolescence. We recommend *Moving into Adolescence: The Impact of Pubertal Change and School Context* if you are seeking a careful comparison of competing hypotheses about self-esteem and body image.

---

both social-learning and symbolic-interaction theory should be construed to predict adolescent self-esteem and its development through parent/adolescent socialization. (See Box 9–2.)

Mattering

In contrast to self-esteem, the concept of mattering has been given little attention. It refers to the degree to which a person feels that he or she counts or makes a difference. Rosenberg (1985) identifies two types: *Societal mattering* involves feelings of making a difference in the broader sociopolitical events of society. *Interpersonal mattering* refers to whether one has an impact on specific significant others. Rosenberg argues that the essential ingredient of interpersonal mattering is feeling that one is the object of another person's attention or notice. Corollaries of mattering include feeling missed if absent, being of concern to others, feeling as if one is someone else's ego extension, and feeling that others depend on one.

What little research is available on this important topic suggests that adolescents who perceive that they matter very little to others are highly depressed, unhappy, and report a wide variety of other negative emotional states. Furthermore, they are prone to considerable tension and general anxiety. Likewise, they express various feelings of hostility, bitterness, and alienation. Such adolescents see themselves as unimportant, unnoticed, peripheral, and irrelevant to others. In Rosenberg's terms, they are dysphoric.

Stability of Self-Concept

A stable self-concept is believed to provide a consistent frame of reference from which to behave or act. It promotes certainty and decisiveness. M. Rosenberg (1985) notes that there is considerable reason to conclude that a shifting or volatile self-concept creates a doubt about the self that is likely to be associated with dysphoria.

Findings from the three large longitudinal studies mentioned earlier suggest that instability is associated more with general anxiety than with depression. Perhaps a better conclusion is that instability creates a volatile self-concept (Markus & Kunda, 1986) that is associated with uneasiness, uncertainty, and psychological discomfort. Early adolescents, in particular, may be at substantial risk when body changes are most pronounced and self-concept is least stable.

Box 9–2   Improving Self-Esteem Among Adolescents

There is a general belief that adolescence is a period of considerable difficulty in establishing self-esteem. Although research data do not fully substantiate this widely held assumption, it is certainly true that some adolescents have lower self-esteem than is desirable for their psychological well-being. What might we do to help raise their self-appraisals? We can suggest the following ideas from several recent research studies:

1. Self-esteem has been proposed to be related to such factors as ability, health, peer-group formation, frustration, relaxation, variety of experience, and self-knowledge. One recent experimental study suggests, however, that self-esteem is primarily improved by participation in community and school experiences. It appears that positive peer-group formation and variety of successful experiences through participation enhance an adolescent's self-esteem (Brennan, 1985).

2. How one thinks can make a difference in how one feels. Recent experimental studies indicate that having students recall positive thoughts and feelings about past events results in elevation of their self-esteem (Anderson & Williams, 1985). Therefore, encouraging adolescents to blend positive social responses with recollections of events can improve self-esteem.

3. Self-esteem is clearly influenced by social relationships. Recent evidence indicates that it may be affected by anticipated loss of a rewarding relationship. Further, that loss of self-esteem, within a social context, can cause anxiety and anger. States of anxiety but not necessarily anger can be due to both loss of esteem and loss of relationship rewards (Mathes, Adams, & Davies, 1985). Therefore, adolescents should be helped to determine whether states of anxiety are caused by a loss of esteem or a loss of a rewarding relationship.

4. Many teenage girls experience low self-esteem because of low assertiveness. Recent assertiveness-training studies indicate that training can enhance self-esteem (Stake, DeVille, & Pennell, 1983). This effect may be due to improved perceptions of one's confidence, abilities, or self-efficacy.

Locus of Control

Another important component of self-concept is the individual's expectations about internal versus external control. Albert Bandura (1977) refers to this element as self-efficacy, and deCharm (1968), as personal causation. Regardless of the differences in definitions by scholars, locus of control refers to whether people believe that outcomes are caused by their personal actions. Rosenberg's (1985) summary of the three large-scale studies indicates that locus of control increases steadily during adolescence. Further, a low sense of locus of control is associated with anxiety, impulsivity, irritability, resentment, alienation, depressive states, and low self-esteem. Thus, lower states of internalized personal control result in dysphoric outcomes in psychological well-being.

Scarr, Weinberg, and Levine (1986) elaborate on the connection between locus of control and self-esteem. Many studies demonstrate that youth who do well in school attribute their academic success to their ability. Failure is attributed to a lack of effort. In general, these adolescents assume they will succeed if they try harder. As such, these youths have a sense of internal locus of control where they believe they are in control of what happens to themselves. Unfortunately, other students believe that failure is due to factors other than themselves. They believe in external forces influencing their success or failure. This is external locus of control. Adolescents with internal locus of control are thought to hold higher self-esteem due to their self-directed efforts. Youths with external locus of control are thought to hold lower self-esteem and to be readily influenced by repeated failure. For further reading on the role of confidence, motivation, and academic achievement among adolescents we refer you to a chapter by Henderson and Dweck (1990).

Vulnerability

Self-concept also includes an individual's degree of sensitivity to critical or negative comments from others. Hypersensitivity, touchiness, and the like are characteristic of a vulnerable adolescent. As Rosenberg (1985) comments, "the hypersensitive person might be described as one with a 'psychological sunburn'; the most delicate touch generates the most acute anguish" (p. 228). As such, a vulnerable adolescent is most sensitive when his or her self-esteem is threatened. Derogation, criticism, scorn, or belittlement can become perilous experiences for the hypersensitive adolescent. But internal threats can also be critical. Inappropriate conduct, lack of self-control, reckless remarks toward others, or poor judgment can cause shame, remorse, or guilt. These negative emotional states can result in equally powerful internal threats to one's self-esteem and corresponding vulnerability.

The little evidence that is available indicates that when we focus on adolescents' sensitivity to criticism as a measure of vulnerability, we find it is negatively related to global self-esteem, but positively related to anxiety and depression (M. Rosenberg, 1985). Therefore, overly sensitive or vulnerable adolescents are easily influenced by threats to their self-esteem. The outcome is depression and anxiety. Further, younger adolescents appear to be somewhat more vulnerable than older ones, with girls about twice as vulnerable as boys. Collectively, these findings suggest that vulnerability heightens and accentuates the dysphoric consequences of low self-esteem. And the effects of vulnerability may be most pronounced during early adolescence.

Self-Consciousness

Duval and Wicklund (1972) were responsible, in particular, for bringing attention to the issue of self-awareness, including the notions of *objective* and *subjective* self-awareness. Self-awareness refers to the degree to which attention on the self is sharp, clear, and obvious. Objective self-awareness focuses on the self to the general exclusion of others, and subjective self-awareness focuses primarily on others with little focus on the self. The emotional state that accompanies self-awareness is usually described as self-consciousness.

Two major camps can be found in social science regarding the implications of self-consciousness. One group suggests that self-awareness is an important positive aspect of good mental health. The other group suggests that low self-awareness and corresponding self-consciousness are ideal; that is, healthy people have low self-consciousness.

Self-consciousness has been shown to be expressed in two general forms. One form involves *public anxiety* in social contexts. Another form involves *preoccupation with the self*. In Rosenberg's (1985) review of the three large studies with adolescent samples, he found that adolescents who were highly preoccupied with themselves were more likely to be anxious or depressed. Similar conclusions were observed for public anxiety as well. Further, we once again find that early adolescents are most likely to be vulnerable to higher states of self-consciousness (see also Hauck, Martens, & Wetzel, 1986). Thus, they are at greater risk for dysphoric mental states of anxiety and depression.

Plane Coordination

Self-concept is an enormously complex phenomenon, with many planes, or levels. We could speak of the plane of reality, the plane of possibility, the plane of self-representation, and so forth. Rosenberg (1985) maintains that the management of the various planes is a central issue in understanding self-concept. For the healthy adolescent, he proposes, there should be a harmony between what the adolescent really is as a person in the eyes of others, how accurately the adolescent sees his or her own characteristics, and the consistency with which the self is presented to others. A false front or facade, with the presenting self different from the experienced self, is thought to be unhealthy.

As we discussed earlier, the debate continues over whether self-image disparity is a developmental issue or one that reflects mental-health problems (Achenbach & Ziegler, 1963; Glick & Ziegler, 1985). Nonetheless, Rosenberg does review literature suggesting that adolescence is associated with greater problems in plane coordination between presented and experienced selves. The broader implications of these findings for understanding self-concept and psychological well-being are yet to be fully understood.

Self-Concept and Self-Esteem: Minority Issues

It is commonly assumed that differences between White and ethnic minority groups in such things as academic success, drug use, or criminal behavior is linked to issues of self-esteem or self-concept. However, the research literature on self-concept, self-esteem, and other constructs of the self is fraught with a host of methodological problems. Consequently, there is often inconsistency in findings between studies comparing ethnic groups, thereby making it difficult to form general conclusions. For example, Powell (1984a, 1984b, 1985) notes that research on self-concept among African-American children falls into three categories: (a) no differences in self-concept between African-American and White children; (b) African-American children have more positive self-concepts than do White children; and (c) African-American children with lower self-concepts are in desegregated schools, rather than integrated schools. Therefore, in conducting research on self-concept and self-esteem among minorities, it is important to be cognizant of the multiple methodological pitfalls widely noted in the research literature (for example, Markstrom-Adams, 1991; Powell, 1985; Spencer & Markstrom-Adams, 1990). In the following section, three potential methodological shortcomings on self-concept and self-esteem research among minorities are identified and discussed.

Selection and Operationalization of the Research Construct

Aspects of the *self,* identified for measurement purposes, should be relevant to the group under investigation. Furthermore, these selected constructs should be defined so as to allow fair assessments of minority self-concept and self-esteem. Drawing a distinction between private versus public components of self-esteem is an example of fair assessment. For example, lower self-esteem among minorities is linked to racist public domain institutions, such as school and work (Martinez & Dukes, 1991). In contrast, assessment of self-esteem in the private domain should be associated with higher self-esteem among minorities. The reason for these findings is that in public domains, racist attitudes of the dominant society prevail. A minority individual who examines the self according to such (racist/public) standards is likely to experience a lower level of self-esteem. In contrast, in the private domain, self-judgments are made according to the standards of one's own minority group. Hence, higher self-esteem is likely. Acknowledging differences in public and private domains allows for recognition of the dual socialization processes experienced by many minority groups. When one's self-esteem is defined according to socialization processes offered by his or her minority culture, there is higher external validity in the research.

For further clarification of this point, it is useful to examine a distinction between the role of cultural factors and the role of environment in self-concept (Iheanacho, 1988). The basic premise given by Iheanacho (1988) is that even though environment influences self-concept, culture does not. Cultural factors do not cause poor self-concept. That is, it is erroneous to assume that positive self-concept does not exist among those who do not belong to the White culture. Every culture has its own forms of richness and provides definitions of what constitutes healthy self-concept. Thus, when studying constructs of self-concept, self-esteem, and self-perception, individuals should be assessed according to their own cultural orientation. For example, to compare a low-income Black adolescent to a middle-class White adolescent is not only methodologically flawed, but it is also unfair. These youths' social, economic, political, and historical worlds differ dramatically and are not directly comparable.

Environmental factors, in contrast, can and do contribute to poor self-concept. For example, ethnic and racial prejudice and discrimination are unfortunate destructive realities in racial relations. Minorities who are stereotyped according to mainstream society's standards are erroneously judged according to their group membership. The harm occurs when the minority individual accepts and internalizes such statements. However, there is ample evidence to suggest that when minority individuals define themselves according to their own group's standards and reflect on the self from the perspective of same-group significant others, self-concept and self-esteem are high.

Differential Subject Selection

To maintain internal validity in minority research, it is important to take great care in defining the sample and in identifying comparison samples. The necessity of between-group comparisons and, sometimes within-group comparisons, illustrate this point. It is usually inappropriate to select subjects merely according to their minority status without distinguishing specific ethnic and racial group affiliations. All minority individuals are not the same, and between-minority group differences should be recognized. Furthermore, within-minority group differences also may exist and should be controlled. For example, in the United States, there are more than 300 Indian tribes, and they can differ greatly one from the other. Thus, it would often be appropriate to select subjects carefully according to specific tribal membership, as opposed to a general American Indian ethnicity.

Careful delineation of the sample and comparison samples requires that potential research confounds or extraneous factors be exposed. Two potential confounds in studies on self-esteem and self-concept are socioeconomic status (SES) and gender. For instance, if a minority group is compared to another group (either White or another minority group) and SES differences exist between groups, the interpretation of research findings would be confounded. Specifically, it would be difficult to determine if the between-group differences are attributable to SES differences or other factors. Thus, researchers should carefully determine the SES of subjects to ensure equivalency or in some other way make comparisons that take SES differences into account.

Gender also should be taken into account when examining self-concept and self-esteem among minorities. Because gender and ethnicity both influence attitudes toward the self, it makes sense to investigate their joint effects (Martinez & Dukes, 1991). For example, research findings support the view that low self-esteem is related to institutionalized racism and sexism (Martinez & Dukes, 1991). Thus, minority women are at greatest risk for the development of poor self-perceptions *if* they accept the dominant society's definitions of their group.

Data Collection Procedures

There are many potential flaws of data collection that can distort research findings on self-concept and self-esteem among minorities. Language barriers are a major consideration in this respect. For example, if researchers administer assessments in English when it is not the primary language of the research subjects, respondents' answers may be invalid due to communication barriers. This issue effects many North American Indian, Hispanic, and Asian adolescents. If items are not clearly understood because of language barriers, minority adolescents may score in a less desirable direction in self-concept and self-esteem. Thus, research findings are misinterpreted, and, in some cases, the minority group is reflected in an erroneous and negative light.

A related problem occurs when self-concept and self-esteem measures designed for and normed on middle-class White populations are administered to minority adolescents. Such instruments are not fair assessments of minority adolescents because they are culturally sensitive only to the White middle-class society.

Researchers, themselves, also may introduce bias in administering and scoring instrumentation. This can be particularly problematic when a White researcher must make subjective decisions concerning subjects' feelings about themselves. Ideally, when subjective judgments are to be made in scoring instruments, those making the judgments should be of the same gender, and ethnic or racial background, of the subjects.

Summary

The prevalence of methodological inconsistencies and pitfalls in research on self-concept and self-esteem among minority adolescents has yielded literature that is inconsistent and biased. Sensitivity to cultural differences and assessing groups according to the standards of their own cultures are steps to take in accurately assessing the self-perceptions of minority adolescents. (Also, see Box 9–3 for material on issues of oppression and resistance.)

Box 9–3   A Model of Resistance for Liberation for African-American Females

Robinson and Ward (1991) identify two major strategies African-American girls and women adopt in their resistance to the realities of an oppressive, demeaning, and judgmental sociopolitical environment. "Resistance for survival" is oriented toward quick fixes that offer short-term solutions to such problems as unplanned pregnancies and substance abuse. Such transient solutions are counterproductive to the development of self-confidence, high self-esteem, and positive identity formation.

In contrast, "resistance for liberation" offers solutions that serve to empower African-American female adolescents through confirmation of positive self-conceptions, as well as strengthening connections to the broader African-American community. The adolescent is encouraged to think critically about herself and her place in the world around her. The following seven principles based on traditional African philosophies are offered as strategies in "resistance for liberation":

Unity
In contrast to isolation and disconnectedness, resistance for liberation/empowerment means unity and connection with the larger African-American people. Such unity transcends demographic parameters of age, SES, geographic origin, and so on. Affiliation with the broader African community is an essential ingredient in positive self-conceptions.

Self-determination
Oppressive definitions of oneself and one's group are confronted and repudiated. For example, the most common portrayal of the African-American female adolescent is of the sexually irresponsible, welfare recipient teen mother. Such a distorted image is one-sided and does not take sociopolitical and economic constraints into account. Images portraying the many admirable traits of African-American girls and women

are frequently disregarded. In contrast, resistance for liberation means "the ability to move beyond the internalization of racial denigration to an internalization of racial pride" (Robinson & Ward, 1991, p. 91).

Collective work and responsibility
A message that African-American adolescents hear from the broader society is that success (based on White, middle-class standards) requires disentanglement from racial allegiances. In resisting this ideology, excessive individualism and autonomy originating in the Eurocentered view must be disclaimed, and an orientation toward connection adopted. The notion of collective interdependence is incorporated in the self-concept of the African-American female adolescent. Although individual achievement is still highly regarded, such efforts are linked to a common destiny of the African-American community.

Cooperative Economics
A highly individualistic orientation is illustrative of the competitive, capitalistic Western society. This ideology is consistent with "resistance for survival" that is oriented toward short-term solutions that meet the immediate economic needs of the self. In contrast, an orientation toward the collective incorporates cooperative economics, economic interdependence, and sharing of resources. The "I" and "we" converge, and notions of "mine" and "yours" are minimized.

Purpose
As a contrast to meaninglessness, purpose in life promotes the interests of both the individual and the collective. There is a resistance to immediate, quick fixes, and an orientation toward delayed gratification to serve long-term commitments. Individual efforts toward achievement and success are given meaning as they are defined in the context of the community.

Conclusion

Self-concept is a multifaceted psychological construct, reflecting the essential ingredients of individuality within society. As a construct it includes both conscious and unconscious components. Furthermore, it clearly has strong implications for motivation, self-esteem, and psychological well-being. High self-esteem, a sense of mattering, low vulnerability, high belief in personal control, reasonable stability, modest self-consciousness, and good harmony between the presented and the extant self are thought to be the most healthy for an adolescent's psychological

---

Box 9–3   A Model of Resistance for Liberation for African-American Females (continued)

Creativity

In implementing creative strategies, the status quo is challenged. Many existing models of understanding are irrelevant and support, at best, "resistance for survival." Creativity is directed toward building new paradigms of understanding that take into account the needs of the larger African community. Dialogue and interconnection are critical in channeling creative abilities to resolving real issues and problems.

Faith

In "resistance for survival" the African-American adolescent female is oriented toward finding solutions to problems in the short term. Thus, permanent changes in her own life and the lives of those around her are thwarted. In contrast, "resistance for liberation" offers a realistic approach that examines the present in the context of the past and future. Faith is necessary in this process because it incorporates an intergenerational perspective that takes into account the history of other African resistors and is oriented toward care of future generations.

Although this model of "resistance for liberation" has been proposed with African-American females in mind, it also applies to adolescent women in other ethnic and racial groups. Many minority groups hold similar values of interpersonal connection and orientations toward both personal welfare and the welfare of the group. A strategy of "resistance for liberation" can have long-lasting impact that can affect subsequent generations of minority group members.

---

well-being. Further, adolescents are most prone to risk for dysphoric mental-health problems during early adolescence which is associated with problems of self-concept and psychological well-being.

It has been argued that the nature of self-concept during childhood and, possibly, early adolescence provides the foundation on which identity formation is based. Whether or not one accepts this notion, identity formation and development are thought by many to be the central developmental task of middle and late adolescence. We turn next to the issue of identity formation.

Major Points to Remember

1. Self-development is grounded in the basic functions of social development. Integrative forces encourage connectedness and maintenance of social roles. Individualistic forces encourage uniqueness, differentiation, and personal identities.

2. Self-development involves the notions of *me,* or self-as-known, and *I,* the self-as-knower. The former is the content of the self, the latter, the ego processes.

3. Symbolic interactionism involves a form of social cognition. It deals with the way a person comes to listen before speaking and learns the role of the reflected other in self-development.

4. Self-image disparity involves the contrasting of the real self and the ideal self. The disparity, once thought to reflect psychopathology, is now thought to reflect complexity of self-image in development.

5. Psychological well-being includes aspects of self-confidence, perceived ability to perform well, self-efficacy, psychological comfort, and feeling good about oneself. Aspects of self-development that are correlated with psychological well-being include self-esteem, mattering, stability, locus of control, vulnerability, self-consciousness, and plane coordination.

CHAPTER

10

Identity Development

A major developmental task during adolescence is the creation of a sense of identity. Society places demands on adolescents to experiment and try various attitudes, styles, and behaviors before selecting an identity based on commitments. In this chapter we examine the meaning of identity, how it is conceptualized, and various factors regarding the facilitation of identity formation and development.

A Theoretical Perspective on Identity Development

In his classic work entitled *Identity:Youth and Crisis* (1986), Erik Erikson laid the foundation for most of the research on adolescent identity development for more than a decade. As we have noted, Erikson views adolescence as a major junction in life in which young people focus intensive energy on issues of self-definition and self-esteem. Through a combination of factors associated with physical change, occupational and social choices, and expectations by parents and peers, the adolescent is thought to engage in a period of "identity crisis." In an accommodation (or integration) process, the adolescent is believed to draw on resolutions from earlier life crises and experiences to bring closure to a search for a sense of personal direction. (See also Grotevant, 1992.) The question "Who am I?" is addressed over and over again during the teenage years.

The Meaning of Identity

But what does the word *identity* actually mean? Is identity fixed? Once we have obtained it, can we ever lose it? Identity is a complex psychological phenomenon. It might be thought of as the *person* in *person*ality. It includes our own interpretation of early childhood identification with important individuals in our lives. It includes a sense of direction, commitment, and trust in a personal ideal. A sense of identity integrates sex-role identification, individual ideology, accepted group norms and standards, self-conception, and much more. Ego identity is a complex role image that summarizes one's past, gives meaning to the present, and directs behavior in the future. It includes a sense of self-direction, individual fidelity, and some basic internalized values. As a psychological construct, identity is a gradual rather than all-or-none development. As children, we learn much about ourselves, our family, work, leisure, religion, politics, and so on. Each of these varying aspects of everday life becomes a meaningful part of who we are to become (Baumeister, 1986).

Identity, therefore, is not formed exclusively in adolescence (Kroger, 1989). Rather, identity is significantly transformed during this period of life. Adolescent identity begins with birth and the development of basic trust. However, during adolescence, concern with identity becomes conscious and strong due to several factors. Most important, the adolescent is confronted with the internal physiological revolution (puberty) that accompanies the maturation of the body. New and erotic sensations accompany changes in the endocrine system, and awareness of bodily changes and sexuality grows (Blos, 1962). The bodily changes are associated with the emergence of a strong self-consciousness, and the new forms of eroticism require the adolescent to cope with emerging sexual impulses that have never before been experienced. Also during this period of the life cycle, the adult world begins to expect more responsible behavior from adolescents, compelling them to consolidate and channel individual ego mechanisms (or personality characteristics) into more advanced forms of competition, achievement, and competence. With this new body awareness and a growing sense of social maturity, adolescents begin to think about their role in society. They become very concerned with how others view individual behaviors. They may even begin to question how an assumed role and newly acquired skills will actually meet the needs of the future.

Most technologically advanced societies recognize the need for a period of growth for adolescents. To assist in the transformation from childhood, adolescents are placed in educational and social environments that allow some degree of experimentation. Erikson (1959) refers to this period as a *psychosocial moratorium:*

> The period can be viewed as a psychosocial moratorium during which the individual through free role experimentation may find a niche in some section of his society, a niche which is firmly defined and yet seems to be uniquely made for him. In finding it the young adult gains an assured sense of inner continuity and social sameness which will bridge what he was as a child and what he is about to become, and will reconcile his conception of himself and his community's recognition of him. (P. 110)

Thus, in Erikson's model, adolescents with a strong sense of ego identity view themselves as distinct individuals and have a consistent self-image. In the search for identity, the adolescent plays at many roles, shifting back and forth in an attempt to find the "real me." This shifting role play is both a conscious and an unconscious ego-identity struggle.

Identity Crisis

In the Eriksonian ego-psychology perspective, identity consists of several inter-related elements (Bourne, 1978a). Identity can be viewed as a *developmental outcome* of early-childhood experiences, as a summary of *adaptive accomplishments,* and as a *structural configuration* of personality. And above all else, identity is thought to be a *dynamic process* of testing, selecting, and integrating self-images and personal ideologies. However, it is thought that to arrive at a wholesome and integrated sense of identity during adolescence, one must experience a "crisis." Unfortunately, the concept of crisis is greatly misunderstood.

Both Erikson (1968) and Allport (1964) have attempted to describe what is meant by crisis in normal development. According to Allport:

> a crisis . . . is a situation of emotional and mental stress requiring significant alterations of outlook within a short period of time. These alterations of outlook frequently involve changes in the structure of personality. The resulting changes may be progressive in the life or they may be regressive. By definition, a person in crisis cannot stand still. . . . He must either separate himself further from childhood and move toward adulthood, or else move backward to earlier levels of adjustment. (P. 235)

Erikson characterizes this experience as a feeling of suspended animation; preceding events are irrelevant to what is to come. The individual is facing a multitude of decisions on vocational choice and training, marriage, and ideology and comes to feel increasingly uneasy, anxious, and compelled to resolve the tension. For most adolescents, coping with this tension results in an altered personality. However, for some the challenge becomes too great. Erikson argues that these youths meet the challenge with regressive behavior or apathy and a kind of "paralysis of will."

Resolution of an identity crisis commonly involves a lot of contemplation.

A state of crisis, with its corresponding search for answers, creates the force behind identity development itself. The best possible outcome occurs when the youth searches for self-definitions and integrates these self-made images into his or her personality makeup. However, some young people are unable to meet the challenge of crisis and regress into a state of *role confusion* (Erikson, 1959). The overall portrait of a role-confused youth is a disturbing one. This adolescent is unable to arrive at a psychosocial self-definition and finds all decision making to be threatening and conflicting. Failure to make decisions creates an ever-growing sense of isolation. These symptoms are accompanied by related feelings of shame, lack of pride, personal alienation, and perceptions of being manipulated by others. The total estrangement of role confusion is reflected in Erikson's (1968) example of Biff's remark in Arthur Miller's *Death of a Salesman:* "I just can't take hold, Mom, I can't take hold of some kind of life" (p.131).

Other adolescents resolve their identity crisis through even less desirable means. Erikson (1959) has alluded to such adolescents as individuals with a *negative* identity. These youths find commitment in undesirable identification with criminal, delinquent, or antisocial groups, cliques, or antiheroes. Parents of adolescents who develop negative identities are thought to be deeply concerned about social status and to prefer facades of social prominence over true involvement and meaningful relationships. Erikson refers to these parents as overpowering and inescapable. They appear to love their children in undesirable ways and continually complain about their relationships with their spouses. It would appear that such parents implore their children to give meaning to their existence while treating them as possessions that must be jealously guarded or be stolen away by others. In particular, the mother appears unable to accept the possibility of the maturing youth's identifying with the father, while the father may actually be jealous of the perceived close relationship between the youth and his or her mother.

Some Important Facilitators of Identity Development

Although an early identification with the mother or the father can either encourage or harm effective identity formation, early identifications are not the exclusive source of ego-identity development. Indeed, Erikson (1959) sees the concept of identification as a limited mechanism within an understanding of the total framework of identity formation. Development of identity is thought to consist of several gradual stages. During infancy and very early childhood, a mutually satisfying relationship between the caretaker (usually the mother) and the child results in the first development of sensations of caring for another (love). Parsons and Bales (1955), in a classic treatise, view this period as a time of oral dependency on the mother and a gradual developmental outcome of a mother/child identity. But as the child's ego growth accelerates, the child becomes more autonomous in interactions with the mother. The child is now capable of what is referred to as parent/self object differentiation. In other words, the child can now love another in addition to being loved. Even so, the major attachment during this period is to the mother.

Erikson (1959) surmises that the success of childhood identification depends on the integration of the child's experience with models who exemplify the hierarchical social structure, particularly within the family. As Parsons and Bales (1955) view it, the major socializing differentiation that the nuclear family provides is role structure on dimensions of *hierarchy of power* and *instrumental* versus *expressive* functions. Hierarchy of power involves superior (superordinate) and inferior (subordinate) statuses. Instrumentality is best conceptualized as adaptive functions with goal-oriented activities, whereas expressiveness is an integrative emotional capacity to experience feelings. Given that mothers are seen as highly expressive and nurturing persons, their major influence on identity formation is thought to be on expressive aspects of identity. In that fathers are viewed as highly instrumental, Erikson has argued that a father's major influence may be on the socialization of instrumental, work-related dimensions of identity. However, with increasing numbers of women finding a visible and successful place in the world of work, it is yet to be seen whether Erikson's early thought is an accurate reflection of a changing society. With the growing evidence that working mothers provide positive role models for the career aspirations of their teenage daughters and the realization that fathers provide important emotional support to their off-spring, we suspect that much is yet to be learned about the instrumental and expressive effects associated with maternal and paternal identifications. For another perspective on personal expressiveness see Waterman (1990, 1992).

Erikson (1959) and others believe that several additional factors encourage identity formation. A positive, rewarding parent/child relationship clearly facilitates a healthy identification with the parent. For example, it has been well documented that a warm and nurturing relationship facilitates a strong father/son identification. In addition, an appropriate sex-typed body image and the ability to integrate this identification with the maturing body during adolescence are thought to be important elements of the sexual aspects of identity formation. Furthermore, specific cultural opportunities and experiences are important in coming to recognize who others view one to be. Varying social experiences in ethnic traditions and rites of passage offer the adolescent an opportunity to develop a sense of continuity with his or her heritage (Phinney & Rosenthal, 1992). Similarly, early social experiences allow a child to develop the social skills that create positive experiences and a feeling of self-confidence and poise.

In a highly influential paper R. W. White (1960) referred to this last factor as the need to develop *competency*. An essential component of a healthy personality is being able to feel effective in one's dealings with the world. Through long hours of play, children and young adolescents alike steadily increase their ability to deal with an ever-enlarging and ever-changing social environment. These play activities foster the development of characteristics such as directedness, selectivity, and persistence while providing a sense of fitness or ability to interact with others in an effective, efficient way. Therefore, for White, competence, as reflected in the adolescent's abilities, skills, and limitations, is the very essence of the foundation for understanding identity development.

Identity Status: Four Levels of Identity Formation

Over the years a number of different conceptualizations regarding measurement of ego identity have been devised (see, for example, Boyd & Koskela, 1970; Bosma, 1992; Matteson, 1977; Rasmussen, 1964; D. D. Simmons, 1970). However, only one conceptualization has caught the attention of a significant number of researchers. Using an extensive interview technique, James Marcia (1966) has been able to identify *crisis* and *commitment* as major variables leading to a state of identity (with personal expressiveness recently added by Waterman, 1992). According to Marcia, "'crisis' refers to the adolescent's period of engagement in choosing among meaningful alternatives; 'commitment' refers to the degree of personal investment the individual exhibits" (p. 551). Thus, a state of crisis is a period of searching for answers, while a commitment is a meaningful choice that guides behavior. In Marcia's interview technique, individuals were questioned about their previous or present experience with searching (crisis) and their commitment on occupational, political, religious, and ideological issues.

James Marcia's conceptualization of the Identity Status Paradigm has stimulated more than two decades of research.

Using reported states of involvement with crisis and commitment, Marcia (1966) developed four types of identity status: *diffusion, foreclosure, moratorium,* and *identity achievement.* These statuses provide a summary label for individuals in different levels of identity formation. Table 10–1 lists these four statuses and shows their relationships to reported crisis and commitment.

Erikson (1968) has protrayed *identity achievement* and *identity diffusion* as polar opposites in identity formation. According to Marcia (1966), an identity-diffusion youth is one who is likely to report having neither experienced a sense of needing to search for personal answers nor made any strong commitment to a given perspective in life. As Marcia states, "he is either uninterested in ideological matters or takes a smorgasbord approach in which one outlook seems as good to him as another and he is not averse to sampling from all" (p. 552).

At the other extreme is the identity-achievement youth. These youths not only report a period of struggle and exploration about occupational, political, and religious matters but bring this struggle to a meaningful closure through decisions on each. Their commitments are strong and well defined. Their pathways are vividly marked. Although identity-achievement youths can be convinced to change their minds, it takes a great deal of effort and thought before they are willing to change commitments.

Intermediate between these two extremes are the *foreclosure* and *moratorium* adolescents. The foreclosure youth shares with the identity-achievement youth a sense of commitment, but the quality of this commitment and the manner in which it is derived vary tremendously. The foreclosure youth does not experience struggle or a state of crisis. Instead, these young people assume a commitment handed to them by others—most notably their parents. Such adolescents are capable of expressing a commitment but cannot describe how they acquired it, or they state that what is good enough for their parents is good enough for them.

Moratorium adolescents are searching for answers to many personal questions. In their search for personal commitment and meaning, they appear to be struggling with unresolved questions and offer to the world a bewildered appearance.

To provide an alternative to Marcia's (1966) interview technique in studying identity formation, a variety of questionnaire items have been developed that indicate identity status (G. R. Adams, Shea, & Fitch, 1979; Bennion & Adams, 1986; Grotevant & Adams, 1984). In Table 10–2 we list a few of those items to further clarify Marcia's four identity-status categories.

Table 10–1   Marcia's four identity statuses

Status	*Past or present crisis*	*Commitment*
Diffusion	No	No
Foreclosure	No	Yes
Moratorium	Yes	No
Identity achievement	Yes	Yes

Source: Adapted from J. Marcia, "Development and Validation of Ego-Identity Status." *Journal of Personality and Psychology,* 1966 *3,* pp. 551–558.

Table 10–2   Sample items from the objective measure of ego-identity status

Status	Item
Diffusion	I haven't chosen the occupation I really want to get into, but I'm working toward becoming a _____ until something better comes along.
	When it comes to religion, I just haven't found any that I'm really into myself.
Foreclosure	I guess I'm pretty much like my folks when it comes to politics. I follow what they do in terms of voting and such.
	I've never really questioned my religion. If it's right for my parents, it must be right for me.
Moratorium	I just can't decide how capable I am as a person and what jobs I'll be right for.
	There are so many different political parties and ideals, I can't decide which to follow until I figure it all out.
Identity-achievement	A person's faith is unique to each individual. I've considered and reconsidered it myself and know what I can believe.
	It took me a while to figure it out, but now I really know what I want for a career.

Using Marcia's (1966) framework for the study of identity formation, in the remaining sections of this chapter we provide a general description of the psychological and social behavior associated with each identity status, examine the functions of identity, explore whether one is fixed in a given identity status or is capable of changing from one category to the next, and return to the influence of the family on identity formation.

Psychological Characteristics and Social Behavior of the Four Identity Statuses

Diffusion

Observations by Logan (1980) suggest that identity-diffusion adolescents use a variety of psychological defenses to control anxiety stemming from an undefined identity. Some adolescents temporarily escape the anxiety of meaninglessness by engaging in *intense, immediate experiences* that heighten their senses and provide an immediate, "right now" sensation. Wild parties, drug usage, fast driving, and other thrills ward off the anxiety associated with identity confusion. Other adolescents move from one peer group to another, establishing a sense of belonging by *peer association.* Still others engage in *fad behavior,* such as the stuffing of small cars with as many people as possible, streaking, or other forms of extreme behavior. Thus, Logan argues, a career of meaninglessness is transformed into a commitment to fads.

Feelings of inferiority, alienation, and ambivalence are often reported by diffused-identity adolescents (see Donovan, 1975a, 1975b). They report poor physical, moral, ethical, personal, and social self-concepts (LaVoie, 1976) while maintaining a high field dependence (Schenkel, 1975). Diffused youths are likely also to manifest cognitive stereotyping behaviors (Streitmatter & Pate, 1989). These findings are noteworthy because a healthy and clear identity relies on a sense of field independence, which allows individuals to sort out, analyze, and structure their environment. Further, for diffused youths, less developed differentiation is observed on such constructs as moral reasoning (Halt, 1979), developmental themes of early childhood (Orlofsky & Frank, 1986), sex-role orientation and resolution of earlier childhood psychosocial crises (Prager, 1983; Selva & Dusek, 1984), cognitive development (Leadbeater & Dionne, 1981; Protinsky & Wilkerson, 1986), stages of ego development (Ginsburg & Orlofsky, 1981), locus of control (Abraham, 1983), and perceptions of the future (Rappaport, Enrich, & Wilson, 1985).

Other investigations indicate that such immaturity in identity formation is associated with tension and anxiety, guilt and insecurity, and suspicion and jealousy in interpersonal contexts (Kahn, Zimmerman, Csikszentmihali, & Getzels, 1985; Vandenplas-Holper & Campos, 1990).

Diffused adolescents appear to be unable to narrow their attention in complex social interactions, perceive the need for considerable control over their environment, and view their social environment as very demanding of their energy and attention (G. R. Adams, Ryan, Hoffman, Dobson, & Nielsen, 1985; Read, Adams & Dobson, 1984). Collectively, these studies and others (for example, Slugoski, Marcia, & Koopman, 1984; Streitmatter, 1989) suggest that diffused adolescents are less mature than expected or desired in their cognitive complexity, emotional development, and general development. Berzonsky (1992) describes diffused adolescents as avoidant oriented. He implies that diffusion is associated with avoiding making decisions for as long as possible. Likewise, other studies of social behaviors indicate that diffused youths may be less cooperative in social interactions (Slugoski et al., 1984), more manipulative and deceptive (Read et al., 1984), more readily influenced by peer pressure (Adams et al., 1985), and more likely to engage in socially deviant behavior (Jones, 1992). Likewise, in studies of interpersonal attraction, diffused subjects are found to prefer others who also do not hold personal commitments (Goldman, Rosenzweig, & Lutter, 1980).

Overall, diffused-identity adolescents present an image of a bleak inner life, barren of loving people (Donovan, 1975a, 1975b). A variety of studies suggests that these adolescents cope with stress through social withdrawal, manipulation, and conformity. Further, diffused youths are the least likely of the four identity-status groups to have immediate or long-term intimate relationships with friends or lovers of either sex (Craig-Bray, Adams, & Dobson, 1988; Fitch & Adams, 1983; Hodgson & Fischer, 1979; Kacerguis & Adams, 1980; Kahn et al., 1985; Marcia, 1976; Orlofsky, 1978; Tesch & Whitbourne, 1982; Whitbourne & Tesch, 1985).

Foreclosure

Foreclosed adolescents, like diffused-identity youths, appear highly impulsive (C. K. Waterman & Waterman, 1974) but are more likely to repress or deny impulsive tendencies (Donovan, 1975a, 1975b). These adolescents pursue a quiet, orderly, and industrious life-style. They tend to endorse authoritarian values, such as obedience, strong leadership, and respect for authority (Marcia, 1966) while maintaining a strong goal orientation. Berzonsky (1992) refers to foreclosed adolescents as normative oriented, where the youth conforms to the expectations and prescription of significant others such as parents. Although many foreclosed youths appear to have lower levels of ego development as a whole, a surprising number parallel the more advanced ego-development levels of moratorium and identity-achievement youths (G. R. Adams & Shea, 1979). Other evidence indicates that these adolescents have a strong need for social approval (Orlofsky, Marcia, & Lesser, 1973) and maintain very dependent (nonautonomous) relationships with significant others (Matteson, 1977; Orlofsky et al., 1973).

In an investigation of the relationship between identity status and interpersonal style (Donovan, 1975a, 1975b), foreclosure was observed to be associated with a loving and affectionate home life. Although warm and gratifying, parental concern may actually stifle autonomous growth for these adolescents. The consequences appear to be inhibited sexual and aggressive impulses. Therefore, these foreclosed youths remain cautious and dependent on others. They are hard working, talkative, and constructive, but they are unlikely to offer creative leadership or direction.

Other studies show that foreclosed youths are less likely to establish a solidarity in group contexts and to express their emotional tension (Slugoski et al., 1984). Gerald Adams and his colleagues have observed that foreclosed late adolescents have relatively constricted personalities, with less competitive striving and fewer analytic capabilities than their peers (Adams et al., 1985; Read et al., 1984). When these findings are placed in the context that foreclosed youths are extreme in their rigidity to their commitments (Rappaport et al., 1985) and are relatively immature in their social-behavior styles, one perceives them as frozen in their developmental progression, rigid in their overcompliance, and generally unadaptive.

Moratorium

Moratorium youths are, as one would expect from their crisis state, the most anxious of the four identity-status groups (Marcia, 1980). However, they maintain a stable sense of self-esteem, similar to that of identity-achievement youths (Marcia, 1980), while tending to function at high levels of both moral reasoning and ego development (G. R. Adams & Shea, 1979; Podd, 1972). They also appear to be highly self-directive (C. K. Waterman, Beubel, & Waterman, 1970) yet open to exploring a host of alternative values (Munro & Adams, 1977b). On the whole, these youths lack well-defined goals and values, are highly explorative, and, as very self-conscious individuals, possess the ability to describe their feelings clearly and deeply (Donovan, 1975a, 1975b). Our recent evidence indicates that moratorium youths are comfortable thinking about themselves and their own ideas and perceive that they are capable of dealing with a demanding interpersonal environment (Read et al., 1984; Adams et al., 1985). Overall, moratorium youths are introspective and explorative, actively monitoring their own thoughts, perceptions, and goals. Berzonsky (1992) describes moratorium youth as information oriented, where decisions are made based on a wide and relevant body of information.

Identity-moratorium adolescents are highly active and social (Donovan, 1975a, 1975b). Their daily activities are less restricted than those of youths in the other statuses. They appear emotionally responsive and capable of expressing their feelings of affection toward others (Donovan, 1975a, 1975b) and are thus capable of intimate interpersonal relationships (Fitch & Adams, 1981; Orlofsky et al., 1973). They use socially mature influence or persuasion behaviors with their peers (Slugoski et al., 1984; Read et al., 1984), and in contrast to their diffused peers they are less inclined to be influenced by undesirable peer pressure (G. R. Adams et al., 1985). In general, moratorium youths, while undergoing extensive searching for personal commitments, appear to be comfortable with others and are generally socially adept and effective.

Little is actually known about the process of a psychosocial moratorium. One can ask, "Are all moratoriums similar in their social process or underpinnings?" Baumeister, Shapiro, and Tice (1985) write that there are two kinds of identity crisis. The *legitimate crisis,* or *identity conflict,* is the product of multiple aspects of the self and incompatible commitments that need reconciliation. The underpinning force is inconsistency between a person's goals or values. In contrast, a *motivation crisis,* or *identity deficit,* is characterized by an inadequately defined self that lacks commitments, goals, or values from which to base decisions, actions, or choices. According to Baumeister and his associates, motivation crises arise when a person lacking guiding commitments struggles to make such commitments. They speculate that an identity conflict (legitimate crisis) results from situational demands that call for reconciliation. An identity deficit (or motivation crisis) is more likely to be produced by factors associated with the normal development of a maturing organism.

Both emotional states and corresponding behaviors are thought to accompany the two kinds of crises. Adolescents experiencing an identity deficit are characterized as engaging in an ongoing personal struggle. Subjectively they are likely to experience feelings of vagueness, preoccupation with unresolved questions, anxiety, feelings of confusion, and self-consciousness associated with rumination, and occasional bewilderment. Baumeister and his associates propose that underlying these subjective experiences is a basic emotional conflict between the desire to obtain commitment and the reluctance to give up any possibilities. Related behaviors can include empathy, supportiveness, and camaraderie among peers with similar identity struggles or exploratory and dramatic attempts to plunge into new activities.

The hallmark subjective experience of identity conflict is the feeling of being in an impossible situation in which one cannot act without betraying oneself or loyalty to another. Feelings of guilt and difficulty in maintaining dignity are common. The sujective experience of being torn between incompatible commitments does not call for new commitments. Rather too many commitments are present, and resolution requires either compromising existing ones or letting go of incompatible ones.

We actually know little about the process of resolving identity crises. Baumeister and his colleagues (1985) suggest that the resolution of an identity deficit can be broken down into a two-step process. The first step involves *values,* and the second addresses *instrumental* issues. The resolution of the first aspect of identity requires rumination about values and beliefs. It requires that the individual examine abstract and vaguely defined constructs, define them, and establish a set of consistent values. Instrumental resolution involves translating the abstract values into goals and corresponding ways of fulfilling them. An identity conflict, in contrast, may simply require resolving which critical value will be assumed over another or which behavior will be acceptable over another. In contrast to the resolution of an identity deficit, it is likely to require only a single step.

Identity Achievement

Identity-achievement youths have the most complex, highly adaptive personality profile of the four identity-status groups. These adolescents have the highest levels of ego development (G. R. Adams & Shea, 1979), moral-reasoning abilities (Podd, 1972; Rowe & Marcia, 1980), self-esteem (G. R. Adams, Shea, & Fitch, 1979; Bruer, 1973), and reflective (or analytic) cognitive sytle (Berzonsky, 1992; Leadbeater & Dionne, 1981; Protinsky & Wilkerson, 1986; C. K. Waterman & Waterman, 1974). Other evidence suggests that identity-achievement adolescents are more future oriented and are more capable of recognizing things to come in their futures (Freilino & Hummel, 1985; Protter, 1973; Rappaport et al., 1985).

In concept-attainment tasks, like those associated with school experiences, identity-achievement youths are capable of outperforming any other identity-status group under stress (Marcia, 1966). In school they often obtain higher grades (Cross & Allen, 1970) and report high satisfaction with their schooling experiences (A. S. Waterman & Waterman, 1970). When placed in high-conformity, stressful situations, identity-achievement youths are inclined to resist the pressure to conform (Toder & Marcia, 1973). Likewise, when they engage in conformity, they commonly do so for the sake of achievement (G. R. Adams et al., 1985). In general, these youths live orderly, active (Donovan, 1975a), and self-directed lives (Donovan, 1975b).

The overall personality and social profile of the identity-achievement adolescent suggests a harmoniousness between individuation and social needs for relatedness (Orlofsky & Frank, 1986). Numerous studies suggest that these adolescents show strong positive characteristics reflecting self-confidence, security, psychological integration, social adeptness, psychological complexity, emotional maturity, and advanced ego development (G. R. Adams et al., 1985; Ginsburg & Orlofsky, 1981; Josselson, 1982; Kahn et al., 1985; Kroger, 1985; Prager, 1982; Rappaport et al., 1985; Selva & Dusek, 1984; Slugoski et al., 1984).

In accord with what A. S. Waterman (1984; 1992) has argued, complexity in levels of individualism in the form of identity is associated with social adeptness, social intimacy, and social relatedness. For example, social-behavioral studies show that identity-achievement adolescents are usually not likely to conform to peer pressure but do conform when it is needed to be successful (G. R. Adams et al., 1985). They are likely to use highly effective social-interaction and social-influence behaviors in working with and dealing with others (Read et al., 1984; Sugoski et al., 1984). And they are the most likely of the four identity-status

Box 10–1   A Study of Differences Among Women's Identities

Ruthellen Josselson (1987) has provided a descriptive portrait of identity development between adolescence and adulthood for a group of women studied first in college and again in middle adulthood. Arguing that no one had looked seriously at how identity is organized for women, she focused her clinical interviews on this select population. Drawing on the hypothesis that career, achievement, and independence are issues of individuality that organize males' identity and that relatedness, connectedness, union, and caring are focal to females' identity, Josselson analyzed the nature of the four identity statuses for women.

Identity-diffusion women appear to fail to internalize important lessons from relationships and social experience. They have poor integration abilities and thus reject little as unacceptable. Hence everything and anything is possibly part of the self. Fragmentation of the self is externalized in the form of interest in helping others. Lacking organizing principles in the self—a reflection of low ego development—these women seek external authority figures to guide their behavior.

Foreclosed women focus much of their attention on family closeness and harmony. They spend considerable energy reproducing the warming lovingness of their childhood with their own family. They have a strong sense of duty, morality, and values. They are hard-working, responsible, and able in their careers. Although not insightful, they are effective. However, foreclosed women reflect in their words and deeds concerns for security and safety reflective of early stages of psychosocial development.

Moratorium women, as a group, struggle to untangle their familial ties and attempt to resolve their guilt for not having lived out family expectations and desires. As a group they need and seek relationships to help them build new identifications. Many use these identifications to move on into an identity-achievement status. Those who remain in moratorium seem to be caught in conflict and are unable to transcend it. Moratorium women need supportive others to help them arrive at self-definitions and differentiation of self. As a whole, moratorium women are insightful, self-reflective, and sensitive people.

Identity-achievement women are distinguished as a group in their independence. They strive to have an effect on their world. They recognize a need to find themselves and their own pathway to self-definition. In contrast to other statuses they have a considerable capacity to tolerate guilt. In their relationships they find men who are ego supports. That is, they form relationships with men who help them become less dependent on their parents and who are supportive of their accomplishments. In total, identity-achievement women balance work, relationships, and personal interests. They are confident, flexible, and successful—at work, in relationships, and at play.

Josselson concludes that women's identity is to a great extent a matter of whom they know and the relational connections they develop. Much of their identity is *anchored* in relationships with friends, mates, children, and partners. Indeed, women find themselves in the web of relatedness.

groups to have made deep commitments to same-sex friends and to have established strong heterosexual relationships (Craig-Bray et al., 1988; Fitch & Adams, 1981; Kacerguis & Adams, 1980; Kahn et al., 1985; Whitbourne & Tesch, 1985). We speculate that commitment to a given self-definition in the form of an identity increases the likelihood that an adolescent or adult will be able to establish positive relationships and commitments to others. As youths with highly differentiated and complex personalities, these young people may have more to give to others in their relationships and may have more coping skills in relating to others. (For a comparison of identity statuses for women see Box 10–1, and for a summary of personality variables that differentiate the identity statuses see Box 10–2). We return to the issue of an association between identity and intimacy later in this chapter.

Box 10–2 **Personality Characteristics of the Identity Statuses**

Mary Mallory (1989) has completed an investigation of perceived personality characteristics for each of the four identity statuses. Among other characteristics, the following four personality or social behaviors are viewed as pertinent to a general prototypical portrait for each status.

Identity Diffusion
Reluctant to Act
Brittle Ego-Defense
Avoids Close Relations
Lacks Personal Meaning

Identity Foreclosure
Overcontrol of Impulses
Moralistic
Sex-Appropriate Behavior
Conventional

Identity Moratorium
Introspective
Values Own Independence
Rebellious, Nonconforming
Basically Anxious

Identity Achievement
Clear, Consistent Personality
Warm and Compassionate
Productive
Values Own Independence

The Functions of Identity

One assumption underlying our discussion of self-concept and identity formation is that personality provides several basic functions for behavior. We propose that identity, as the central core of personality, maintains the following essential functions: First, it provides the *structure* for understanding who we are and the substance to the question "Who am I?" It is the organized *me*, in James's terms. Second, it is the mechanism, or the ego structure, that provides *meaning* and *direction* through the construction of reality. Third, an identity enables a persson to make choices based on alternatives, thereby providing a sense of personal control, or *free will*. Fourth, identity functions to provide an *integration* or consistency between values, beliefs, or commitments. And finally, an identity enables a person to realize his or her *potential*. That is, it provides a personal sense of future goals.

Collectively, these basic functions allow for a central, or core, identity that gives meaning, direction, goals, and commitments to human life. These aspects of identity compel an individual to strive for consistency. Likewise, they influence a person's behaviors, social relationships, and social interdependence. Therefore, our interest in the self and in identity is paramount during adolescence. It is paramount because society provides for central changes in the development of identity during adolescence. Let us now turn to the evidence on identity development during adolescence.

Identity Statuses as Developmental Stages

Marcia's original work presented identity statuses as categories reflecting individual differences between adolescents at a single point in time. He wrote later, however, that identity statuses should not be viewed as a static quality and that identity should be viewed in more fluid and developmental ways (Marcia, 1976). Early in this line of thinking several cross-sectional and longitudinal research studies were completed to assess the developmental relationship between the four identity statuses (Marcia, 1976; Meilman, 1979; A. S. Waterman et al., 1974; A. S. Waterman & Goldman, 1976). These data clearly indicated transformation over time in identity status.

A careful review of the findings on identity development during early adolescence found that the four identity statuses could be detected in youths as early as the sixth grade but that the quality and nature of each of the identity statuses might be specific to a given age (Archer & Waterman, 1983). More importantly, however, all of the studies indicated that with increasing grade level or age, the number of identity-achievement and moratorium youths increased, and the number of foreclosure and diffusion youths decreased. Another comprehensive review of identity development from adolescence into adulthood drew a parallel conclusion (A. S. Waterman, 1982). Further, few consistent sex differences seem to be observed in patterns of identity development (Archer, 1989).

Change in development over time can come in three forms. First, change can come in the form of *consistent advancement* toward higher statuses. For example, a diffusion-status person could become foreclosed or move into moratorium. Second, theoretically *inconsistent change* could occur. It would be theoretically impossible for an identity-achievement person, who has experienced a crisis and made a commitment, to become diffused again or for a moratorium-status adolescent to become foreclosed, since foreclosed youths never experience crisis. Finally, it would be theoretically possible for an adolescent to experience a state of *regression;* that is, an adolescent could cope with the stress of change by temporarily behaving in ways associated with an earlier stage of development. A moratorium youth might act like a diffusion-status adolescent for a brief period before coming out of his or her cocoon and becoming an identity-achievement person. In the psychoanalytic perspective, this process is termed regression in the service of the ego.

To test these assumptions, changes in identity status for a large number of college students were compared over the course of a year (G. R. Adams & Fitch, 1981). In most cases there was either consistent change toward more advanced stages or regression to earlier stages. Additional elaboration on this line of research (G. R. Adams & Montemayor, 1988) has delineated several basic trajectories in identity development over a three-year period. Five basic patterns were documented (see Figure 10–1). The majority of students (50%) manifested progressive differentiation and growth in individuality. However, approximately 20% showed an uneven pattern reflective of tumultuous (up-and-down) identity resolution; these trajectories are labeled "progressive/regressive" and "regressive/progressive." Relatively few students remained stable (15%) or manifested consistent regressive development. The uneven, tumultuous patterns may reflect the consequences of an ineffective or unsupportive environment, as suggested by other studies (for example, G. R. Adams & Fitch, 1983), while consistent regression may be indicative of either a negative identity resolution or identity disorders.

It is unclear whether those youths who enter the work force on graduation from college are likely to continue to advance in identity status. Some research data (Munro & Adams, 1977b) suggest that adolescents entering the work force on graduation from high school may be more advanced than those who go on to college. However, whether, four years later, these working youths will maintain

Figure 10–1
Trajectories in identity development beginning with the freshman year in college. (Source: G. R. Adams & Montemayor, 1988.)

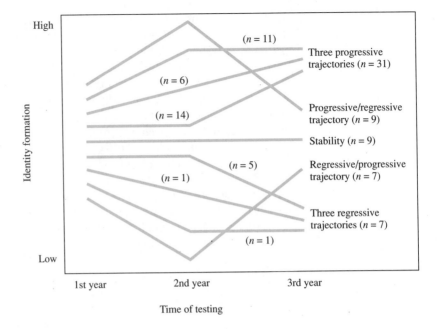

advanced identity status is unknown. We suspect that the college environment is more challenging than the typical setting for unskilled or semiskilled work. Therefore, it is reasonable to speculate that the demands of an intellectual dialogue in an academic setting are more conducive to exploring issues that are associated with the establishment of higher levels of identity. (See Costa & Campus, 1990.)

These and other data reviewed in this chapter provide evidence for the belief that identity formation is a central element of the adolescent experience. However, identity formation must be viewed, as Erikson (1968) has argued, as being "at its best . . . a process of increasing differentiation" (p. 23)—that is, as a gradual process of evolution from a simple role confusion to a highly complex and committed role structure. (For further information about identity as it relates specifically to ethnicity see Box 10–3.)

The Question of Necessary or Sufficient Conditions for Identity Change

When a personality construct is thought to be developmental, the question of what causes the change naturally arises. When adolescents and teachers part at the end of spring for summer vacation and are reunited in fall for the beginning of a new school term, it is common to hear such conversation between the two as "John, you've really changed since your sophomore year. It's good to see such positive changes!" But what causes these behavioral changes? Are there absolutely necessary conditions, for example, for identity development, or are there only sufficient conditions that encourage but do not cause identity-status change?

Box 10–3   Ethnic Identity Development

Jean Phinney (1990) has provided considerable enlightenment on the current understanding of ethnic identity formation. According to her review, there are many components of ethnic identity. These components include:

1. Ethnicity and ethnic self-identification
2. Sense of belonging
3. Positive and negative attitudes toward one's ethnic group
4. Ethnic involvement (social participation and cultural practices)

Much of the published research focuses on self-identification or self-labeling. Self-labeling can vary by choice. For example, having ancestry from Mexico can be associated with self-labels such as Latino, Chicano, Hispanic, or Mexican American. Use of such self-labels may be associated with the degree of a sense of belonging. Likewise, self-labeling can reflect positive and negative attitudes. Positive attitudes include pride, satisfaction, or contentment. Negative attitudes can reflect feelings of inferiority or even the desire to hide one's own ethnic heritage. To understand ethnic involvement one must study the language, friendship, religious affiliation and practices, social groups, political ideology, residence, home and family living.

Phinney and Alipuria (1990) have developed a scale to measure ethnic identity. The Multigroup Ethnic Identity Measure (Phinney, 1990) can be used to assess the status and transformation of identity among Asian-American, African-American, Mexican-American, and White adolescents. It is comparable in format to the Objective Measure of Ego Identity Status (Adams, Bennion, & Huh, 1989) but exclusively focused on ethnic identity.

Three important research projects suggest sufficient conditions for advanced identity statuses. One project (Rowe & Marcia, 1980) addressed the question of whether formal logical thought is a necessary precondition for advanced identity status (also see, for example, W. M. Berzonsky, Weiner, & Raphael, 1975; Cauble, 1976; Enright, Ganiere, Buss, Lapsley, & Olson, 1983; Leadbeater & Dionne, 1981; Protinsky & Wilkerson, 1986; J. Wagner, 1976). The results indicate that the relationship between the two psychological variables is replicable. Even so, we must conclude on the basis of other research that individuals with an identity-achievement status have not necessarily developed the capacity for formal logical thinking (see Rowe & Marcia, 1980). Thus, cognitive development may enhance but not cause advanced identity development.

Another important project (a series of studies reported by A. S. Waterman & Archer, 1979) suggests that a related cognitive process may similarly enhance but not cause advancement in identity. Believing that expressive writing functions as an aid in resolving identity crises, these researchers explored the relationship between identity status and writing expressive poetry or keeping a journal. For both high school and college-age research subjects, expressive poetry but not journal writing was consistently predictive of higher identity statuses. The capacity of a poetry-writing history to foster an increased self-awareness is illustrated by the following excerpt from this research report:

> When I thought of something that was puzzling to me I would try to solve it in a song. Like each song is a question. . . . There are more question marks in a song than periods. . . . When you try to write your thoughts down, you straighten them out and you realize something about yourself that you did not know before. (P. 339)

Gerald Adams and Fitch (1983) examined what characteristics of an educational experience enhanced growth in identity during the college years. Assessments of the social-psychological environment of several departments were obtained and tested for their predictive usefulness in understanding growth in identity. Departments that required a critical examination of issues, focused on multiple perspectives, and provided opportunities for a broad analysis of issues enhanced growth in identity. This third study suggests that growth in identity may require a social-cognitive dialectic process of analysis, counteranalysis, and a certain degree of cognitive dissonance.

Finally, Markstrom-Adams (1988) has reviewed several studies that examined the effects of social-perspective-taking training on identity formation (for example, Enright et al., 1983; Enright, Olson, Ganiere, Lapsley, & Buss, 1984). She concludes that high school and college students who receive such training show greater advancement in identity development than those who receive training in formal-operational thought. Thus, important social-cognition links appear to exist between perspective taking and identity development. Adams speculates that the processes of cognitive differentiation (seeing the parts of a whole) and integration (putting the parts into a complex, organized whole) facilitate identity exploration. Indeed, Slugoski and her colleagues (1984) have found that psychological integration has a salient role in ego-identity formation. (See also Ganiere & Enright, 1989). These findings suggest that a training program based on differentiation and integration can have an important facilitating effect on identity development. For further reading on intervening factors associated with the promotion of identity, interested readers should see Markstrom-Adams (1992).

Minority Adolescents and the Identity Statuses

Several studies on identity formation based on the identity status model have been conducted among minority groups. Abraham (1983) reports that Anglo-Americans are more likely to be classified in diffusion than are Mexican Americans. In a later investigation (Abraham, 1986) she finds that Mexican Americans are more foreclosed in ideological identity than Anglo-American youths. Streitmatter (1988) reports that Anglo-American adolescents score significantly lower on both interpersonal and ideological foreclosure in comparison to a minority adolescent category (comprised of Hispanic, African American, American Indian, and Asians). Likewise, Hauser (1972a, 1972b) has found the identity pattern of African-American adolescent boys to be characterized by foreclosure. Consistent with these findings, Markstrom-Adams and Adams (1992) report that African Americans, American Indians, and Mexican Americans scored significantly higher on ideological foreclosure. Rotheram-Borus (1989) found that in comparisons between Black, Puerto Rican, Filipino, and White high school students, White students at higher grade levels scored higher on moratorium.

In summary we can conclude that, in several instances, foreclosure appears to be a particular status characteristic of ethnic minority groups (Abraham, 1986; Hauser, 1972a, 1972b; Markstrom-Adams & Adams, 1992; Streitmatter, 1988). It appears that exploration in identity does not occur for minority adolescents to

---

Box 10–4   Identity Formation Among Biracial Adolescents

The task of identity formation is complex for any adolescent, but it is particularly complicated for the biracial adolescent. In particular, Overmier (1990) delineates five areas of conflict regarding identity formation among biracial adolescents.

1. *Racial Identity*   This is the core conflict for biracial adolescents. Ideally, an adolescent forms a separate sense of identity that is comprised of an integration of both racial backgrounds. However, the tendency is to overidentify with the parent with whom one shares the most characteristics.

2. *Social Marginality*   Even though many biracial children experience positive social relations in childhood, problems related to fitting in often emerge in adolescence. The biracial adolescent may have difficulty in finding a peer group that is comfortable with his or her biracial status. A fear of social rejection may lead the biracial adolescent to overconform to peer pressure and to engage in problematic behavior.

3. *Sexuality*   Confusion in overall identity formation among biracial adolescents may extend to confusion in gender identity and sexual orientation. These difficulties may extend from the failure to have identified with the same-sex parent.

4. *Autonomy*   Individuation for biracial adolescents may be hindered. Social marginality, combined with parental efforts to protect the adolescent from the pains of social rejection and prejudice, may result in the adolescent's remaining dependent on the family for a longer period of time.

5. *Aspirations*   Given the realities of prejudice and discrimination, most biracial adolescents know that there are barriers to accomplishing their aspirations. The biracial teen's identification with one or the other side of their racial heritage is likely to have an effect on how aspirations are experienced.

Given such considerations in biracial identity formation, Overmier (1990) goes on to summarize from Gibbs (1987) five recommendations to facilitate the treatment process for biracial teenagers. First, therapists need to allow adolescents to express their feelings about their biracial identity. Second, the therapist should encourage the development of self-esteem among biracial clients, independent of ethnic background. Third, assist adolescents in exploring the connections between confusion about racial identity and other aspects of development. Fourth, encourage teenagers to explore both forms of ethnicity that comprise the biracial background. Fifth, include parents and siblings in therapy with biracial adolescents.

---

the degree it does for White adolescents. It may be that the effects of prejudice and discrimination experienced by minority adolescents diminish opportunities for exploration in identity. Along with such discouragement to examine identity options in the broader society, some minority adolescents may be socialized by their significant others to form their identities in the contexts of their groups. It was noted in chapter three that a strong emphasis on family and connectedness is evident among many minority groups. Thus, in such contexts, foreclosure would be indicative of a healthy and desirable outcome in identity. (See Box 10–4 on information about identity formation and biracial adolescents.)

The Question of Identity as a Correlate of or Precursor to Intimacy

Erikson (1968) has proposed that the resolution of role confusion versus identity achievement is a normative life crisis during adolescence. However, during late adolescence a related crisis, intimacy versus isolation, emerges. Erikson believes that it is beneficial for adolescents to resolve the identity crisis to ensure a sound foundation for relationship development. Most of us can remember hearing similar insights in such parental remarks as "How can you ever expect to really know someone else without really knowing who you are?"

A series of studies suggests that a clearly self-determined commitment in identity is both a correlate and a precondition of intimacy formation. Although some research shows that women develop competence in intimate relationships earlier than men (Fischer, 1981), other cross-sectional and longitudinal data indicate that both men and women in higher identity statuses are likely to have more committed, intense, and mature same-sex and heterosexual relations (see, for example, Fitch & Adams, 1981; Kahn et al., 1985; Tesch & Whitbourne, 1982). According to one study (Hodgson & Fischer, 1979), the relationship between intimacy and identity achievement may be stronger for males than females, but other data are inconsistent with that conclusion. For example, occupational identity is an important correlate of mature intimate relations for both sexes (Kacerguis & Adams, 1980).

Several studies provide strong evidence for the measurement of identity and intimacy as valid constructs that are interrelated (for example, Craig-Bray & Adams, 1986). But only recently have we looked closely at the potential distinction between ideological and social identity as predictors of same-sex and opposite-sex intimacy during adolescence. The theoretical work of Erik Erikson, based on a male bias, proposes that ideological content is important for predicting males' social intimacy. Recent feminist arguments suggest that interpersonal, or social, identity is more important for predicting women's social-intimacy behaviors (Gilligan, 1982). To assess this possibility, Craig-Bray and her associates (1988) assessed this distinction in theoretical predictions. The first general finding was that identity development might have a primary predictive influence on social intimacy in same-sex relationships during adolescence and that only later in young adulthood might it have a major association with opposite-sex

Identity formation provides the foundation for being able to establish intimacy and make sacrifices for the sake of another.

relationships. Second, the findings suggested that both ideological and social contexts of identity were important for predicting social intimacy for both males and females.

Most recently Dyk and Adams (1988) have tested the notion that women's psychological development occurs "in a different voice" (Chodorow, 1978; Gilligan, 1982), with identity formation anchored in social relationships, and that males' identity is based on an instrumental process of separation/individuation. Using a cross-lagged longitudinal study involving college males and females, we tested the two theories for their validity. When gender comparisons were made, controlling for sex-role orientatin, identity formation was predictive of later intimacy development for both males and females. However, sex-role orientation mediated the identity/intimacy association. For males, interest in feminine tasks enhanced the identity/intimacy association. However, both masculine- and feminine-focused males were observed to maintain the separation/individuation process of identity functioning as a precursor to intimacy. For women, femininity was associated with the hypothesized fusion between identity and intimacy. Nonetheless, women with masculine interests revealed a male tendency to separate identity as a precursor to intimacy. Therefore, findings are emerging to support potentially different associations between identity and intimacy for men and women. However, these differences may be mediated by issues of sex roles and their development. We examine such sex-role issues in the next chapter.

Family Contributions to Identity Formation

Earlier in this chapter we review some evidence suggesting that certain family-variables affect identity formation. Several reviews of the relationship between identity formation and family relations offer further confirmation of the importance of the family in identity development (Grotevant, 1983; Marcia, 1980; Matteson, 1977). A synopsis of these reviews indicates that somewhat different parental factors are associated with each identity status. Diffusion youths appear to come from more rejecting and detached families. Often the father is absent through separation or divorce. The fathers who are at home may not be very encouraging of their adolescents and may show some signs of negativity.

Foreclosure youths appear to come from strongly child-centered families in which the parents may be intrusive and possessive with their children. However, the parents of foreclosed adolescents appear highly encouraging and supportive, with one or both parents assuming a dominant leadership role in the home. Family members express very low levels of emotion and appear to show little encouragement of individual differences. There is some evidence of strong pressures to conform to family values and beliefs.

Moratorium youths, particularly males, struggle to separate themselves from their mothers. The homes of these youths are generally active ones. Autonomy and self-expression appear to be encouraged, as are individual differences.

Finally, identity-achievement youths view their parents in positive but occasionally ambivalent terms. These youths seem to come from homes with high praise, minimal parental control and secure attachments (Kroger & Haslett, 1988).

Family relations play a major role in determining identity formation. Family communications provide the foundation for self development.

One investigation suggests that identity-achievement males, in particular, are as likely to come from homes with fathers absent as from homes with fathers present (Crossman, Shea, & Adams, 1980). Indeed, a slightly higher proportion of identity-achievement males may come from single-parent homes in which the mothers provide important early experiences for their sons' occupational-identity development.

Three studies have examined adolescents' and parents' perceptions of family relationships among the four types of identity statuses (G. R. Adams, 1985; G. R. Adams & Jones, 1983; Campbell, Adams, & Dobson, 1984). As Figure 10–2

Figure 10–2
A summary of family
correlates associated with
individual differences in
identity formation during
middle and late
adolescence. (Source:
Conclusions drawn from
G. R. Adams, "Family
Correlates of Female
Adolescents' Ego-Identity
Development." *Journal of
Adolescence,* 1985, *8,* pp.
69–82; E. Campbell, G. R.
Adams and W. R. Dobson
"Familial Correlates of
Identity Formation in Late
Adolescence: A Study of
the Predictive Utility of
Connectedness and
Individuality in Family
Relations," *Journal of
Youth and Adolescence,*
1984, 13, pp. 509–525;
and G. R. Adams & R. M.
Jones, "Female
Adolescence Identity
Development,"
*Developmental
Psychology,* 1983,
19, pp. 249–256.)

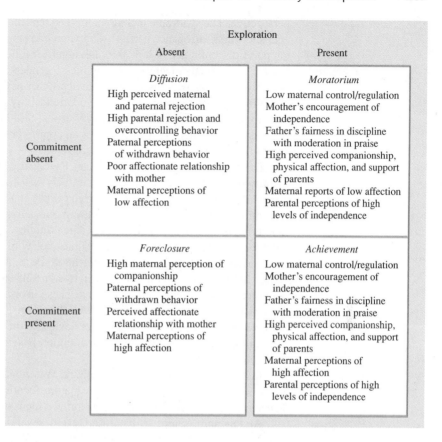

indicates, the data corroborate the conclusions drawn from previous reviews. Diffused youths experience rejection and low levels of affection. Foreclosed adolescents have affectionate and possible "emotionally enmeshed" family lives. Moratorium and identity-achievement youths come from homes that are affectionate and encouraging and provide strong independence training. Finally, Gerald Adams and Montemayor (1988) have also completed several longitudinal studies showing that a warm home life that allows for a moderate degree of disagreement creates an environment for psychological growth in individuation (see G. R. Adams, Dyk, & Bennion, 1987; Bosma & Gerrits, 1985). For additional evidence confirming the conclusion that family relationships differentially predict identity statuses see Kamptner (1988) and Papini, Micka, and Barnett (1989).

Normality versus Pathology in Identity

From his beginning work, Erikson was interested in abnormality in identity formation. In his early work he focused on *acute identity diffusion.* Yet even though Erikson has written on this issue, surpirsingly little research has been completed on the distinctions between normality and pathology in identity. More recently, Akhtar (1984) described the syndrome of identity diffusion from a psychiatric perspective. The syndrome includes a marked tendency to manifest contradictory character traits (arrogance versus timidity, greed versus self-denial, and the like); temporal discontinuity in how the individual sees the past, present, or future; a lack of authenticity; feelings of emptiness; gender- or sex-role diffusion; and possibly problems with a sense of ethnicity. Other psychiatric classifications can result in such diverse categories as psychotic identity disturbances, multiple personality disorders, or adolescent identity crises. Still other professionals suggest that a narcissistic personality disorder is an appropriate definition for identity diffusion (see G. R. Adams & Markstrom, 1987).

The nomenclature of the American Psychiatric Association indicates that identity-diffused adolescents are excessively self-focused and self-conscious. Gerald Adams, Abraham, and Markstrom (1989) conducted research designed to determine whether excessive self-focusing and self-consciousness were evident among identity-diffused adolescents. Three studies were completed to investigate the self-focusing and self-conscious behaviors of diffused, foreclosed, moratorium, and identity-achievement adolescents. Consistently evidence was found linking identity diffusion with overly self-focused behavior, self-consciousness, and extreme self-awareness. These investigations may open broader clinical research attention to the central characteristics of acute identity disorders. When does self-focusing behavior deviate to the point of becoming a disorder during adolescence? Far too little attention has been given to this important research question.

Recent pioneering work by Archer and Waterman (1990) has focused on the identification of subtypes of the least mature identity status—diffusion. Given Erikson's (1968) concerns about diffusion, we focus on this status.

Archer and Waterman have delineated several identity status types that may be dysfunctional. The *apathetic* identity diffusion youths appear to show no interest in making commitments, and their indifference may be used to protect their self-esteem. The *alienated* identity diffusion adolescents are likewise not interested in forming commitments. Further, they may manifest anger toward community or cultural leaders. This anger is likely to be masking anxiety over inability to successfully address the identity formation task. *Pathological* identity diffusion youths are manifesting a severe dysfunction usually associated with organic (neurological or physiological) or developmental disturbances. *Marginally involved* identity diffusion adolescents hold marginal interest in identity-related values, beliefs, or goals. As Archer and Waterman state, "They are lacking in a sufficient investment in their choice to warrant labeling them as having identity commitments. . . . Their ideas are 'good enough' until, and if, something better comes along" (p. 104). *Commitment-avoiding* identity diffusion adolescents are committed to not being committed. These youths are experimenting with choices in values or beliefs but are unwilling to commit themselves. Possibly these youths fear that a commitment would be unsatisfying. At this point, these initial descriptions of dysfunctional diffusion Archer and Waterman have provided are all we have. Researchers need to learn much more concerning identity diffusion adolescents' general character, behavior, and developmental pathways.

Major Points to Remember

1. Identity formation is a dynamic process of structuring elements of personality that summarize individual accomplishments.

2. An identity crisis is a period of intense exploration and searching for acceptable commitments.

3. Four labels for the stages in identity formation are diffusion, foreclosure, moratorium, and identity-achievement.

4. Over the course of the high school and college years, both male and female adolescents are inclined to progress from diffusion to more advanced identity statuses.

5. To date we are unaware of any absolutely necessary precondition for an advanced identity status.

6. An advanced identity status has been shown to be a possible correlate but not a cause of intimacy development.

7. Each of the four identity statuses is associated with specific family-relations styles. Diffused youths appear to come primarily from detached familes, while foreclosed adolescents come from extremely warm, overly indulgent, child-centered families. Moratorium youths appear to come from warm but highly independent families. Finally, identity-achievement adolescents come from highly interactive families in which the parents use minimal control and high praise.

8. Progressive identity development is associated with greater perspective-taking skills.

9. Advanced identity formation appears to be predictive of developing social intimacy. Some gender role differences may exist in the identity/intimacy association.

10. A variety of identity diffusion types may be dysfunctional. These types have been labeled alienated, apathetic, pathological, marginally involved, and commitment-avoiding.

CHAPTER

11

Gender Differences and Sex-Role Development

Evidence confirms that notions of womanhood and manhood, sex-role behaviors, and attitudes about the roles of men and women are changing. Adolescents find themselves coming of age in a changing society with a variety of public forces (the women's movement, the news media, conservative religious groups, and so forth) proposing either a return to the "good old days" of sex roles and attitudes or a further liberalization toward egalitarian role sharing.

Simply put, egalitarianism implies the equal sharing of roles and behaviors. Boys can select to do both "male" and "female" things; girls can likewise make such a selection. In this perspective, choice is based on interest, not gender. Further, it is assumed that a balance will occur between couples in their behaviors and accepted roles.

In this chapter we explore some evidence indicating that society is liberalizing in its views about sex roles and examine what benefits and costs adolescents might anticipate as they grow toward adulthood. In other words, we examine the question of gender differences and sex-role development. The question of *gender differences* focuses on whether there are biological or genetic distinctions between boys and girls beyond their obvious physical differences. The question of *sex-role development* focuses on the degree to which male and female adolescents *internalize* corresponding *societal characteristics* thought to be associated with being female or male.

The Movement Toward Role Sharing

One way to document whether society is moving toward an egalitarian role-sharing perspective is to examine demographic changes in the general population. In the past, women's identity focused on marriage and work in the home. Their duties were to be homemakers and wives. A close look at a woman's job description would find such a traditional wife cooking, washing, caring for the children and husband, providing a taxi service, and performing assorted domestic tasks (Bernard, 1974). Although none of these activities is demeaning, their low prestige value has perpetuated the belief that so-called women's work is inferior to men's work. If all women were still expected to engage in only these behaviors, then clearly we would have progressed no further than our early ancestors toward equity in sex-role behavior.

In general, the evidence points to the broadening of women's role in modern society. As one example, women are marrying later, thus giving themselves more time during late adolescence for schooling and work experience (Thomas P. Gullotta, Adams, & Alexander, 1986; G. L. Lewis, 1978). With more education and work experience, women are likely to enter marriage expecting to share decision making with their spouses.

Changes in societal expectations about sex-role behavior can also be determined by interview and survey techniques designed to detect cultural lag or change. For example, one study found that individuals (aged 18 to 65) were more accepting of a wife's earning extra money for the family than were respondents from an earlier era (Albrecht, Bahr, & Chadwick, 1979). Even so, the working wife is still expected to fill the role of homemaker, child-care provider, and, to a somewhat lesser extent, maintainer of kinship ties. Although retaining some traditional practices, younger respondents are more accepting of changes in family life-styles than are older respondents surveyed at the same time—more accepting of communal family arrangements, egalitarian dual-career families, part-time employment, and part-time child-care duties for both spouses. Further, these attitudes may bear on the emotional health of married women, in that prestigious and enjoyable work improves women's and men's mental health and psychological well-being. However, a husband who disapproves of his wife's employment can reduce the beneficial effects of employment for her. But a man who supports his wife's work and can contribute to child care promotes family well-being (Kessler & McRae, 1982).

Other studies have compared the attitudes and beliefs of parents and their children over several decades. Roper and LaBeff (1977), for example, sampled the views of adolescents and their parents in 1934 and in 1974. In 1974 both adolescents and parents accepted feminist or egalitarian role-sharing ideals for husbands and wives. Strong changes occurred on issues associated with economic and political or legal matters: women had made substantial gains through acceptance of equal rights. However, less movement toward egalitarianism was noted on the issue of household responsibilities. Roper and LaBeff suggest that although women are more likely than men to endorse the egalitarian role-sharing ideals of the feminist movement, both sexes remain relatively traditional in their beliefs about a woman's responsibility for home management and child care. As other studies have yielded similar findings, it must be concluded that only modest change toward egalitarianism can be found from such survey data (Scanzoni, 1976; Scanzoni & Fox, 1980; Tomeh, 1978).

Some people believe, however, that we can learn more about changing sex roles in society by studying young persons than by studying their parents (Carter & Patterson, 1982). Adults have completed their most dramatic socialization process and are more likely to be committed to firm sex-role notions. Children, however, are still experiencing intense socialization forces from family members, teachers, television, peers, and social institutions (for example, see Morgan, 1987, for a study of television viewing and its effects on sex-role attitudes and behaviors). Hence, comparing different generations of youths may provide the most compelling information on changes in attitudes toward sex roles.

In fact, there is some support for this assumption. In one comparison of high school seniors' responses between 1964 and 1975 on sex-role orientation in occupational choices, Lueptow (1981) concluded that 10% to 20% of these adolescents had liberalized their notions in an egalitarian direction. Although many adolescents remain highly traditional, the orientation of girls toward a limited number of traditional female sex-typed occupations has lessened. Additional evidence gathered by Kreidberg, Butcher, and White (1978), Kenkel and Gage (1983), and Herzog and Bachman (1982) corroborates this conclusion.

Using a longitudinal data source, Thornton, Alwin, and Camburn (1983) found a definite trend toward egalitarian sex-role concepts among females during the 1970s and the 1980s. They discovered that acceptance of egalitarianism correlated with being younger, having more education, and having spent more time in the labor force; church attendance and a fundamentalist religious identification fostered the maintenance of traditional sex-role attitudes. Furthermore, it appears that mothers' sex-role attitudes are important in shaping the attitudes of their children. Egalitarian mothers are likely to have egalitarian children.

In summary, demographic, survey, and interview data from children, adolescents, and adults suggest that society is slowly moving toward egalitarianism in sex-role orientation. The evidence indicates, however, that change is at best gradual and is inching rather than racing along.

Shifts in Motives and Values

One must likewise ask if shifts are occurring in sex-role attitudes. Using data from studies completed in 1957 and 1976, Veroff, Depner, Kulka, and Douvan (1980) compared men's and women's responses on four basic motives: (1) the need for achievement, or the importance of meeting standards of excellence; (2) the need for affiliation, or the importance of maintaining emotional connections with others; (3) the fear of weakness, or concern about maintaining one's status through another person; and (4) the hope for power, or the importance given to having an impact through one's own actions. Need for achievement and desire for power are associated with traditional views of masculinity; need for affiliation and fear of weakness are more closely associated with issues of femininity.

Four important conclusions emerge from this study. First, reported achievement motivation increased from 1957 to 1976 for women but not for men. Second, men diminished in their affiliation motivation, while women remained stable over the two decades. Third, both men and women showed significant increases in their concerns about weakness. Finally, men showed an increase in hope for power, but women did not.

This study suggests that gradual change toward egalitarianism is associated with parallel changes in men's and women's motives. Women are showing an increasing need for achievement. Their patterns of employment and reported motives reveal more interest in long-term professional careers. They report increased interest in contributing to society and in meeting standards of excellence that underlie their intentions. Men, by comparison, show little substantial change in such motivations. While women are increasing their achievement needs and making employment gains, however, men are showing increased interest in power and are decreasing their affiliative needs. These latter findings may reflect a threat perceived by men posed by the changes in women's needs. By increasing their power over another and decreasing their desire to affiliate, threatened males may be attempting to maintain control without emotional costs.

Studies such as these and others suggest that egalitarianism and role-sharing interests are accompanied by shifts in motives, values, and other psychological facets of development and behavior (see, for example, Bryant & Veroff, 1982). As adolescents develop in a culture with changing motives and values, many effects, as yet not fully understood, are likely to influence their ultimate developmental patterns. At best, as we have said, one can hypothesize that the more liberal the parents, in particular the mother, the greater the likelihood of the adolescent (boy or girl) developing egalitarian attitudes and a role-sharing attitude.

Benefits and Problems from Change

Relatively few investigations have examined the potential benefits and problems associated with the gradual societal changes in egalitarian attitudes. Elsewhere we have reviewed the implications for family life (Gullotta et al., 1986). Extrapolations from this review suggest several benefits for adolescents. First, the parents of adolescents with egalitarian attitudes are likely to engage in a mixture of behaviors defined as masculine and feminine. They thus illustrate role-modeling flexibility, adaptability, and fluidity in behavior for emulation by their children. Second, the freedom from traditional views of sex-role behavior may create an open environment for experimentation and personal expression of whatever is appealing to the youth, regardless of gender. And third, given that egalitarian couples are generally happier, adolescents are likely to view role-sharing behaviors within the context of positive affect and joy. This context may create a reinforcement process in which positive emotional states are associated with the personal freedom of an egalitarian viewpoint.

Problems are likely, too. Egalitarian attitudes are apt to result in dual-career families and parents who either commute long distances to work or live part of the time separated. This situation may mean less parental contact for the adolescent. Egalitarianism may also be seen as flexibility without traditional psychological boundaries and may create uncertainty and confusion for early adolescents in particular. And peers who have been reared more traditionally may not respond favorably to egalitarian adolescents at school or in the neighborhood.

Conceptualizing Gender Differences

Some psychologists and psychiatrists argue that gender differences are inevitable because of biological destiny. Others argue that the concept of differences has resulted in discriminatory perceptions, and even behaviors, toward females. Still others argue that no meaningful or real differences actually exist.

At the simplest level, differences that are detected between male and female adolescents can simply be genetic. That is, the chromosomes that determine whether one is phenotypically referred to as a female or as a male also determine gender-specific behaviors. This explanation is readily used in the animal kingdom to explain differences between males and females in courtship, aggression, parenting, and other behaviors of a social nature. One can question, however, to what degree this perspective is useful in understanding human behavior (see Montemayor, 1990).

Another viable perspective is suggested by sociobiology (for example, E. O. Wilson, 1975). This conceptualization, sometimes called human ethology, argues, in general terms, that genetically based evolutionary factors are predictive of basic differences between genders and even races. Ethologists support such assumptions through genetic studies with both animals and human beings. Human ethologists argue that basic genetic differences are predictive of dyadic "dominance behaviors" that occur within social groups, resulting in hierarchical status differences. Hence, some individuals have a higher social status because

Gender differences can be based on biological or sociocultural factors. Differences are obviously seen in group behavior.

of a genetically determined higher frequency of dominance behavior. Studies with birds and with primates and other mammals are cited to support the existence of dominance, in humans and animals alike. Perhaps the most notable and interesting ethological work with adolescents is being undertaken by Savin-Williams (1979).

The basic conceptualizations suggested by geneticists and ethologists are similar, yet these two groups have distinctively different viewpoints of the underpinnings of gender differences. The *genetic hypothesis* assumes that chromosomal differences cause basic physiological, biochemical, or neurological differences that result in different functional behaviors. The *ethological perspective* recognizes that basic biological/genetic differences exist. It adds that through a process of evolutionary development these differences evolve. Finally, it posits a biosocial connection by which differences in social status emerge and influence behaviors in mate selection, aggression, and so forth.

It might be argued that in our primitive past dominance in the form of threat and appeasement assured access to food and sex. Savin-Williams suggests, however, that through an evolutionary process the need for dominance and its corresponding high social ranking are more directly linked with the need to maintain self-esteem, self-respect, and self-worth. By elevating one's social status, one is thought to correspondingly elevate one's prestige, social worth, and self-appraisal. Thus, we can infer from this perspective that differences between males and females may be due to biological underpinnings that result in different forms of dominance-related behaviors for males and females. Ethologists have tentatively suggested that males gain social dominance and status through physical and aggressive behaviors, whereas females use more interpersonal or social-influence behaviors.

We look next at three behaviors that have been broadly studied and that seem to be supportive of this biosocial conceptualization of gender differences. We document that systematic and consistent differences are found between males and females in aggression, "influenceability," and social-relation skills.

The magnitude of these differences remains uncertain, however. We further agree with Maccoby (1990) that differences may be mostly due to situational contexts in which they are observed.

Aggression

Several major reviews of research on aggression have concluded that males, at all ages, are more physically aggressive than are females (see, for example, Eron, Walder, & Lefkowitz, 1971; R. Johnson, 1972; Maccoby & Jacklin, 1974). Caution must be maintained about this general assumption, since females have been shown to be more aggressive in some family-conflict situations (Lips & Colwill, 1978), but the general rule that males are more aggressive than females still appears to hold.

A number of explanations have been advanced for this commonly replicated finding. Some have argued that an evolutionary explanation can explain the difference. Because males are stronger and larger, they historically may have become more aggressive than females to assure survival of the group or tribe. However, such an explanation is difficult to defend with data. Conversely, more popular explanations of sex differences in aggression have been based on physiology. For example, some studies suggest that aggression is associated with the male Y chromosome (Lips & Colwill, 1978). However, the findings in support of this argument are very mixed, and we do not accept them. Another argument is that the male hormone called androgen causes the difference. Indeed, castration of animals is one way of controlling their aggression. Yet another argument is that the Y chromosome may be associated with a preparedness to learn aggressive behavior, while the female X chromosome may have an inhibitory mechanism that minimizes aggressive learning.

Regardless of which hypothesis, if any, emerges as the strongest explanation for the sex difference in aggression, we can only speculate that physiological mechanisms are part of the reason and that environmental factors support the physiological mechanisms. No doubt learning mechanisms either support or supplement the physiological properties behind aggression in highly complex and interacting ways.

Influenceability

While males are thought to be more aggressive, women are commonly seen as more influenceable. In other words, in conformity or persuasion situations women are thought to be more readily swayed by another's position. Indeed, a review of 61 persuasion studies, 64 conformity studies involving group pressure, and 23 conformity studies not involving group pressure showed that at varying ages women are consistently more readily influenced by social pressure than are men (Eagly & Carli, 1981: see also Eagly, 1987). We contend that such a finding might be expected with adolescent populations, given that several of Gerald Adams' studies comparing adolescent boys and girls on empathic abilities and tendencies have consistently shown females to be significantly more empathic (Adams, 1981b; Adams, Schvaneveldt, & Jenson, 1979). Due to their strong empathic tendencies, females may find themselves experiencing an emotional attachment to or identification with another that enhances their tendency to be influenced by that person (see also Camarena, Sarigioani, & Petersen's [1990] study on gender-specific pathways to intimacy). This assumption is bolstered by other evidence indicating that females report a need to feel emotionally attached to (love) another person before they feel they can share things about themselves. Conversely, for males, self-disclosure apparently precedes the development of an emotional attachment (G. R. Adams & Shea, 1981).

Capacity for Friendship and Intimate Relations

Although both males and females obviously develop friendships beginning in infancy and continue to do so throughout the life cycle, there is growing evidence that females are more capable of developing and maintaining intimate relations. Judith Fischer (1981) has reviewed numerous studies that support this notion for adolescence. Her review indicates that girls demonstrate friendships of greater depth and intimacy than do boys in self-disclosure patterns (Rivenbark, 1956), show greater depth in the topics disclosed to others (Mulcahey, 1973), use friends for greater support and sharing (Douvan & Adelson, 1966), and establish more committed and mature intimate relations than do males in late adolescence (Hodgson & Fischer, 1979). Fischer also reports data supporting the notion that females develop skills in relating to others earlier than do males. Other findings indicate that interpersonal competence is correlated with friendship intimacy during adolescence; and that friendship intimacy is predictive of adjustment. These findings are observed for middle but not early adolescents (Buhrmester, 1990).

The gender differences we have discussed have been found relatively consistently between male and female children, adolescents, and adults. These differences are likely to be based on both biological and psychological mechanisms that are gender specific but are influenced by several complex social factors. Nonetheless, they clearly demonstrate that working with adolescents requires a recognition that certain average differences are likely between males and females. See Box 11-1 for a further discussion on gender differences.

Theories of Sex-Role Development

To this point we have focused on gender differences. However, many of the differences between boys and girls are based on their acceptance of what they and society judge to be appropriate sex-typed behavior. This process of identifying and accepting specific sex-typed behavior based on societal standards results in a *sex-role identity*. We now examine the theories used most frequently to explain sex-role development, followed by an overview of the basic personality, behavioral, and family-life correlates of sex roles.

Social-Learning Theories

Many psychologists have presented a social-learning explanation of sex-role development. The basic argument is that boys learn boy things and girls learn girl things through society's encouragement of them to engage in sex-appropriate behavior. A combination of *reinforcement* and *punishment* is used to encourage gender-appropriate conduct. Most social-learning theorists argue that children and adolescents observe appropriate role models engaging in gender-appropriate behavior. They are reinforced for their imitation of such behavior, whereas they

---

Box 11–1   An Explanation for Gender Differences

Eleanor Maccoby (1990), a prominent developmental psychologist, has provided a compelling account for why boys and girls differ in their gender relationships. Focusing on the common observation that children prefer same-sex playmates, she offers one explanation for attraction to same-sex playmates and the avoidance of opposite-sex peer groups.

Maccoby suggests that the rough-and-tumble play of boys and their orientation toward competition and dominance are aversive to most girls. Furthermore, girls commonly find it difficult to influence the behavior of boys. Therefore, Maccoby offers the hypothesis that girls find it aversive to try to interact with boys, given their general unresponsiveness and relatively antagonistic behaviors, therein avoiding opposite-sex play groups.

She goes on to argue that two distinct cultures emerge during the course of growing up. The male culture (all-male groups) involves such behaviors as interruption of another, use of commands, threats, or boasts of authority, refusal to comply, offering information, heckling a speaker, and topping another's story. The female culture (all-female groups) manifest behaviors such as expressing agreement, pausing for a speaker, taking turns in speaking, and acknowledging a point of view. Maccoby suggests that the male culture has primarily an egoistic function, while the female culture has a socially binding function.

As boys and girls mature into men and women the two cultures are increasingly likely to interact. What happens? Often the cultures clash. To quote Maccoby (1990):

> People of both sexes are faced with a relatively unfamiliar situation to which they must adapt. Young women are less likely to receive the reciprocal agreement, opportunities to talk, and so on that they have learned to expect when interacting with female partners. Men have been accustomed to counter-dominance and competitive reactions to their own power assertions, and they now find themselves with partners who agree with them and otherwise offer enabling responses. (P. 517)

Can you guess which of the two groups might find it hardest to adjust? Maccoby argues that in heterosexual relationships the men will find it easier to adapt than the women. Do you agree with this conclusion?

---

are punished for engaging in opposite-gender conduct and activities. Underlying this theoretical perspective is the notion that one can then change an adolescent's sex-role behavior by changing role models, modifying reinforcements, and so forth. Furthermore, because each culture role-models different images or messages, differences in sex-role behavior are thought to be accounted for by the nature of the roles being modeled.

This straightforward social-learning perspective is fundamentally behaviorist. In the extreme form the behaviorist perspective focuses on stimuli and responses while ignoring any mediating organismic or personality variables, such as temperament or cognitive capacity. However, a *cognitive social-learning* camp has emerged, which recognizes that mental processes play an important role in sex-role development. In particular, it is assumed that as children or adolescents experience the consequences of their actions, they form expectancies about the likely consequences of future behaviors. Therefore, as expectancies emerge through reinforced or punished actions, they come to guide behavior.

Cognitive-Developmental Theories

In contrast to social-learning theories, cognitive-developmental theories focus on the youth's concepts about masculinity, femininity, and gender-appropriate conduct. Thought is given importance over actual behavior (Huston, 1983). In these theories the ways in which children organize their thoughts about sex roles are viewed as organizing schemata (thought processes) that guide them in selecting information from their environment and actively organizing it. From a developmental perspective the schema concerning sex-role behaviors and attitudes changes as children mature, with both innate development and environmental (or experiential) learning recognized as important influences on how youths think about sex typing.

Several cognitive-developmental theories have been developed to describe sex-role development. Kohlberg (1969) argued that the basis for sex typing was children's cognitive organization of their world. He viewed children as having a gender identity early on. This identity provides the basic self-categorization of what a boy or a girl is. The gender-identity schema serves the role of selecting and organizing information about what is gender appropriate. As the schema becomes stable or constant in a child's mind, it becomes an increasingly dominant organizer of social information, which is influenced by the sex-stereotyped information and social roles the child observes. The major point is that a child has a relatively innate view of what gender identity is and that this identity functions to select and organize information. Although societal factors influence the child's standards, the child's own thinking processes are more powerful in determining attitudes, preferences, or values about sex roles.

J. H. Block (1973) has proposed a similar developmental theory based on stages of ego development. She draws on notions of *agency* and *communion* in describing sex-role development. *Agency* refers to the tendency to be individualistic or self-assertive; *communion* refers to interpersonal harmony, altruism, cooperativeness, and group consensus. In Block's developmental framework, younger children are more "agentic," then move toward conformity with roles that are sex appropriate, and only in latter years, when they are capable of introspection and self-consciousness, come to integrate aspects of masculinity or femininity in the form of an androgynous sex type. As Huston (1983) indicates, in an analysis of Block's theory, the content of sex roles is viewed as being mostly determined by the child's cultural and social experience, although maturational variables provide the basic underpinnings for the structure of how children think about sex-typed content.

In all cognitive-developmental theories the youth moves from an oversimplified, underdeveloped, or disorganized state of sex-role perceptions into a pattern of conformity to gender-specific societal standards, with final movement to greater selection, choice, and integration of both masculine and feminine characteristics. In recent years cognitive-development theories have been further elaborated using information-processing theories. Information-processing models such as those proposed by Bem (1981) or Martin and Halverson (1981) hold that schemata consist of a set of expectations that guide and organize an individual's perceptions. The sex-role schema serves as anticipatory thinking structures that compel the individual or youth to seek information that is consistent with the currently held sex-typing attitude; information that is inconsistent with a current schema is ignored, transformed, or somehow reorganized. Indeed, a sex-role schema is thought to be relatively stable and not easily modified. This view of sex-role development presents the individual as a very active constructionist of his or her own perceptual realities.

Psychoanalytic Theory

In addition to the cognitive and information-processing theories of sex-role development, one of the oldest theories of sex typing was proposed by Sigmund Freud. His perspective was a combined emotional and social-cognitive one. He believed that the foundation of sex-role development began with a child's sexual interest toward a parent. According to psychoanalytic theory, a boy sexually desires his mother and envies his father for the father's possession of her time and attention. Thus, the father is the target of the boy's hostility, and the mother is the target of his sexual impulses and interest. Recognizing, however, that his impulses must go unfulfilled and aware that an expression of those feelings could result in the loss of either or both parents' love, the boy represses his impulses. As a defense against the threat of these sexual and hostile impulses, the child engages in an identification process. Through this process, the child is thought both to internalize the moral standards of the more threatening parent and to transform his or her personality through socialization.

Figure 11–1 contrasts the three basic theoretical perspectives that are used to explain sex-role development during childhood and adolescence. Although many psychologists and educators use the psychoanalytic theory to explain sex-typed identity, very little strong empirical evidence can be found to support it (Damon, 1983). Indeed, the evidence suggests that once a child has developed a stable gender identity, he or she will spontaneously seek out and develop sex-appropriate values and standards. Furthermore, because youths perceive what is similar to them as good, they will probably identify with the

Figure 11–1   Three Theoretical Models Explaining Sex-Role Development.

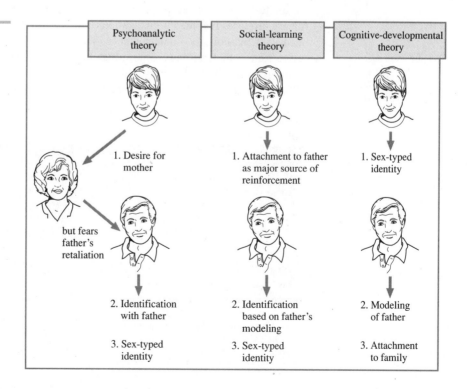

same-sex parent as a model. This identification process is completed when the youth develops a strong and lasting emotional attachment to the same-sex parent. This attachment encourages conformity to that parent's standards and role-modeled behaviors.

Correlates of Sex Roles

Sandra Bem's (1974) classic analysis of sex-role development provides a description of four basic sex types. Using information regarding the characteristics of *masculinity* and *femininity* (see Table 11–1), she has compared four basic groups (see Figure 11–2). As the figure indicates, a *feminine* person is high on femininity but low on masculinity. A *masculine* person is high on masculinity and low on femininity. But two additional sex types can also be identified. A person low on both femininity and masculinity can be theoretically observed and is called *undifferentiated*. A person high on both masculinity and femininity is referred to as *androgynous*. (See Box 11–2 for a possible biological link to sex roles.)

In recent years, as old views of masculine and feminine sex types have been challenged (Huston, 1983), new and broader definitions of sex typing have emerged. Arguments have been advanced that the traditional concepts of task competence associated with masculinity and emotional expressiveness associated with femininity need not be rigidly defined by gender. Rather, Bem and others have argued that both males and females may internalize psychological attributes that are associated with instrumental and expressive characteristics and competencies. In the past psychologists argued that masculinity for males and femininity for females were the preferred, if not the ideal, sex typing. Contemporary theory proposes that the internalization of the socially desirable attributes associated with masculinity—independence, self-confidence, and activity—and those associated with femininity—nurturing, helping, and kindness—in the form of *androgyny,* results in a healthy and adaptive sex-role concept for boys and girls. What, then, does the research literature indicate regarding this assumption?

Table 11–1 Masculine and Feminine Characteristics

Masculine	Feminine
Aggressive	Dependent
Competitive	Compliant
Logical	Emotional
Rough	Gentle
Loud	Quiet
Objective	Subjective
Uncaring	Caring
Blunt	Tactful
World oriented	Home oriented

Source: Derived from I. K. Braverman, D. M. Braverman, F. E. Clarkson, P. S. Rosenkrantz, & S. R. Vogel, "Sex Role Stereotypes and Clinical Judgments of Mental Health." *Journal of Consulting and Clinical Psychology,* 1970, *34,* pp. 1–7; E. Maccoby and C. N. Jacklin, *The Psychology of Sex Differences.* Stanford, Calif.: Stanford University Press, Copyright © 1974; and S. Weitz, *Sex Roles.* New York: Oxford University Press. Copyright © 1977.

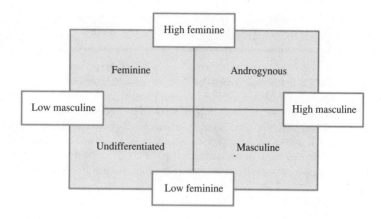

Figure 11–2 Bem's Categorization of Four Sex Types. (From "The Measurement of Psychological Androgyny," by S. L. Bem, *Journal of Consulting and Clinical Psychology,* 1974, *42,* 155–162. Copyright 1974 by the American Psychological Association. Reprinted by permission.)

Sex Roles and Personality

A perusal of the research literature looking at the personality correlates of sex typing provides general support for the notion that undifferentiated adolescents have the least desirable personality profiles and that masculine, feminine, and androgynous adolescents have more socially desirable personalities. Distinctions between the latter three sex types are somewhat less clear. However, a select series of studies suggests that androgyny may be more desirable than masculine and feminine sex types.

For example, K. Wells (1980) has assessed the adjustment of high school students based on sex-role development. In this study androgynous youths, particularly adolescent males, maintained better social adjustment than other youths. Other research suggests that highly feminine females are significantly inhibited in their individuality, achievement, and expression of autonomy (J. R. Block, Von der Lippe, & Block, 1973), with highly masculine males being more prone to neurosis and high anxiety (Hartford, Willis, & Deabler, 1967). Behavioral research has found that more feminine individuals (both boys and girls) are less prone to loneliness (Wheeler, Reis, & Nezlek, 1983). Feminine individuals, as expected, are more interpersonally focused, thus decreasing the amount of time they spend alone and the likelihood of their being lonely.

Clinical investigations of sex typing and adaptational or dysphoric characteristics have also provided important evidence of the personality correlates of sex roles. For example, J. S. Shaw (1982) has shown that androgynous people perceive potentially disruptive life events as less stressful than other sex types. In a mixed finding, Frank, McLaughlin, and Crusco (1984) provide evidence that when dysphoric states of stress (reflected by somatization, obsessiveness, sensitivity, depression, anxiety, fears, and hostility) were assessed, masculine women reported relatively low and feminine men relatively high degrees of distress. Thus, masculinity may be an enhancing factor for women in this regard, while femininity may be a detrimental factor for males. Overall, however, a number of investigations reveal that undifferentiated adolescents are least likely to report socially desirable characteristics on self-concept and identity development measures (Schiedel & Marcia, 1985; Selva & Dusek, 1984; Ziegler, Dusek, & Carter, 1984). And androgynous youths consistently

Box 11–2   A Biological Connection with Sex Roles

The natural production of the male steroid known as testosterone in the testes and in females' ovaries and adrenal glands has been shown to be associated with a masculinizing effect resulting in increased body hair, muscular structure, and sex drive. Animal researchers have found that it is associated with aggressiveness, particularly for males. Baucom, Besch, and Callahan (1985) have tested the association between testosterone concentrations and sex roles. Measuring the testosterone concentration of saliva samples provided by females, they computed a correlation between the measurement and assessments of masculinity and femininity. These investigators observed that undifferentiated females had higher levels of testosterone than did feminine sex-typed women. Further, women with higher levels of masculinity (androgynous and masculine sex typing) had higher testosterone levels than did feminine sex-typed peers.

Likewise, self-reported data indicated that females with higher testosterone concentrations perceived themselves as self-directed, resourceful, action-oriented persons. In comparison, lower testosterone concentration was associated with self-perceived conventionality, well-socialized and caring/nurturing attitudes, and moodiness.

Studies such as these suggest a biological link between hormones and psychological mechanisms such as sex roles. Furthermore, these findings provide important information supporting an ethological view of relationships between biological and psychological processes. If these investigators had studied prepubescent, pubescent, and menopausal women, what association between hormone production and sex roles might we expect to observe? Can you think of other critical tests of the biological/psychological connection's influence on sex roles and related social behaviors or constructs?

show the highest or most advanced development of identity, self-esteem and self-concept (Lamke, 1982; Lamke & Abraham, 1984; Mullis & McKinley, 1989). Likewise, the more positive outcomes for the androgynous youths appear to be associated with desirable or positive resolutions of earlier life crises associated with the formation of trust, autonomy, industry, and identity (Ziegler & Dusek, 1985).

When these and other findings are examined in the context of studies (Hiller & Philliber, 1985) showing that measures of sex-role development such as the one Bem used (1974) are primarily assessing aspects of assertiveness (dominant, forceful, aggressive, strong, assertive) and sensitivity (sensitive, sympathetic, tender, warm, gentle, affectionate), it becomes clear why corresponding personality characteristics are observed. Furthermore, the findings appear generally to support the notion that androgynous adolescents are likely to have more adaptive, flexible, socially adept, and mature personalities than are the other three basic sex types.

Sex Roles and Social Behavior

Perhaps the most important aspect of masculine, feminine, and androgynous characteristics is their significance for social behavior. An individual can maintain either a self-assertive or an integrative pattern of interacting with others. Indeed, aspects of self-assertion and integration/nurturance are thought to be equally important aspects of social competence. *Self-assertion,* the traditional masculine pattern, involves assertiveness, independence, and dominance. *Integration,* the traditional feminine pattern, is a more expressive role that promotes intimacy, nurturance, and cooperation in the form of social unity and connectedness. An individual can possess both self-assertive and integrative patterns of behavior and therein be androgynous.

In recent years some scholars have suggested that androgynous men and women may be more competent than traditionally sex-typed persons (Bem, 1977; Orlofsky, Aslin, & Ginsburg, 1977; Spence & Helmreich, 1979). In one review of this hypothesis, Ford (1981) proposed six major criteria of competence: self-esteem, mental health and psychological adjustment, physical health, psychological development, achievement motivation, and social competence. This review presents four basic conclusions:

1. Androgynous people generally score high on self-esteem, but not much higher than masculine people. Both these groups generally have higher self-esteem than do the feminine groups.

2. Androgynous and masculine people are likely to have positive mental health and better psychological adjustment than are feminine people.

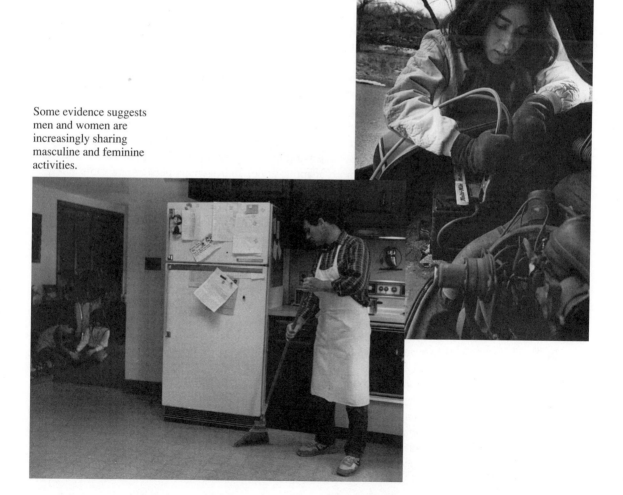

Some evidence suggests men and women are increasingly sharing masculine and feminine activities.

3. Androgynous and masculine characteristics are predictors of mature identity development, sexual maturity, and achievement motivation.

4. Androgynous and masculine characteristics are strong predictors of assertiveness, independence, dominance, positive interpersonal adjustment, social poise, and certain aspects of leadership, while androgyny and femininity are associated with other competence criteria such as nurturance and solidarity.

From this review we can see that self-assertion blended with integration, and at times self-assertion alone, are strongly associated with behavioral competencies. (This conclusion is, in general, supported by a review of sex-role research by Markstrom-Adams, 1989). Further evidence supporting this conclusion can be found in the results of several investigations. For example, a series of experimental studies on the flexibility of androgynous youths has indicated that androgynous males and females are capable of changing their behavior to suit the situation (Bem, 1975; Bem, Martyna, & Watson, 1976). In two experiments reported by Bem (1975), androgynous subjects were able to display "masculine" independence in a pressure-to-conform setting and to display "feminine" playfulness with a kitten in another condition. All these studies suggest that androgyny is a very flexible sex-role identity that allows fluidity in numerous social settings.

As we have reported, androgynous boys, girls, men, and women have a stronger capacity for establishing intimate relations. But there are further implications of an androgynous identity. Sex-role identity may have a direct bearing on the type of persuasion techniques used in romantic or intimate relations. While masculine individuals apparently use more direct strategies, such as telling their partner to do something, feminine persons are more likely to use indirect strategies, such as pouting. However, in accordance with their more flexible and possibly more adaptive style, androgynous persons are more likely to see themselves using persuasion, bargaining, or positive affect to get their way (Falbo & Peplau, 1979).

The Influence of Society

Little research has been conducted on how societal forces influence sex-role identity over time. However, J. H. Block (1973) has argued that society tends to encourage a more androgynous sex-role identity for boys as they get older but reinforces a very narrowly defined feminine orientation for girls as they mature. Some data (C. J. Mills, 1981) support this general notion, but other data from life-span samples provide mixed evidence. For example, Spence and Helmreich (1979) compared scores on masculinity and femininity scales for male and female high school students, college students, parents of elementary school children, and parents of college students. In contrast to Block's assertion, with advancing age, masculinity responses increased, while females showed no developmental pattern. Similarly, at all ages females were more supportive of egalitarian (role-sharing) roles for men and women than were males. Conversely, using better measurement techniques, Hyde and Phillis (1979) compared the scores of subjects aged 13 to 85 on an actual androgyny measure. These researchers report that the percentage (frequency) of androgynous identities was lower for males aged 13 to 40 than for males 41 and older. Females showed just the opposite pattern; more androgynous females were found in the younger group. However, recent replication studies show both genders become more feminine with age (Hyde, Krajnik, & Skuldt-Niederberger, 1991). Clearly, these data hint that maturational changes or environmental influences may change one's sex-role preference or orientation.

Indeed, the results of a very creative study by Abrahams, Feldman, and Nash (1978) suggest that we are likely to identify with the sex-role orientation that best fits our life situation. These researchers hypothesized that when individuals who were cohabitating (living together), married without children, married and expecting a child, or married with children were compared, major differences in sex-role preference would be found. The general logic was that the first two life situations would heighten androgynous (role-sharing) tendencies but that in the last two situations a greater division of labor would occur. The male would see himself as having to emphasize his career and financial responsibilities, and the female would emphasize child care and housekeeping. The results of the study supported this general notion. A much greater likelihood of identifying with an androgynous sex role was found in the first two life situations.

Thus, major life experiences may require or reinforce certain masculine or feminine identities. Males and females can be expected to express sex-role identities that are best suited for general social adjustment to their life situation. For early adolescents, this is likely to mean a very masculine orientation for most boys and a feminine one for girls. When subjects aged 7, 10, and 14 were compared on their perceptions of dominance and nurturance in male and female figures, a developmental trend toward increased attribution of dominance to males and nurturance to females was found with advancing age (Rothbaum, 1977). Other evidence suggests that adolescence proper (high school age) is the period of most stereotyping based on sex-role perceptions of masculinity and femininity (Urberg, 1979), with girls showing both major concern about achievement and identification with stereotyped cultural sex roles (Beech & Schoeppe, 1974). (See Box 11–3.) However, as the adolescent matures during the college years, new life events may substantially change the more traditional masculine or feminine sex-role orientation toward a more egalitarian androgynous preference. Furthermore, the life-span research reviewed here suggests that this pattern fluctuates depending on what life situations emerge during adulthood. (See Boxes 11–4 and 11–5 for discussions of cultural features and sex role behavior development.)

John Hill and Lynch (1989) argue that an acceleration of gender-differential socialization during adolescence accounts for increases in boys' identification with masculine characteristics and girls' identification with feminine characteristics. According to Hill and Lynch, the research literature suggests that substantial and widening gender differences emerge during adolescence in self-consciousness, achievement, self-concept and self-esteem, friendships and intimacy, activity levels, and aggression. These widening gender differences

Box 11–3   Cross-Cultural Comparison of Sex Roles

David Tzuriel (1981) has examined the cultural context of sex roles. He hypothesized that a traditional Oriental adolescent group would be less androgynous than a Western more egalitarian group. Comparisons of 11th- and 12th-grade students (571 boys and 636 girls) in 22 religious and secular schools in Israel, however, revealed that more androgynous and less traditional sex-typed adolescents were observed in the Oriental group than in the Western group. The author suggests that the Oriental group is not living in cultural isolation or alienation from the dominant Western culture. However, he does not explain why the Oriental group is not merely equivalent to the Western group. What factors should we consider in understanding why differing minority groups might vary in their sex-role identities? Consider having members of your class or invited panel members discuss cultural factors that are operating to encourage or discourage androgyny, masculinity, or femininity in your own immediate community.

(gender intensification) may be due to changes accompanying pubescence. As boys and girls move into their adolescent growth spurt, they may become anxious and self-conscious about their appearance. In turn, they may draw on stereotypical perceptions and behaviors to provide a degree of assurance or security. This tendency seems particularly evident for girls. For boys, puberty may be associated with more tolerance from adults for independence and more punishment for any form of emotional display. Indeed, fathers may not only be less protective of their maturing sons but may also actually encourage certain forms of sexual conquests as their sons attain adultlike physical stature. However, recent longitudinal research, comparing pubertal timing (early, on time, late) found that masculine sex role attitudes increased from the 11th to 13th years of age, but pubertal timing did not predict gender intensification (Galambos, Almeida, & Petersen, 1990).

Implications of Androgyny

Let us risk, for a moment, the possibility that you will strongly disagree with us and speculate on some possible implications of androgyny for adolescents. Keep in mind that we are speculating on the basis of our own clinical and educational experiences more than on the basis of hard data about implications.

First, we suspect that androgynous boys and girls both have an uncomfortable adolescence. The general extremes in sex-role identity during this period make androgynous adolescents a relatively small cluster of youths in a large population of more traditionally oriented adolescents. The androgynous youths are therefore likely to be, at times, kidded or hassled by peers, teachers, and even parents. At times they are likely to be labeled and even criticized. But their flexibility and multiple interests and aptitudes will also enable them to adapt to their surroundings. An androgynous male adolescent may be just as likely to be a football player as the lead in the school play. The androgynous girl may be on the debate team, play basketball, and love home economics or typing courses.

Box 11–4   The Roots of "Machismo"

Macho is taken from the Spanish word *machismo* and "means the essence or soul of masculinity" (Mosher & Tomkins, 1987, p. 65). Machismo and the patriarchal ideology are commonly associated with Mexican American and other Hispanic families. Some evidence suggests these concepts may be gradually decreasing in their influence among Mexican American families (Ramirez, 1989). Furthermore, the concept of machismo is found among men from a variety of racial and ethnic backgrounds. It is important to address the development of this attitude because of its detrimental effect not only on women, but on the macho male.

Mosher and Tomkins (1987) define machismo as "a system of ideas forming a world view that chauvinistically exalts male dominance by assuming masculinity, virility, and physicality to be the ideal essence of real men who are adversarial warriors competing for scarce resources (including women as chattel) in a dangerous world" (p. 64). According to Mosher and Tomkins (1987), a macho approach toward life is perpetuated through the following seven socialization dynamics:

First, beginning in infancy and continuing over the course of childhood, parents attempt to socialize the male children into becoming a "real man" through the failure to relieve the male child's distress until it is expressed as anger.

Second, the expression of fear in boys is suppressed by parents through a variety of tactics. For example, boys are forced to stay in the feared situation until habituation reduces the fear. Ideally, in response to perceived threat and danger, fear will be replaced by excitement.

Third, parents exhibit disgust toward the child's fear. Eventually, the boy will feel self-disgust and self-contempt in response to his distress and fear. A "real-boy" counters fear and distress with anger and aggressive counteraction.

Fourth, the boy feels pride for his ability to subjugate his fear and distress. Subsequently, he feels disgust and contempt for those who cannot do the same.

Fifth, due to the socialization practices of parents, a hostile-dominant interpersonal style predominates in the male offspring. Anger, pride, excitement, and other forms of "superior masculinity" are used to dominate others considered weaker, inferior, and submissive.

Sixth, the boy discovers that a strategy involving surprise heightens his own feelings of excitement, as well as inducing fear in others and gaining dominance over them.

Seventh, the macho male is suspicious of relaxed enjoyment, and engages in continual seeking after excitement. Joy only comes from victory.

The roots of machismo are thus firmly embedded in childhood. Significant during adolescence is the transition from "real boy" to "real man" that occurs through processes of socialization and enculturation in the male peer group. Judgments on the adolescent boy's transition into the "real man" are made by the male peer group in the fight scene, the danger scene, and the callous sex scene. The fight scene refers to the adolescent boy's fight to gain admission to the male peer group. Acceptance and friendship are rewards for boys who demonstrate courage and toughness. The danger scene is evidenced by the necessity to engage in reckless behavior and to take on the challenge of "the dare." Engaging in sexual intercourse as a means to prove one's masculinity and subsequently to boast of such exploits in the male peer group is necessary to pass tests in the callous sex scene.

Machismo demands a high price from the boys and men who adhere to its tenets. Any affect that hints of weakness and vulnerability is denied and dismissed. Honest emotions are suppressed and replaced by anger and feelings of power and superiority over others. Even positive feelings are suppressed since they are only derived from experiences of success, victory, and dominance. Self-awareness is limited because the self is defined only according to traits that support the superior notions of masculinity. Relationships lack true mutuality and reciprocity; thus, the development of intimacy is hindered.

If, as according to Mosher and Tomkins (1987), the roots of machoism are laid in childhood by parents and perpetuated in adolescence by the male peer group, how might intervention be directed toward promoting greater androgyny among male adolescents?

Box 11–5   Empowerment and Minority Female Youths

As noted in Box 9–3 "A model of Resistance for Liberation for African-American Females;" empowerment is a critical goal to incorporate in intervention strategies directed toward minority adolescent females. Empowerment is a concept central to the discussion of sex roles in this chapter. In particular, Parsons (1988) presents an intervention focused on empowerment for role alternatives among low income minority young women. Two aspects of empowerment that affect minority females include limitations in internal locus of control and constraints posed by sexism, racism, and classism in U.S. society. Limitations in both sources of empowerment contribute to limited recognition of role alternatives among low income minority adolescent females. Although Parsons (1988) focuses on the implications of this discussion in respect to adolescent pregnancy, limited conceptions of empowerment may contribute to other concerns of adolescence. For example, a weak sense of empowerment among low income minority adolescent females may contribute to feelings of hopelessness and depression, less than satisfactory career options, and engagement in deviant behavior.

Parson's (1988) empowerment intervention involves small groups of adolescent minority females (8 to 12 persons in a group) meeting for 90 minutes once a week over a period of several weeks. The goals of the program are to broaden the participants' knowledge of roles for women, to increase knowledge and resources of women's role alternatives, and to foster an active problem-solving orientation. Intervention is aimed at change in participants' own attitudinal and belief systems, as well as knowledge about and access to resources in the powerful societal systems with which the adolescents interact (for example, the health system and the school system). A variety of approaches are incorporated in the intervention, for example, role plays, educational games, information presented by professionals, group discussions, and field trips.

Posttest evaluation of this program reveal that participants became less traditional in their value systems, increased in their knowledge of role alternatives for women, and increased in perception of control. Apparently, empowerment strategies are effective when intervening with minority adolescent women. Further studies are required to assess the long-term effects of such programs on minority women's personal goal setting and career development.

Second, we suspect that androgynous youths are likely to be admired by many teachers who see them as having more complex and richer personalities. Having a mixture of male and female sex-role characteristics can help them develop relationships with both male and female teachers, particularly if the androgynous youths have both achievement and nurturant capacities.

Third, we suspect that androgynous youths will have a richer educational experience. With their multiple interests, such youths may well experience a wider range of curricula, extracurricular activities, and possibly school-leadership roles. We are not implying that there will be no hardship associated with these experiences, but the dividends may far exceed the costs.

Little research is available on the implications of an androgynous sex-role identity for adolescents as they move into adulthood. Some dated research from the Berkeley Growth Studies suggests that a highly masculinized adolescent may be very well suited for the adolescent world but that such an extreme sex-role identity may be counterproductive in an adult world that is more androgynous (that is, for the more prestigious, high-paying jobs).

Sex Roles and Family Life

The place of sex roles in family life has been discussed by both sociologists (Scanzoni & Fox, 1980) and psychologists (Huston, 1983). A growing body of research indicates that various parental childrearing or socialization factors contribute to an adolescent's sex-role development (see Huston & Alvarez, 1990). According to Lidz (1963) an optimal development for children occurs in families where mothers and fathers assume their respective gender-linked roles of femininity and masculinity, in an atmosphere of mutual care, love, respect, and support. Evidence from M. M. Klein and Shulman (1981) supports this general assumption. Masculine fathers and feminine mothers who were rearing their family within a well-adjusted and happy marriage had adolescents who were likely to be androgynous. Likewise, Ziegler and Dusek (1985) report that parental acceptance fosters a more flexible or androgynous sex role. A firm and controlling parental style is believed to restrict masculine sex-role development be fostering dependence and other basically traditional feminine traits. It is only fair, however, to note that several researchers challenge such findings, based on complex data analyses and survey research (Costos, 1986; Lamke & Filsinger, 1983). Likewise, influences of mothers on daughters seem to be more consistently observed than influences of fathers on sons (Affleck, Morgan, & Hayes, 1989; Chandler, Sawicki, & Stryffeler, 1981; Costos, 1986; Notar & McDaniel, 1986; M. D. Smith & Self, 1980). Mothers' attitudes about sex roles, work, and career may, in particular, be predictive of androgynous and role-sharing attitudes by adolescent daughters (see also Corder & Stephan, 1984). Unfortunately, family decisions associated with career goals still favor sons over daughters in families with male and female adolescents (Peterson, Rollins, Thomas, & Heaps, 1982).

A common assumption by clinicians has been that divorce disrupts the modeling of appropriate sex-role behavior by a male or female role model. It is assumed that custodial mothers are unlikely to adequately role model self-assertion and integration to their sons, therefore placing them at a disadvantage for internalizing androgynous characteristics. However, a study by Kurdek and Siesky (1980a) revealed that youths from divorced homes were actually more androgynous than were adolescents from intact homes. This finding questions the notion that males in divorced homes are at risk for feminization. Perhaps single mothers work harder to ensure role-modeled self-assertive and integrative behaviors for their boys and girls, recognizing the risk their youths may be in, given their family living conditions.

In general, the research literature indicates that androgynous people are more competent, confident, spontaneous, and self-accepting. Likewise, they appear to have greater capacity for intimate contact (Bailey & Prager, 1984; Ickes & Barnes, 1979). But androgyny has still other implications for family life or interpersonal relationships. Falbo and Peplau (1979) have found that sex-role orientation has a direct implication for the type of power or persuasive technique a person will use in romantic or intimate relations. Their study suggests that masculine people employ more direct strategies, such as telling their partner to do something, which is consistent with a self-assertive interpretation of masculinity. Feminine people are more likely to use indirect and subtle techniques of an integrative nature. Androgynous people are more likely to use persuasion, bargaining, or positive affect—a combination of self-assertion and integration.

We conclude that the implications of sex-role development for family life are multiple. Parental socialization practices appear to enhance the process of developing a sex-role identity, although this identity may not be a direct function of the parent's sex role itself (Baumrind, 1982). Maternal socialization practices may have more of an influence on daughters' sex-role development than do fathers' socialization on sons' behaviors. Masculine and androgynous characteristics appear to be most strongly associated with competence. And competence can be reflected in behaviors that enhance social relationships and the quality of intimacy.

Major Points to Remember

1. Societal practices encourage a strong differentiation between boys and girls. Contemporary society is changing in its attitudes, however.
2. Some have argued that society is becoming increasingly liberalized. However, research evidence suggests that attitudes about men's and women's roles are changing only gradually.
3. Sex differences involve differences in behavior thought to be based on a highly complex interaction between biochemistry, genetic differences, and socialization processes. Sex-role identity involves the internalization or adoption of behaviors thought appropriate for masculine, feminine, or androgynous behavior.
4. Most adolescents identify with or prefer either a masculine or a feminine sex-role identity. A mixture of the two qualities is relatively rare in adolescence proper but begins to emerge during late adolescence, especially in boys.
5. Androgynous boys and girls seem to be somewhat better socially adjusted and have a greater capacity for forming friendships.
6. The process of identifying and accepting specific sex-typed behavior based on societal standards of maleness and femaleness results in a sex-role identity. Social learning theories focusing on reinforcement, punishment, and identification of role models were early frameworks for understanding sex-role identity. More contemporary cognitive development theories focus on thought processes, organizational schemata, maturational factors, and organismic variables to explain sex-role development and behaviors.
7. Bem's use of feminine and masculine characteristics to identify masculine, feminine, androgynous, and undifferentiated sex types has resulted in further refinements of sex-role development. Considerable data suggest that androgynous people are the most competent, with masculinity associated with self-assertiveness and femininity with nurturance and integrative social behaviors.
8. Parental socialization styles that include gender-linked roles of femininity and masculinity are thought to be optimal conditions for encouraging

androgyny in adolescents. Further, mothers may be more central in determining androgynous and role-sharing attitudes than are fathers. Finally, single mothers may work harder to ensure role modeling of self-assertiveness and integrative behaviors for their children, thereby having more androgynous adolescents.

9. Survey and interview data suggest a gradual movement in society toward an egalitarian, role-sharing view of family roles and living. Analyses of shifts in motives and values in need for achievement, need for affiliation, and related social constructs indicate that as females are making gains in need for achievement, men are responding with increased interest in need for power.

10. Benefits and problems are associated with the gradual changes toward increased egalitarianism for adolescents. Primary benefits may come in role modeling of flexibility, adaptability, and fluidity in behavior. Central problems may be limited contact with parents, lack of boundaries regarding gender-related psychological functions, and possible confusion regarding social roles of a traditional nature.

Adolescent Sexual Behavior and Development

A dolescence is filled with concerns about relationships, intimacy, and a growing interest (some would say obsession) with sexuality. In this chapter we examine some of the issues that today's youths confront as their sexuality emerges.

Adolescent Sexuality: Two Perspectives

There are at least two common perspectives of adolescent sexuality. The first understands young people as responding to instinctual, biologically driven sexual impulses. The second position understands adolescent sexuality as socially shaped and learned behavior.

Supporters of the first view argue that the same hormones that trigger the development of secondary sex characteristics in young people are also responsible for their sexual behavior. For example, several studies measuring male testosterone levels suggest that as the level of testosterone increases, so does male sexual activity (see B. C. Miller & Fox, 1987). Even though Sigmund Freud (1933, 1953) was not a biologist, his theory of human behavior certainly contained biological premises. In his view, unconscious innate drives move the young person toward genital sexuality. Indeed, were it not for the superego, the id in all of us would operate unrestrained. To illustrate, imagine all human behavior mirroring that found in those forgettable teenage exploitation films released at Easter break that depict young men and women dressed in little or nothing acting out instinctual mating rituals, and you have the essence of Freud's perspective.

Hirschi (1969) believes that deviant behavior (including adolescent sexual behavior) is the result of inadequate societal controls. This position (called social-control theory) maintains that schools, religious groups, and the family are responsible (due to weakened social bonds) when young people become prematurely sexually active. Examples of a societal control problem are readily identifiable. Miller and Bingham (1989) indicate that adolescents raised in a single-parent home are more likely than their peers from intact families to have nonmarital sexual intercourse. Newcomer and Udry (1987) suggest this early sexual behavior is due to reduced monitoring or limited supervision. However, Thorton and Camburn (1987) imply that divorced mothers may be less religious and hold more sexually permissive attitudes. Therefore, mother's role modeling may indicate more acceptance of nonmarital sexual behavior. The consequences might be that adolescents interpret this as parental acceptance of nonconventional behavior. To be fair, however, we have to recognize these interpretations of the data as being highly speculative. No "direct" evidence is available to support this tentative conclusion.

Proponents of this second position view sexual behavior as more socially learned than internally driven. According to social-control theory, society communicates its behavioral expectations through parents, the arts, the media, and other sources. These communications are then imitated by young people. For example, several researchers have used social-control theory to explain the finding that daughters living in single-parent families in which the parent is dating

---

Box 12–1   Intimacy: A Cross-Cultural Perspective

What does the word *intimacy* mean to you? Does it suggest very personal conversations with a loved one? Does it imply closeness and warmth with a significant other? Do you associate it with thoughts of romantic love? If you do, these are very Western ideas. In other parts of the world, they don't apply.

For example, in Bangladesh the concept of romantic love and the intimacy Westerners associate with it are foreign ideas. Most marriages in that Islamic nation are arranged. The average age of a young woman entering matrimony is 14, and it is expected that she will bring to the marriage not only the ability to bear children but also a dowry. Once married, this child bride can expect to have less food, poorer health care, and a lower standard of living than her husband (Mydans, 1988). Given these realities, do you believe it possible for such relationships to achieve a Western kind of intimacy?

Source: Mydane, S. (1988, April 17). "In Bangladesh, women can't go home again." NY Times, p. 8.

---

are often more sexually active than are daughters from two-parent families (see B. C. Miller & Fox, 1987). The implication, of course, is that the daughters in these families are modeling the behavior of their parent.

Intimacy

The need for closeness, a sense of emotional feeling for another, and the ability to share feelings honestly are some of the attributes of intimacy. (See Box 12–1.) It reflects a deep emotional involvement with another. As young people approach adolescence, their gradual drift away from their parents encourages them to seek peers with whom to share their innermost thoughts. This desire to share must be balanced, as Mitchell (1976) writes, against possible exploitation. Nevertheless, young people risk hurt feelings and rejection in order to form close relationships and romantic involvements that blossom sometimes only briefly. Mitchell understands intimacy to be "interwoven with the impulse for sexual expression" (pp. 442–443). He suggests that strong emotions for an individual, when coupled with physical contact, lead many young people to conclude that they are "in love"—a phrase that many adults tend to reject with such disparaging remarks as "Why, it's only puppy love" or "It's only a summer crush." Such remarks Mitchell correctly judges to be unfair value judgments of the sincerity and depth of the emotional feeling young people can have for each other even if the relationship is brief.

If the need for intimacy becomes coupled with physical sexual drives, as it does in adolescence, a conflict must inevitably arise between earlier parental and societal teachings about the standards for sexual intimacy (touching, caressing, fondling, body contact) and the young person's desire for that contact. The *traditional standard* forbids sexual intimacy (intercourse) until marriage. A variation of the traditional standard, the *double standard,* demands virginity from females but permits males to have sexual experiences with women. Thus, it is not unusual or surprising to find early studies reporting that the major reason young women gave for stopping short of intercourse was "morals" (see, for example, Ehrmann, 1959).

Reiss's (1967) work documents a shift in moral and sexual standards to a new position that condones intercourse for an engaged woman. More important, Reiss has observed a gradual movement away from traditional standards of approving sexual intimacy only with marriage or the promise of marriage to a new set of standards based on the degree of affection existing between two partners. To the abstinence standard and the double standard Reiss adds *permissiveness with affection* and *permissiveness without affection* as two new standards of male/female sexual intimacy. The emergence of these standards, wherein a couple decides to pursue a sexual relationship with or without emotional commitments, indicates an increasing regard for the quality of the relationship, whether based on affection or mutual physical desires.

In an attempt to clarify the moral reasoning of relationships, D'Augelli and D'Augelli (1977) offer a concept they call *relationship reasoning*. Described as a personality variable, it is an individual's "unique way of reasoning about interpersonal relationships" (p. 61). It reflects the current and future decisions an individual makes about a relationship—its initiation, development, or termination.

D'Augelli and D'Augelli (1977) propose that relationship reasoning has three levels. The first, *egotistic reasoning,* is an individual's conceptualization of the relationship in terms of a cost/benefit ratio. This individual sees interactions in the here and now and pays little attention to long-term interpersonal rewards. The ideal relationship is one that provides immediate gratification for the individual.

The second level, *dyadic reasoning,* is based on a partner's view of the relationship and is in keeping with traditional societal role expectations. These individuals will, if necessary, sacrifice personal rewards to "support the couple's socially defined conception of the relationship" (p. 62). The ideal relationship is one that offers the best opportunity for meeting a partner's expectations in the relationship.

The last level, *interactive reasoning,* is founded on each partner's needs and feelings. The D'Augellis (1977) describe it as "dynamic and fluid." This is the most open and egalitarian of the three levels, with both partners contributing to decision making.

Certainly, whether one finds a comfortable label for oneself in Reiss's (1967) four-part system or Jurich and Jurich's (1974) five-part system of sexual conduct (see Table 12–1), the sexual behavior of adolescents is affected by their memberships in countless institutions. Their behavior is shaped not only by their own needs but also by their upbringing. For example, several studies show that the higher the degree of religiosity, the greater the chances that premarital sexual activity will *not* occur (Ehrmann, 1959; Jurich & Jurich, 1974; Reiss, 1967).

One attempt to address the moral issues, by Mitchell (1975), examines the impact these institutions have on the adolescent and the conflict they produce when the young person suddenly perceives the world as no longer having absolute answers. Facing issues of conformity, double standards, and independence, the adolescent must also face sexuality as one of these growth dilemmas. The issue becomes how a young person balances moral teachings against the natural desire to engage in sexual activity. Inevitably, according to Mitchell, the young person disobeys the moral rule and experiences guilt. As Mitchell observes, "When the moral rule states that sexual behavior is taboo, the stage is

Table 12–1   Two Sexual-Conduct Systems

Reiss	*Jurich and Jurich*
Traditional standard Sexual intercourse is not permissible for either sex until marriage.	**Traditional standard** (same)
Double standard Sexual intercourse before marriage is permissible for males but not for "good" females.	**Double standard** (same)
Permissiveness with affection Sexual intercourse before marriage is permissible if the couple is "in love."	**Permissiveness with affection** (same)
Permissiveness without affection Sexual intercourse is permissible for physical pleasure; "love" need not be involved.	**Permissiveness without affection** (same)
	Nonexploitative permissiveness Sexual intercourse is permissible provided both partners operate from a mutual understanding: "love" need not be involved.

Source: I. Reiss, *The Social Context of Premarital Sexual Permissiveness.* New York: Holt, Rinehart & Winston. Copyright © 1967; and A. Jurich & J. Jurich, "The Effect of Cognitive Moral Development upon the Selection of Premarital Sexual Standards." *Journal of Marriage and the Family,* 1974, 35, pp. 736–741.

set for conflict. The adolescent must learn to live with the fact that moral beliefs do not always correspond with personal desires" (p. 443). The resolution of this situation occurs during adolescence. It is a natural process of "experimentation, trial and error, and introspection" (p. 443). Mitchell's view of adolescent sexual growth is, then, a healthy one recognizing that behavior is flexible and subject to change as the young person matures. For more information on promoting healthy adolescent sexuality we refer to Blau and Gullotta (1993) and Chilman (1990).

Learning the Language

In some respects we have progressed a bit too fast in this section, moving from the need for being close all the way to sexual relations. In between are numerous staging points, from learning about sex to dating rituals to actual sexual behavior. We examine these aspects of the adolescent sexual experience in the rest of this chapter.

To begin, where do adolescents go for information about their sexuality? Dickinson (1978) and others (McNamara, King, & Green, 1979; Nadelson, Notman, & Gillon, 1980; Thornburg, 1981) suggest that young males go to their friends. Dickinson studied two groups of young people ten years apart in a small southern community in an attempt to learn where adolescents go for sex information. He found that in 1964 the major source of sex information for White males, White females, and Black males was the peer group. Only Black females depended as much or more on sex-education materials or their mothers' advice. Dickinson's sample from 1974 showed some rather dramatic changes. Although mothers remained an important information source for girls of both races, girls turned much more toward their peers for information, Blacks especially so. White males and Black males also depended significantly more on friends and relied less on sex-education materials than in the past.

Of further interest in this study and others (Handelsman, Cabral, & Weisfeld, 1987) is students' expressed desire for their parents to be the source of sex information. Although this desire for parental teaching diminished over the two sample dates, their wanting information from one or both parents still far outdistanced wanting information from either books or peers. Dickinson (1978) agrees with others (Sorensen, 1973; Gullotta, Adams, & Montemayor, 1993) that adolescents want to be able to talk about sex with their parents. He speculates that parental inhibitions may forestall such open communications and may encourage young people to consult their peers.

But consult their peers about what? A study of young adolescents' sexual interests (Rubenstein, Watson, Drollette, & Rubenstein, 1976) provides one answer to this question. This study suggests that young male and female adolescents are interested in similar issues, as the following list of areas of highest interest for each sex indicates:

Girls	*Boys*
1. Birth control	1. Venereal disease
2. Abortion	2. Enjoyment of sex
3. Birth-control pill	3. Sexual intercourse
4. Venereal disease	4. Birth control
5. Pregnancy	5. Love
6. Love	6. Oral intercourse
7. Fear of sex	7. Pregnancy
8. Rape	8. Abortion
9. Enjoyment of sex	9. Guilt about sex
10. Sexual intercourse	10. Birth-control pill
11. Sex offenses	11. Fear of sex
12. Prostitution	12. Sex offenses
	13. Prostitution

The researchers judge these young people to have a surprisingly high level of interest in the adult behavior of sexual intercourse "not as an isolated act, but with its interpersonal consequences and context" (Rubenstein et al., 1976, p. 494). They go on to observe that some variations imply that females are more consequence-oriented than males, who seem to express a more pleasure/punishment orientation.

The interest of young people in sexual intercourse and its context within a relationship raises the question of how these concerns are addressed. Given that parents are not frequently consulted on such issues and that the peer group may not be able to provide the most accurate information on this subject, where does

---

Box 12–2   Homosexuality: Some Questions and Answers

1. Are homosexual experiences a common life experience for adolescents? Many studies report that approximately 1 boy in 10 and 1 girl in 20 has a homosexual experience in early adolescence (see, for example, M. Glasser, 1977).
2. Does a homosexual experience in early adolescence mean that one will grow up as a homosexual? No. According to one report, 4% to 10% of young people today will prefer homosexuality to heterosexuality (cited in Holden, 1992).

3. Is homosexuality a sign of emotional illness? In the words of Eli Coleman (1978), "The illness model of homosexuality is no longer viable. It has been put to rest by the flood of research that has found that homosexuality *per se* is not pathological. The main difference between homosexuals and heterosexuals is their choice of affectional and sexual preference" (p. 355).

---

one go? We might suggest with a sigh of relief that since the 1970s the books on sex education have been moved out of the closed stacks and onto the shelves. But will most books provide the information young adolescents seek?

Rubenstein, Watson, and Rubenstein (1977), in an evaluation of sex-education books based on their earlier work with adolescents' sexual interests, suggest not. Nearly a quarter of the books they studied did not discuss issues such as pregnancy, sexual intercourse, or even the word *love*. Slightly more than half had discussions on venereal disease, birth control, abortion, or guilt about sex. Topics such as enjoyment of sex or homosexuality appeared in fewer than half the texts reviewed. (See Box 12–2.) The authors further complain that a "scientific" basis for discussions in many of these texts was woefully lacking in many instances.

Their overall conclusion, that much remains to be done in improving the quality of sex-education materials must be balanced against their dated sample of books. Because the books examined were published between 1954 and 1971, they are not a fair representation of publications available today. In writing this chapter, we had an opportunity to examine several books published since 1983. Although some have the failings of their predecessors, others, such as Ruth Bell's *Changing Bodies, Changing Lives* (1987), show a more contemporary attitude toward adolescent concerns. For instance, in a chapter entitled "Exploring Sex with Someone Else," Bell offers this frank and honest advice about oral sex:

> Oral sex means using your mouth and tongue to stimulate sexually, usually by kissing and sucking their genitals. It is a kind of lovemaking that many people find very pleasurable and exciting (and it doesn't risk pregnancy). Many others don't feel comfortable with it at all and never have oral sex; or even if they have oral sex, they don't enjoy it. The important thing to remember is that what you do should feel right for *you*. If you don't want to have oral sex, you shouldn't. It isn't your "duty" to do it. You needn't let yourself be pushed into it, and you shouldn't push anyone else into it. (Bell, 1987, p. 99)

Dating

When a boy and a girl plan to meet alone or in a group at some place at some time, a date has been arranged. Confront young adolescents with this information and most will blush, stammer, and protest that it is just "the gang" getting together. To the critics who comment that young people are dating too soon in our society, Kett (1977) offers evidence that young Americans courted in the earliest colonial times. Nor can one escape the fact that the Puritans practiced a "dating" behavior made necessary by the living conditions called *bundling,* in which males and females visited in one another's beds separated by a plank. As Rothman (1987, p. 46) shares, the late 1700s was "a low point in premarital sexual restraint." She believes bundling was partly responsible for the early arrival of children in nearly one-third of the new colonial marriages of that time.

Models of Dating Behavior

In the United States today, dating appears to follow a pattern. Dunphy (1963) suggests a model in which boys and girls come together in groups and then in couples in five stages. Early adolescence is marked by small, unisex groups with three to nine members. These boy groups and girl groups in Stage 1 "hang around" separately and engage in some activities but mostly talk. As these unisex groups grow older, they increasingly make contact with and talk to one another (Stage 2). In Stage 3 the unisex groupings begin to break down, with the leaders of each group forming heterosexual relationships, but it is not until Stage 4 that the groups fully integrate. In Stage 5 the groups begin to disintegrate, and the couple emerges as the dominant relationship form.

Feinstein and Ardon (1973) offer a four-stage model based on psychoanalytic dynamics for examining dating behaviors. Between the ages of 13 and 15, the

Early dating patterns
begin in group behavior.

adolescent is in the stage of *sexual awakening.* This period is marked by a decrease in hostility between the sexes and the emergence of kissing and light petting. (You might recall E. Maccoby's comments on male versus female cultures and behavioral differences that need to be compromised during sexual awakenings. This compromise appears to be no small task.) The reason for these developments is that the Oedipal conflict (the young person's sexual desire for a parent) has been resolved enough to allow the adolescent to find a suitable replacement.

Between the ages of 14 and 17, the stage of *practicing,* young people are likely to experience a succession of short-term relationships of high emotional intensity. This stage corresponds to Dunphy's (1963) Stage 4, in which dating can occur individually or in groups but the primary emphasis is on the group. The adolescent at this stage is "solidifying" the resolution of the Oedipal conflict. For males, this solidification occurs in their increased identification with the father and the weakening of the relationship with the mother. Increasingly, the adolescent is becoming more comfortable in relationships with the opposite sex.

It is in the third stage, the *acceptance of sex roles,* between the ages of 16 and 19, that the adolescent is able to settle into a more stable dating pattern. This period is marked by increased experimentation with long-term relationships and corresponding increases in sexual experimentation. Feinstein and Ardon (1973) comment that anxiety typically increases during this period as parental controls weaken and the adolescent learns to handle self-control and personal issues while establishing dyadic relationships.

The last stage, the *development of a permanent object choice,* occurs between the ages of 18 and 25. This stage marks the "closure of the ego processes," wherein the young person has successfully resolved parental issues of desire, authority, and values. The individual is thus able to settle on a "love object" and invest in that relationship. Keep these two models in mind as we examine the dating process.

Dunphy's Stage 1, for instance, is nondating unisex groupings. A study of preadolescents' views on dating (Jackson, 1975) suggests that the overwhelming majority of young people have no idea of dating as a means of developing male/female relationships. Rather, their conceptualizations closely approximate the crowd-orientation phase of Dunphy's model, with preadolescents choosing group settings for contact with members of the opposite sex.

As young people grow older and their interest in the opposite sex increases, in Dunphy's model the leaders of the unisex groupings are the first to create heterosexual relationships. Though we may like to think that charm and honesty are the attributes most sought after in a dating partner, they are not. In several studies physical appearance emerges as the dominating influence. For instance, Mathes (1975) examined a matched college dating population to determine the effect of high anxiety on hindering the development of a relationship over the course of five dates. Although he expected physical attractiveness to be important initially, he believed that personality factors would assume increasing importance as the dates proceeded. His belief that highly anxious people would have greater difficulty in maintaining a dating relationship was not upheld. The initial importance of physical attractiveness remained throughout the study the primary factor influencing how well liked a dating partner was.

Some clues to the emphasis on appearance can be found in a paper by Herold (1974). From the research on college dating to that time, he proposes a three-stage process by which one dating partner evaluates the other. In the first stage, he suggests, one chooses a date largely on looks. Next, one compares the dating partner's social sophistication against one's own self-perceived savoir-faire. Finally, the college student assesses personality traits of honesty, reliability, and stability to assess the dating relationship. If the partner is attractive, has a pleasing personality, and has integrity, the relationship is very likely to continue. If, however, integrity is lacking, the student must balance its absence against the two other powerful factors of appearance and personality. Herold observes:

> Although students give a higher ranking to a trait such as honesty than to physical appearance, the dishonest person who has good looks and social sophistication is likely to date frequently, whereas the person who is honest and dependable, but lacks in good looks and charm, is less likely to date. Indeed, many students would not date at all rather than date someone who is considered to be physically unattractive and/or socially unsophisticated. (P. 119)

For advanced reading on research and theory on mate selection and premarital relationships, we refer interested readers to Surra (1990).

Dating Expectations

Given that by age 16, over 85% of adolescents report having their first date, what expectations are generated when two persons agree to a date (Thornton, 1990)? It appears that clothing, physical touch, reputation, and the location of the date provide strong cues for males. This is not necessarily the case with young women. For example, research suggests that young men view young women's tight jeans, low-cut blouses, or shorts as indications of desired sexual activity. But most young women attach no such sexual connotations to their dress. Rather, they view their clothing as an attempt at being fashionable (Zellman, Johnson, Giarruse, & Goodchilds, 1979). The same is true for touch. Males perceived being tickled and having their hair stroked by a dating partner as an encouragement to make sexual advances. Females did not share the same perception (Zellman et al., 1979).

On issues such as your date's reputation and the location of the date, there was agreement between the sexes. For both sexes having a reputation as being sexually active was likely to create expectations of sexual activity on a date. Likewise, males and females agreed that going to a young man's home when his mother and father weren't home clearly implied the expectation of sexual activity (Miller, Christopherson, & King, 1993; Zellman et al., 1979).

These findings should generate concern. It appears that male and female young people are at considerable risk for misunderstandings with regard to sexual activity on a date. Such misunderstandings can lead to tragic situations (see Box 12–3).

As intimacy grows in the dating relationship, it is hypothesized that the desire increases to express feelings physically in both Dunphy's (1963) or Feinstein and Ardon's (1973) model. (See Box 12–4 for an example of a

Box 12–3   Courtship Violence

Consider the words *romance, courtship,* and *love.* What images do these words convey to you? Are they images of two lovers walking hand in hand, of kindness and gentleness, of caring and concern? Or are your images of a couple pushing, grabbing, shoving, slapping, kicking, biting, and hitting each other? Most of us have assumed that courtship violence was a rare event. Only recently has society begun to realize that violence is not a stranger to courtship.

For example, it has been estimated that 15% to 25% of women will be raped during their lifetime. Nearly 59% of these individuals will know their attacker (Rickel & Hendren, 1993).

Although the extent of courtship violence is uncertain, two studies, one of college students and the other of high school students, found that 22.3% of the 355 college students and 13.1% of the 644 high school students admitted to some form of violence (Cate, Henton, Koval, Christopher, & Lloyd, 1982; Henton, Cate, Koval, Lloyd, & Christopher, 1983).

Preliminary findings suggest that many of the patterns of abuse evident in other forms of family violence also appear to be present in courtship violence. For example, it appears that the abuser and the abused often share the belief that the violent act was spontaneous, not premeditated. Violence does not necessarily end the relationship—many relationships continue. Disturbingly many male attackers see their victim as "deserving" the assault (Rickel & Hendren 1993). Finally, preliminary evidence suggests that individuals in violent relationships view themselves as "handicapped"—that is, as having "fewer alternative partners than those who broke up" their violent courtship (Cate et al., 1982, p. 88). The issue that we would like you to address is, How might courtship violence be prevented?

Other findings reveal that a history of victimization is predictive of courtship aggression (Gwartney-Gibbs, Stockard, & Bohmer, 1987) and, strange as it might seem, couple violence may stimulate greater couple commitment (Billingham, 1987). For further advanced reading we suggest articles by Lloyd (1991); Stets and Henderson (1991); Boeringer, Shehan and Akers (1991).

---

troubled client who was counseled by Tom Gullotta.) Through questioning more than 300 college students, Knox and Wilson (1981) found that the two sexes substantially agreed on the length of time a relationship needs to exist before kissing is considered appropriate. The majority of both sexes find kissing to be permissible on the first date, with near-universal agreement that it may occur on the second date. This level of agreement quickly descends into disagreement between the sexes when other sexual behaviors (particularly intercourse) are considered, with males believing these sexual behaviors appropriate sooner than females.

According to another study of behavioral expectations in the dating process (McCabe & Collins, 1984, cited in Miller et al., 1993), Australian adolescent expectations also changed as the relationship continued, with males and females becoming increasingly sexually liberal. For instance, "necking" was practiced by 47% of couples after the first date, 82% after several dates, and 88% when young people were going steady. Regarding the behavior of mutual masturbation, 18% of couples engaged in the behavior after the first date, 45% after several dates, and 64% who were going steady.

These findings were generally echoed in an earlier study by Collins, Kennedy, and Francis (1976), which observed that older women's sexual liberalism increased with their age.

The authors of this study propose two different explanations for women's increasing sexual permissiveness. The first is that as the female becomes aware

Box 12–4   Still a Virgin at 16

Jim came into the office asking if I could see him for a few minutes. He appeared terribly upset as he accepted my offer to sit down. When I asked this 16-year-old what was wrong, he shook his head and said in a low, serious voice, "I think I'm queer."

When I asked him what he meant by *queer,* he related to me an incident that had occurred over the weekend. He had asked a girl in his class out for a date. She had accepted the invitation and suggested that they catch a movie at a local drive-in. At the drive-in, Jim related, she suggested they both move to the back seat, where it was more comfortable. At this point in his story, Jim began to shake his head again. Letting out a slow sigh, he mumbled, "I must be queer. You see, when we got in the back seat, she began to tickle me, and I kinda returned the tickling. Well, that went on for a while and then she kissed me."

"That's nice," I said.

"No, you don't understand," Jim said. "She *really* kissed me. Hey, but that wasn't all. Here she is making out like there's no tomorrow when she puts her hand on my joint and starts rubbing it! I didn't know what to do. I sat there dumbfounded, not believing what was going on. So I asked her to stop, and I told her that I liked her a lot but that I wasn't ready yet. I said I just wanted to be her friend right now."

"What was her response to that?" I asked.

Jim said she appeared a little embarrassed but agreed. The rest of the evening was uneventful. The film was watched, hamburgers were eaten, and a good-night kiss was exchanged. Later that same evening Jim began to question his "manliness." By Monday morning he had convinced himself that he was a homosexual.

I reassured Jim that he was not a homosexual on the basis of that incident. I helped him see that his upbringing in a deeply religious family and his own sincere beliefs about the emotional feelings one needs to have for a person before permitting sexual intimacy to occur would have made it wrong for him to continue. As we talked, it was evident that Jim was seeking reassurance that he had behaved properly within his own value system as opposed to being "one of the boys" or a "stud." Jim left an hour or so later believing that maintaining his values had been the proper thing to do.

Do you think that young people are being pressured into sexual activity at an earlier age? Should a counselor have shown greater concern over Jim's refusal to become sexually intimate?

---

of male expectations, her behavior correspondingly alters. This shift in her behavior, they suggest, occurs with her increasing realization of the psychobiological orientation of the male. The second explanation is a "sexual renaissance" in women's thinking. In this regard, the gradual change in behavior from a traditional sexual orientation to "permissiveness with affection" suggests that women may be shedding the cultural inhibitions against their own sexuality. In the next section we examine the evidence for this position and for observations that young people in our society are in the midst of implementing a sexual revolution.

Contemporary Sexual Behavior

In her book *Male and Female* (1949), Margaret Mead described dating behavior in the United States as a highly elaborate game in which young people are confronted with balancing their sexual needs against society's prohibition of sexual intercourse. Mead found the resolution of this dilemma (as does E. Hamilton, 1978, cited earlier) to be in petting:

Box 12–5   Scientists Rely on *Redbook, Cosmopolitan,* and *Playboy*

One of the most frustrating situations confronting scientists working on the prevention of acquired immune deficiency syndrome is the lack of accurate information on the sexual behaviors of Americans. The data that are being used to project the incidence of AIDS in the United States are based on the work of Alfred Kinsey collected in the late 1930s and early 1940s. More recent data, collected by the Kinsey Institute in 1970, have been unavailable to the public and will remain so until the study's authors resolve the "critical" issue of who will be listed as the senior author. In the meantime, consumer surveys that appeared in magazines such as *Redbook, Cosmopolitan,* and *Playboy* are being used by scientists.

Source: W. Booth, "The Long, Lost Survey on Sex," *Science,* 1988, *239* (4844), pp. 1084–1085.

The curious adjustment that American culture has made to this anomalous situation is petting, a variety of sexual practices that will not result in pregnancy. Technical virginity has become . . . less important, but the prohibition of extra-marital pregnancy remains. Petting is the answer to the dilemma. But petting has emotional effects of its own. It requires a very special sort of adjustment in both male and female. The first rule of petting is the need for keeping control of just how far the physical behavior is to go; one sweeping impulse . . . and the game is lost . . . . The controls on this dangerous game . . . are placed in the hands of the girl. The boy is expected to ask for as much as possible, the girl to yield as little as possible. (P. 290)

In an investigation by Robinson and associates (1991), examining 20 years of the sexual revolution, it has been observed that continuing liberalization in sexual attitudes are observed for both men and women, with the largest shift for women. However, fewer women now endorse promiscuity, with greater disapproval of promiscuous females than males. (For a recent summary of adolescent sexual behavior we also refer you to Brooks-Gunn and Furstenberg [1989] and Miller, Christopherson, and King [1993].)

Certainly, we are confronted with a barrage of messages implying that chastity is an ancient relic of former generations. One might imagine that adolescent sexual behavior is one area for which there exists a well-documented base of empirical knowledge. Frankly, nothing could be further from the truth. In fact, it is rather shocking to find that the entire area of research on adolescent sexuality is fraught with methodological problems. In this section we examine several sexual behaviors—masturbation, kissing and petting, and intercourse—in light of the extremely small body of research available. (See Box 12–5.)

Masturbation

Masturbation has been thought to result in insanity, blindness, pimples, infections, and weakening of the brain, and, most frightening of all, it tends to cause that dread disease in which the penis drops off (see Figure 12–1). Although we may be amused at these myths of yesteryear, painful consequences awaited the young lad (masturbation was viewed as primarily a male disorder called spermatorrhea) caught by his parents in the act of "self-abuse," as this passage from the 1887 edition of *The Practical Home Physician* indicates:

Figure 12–1 The imagined results of masturbation, circa 1895. Pictures such as these regarding the crippling effects of masturbation appeared regularly in 19th-century medical books. (Source: Pierce, R. V. (1985) *The People's Common Sense Medical Advisor.* Buffalo, NY: World's Dispensary Printing Office.)

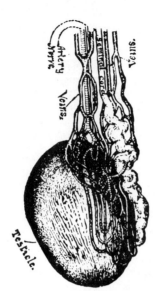

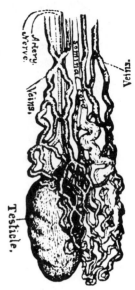

The Testicle in a healthy condition.   A Testicle wasted by Masturbation.

As for the treatment of masturbation no rules can be given. The habit must of course be stopped as soon as possible. . . . In some cases it may be absolutely necessary to employ mechanical means for preventing the practice in individuals who are too young to summon the moral strength necessary to overcome the habit. If any such mechanical means must be used, the most effectual is probably the application of a small Spanish fly-blister plaster to the parts in such a way as to keep them constantly so tender that the child is restrained by pain from meddling with them. (Lyman, Fenger, Jones, & Belfield, 1877)

The passage of time fortunately has persuaded most parents and adolescents to view masturbation for what it is—a normal, natural, pleasurable, satisfying sexual behavior. The level of male self-reported masturbation has remained relatively unchanged over the past 40 years. Several studies suggest that 80% of all males have masturbated by age 14 (Kinsey, Pomeroy, & Martin, 1948; G. Ramsey, 1943; Sorensen, 1973). By the age of 18, the percentage increases to more than 90% (Kinsey et al., 1948).

For females, change in masturbation practices has been noted in the research literature. Kinsey, Pomeroy, Martin, and Gebhard reported in 1953 that by age 15, some 20% of the females in their study had masturbated and that the percentage had increased to a third by age 19. These figures may be gradually changing, however; according to Dupold and Young's (1979) review of the literature, female acceptance of masturbation seems to be growing. Indeed, a more recent study by M. D. Newcomb (1984) of 115 sexually active women with a mean age of 25 revealed that the average age of first masturbation was just under 14 years and that young adults reported masturbating approximately seven times a month.

Box 12–6   You Would If You Loved Me!

Mead (1949) wrote of the girl in the adolescent relationship as being in the driver's seat in determining how sexually advanced a relationship becomes. This is unquestionably a difficult seat to be in, as the male attempts to use every ploy imaginable to convince the girl to "surrender." It may be that this situation is changing, and then again it may not be. Regardless, we would like you to make a list of the various lines you have either heard or used in your dating career. Here are several drawn from a book by Sol Gordon (1978) entitled *You Would If You Loved Me*.

- Let's make tonight something to remember.
- I really give a great back rub—but you have to undo your bra.
- I promise I won't hurt you.
- I want to make you feel like a woman (man).
- When's your mother coming home?
- I just want to hold you all night.

What might your response be to these lines and those on your own list? Do you believe that the girl is still the brake in adolescent sexual relationships?

From Kissing to Petting

Although masturbation is probably the first sexual experience in many adolescents' lives, kissing is, with the possible exception of hand holding or slow dancing, the first sexual contact with a person of the opposite sex. Dupold and Young (1979) report that by middle adolescence it is a "nearly universal phenomenon," with few reported differences between sexes or races.

The touching of lips opens new possibilities in the dating relationship. The tongue can now be used to tickle the ear lobe, or it can be used in a French kiss, in which the tongue is thrust into the mouth of the partner in what many consider a symbolic act of intercourse. Mead's (1949) rules of dating diplomacy, if we applied them here, would set the French kiss as the second way station (the first being the kiss itself). Should a girl accept or return a French kiss, the male is permitted to become increasingly sexually aroused. Should a girl keep her teeth firmly clenched, the male is given the clear indication that she does not seek further intimacy. (See Box 12–6.)

This further intimacy is considered petting. There are several definitions of light and heavy petting. Some consider light petting to be activity outside a partner's cloths. (Squeezing of a female's breasts through her garments or the gentle rubbing of the genitals against a partner's leg) and heavy petting to be the direct caressing and touching of a partner's body. Others define light petting as activity restricted to above the waist (which may or may not involve direct body contact) and heavy petting to be activity below the waist involving genital contact short of intercourse. Examining data from Smith and Udry (1985) and Dupold and Young's (1979) work, reveals that no remarkable changes have occurred in the reported frequency of petting behaviors during the past 30 years. Studies seem to show that about 60% of the adolescent population by age 15 has been involved in light petting and about 30% in heavy petting. Where changes have occurred in the past three decades, they have been in the under-15 group. It seems that both males and females are starting to pet earlier than their parents did.

Sexual Intercourse

Although much has been written over the past 20 years about the suspected adolescent sexual revolution in the United States, our knowledge remains very limited. Attempts during the 1980s to support extensive surveys to better understand adolescent sexuality were neither supported nor funded by the United States federal government. Therefore, even though we suspect changes have occurred, current data to confirm those suspicions not only remain elusive but also generate more questions than answers.

We suspect that young people are more open in discussing sexual issues and possess more liberal attitudes than their parents when they were young. But then, today's society, in general, is more open about sexuality. From soap operas, tampon commercials, and contraceptive advertisements on television to films and talk shows, Americans are publicly discussing what was once not even mentioned in private conversations between husband and wife. If a sexual revolution is occurring, or, for that matter, has occurred, then we should be able to observe considerable change in adolescent behavior since Kinsey and his colleagues (1948, 1953) and later Sorensen (1973) published their findings.

Adolescent-Female Coital Behavior

As Table 12–2 shows, the studies published in the 1970s containing data on sexual intercourse for adolescents (aged 13 to 19) do show a growth in the incidence of coitus. Kinsey and associates (1953) reported that 2% of females between the ages of 13 and 15 had engaged in sexual intercourse with a male. Several studies in the 1970s all show marked increases in adolescent females in this age range admitting to coitus, with Sorensen's (1973) 30% considerably higher by at least 10% than other estimates.

By later adolescence (16 to 19 years of age), the incidence of coitus for females in Kinsey's (1953) data was 18%. This percentage grew also in the 1970s, with Sorensen's (1973) 57% considerably higher again by at least 19% than were other estimates.

Table 12–2   Incidence of coitus in early and later adolescence

Reports	Females 13–15	Females 16–19	Males 13–15	Males 16–19
Kinsey, Pomeroy, and Martin (1948)	—	—	10%	42%
Kinsey, Pomeroy, Martin, and Gebhard (1953)	2%	18%	—	—
Vener, Stewart, and Hager (1972)	10%	25%	24%	34%
Sorensen (1973)	30%	57%	44%	72%
Vener and Stewart (1974)	17%	33%	33%	36%
P. Miller and Simon (1974)	7%	22%	9%	21%
S. L. Jessor and Jessor (1975)	—	38%	—	27%
A. Thornton (1990)	9%	54%	22%	64%
C. D. Hayes (1987)	5.4	58%	17%	78%

Source: Adapted from "Sex in Adolescence," by R. Hopkins, *Journal of Social Issues,* 1977, *33*(12), 67–85. Reprinted by permission.

Provocative dressing during adolescence may cause miscommunication between girls and boys. Although perhaps fashionable, certain forms of dress may be interpreted by boys as communicating sexual availability.

Now compare these figures with data reported by Hayes (1987) and Thornton (1990). For 13- to 15-year-olds, coital behavior approximates 1970s studies other than Sorensen's. Certainly, these lower figures provide no ringing confirmation of increased early adolescent female promiscuity in the 1980s. For 16-to 19-year-olds, Hayes's (1987) 58% and Thornton's (1990) 54% more closely approximate Sorensen's 57% estimate for female coital activity. Still, if a sexual awakening had been under way, shouldn't these figures have been higher?

Adolescent-Male Coital Behavior

For young adolescent males between the ages of 13 and 15, Kinsey and colleagues (1948) found that 10% had experienced coitus. With one exception, studies in the 1970s saw this percentage double, triple, or in the cases of Sorensen (1973) more than quadruple (44%).

For adolescent males between the ages of 16 and 19, Kinsey and his associates (1948) reported 42% had experienced sexual intercourse. Interestingly, with the exception of Sorensen's data showing 72% as experiencing coitus by age 19, all the other 1970s studies report figures actually lower than Kinsey's—21% (P. Miller & Simon, 1974); 27% (S. L. Jessor & Jessor, 1975);—and 34% and 36% (Vener & Stewart, 1974; Vener, Stewart, & Hager, 1972).

Now compare these figures again with data reported by Hayes (1987) and Thorton (1990). For 13- to 15-year-old males, reported coital behavior is less than reports from three other 1970s studies. Media perceptions of excessive early adolescent male sexual behavior do not appear to be confirmed by this data. For 16- to 19-year-olds, Hayes's (1987) 78% and Thorton's (1990) 64% approximate Sorensen's 72% estimate for male coital activity. Still, if a sexual awakening had been under way, shouldn't these figures have been considerably higher?

Before we draw conclusions from these reports, we should consider a Harris and Associates (1986) poll of 1,000 adolescents between the ages of 12 and 17, which was concerned with coital behavior. As might be expected, coital activity increased with age, so that roughly 7% of the sample's 12- to 13-year-olds had had intercourse. This figure grew to 25% by age 15 and leveled off at 51% for 17-year-olds. These data are not surprisingly different from that reported earlier. Racial, regional, and situational factors also influenced coital activity. White young people had the lowest level of sexual activity, followed by Hispanic and then Black adolescents. Sexual activity was reported highest in the East, followed by the South, the West, and the Midwest. Finally, as socioeconomic status declined, sexual activity increased. Young people living in a single-parent household reported a higher incidence of coital activity, while adolescents who attended church, did well in school, and were in academic rather than vocational tracks reported lower activity.

These last findings support numerous other studies that have also reported the situational factors that encourage early coital activity (Billy, Rodgers, & Udry, 1984; M. Coleman, Ganong, & Ellis, 1985; R. Jessor, Costa, Jessor, & Donovan, 1983; B. C. Miller, Christensen, & Olsen, 1987; Miller & Heaton, 1991; Miller & Moore, 1990; B. C. Miller, McCoy, & Olson, 1986; B. C. Miller, McCoy, Olson, & Wallace, 1986; Newcomb, Huba, & Bentler, 1986; Thornton & Camburn, 1989). Our review of these studies found that:

1. Early dating experiences increase the likelihood of coital activity by middle adolescence.
2. Parental expectations of high academic performance and consistent religious participation discouraged coital activity.
3. A positive family-youth relationship discouraged coital activity. However, Fisher (1989) reports that greater sexual communication between adolescents and their parents may actually be associated with sexual intercourse experience for daughters.
4. Discipline, if too permissive or overly strict, encouraged coital activity.

As we review these findings, the cautions of Hopkins (1977) remind us that it is very likely that each study suffers from at least one of the following problems:

1. Many studies lose sizable portions of their original sample to parental objections. Hopkins speculates that parents who permitted their children to participate may be more "liberated" than those who did not. He argues that if so, the sample may well be more "liberated" than their nonparticipating peers.
2. Today's young people, in an attempt to fit themselves into societal expectations for their behavior, may overreport their sexual activity, whereas earlier generations may have attempted to minimize their experiences.

3. Although *virginity* and *sexual intercourse* may be clearly understandable terms to researchers, these words may have entirely different meanings for some adolescents. Vener and Stewart (1974) report that some young people in their pilot study, for instance, felt that "socializing with the opposite sex" (p. 729) is equivalent to sexual intercourse.

With these limitations, the clearest conclusion that can be drawn is a desperate need for additional research. It is unfortunate that policy makers and scholars have not had access to accurate data that could have helped to shape funding and programs to assist youth over the past two decades. Science does not exist in the absence of evidence. Rather, instead of science, divination has seemingly influenced our attitudes about adolescents' sexuality.

As for whether a sexual revolution has occurred, we suspect that over the past two decades a gradual shift toward permissiveness with affection has become the standard and not a free-love stampede. Indeed, as concern about HIV retrovirus continues to grow in the United States and Canada, we suspect that within certain subgroups of the adolescent population sexual activity will potentially decline in the coming years. Whether our suspicion will ever be confirmed by research data awaits that yet-to-be-funded longitudinal study on adolescent sexual attitudes and behavior.

Ethnic Differences in Sex Behavior

In general, adolescents, regardless of ethnicity, are gradually having their first sexual experience at an earlier age (Wyatt, 1989). However, there are differences in the frequency, rate, and timing of sexual intercourse among ethnic groups. Perhaps these differences would be meaningless if the consequences of teenage sexual intercourse were not so potentially serious for the future of the teenager. Issues of pregnancy, health, education, and even life-threatening illnesses are part of the larger issues associated with contemporary sexual behavior (Brooks-Gunn & Furstenberg, 1989).

Various investigations reveal that African-American adolescents are more likely to be sexually active than are White teenagers, while Mexican-American youths are less likely to be sexually active than either of the other two ethnic groups. The normative sequence of sexual initiation may vary, however, by ethnic group. Miller, Christopherson, and King (1993) offer an overview summary of certain aspects of adolescent sexual behavior:

> Contemporary adolescents typically engage in a series of sequenced heterosexual behaviors that begins with kissing, proceeds to petting, and eventually includes coitus in the midteenage years, on the average. These behaviors tend to be cumulative, especially among whites, and among all races the tendency is for sexual behaviors to be expressed between partners who feel some degree of affection or commitment toward each other. Black adolescents have sexual intercourse sooner than nonblacks, on the average, but by the late teens the large majority of all adolescents have had sexual intercourse. The younger the age of first sexual intercourse, the greater the number of sexual partners, and the greater the risk of negative consequences of adolescent sexual behavior. (P. 72)

It is quite difficult to understand the major factors that distinguish the differences that exist in sexual behavior between majority and minority groups in North America during early and middle adolescence. Ethnic issues are intertwined with economic, social, historical, racial, political, and educational factors that make it difficult to determine if actual ethnic group differences do indeed exist. To address the issues of group differences one must, minimally, attempt to separate out the contribution of economic (have versus have not) factors from minority group status.

Furstenberg, Morgan, Moore, and Peterson (1987) suggest four possible models to explain the observation that national samples of youth consistently demonstrate that Blacks are approximately four times more likely than Whites to report having premarital intercourse in the middle teenage years. One model suggests that the earlier age of menarche among Black females may increase their risk of sexual intercourse due to hormonal influences. Another perspective focuses on the disadvantaged socioeconomic position of Blacks. It is argued that economic and social advancement is limited for Black disadvantaged groups, therefore such limitations make it less costly to experience early parenthood. If the first model is true, then early age of menarche, regardless of ethnicity, should be a stronger predictor of sexual behavior than is ethnicity. If the second model is correct, then comparable socioeconomic conditions should attenuate (or diminish) ethnic or racial differences in sexual behavior.

Furstenberg and associates also suggest that such factors as different sexual norms, greater tolerance about early childbearing, poorer school performance or achievement interests by the adolescent, or even less effective monitoring or supervision in single-parent households due to limited economic, energy, or supporting resources may be more influential than is ethnicity in predicting teenage sexual behavior.

In a highly sophisticated analysis of a national sample of 15- to 16-year-old White and Black teenagers, Furstenberg and associates observe that several contextual factors account for many of the differences between Black and White teenagers in sexual behavior. Some evidence suggests that socioeconomic factors, as measured by mother's education, partially account for the difference. However, other evidence suggests that peer group influences may be an even stronger factor. For example, for African-American youths attending a predominantly Black school, the chances are more than double of having sexually active friends who role model or encourage early sexual behavior. In contrast White teenagers attending a mostly White school, actually have lower odds of having sexually active friends. Possibly the enormous peer pressure on Black males to engage in sexuality as part of their peer culture may have a greater influence on the incidence of higher coital behavior in predominantly all-Black educational settings. Black male youths, to show their masculinity, may encourage—even demand—sexual participation by their female peers. In contrast, White males may be less demanding due to either different sexual norms or higher achievement interests and be less forceful in their sexual demands.

Findings such as these, and others reported by Furstenberg and associates, have inspired other investigators to examine variations of the explanatory models suggested in their work to explain possible ethnic or racial group differences in teenage sexual behavior. We conclude this section with an examination of two such attempts that compared White adolescents with either African-American or Mexican-American youths to further demonstrate that although ethnic differences may exist, much of the differences may be accounted for by various contextual factors.

Perhaps the two most widely examined explanatory models for studying racial differences in sexual behavior include the "demographic characteristic" hypothesis or the "minority status" hypothesis. The demographic characteristic hypothesis suggests that any observed differences between groups is not due to minority status but rather to accompanying social, economic, or demographic factors associated with minority group membership. The minority status hypothesis, in contrast, indicates that minority group membership has an independent effect above and beyond socioeconomic factors. These effects are thought to be due to cultural, attitudinal, or normative factors associated with each ethnic group or community. To assess the relative validity of these two contrasting hypotheses researchers compare ethnic groups while controlling for socioeconomic factors.

When Aneshensel, Fielder, and Becerra (1989) control for socioeconomic factors in their comparison of Mexican-American and White female adolescents regarding their sexual behavior, they observe that although certain rates of sexual behavior are reduced by controlling for socioeconomic factors the "minority status" hypothesis remains supported, suggesting certain social, attitudinal, or behavioral factors associated with being Hispanic account for the lower rate of most sexual behaviors among Hispanic adolescent females. The authors point to factors associated with religion, values regarding abortion, mother's education and availability, and other factors to account for fewer sexual behaviors for the Hispanic youths.

Furthermore, Wyatt (1990) has completed a large survey study of Black and White youths in the Los Angeles area. She controlled for socioeconomic factors and found that few ethnic-related differences were observed in this sample. At the conclusion of her study, Wyatt (1990) states:

> the occurrence of adolescent sexual behavior hasn't changed, but the age of onset has. We have begun to refine the contributors to early onset and have found that ethnicity as a variable is less significant than SES, the presence and consistency of parents in the home, women's sexual abuse histories, and the age of onset of sexual behaviors that precede intercourse. These findings also highlight the value of educating children about the advantages of delaying coitus and offering them a realistic appraisal of the consequences of sexual activity. Adolescents are not likely to refrain from sex, but the more their decision making is based on their own desire for sex, the more likely they may be to accept the responsibility that comes with being sexually active." (P. 202)

Although the investigations summarized in this section vary as to whether the demographic characteristic or the minority status hypothesis most clearly explains the differences between ethnic groups in sexual behavior, it becomes clear that as one works with various adolescent populations it is important to recognize that certain differences in sexual behavior may be due to biological, social, cultural, and/or economic factors. As professionals, we believe that certain values, attitudes, and norms associated with one's ethnic group membership, coupled with economic, political, and social conditions, are more likely to explain differences in sexual behavior among racial groups than are biological or genetic factors.

Homosexuality

According to Savin-Williams and Rodriguez (1993) heterosexism so dominates the visibility of sexual behavior in most textbooks on adolescent psychology that homosexuality in its various forms—lesbian, bisexual, gay—remains relatively invisible. However, a 1986–1987 representative sample of approximately 35,000 junior and senior high school students reveals that 1% of the sample admits to at least one homosexual encounter, while far more report predominantly homosexual fantasies (2.6%) and homosexual attractions (4.5%). (For a detailed account of the prevalence and patterns of same-gender sexual contacts among men, we refer to Fay, Turner, Klassen, & Gagnon, 1989).

Savin-Williams and Rodriguez (1993) indicate that at an early age lesbians, bisexuals, and gays perceive themselves as "different." This feeling of being different is associated with a lack of erotic and intimate interests in persons of the other sex. In time, early denial of interest in the same sex gives way to confrontation of feelings of sexual attraction to the same sex. Frequently, this awareness is initially associated with self-devaluation and self-derogation. Many homosexual youths will defend through the process of "passing" as a heterosexual.

Over the history of humankind these "different" feelings have been viewed as sick, evil, and threatening in many parts of the world. Indeed, the struggle over allowing gays to serve in the U.S. military illustrates the depth of homophobia that exists in the U.S. However, although not immune to bigotry or hatred, Canada and other nations do not discriminate against homosexuals in their military forces.

A recurrent charge against homosexuality is that it is a chosen life-style. That is, homosexuals could become "straight" if only they chose to do so. However, as we discuss in Chapters 2 and 13, the study of the influence of genetics on human behavior remains in its infancy. Previous efforts linking specific behaviors to certain genes or groups of genes have yet to survive replication attempts. Still, it is not completely unreasonable to assume that genetic or biochemical differences in the human body may expose an individual to a greater probability of developing certain behaviors, such as homosexuality, in a complex and as yet not understood interaction with external environmental stimuli.

Based on his research, LeVay (1991) speculates, for example, that homosexuality in men may be tied to the genes responsible for prenatal brain development—in particular, those genes that provide instructions to the hypothalamus. His work reveals that certain cell groupings in the hypothalamus differ between homosexual and heterosexual men. He speculates that this difference influences sexual preference. New twin studies by Bailey and Pillard (cited in Holden, 1992) give a broad range from 30% to 70% of the possible influence of genetics on homosexual behavior. This expansive range suggests the crudeness of the science of the field. Furthermore, it underscores our earlier observation that envi-

---

Box 12–7   **Adolescent Sexual Behavior and Drug Involvement**

In Chapter 15 we examine drug abuse and its ramifications for adolescent behavior and development. In regard to drug involvement and sexual behavior, Rosenbaum and Kandel (1990) report that the use of cigarettes, alcohol, marijuana, and other illicit drugs increases the likelihood of early nonmarital sexual activity. The greater the extent of drug involvement, the greater the probability of early sexual experience. In general, the same pattern is observed for White, African-American, and Hispanic ethnic groups.

Can you think of possible reasons for the association between drug involvement and sexual behavior?

---

ronmental influences would inversely account for the remaining unanswered percentage of the variance. That is, learned behavior and biology are dynamic interactive forces.

D'Augelli (1993) argues that adolescents and adults who self-identify as bisexual, lesbian, or gay experience major stressors in the management of their sexual orientation. They are at particular risk for serious bouts of depression and for suicidal behavior. Widespread stigmatization due to negative attitudes, harassment, and even interpersonal violence directed at the homosexual community reenforces the self-derogation, so commonly seen in this population of adolescents.

D'Augelli (1993) suggests that schools need to have safe settings such as university dorms that reduce harassment and victimization. Institutions need to be intolerant of harassment and victimization of homosexuals. Supporting organizations, focusing on the needs of lesbian, gay, and bisexual youths, should be fostered and supported. Further, just as feminists argue for increased visibility of the achievement of women in the educational curriculum, so too should material on homosexuality, homophobia, and related issues be included in educational curriculum materials.

Implications

What are some of the implications that one might draw from this overview? First, there are enough threads of evidence to suggest that young people are moving toward a standard of "permissiveness with affection." Second, this gradual shift is more accelerated for women more than for men. Whether, as some argue, the Pill has provided the impetus for change (a position we do not readily support) or whether it has been a by-product of the women's movement, today's adolescent females are beginning to approach parity with adolescent males in a number of sexual behaviors. (See also Box 12–7 for a contemporary discussion about drug involvement and adolescent sexuality.)

Should we be alarmed by this revelation? We believe that there is no cause for alarm over the desire young people have for one another. It is very hard, in fact, to imagine sexual intimacy as not being one of the most satisfying and enjoyable experiences of life so long as both partners are willing participants.

The changes that need to occur are not with our young people but with the handling of the entire issue of sexuality by adults. It is in adults' fear and their

Changing sexual standards and incurable diseases make it important to use such devices as condoms. However, it is often embarrassing for adolescents to purchase condoms.

inability to discuss sexual issues with young people that they commit perhaps the greatest error of all. This error is immersing young people in ignorance, so that experimentation and peer advice replace knowledge.

Knowledge in this area is equated with sex education. Opponents of sex education contend that by informing young people about themselves and their bodies, sex education contributes to increased sexual activity. Spanier's (1976) work helps place these arguments against sex education in a clearer perspective. By questioning a sample of more than 1,000 college students, Spanier traced a network of variables that influence sexual behavior. He reports that the earlier the socialization process of peer interaction and dating begins for young people, the sooner sexual intimacy occurs, in part because society immerses young people in an environment that says that sex is pleasurable.

Box 12–8   Commandments for Parents Providing Sex Education

1. Thou shalt not separate sex education from any other education, but realize that sex education starts in the cradle.
2. Thou shalt realize that skin and hands are our most important sex organs.
3. Thou shalt neither curb spontaneous sex expressions of the child, nor ever stimulate them artificially.
4. Thou shalt answer every question of the child according to truth, wherever possible immediately but always according to the emotional and spiritual level of the child; never answer more than was asked for.
5. Thou shalt realize that a living example carries more weight than words.
6. Thou shalt realize that sex information at school can never be anything but an addition to sex education in the family.

7. Thou shalt realize that overstressing of the biological aspects of sexuality must lead to underestimating of the emotional and relational aspects.
8. Thou shalt teach that sexual exploitation of another human being is equally as reprehensible as any other form of exploitation.
9. Thou shalt teach your children that the stem "co" in coitus means "together": being together, belonging together, becoming one and thus pre-supposes an intimate relationship.
10. The Pill: rather a year too early than one night too late.

Note: In an era when AIDS has redefined the meaning of sexual activity, we would add an 11th commandment: thou shalt, if a male, use a latex condom out of respect for your partner and, if a female, use spermicidal foam out of respect for your partner. If this commandment is followed faithfully, thou shalt live.

Source: From "10 Commandments for Parents Providing Sex Education," by C. Van Emde Boas, *Journal of Sex Education and Therapy,* 1980, 6, *1,* 19. Reprinted by permission.

The opponents of sex education have a point. Information—any information—is likely to stimulate increased interest in experimentation with sexual behaviors. Perhaps if we could shut down the media, postpone any male/female contact until late adolescence, and purge libraries of all romantic novels, we might be able to stall acquisition of the knowledge that sexual intimacy in its many forms is pleasurable.

But would keeping accurate sex information from adolescents curb their behavior? Spanier (1978) clearly indicates that there exists no relationship between sex education and premarital sexual activity. He reports no differences in degree of sexual activity between young people who had attended sex-education courses and those who had not. Furthermore, he reports that the provision of birth-control information does not increase sexual activity in adolescents. In another study of 113 urban high school students, Handelsman and her associates (1987) found no relationship between the source of sex information and later sexual activity. Other reports by Furstenberg, Moore, and Peterson (1986) and Blau and Gullotta (1993) lend further support to this finding.

If you draw the same conclusion that we do, that adolescent sexual intimacy is reasonably probable, then the provision of honest, unprejudiced information is essential. (See Box 12–8.) Indeed, with the threat of AIDS growing, knowledge is essential. The issue is not preventing sexual activity but ensuring that people can decide for themselves whether they are emotionally ready and willing and medically protected to engage in such activity.

Major Points to Remember

1. Intimacy involves the need for closeness, a sense of emotional feeling for another, and the ability to share feelings. The need for intimacy is balanced against parental and societal teachings about the standard for sexual intimacy.

2. There are essentially four standards of sexual intimacy: the traditional standard, the double standard, permissiveness with affection, and permissiveness without affection.

3. The overwhelming majority of adolescents learns about their sexual being from experimentation and from their peers.

4. Dating originates as the result of a gradual process beginning with small uni-sex groups and ending in couples. Incidentally, the adolescents most likely to date are not those with the best personality but those with the best looks. More interesting still is that as the age of males and females increases, their understanding of one another's sexual expectations becomes more accurate.

5. Mead suggests that Americans play an elaborate dating game in which females are expected to be solely responsible for how far the relationship goes.

6. Although male masturbation rates remain relatively unchanged, there is evidence that female masturbation rates are increasing.

7. Petting appears to be on the increase, with most adolescents reporting involvement in light petting by age 15.

8. Surprisingly, despite rumors of a sexual revolution, there is little evidence that one has occurred. There has been an unmistakable change in attitudes, but this does not appear in behavior.

9. Although it is true that sex education increases interest in sex, it does not follow that sex education encourages premarital sexual activity.

PART FOUR

Dealing with Issues of Concern: Intervention and Prevention

CHAPTER

13

Helping Adolescents: Intervention and Prevention

- Cardinal Rules

- Treatment and Rehabilitation

- Does Treatment Work?

- Psychotherapy with Ethnic Minorities

- Primary Prevention and Its Technology

- Does Prevention Work?

- The Promise of Prevention in Working with Adolescents

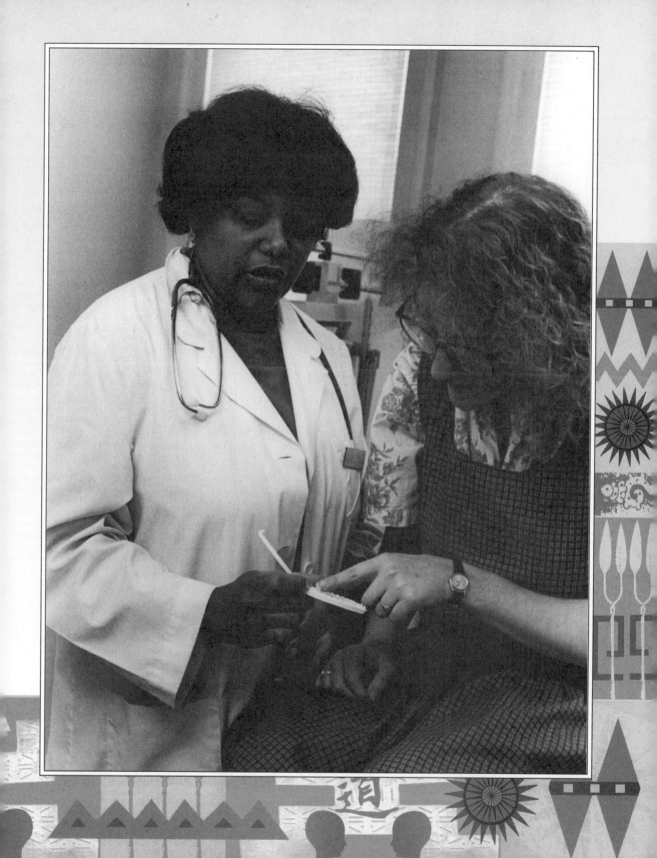

Not long ago a major association of mental-health professionals held a conference to discuss the proliferation of new therapies. In writing a chapter on therapy for adolescents, many authors might take a similar approach and merely describe the enormous variety of therapies now available. We have taken a different route. This chapter does not contrast the advantages of, say, primal-scream therapy and reality therapy, nor does it state that Freud is inferior to Carl Rogers or he to Erik Erikson. Instead, we have drawn on our own experience to share our beliefs about working with young people.

We have organized this personal statement into three sections. The "Cardinal Rules" section shares the secret of success in working not only with adolescents but with people of any age. The second section, on treatment and rehabilitation, describes what our society has emphasized for many years: the correction of already existing problems. In this section we briefly touch on the major types of therapies available but, as just promised, avoid the multitude of variations. Next we examine the concept of prevention, an area of tremendous promise in the mental-health field that is only now coming into its own alongside treatment and rehabilitation. Prevention programs aimed at alleviating or removing the causes of troubled adolescent behavior are now under way, and at the end of this section we look at the promise of such programs for reducing the need for treatment and rehabilitation by preventing adolescent dysfunctions in the first place.

Cardinal Rules

The formula for success in working with adolescents is simple, although combining the ingredients in the proper amounts can at times be puzzlingly complex. There are five essential, interrelated ingredients in helping adolescents decide to change their behavior. The first of these is *trustworthiness*. The adolescent must be able to trust the mental-health worker, for young people do not share feelings that show their vulnerabilities and weaknesses with individuals who they feel will treat those feelings insensitively.

The second quality that a mental-health professional must have is *genuineness*. We believe that no other age group is so perceptive in "reading" other people. If mental-health workers are not genuine in their concern for and love of young people, their effectiveness will be severely impaired. As one hospitalized young man, fighting back tears, angrily exclaimed after his therapist refused to give him permission to see an injured pet, "That artificial dude knows or cares shit about me! That —— —— comes in here with that goddamn —— pipe stuck in his mouth. Who does he think he is? He don't care for nuthin'."

Genuineness helps establish an atmosphere in which trust can grow. Feigning genuineness is more damaging to a therapeutic relationship than expressing the inability to be "real" with that adolescent and withdrawing from the relationship.

The third quality that a mental-health worker must have is *empathy,* the ability to feel for the young person. Empathy, incidentally, is not to be confused with sympathy. The word *sympathy* implies agreement and commiseration for the individual as a person but not necessarily condoning that individual's behavior in a given situation.

The fourth ingredient is *honesty*. Without honesty there can be no relationship. Honesty means that if the professional disapproves of an action by the client, the professional is able to express that feeling in a way that does not pull the relationship apart. The notion that any mental-health worker can remain impartial in a therapeutic relationship is, in our estimation, poppycock. We believe that expressing sadness, dissatisfaction, worry, or pleasure over the behavior of a young person is far better than attempting to hide it, for we contend that such feelings cannot be hidden. We believe that professionals who fail to express these feelings directly work against themselves by building a barrier to the development of a trusting and genuine relationship.

Like the scarecrow in *The Wizard of Oz* you are probably remarking how simple this recipe is, and thinking "Why, I should have thought of that myself."

Without trustworthiness, genuineness, empathy, and honesty, behavioral change will not occur. However, these four ingredients are useless without a fifth one to hold them all together. This ingredient is the adolescent's *perception* of the mental-health worker as trustworthy, genuine, empathic, and honest. Our experience has shown that regardless of how trustworthy, genuine, empathic, and honest a mental-health professional is, if the client does not perceive the professional as having those qualities, change will not occur (Rogers, 1965).

Treatment and Rehabilitation

By merging two operational definitions that the federal government uses in mental-health information systems, we can obtain a fairly inclusive definition of the term *therapy*. Therapy involves the ability to determine the mental-health status of clients and provide them with the help necessary to improve their coping abilities. Therapy occurs in face-to-face encounters between a therapist and a client who suffers from some difficulty, according to the client or the therapist or both. Before we examine the major schools of treatment, it might be helpful to look at how this interaction takes place.

Categories of Therapy

There are four basic categories of therapy. The first and perhaps still the most common is *individual therapy*. The client and the therapist explore together in private the feelings, emotions, and attitudes of the client.

The second category of therapy, which is becoming increasingly popular, is *family therapy*. Depending on the circumstances, the therapy may be limited to the adolescent and his or her parents, or it may include other family members as well. We admit to a bias in favor of this type of therapy. Our experiences in working with young people have demonstrated time and again the usefulness of being able to gather family members together to explore what are seen to be family, not individual, problems. In family therapy the difficulty is perceived to exist not solely with the individual but also with the system from which that individual comes.

The third category is *group therapy*. Within a small group of people (normally no more than ten), the therapist interacts with each individual and encourages them to interact with one another. The groups usually, but not always, consist of clients experiencing similar problems.

The last category is *couple therapy.* Not really family therapy because other members of the family are not included, couple therapy is the working through of problems between two individuals (who need not be related) with a mental-health worker.

Therapy Locations and the Medical Model

The terms *treatment* and *rehabilitation* often relate to the locations in which therapy is undertaken. The first term suggests to most mental-health workers an *outpatient* setting. This setting may be a child-guidance clinic, a youth-service bureau, a family-service agency, or a community mental-health center. The second term suggests an *inpatient* setting, such as a hospital or a residential school.

The above remarks reflect an orientation influenced by what is commonly called the *medical model.* In this model emotional difficulties are treated as diseases. Although the model has justly come under severe criticism in recent years (Albee, 1980), it is still the most commonly used explanation of illness in the field of mental health. For that reason we briefly discuss it here.

In the medical model dysfunctional behavior is considered to be disease. From this perspective each dysfunctional behavior has a specific cause and a specific set of symptoms associated with it. Taken it its most extreme form, the medical model suggests that *all* dysfunctional behavior is biogenic: that is, *all* dysfunctional behavior can be explained by a physical malfunction within the body.

To see how the medical model works, let's for a moment examine the physical disease called a staphylococcal infection from this perspective. The staphylococcus is a bacterium frequently found in purulent infections. If left untreated, it can result in life-threatening physical disorders. For example, the presence of a sore throat (or other pus-containing irritation) and a fever would provide diagnostic indications signaling a warning that the staphylococcus bacterium might be present. Using this information, the physician would swab the infected area and test for the presence of the bacterium, and if it was found, antibiotics would be prescribed.

Treatment in this model involves a diagnosis that the conditions present in a disease are evident in the individual. Our client would already be showing early clinical signs of the disease: fever, soreness in the infected area, or pus. In this situation, efforts would be taken to confirm the diagnosis and to stop the disease before it progressed further. It is this action to stop the progress of the disease before its final stage that is called treatment.

Within the medical model, rehabilitation occurs after the disease has been brought under control. In our illustration, if the bacterium had not been detected and had resulted in nephritis (a potentially serious inflammation of the kidneys), efforts would be made to restore as much functioning as possible. This attempt to restore functioning is called rehabilitation.

The medical model operates on the principle that before actions can be taken to restore health, the cause of the illness must be understood. Once the defect, or malfunction, has been identified, it can be corrected. Operating from this premise, many within the medical community in the mid-19th century searched for germs in a futile attempt to find an explanation for dysfunctional behavior. This exploration was replaced in the 20th century by a search for viruses, chemical imbalances, and, presently, genes, which some psychiatrists believe are responsible for some dysfunctional behavior. The limitation of such approaches is that the majority of emotional problems are not diseases that can be traced to some microorganism, chemical, or other single cause.

It is true that in the dementia that often accompanies syphilis and acquired immune deficiency syndrome a spirochete, in the case of syphilis, and a retrovirus, in the case of AIDS, are the culprits. Furthermore, some evidence suggests that some incidents of manic-depressive illness may be genetic in origin (Egeland et al., 1987). Egeland and his associates suggest that a manic-depressive gene may be tied to chromosome 11. We express caution in reporting these last findings, however, for three reasons. First, it appears in this preliminary report that the inheritance of this gene does not necessarily mean that the individual will experience the disorder. Therefore, obviously other factors must also be at work. Second, two other research groups working with manic-depressive populations have been unable to find this marker gene in their samples (Kolata, 1987b). Finally, with astounding regularity we have observed claims that the biogenic origins of delinquency, alcoholism, schizophrenia, and a score of other behavioral miseries have been discovered. To this date, the evidence for those arguments has not been overwhelming. The problem with biogenic explanations is that nearly all emotional problems are "problems in living, problems often created by blows of fate, by the damaging forces of a racist, sexist, ageist society" (Albee, 1980, p. 76; see also Albee, 1985a, 1985b).

There is a third level of intervention, which does not occur after the fact or during the fact but before the fact. This third level is *primary prevention*. But before we explore it, we need to look briefly at the groupings of therapies presently is use.

Schools of Therapy

In 1977 the National Institute of Mental Health developed a publication that has been reprinted many times since to assist individuals in their search for the "right therapy" (Parloff, 1977). This section draws on the Institute's five primary groupings of therapies: analytical, behavioral, humanistic, transpersonal, and biogenic. Although these groupings are by no means all-inclusive, they do provide a way of categorizing the philosophical underpinnings of various therapies.

Analytically Oriented Therapy

The first grouping is derived from classical psychoanalysis. This perspective focuses on the interactions of instinctual desires, anxieties, and defenses. It places considerable importance on the conflicts between opposing wishes, the anxiety caused by those wishes, and the defenses that arise against wishes that have created anxiety. Furthermore, it is believed that most of this process occurs without the individual's conscious knowledge.

According to psychoanalytic therapists, emotional difficulties arise out of early experiences buried in the unconscious and can be resolved by bringing these experiences into consciousness. Helping clients become more aware of themselves is thought to enable them to change their behavior. Thus, these therapists do not attempt to change their clients' behavior directly but to increase their understanding of themselves and, in so doing, allow behavioral change to occur through a gradual self-made transformation.

Psychoanalytic theory has literally changed our understanding of human behavior. For example, it was psychoanalysts who first suggested how past experiences could explain an individual's present behavior. It provided the first explanation of dysfunctional behavior that did not have biogenic origins, and it introduced a whole new set of meanings into Western society (for example, concepts such as repression, rationalization, and libido).

However, even though the contributions of psychoanalytic theory to the understanding of human behavior cannot be overestimated, this therapy is not without its problems. First, there is the lack of experimental support for many of its tenets. It is a theory whose assumptions rest on a limited number of clinical cases. Second, there is an overdependence on inference. To illustrate this last point, there is a story that the founder of the psychoanalytic movement, Sigmund Freud, was once confronted by a follower who declared that one of Freud's favorite pastimes, smoking a cigar, was a phallic activity. It is reported that Freud responded, with cigar in hand, "Sometimes a good cigar is just a good cigar" (Meltzer, 1987, p. 215). A theory that assumes that obvious behavior does not represent obvious behavior is prone to error. Finally, the view that all human behavior is driven by the deterministic instinctual drives of sex and aggression or that early childhood experience dooms a person to an inescapable adult life outcome has found less favor in recent years.

Behavior Therapy

There are four basic tenets underlying behavioral psychology. First, behaviorists view their role as studying the responses people make to the stimuli in their environment. Second, behaviorists use empirical methods to gather data in order to study human behavior. Next, they believe that all behavior can be predicted and ultimately controlled. This belief is rooted in the fourth tenet, that the primary component of all human behavior is learning. Thus, behavioral therapists are not concerned with their clients' self-awareness but with their overt behavior. Using learning theory, behaviorists study the events that lead to and directly follow a maladaptive behavior and attempt to intercede in that course of events to break a learned response pattern (see Box 13–1).

The behavioral model has made important contributions to the understanding and treatment of dysfunctional behavior. The most important contribution has been the establishment of research protocols in assessing treatment protocols. The establishment of these protocols has introduced the scientific method into treatment. Phrases such as *treatment goals* and *baseline counts of behavior* are examples of the behaviorists' influence on treatment. Behaviorists can justly lay claim to being responsible for providing the means by which all treatment plans are now held accountable.

The behavioral model is not without its critics, however. Where the medical model sees dysfunctional behavior as biogenic in origin and the psychoanalytic model views this behavior as rooted in unconscious childhood experiences, the

---

Box 13–1   Cognitive-Developmental Behaviorism and Its Application to Intervention and Prevention

In recent years mental-health professionals have turned with increasing interest to attempting to understand the interrelatedness among behaviorism, cognition, and human development. Cognitive-developmental theorists such as Mischel (1973, 1979) and Bandura (1977, 1982) contend that people react less to external stimuli in the environment than to their individual processing of those stimuli. This theoretical offshoot of behaviorism offers a more intricate and complex view of human behavior than traditional stimulus/response theory.

Mischel, for example, suggests that five mediating variables help shape a response to a given stimulus. The first variable, competencies, represents the past repertoire of skills that individuals call on when dealing with both familiar and novel situations. The second, encoding, involves the manner in which young people perceive and categorize their life experiences. The next, expectancies, represents the predicted outcome (whether pleasant or unpleasant) of some event based on previous learning. The fourth, values, stands for the different weights that individuals assign to life events. And the last, plans, governs the rules that humans use to lead their lives.

Rather than the five mediating variables Mischel proposes, Bandura suggests that expectations govern an individual's response to a particular situation. Expectations can take one of two forms. The first, an outcome expectation, is the belief that a certain behavior will lead to a person's predicted outcome of that event. The second, an efficacy expectation, involves a person's belief that he or she will be able to execute the behavior successfully.

The premise of mental-health professionals using these models is that behavior results from not only external but also internal reinforcers. Thus, to change behavior, external as well as internal contingencies need to be manipulated. From an interventionist's position, this manipulation involves the use of social-learning models. From a preventionist's position, it involves the application of each of prevention's four tools: education, promotion of social competency, community organization/systems intervention, and natural care giving. Both approaches are directed toward a cognitive restructuring of a young person's understanding of events and his or her self-reinforcing behaviors. In each of the chapters that follow, examples of these applications will appear.

---

behaviorist sees learned habits. This world view expressed as "what you see is what is there" has been criticized as being oversimplified. For example, Watson's (1914) view that behaviorists would someday be able to take society's worst social failure, "pull him apart, psychologically speaking, and reconstruct him anew" is not widely shared today. The second major criticism is that behavioral theory is deterministic. If all behavior is in response to the stimuli present in the environment, free will does not exist. This is a world view that also is not currently held in favor.

Humanistic Therapy

Humanistic approaches to treating dysfunctional behavior emerge from a basic belief in the goodness of humans. Rather than viewing dysfunctional behavior as a physical disease or viewing humans as being driven by instinctual urges or as being merely reactors, humanists understand people to be basically good, rational, and interested in that collective community known as society. They believe that conflicts in life occur when people cannot realize their potential. Accordingly, therapists like Carl Rogers try to help their clients achieve self-acceptance, self-satisfaction, and their own potential as fully functioning individuals. Humanistic therapy and analytically oriented therapy both emphasize self-discovery, but the kinds of discovery differ. At the risk of some legitimate criticism, one might think of humanists as focusing on humanity's most positive attributes and of psychoanalysts as tending to focus on the more base instinctual drives.

Perhaps the single most important contribution that the humanist model has made to our understanding of dysfunctional behavior is its firm belief that humans are actors. We can change our lives. This perspective has encouraged therapists to urge clients to take control of their lives and destiny.

Given the humanist view that the focus in treatment is what the client thinks about his or her own life, it is not surprising that critics contend that humanists ignore the science of human behavior. For example, how can one ignore the wealth of information contained in this book to be solely concerned with the uniqueness of the individual, his or her human potential, and his or her freedom? Disturbing as it might be to many of our colleagues, this world view is held in favor by many.

Transpersonal Therapy

The fourth grouping is "not content with the aim of integrating one's energies and expanding the awareness of oneself as an entity separate from the rest of the universe [as are humanists]" (Parloff, 1977, p. 8). Rather, transpersonal therapists, or existentialists, focus their attention on the major challenge facing humanity in the 20th century: living in an amoral, technological society. Transpersonal therapy is concerned with a search for meaning and the ability of people to live their lives according to their own principles. Whereas humanists focus on individuals and their needs, existentialists are concerned with the individual's relationship to the human condition and the question of individual responsibility. Transpersonal approaches do not share a common set of theoretical concepts. Rather, they assume that all humans have large untapped pools of spiritual abilities. Examples of transpersonal approaches include Zen, psychosynthesis, yoga, Buddhism, and transcendental meditation.

The primary contribution that transpersonal therapy has made is in raising issues of major human concern. Like the humanists, existentialists are accused of an unscientific approach.

Biogenic Therapies

The final grouping focuses on biological explanations for dysfunctional behavior and on the use of genetic research, surgical, or chemical interventions to understand or treat those dysfunctions. It contains several widely varying and often competing approaches to treating dysfunctional behavior. Nevertheless, they all view the problems that humans experience from a biological perspective.

The first of these perspectives focuses on genetics. This perspective maintains the position that genes, not the environment, control behavior. Scientists search the human genome for possible DNA (deoxyribose nucleic acid) aberrations that might explain dysfunctional behaviors like alcoholism, criminal misconduct, or schizophrenia. The primary methods to undertake these investigations are the use of twin and adoptee studies (Gullotta, 1994).

In the first instance, if a genetic marker exists for some behavior, then identical twins, who have the same genes, would be expected to exhibit similar histories for developing (or not developing) that specific dysfunctional behavior. The second method is to study the adopted children of parents who suffered from the dysfunctional behavior under investigation. Again, if a genetic marker exists, then in numbers higher than would otherwise be expected by chance the adopted child of that affected biological parent should develop similar behaviors. Of course, and even geneticists would reluctantly admit it, living conditions complicate the picture considerably, and twin studies have difficulty accounting for varying environmental conditions. "Heritabilities for behavior [in the best of studies] seldom exceed 50%," (Plomin, 1990, p. 187) providing enormous opportunities for living situations to affect the ultimate outcome.

It is reasonable to believe that genetic or other biochemical factors increase the risk of some individuals for some behaviors. Depression, schizophrenia, and some learning disabilities like attention deficit disorder *may* have partial genetic explanations. Nevertheless, as noted in this chapter, confirming reports locating specific genes for specific behaviors have routinely failed to withstand replication. Furthermore, even if a specific gene were identified, the fact that countless "at risk" individuals never proceed to develop the dysfunctional behavior suggests that a complex interaction of environment and chemistry are under way. Given that at present no engineered retrovirus exists to alter DNA for behavioral purposes, attention, we believe, needs to be focused on the factors explaining how individuals "escaped" the DNA script provided them at conception.

The second perspective is biochemical neurology. This approach maintains that dysfunctional behavior is the result of chemical imbalances within the body. It believes that medications can correct these chemical imbalances.

The final perspective is psychosurgery. This perspective maintains that surgical removal or destruction of brain tissue will correct dysfunctional behavior. (For a fascinating but deeply disturbing history of psychosurgery, read *Great and Desperate Cures* by Elliot Valenstein, 1986).

With the exception of psychosurgery, whose popularity waned with the introduction of the phenothiazines in the 1960s, biogenic approaches are attracting increasing attention. These approaches can be credited with drawing the public's attention to the fact that the mind and body reside in the same space and that it is likely that the two interact.

Nevertheless, as critics point out, the evidence for attributing dysfunctional behaviors solely to organic causes is weak. Further, critics question whether society should seek the *Brave New World* that the biochemical-neurology approach promises to deliver.* Where is the difference, they ask, between plucking out portions of the brain tissue (lobotomy or psychosurgery) and chemically straight-jacketing individuals? Are we really addressing the issue of a client's dysfunctional behavior with medications, they ask, or are we masking poor schools or incompetent parenting behavior instead?

---

*The novel *Brave New World,* by Aldous Huxley, examines the incompatibility of individual freedom and a society made "trouble-free" by science.

Does Treatment Work?

Several recent reviews of treatment outcome studies with children and adolescents provide some clues as to the effectiveness of psychotherapy with young people (Kazdin, 1987; Mann & Borduin, 1991; Weisz, Weiss, Alicke, & Klotz, 1987). Collectively these studies find evidence to suggest that psychotherapy works. Mann and Borduin (1991), for example, conclude that cognitive therapies such as analytically oriented or humanistic treatment models can be successful with formally operational youth. Approaches that use behavioral techniques can be effective in improving social skills, problem solving, and communication abilities of young people. It should be noted that Mann and Borduin encourage multisystem approaches to improving the functioning of dysfunctional youth. This suggestion is made because no single therapeutic model was found to be successful for all youth in all circumstances.

This last statement underscores the cardinal rules described in this chapter. It may not be so much the theoretical underpinnings of the therapeutic approach as the interpersonal relationship between client and therapist that matters. This alliance founded on mutual agreement regarding goals, behavior changes, and respect for each other spell, in our experience, the difference between change and stagnation (Marziali & Alexander, 1991).

Psychotherapy with Ethnic Minorities

Respect for each other includes, among other things, care in understanding and using a person's culture to assist in the healing and recovery process. Indeed, the American Psychological Association, in its 1990 council meetings, approved guidelines for working with ethnic minorities. These guidelines urge psychologists and other mental health providers to assume the responsibility for (1) educating their minority clients about the intervention process; (2) being personally informed of the relevant research and therapeutic practices for minority groups; (3) recognizing the importance and role of culture and ethnicity in understanding psychological processes; (4) respecting the role of family, community, values, and beliefs of the minority client's culture; (5) respecting minority religious and spiritual beliefs and their role in psychological recovery; (6) considering the sociopolitical factors of each person's case in making assessments and designing interventions; and (7) striving to eliminate forms of prejudice, bias, or discrimination in therapeutic practice.

Lillian Comas-Diaz, at the Transcultural Mental Health Institute in Washington, D.C., indicates that in 1990 one in four persons can identify themselves as a person of color or minority in the United States, and by the year 2056 the average resident will trace his or her descent to almost anywhere but White Europe (Henry, 1990). This trend is sometimes called the *browning of America* (Gibbs & Huang, 1989), referring to this group as people of color. Comas-Diaz (1992) suggests that the future of psychotherapy with ethnic minorities will result in the development of culturally specific psychotherapies for minorities. She cites existing or emerging programs for American Indians/Alaska Natives (Trimble & LaFromboise, 1985), Asian American/Pacific Islanders (Leong,

1986), African American/Blacks (Lee, 1990), and Hispanic/Latinos (Levine & Padilla, 1980). Likewise, she reports on therapeutic programs for Asian and Latino refugees (Rozee & Van Boemel, 1989; Garcia & Rodriguez, 1989). Also, Comas-Diaz suggests that psychotherapy for minorities will include generalized cross-cultural skills applicable to many ethnic groups.

The growing cultural revolution associated with the browning of America is likely to bring a kaleidoscopic impact on psychotherapeutic constructs. Once again, Comas-Diaz (1992) suggests a multitude of changes in fundamental therapeutic values and foci that are likely to come from the ethnocultural backgrounds of ethnic minorities. For example, instead of setting a premium on independence, greater attention will be given to the importance of interdependence. More attention will be given to the role of coping through faith and prayer. The concept of health will incorporate notions of balance and harmony within the different aspects of self (for instance, Yin and Yang). The value of developing the self through spirituality, social, physical, or emotional dimensions will become more broadly recognized and implemented. The theme of interconnectedness, family, community, and even cosmos will be expanded and a broader contextual definition of self will become prominent in therapy for ethnic minorities. This definition will likely include elements of the self in relationship with others, self in relationships with the world, and self in relationship with the cosmos.

Many challenges face those entering the therapeutic practice with adolescents. It will require a greater appreciation and understanding of ethno/socio/-politico/cultural contextualism.

Primary Prevention and Its Technology

The concept of prevention is far from new. The thought that emotional distress might be avoided and mental health encouraged can be traced back to the ancients. However, the idea of prevention as an attainable goal emerged only

George Albee is a major figure in the prevention movement in the United States and Canada.

recently as the result of the failure of the treatment model to reduce the ever-growing number of seriously emotionally ill individuals in our society (Albee, 1980, 1985a). Prevention has evolved since the early 1960s, when Gerald Caplan (1961, 1964, 1974) introduced a model suggesting that emotional illness could be prevented. That three-tier model of primary, secondary, and tertiary prevention, similar to the prevention model found in public health, has been pruned and refined. Secondary-prevention activities—attempts to reduce the length of time an individual or family experiences an emotionally distressful situation—are now called *treatment activities*. Tertiary-prevention activities—attempts to prevent the recurrence of a debilitating problem and to restore as high as possible a level of individual and family reorganization—are now called *rehabilitation activities*. Prevention has emerged in a hybrid form called *primary prevention*.

The goal of primary prevention remains basically unaltered from Caplan's (1974, pp. 189–190) original purpose of reducing "the incidence of new cases of mental disorder in the population by combating harmful forces which operate in the community and by strengthening the capacity of people to withstand stress." Parameters for this goal have now been established. Primary prevention focuses on groups (not individuals) and the specific problems those groups experience (Klein & Goldston, 1977). Prevention is proactive; that is, it builds new coping resources and adaptation skills and thus promotes emotional health (Albee & Gullotta, 1986). Finally, prevention activities are planned interventions that can be observed, recorded, and evaluated for effectiveness (Cowen, 1982b; Kelin & Goldston, 1977).

From this general conceptualization, different strategies emerge. They all involve each of us as an active participant in preventing illness and promoting health. Prevention advocates reject the claim "that major [emotional] illness is probably in large part genetically determined and is probably, therefore, not preventable, at most modifiable" (Lamb & Zusman, 1979, p. 1349). Rather, prevention takes the position that emotional problems are not diseases that can be traced to some microorganism or DNA thread, but are problems in living often created by blows of fate. Prevention views dysfunctional behavior, whether individual or family, as an outgrowth of multiple factors interacting to place groups of individuals at risk. One of these factors is the impact of stress on each person's life. From stress theory, the idea emerges that harmful stress (distress) might be managed, avoided, or eliminated. Thoughts also develop that you and I, our family, and our friends can gather strength to first cope with and then adapt to circumstances that cruel twists of fate fling across the path that humans walk (Hollister, 1977). How might we handle these problems in living? The answer is found in the technology that preventionists use to promote emotional health and to discourage emotional illness in society.

The technology of prevention consists of four tools that are used to fashion a healthier environment (Gullotta, 1987, 1992; Gullotta, Adams, & Alexander, 1986). These tools are *education, community organization/systems intervention, competency promotion,* and *natural care giving.* These tools have overlapping boundaries, and well-planned prevention programs practice elements of all four. (See Table 13–1.)

Table 13–1   The tools of prevention: selected examples and desired outcomes

Tool	Examples	Desired outcomes
Education		
• Public information	Public-service announcement, printed material, films, curricula	Avoid harmful stressors, manage stressors
• Anticipatory guidance	Career guidance	Manage stressors, build resistance to a stressor, avoid harmful stressors
• Behavioral approaches	Biofeedback, yoga, meditation	Manage stressors, avoid harmful stressors
Community organization/ systems intervention		
• Modification or removal of institutional barriers	Institution of new practices such as pass/fail system to replace letter grades; or a change in old practices such as permitting pregnant adolescents to attend class	Eliminate stressors
• Community resource development	Neighborhood associations, rehabilitation of housing stock	Eliminate stressors, manage stressors, avoid stressors
• Legislative or judicial action	Civil rights legislation, consumer-protection laws	Avoid stressors, eliminate stressors, manage stressors
Competency promotion		
• Active approaches	Wilderness schools: art, theater programs	Build resistance to a stressor
• Passive approaches	Affective education, assertiveness training	
Natural care giving		
• Indigenous care givers	Coaches, lawyers, friends	Manage stressors, build resistance to a stressor
• Trained indigenous care givers	Clergy, teachers	Manage stressors, build resistance to a stressor
• Mutual self-help	Alateen	Manage stressors, build resistance to a stressor

Education

Of all the tools of prevention, education is the most widely used. The belief behind education is that by increasing our knowledge we can change attitudes and behavior that hurt ourselves or others. Education can be used to ease the passage from one life event to another; information can be given to individuals to enhance their well-being. Whether in the form of the spoken word, a visual image, or printed material, education uses three techniques.

The first of these is *public information*. This information awakens, alerts, and sensitizes us to hazardous situations that can affect our lives. For example,

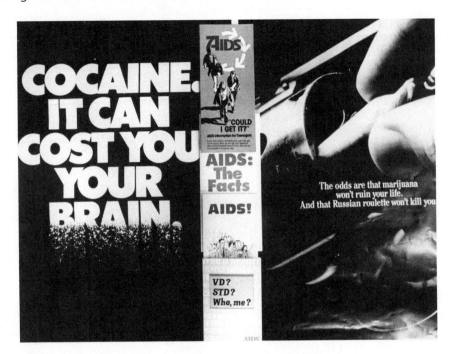

Consider these messages. What prevention tool do they illustrate?

public-service announcements about cigarette smoking are attempts to enlighten the public and to promote health. Education also includes books (like this one) that encourage you to take responsibility for your own life while sharing with you the findings that the social sciences can offer about individuals, relationships, and the family. Here, the intention is to alert you not only to potential hazards but also to health-promoting activities as well. Public information can include films, role plays, and classroom activities to impart to the learner new or improved skills for handling life.

Research is very clear on the point that all animals, including humans, desire some warning about an event before it happens (see Elliott & Eisdorfer, 1982). The time between the warning and the actual occurrence permits us to gather emotional resources to handle the event. Preventionists call the educational technique that builds these resources *anticipatory guidance*. Anticipatory guidance may take as simple a form as printed material that explains an upcoming life event, like the booklets that explain what to expect in the transition to college life. Or it may involve a mixture of print, film, and lecture material, like that used by health organizations teaching teenage expectant parents about childbirth and the infant.

Finally, some educational approaches use *behavioral techniques* to promote increased self-awareness. This category includes such approaches as biofeedback, progressive relaxation, and Eastern meditational philosophies. These techniques provide informational feedback that permits individuals to acquire the skills to cope with life.

Community Organization/Systems Intervention

The ability to live life effectively is sometimes impeded by forces beyond one's personal control. Such forces limit access to life options and opportunities. The second tool of prevention is used to redress these inequities. Obstructions can be removed in any of three ways.

Where obstructions exist because of the institutional practices or policies of an organization, individuals can work to *modify or remove institutional barriers.* One successful example has been the pressure exerted by health officials to include information about AIDS in the public school health curriculum.

Education programs serve an important role in primary prevention.

A second area for community organization/systems intervention (CO/SI) is *community resource development*. Here the activity is focused on achieving a more equitable distribution of power to improve the standard of living of a group of people within a community. Neighborhood associations and community-owned, community-directed operations to rehabilitate housing stock are two examples.

The third activity within the domain of CO/SI activity is *legislative or judicial action*. This is the most controversial of the three approaches, because it involves a change in the balance of political power in the direction of empowering the weak. And lately the buzzword *empowerment* has fallen on hard times. Those who need to be "empowered" have fallen even harder. The preventionist recognizes that the young people who fill the rosters of clinics and hospitals come predominantly from the leagues of the powerless, the disenfranchised, the helpless, and the hopeless. Lack of power itself has been suggested as a major stress in these people's lives: "Every research study we examined suggested that major sources of human stress and distress generally involve some form of excessive power [over the powerless]. . . . It is enough to suggest the hypothesis that a dramatic reduction and control of power might improve . . . mental health" (Kessler & Albee, 1977, pp. 379–380). If one of the keys to explaining dysfunction is a lack of power, then organizing and mobilizing a group for the purposes of acquiring power in a free society is a necessary and legitimate function of prevention activity. Such initiatives have been undertaken by the American Civil Liberties Union, Mothers Against Drunk Drivers, the National Organization for Women, and the National Association for the Advancement of Colored People, among others. These organizations are attempting, through legislative and judicial means, to put teeth into the phrase *equality of opportunity*.

Competency Promotion

Competency-promotion activities develop a feeling of being a part of, rather than apart from, society. They encourage feelings of worth, care for others, and belief in oneself. Encouraging such pride promotes increased self-esteem, an internal locus of control, and community interest rather than self-interest.

To be socially competent, three factors must be present. First, socially competent people *belong*. That is they are members of a society and have recognized roles and positions in that society. Next, socially competent people are *valued*. That is they have worth not in the sense of wealth but in respect. They are desired members of that society. Third, they have the opportunity and exercise that opportunity to *contribute*. Unless people can add their thoughts, their labor, and their energy to the society they belong to, they cannot be considered a part of that society (Gullotta, 1990). Activities such as affective education and assertiveness training are both education and competency-promotion tools. They are also examples of *passive approaches* to competency promotion. Passive approaches involve group classroom activities. They differ from the activities typically undertaken by wilderness schools, Scouting, 4-H, and arts programs. These programs teach skills like climbing, canoeing, or stage-set construction and acting but emphasize, first and more importantly, interpersonal and community relationships. Because these activities involve action and are usually directed toward accomplishment of some task, they are called *active approaches.*

Natural Care Giving

On almost every issue, adults and youths turn not to professionals but to friends or others (coaches, the clergy, teachers, and so on) for advice and guidance. Natural care giving recognizes the ability within each of us to help a fellow human being. It extends beyond activities like those of helping another in similar straits (mutual self-help groups) to acknowledge the responsibility each of us has to fellow human beings (Cowen, 1982a). Natural care giving involves behavior such as the sharing of knowledge, the sharing of experiences, compassionate understanding, companionship, and, when necessary, confrontation. Such care giving is a reference point for people to acknowledge that they are an important part of an emotional network (system) that extends beyond family members and friends to all people.

Some of us may choose professions in which we become *trained indigenous care givers,* such as teachers and the clergy. Others of us will at some time in our lives join a *mutual self-help group* to give and receive help from others who find themselves in similar straits—for example, as a child of an alcoholic parent or as an individual recovering from a serious physical or emotional illness. Regardless of the circumstance, it is vital to remember that each of us is an *indigenous care giver* with a responsibility to assist his or her fellow human beings.

Does Prevention Work?

In 1981 the American Psychological Association established a task force to identify and describe effective models of primary prevention. This effort has been published in a book, *14 Ounces of Prevention: A Casebook for Practitioners* (Price, Cowen, Lorion, & Ramos-McKay, 1988). According to a summary by Conyne (1991) the common denominators for success include six fundamental factors. Once again, we see that ethnocultural factors are recognized as an important component. The fundamental features of a successful primary prevention program are thought to include:

- Building a data base on the risks and problems experienced by the target group
- Designing programs that accomplish long-term change that assists individuals in altering their lives in facilitative ways
- Teaching new concrete skills that enhance coping with such things as decision making, communication, assertiveness, or self-management
- Maintaining responsiveness and sensitivity to cultural and ethnic variations within a population
- Using program evaluation techniques to document successful outcomes and program effectiveness

In that recent epidemiological data suggest that 15% to 22% of the roughly 63 million children and adolescents in the United States have mental health

---

Box 13–2   Primary Prevention Among Adolescent Refugees

Refugees are immigrants who have had to flee their home due to persecution for their beliefs, politics, or ethnicity. Many refugees have experienced war, torture, repression, oppression, human rights violations, and other horrific events. Therefore, countries such as the United States and Canada, which are open to immigration by refugees, need to promote primary prevent programs at the community, national, and even international level. Few materials are available on recommended models to prevent stress associated with culturation among already stressed refugees. Fortunately, Williams and Berry (1991), a research team from the United States and Canada, have provided a model based on notions of acculturation and adaptation.

Acculturation and adaptation deal with changes that groups and individuals must make when they move to another culture. Group-level acculturation focuses on changes associated with economic, technological, social, cultural, and political change. Individual-level acculturation includes changes in behavior, values, attitudes, and personal or social identity. To facilitate acculturation, professionals must adopt a cross-cultural perspective that includes the understanding of the acculturating group's sociocultural history. Furthermore, the acculturation process should be viewed as including an "interaction" between cultures—not just a process within the ethnic minority/refugee group. Finally, note that there are wide individual differences in psychological acculturation (individual-level acculturation) that will be accompanied by varying levels of acculturative stress.

Acculturation can enhance one's life or it can disrupt one's physical well-being and mental health.

When acculturative stress is high, the individual may experience societal disintegration where old social norms and order disappear and the individual feels stressed by such change. Former patterns of authority, welfare, and relating with others may be virtually gone, leaving the individual feeling hostile, uncertain, depressed, or confused in identity. Feelings of marginality and alienation, anxiety, and psychosomatic complaints are not uncommon among refugee family members.

Williams and Berry (1991) suggest the following chain of reactions in their model of acculturative stress:

ACCULTURATION EXPERIENCE →
STRESSORS → ACCULTURATIVE STRESS

The degree to which an adolescent may cope with this chain of events and processes is based on a series of complex factors. Among many factors include the (1) degree of loss of status to the family due to socioeconomic factors, (2) the tolerance for or acceptance of the culture of the group within the new community, (3) the availability of a network of social and cultural group support for the refugee, (4) the occurrence of prejudice, discrimination, or exclusion as barriers to acculturation, (5) prior intercultural exposure or encounters, (6) attitudes toward the acculturation process, and (7) skills in coping strategies.

Professionals working with such adolescent refugees have a substantial challenge. However, models of primary prevention for working with refugees are providing a foundation for effective application of psychological theory and practice.

---

problems (National Advisory Mental Health Council, 1990) there appears to be ample need for primary prevention efforts. Family, school, and community-oriented prevention efforts that have documented success can now be identified (Weissberg, Caplan, & Harwood, 1991), and many programs attempt to be sensitive to the ethnocultural needs of minority youths (Bobo, Cvetkovich, Gilchrist, Trimble, & Schinke, 1988; Neighbors, 1990; Ashby, Gilchrist, & Miramontez, 1987; Dressler, 1987; Stuart & Gokiert, 1990; Tsui & Sammons, 1988). For additional reading refer to Bond and Compas (1989). Also see Box 13–2 for information about prevention and refugee adolescents.

The Promise of Prevention in Working with Adolescents

The goal of prevention is not to eliminate all these stresses. Life without any stress is death. Each of us experiences stress with every life change. The goal of prevention is to help ensure that stress does not create distress, which contributes to emotional suffering. Prevention specialists should work to help people manage stress, avoid or eliminate those stresses that are distressful, and strengthen stress-resistance abilities (Hollister, 1977).

In recent years the strengthening of stress-resistant abilities has been the focus of several investigations (Bloom, 1990; Downs, 1990; Luthar & Zigler, 1991; Schinke, McAlister, Orlandi, & Botvin, 1990; Work, Cowen, Parker, & Wyman, 1990). The riddle these scholars have sought to solve may be expressed as follows:

Who becomes dysfunctional?

Who doesn't?

Why?

Their preliminary findings suggest that nonsupportive families and institutions with failure experiences in settings such as school place youth as risk—particularly young people who are temperamental and male. Stress-resilient youth use a variety of mechanisms to succeed, including humor, higher intelligence, an internal locus of control, and involvement with supporting, caring, and empathic adult role models.

In adolescence the circumstances under which a particular stress occurs may change, but the stresses themselves remain constant. Pause for a few moments to consider how you might use each of the tools of prevention to improve the conditions under which each of these stresses occurs. Are some of the stresses imposed by the structure of society? (For instance, would the passage of the Equal Rights Amendment have removed stress on women that is structurally imposed by society?) If so, can they be eliminated through political action? Are other stresses inevitable? If so, can we help adolescents at highest risk avoid them, those at lesser risk manage them, and still others combat them successfully? As you read this text, ask these questions about each of the issues we raise, and don't be afraid to work out possible answers where we have not. (See Box 13–3.)

In the chapters that follow we shall examine several problem behaviors. We shall refer to the material in this chapter and other chapters in an attempt to make sense of acts that harm not only oneself but also others. It has been brought to our attention that this book concludes with very somber subjects. It is not our intention to depress you as you study explanations for problem sexual behaviors, substance abuse, eating disorders, delinquency, and suicide. Instead, our intention is to motivate you to act to reduce the incidence of these behaviors, and we hope that you will be so motivated.

Box 13–3   A Primary-Prevention Work Sheet

The following work sheet was first used by Klein and Goldston (1977) at an NIMH-sponsored workshop and then adapted by George Albee for use in teaching students about prevention. We have further refined it and strongly encourage you to use it after reading each of the remaining chapters in this book. The task at the end of each chapter is to design for yourself or an "at-risk" group a prevention program to promote health and reduce distress.

1. If this is a program for an "at-risk" group, describe the group as fully as possible.

   _____

   _____

2. In this exercise, what are the major stressors affecting you or the "at-risk" group?

   _____

   _____

3. In this exercise, what problems do you wish to manage, avoid, or eliminate? What competencies do

you wish to enhance that will build resistance to the stressors identified in question 2?

   _____

   _____

4. Describe the prevention initiatives you would use to address the problems and promote the competencies identified in question 3.

   _____

   _____

5. Do your initiatives have ethical or political implications? Are some initiatives easier to implement than others?

   _____

   _____

6. Taking into account the ethical and political implications of your initiatives, combine those initiatives that appear most feasible and describe your prevention program.

   _____

   _____

Major Points to Remember

1. The secret of working with adolescents is being trustworthy, genuine, empathic, and honest. For this formula to work, the adolescent must perceive the mental-health worker as having these qualities.
2. Therapy involves diagnosing a client's emotional problem and, where appropriate, acting to correct that problem by increasing the individual's capacity to cope with life.
3. The four basic categories of therapy are individual, family, group, and couple therapy. The two primary locations in which therapy takes place are treatment (outpatient) settings and rehabilitation (inpatient) settings.
4. The medical model is a disease-based model in which illness passes through certain predictable stages. Although useful for physical illness, this approach has certain inherent weaknesses when applied to emotional problems.
5. Most of the many kinds of therapies can be grouped into five schools: analytically oriented therapy, behavior therapy, humanistic therapy, transpersonal therapy, and biogenic therapies.
6. In primary prevention, emotional illness is avoided and mental health encouraged. Prevention is proactive and emphasizes groups rather than individuals.

7. There are four prevention tools: education, community organization/systems intervention, competency promotion, and natural care giving.
8. Stress accompanies any change in life. Excessive stress causes distress, which contributes to emotional suffering.
9. The tools of prevention help individuals manage stress, avoid or eliminate stresses, and strengthen stress-resistance skills.
10. Prevention's promise for working with adolescents is that it can help to ease the life-transition points.

CHAPTER

14

Problems of
Adolescent Sexuality

- Adolescent Pregnancy

- Ethnic Differences

- Implications for Treatment and Prevention

- Contraception

- Factors Involved in Not Using Contraceptives

- Venereal Diseases

- Adolescent Prostitution

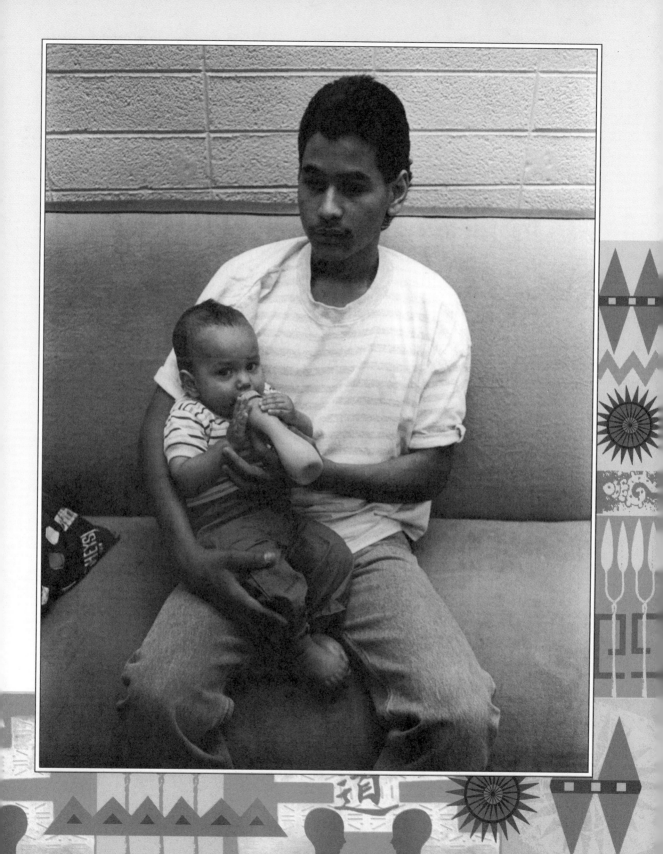

The topics for this chapter remind us in some ways of one of those classic black-and-white horror films. You remember: The monster is hidden from view during the day but emerges at night to stalk the streets. Roaming without restraint, it remains loose until morning breaks the grip of night and then, unable to stand the sun's penetrating and purifying light, withdraws into its shelter until dusk again falls. We admit that this sounds flowery and moralistic, but then most horror films and most sexual advice are flowery and moralistic.*

In the past each issue we examine in this chapter was considered to be relevant to only a few severely disturbed people who existed on the fringes of society. Recently we have begun to appreciate that adolescent pregnancy, venereal diseases, and prostitution are not unique to a few but are experienced by millions of sexually active young people each year. In this chapter we examine these problems and, where appropriate, discuss what actions can be taken to prevent or treat them.

Adolescent Pregnancy

"Most teen pregnancies are products of caring relationships in which the couple decided to make physical commitments—but got caught" (Cartwright, 1980). When the traditional or double standard of sexual behavior was still in vogue, the teenage couple who had conceived a child had few choices, and all of them difficult. Although the couple could marry, most often the girl quietly withdrew from school and, amid neighborhood rumors, disappeared to stay with a relative or at a home for unwed mothers to await the birth of the infant. Once delivered, the infant was given up for adoption. This pattern has recently begun to change; and although the choices remain difficult, there are more options than existed in 1970.

Some of these changes involve new methods of preventing conception (the Pill, foam). Others involve wider accessibility to already known birth-control devices (condoms). There has also been a liberalization of our attitudes. We are now able to discuss sexual issues, and old standards for women are giving way to new codes of sexual conduct. Some groups argue that these changes have resulted in an "epidemic" of adolescent pregnancies. The term *epidemic* can be understood to have several meanings. Among these would be births to *unmarried* adolescents. In 1960, for example, 85% of births to adolescent women were to married teenagers. In contrast, by 1988 this percentage had decreased to fewer than 33% (Jorgensen, 1993). Several researchers argue, in response, that there has been no increase in the number of adolescent women giving birth to children (Chilman, 1983; Vinovskis, 1981). Rather, they contend, the issue is one of demographics; that is, fewer women above the age of 20 are having children. The result is that it appears that adolescent birthrates are on the rise when, in fact, until recently births to adolescents had declined. In 1952, for example, the overall U.S. birthrate was 86 in 1,000 among women 15 to 19 years old. In 1972 the rate was 62 in 1,000, and in 1983 there were 52 births per 1,000. In recent years the figure of 52 births per 1,000 has varied slightly. For the latest year for

*Notice, the next time you go to the movies, who escapes the clutches of evil. Typically, it is the character who is pure in mind, body, and spirit.

which data is available, 1988, the figure stood at 54 per 1,000 (U.S. Census, 1991). Regardless of one's position on whether the adolescent pregnancy rate is high, there is no disagreement that an estimated one adolescent female in ten will conceive this year, or about 1 million pregnancies; of this number about 478,000 young women are expected to carry their infants to term (Jorgensen, 1993; Roosa, 1991).Finally, two other changes are occurring. Fewer young women are leaving home to have their babies. More interesting still is that fewer are giving up their infants to family agencies for adoption (Farber, 1991). Can we conclude that society has cast off its prohibitions and embraced these young people? Is adolescent pregnancy less stigmatizing than it was 10, 15, or 300 years ago?

To be frank, we find it difficult to imagine that any behavior with media headlines like *casualty figures, epidemic,* or *national disaster* can be considered desirable in society's eyes. Information from the Office of Technology Assessment (1991) for the U.S. Congress that the United States spent at least $20 billion in 1988 on AFDC, Medicaid, and food stamps to support adolescents with children does little to endear these teenagers and their children to the public. Additional information that the cost to the United States of 385,000 children born to teenage mothers in 1985 over the next twenty years may exceed $6 billion in welfare payments engenders further disrespect ("Cost of Teenage Pregnancies," 1987). Nor do we find evidence to suggest that the immediate family or society at large has become any more understanding of the problems these young people face. The consequences of adolescent pregnancy clearly remain painful (Bergman, 1980; Black & DeBlassie, 1985; Dryfoos, 1990; Hechinger, 1992; Jorgensen, 1993; Kenney, 1987; McClellan, 1987; C. H. Wright, 1980).

Knowing how far to go in a sexual relationship is a common challenge for teenagers.

Many young pregnant women drop out of school, and few ever return to complete their education. Handicapped by a poor education, few are ever satisfied with the jobs they are capable of getting. Most find their freedom severely limited by their new family responsibilities. For those who marry the father of the infant, marital satisfaction is lower than in nonadolescent marriages, and the divorce rate is twice as high. Finally, family size tends to be larger than with other marriages, with the children of adolescent parents experiencing greater health risks, such as low birth weight and premature birth. (Black & DeBlassie, 1985; Dillard & Pol, 1982; Dryfoos, 1990; Elster & McAnarney, 1980; Hechinger, 1992; G. H. Henderson, 1980; Jorgensen, 1993; Jorgensen & Alexander, 1981; Merritt, Lawrence, & Naeye, 1980; Nye & Lamberts, 1980; Office of Technology, 1991; D. B. Schwartz; Walters, & Walters, 1980).

If these are the unpleasant consequences of adolescent pregnancy, what, then, are the antecedents? In the following sections we examine the literature on the teenage girl/mother, her family, the boy/father and adolescent marriage.

The Girl/Mother

Since Sigmund Freud postulated that the sex drive is one of two instinctive universal human urges (the other being aggression), it is certainly understandable that there are numerous psychoanalytic explanations for adolescent pregnancy in the literature. One of the most common themes is the Oedipal nature of intercourse for adolescent girls. Several studies using clinical populations suggest that the adolescent girl, desiring sexual relations with her father, pushes back those incestuous feelings and engages in sexual intercourse with a surrogate (Babikian & Goldman, 1971; LaBarre, 1968).

According to an investigation of the factors contributing to a high risk of pregnancy among mentally ill adolescent girls (Abernethy & Abernethy, 1974), girls at high risk have much poorer relationships with their mothers than with their fathers. In a small, clinical subject sample, the authors find that paternal relationships are "associated with a higher incidence of incest or quasi-incestuous relationship" (p. 447). They suggest that the poor mother/daughter relationship pushes the daughter into an intimate relationship with her father. Seeking to control these sexual desires, the adolescent becomes sexually promiscuous, displacing her urges onto a "safer" male.

Other psychoanalytic explanations for adolescent pregnancy are that pregnancy is a struggle against a pre-Oedipal, homosexual liaison with the mother (Blos. 1967) and that pregnancy is a substitute for the female's missing penis (Clothier, 1943).

Beginning in the 1970s studies started to offer more than a one-dimensional view of adolescent pregnancy. For example, half of one research sample showed few, if any, signs of deviancy; these girls were typical outgoing, open, and enthusiastic adolescents (Kane, Moan, & Bolling, 1974). Similar findings emerged from detailed psychiatric observations of 61 pregnant adolescents (Percy-Reyes & Falk, 1973, cited in Shaffer, Pettigrew, Wollkind, & Zaijicek, 1978). In this study 27% of the highly selective population proved to be normal, well-adjusted young people. The remainder had many difficulties with their families and showed signs of emotional disturbance, but it is important to note that not all the girls in this study had these problems. Several recent reviews of the literature tend to reinforce this suggestion that there may be no psychological differences between pregnant and nonpregnant girls (McKenry, Walters, & Johnson, 1979; Phipps-Yonas, 1980; Shaffer et al., 1978). (There are, however, psychological variables in young people's decisions whether to use contraceptives; this issue will be taken up later in the chapter.)

Some of the work on pregnant adolescents shows that they may have deep emotional problems. However, many of the authors of these studies properly caution their readers that the sample for observation was drawn from a small, highly selective group, so that the findings cannot be generalized to the overall population. Are all pregnant adolescents emotionally disturbed? We suggest not. There is a growing body of evidence to support the student comment quoted at the beginning of this section that often the caring relationship between two people simply ends unexpectedly in pregnancy (Gullotta et al., 1986). The reactions of the girl's family to this news and their contribution to this situation are investigated next.

The Girl/Mother's Family

There is considerably greater agreement in the literature on the families of most pregnant adolescents. Several common themes emerge from these studies. The home is described as a very stressful place, with the parents reported in some cases to be alcoholics or assaultive (Franklin, 1988; LaBarre, 1968; McCullough & Scherman, 1991; Robbins, Kaplan, & Martin, 1985; Russ-Eft, Sprenger, & Beever, 1979; Science, 1991a). Single-parent families abound (Babikian & Goldman, 1971; Barnett, Papini, & Gbur, 1991; Boyce & Benoit, 1975; LaBarre, 1968; Russ-Eft et al., 1979). Mother/daughter relationships, at least before pregnancy, are often described as strained (Babikian & Goldman, 1971; LaBarre, 1968). Agreement on this last point is not universal, however. In one study (Uddenberg, 1976), pregnant adolescents with unstable homes reported closer relationships with their mothers than with their fathers. The author of this study suggests that this inability to relate in a positive manner to the father carries over into other relationships with men. Other reports indicate that physical or emotional illness marks many of these families (LaBarr, 1968; Russ-Eft et al., 1979).

Because of the suggestion that adolescent pregnancy may be the result of an unresolved Oedipal conflict, the descriptions of mother/daughter relationships before and after conception are particularly interesting. Most studies report a vast improvement in tense and conflict-ridden relationships after conception. The grandmother-to-be in these reports seems to, midway through the pregnancy, share in her expectant daughter's experience. In one recent study 60% of the adolescent mothers continued to live at home with their mother. Although the new grandmothers reported becoming upset at learning of their daughter's pregnancy and younger grandmothers in their 20s and 30s reported the role as burdensome and stressful, still these women extended help and support to their daughters and grandchildren. This help and support could be considered vital to the well-being of the infant for, in the opinion of the researchers, these new grandmothers were more responsive to the child's needs and caring than the adolescent mother (Chase-Lansdale, Brooks-Gunn, & Palkoff, 1991). Whether the adolescent's mother is reliving her own pregnancy, or whether this situation creates an environment in which daughter and mother can share experiences and in so doing improve their relationship, is unclear (E. W. Smith, 1975; Townsend & Worobey, 1987; Wise & Grossman, 1980).

In general, the picture that develops of the girl/mother and her family suggests a fair amount of family stress. Several studies have found a higher incidence of separation or divorce and strained mother/daughter relationships. Until recently, little attention was paid to the boy/father. In the next section we look at him and adolescent marriage.

Boy/Father and Adolescent Marriage

Perhaps it is society's double standard that has allowed males to be ignored in studying the problems created by adolescent pregnancies. Society has tended to view the young male's involvement in this situation as the sowing of wild oats. Although the male bears the responsibility for planting the seed, society has reasoned that it is the girl who allows it to be planted. Further, should conception occur, it is she, of course, and not the male, who bears the unmistakable signs of pregnancy. Finally, it is also clear that when marriage has not been an option, the girl's family has taken every measure available to separate the young lovers.

Few research reports exist on the boy/father (Meyer, 1991). In part, this is because the fathers of children born to adolescent women are often not adolescents but older men (Hardy & Duggan, 1988). The few studies that do exist portray a young man in many ways less prepared than his child bride for the responsibilities of marriage. Although several reports describe him as involved with and concerned over his family's welfare (Cannon-Bonventure & Kahn, 1979; Connally, 1978; Earls & Siegel, 1980), others describe him as flighty, childish, and irresponsible (Earls & Siegel, 1980; Inselberg, 1961; Walters & Walters, 1980). In either description the young man is less than fully prepared to assume the responsibilities of a father. Poorly educated with few, if any, financial resources, the boy/father in any case is an inadequate family provider (Barret & Robinson, 1982; Dryfoos, 1990; Hardy & Duggan, 1988; Smollar & Ooms, 1987; O. E. Westney, Cole, & Munford, 1986). For example, one study reports that adolescent fathers who marry the mother of their child have fewer years of education, poorer jobs, and lower incomes than other young men (Teti, Lamb, & Elster, 1987). Additional work by P. A. Robinson (1988) confirms these findings and suggests further that the adolescent father is ignorant in many areas of human sexuality, as well as depressed.

Thus, it probably should not be too surprising to learn that adolescent marriages have a greater chance than others of ending in divorce (Dowling, 1987; Furstenberg, 1976; Russ-Eft et al., 1979). Nor should it be surprising that financial problems in part related to poor education and inadequate job skills plague these marriages (Cannon-Bonventure & Kahn, 1979; Dowling, 1987; Nye & Lamberts, 1980; Office of Technology, 1991).

De Lissovoy's (1973) longitudinal study of adolescent marriages provides an intimate glimpse of the lives of these people, whom he calls the "insignificant Americans." The 48 couples in his sample were from small-town or rural families of blue-collar heritage. Troubled, isolated, and, in the author's words, "unrecognized by the local community," they had few resources and little hope for a better future.

The typical "honeymoon" excitement during the first few weeks of a new marriage did not exist in the De Lissovoy study, as financial troubles were evident from the first day of most marriages. As one young parent said in another study, "Once we didn't have enough money for food. I ran out of food stamps. . . . The check always runs out and there's never any money for extras" (Cannon-Bonventure & Kahn, 1979, p. 18).

De Lissovoy (1973) reports that while the husbands remained "boys," engaging in sports with their former schoolmates, the wives felt lonely and alienated. This reported loneliness originated from feelings of being dropped by their friends and the time needed to care for their infants. Such reports of wives' loneliness are common in the literature: "I didn't know where to look for friends, and the time it took just to think of some old friends to call! It seemed like they had all just gone away to school somewhere or were just too busy" (Cannon-Bonventure & Kahn, 1979, p. 18).

Additional problems exist in such areas as frequency of sexual relations and childrearing. In the DeLissovoy (1973) study the wives tended to report that their husbands wanted sexual relations more often than they did. In childrearing the parents' expectations for their children were unrealistic. Parents in this study had little knowledge of child development and were overly optimistic about what their children could do. Such expectations lead De Lissovoy to speculate that such families may become "impatient" and "intolerant" with their offspring. The impatience is complicated by a lack of available and affordable child care, and with that comes an increased risk of child abuse (Bolton, Laner, & Kane, 1980; Fox, Baisch, Goldberg, & Hockmuth, 1987; Ketterlinus, Lamb, & Nitz, 1991; Sahler, 1980).

> My husband had to leave his job because I had no babysitter [and I had to go to work]. . . . He did not go to work and I feel bad because I have to take care of everything. . . . I would take her to my friend's house but I could smell her house a block away. Once I let her do it, but she didn't feed [my baby] or change her. (Cannon-Bonventure & Kahn, 1979, p. 18).

Despite the formidable problems these couples faced, leading De Lissovoy (1973) to observe that they reached the "middle years of marriage in 30 months" (p. 249), there were also strengths. These included the use of the church for emotional support, the building of strong bonds with in-laws, and, in many of these marriages, a true caring for each other. Three years after De Lissovoy began his study, 77% of the marriages remained intact. While confirming many of the problems that plague the adolescent marriage, this study suggests that despite incredible odds, some adolescent marriages can survive, at least for a while.

Other research data support parts of De Lissovoy's classic study. In two urban samples of pregnant adolescents, most boy/fathers did not desert the girl/mothers but remained involved with the mother and child (Lorenzi, Klerman, & Jekel, 1977; P. B. Smith, Munford, & Hammer, 1979). Other studies report the majority of males willing to provide financial child support (P. A.

Robinson, 1988; O. E. Westney, Cole, & Munford, 1986) and anxious not to leave the decision of parenthood solely to the girl/mother (Redmon, 1985). Although unquestionably these young people, married or not, faced overwhelming problems in maintaining their relationship, it is important to note that at least in some of these studies, many of the couples reported caring for each other.

There can be no doubt that adolescent marriages begin with a poor prognosis for success. Nor can there be any doubt that the burden of pregnancy still descends heavily on the female. What does begin to emerge in all these studies is some appreciation of the factors weighing against the young couple

Finally, two other longitudinal studies provide additional insight on the long-term prospects of early childbearing. The first, a 17-year longitudinal study of slightly more than 300 mostly Black women who became pregnant in the mid-1960s, provides small encouragement to the belief that early adversity can be overcome later in life. Compared to the five-year follow-up in 1972 when one-third were receiving welfare and only half had graduated from high school, the 1984 data reported that significantly more women had returned to finish high school or its equivalent. Similarly, many more had left welfare programs, and were employed in stable jobs. Even so, only slightly more than one-third were married, and in comparison to other groups of Black women who had delayed childbearing, these individuals were not as successful (Furstenberg, Brook-Gunn, & Morgan, 1987).

The second study was a 20-year follow-up of 154 Black women who also became pregnant as teenagers in the 1960s. The researchers reported that at the follow-up 62% had completed a high school education or its equivalent and were either employed or married. Using this standard as a "success" measure, the researchers were interested in understanding what factors enabled success. Five common elements were identified.

First, successful subjects were further along in their high school studies when they became pregnant than other subjects. Next, women who succeeded had participated in life skills training sessions during their initial pregnancy. (See Box 14–1.) These women returned to school after the birth of the first child and importantly avoided a second pregnancy for at least two years after the birth of the first child. Fourth, they were not socially isolated after the first pregnancy and able to reintegrate quickly into society. Finally, successful women had smaller families than unsuccessful subjects. Family size for successful women numbered two to three children as compared to several children for other subjects (Horwitz, Klerman, & Jekel, 1991).

Ethnic Differences

The best evidence suggests that irrespective of ethnic group, family type, or caregiving arrangements, infants and children show declines in positive development during early childhood and beyond (for example see Field, Widmayer, Adler, & DeCubas, 1990; Furstenberg, Brooks-Gunn, & Chase-Lansdale, 1989) due to teenage pregnancy. Given that by age 18, 24% of all women will become pregnant in the United States and that 40% of Whites and 63% of Blacks will be pregnant by age 20 (Hayes, 1987), it is no wonder that government officials are

---

Box 14–1   Young Parents Programs

Barbara Sheffey has been a community worker for Child and Family Agency for nearly two decades. This gracious, lovely grandmother has worked during those years with young teenage women who become pregnant and decide to carry to term. She exemplifies the best characteristics of a helping professional. Warm, trustworthy, empathic, and no nonsense, Barbara has seen hundreds of young women enter adulthood prematurely and has held their babies as mother struggled to complete her education.

Barbara is employed for the agency Thomas Gullotta directs in a service called the Young Parents Program. Located in the high school, young women are able to continue with their education after their pregnancy while their infants are cared for at a nursery located in or near the school. Primary medical care for the infants and mothers is provided by the school-

based health center located at that site. Mental health counseling services, should they be needed, are also provided by the school-based health center. "Concrete" social service help in enrolling for city, state, and federal aid programs is also provided on-site by Barbara who will transport child-mother and infant, if necessary, to ensure both receive quality care.

Most important, Barbara feels the Young Parents Program offers these young women the social support and child development information needed to have a better chance at making it. Quiet talks, tears, and laughter make up Barbara's day. That also includes following up on child-mom and infant when they fail to arrive at school on a given day. "Can't miss school, you know, too much at stake for that little baby," she'll say—a statement we would all agree with.

---

concerned about pregnancy and its consequences for children—especially among minority groups with very high pregnancy rates overall. Fortunately, some evidence suggests that some of the detrimental effects of early childrearing can be offset by social and educational programs (Furstenberg et al., 1989); however, the costs are relatively high, and society remains uncertain as to its moral and financial commitment to such programs.

Important qualitative research, using ethnographic techniques, has been completed to identify possible themes associated with teenage pregnancy among both Black (Boxhill, 1987) and Hispanic (de Anda, Becerra, & Fielder, 1990) adolescent populations. Research with Black adolescent females who were either pregnant or were currently teenage parents indicates these youths feel let down by their parents, having had experienced consistent conflict, fighting, and avoidance between themselves and their parents. Although they love their parents, these Black teenagers viewed their parents as ineffective and unable to control their own destiny, not alone that of the behavior and well-being of the family and its members. Likewise, pregnant Black teenagers saw their personal relationships as always requiring taking and little giving in return. They indicate they avoid committing to lasting relationships because of a history of unhappiness and broken expectations. Relationships with peers and parents are viewed as punitive, insincere, and ineffective. Most of the teenagers viewed themselves as caught in a life transition where they were either too young or too old. A mosaic of such feelings are expressed in the themes of the following comments from numerous pregnant Black teenagers:

> I am too young to have to make all these decisions. I am too old to have to ask for advice. I should be able to figure things out on my own. I am too young to have to be

in control of everything. I am too old to have to depend on my parents. I am too young to get a job. I am too old to take hand-outs. I am too young to have to be grown-up. I am too old to do childish things. I am too young to know the answers. I am too old to be so confused. I am too young to be a mother. I am too old to be told what to do. (Boxhill, 1987, p. 47)

Collectively, feelings of family conflict and disappointment, dissatisfaction about personal relations with peers and at home, and the perceptions of being marginalized between childhood and adulthood leave pregnant Black teenagers unprepared for effective parenting.

Mexican-American pregnant teenagers portray a somewhat different picture (de Anda et al., 1990). Interviews with Mexican-American adolescents reveal a picture of warm recollections of early childhood, damaged by the loss of a parent due to divorce (mostly) or death. Perceptions of loss of a special person and loss of protection permeate these adolescents' images. Conflict over the choice of friends, based on parental preference, is commonly observed—particularly with mothers. Relationships with fathers are often conflict-free but distant and alienated. Therefore, the lives of pregnant Hispanic teenagers are filled with arguments, name calling, and disobedience, with temporary running away common. The social lives of these youths are usually filled with continuous involvement in peer activities, including varying degrees of hanging around together, cruising, shopping, going to movies or beaches, attending parties or dances. Most pregnant Hispanic youths report having limited experience with relationships with males. They tend to have relatively few sexual encounters and are involved in a meaningful and reasonably committed relationship. Usually when they discover they are pregnant, their boyfriends propose marriage and assume some responsibility for their sexual behavior.

According to Zayas, Schinke, and Casareno (1987), parental commitment by Hispanic fathers may be due, in part, to the gender-specific role of *machismo*. To be machismo means to be an adequate and gentle protector, provider, and nurturer of one's children. This involves assuming responsibility for one's masculine (sexual) behavior. Likewise, the macho role compels the male adolescent to avoid bringing shame *(verguenza)* to the family by neglecting one's duties and responsibilities to one's mate, offspring, and mate's family. Therefore, in contrast to Black females, who might experience sexual demands with marginal responsibility for parenting (due to economic limitations and other problems) from their male partners, Hispanic females may experience greater paternal support and involvement by their mates.

De Anda and associates (1990) have also interviewed White pregnant adolescents and adolescent mothers. The lives and perceptions of White youths are quite different from those of Black and Hispanic adolescents. Pregnant White adolescents commonly come from homes where parents did not live together and, in turn, experience more parental figures due to cohabitation, remarriage, or visiting male figures. They are much more likely to experience more frequent moves and changes in parental figures and to have considerable conflict with parents over friends, home responsibilities, and parental control. Their social lives are active and peer dominated. Common social activities include gatherings at friends' houses and hanging out or "ditching" school together. White adolescents who become pregnant are likely to have had more sexual experience and to have initiated sexual relations with their boyfriends very early in their relationship. Many of the fathers are hesitant to assume fathering roles due to personal ambition or economic/social implications. Perhaps this accounts for why so many White adolescent females, in comparison to Hispanic youths, choose abortion as a means of dealing with the pregnancy.

In conclusion, varying social and cultural conditions may surround teenage pregnancy for adolescents from different ethnic groups. Cultural values, varying degrees of parental support/conflict, paternal involvement by boyfriends, and social expectations may vary for each group, making it important for professionals working with programs associated with teenage pregnancy to disentangle the sociocultural factors in working with pregnant teenagers of varying races or ethnic groups.

Implications for Treatment and Prevention

Two treatment approaches can be used to improve the life conditions of these young people once conception has occurred. Both are highly controversial and emotionally charged. The first is to provide easily accessible, low-cost or no-cost abortions to young people without the need for parental consent. Since 1973, when the U.S. Supreme Court legalized the procedure (with some restrictions), millions of unwanted pregnancies have been terminated by young people who felt that they could not properly care for a child. (Cates, 1982). (See Box 14–2.)

The second approach involves society's revaluing all children, but particularly the children of adolescents, as national resources and providing them with the means to grow up in a healthy home environment. We have noted the problems that the adolescent faces in attempting to rear a child. Support programs and financial aid would be necessary to ensure that the mothers and fathers could complete their own education and provide food, shelter, clothing, and medical attention for their infant above today's welfare standards. Although many opponents of this suggestion would argue that we would be rewarding adolescents for their irresponsible behavior, we argue that we should not be destroying their lives—and, more important, the lives of their children—because they had a child in adolescence.

Prevention is no less controversial. Sex education should be a mandatory part of all school curricula. It should begin in elementary school and should be directed at more than simply providing information. Courses should attempt to encourage young people to be more comfortable with their sexuality. In high school these courses should include substantial information on family life, child care, responsible decision making, and parenting.

Finally, we need to make available to sexually active young people the means to prevent conception. The first step is to inform them of birth-control methods in school The next is to make sure that young people have access to them.

These are not easy or uncontroversial proposals. But if we are serious about wanting to diminish the number of unwanted pregnancies and improving the life

---

Box 14–2   A Decision on Abortion

Since the Supreme Court decision of 1973, an abortion during the first few months of pregnancy is a personal matter between a woman and her doctor. Abortion differs from contraception in that abortion terminates a pregnancy, while contraception prevents it. Studies suggest women experience the greatest psychological distress before an abortion occurs. Severe negative psychological responses have not been reported frequently in the literature. Latest available data for the year 1987 report that 60% of the 1,559,000 abortions were performed on women under the age of 25. Eighty-two percent of these women were not married. Sixty-nine percent were White (Adler, David, Major, Roth, Russo, & Wyett, 1990). Nevertheless, the decision to terminate a pregnancy is always a very difficult one for any woman but is more so for the adolescent. The adolescent is confronted not only with the pro-life movement's argument against abortion but with tremendous personal stress, as the following case involving a client of Tom Gullotta's illustrates:

> Sherry was a 17-year-old who became pregnant a few months into her senior year of high school. When she came to my office seeking help in deciding what to do, she was, by her best estimate, five to six weeks pregnant. She informed me that she and Donald, her boyfriend, had been going steady for a year but had no plans to marry. Both wanted to go to college. Since he had learned about the pregnancy (which she had confirmed for herself by using an over-the-counter pregnancy-testing kit), Donald had been encouraging her to have an abortion. According to Sherry, their relationship was not going well; she felt that he did not care about her but was worrying only about himself. (I had no chance to meet with Donald, but Sherry did tell me later that they had broken up.) Sherry said she had not been able to discuss her problem with her parents, whom she described as rather strict religious types. She remarked, "If my parents knew, they would *die!*"
>
> Sherry was clearly under tremendous stress. She had not been sleeping well and had lost weight. She also reported feeling depressed and "crying for no reason." I asked what she wanted to do. She said she had thoroughly researched the issue herself at

the library and had concluded that having a child would not be a good decision at this time. After further exploring this issue with her, I felt that she had, as best one could, reached a difficult decision that for her was correct.

I transferred this case to the local Visiting Nurses Association, which had a nurse specialist in adolescent health problems. In our particular area, doctors would not perform an abortion on a minor without parental permission. As Sherry absolutely refused to inform her parents of her situation, arrangements were made to have the operation performed out of state with continuing care done through the VNA.

The treatment Sherry received was a suction abortion, or vacuum "curettage." This technique is the procedure of choice for abortions in the first months of a pregnancy. It involves the insertion of a flexible tube into the uterus. Suction from the tube gently loosens the fetal tissue from the uterine wall and removes it. This type of procedure can be performed in a doctor's office, as was done in Sherry's case. She experienced some discomfort for the next few days, but it was relieved with medication.

If Sherry had waited beyond the 10th to 12th week to have the abortion, the procedure would have been much more complex, and the possibility of complications would have increased tremendously. Abortions performed after this period involve the use of vaginal suppositories of prostaglandin E2 or the injection of a saline solution into the uterus to induce labor. These procedures require a short stay in a hospital. The period of recovery is longer, and most clinicians find the emotional trauma more pronounced. We strongly encourage young women having an abortion in the second trimester to accept the follow-up care offered for assistance in dealing with the natural feelings of anger and depression that follow many abortions performed during this stage of pregnancy.

Do you believe that it was the correct decision to support Sherry's decision to terminate her pregnancy? What other interventions might have been used? What are the ethical and moral issues involved in handling a case like this?

Box 14–3 The Spermicidal Effectiveness of Coke

Since its introduction in 1886 as a patent medicine reputedly able to cure the world's ills. Coca-Cola has been used, among other things, as a contraceptive. Its use as a birth-control douche continues to this day in some Third World nations. Thus, it was only a matter of time before science would ask the question "Is Coke the real thing?" In a letter to the editor of the *New England Journal of Medicine* a group at Harvard Medical School reported the results of mixing sperm samples with Diet Coke, Classic Coke, and New Coke. The researchers found that no sperm were swimming after a one-minute exposure to Diet Coke. 8.5% were moving after a one-minute exposure to Classic Coke, and 41.6% were still moving upstream after a one-minute exposure to New Coke. Apparently, Pepsi is not interested in the douche possibilities of its product and has not challenged Coke's supremacy in this area.

Source: (Adapted from S. A. Umpierre, J. A. Hill, & D. J. Anderson, "Effect of 'Coke' on Sperm Motility," *New England Journal of Medicine,* 1985, *313* (21), p. 1351.)

---

chances of infants born to adolescent parents, the solution is not moralistic platitudes. We cannot expect platitudes that have been unsuccessful in the past to succeed now.

Contraception

The desire to prevent conception dates back thousands of years. The means to do it effectively and safely, however, have been available to adults only in the last three decades and to many adolescents only since 1977 (Beiswinger, 1979). We can vividly remember from our own adolescence the unsuccessful attempts by friends to purchase condoms and the use of clear plastic wrap as a substitute. Girls fared no better; their contraceptive knowledge was based largely on hearsay offering such bits of wisdom as that douching with soda pop after intercourse prevents conception. (See Box 14–3.)

It was not until 1977, when the U.S. Supreme Court overturned New York's law prohibiting the sale of birth-control devices to minors, that the means of birth control were accessible to many young people. Why, then, with the means available to prevent unwanted births, are we experiencing a so-called epidemic of adolescent pregnancies? In this section we discuss the means of birth control presently available to adolescents; in the following section we examine some possible reasons that many adolescents do not use them.

Birth-control methods range from the highly effective to the highly ineffective. Some require a prescription, others can be purchased over the counter in drugstores, and still others involve timing or other techniques. Table 14–1 presents an overview of birth-control methods and their advantages and disadvantages.

The Pill

The most commonly used birth-control method is the oral contraceptive. So widespread is its use that most individuals immediately recognize it by no other name than "the Pill." Containing progesterone and estrogen compounds in varying amounts depending on the brand, the Pill works by preventing the release of

Table 14–1   Methods of contraception

Method	The Pill	The minipill	Intrauterine devices (IUD)
What is it?	Pills with two hormones, an estrogen and progestin, similar to the hormones a womena makes in her own ovaries.	Pills with just one type of hormone: a progestin, similar to a hormone a woman makes in her own ovaries.	A small piece of plastic with nylon threads attached. Some have copper wire wrapped around them. One IUD gives off a hormone, progesterone.
How does it work?	Prevents egg's release from woman's ovaries, makes cervical mucus thicker, and changes lining of the uterus.	It may prevent egg's release from woman's ovaries: it makes cervical mucus thicker and changes lining of uterus, making it harder for a fertilized egg to start growing there.	The IUD is inserted into the uterus. It is not known exactly how the IUD prevents pregnancy.
How reliable or effective is it?	97% if used consistently, but much less effective if used carelessly.	97% if used perfectly, but less effective if used carelessly.	94% if patient checks for string regularly.
How would I use it?	Either of two ways: 1. A pill a day for 3 weeks, stop for one week, then start a new pack. 2. A pill every single day with no stopping between packs.	Take one pill every single day as long as you want to avoid pregnancy.	Check string at least once a month right after the period ends to make sure your IUD is still properly in place.
Are there problems with it?	Must be prescribed by a doctor. All women should have a medical exam before taking the pill, and some women should not take it.	Must be prescribed by a doctor. All women should have a medical exam first.	Must be inserted by a doctor after a pelvic examination. Cannot be used by all woman. Sometimes the uterus "pushes" it out.
What are the side effects or complications?	Nausea, weight gain, headaches. missed periods, darkened skin on the face, or depression may occur. More serious and more rare problems are blood clots in the legs, the lungs, or the brain, and heart attacks.	Irregular periods, missed periods, and spotting may occur and are more common problems with minipills than with the regular birth-control pills.	May cause cramps, bleeding, or spotting; infections of the uterus or of the oviducts (tubes) may be serious. See a doctor for pain, bleeding, fever, or a bad discharge.
What are the advantages?	Convenient, extremely effective, does not interfere with sex, and may diminish menstrual cramps.	Convenient, effective, does not interfere with sex, and has less serious side effects than birth-control pills.	Effective, always there when needed, but usually not felt by either partner.

Table 14–1   Methods of contraception (continued)

Method	Diaphragm with spermicidal jelly	Spermicidal foam, jelly, or cream	Condom ("rubber")
What is it?	A shallow rubber cup used with a sperm-killing jelly or cream.	Cream and jelly come in tubes: foam comes in aerosol cans or individual applicators and is placed into the vagina.	A sheath of rubber shaped to fit snugly over the erect penis.
How does it work?	Fits inside the vagina. The rubber cup forms a barrier between the uterus and the sperm. The jelly or cream kills the sperm.	Foam, jelly, and cream contain a chemical that kills sperm and acts as a physical barrier between sperm and the uterus.	Prevents sperm from getting inside a woman's vagina during intercourse.
How reliable or effective is it?	About 94% effective if used correctly and consistently, but much less effective if used carelessly.	About 79% effective if used correctly and consistently, but much less effective if used carelessly.	About 88% effective if used correctly and consistently, but much less effective if used carelessly.
How would I use it?	Insert the diaphragm and jelly (or cream) before intercourse. Can be inserted up to 6 hours before intercourse. Must stay in at least 6 hours after intercourse.	Put foam, jelly, or cream into your vagina each time you have intercourse, not more than 30 minutes beforehand. No douching for at least 8 hours after intercourse.	The condom should be placed on the erect penis before the penis ever comes into contact with the vagina. After ejaculation, the penis should be removed from the vagina immediately.
Are there problems with it?	Must be fitted by a doctor after a pelvic exam. Some women find it difficult to insert, inconvenient, or messy.	Must be inserted just before intercourse. Some find it inconvenient or messy.	Objectionable to some men and women. Interrupts intercourse. May be messy. Condom may break.
What are the side effects or complications?	Some women find that the jelly or cream irritates the vagina. Try changing brands if this happens.	Some women find that the foam, cream, or jelly irritates the vagina. May irritate the man's penis. Try changing brands if this happens.	Rarely, individuals are allergic to rubber. If this is a problem, condoms called "skins," which are not made out of rubber, are available.
What are the advantages?	Effective and safe.	Effective, safe, a good lubricant, and can be purchased at a drugstore.	Effective, safe, can be purchased at a drugstore: excellent protection against sexually transmitted infections.

Table 14–1   Methods of contraception *(continued)*

Method	Condom and foam used together	Periodic abstinence (natural family planning)	Sterilization
What is it?		Ways of finding out days each month when you are most likely to get pregnant. Intercourse is avoided at that time.	Vasectomy (male). Tubal ligation (female). Ducts carrying sperm or the egg are tied and cut surgically.
How does it work?	Prevents sperm from getting inside the uterus by killing sperm and preventing sperm from getting out into the vagina.	Techniques include maintaining chart of basal body temperature, checking vaginal secretions, and keeping calendar of menstrual periods, all of which can help predict when you are most likely to release an egg.	Closing of tubes in male prevents sperm from reaching egg; closing tubes in female prevents egg from reaching sperm
How reliable or effective is it?	Close to 100% effective if both foam and condoms are used with every act of intercourse.	Certain methods are about 80% if used consistently. Other methods are less effective. Combining techniques increases effectiveness.	Almost 100% effective and *not* usually reversible.
How would I use it?	Foam must be inserted within 30 minutes before intercourse, and condom must be placed onto erect penis before contact with vagina.	Careful records must be maintained of several factors: basal body temperature, vaginal secretions, and onset of menstrual bleeding. Careful methods will dictate when study of these intercourse should be avoided.	After the decision to have no more children has been well thought through, a brief surgical procedure is performed on the man or the woman.
Are there problems with it?	Requires more effort than some couples like. May be messy or inconvenient. Interrupts intercourse.	Difficult to use method if menstrual cycle is irregular. Sexual intercourse must be avoided for a significant part of each cycle.	Surgical operation has some risk but serious complications are rare. Sterilizations should not be done unless no more children are desired.
What are the side effects or complications?	No serious complications.	No complications.	All surgical operations have some risk, but serious complications are uncommon. Some pain may last for several days. Rarely, the wrong structure is tied off, or the tube grows back together. There is no loss of sexual desire or ability in vast majority of patients.
What are the advantages?	Extremely effective, safe, and both methods may be purchased at a drugstore without a doctor's prescription. Excellent protection against sexually transmitted infections.	Safe, effective if followed carefully; little if any religious objection to method. Teaches women about their menstrual cycles	The most effective method; low rate of complications; many feel that removing fear of pregnancy improves sexual relations.

Sources: U.S. Public Health Service. (1978). *Family planning methods of contraception* (DHEW Publication No. HSA 78-5646). Washington, D.C.: U.S. Government Printing Office; Roberts, L. (1990). United States lags on birth control development. *Science, 248,* 909.

the egg, so that fertilization does not occur. In the typical schedule of use, a pill is taken after the fifth day of the start of menstruation for 21 days and then stopped for 7. During this "off" week, menstruation (sometimes called withdrawal bleeding because ovulation has not happened) occurs. Some drug companies market their birth-control pills in a 28-day package containing specially marked placebos (often containing vitamins and iron) to take during the off week. The advantage this particular course offers is in establishing the routine of taking a pill every day.

The Pill has several advantages over other birth-control methods. Not only is it considered highly effective (it has a reported reliability rate of up to 97%), but it is simple and convenient to use. It does not, as many other contraceptive methods do, require special preparations before intercourse. It also normalizes the menstrual cycle and has been reported to decrease adolescent acne.

But the Pill does have drawbacks. The most common complaints are nausea, weight gain, headaches, and depression. Less common but certainly more serious problems may also arise. Studies indicate that women on the Pill stand a small but nevertheless significantly greater chance than non-Pill users of developing blood clots in the legs, lungs, or brain. There is also some concern that prolonged estrogen use may increase the chances of developing cancer. At this point there is no clear evidence of a cancer/estrogen connection in humans, but women with a family history of cancer should not consider the pill. Women with any of the following conditions should also not take the pill:

1. Undiagnosed uterine bleeding
2. Pregnancy
3. History of thromboembolism or thrombotic disease
4. Active acute or chronic liver disease
5. Breast cancer
6. Estrogen-dependent neoplasia [tumor growth] (Greydanus, 1980. p. 53)

Since the Pill requires a prescription, we agree with others that the woman should insist on a physical examination and a thorough discussion of the advantages and disadvantages of the Pill with her physician before starting to take it (Allgeier & Allgeier, 1984; Ammer, 1983; Greydanus, 1980).

Intrauterine Devices (IUDs)

Credit for the discovery of the IUD has been traced back in some texts to before the time of Hippocrates and in others to camel drivers who apparently placed stones in the uteri of camels to prevent them from getting pregnant. IUDs were popular through the 19th century but fell into disfavor until the early 1960s. Recently, the use of IUDs has again declined as more women have reported serious health problems associated with their use.

Made of plastic, sometimes with small amounts of copper added, the IUD has certain advantages over the Pill. Properly placed in the uterus by a gynecologist, the IUD eliminates the worry of remembering to take the Pill. Because it is a mechanical device, which many researchers speculate acts to produce a mild inflammation of the uterus and thereby prevents the egg from becoming implanted on the uterine wall, the IUD does not pose the chemical risks or produce the physical complaints associated with the pill. With a reported effectiveness rate of 94%, the IUD would seem to be an ideal birth-control device.

Unfortunately, that is not true. One major disadvantage of IUDs is that somewhere between 4% and 20% of the women who have them inserted are not able to retain them. The expulsion of the IUD is rarely felt, leading most doctors to advise women using IUDs to check frequently to be sure that the IUD is still there. Second, those women who become pregnant with an IUD *in place* stand a greater chance of miscarriage. Third, women who have not had a baby may not be able to accommodate an IUD, or it may be highly uncomfortable. Finally, there is a risk (a chance of approximately 1 in 1000) that the uterus will be perforated (Allgeier & Allgeier, 1984; Ammer, 1983; Greydanus, 1980).

The Diaphragm

Developed at the end of the 19th century, the diaphragm was the most commonly used form of mechanical birth control until the development of the IUD. The diaphragm is a concave, round, rubber disk with a flexible, metal-spring rim. Before intercourse the woman places spermicidal cream or jelly over the disk and then carefully inserts the disk into the vagina to fit over the cervix. When properly placed, the diaphragm prevents sperm from entering the cervical canal. The cream or jelly used with the diaphragm acts to destroy the sperm.

The diaphragm is an effective (94% reliability rating), safe means of birth control. Using it does require more attention than either the Pill or the IUD. Although the diaphragm can be inserted up to six hours before intercourse, not all decisions to have intercourse are made in advance. Interrupting lovemaking to insert the diaphragm may be considered awkward or embarrassing by many adolescents who enjoy the spontaneity of the decision to engage in sexual intercourse. In addition, the requirement that the diaphragm be left in place for at least six hours after intercourse is considered undesirable by many adolescents. There are some complaints that the cream or jelly that must be used causes irritation. This can be controlled in most cases by simply changing brands.

As with the pill and the IUD, the diaphragm is a prescribed form of birth control requiring a doctor to fit the diaphragm properly (Allgeier & Allgeier, 1984; Ammer, 1983; Greydanus, 1980). Women with any of these conditions should not use a diaphragm:

1. Short anterior vaginal wall
2. Severe retroversion (backward tilting of uterus)
3. Severe anteversion (forward tilting of uterus)
4. Perineal tears
5. Vesicovaginal (or rectovaginal) fistulas
6. Complete uterine prolapse
7. Allergy to rubber or spermicides (Greydanus, 1980, p. 59)

Spermicidal Foam, Jelly, Cream, and Suppositories

Available over the counter are several brands of foam, jelly, cream, and suppositories that destroy sperm on contact. Most commonly used is the foam. The consistency of shaving cream, the foam is inserted into the vagina with an applicator just before intercourse.

Foam is considered less effective than the contraceptive methods already discussed but more effective than spermicidal cream, jelly, or suppositories (79% reliability rating by most reports, versus 70%). The effectiveness of foam is dependent on how well the chemical spreads through the vagina. To be most effective, the foam should be inserted no more than 15 minutes before intercourse. Many adolescents find this aspect of using foam inconvenient (Allgeier & Allgeier, 1984; Ammer, 1983; Greydanus, 1980). However, all the vaginal contraceptives have a number of advantages (Greydanus, 1980):

1. They provide effective contraception, especially if used in conjunction with a condom or diaphragm.
2. They allow the couple to share contraceptive responsibility if used in conjunction with a condom.
3. No prescription is needed.
4. They are relatively inexpensive.
5. There are few side effects.
6. They serve as vaginal lubricants to reduce dyspareunia (painful intercourse).
7. They may provide some protection against venereal disease because of bactericidal action on *Treponema pallidum* and *Neisseria gonorrhoeae*.*
8. They are useful for young women who have only sporadic intercourse.

The Condom

Made of rubber or the intestines of sheep or other animals, the condom (rubber, prophylactic, skins, French letter) is made to fit over an erect penis. When put on *before* the penis ever enters the vagina, the condom is an extremely effective (88%) birth-control device. When the condom is combined with foam, its effectiveness in preventing conception comes close to 100%. As with all birth-control methods, improper use of the condom accounts for most failures.

The latex condom offers many advantages. It is available over the counter and comes in a variety of forms, some of which may enhance the woman's enjoyment of sexual intercourse. It is inexpensive and easy to use. It offers excellent venereal-disease protection, including protection against the AIDS retrovirus. Other advantages include:

1. No side effects
2. May prolong coitus by delaying ejaculation
3. Allows the male to share in the responsibility for contraception
4. May contribute to reduced incidence of cervical cancer
5. Can assist in relieving dyspareunia (Greydanus, 1980. p. 60)

The primary complaint about condoms is that they diminish the male's sexual pleasure ("It's like taking a shower in a raincoat"). However, with recent improvements in manufacturing processes, this complaint is not valid. Take very

---

*Reports from the Centers for Disease Control in Atlanta suggest that spermicidal foams are effective in killing the virus responsible for acquired immune deficiency syndrome (AIDS). Sexually active individuals interested in avoiding a fatal encounter with AIDS should, among other things, always use spermicidal foam *and* latex condoms.

seriously the precautionary advice that condoms should be of the lubricated latex variety; they should have a reciprocal end to reduce chances of leakage or breakage; and they should contain a spermicide. *That spermicide will assist in protecting both partners from the other partner's possibly infected bodily fluids.* Finally, condoms should be kept in a cool place, out of direct sunlight, and used within one year or replaced. For the sexually active adolescent, condoms literally are a matter of life and death (Bergman, 1980; Leukenfeld & Haverkos, 1993).

Other Methods

Three other methods of contraception deserve mention in this section. They are the rhythm method, withdrawal, and douching. The only method of birth control for Catholic women approved by their church, the rhythm method assumes that only one egg is released for fertilization during each menstrual cycle. By having sexual intercourse only when the egg cannot be fertilized, conception can be avoided. There are three ways to determine this period: a formula based on a record of menstrual cycles, basal body temperature, and the symptothermic method. The first two are less reliable than when combined to create the symptothermic method. Essentially this method works by women's learning to recognize the changes in their cervical mucus that occur during the monthly cycle, together with taking their temperatures with a special (basal) thermometer. If carefully practiced, the rhythm method can be effective, but it requires training, motivation, and, above all, partner cooperation. Without these elements, "mistakes" are almost certain to occur.

Withdrawal is the pulling of the penis out of the vagina before ejaculation. For this method to be effective, no semen can be deposited even on the lips of the vagina. As sperm may leak out at any time during the act of intercourse before ejaculation, withdrawal can be considered better than doing nothing, but certainly not much better.

The use of douching involves the belief that after intercourse, sperm can be washed out of the vagina. The primary problem with this method is that sperm are much faster than the woman's ability to rid herself of them. It is impossible to clean oneself fast enough to eliminate all of the millions of sperm deposited in the vagina (Allgeier & Allgeier, 1984; Greydanus, 1980).

Summary of Birth-Control Methods

Each method discussed, with the exception of the last two, offers substantial protection from unwanted conception when used properly. Some methods, such as the rhythm technique, involve extensive planning and knowledge about one's own body. For this reason, rhythm may not be the best method for adolescents who cannot commit themselves to keeping accurate daily temperature charts or who find self-inspection awkward or messy. Other methods, such as the Pill and the diaphragm, are less troublesome and more easily used but involve a physical examination and prescription by a doctor. Some adolescents may find this aspect embarrassing. We encourage those young people who do not feel comfortable with their family doctor to seek out the Planned Parenthood office in their area. This organization has been in the forefront of advocating young people's rights to a choice on contraceptive use. The personnel are very willing to help young people in deciding for themselves which contraceptive is most appropriate for them.

Foam and condoms, particularly when used together, offer the adolescent the means to control conception without visiting a medical facility or a family-planning clinic. With new developments in condoms for his increased sensitivity and some types ribbed to increase his partner's pleasure, the condom should be seriously considered for use by the sexually active male. Foam, although not as effective as other means, provides reasonable assurance that an unwanted conception will not occur. When used together, they are almost 100% effective in preventing pregnancy.

Factors Involved in Not Using Contraceptives

Given that it is possible to prevent conception, why are young people becoming pregnant? Four general explanations have been proposed for why some adolescents do not use contraceptives. Prudence Rains first suggested in her book *Becoming an Unwed Mother* (1971) that the primary reason most young women do not use contraceptives is that they have not accepted their sexual behavior as correct. The second explanation is that young people do not have adequate access to either birth-control information or contraceptive devices. The third explanation, offered by Furstenberg (1971), is that the depth of the relationship may determine whether contraceptives are used. Thus, couples who have been going together and are "serious" are more likely to use contraceptives than are people in a relationship that could be categorized as a one-night stand. The final perspective is that contraceptive nonusage is intentional. A closer look at each of these perspectives is warranted in order to gain a fuller appreciation of how these factors operate independently and collectively to effect a conscious or an ignorant decision not to use contraceptives.

The Emotional Development Perspective

The results of several studies support Rains's (1971) suggestion that contraceptive usage is a function of accepting one's own sexuality (see, for example, Goldsmith, Gabrielson, Gabrielson, Matthews, & Potts, 1972; I. L. Reiss, Banwart, & Foreman, 1975; Schneider, 1982). Ira Reiss and his associates suggest that young women who use contraceptives believe that it is their right to choose their own sexual life-style. They also appear to view themselves as more attractive than nonusers do. This positive self-image, the researchers believe, acts to encourage "one to be contraceptively safe, perhaps because one expects that attractiveness to males will lead to full sexual relationships" (p. 625).

Lundy's (1972) study of 600 unmarried female college students expands on the notion of the influence of self-image. He reports that contraceptive users are more accepting of responsibility and less rigid in their thinking than are nonusers. Interestingly, Lundy did not find significant differences in self-esteem; he had expected sexually active females to feel less positive about themselves than sexually inactive females because of the double standard. This finding lends credence to the suggestion that society is moving away from the double standard to a standard of permissiveness with affection. In a more recent study Plotnick &

Pregnancy is a major concern for adolescents who are sexually active.

Butler (1991) find that higher self-esteem, positive attitudes about school, and future thoughts about college decrease the risk for pregnancy.

Some authors suggest that the inability to accept one's sexuality may be a function of age. Using a cognitive-development model, they point out that the young adolescent is in between concrete and formal operations. The ability to look at the future and take the necessary precautions to avoid pregnancy is a characteristic of formal operations. Thus, caught between formal and concrete operations, young adolescents are hindered in making decisions on sexual matters (Cobliner, 1974; Cvetkovich, 1975; Dembo & Lundell, 1979; Franklin, 1988; Gullotta, Adams, & Alexander, 1986; Hart & Hilton, 1988; Pestrak & Martin, 1985).

Still others suggest that societal expectations strongly influence female sexual behavior. Although we may be gradually changing to a more egalitarian system of male/female sex roles, this change is not yet complete. Thus, for many young females, planning their sexual encounters is unacceptable, for this "aggressiveness" might be perceived by their partner (or in their own minds) as suggesting loose morals associated with "common" women (Chilman, 1973, 1980; Dembo & Lundell, 1979).

Lack of Information

Ignorance of one's own body, of how it functions and how pregnancy occurs, is one of the most frequently cited reasons for adolescent-pregnancy rates. A number of studies have documented that adolescents operate under a large number of misconceptions about sexual issues. These include: Pregnancy cannot occur in the middle of the menstrual cycle (Babikian & Goldman, 1971; Kanter & Zelnick, 1972); Pregnancy occurs only to those who want to become pregnant (Babikian & Goldman, 1971; Zelnick, 1979); and Pregnancy cannot occur if one is too young (Furstenberg, 1970; Kanter & Zelnick, 1973). These misconceptions, coupled with studies showing that adolescents have little factual information on child bearing (Walters, McKenry, & Walters, 1979) and that males express the belief that contraceptives are "her problem" (Finkel & Finkel, 1978), underscore the need for education on sexual matters (Freeman et al., 1980; Blau & Gullotta, 1993).

Relationship Factors

Several studies indicate that contraceptive use increases as the relationship lengthens. One reason may be the couple's realization that the frequency of their sexual relations increases the probability of conception and that precautions thus need to be taken (DeAmicis, Klorman, Hess, & McAnarney, 1981; Jorgensen, King, & Torrey, 1980; Kanter & Zelnick, 1973; Reiss et al., 1975).

Other motivations as well may encourage contraceptive use by adolescents. According to one study (Hornick, Doran, & Crawford, 1979), such "internal" variables as the stability of the relationship, strong feelings for the partner, and self-esteem may influence the female to use contraceptives. Adolescent females most likely to use them come from well-educated, middle-class families and have stable dating relationships. Those least likely to use them are young women who date several people. In contrast, contraceptive use by adolescent males is affected by "external" forces related to parental permissiveness and dating experience. The earlier a male dates, the more likely it is that he will use a contraceptive. Males with parents who would not be upset by learning that their sons are sexually active are reported to use contraceptives least. As parental permissiveness decreases and the attitude that "planning" intercourse is acceptable increases, male contraceptive use increases. A study of 283 college students confirms many of these findings (Lowe & Radius, 1987). The authors suggest that easy access to contraceptives encourages use, that open communication by the couple encourages use, and that a liberal ideology encourages use. Disturbingly, 57% of this college sample reported not using a contraceptive at the time of first coitus in a new relationship.

Similar reports of contraceptive nonuse can also be found in Jorgensen's (1993) review of the literature. He estimates that only 48% of sexually active adolescents regularly use contraceptives. This figure may be optimistically high. One recent study of 1880 15- to 19-year-old males reported that roughly one-third of these adolescents used condoms. Of additional concern was the finding that 73% of the female partners in this study did not expect contraceptives to be used. Factors determining male condom use were fear of pregnancy, fear of AIDS, and respect for the sexual partner (Pleck, Sonenstein, & Kie, 1991).

Intentional Contraceptive Non Usage

Given the availability of condoms, foam, and vaginal sponges in drug stores, supermarkets, and discount stores, unintended pregnancies need not occur; and yet they do. Many scholars believe that a percentage of these pregnancies are intentional. That is, the young woman wanted to become pregnant. The reasons to explain this behavior can be found in deprived childhoods filled with abuse, emotional neglect, and troubled families (Jorgensen, 1993; Miller, Christopherson, & King, 1993; Rickel & Hendren, 1993). These young women have histories of poor school performance, truancy, drug use, running away from home, and fights (Elster, Ketterlinus, & Lamb, 1990). With a low sense of self-esteem and depression (*Science,* 1991a), early sexual behavior becomes, as one young woman of twelve once told Thomas Gullotta, "a feeling"—a feeling, we would observe, that occurs in a world devoid of success, social support, and emotional love. In such a world, the temporary physical pleasure of sex poorly replaces the emotional needs of the adolescent. In such a world, having a baby is something to love, to cherish, and to establish an identity around. Tragically, for the child and its child/mother these hopes for identity are rarely, if ever, fulfilled.

Summary

Clearly, no single explanation accounts for all lack of use of contraceptives among adolescents. However, when taken together, the four explanations discussed in this section provide a picture of young people who are poorly informed or misinformed about their sexuality and who are uncomfortable with themselves as sexual beings. Conditions such as these contribute not only to unwanted pregnancies but to illness as well. In the next section we examine a problem more serious than not using contraceptives—venereal diseases.

Venereal Diseases

Venereal diseases are infections almost always transmitted in sexual intercourse (vaginal, anal, and oral are all included). The organisms that cause venereal diseases are extremely sensitive to light, air, and the absence of moisture. Only in dark, warm, moist areas can the VD organisms survive. (Thus, stories of contracting AIDS from toilet seats are sheer fantasy.) As luck would have it, the human body offers perfect conditions for this group of diseases to flourish. Once inside the body, syphilis, gonorrhea, herpes simplex virus types 1 and 2, chlamydia, and the human immunodeficiency virus (HIV) have an ideal environment in which to grow and multiply. Unchecked, these diseases can cause serious and permanent damage or even death. In pregnant women these diseases can be passed on to the unborn child. (See Table 14–2.)

Syphilis

Referred to by adolescents as bad blood, syph, and the pox, syphilis may have been a gift from the New World. There is no evidence that syphilis existed in Europe before Columbus's voyage, but by 1497 the disease was running rampant, decimating the population. Columbus himself is believed to have died of the disease. At that time the names given to the disease represented a kind of political slur against a neighboring state. The French called it the Neapolitan disease. The Italians returned the favor by referring to it as the French pox. It was not until 1530 that an Italian physician, Girolamo Fracastoro, gave this disease its present name in a poem in which a shepherd named Syphilus was struck with the plague that came to bear his name. The infectious agent that causes syphilis was discovered in 1905. It was a discovery that at the time was equivalent in magnitude to the finding of the retrovirus responsible for AIDS. At the turn of the century one-third of all hospital beds in the United States were filled with patients suffering from syphilis. Indeed, so serious was the threat of this disease that in 1918 the United States imprisoned 20,000 suspected prostitutes in a futile attempt to reduce the military's exposure to the disease (Brandt, 1988).

Syphilis is caused by a very tiny, slender, corkscrew-shaped bacterium (*Treponema pallidum*) called a spirochete. It is nearly always spread by direct contact from a carrier of the disease to a noncarrier by sexual intercourse. When a noninfected individual's broken skin touches a syphilitic lesion, syphilis can be transferred. Once infected, the individual left untreated goes through three stages of the illness plus a latent period.

The first, or primary, stage appears three or four weeks after exposure to the disease in the form of a hard, often painless, open sore called a chancre. Chancres can appear singly or in groups. Ranging from one-eighth of an inch to an inch in diameter, they look like small craters. The surfaces of these craters appear red, raw, and at times crusted. In men they appear most often on the shaft of the penis, and in women they appear (without their notice) within the vulva, on the walls of the vagina, or on the cervix. Typically, these chancres disappear a few weeks after their first appearance, leading the infected individual to believe that the problem has gone away. It has not. The disappearance of these painless sores signals the entrance of the disease into its second stage.

Table 14–2   Overview of Selected Sexually Transmitted Diseases and Syndromes

Agent	Disease or syndrome	Typical presenting signs and symptoms	Examples of potential complications/sequelae
Bacterial Agents			
Neisseria gonorrhoeae	Gonorrhea	Abnormal vaginal or penile discharge, abdominal pain; may be asymptomatic	Disseminated gonococcal infection (e.g., septicemia), PID, infertility, epididymitis
Chlamydia trachomatis	Chlamydial infections: Nongonococcal urethritis	Dysuria, urinary frequency, abnormal penile discharge; may be asymptomatic	Urethral stricture, prostatitis, epididymitis
	Mucopurulent cervicitis	Abnormal endocervical discharge; may be asynptomatic	Endometritis, salpingitis, infertility, adverse obstetric outcomes
Treponema pallidum	Primary syphilis	Chancre	Late (teriary) syphilis and sequelae, neurosyphilis
	Secondary syphilis	Skin rash, mucous patches, lymphadenopathy, condyloma lata	
Viral Agents			
Herpes simplex virus (HSV) 1	Nongenital herpes	Blisters on eyes or other facial regions	Aseptic meningitis, recurrent HSV infection
Herpes simplex virus (HSV) 2	Genital herpes	Blisters, genital ulcers, stomatitis, and oral lesions	Disseminated infection, recurrent HSV infection
Human immunodeficiency virus (HIV)	HIV infection	Generalized lymphadenopathy, weight loss, night sweats, intermittent fever, malaise, diarrhea; may initially be asymptomatic	Full-blown AIDS
	Acquired immunodeficiency syndrome (AIDS)	Symptoms of opportunistic infections such as pneumocystic pneumonia, or Kaposi's sarcoma	Death

Source: Office of Technology Assessment, 1991, based on U.S. Department of Health and Human Services, Public Health Service, Centers for Disease Control, "Sexually Transmitted Disease Summary: 1990," Atlanta, Ga., June 1990.

In the second stage, the effects of syphilis on the body are more pronounced. Two to six months after exposure, the individual may complain of fever, loss of appetite, headaches, or a sore throat. However, the symptom most significantly associated with secondary syphilis is one of two types of skin rashes called macular syphilide and papular syphilide. In the first type small, round, shiny, red spots appear on the upper body and arms. These spots may be so light that they are hardly noticeable, and they may disappear in a few days. The second type is more prominent. Papular syphilide appears as raised red spots and covers the entire body, including the soles, palms, and face. Hair loss can occur, with hair falling out in patches. But even in this most infectious stage of syphilis, the symptoms disappear after several weeks. Syphilis now enters the latent period.

In this period all symptoms disappear as the disease becomes spontaneously cured,* remains latent, or invades the others organs of the body, such as the eyes, heart, brain, and spinal cord. In the latent period, the disease can no longer be transmitted from one sexual partner to another, but pregnant women can transmit it to the fetus. After one or several years, if the disease has been invading other body tissues, the last stage occurs..

In this late, or tertiary, stage extremely serious health problems appear. Depending on which body organ has been attacked, the individual may experience blindness, insanity, paralysis, or severe heart problems. It is the heart problems that most frequently cause death (Ammer, 1983; Leukenfeld & Haverkos, 1993, Lumiere & Cook, 1983; Nettina, 1990). For the year 1990, 50,224 cases of syphilis were diagnosed in the United States. Of this number 1,195 were males between the ages of 10 and 19 and 3,592 were females between the same ages (Leukenfeld & Haverkos, 1993).

Gonorrhea

Called, among other things, the drip, clap, dose, or strain, gonorrhea infects more than 225,000 adolescents each year. Of this number for the year 1990, 120,000 were males between the ages of 10 and 19 and 105,206 were females between the same ages (Leukenfeld & Haverkos, 1993).

For several years, gonorrhea has held the dubious distinction of being the most reported infectious disease in the country, exceeding the combined reported cases of chicken pox, measles, mumps, and rubella (Silber, 1981). It is caused by the bacterium *Neisseria gonorrhoeae* and affects the mucous membranes of the genitalia, throat, or rectum.

After sexual contact (anal, oral, or vaginal) with an infected individual, the disease appears in one day to two weeks in its first form. In males this is a yellowish, puslike discharge from the penis. Other symptoms include a burning sensation when urinating and a sensation of itching within the urethra. Sympotoms in women may be nonexistent in the earliest stage of this disease. As many as 80% of the women infected with gonorrhea have no early symptoms. Those who do have a yellowish-green vaginal discharge. If unnoticed or left untreated in this early stage, gonorrhea may affect other parts of the body.

In its most advanced stages the disease in males can cause chronic infection of the urethra, resulting in the inability to urinate, or it can cause sterility. In women the disease can spread through the uterus and Fallopian tubes, causing

---

*Spontaneous cures resulted from patients' experiencing an extremely high fever. It appears that the fever and the body's reaction to it often destroyed the spirochete. From the 1920s into the 1940s syphilitic individuals were intentionally infected with a mild form of malaria to induce this condition (Valenstein, 1986)

sterility. Infections resulting from this disease can lead to heart problems, blindness, and arthritis in both males and females. Until recently, infants could be contaminated by the disease at birth in their passage through the infected birth-canal. The result of this passage through the infected area was blindness. This problem has been successfully prevented by the application of small amounts of silver-nitrate drops or penicillin ointment to the eyes of these infants (Ammer, 1983; Lumiere & Cook, 1983).

Herpes

Herpes takes its name from *herpein* (Greek), "to creep." In its latent stage, the herpes virus most often resides at the base of the spine or recessed in the fifth cranial nerve. When the carrier's resistance is lowered by fatigue, stress, or illness, the virus "creeps" down the nerve fibers at the rate of 1 inch in 16 hours and erupts in a painful sore that appears most often on the lips, inside the mouth, or on the genitals. The venereal forms of the virus are herpes simplex virus type 1 (HSV 1) and herpes simplex virus type 2 (HSV 2) (Gregg, 1983). There are more than 50 kinds of herpes viruses (Langston, 1983). The most common are herpes simplex types 1 and 2, which infect the genitals, skin, eyes, mouth and brain; herpes zoster, which causes shingles and chicken pox; cytomegalovirus, which causes blindness or mental retardation in babies; and Epstein-Barr virus, which causes mononucleosis and some forms of cancer.

It was once incorrectly believed that herpes type 1 occurred only above the waist and type 2 only below the waist. Because of oral contact with various parts of the body, both types are increasingly found almost anywhere. (See Table 14–3.)

Not to be confused with cold sores or fever blisters, herpes simplex type 2 blisters (often accompanied by a fever and chills) appear anywhere from one day

Table 14–3   Estimated frequency and location of herpes simplex type 1 and type 2 infections.

Location of primary or recurrent disease	Most frequent herpes type	Etimated cases per year in United States
Primary		
Mouth	95% type 1	500,000
Eye	95% type 1	Unknown
Recurrent		98 million
Mouth	95% type 1	280,000–300,000
Eye	95% type 1	
Primary		
Genitals	60%–90% type 2	20,000–500,000
Fingers	80% (?) type 2	Unknown
Recurrent		
Genitals	70%–85% type 2	3–9 million
Fingers	15%–30% type 1	
	Often type 2	Unknown

Source: Copyright © 1983 by Deborah P. Langston, From *Living with Herpes,* by Dr. Deborah P. Langston, M. D., published by Doubleday. Reprinted by permission of the author.

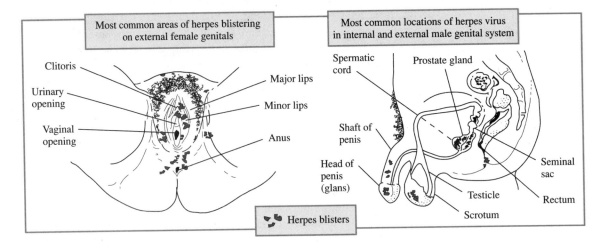

Figure 14–1   Areas of female and male genitals commonly infected with herpes simplex type 1 or 2. (*Source:* Zelnick, M., & Kantner, J. F. (1980). Sexual activity, contraceptive use and pregnancy among metropolitan-area teenagers: 1971–1979. *Family Planning Perspectives, 12,* 230–237.)

to about three weeks after contact. (Figure 14–1 shows the most common locations.) The sores and flulike symptoms disappear over the course of a few days to several weeks, as the virus retreats along the nerve fibers to wait to erupt again at some future date. During an outbreak of HSV 1 or 2 the disease is highly contagious because the sore or sores are constantly shedding the virus. Caution needs to be exercised at this time, because one can inadvertently give the virus to others or spread it to other parts of one's own body. For example, inserting contact lenses after touching a herpes sore without washing one's hands with soap and water may transmit billions of active viruses to one's eyes (Bettoli, 1982). Recent medical reports also suggest that it is possible to experience an asymtomatic shedding of the virus. That is, the virus may be present and active without noticeable side effects. Thus, caution must be exercised by known carriers of the virus (Brock, Selke, Benedetti, Douglas, & Corey, 1990).

Unlike other venereal disease organisms, which cannot live outside the body, HSV 1 and 2 can survive for several hours on such surfaces as the human skin, clothing, and plastic (Turner, Shehab, Osborne, & Hendley, 1982). In fact, the National Institutes of Health once reported that three elderly women had contracted the disease while soaking in a hot tub. Although viruses cannot live in the chemically treated water in a hot tub, they did survive long enough on the tub rim to infect these three individuals ("Highlights," 1984).

Additional concern is warranted for pregnant women who have genital herpes. For instance, genital herpes increases the risk of spontaneous abortion or premature delivery. There is also a risk of 40% to 60% that a woman delivering vaginally who is experiencing an outbreak of genital herpes at the time of delivery will infect her infant (Bettoli, 1982).* Finally, evidence is accumulating that women with genital herpes run eight times the normal risk of developing cervical cancer.

_____

*A woman with genital herpes need not fear infecting her unborn infant provided she fully informs her physician of her condition. Should an outbreak of HSV occur near or during the birth process, the child can still be safely delivered by a cesarean section.

Although genital herpes cannot be cured at this time,* it can be managed. The drug acyclovir has been approved for topical and oral applications and has been shown to be effective in speeding the healing of HSV sores (Corey & Holmes, 1983).

Meanwhile, the following suggestions will minimize discomfort for the herpes sufferer and reduce the probability of spreading the disease to others. During an outbreak of genital sores, avoid intercourse (oral, anal, or vaginal) for 14 days. When the HSV is active, take particular care not to touch the sores. Should you touch a sore, wash your hands immediately, and do not touch your eyes. To prevent recurrences, get ample rest and good nutrition and engage in stress-reduction techniques. We urge women sufferers to receive an annual medical exam that includes a pap smear. Herpes, though painful for one's body and soul, can be lived with successfully with some care and effort (Lenard, 1982).

Chlamydia

This little-known disease is suspected of infecting 3 to 4 million individuals a year. Once believed to be a virus, it is a highly contagious infection caused by obligate, intracellular organisms classified as bacteria (Leukenfeld & Haverkos, 1993). Chlamydia is transmitted through sexual intercourse. It is a difficult disease to diagnose because it often produces no symptoms in its early stages. If symptoms appear (approximately three weeks after exposure), the most often-reported complaints are, for women, a slight vaginal discharge and pain during coitus and, for men, pain on urination and a urethral discharge. To complicate matters further, if symptoms do appear, they are often mistakenly attributed to some other malady.

Chlamydia is responsible for about half of the cases of pelvic inflammatory disease in women. In addition the disease can be transmitted to infants as they pass through the birth canal. Roughly 120,000 infants in the United States each year develop eye infections or pneumonia as a result of chlamydia. Left untreated, a male may become sterile.

Chlamydia can be treated successfully in its early stages with antibiotics. More important, it can be prevented. The use of condoms and spermicidal foam offers excellent protection against the disease (Ammer, 1983; Kronholm, 1986; Leukenfeld & Haverkos, 1993; Lumiere & Cook, 1983).

Acquired Immune Deficiency Syndrome (AIDS)

The story of this last venereal disease begins in March 1981, when a group of epidemiologists at the Centers for Disease Control in Atlanta noticed something unusual. In the Los Angeles area five homosexuals had died during the previous 18 months of a rare protozoan infection that causes pneumonia. Intrigued by their finding, the researchers were also surprised, on further investigation, to dis-

---

*Recently *Science* (1989) reported on the clinical effectiveness of capsaicin for the treatment of herpes. This chemical found in chili peppers appears to prevent reinfection in mice for up to two months. Incidentally, until more is known about the drug and its effect on humans, readers should not try home experiments as the application of chili peppers to sores will only increase discomfort and discourage healing.

cover that an unusually large number of homosexuals had died from a very rare skin malignancy called Kaposi's sarcoma. Both diseases had been known to strike people undergoing immunosuppressive therapy (typically to prevent the body's rejection of a transplanted organ). But why would these diseases attack these two groups and , as time went on, other people? The answer to this riddle, called acquired immune deficiency syndrome (AIDS), can be found in a virus (HIV) that destroys the body's ability to ward off disease (*AIDS Information Bulletin,* 1983; Culliton, 1984; *Facts about AIDS,* 1983; Leukefeld & Fimbres, 1987; Leukefeld & Haverkos, 1993; Runck, 1986; West, 1983).

HIV is a retrovirus. Regular viruses, like the ones that cause the flu, are made of DNA (deoxyribonucleic acid), the genetic material that is the building block of all living things. DNA viruses operate by infecting the body, penetrating a cell, and using the cell's machinery to make more viruses. Eventually the cell bursts, sending additional virus copies into the body to infect other cells. This process continues, causing the misery we all associate with colds and the flu, until the body's immune system stops the viral infection.

Retroviruses differ from regular viruses in a significant, insidious, and disturbing way. Rather than being composed of DNA, retroviruses are made up of RNA (ribonucleic acid). RNA has the function of serving as DNA's messenger in communicating the instructions that determine the makeup of every cell in our body. Thus a retrovirus—unlike a regular virus, which the immune system of the body can detect, attack, and destroy—alters the original DNA blueprint to become a permanent part of the cell's genetic code. A retrovirus infection is lifelong. An AIDS infection is lifelong. As part of the genetic DNA blueprint, the virus continues to multiply, spreading throughout the body, and is found in semen, blood, saliva, tears, and other body fluids.

The retrovirus that is responsible for AIDS is so deadly because it sets up home in the T and B blood cells that orchestrate the body's immune defense system. These cells are destroyed as the disease progresses, making its victims vulnerable to a host of cruel opportunistic diseases (D. M. Barnes, 1986a, 1988; Curran et al., 1985; Runck, 1986).

Despite the intensive efforts of hundreds of research centers around the world, no cure or preventive vaccine has been developed to control one of the deadliest diseases that humankind has ever encountered. HIV has been reported in almost every country. (See Box 14–4.) As of the fall of 1993 more than 200,000 people in the United States had been diagnosed as having AIDS, and nearly half that number had already died. It is estimated that 1.5 million people in the U.S. have been infected by HIV. This number is certain to grow in the coming years. Although the risk to heterosexuals is increasing as the disease spreads beyond the high-risk populations, the majority of reported AIDS cases remain either intravenous drug users or homosexual/bisexual males and their partners. The remaining at-risk population includes recipients of contaminated blood transfusions and infants born to infected mothers (D. M. Barnes, 1986b; Booth, 1988a; Drotman, 1987; Leukenfeld & Haverkos, 1993; Runck, 1986; Scitovsky & Rice, 1987).

HIV is transmitted in the following ways: by sexual intercourse, the sharing of unsterilized needles between drug users, contaminated blood transfusions, and

Box 14–4   The Treatment of AIDS Victims: A Cross-Cultural Perspective

A generation of people is judged in history by how it responded in a crisis. It is judged by how it cared for those in need and how it resisted the urge to persecute others. Thus, we remember the Puritans for, among other things, the Salem witchcraft trials. We remember the British during the Second World War for their courage, and we remember the Shakers for their kindness toward orphans. How will this generation be remembered in regard to its treatment of AIDS victims? Early evidence suggests that countries are responding in different ways. In some nations, like the United States, strong debates are under way regarding the conflict between individual rights and societal rights. To their credit, the American people have so far protected the human rights and human dignity of AIDS victims. This has not been the case in some other nations.

In Cuba, for example, the government has tested every man, woman, and adolescent over the age of 15 for HIV. In a nation that denies having a problem with the retrovirus, the testing of 7 million people is, to say the least, a bit unusual. What is more disturbing, however, is that those who test positive are removed from their homes and isolated. Reports from Cuba suggest that the isolation facility, which is ten miles south of Havana, is clean and that medical care is provided (Betancourt, 1988).

Other nations fall between these two extremes in respecting individual rights. We ask that you consider the issues. What are your thoughts on the subject?

an infected mother's giving birth. The disease progresses in the following manner. In the beginning, an exposed individual tests positive for AIDS antibodies but otherwise appears healthy. At one time the word *dormant* was used. However, recent research suggests that the retrovirus is multiplying rapidly in sites within the lymph nodes and related organs like the spleen, tonsils, and adenoids (Temin & Bolognesi, 1993). As the disease weakens the immune system, individuals begin to experience noticeably swollen glands, near-constant fevers in excess of 100 degrees, persistent diarrhea, and chronic fatigue. (See Table 14–4.)

As the disease destroys the immune system, the body becomes vulnerable to any number of opportunistic diseases. It is these infections that kill an AIDS carrier. Currently, there is no reliable estimate of how many individuals infected with the HIV retrovirus will develop AIDS. The most recent data place the risk of developing AIDS from the date of a HIV positive test at 2% after 2 years, 35% from 2 to 7 years, and 50% after 10 years (Brookmeyer, 1991).

As there is a latent period from a few months to several years between testing HIV-positive and the onset of symptoms, individuals may transmit the disease without realizing that they are carriers (Centers for Disease Control, 1983a, 1983b; Runck, 1986). Although the retrovirus has been found in tears, saliva, and other bodily fluids, infection appears to require direct blood-to-blood transmission. *No evidence exists to suggest that AIDS can be transmitted by casual or even close daily contact with AIDS victims.* Various drugs, such as AZT, Videx (ddl), nevirapine, and U-90, 152 are being used to provide some help to patients struggling with AIDS (Kolata, 1987a; *Science,* 1991). Until such time as a cure or vaccine is developed, we strongly urge sexually active individuals to take the following steps to help prevent the spread of this fatal disease (Koop, 1987; Leukenfeld & Haverkos, 1993; Runck, 1986):

Table 14–4   CDC Classification for AIDS

Group 1: Acute Infection
This represents a transient state that is probably related to acute viremia. Patients are initially seronegative. Symptoms appear approximately two to eight weeks after infection, remain for one to three weeks, and then resolve. The symptom complex resembles that of mononucleosis with fatigue, weakness, fever, sweats, headache, still neck, cranial nerve palsies, muscle pain, sore throat, diarrhea, and a fleeting rash. The neurologic symptoms are transient and may represent a transient aseptic meningitis.

Group 2: Asymptomatic Infection
These patients are seropositive but have no clinical manifestations of the disease.

Group 3: Persistent Generalized Lymphadenopathy
These patients have chronically enlarged lymph nodes, defined as > 1 cm in more than two groups of nodal chains. The enlarged lymph nodes last longer than three months and are painless. They tend to wax and wane in size.

Group 4: Other HIV Disease
Subgroup A: Constitutional Symptoms
These include: (1) Fever of greater than one-month's duration. (2) weight loss of > 10% of total body weight, persistent diarrhea, night sweats, malaise, and fatigue.

Subgroup B: Neurologic Disease
This is secondary to CNS infection of malignancy and has been termed AIDS-dementia. Approximately 50% of all AIDS patients are affected.

Subgroup C: Secondary Infectious Diseases
Included in this group are the opportunistic infections.

Subgroup D: Secondary Cancers
Kaposi's sarcoma, non-Hodgkins' lymphoma, and primary CNS lymphomas.

Subgroup E: Other
Any other disease in an HIV-positive patient.

Source: Office of Technology Assessment (1991). *Sexually Transmitted Disease Summary: 1990* Atlanta, Ga., June 1990.

1. Avoid sexual contact with persons who are HIV-positive or have AIDS.
2. Avoid engaging in sex with multiple partners or with others who have multiple partners.
3. Avoid sex with intravenous drug users.
4. Homosexuals should not use amyl nitrate to facilitate lovemaking. This drug is an immunosuppressant, the worst possible agent to have in your body.
5. Avoid sexual practices that damage body tissues (for example, anal intercourse).
6. *Insist that you and your sexual partner use latex condoms and spermicidal foam!*

The Treatment and Prevention of Venereal Diseases

Before the development of penicillin and other antibiotics, syphilis and gonorrhea sufferers were treated with mercury, arsenic, and other assorted home remedies. Syphilis, gonorrhea, and chlamydia can be successfully treated. Herpes, while it has no known cure, can be treated to reduce the uncomfortable effects of an attack and prevent a secondary infection. These diseases need not be damaging, even to the fetus, if the sexually active adolescent who has the slightest suspicion of venereal disease seeks medical help. It is natural for adolescents to be embarrassed over suspecting themselves of being infected, but with helpful, youth-oriented programs in family-planning clinics, local health departments, and Planned Parenthood offices, they need not fear ostracism or unsympathetic care. These organizations recognize and appreciate the adolescents' dilemma and treat their their clients with respect and dignity.

The astute reader will have noticed that we have not included AIDS in the above paragraph. Adolescents must recognize that *the only way to beat AIDS is to prevent AIDS*. In the process of preventing AIDS, the adolescent will also prevent other venereal diseases. It is nice to encourage, and we certainly would encourage young people to consider, sexual abstinence. Assuming one is not an illegal IV drug user, abstinence is the only 100% guaranteed method for avoiding venereal disease. However, until such time as the majority of the adolescents in the United States who are sexually active elect abstinence, we will urge that sexually active adolescents practice safe sex. Safe sex is more than latex condoms. Safe sex is latex condoms and foam. The condom works by providing a barrier to keep infected and uninfected areas from touching. In the event that the condom fails, foams such as Delfen, Emko, Ortho, Conceptrol, and others, used before intercourse, reduce the chances of becoming infected. The foam is not only an effective spermicide but is also effective against the organisms and viral agents discussed in this chapter that cause venereal disease. But safe sex is more than latex condoms and foam; it is knowing your partner and your partner's sexual history. The mind set for adolescents to have is that they are having sex not only with their partner but also with whomever their partner has ever had sex. Incidentally, that mind set tends to encourage condom and foam use. Finally, adolescents need to learn to check sexual partners for signs of venereal disease before engaging in intercourse. We encourage foreplay, mutual showers, and a thorough exploration of each other's bodies before intercourse. If something doesn't look right, we urge them to ask about it. We want them to remember that if they decide to become sexually active, it is their responsibility to protect themselves. (See Box 14–5.)

Adolescent Prostitution

Americans are apparently fascinated with adolescent prostitution, given the number of recent films and television programs devoted to the subject. Pictures like *Angel, Taxi Driver, Hardcore, Pretty Baby,* and *Indecent Proposal* all focus on the behavior of young girls who willingly or unwillingly are thrust into situations in which they exchange sexual favors for money. Other than these Hollywood versions of life on the streets, what do we know of prostitution? First, it is as old as recorded history. Second, child prostitution is not unique to this century. In England before 1814, for example, girls were officially allowed to become prostitutes at the age of 12; the age was changed to 13 in 1875 and to 16 in 1885 (Baizerman, Thompson, & Stafford-White, 1979; Downs & Hillje, 1993).

Box 14–5   AIDS: Questions and Answers

In 1981, we began to include in our class lectures a brief discussion about AIDS. Needless to say, as HIV began to threaten humanity, the amount of time we devoted to the subject grew. The following are the most frequently asked questions that come out of those classes and our responses.

Q: What are my chances of contracting AIDS?

A: One study has calculated the risk from a single act of intercourse at one in five billion, assuming that a latex condom is used and the sexual partner is "low risk." The risk increases dramatically if the partner is a prostitute, bisexual, homosexual, an IV drug user, or if a condom is not used.

Q: If I test positive for the retrovirus, does that mean I will die?

A: Frankly, no one knows for sure. One recent study in *Science* reported that a sample of 84 homosexual and bisexual men who had tested positive for HIV all went on to develop AIDS. Discouraging as this information is, it cannot be generalized to the entire HIV-positive population. It is believed that 1.5 million people in the United States and 10 million worldwide are carrying the virus. Most of these people are now healthy. It is important to understand that a positive test result is not a diagnosis of AIDS. Furthermore, it does not mean the individual will develop AIDS. Rather it is a sign that the individual has been exposed to the retrovirus. There may be individual factors involving life-style, heredity, or something else that provide immunity against the virus for that individual. The important thing to remember is that once infected, always infected. Caution must be exercised to ensure that the virus is not spread further.

Q: Why don't we quarantine HIV-positive people and AIDS victims from the rest of society? Aren't they a health risk?

A: Providing the HIV-positive individual or AIDS victim is not engaging in illegal IV drug use or unsafe sexual practices, there is no need to remove him or her from society. The retrovirus is very difficult to contract. It requires direct contact between HIV-carrying fluids and the blood of another individual. In fact, as of the spring of 1993 there had been no reports of any one contracting the retrovirus from

any activity short of blood-to-blood contact. Even so, until more is understood about the virus, oral intercourse is being discouraged by health authorities.

Q: Should I worry about having oral sex if this retrovirus is so hard to catch?

Q: As we noted earlier, HIV is present in all body fluids. The concentration of the retrovirus in saliva or tears is quite low in comparison to the concentration in either blood or semen. In studies of health workers and family members in "casual" contact with an AIDS victim, there does not exist a single case of transmission. The few reports that do exist of health workers who have tested positive for the retrovirus are the result of blood-to-blood exposure in which the worker was exposed to large amounts of retrovirus-carrying material. By that we mean needle pricks where the risk has been calculated at 1 in 200 episodes, exposure in the research laboratory by spilling retrovirus samples on broken skin, or exposure in an emergency situation in which the health worker trying to control a victim's bleeding had a break in the skin that came in contact with the victim's blood. These facts are extremely encouraging and support the contention that this is a very difficult disease to catch. However, until more is known regarding the pathogenicity of the retrovirus, health officials advise avoiding the exchange of bodily fluids including the fluids generated in oral sex.

Q: I've heard that you can go crazy from AIDS.

A: Sadly, the retrovirus does travel to the brain. The term *AIDS dementia complex* describes the condition that results from that infection. Symptoms range from forgetfulness and a loss of balance to severe depression and incontinence.

Q: I heard that the virus was a biological-warfare experiment that got out of hand. Is this true?

A: It is true that some elements in the former Soviet Union had reported that AIDS was a U.S. biological warfare experiment gone-wrong. However, there is no evidence to support this contention. The evidence strongly suggests that AIDS originated in Africa. It has been found that the African green monkey carries a retrovirus almost identical to HIV. Some suggest that this retrovirus crossed the species

Box 14–5   AIDS: Questions and Answers *(continued)*

barrier and infected humans. Of particular interest are published reports of serum and tissue samples collected from Africans in the 1970s and as early as 1959 that have tested positive for HIV. In large part this would explain the pandemic spread of the disease in central Africa.

Q: If the retrovirus has been found in frozen serum and tissue samples dating back 30 years, why has it only recently appeared in developed nations?

A: Recognizing that we are now speculating and that no one knows for sure, we surmise that the retrovirus may have been spread from infected Africans to French-speaking Haitians who went to central Africa to work in the 1960s after the colonial powers withdrew. Infected Haitians returning home may have passed the retrovirus to vacationing homosexuals from the United States. The disease spread rapidly among homosexuals, because they tended to maintain a closed community and because many had numerous sexual partners. The second possible explanation is that for many years the United States purchased human blood from Africa.

Q: I heard AIDS came from a polio vaccine; is this true?

A: In the March 1992 issue of *Rolling Stone,* Tom Curtis reported the theory of Blaine Elswood and Raphael Stricker that the AIDS virus might have crossed the species barrier from monkeys to people through a tainted polio vaccine. It is a fact that some early polio vaccines were manufactured using monkey tissue. It is also true that simian immunodeficiency virus (SIV) is a relative of the human AIDS virus. Furthermore, in the July 31, 1992, issue of *Science,* it was reported that the Centers for Disease Control had identified two cases in which SIV had infected laboratory workers. It should be noted that in both instances the contact was blood to blood.

Q: Does this mean science fiction has become science fact? We've created the seeds of our own self-destruction as a species!

A: Whoa, don't go "B" movie quite yet. First, it is a hypothesis. Second, many authorities deny its feasibility. Third, other SIV possibilities also exist. For example, given that two laboratory workers contracted SIV after direct blood-to-blood exposure to contaminated blood products, why could not that

have been the means for exposing countless others in Africa. How? Well, monkey meat is a food source in equatorial Africa. Contact with contaminated meat might have transmitted SIV to humans.

Q: Are adolescents as a population really at risk for AIDS?

A: Most certainly, sexually active adolescents are at high risk for the disease given their failure to practice safe sex. It appears that at best 50% of sexually active adolescents practice partially safe sex with the use of a condom. Disturbingly, some studies report that as high as three-quarters of sexually active adolescent females do not insist on safe sex.

Q: If the HIV retrovirus is so dangerous, why don't we test everyone?

A: First, it would not be cost effective. Second, just because you tested negative for the virus today does not mean that if you have been exposed that six months from now you would not test positive. The better approaches to spending those dollars, providing you are not in a high-risk group, are for preventing the spread of the disease and for developing a vaccine and cure for this deadly disease.

Q: Does that mean no one should be tested?

A: If you believe yourself to be in a high-risk group (homosexual, bisexual, IV drug user, an individual with multiple sex partners who has not practiced safe sex, hemophiliac, or the partner of a member of the aforementioned groups) you should seriously consider being tested.

Q: I have heard that my risk for HIV infection is not great if I am male and exclusively heterosexual. And yet I read about sports stars and others who have become infected with the HIV retrovirus. It doesn't make sense.

A: This is a difficult question to answer. If I told you your risk to receiving the AIDS retrovirus was 1 in 40,000 which is the latest estimate, then you would feel quite comforted. That is unless you happened to be the 1 in 40,000. It appears that it is harder for a male to receive the retrovirus from a woman than it is for a woman to receive it from a man. However, as you increase the number of sexual partners, the number of times unsafe sex occurs, and practices that increase the chance of the transmission of blood, risk increases.

Box 14–5   AIDS: Questions and Answers *(continued)*

Q: Why am I a greater risk if I am a female?

A: It is into your body the male ejaculates. This fluid which may contain the retrovirus has a longer opportunity to find damaged tissue than the fluid your body deposits on the circumcised penis. Risk increases dramatically for males if they are not circumcised. Therefore, it is in your best interest to insist on safe sex or no sex.

Q: What if my male partner has the HIV retrovirus and I am pregnant by him or want to become pregnant by him? What is my risk and the risk for my baby?

A: First, please talk to your doctor. These are questions best answered by an expert. If your sexual experiences did not involve blood-to-blood contact then there is a good probability you are not infected. Can you carry a child from an HIV-infected individual? A report in *Science* suggests that it is the ejaculated fluid and not the sperm that carries the retrovirus. If this report is correct, then it is conceivable that someday sperm free of fluid could be artificially implanted. But again, these are tentative findings and should be discussed with your doctor.

Q: If my partner and I are infected with the virus will our child be infected?

A: Not necessarily. More than 40% of children born to HIV-infected individuals do not test positive for the virus. Recent thinking suggests that the retrovirus may be transmitted to the infant during its passage through the birth canal. If so. medical procedures

may be developed to avoid its transmission. However, again, we urge you to seek good medical advice before making any decisions.

Q: Can I become infected with HIV by French kissing?

Q: Although the retrovirus can be found in low concentrations in saliva, it is considered unlikely.

Q: Why should I worry about AIDS? Modern medicine will develop a cure for this problem.

A: The most optimistic reports are that a vaccine is a decade away. Furthermore, AIDS is caused by a retrovirus that appears in several genetic variations. Thus, one vaccine—even several vaccines—may not be enough to provide immunity. If you plan to become sexually active before a cure is found, I would encourage worry. Worry motivates you to exercise caution and motivates you to protect yourself and your partner.

Q: OK, I'm worried. What advice would you offer?

A: For those seeking complete protection, celibacy or practicing masturbation (providing you are not an illegal IV drug user) are the two most certain means of avoiding the retrovirus. As one strays from this path, the risk increases. Ways of reducing the risk are to know your partner's previous sexual history, avoid sexual practices that damage tissues (for example, anal sex), avoid the exchange of body fluids containing blood, and, most of all, use a latex condom and foam.

Sources: Barnes, 1986a, 1986b; Buckingham & Van Gorp, 1988; Curran et al., 1985; Kanki, Alroy, & Essex, 1985; Lui, Darrow, & Rutherford, 1988; Marx, 1986; Piot et al., 1988; Price et al., 1988; Runck, 1986. Viscarello, 1990; Guilian, Vaca, & Noonan, 1990; *New York Times* Service, 1990; Davidson & Grant, 1988; Goodman & Cohall, 1989; Bloom & Glied, 1991; *Science,* 1989; Marx, 1989; Segest, Mygind, Harris, & Bay, 1991; Moore & Rosenthal, 1991; Palca, 1991, 1992; Catania et al., 1992; Fox, 1992; Curtis, 1992; Select Committee on Children, Youth, and Families, 1992.

Then as today, young people exchanged sexual services for money, with the fee dependent on the service rendered. Today in some parts of the United States manual masturbation (a "hand job") might cost as little as $25 while on either coast the charge may be as high as $50. A "French massage" (oral sex) can vary from $50 to $75, and "half and half" (a progression from manual stimulation to oral or vaginal intercourse) can cost from $75 to several hundred dollars.

In a review of the literature Rickel and Hendren (1993) and others (M. E. Brown, 1979; Caplan, 1984; Newton-Ruddy & Handelsman, 1986; Vitaliano, Boyer, & James, 1981) suggest several explanations for juvenile prostitution. Rickel and her associate Hendren report that family relationships are strained and that parental sexual abuse is common. they speculate that "normlessness," poor education, and poor employment prospects also help push a young person onto the streets. Other factors may contribute to a decision to stay there. For example, Caplan (1984) observes that pimps often fulfill parental needs for these young girls, and Brown (1979) notes that an element of adventure is involved and that the financial rewards of prostitution can be high. Few other jobs pay from $200 to $1000 a day tax-free, and for the adolescent on the run who needs cash quickly, prostitution offers a means to acquire it:

> Listen, man, I'm 14 years old. Can't even work yet. But I gotta have money. Nobody's gonna take care of me. So I visit Danny [a store manager] and look, you know, sexy. Well, he gets turned on and starts squeezing me. So I says, "I'll blow ya if I can have those jeans over there." Christ, he threw the stuff I wanted at me—he wanted it so bad.

Other factors, such as early forced sexual relations, association with delinquent peers, and drug abuse, can combine with a sense of powerlessness, anger, and hatred to push an adolescent into prostitution. Many studies report strong antifather feelings expressed by prostitutes who, it these authors' judgment, are "symbolically castrating them" (Brown, 1979, p. 672).

Baizerman, Thompson, and Stafford-White (1979), in an article based on their professional contacts with teenage prostitutes, provide support for Brown's

Adolescent prostitution is a major problem in many large cities in the United States and Canada.

(1979) observations. To the possible surprise of many, they note that many young prostitutes, without their parents' knowledge, service businessmen after school.

In a study of Canadian youth similar findings appear. In a sample of 100 male and female prostitutes, young people reported very negative feelings toward their families. These feelings contributed to their decision to leave home at an early age. In the case of females, that average age was less than 14 years old. This unhappiness with family life in many instances involved sexual abuse by a close family member. Finally, the authors suggest that different motivational factors may affect the decision of males to enter into prostitution. They raise the question for further study of whether, "for males, sexual preference [homosexuality] may influence entry into prostitution" (Earls & David, 1990, p. 10).

Brown (1979) and Baizerman and his colleagues (1979) do not find the outlook for preventing teenage prostitution particularly bright. They note that such factors as societal rejection, poor family life, and the plain fact that prostitution pays so well combine to encourage rather than discourage it. Baizerman and his associates propose a combined approach of education and shelter homes to help young people in or at risk of prostitution. Education would focus on a "nonscare approach" of information and discussions with teenage prostitutes. Shelter homes would offer girls wanting to get out of prostitution the medical, legal, and educational/vocational help necessary to work in some other area.

The solutions to the problems described in this chapter are not simple, nor are they easy. Attacking these situations constructively calls first for a realization that such behaviors exist and cannot be stopped with moralistic statements. Only then can society begin to address the needs of these young people.

Major Points to Remember

1. Although birth-control methods are widely available, this year more than one in ten adolescents will give birth to a child.
2. The problems facing the expectant teenager are many, including poor future educational employment prospects, lower marital satisfaction, and a high divorce rate.
3. Researchers are divided on why some adolescents become pregnant and others don't. Some investigators find evidence for psychological explanations, while others state that it is really nothing more than dumb, blind, unfortunate luck.
4. The family life of many adolescents who become pregnant has been described as very stressful before the pregnancy, but the relationship between the adolescent and her mother is thought to improve during the time the adolescent is pregnant.
5. Until recently, little attention has been paid to the adolescent father. Although he appears to be less prepared than his sexual partner for parenthood, he has been found to be caring and concerned in most studies.

6. Although contraceptive knowledge dates back thousands of years, it is only in the past two decades that many adolescents have had access to birth-control devices. Even so, few teenagers use them.

7. Explanations for not using contraceptives include feeling uncomfortable about one's sexuality, lack of information, relationship factors, and a desire to become pregnant.

8. The organisms that cause venereal diseases are highly vulnerable to light, air, and dryness. As luck would have it, the human body is dark, without air, and moist, providing the perfect incubator for the growth of these extremely harmful diseases.

9. Venereal diseases could be brought under control if only sexually active individuals would combine the use of condoms with vaginal foams.

10. Sexual responsibility is a shared responsibility.

11. Strained family relationships, often including parental sexual abuse, the desire for adventure, and the economic lure are some of the factors that draw young people into prostitution.

Drugs

The recovery of the sick is often delayed, sometimes entirely prevented, by the habitual use of tobacco or opium. . . . The use of tobacco is a pernicious habit in whatever form it is introduced into the system. Its active principle, Nicotine, which is an energetic poison, exerts its specific effect on the nervous system, tending to stimulate it to an unnatural degree of activity, the final result of which is weakness, or even paralysis. The horse, under action of whip and spur, may exhibit great spirit and rapid movements, but urge him beyond his strength with these agents, and you inflict a lasting injury. Withhold the stimulants, and the drooping head and moping pace indicate the sad reaction which has taken place. This illustrates the evils of habitually exciting the nerves by the use of tobacco, opium, narcotic, or other drugs. . . . Tobacco itself, when its use becomes habitual and excessive, gives rise to the most unpleasant and dangerous pathological conditions, oppressive stupor, weakness or loss of intellect, softening of the brain, paralysis, nervous debility, dyspepsia, functional derangement of the heart, and diseases of the liver and kidneys. . . . A sense of fainting, nausea, giddiness, dryness of the throat, tremblings, feelings of fear, disquietude, and general nervous prostration must frequently warn persons addicted to this habit that they are sapping the very foundation of health. . . . Dr. King says, "A patient under treatment should give up the use of tobacco, or his physician should assume no responsibility in his case. . . ." The opium habit, to which allusion has also been made, is open to the same objections. (Pierce, 1895, pp. 384–385)

The preceding passage illustrates one of the problems in writing a chapter on substance use. The author of that passage, R. V. Pierce, M.D., of the Invalid's Hotel and Surgical Institute and president of a mail-order patent-medicine firm specializing in such remedies as Dr. Pierce's Favorite Prescription and Dr. Pierce's Compound Extract of Smartweed, is not unlike many writers and researchers both then and now who carry their personal convictions about substance use over into their work. The result is confusion, misrepresentation, and the creation of a credibility gap so wide that many young people and adults beginning to experiment with alcohol or drugs reject any and all findings that portray one or the other in an unfavorable light.

In this chapter we attempt to unravel myth from reality, fantasy from fact, for the substances alcohol, tobacco, marijuana, inhalants, steroids, hallucinogens, stimulants, barbiturates, cocaine, and heroin. In the process we examine the factors that influence some young people to use, others to abuse, and still others to become psychologically and/or physically dependent on alcohol and drugs. Finally, we examine the implications for treating and preventing substance abuse and dependence.

Historical Overview

Although today's newspapers and magazines may constantly run headlines expressing fear and consternation over the use and abuse of drugs and alcohol by adolescents, the use of these and other substances by young people has never been uncommon. This behavior was not condoned or accepted, but the problem was viewed as a moral or legal concern rather than as a mental health issue. In fact, much of the addiction to narcotics by youths in the 19th century (and addiction was common) can be traced to the family and its use of store-bought patent medicines or home-brewed recipes. Most of these contained liberal amounts of opium, which was then easily obtainable (Gullotta & Blau, 1995; Jaffe, 1979).

For instance, sandwiched between the "saloon department" and "the Tanner's, Shoe, and Harness Maker's department" in the 1866 edition of *Dr. Chase's Recipes; or Information for Everybody: An Invaluable Collection of about Eight Hundred Practical Recipes,* the good doctor offered these recipes to mom for her family:

> For Nervousness—Nervous Pill—Morphine 9 grs.; extract of stramonium and hyoscyamus, of each 18 grs.; form into pill-mass by using solution of gum arabic and tragacanth, quite thick. Divide into 40 pills. Dose—In case of severe pain or nervousness, 1 pill taken at bedtime will be found to give a quiet night of rest. The advantage of this pill over those depending entirely upon opium or morphine . . . is that they may be taken without fear of constipation.

> For the common cold—Linseed-Oil, honey, and Jamaican rum, equal parts of each; to be shaken when used.

> Or for the children—Cough Candy—Tincture of squills 2 ozs.; camphorated tincture of opium, and tincture of tolu, of each 1/4 oz.; wine of impeca 1/2 oz.; oils of gaultheria 4 drops, sassafras 3 drops, and of anise seed oil 2 drops. . . . Druggists will get confectioners to make this for a trifle on the pound over common candies. . . .

> And the Pill for Painful Menstruation—Extract of Stramonium and sulphate of quinine of 16 grs.; macrotin 8 gr.; morphine 1 gr.; make into 8 pills. Dose—one pill, repeating once or twice only, 40 to 50 minutes apart, if the pain does not subside before this time. (Chase, 1866, pp. 149, 171–172, 212)

Before we begin to examine individual substances, we need to clarify some terms. By *substance use* we mean the infrequent and limited intake of alcohol or drugs. *Substance abuse* is the frequent and excessive use of alcohol or drugs such that there is an impairment in the physical, mental, or social functioning of the individual. *Substance dependence* is synonymous with *addiction*. It is characterized by the need to use alcohol or drugs on a continuous basis to meet psychological or physical needs and to avoid the discomfort of its absence (withdrawal).

Alcohol

Consider the following facts:

1. The National Institute on Alcohol Abuse and Alcoholism (NIAAA) estimates that 4.6 million teenagers aged 14 to 17 experience serious alcohol-related problems (Johnston, O'Malley and Bachman, 1991).
2. In college, 41% of the student population drinks heavily (Johnston, O'Malley and Bachman, 1991).
3. Motor vehicle accidents involving alcohol are the leading cause of death for young people in the United States aged 15 to 19, accounting for 45% of fatalities in this age group (U.S. Department of Health and Human Services, 1985).

4. Of the 1990 senior class, 89.5% reported using alcohol at least once in their life. This is the first time in 15 years that the figure fell below 90% (National Institute on Drug Abuse, 1991).

5. While the percentage of seniors in the class of 1990 consuming five or more drinks in the last 30 days is the lowest it has ever been, the figure is still slightly less than a third of the total class population (32.2%) (National Institute on Drug Abuse, 1991).

Given these findings, why, to paraphrase an advertising campaign, is drinking so "downright uptight"? If the federal government's estimates of the enormous cost of alcohol-related problems are accurate, then society lost nearly $117 billion in 1983 and $136 billion in 1990, and will lose a projected $150 billion in worker productivity and health care expenses due to alcohol misuse in 1995 (Secretary of Health and Human Services, 1990). These data certainly lend a second, more serious meaning to W. C. Field's famous film short *The Fatal Glass of Beer.*

At one time alcohol consumption was prohibited in the United States, but that well-known 13-year experiment in sobriety failed. It failed because the simple truth is that drinking makes most people feel good. Furthermore, most people do not abuse or become dependent on alcohol (Nicholson, 1995). Given its unique status in our society (the cocktail hour, the Sunday champagne brunch, the Western saloon, wine tasting parties, the corner bar of countless television shows), it is understandable, but not pardonable, that most Americans view other drugs as evil or corrupting and alcohol as acceptable despite overwhelming evidence to the contrary.

Initiation into Drug Use: The Alcohol Connection

Popular belief spurred by anxious and well-meaning individuals suggests that a causal relationship exists between the use of marijuana and other drugs such as cocaine and heroin. The argument is that the use of one drug inevitably creates the need to use a second drug and then a third drug and so on. Interestingly, most proponents of this stage theory begin their argument with marijuana and ignore the possibility that most marijuana users first used alcohol. Such a finding would seriously question the validity of the marijuana stepping-stone theory, since most alcohol users do not move on to marijuana and then to other drugs.

In a series of articles Kandel (1981a) and her associates (Kandel & Faust, 1975; Yamaguchi & Kandel, 1984) have repeatedly demonstrated that, "drug use begins specifically with beer and wine. These are the 'entry drugs' into the continuum of drug use" (1975, p. 931). One of their early studies established an order that most adolescents follow in using drugs. This model suggests that the adolescent begins to experiment with socially approved drugs such as beer and wine. For many young people, this first level is the last level; no further drug use occurs. Other young people take a second step, to cigarettes and hard liquor. Interestingly, evidence on the tobacco/alcohol connection suggests that those who begin with cigarettes are likely to use hard liquor but that those who begin with hard liquor are very unlikely to begin cigarette smoking. "Thus, while drinking can proceed without smoking, smoking is almost always followed by drinking hard liquor. Joint use of hard liquor and cigarettes is associated with the highest rates of entry into illicit drugs. . . . Almost no adolescent proceeds to other drugs without first trying marihuana" (1975, p. 931).

Kandel and Faust emphasize that while "the data show a very clear-cut sequence in the use of various drugs, they do not prove that the use of a particular drug infallibly leads to the use of other drugs higher up in the sequence" (p. 931). Many youths in their study stopped at one of the three lower levels of involvement, with only a minority proceeding to drugs beyond marijuana.

Table 15–1 compares the use of alcohol and other drugs between 1975 and 1990. The figure shows the percentage of high school students who reported having used the listed drugs at any time during their lifetime. Alcohol received by far the heaviest use (89.5%), followed by tobacco (64.4%) and marijuana (40.7%).

A developmental model to account for adolescent drug use has been derived from Kandel and Faust's study (Kandel, 1981a; Kandel, Treiman, Faust, & Single, 1976). Kandel and her associates propose that young people who begin to use alcohol are more socially advanced than their peers. They have adopted adult standards of social behavior and are imitating their parents' drinking behaviors. Adolescents who make the step from alcohol to marijuana do so with their peers. These young people are described as having anti-Establishment feelings toward their parents, school, church, and community. The final move from marijuana to other drugs occurs for those who experience strong feelings of depression and alienation from family, friends, and the community. Support for this stage theory of drug use can be found in a number of studies (Biddle, Bank, & Marim, 1980; Mills & Noyes, 1984; Johnson, et al., 1990; Perry & Murray, 1985; Stumphauzer, 1980; L. S. Wright, 1985b).

In brief, it appears that the chances are good that the illicit-drug user first experimented with beer or wine, tobacco, and hard liquor. This finding does not, however, establish a causal connection between the use of these substances or marijuana and the use of other drugs. Substance use on one level does not necessarily suggest movement to other illicit drugs. In the next section we take a closer look at the research in an attempt to explain why young people drink.

Sociological and Psychological Viewpoints

By the time U.S. young people graduate from high school, nearly 90% will have tried alcohol and 41% will have gotten drunk at least once. About 5% will continue to get drunk frequently throughout adolescence. Despite these statistics, studies show, most of these youthful drinkers will not become alcohol abusers or dependent in the future (National Institute on Alcohol Abuse and Alcoholism, 1984; National Institute on Drug Abuse, 1991).

Table 15–2 compares drug use by high school seniors over several years. Note the differences in levels of use from the lifetime use recorded in Table 15–1.

In one study 44% of a college sample were described as problem drinkers—that is, substance abusers (Fillmore, 1974). Two decades later, of the 200 college students involved in that study, the number of problem drinkers had decreased to 19%. This and other studies with similar findings have led some researchers to conclude that "drinking is a part of growing up and will decrease with age and maturity" (O'Gorman, Stringfield, & Smith, 1976, p. 9). (See Table 15–3.)

Table 15–1   Trends in Lifetime Prevalence of Twenty Types of Drugs

	Percentage who ever used							
	Class of 1975	Class of 1976	Class of 1977	Class of 1978	Class of 1979	Class of 1980	Class of 1981	Class of 1982
Approx. N =	9400	15400	17100	17800	15500	15900	17500	17700
Any Illicit Drug Use[a]	55.2	58.2	61.6	64.1	65.1	65.4	65.6	65.8
Adjusted Version[b]	—	—	—	—	—	—	—	64.4
Any Illicit Drug Other Than Marijuana[c]	36.2	35.4	35.8	36.5	37.4	38.7	42.8	45.0
Adjusted Version[b]	—	—	—	—	—	—	—	41.1
Marijuana/Hashish	47.3	52.8	56.4	59.2	60.4	60.3	59.5	58.7
Inhalants[d]	NA	10.3	11.1	12.0	12.7	11.9	12.3	12.8
Inhalants Adjusted[e]	NA	NA	NA	NA	18.2	17.3	17.2	17.7
Amyl/Butyl Nitrites[f,g]	NA	NA	NA	NA	11.1	11.1	10.1	9.8
Hallucinogens	16.3	15.1	13.9	14.3	14.1	13.3	13.3	12.5
Hallucinogens Adjusted[h]	NA	NA	NA	NA	17.7	16.6	15.3	14.3
LSD	11.3	11.0	9.8	9.7	9.5	9.3	9.8	9.6
PCP[f,g]	NA	NA	NA	NA	12.8	9.6	7.8	6.0
Cocaine	9.0	9.7	10.8	12.9	15.4	15.7	16.5	16.0
"Crack"[i]	NA	NA	NA	NA	NA	NA	NA	NA
Other cocaine[j]	NA	NA	NA	NA	NA	NA	NA	NA
Heroin	2.2	1.8	1.8	1.6	1.1	1.1	1.1	1.2
Other opiates[k]	9.0	9.6	10.3	9.9	10.1	9.8	10.1	9.6
Stimulants[k]	22.3	22.6	23.0	22.9	24.2	26.4	32.2	35.6
Stimulants Adjusted[b,k]	NA	NA	NA	NA	NA	NA	NA	27.9
Crystal Methamphetamine[l]	NA	NA	NA	NA	NA	NA	NA	NA
Sedatives[k,m]	18.2	17.7	17.4	16.0	14.6	14.9	16.0	15.2
Barbiturates[k]	16.9	16.2	15.6	13.7	11.8	11.0	11.3	10.3
Methaqualone[k,m]	8.1	7.8	8.5	7.9	8.3	9.5	10.6	10.7
Tranquilizers[k]	17.0	16.8	18.0	17.0	16.3	15.2	14.7	14.0
Alcohol	90.4	91.9	92.5	93.1	93.0	93.2	92.6	92.8
Cigarettes	73.6	75.4	75.7	75.3	74.0	71.0	71.0	70.1
Steroids[f]	NA	NA	NA	NA	NA	NA	NA	NA

Notes: Level of significance of difference between the two most recent classes: s = .05, ss = .01, sss = .001. NA indicates data not available.

[a]Use of "any illicit drugs" includes any use of marijuana, hallucinogens, cocaine, and heroin, or any use of other opiates, stimulants, barbiturates, methaqualone (excluded in 1990), or tranquilizers not under a doctor's orders.

[b]Based on the data from the revised question, which attempts to exclude the inappropriate reporting of non-prescription stimulants.

[c]Use of "other illicit drugs" includes any use of hallucinogens, cocaine, and heroin, or any use of other opiates, stimulants, barbiturates, methaqualone (exluded in 1990), or tranquilizers not under a doctor's orders.

[d]Data based on four questionnaire forms in 1976–1988; N is four-fifths of N indicated. Data based on five questionnaire forms in 1989–1990; N is five-sixths of N indicated.

[e]Adjusted for underreporting of amyl and butyl nitrites. See text for details.

[f]Data based on a single questionnaire form; N is one-fifth of N indicated in 1979–1988 and one-sixth of N indicated in 1989 and 1990.

[g]Question text changed slightly in 1987.

Table 15–1   Trends in Lifetime Prevalence of Twenty Types of Drugs *(continued)*

			Percentage who ever used					
Class of 1983	Class of 1984	Class of 1985	Class of 1986	Class of 1987	Class of 1988	Class of 1989	Class of 1990	'89–'90 change
16300	15900	16000	15200	16300	16300	16700	15200	
64.1								
62.9	*61.6*	*60.6*	*57.6*	*56.6*	*53.9*	*50.9*	*47.9*	*– 3.0ss*
44.4								
40.4	*40.3*	*39.7*	*37.7*	*35.8*	*32.5*	*31.4*	*29.4*	*– 2.0s*
57.0	54.9	54.2	50.9	50.2	47.2	43.7	40.7	– 3.0ss
13.6	14.4	15.4	15.9	17.0	16.7	17.6	18.0	+ 0.4
18.2	*18.0*	*18.1*	*20.1*	*18.6*	*17.5*	*18.6*	*18.5*	*– 0.1*
8.4	8.1	7.9	8.6	4.7	3.2	3.3	2.1	– 1.2s
11.9	10.7	10.3	9.7	10.3	8.9	9.4	9.4	– 0.0
13.6	*12.3*	*12.1*	*11.9*	*10.6*	*9.2*	*9.9*	*9.7*	*– 0.2*
8.9	8.0	7.5	7.2	8.4	7.7	8.3	8.7	+ 0.4
5.6	5.0	4.9	4.8	3.0	2.9	3.9	2.8	– 1.1
16.2	16.1	17.3	16.9	15.2	12.1	10.3	9.4	– 0.9
NA	NA	NA	NA	5.4	4.8	4.7	3.5	– 1.2ss
NA	NA	NA	NA	14.0	12.1	8.5	8.6	+ 0.1
1.2	1.3	1.2	1.1	1.2	1.1	1.3	1.3	0.0
9.4	9.7	10.2	9.0	9.2	8.6	8.3	8.3	0.0
35.4	NA	NA	NA	NA	NA	NA	NA	NA
26.9	*27.9*	*26.2*	*23.4*	*21.6*	*19.8*	*19.1*	*17.5*	*– 1.6s*
NA	NA	NA	NA	NA	NA	NA	2.7	NA
14.4	13.3	11.8	10.4	8.7	7.8	7.4	5.3	– 2.1ss
9.9	9.9	9.2	8.4	7.4	6.7	6.5	6.8	+ 0.3
10.1	8.3	6.7	5.2	4.0	3.3	2.7	2.3	– 0.4
13.3	12.4	11.9	10.9	10.9	9.4	7.6	7.2	– 0.4
92.6	92.6	92.2	91.3	92.2	92.0	90.7	89.5	– 1.2
70.6	69.7	68.8	67.6	67.2	66.4	65.7	64.4	– 1.3
NA	NA	NA	NA	NA	NA	3.0	2.9	– 0.1

[h]Adjusted for underreporting of PCP.
[i]Data based on two questionnaire forms in 1987–1989; N is two-fifths of N indicated in 1987–1988 and two-sixths of N indicated in 1989. Data based on six questionnaire forms in 1990.
[j]Data based on a single questionnaire form in 1987–1989; N is one-fifth of N indicated in 1987–1988 and one-sixth of N indicated in 1989. Data based on four questionnaire forms in 1990; N is four-sixths of N indicated.
[k]Only drug use which was not under a doctor's orders is included here.
[l]Data based on two questionnaire forms; N is two-sixths of N indicated.
[m]Data based on five questionnaire forms in 1975–1988, six questionnaire forms in 1989, and one questionnaire form in 1990. N is one-sixth of N indicated in 1990.
Source: Research Triangle Institute. (1984). *Economic costs to society of alcohol and drug abuse and mental illness.* Chapel Hill, NC: Author.

Table 15–2   Trends in Annual Prevalence of Twenty Types of Drugs

	Percentage who used in last twelve months							
	Class of 1975	*Class of 1976*	*Class of 1977*	*Class of 1978*	*Class of 1979*	*Class of 1980*	*Class of 1981*	*Class of 1982*
Approx. N =	9400	15400	17100	17800	15500	15900	17500	17700
Any Illicit Drug Use[a]	*45.0*	*48.1*	*51.1*	*53.8*	*54.2*	*53.1*	*52.1*	*50.8*
Adjusted Version[b]	—	—	—	—	—	—	—	*49.4*
Any Illicit Drug Other Than Marijuana[c]	*26.2*	*25.4*	*26.0*	*27.1*	*28.2*	*30.4*	*34.0*	*33.8*
Adjusted Version[b]	—	—	—	—	—	—	—	*30.1*
Marijuana/Hashish	40.0	44.5	47.6	50.2	50.8	48.8	46.1	44.3
Inhalants[d]	NA	3.0	3.7	4.1	5.4	4.6	4.1	4.5
Inhalants Adjusted[e]	*NA*	*NA*	*NA*	*NA*	*8.9*	*7.9*	*6.1*	*6.6*
Amyl/Butyl Nitrites[f,g]	NA	NA	NA	NA	6.5	5.7	3.7	3.6
Hallucinogens	11.2	9.4	8.8	9.6	9.9	9.3	9.0	8.1
Hallucinogens Adjusted[h]	*NA*	*NA*	*NA*	*NA*	*11.8*	*10.4*	*10.1*	*9.0*
LSD	7.2	6.4	5.5	6.3	6.6	6.5	6.5	6.1
PCP[f,g]	NA	NA	NA	NA	7.0	4.4	3.2	2.2
Cocaine	5.6	6.0	7.2	9.0	12.0	12.3	12.4	11.5
"Crack"[i]	NA	NA	NA	NA	NA	NA	NA	NA
Other cocaine[j]	NA	NA	NA	NA	NA	NA	NA	NA
Heroin	1.0	0.8	0.8	0.8	0.5	0.5	0.5	0.6
Other opiates[k]	5.7	5.7	6.4	6.0	6.2	6.3	5.9	5.3
Stimulants[k]	16.2	15.8	16.3	17.1	18.3	20.8	26.0	26.1
Stimulants Adjusted[b,k]	*NA*	*NA*	*NA*	*NA*	*NA*	*NA*	*NA*	*20.3*
Crystal Methamphetamine[l]	NA	NA	NA	NA	NA	NA	NA	NA
Sedatives[k,m]	11.7	10.7	10.8	9.9	9.9	10.3	10.5	9.1
Barbiturates[k]	10.7	9.6	9.3	8.1	7.5	6.8	6.6	5.5
Methaqualone[k,m]	5.1	4.7	5.2	4.9	5.9	7.2	7.6	6.8
Tranquilizers[k]	10.6	10.3	10.8	9.9	9.6	8.7	8.0	7.0
Alcohol	84.8	85.7	87.0	87.7	88.1	87.9	87.0	86.8
Cigarettes	NA	NA	NA	NA	NA	NA	NA	NA
Steroids[f]	NA	NA	NA	NA	NA	NA	NA	NA

Notes: Level of significance of difference between the two most recent classes: s = .05, ss = .01, sss = .001. NA indicates data not available.

[a]Use of "any illicit drugs" includes any use of marijuana, hallucinogens, cocaine, and heroin, or any use of other opiates, stimulants, barbiturates, methaqualone (excluded in 1990), or tranquilizers not under a doctor's orders.

[b]Based on the data from the revised question, which attempts to exclude the inappropriate reporting of non-prescription stimulants.

[c]Use of "other illicit drugs" includes any use of hallucinogens, cocaine, and heroin, or any use of other opiates, stimulants, barbiturates, methaqualone (excluded in 1990), or tranquilizers not under a doctor's orders.

[d]Data based on four questionnaire forms in 1976–1988; N is four-fifths of N indicated. Data based on five questionnaire forms in 1989–1990; N is five-sixths of N indicated.

[e]Adjusted for underreporting of amyl and butyl nitrites. See text for details.

[f]Data based on a single questionnaire form; N is one-fifth of N indicated in 1979–1988 and one-sixth of N indicated in 1989 and 1990.

[g]Question text changed slightly in 1987.

Chapter 15 Drugs **415**

Table 15–2 Trends in Annual Prevalence of Twenty Types of Drugs *(continued)*

			Percentage who used in last twelve monthes					
Class of 1983	*Class of 1984*	*Class of 1985*	*Class of 1986*	*Class of 1987*	*Class of 1988*	*Class of 1989*	*Class of 1990*	*'89–'90 change*
16300	15900	16000	15200	16300	16300	16700	15200	
49.1								
47.4	*45.8*	*46.3*	*44.3*	*41.7*	*38.5*	*35.4*	*32.5*	*– 2.9ss*
32.5	—	—	—	—	—	—	—	
28.4	*28.0*	*27.4*	*25.9*	*24.1*	*21.1*	*20.0*	*17.9*	*– 2.1ss*
42.3	40.0	40.6	38.8	36.3	33.1	29.6	27.0	*– 2.6s*
4.3	5.1	5.7	6.1	6.9	6.5	5.9	6.9	*+ 1.0s*
6.2	7.2	7.5	8.9	*8.1*	7.1	6.9	7.5	*+ 0.6*
3.6	4.0	4.0	4.7	2.6	1.7	1.7	1.4	*– 0.3*
7.3	6.5	6.3	6.0	6.4	5.5	5.6	5.9	*+ 0.3*
8.3	*7.3*	*7.6*	*7.6*	*6.7*	*5.8*	*6.2*	*6.0*	*– 0.2*
5.4	4.7	4.4	4.5	5.2	4.8	4.9	5.4	*+ 0.5*
2.6	2.3	2.9	2.4	1.3	1.2	2.4	1.2	*– 1.2ss*
11.4	11.6	13.1	12.7	10.3	7.9	6.5	5.3	*– 1.2ss*
NA	NA	NA	4.1	3.9	3.1	3.1	1.9	*– 1.2sss*
NA	NA	NA	NA	9.8	7.4	5.2	4.6	*– 0.6*
0.6	0.5	0.6	0.5	0.5	0.5	0.6	0.5	*– 0.1*
5.1	5.2	5.9	5.2	5.3	4.6	4.4	4.5	*+ 0.1*
24.6	NA	NA	NA	NA	NA	NA	NA	NA
17.9	*17.7*	*15.8*	*13.4*	*12.2*	*10.9*	*10.8*	*9.1*	*– 1.7ss*
NA	NA	NA	NA	NA	NA	NA	1.3	NA
7.9	6.6	5.8	5.2	4.1	3.7	3.7	2.5	*– 1.2s*
5.2	4.9	4.6	4.2	3.6	3.2	3.3	3.4	*+ 0.1*
5.4	3.8	2.8	2.1	1.5	1.3	1.3	0.7	*– 0.6s*
6.9	6.1	6.1	5.8	5.5	4.8	3.8	3.5	*– 0.3*
87.3	86.0	85.6	84.5	85.7	85.3	82.7	80.6	*– 2.1s*
NA	NA	NA	NA	NA	NA	NA	NA	NA
NA	NA	NA	NA	NA	NA	1.9	1.7	*– 0.2*

[h]Adjusted for underreporting of PCP. See text for details.

[i]Data based on a single questionnaire form in 1986; N is one-fifth of N indicated. Data based on two questionnaire forms in 1987–1989; N is two-fifths of N indicated in 1987–1988 and two-sixths of N indicated in 1989. Data based on six questionnaire forms in 1990.

[j]Data based on a single questionnaire form in 1987–1989; N is one-fifth of N indicated in 1987–1988 and one-sixth of N indicated in 1989. Data based on four questionnaire forms in 1990; N is four-sixths of N indicated.

[k]Only drug use which was not under a doctor's orders is included here.

[l]Data based on two questionnaire forms; N is two-sixths of N indicated.

[m]Data based on five questionnaire forms in 1975–1988, six questionnaire forms in 1989, and one questionnaire form in 1990. N is one-sixth of N indicated in 1990.

Source: Research Triangle Institute. (1984). *Economic costs to society of alcohol and drug abuse and mental illness.* Chapel Hill, NC: Author.

Table 15–3   Trends in Thirty-Day Prevalence of Twenty Types of Drugs

	Class of 1975	Class of 1976	Class of 1977	Class of 1978	Class of 1979	Class of 1980	Class of 1981	Class of 1982
Approx. N =	9400	15400	17100	17800	15500	15900	17500	17700
Any Illicit Drug Use[a]	*30.7*	*34.2*	*37.6*	*38.9*	*38.9*	*37.2*	*36.9*	*33.5*
Adjusted Version[b]	—	—	—	—	—	—	—	*32.5*
Any Illicit Drug Other Than Marijuana[c]	*15.4*	*13.9*	*15.2*	*15.1*	*16.8*	*18.4*	*21.7*	*19.2*
Adjusted Version[b]	—	—	—	—	—	—	—	*17.0*
Marijuana/Hashish	27.1	32.2	35.4	37.1	36.5	33.7	31.6	28.5
Inhalants[d]	NA	0.9	1.3	1.5	1.7	1.4	1.5	1.5
Inhalants Adjusted[e]	*NA*	*NA*	*NA*	*NA*	*3.2*	*2.7*	*2.5*	*2.5*
Amyl/Butyl Nitrites[f,g]	NA	NA	NA	NA	2.4	1.8	1.4	1.1
Hallucinogens	4.7	3.4	4.1	3.9	4.0	3.7	3.7	3.4
Hallucinogens Adjusted[h]	*NA*	*NA*	*NA*	*NA*	*5.3*	*4.4*	*4.5*	*4.1*
LSD	2.3	1.9	2.1	2.1	2.4	2.3	2.5	2.4
PCP[f,g]	NA	NA	NA	NA	2.4	1.4	1.4	1.0
Cocaine	1.9	2.0	2.9	3.9	5.7	5.2	5.8	5.0
"Crack"[i]	NA	NA	NA	NA	NA	NA	NA	NA
Other cocaine[j]	NA	NA	NA	NA	NA	NA	NA	NA
Heroin	0.4	0.2	0.3	0.3	0.2	0.2	0.2	0.2
Other opiates[k]	2.1	2.0	2.8	2.1	2.4	2.4	2.1	1.8
Stimulants[k]	8.5	7.7	8.8	8.7	9.9	12.1	15.8	13.7
Stimulants Adjusted[b,i]	*NA*	*NA*	*NA*	*NA*	*NA*	*NA*	*NA*	*10.7*
Crystal Methamphetamine[l]	NA	NA	NA	NA	NA	NA	NA	NA
Sedatives[k,m]	5.4	4.5	5.1	4.2	4.4	4.8	4.6	3.4
Barbiturates[k]	4.7	3.9	4.3	3.2	3.2	2.9	2.6	2.0
Methaqualone[k,m]	2.1	1.6	2.3	1.9	2.3	3.3	3.1	2.4
Tranquilizers[k]	4.1	4.0	4.6	3.4	3.7	3.1	2.7	2.4
Alcohol	68.2	68.3	71.2	72.1	71.8	72.0	70.7	69.7
Cigarettes	36.7	38.8	38.4	36.7	34.4	30.5	29.4	30.0
Steroids[f]	NA	NA	NA	NA	NA	NA	NA	NA

Notes: Level of significance of difference between the two most recent classes: s = .05, ss = .01, sss = .001. NA indicates data not available.

[a]Use of "any illicit drugs" includes any use of marijuana, hallucinogens, cocaine, and heroin, or any use of other opiates, stimulants, barbiturates, methaqualone (excluded in 1990), or tranquilizers not under a doctor's orders.

[b]Based on the data from the revised question, which attempts to exclude the inappropriate reporting of non-prescription stimulants.

[c]Use of "other illicit drugs" includes any use of hallucinogens, cocaine, and heroin, or any use of other opiates, stimulants, barbiturates, methaqualone (exluded in 1990), or tranquilizers not under a doctor's orders.

[d]Data based on four questionnaire forms in 1976–1988; N is four-fifths of N indicated. Data based on five questionnaire forms in 1989–1990; N is five-sixths of N indicated.

[e]Adjusted for underreporting of amyl and butyl nitrites. See text for details.

[f]Data based on a single questionnaire form; N is one-fifth of N indicated in 1979–1988 and one-sixth of N indicated in 1989 and 1990.

[g]Question text changed slightly in 1987.

Table 15–3   Trends in Thirty-Day Prevalence of Twenty Types of Drugs *(continued)*

			Percentage who used in last thirty days					
Class of 1983	*Class of 1984*	*Class of 1985*	*Class of 1986*	*Class of 1987*	*Class of 1988*	*Class of 1989*	*Class of 1990*	*'89–'90 change*
16300	15900	16000	15200	16300	16300	16700	15200	
32.4	—	—	—	—	—	—	—	
30.5	*29.2*	*29.7*	*27.1*	*24.7*	*21.3*	*19.7*	*17.2*	*– 2.5sss*
18.4	—	—	—	—	—	—	—	
15.4	*15.1*	*14.9*	*13.2*	*11.6*	*10.0*	*9.1*	*8.0*	*– 1.1s*
27.0	25.2	25.7	23.4	21.0	18.0	16.7	14.0	– 2.7ss
1.7	1.9	2.2	2.5	2.8	2.6	2.3	2.7	+ 0.4
2.5	*2.6*	*3.0*	*3.2*	*3.5*	*3.0*	*2.7*	*2.9*	*+ 0.2*
1.4	1.4	1.6	1.3	1.3	0.6	0.6	0.6	0.0
2.8	2.6	2.5	2.5	2.5	2.2	2.2	2.2	0.0
3.5	*3.2*	*3.8*	*3.5*	*2.8*	*2.3*	*2.9*	*2.3*	*– 0.6*
1.9	1.5	1.6	1.7	1.8	1.8	1.8	1.9	+ 0.1
1.3	1.0	1.6	1.3	0.6	0.3	1.4	0.4	– 1.0ss
4.9	5.8	6.7	6.2	4.3	3.4	2.8	1.9	– 0.9sss
NA	NA	NA	NA	1.3	1.6	1.4	0.7	– 0.7sss
NA	NA	NA	NA	4.1	3.2	1.9	1.7	– 0.2
0.2	0.3	0.3	0.2	0.2	0.2	0.3	0.2	– 0.1
1.8	1.8	2.3	2.0	1.8	1.6	1.6	1.5	– 0.1
12.4	NA	NA	NA	NA	NA	NA	NA	NA
8.9	*8.3*	*6.8*	*5.5*	*5.2*	*4.6*	*4.2*	*3.7*	*– 0.5*
NA	NA	NA	NA	NA	NA	NA	0.6	NA
3.0	2.3	2.4	2.2	1.7	1.4	1.6	1.0	– 0.6
2.1	1.7	2.0	1.8	1.4	1.2	1.4	1.3	– 0.1
1.8	1.1	1.0	0.8	0.6	0.5	0.6	0.2	– 0.4s
2.5	2.1	2.1	2.1	2.0	1.5	1.3	1.2	– 0.1
69.4	67.2	65.9	65.3	66.4	63.9	60.0	57.1	– 2.9s
30.3	29.3	30.1	29.6	29.4	28.7	28.6	29.4	+ 0.8
NA	NA	NA	NA	NA	NA	0.8	1.0	+ 0.2

[h]Adjusted for underreporting of PCP. See text for details.
[i]Data based on two questionnaire forms in 1987–1989; No is two-fifths of N indicated in 1987–1988 and two-sixths of N indicated in 1989. Data based on six questionnaire forms in 1990.
[j]Data based on a single questionnaire form in 1987–1989; N is one-fifth of N indicated in 1987–1988 and one-sixth of N indicated in 1989. Data based on four questionnaire forms in 1990; N is four-sixths of N indicated.
[k]Only drug use which was not under a doctor's orders is included here.
[l]Data based on two questionnaire forms; N is two-sixths of N indicated.
[m]Data based on five questionnaire forms in 1975–1988, six questionnaire forms in 1989, and one questionnaire form in 1990. N is one-sixth of N indicated in 1990.
Source: Research Triangle Institute. (1984). *Economic costs to society of alcohol and drug abuse and mental illness.* Chapel Hill, NC: Author.

Scholars have suggested a number of reasons for becoming intoxicated (Finn, 1979; St. Pierre & Miller, 1986). These include such "healthy" purposes as occasional desires to escape responsibilities as in "letting off steam," celebrating a special event such as a sports victory or holiday, or the wish to have a pleasant sensation. Less healthy or justifiable reasons include the desire to avoid the emotional pain associated with growing up, to encourage sexual misconduct, or to compensate for feelings of inadequacy.

Other possible reasons for increased adolescent alcohol use can be found in the changes that have occurred in the United States and Canada since World War II. A changing society has brought about revolutions in communications (television, instant worldwide satellite communication, home computers), in industry (increased automation, more leisure time, the demand for more specialized skills), and in marketing (who can resist the opportunity for the all-but-promised sex that goes with the night and a Michelob, for instance, and who would not want to celebrate Miller time?).

The drinking behavior of adolescents can be viewed as being in step with the increased permissiveness of the times. Nevertheless, whether the figure is 19%, 10%, or 5%, tens of thousands of young people do become alcohol dependent each year, a fact leading Finn (1979) to conclude that "interpretations of youthful intoxication must be individualized . . . [within] the context in which a youngster gets drunk" (p. 830). (See Table 15–4.)

A great deal of research has been conducted on the factors that contribute to making a young person vulnerable to becoming alcohol dependent. For instance, the results of a longitudinal study that followed several hundred male children over 30 years (M. C. Jones, 1968) suggest that those who become alcohol dependent are extroverted, worried over their masculinity, and rebellious as children. Karl Menninger (1965) and others (Johnson et al., 1990; Newcomb & Bentler, 1989) viewed the alcohol-dependent individual as a depressed failure seeking to escape the problems of living. Menninger speculated that alcohol dependence was a subtle form of suicidal behavior.

Numerous studies show that alcohol-dependent adolescents do poorly in school (G. M. Barnes, & Welte, 1986; Gersick, Grady, Sexton, & Lyons, 1981; Johnson et al., 1990; Newcomb & Bentler, 1989); are likely to be involved in deviant activities (Braucht, 1982; Dawkins & Dawkins, 1983; Rua, 1990); are nonreligious or at least less religious than their peers (Thomas & Carver, 1990); are likely to be using other illicit drugs (Vicary & Lerner, 1986); and are influenced more by their peer group than by their families (Department of Health and Human Services, 1991a; Selnow & Crano, 1986; Stein, Newcomb, & Bentler, 1987; Swaim, Oetting, Edwards, & Beauvais, 1989).

A composite picture, then, of alcohol-dependent adolescents is one of low-achieving, delinquent individuals. Not highly religious, they are likely to be using other drugs and are influenced more by their peers than by their families. Having feelings of rootlessness, depression, and failure, alcohol-dependent adolescents are seen as committing a form of suicide by their use of alcohol.

A Family Perspective

There is considerable evidence that parents have a strong influence on the drinking habits their children will eventually acquire. As discussed in Chapter 3 the family is the primary socialization agent for young people. No other institution maintains the length or depth of contact that the family does with its children.

G. M. Barnes (1977) uses this perspective to suggest that "problem drinking is a manifestation of incomplete, inadequate socialization within the family" (p. 573). Two recent studies support this conclusion. The first, by Vicary and Lerner (1986), draws from a 30-year longitudinal study of 133 White, middle-class subjects and their parents. It documents abuse of alcohol by those subjects who were rejected by their mothers or whose families experienced conflict over childrearing practices or exercised inconsistent or restrictive discipline. The second study, by Hundleby and Mercer (1987), draws on a Canadian sample of 2048 Ontario school children. In this sample lack of parental affection, concern, or involvement in these young people's lives significantly contributed to their substance misuse.

The profile of the alcohol-dependent adolescent's family that emerges from these and other studies (Johnson et al., 1990; Newcomb & Bentler, 1989; Tudor, Peterson, & Elifson, 1980) is of poor parental control over the adolescent and a distant relationship between teenager and parents. Families with affectionate, child-centered parents, on the other hand, are much less likely to have adolescents who use illegal substances (J. S. Brook, Gordon, & Brook, 1980; Johnson, et al., 1990).

Despite the poor relationship between alcohol-dependent adolescents and their parents, these researchers have found that the parents often condone, if not encourage, their adolescents' drinking (Barnes & Welte, 1986; McDermott, 1984). Seligman (1986) illustrates this last point in his clinical report of working with such a family. He reports that the family arrived at the second session amused, reporting that their son had taken money that his father had given him and "'blown it on a boozing binge with his friends.' Father's complaint, made in a half-jocular indulgent tone, was that Ricky had stayed out without telephoning to say where he was" (p. 234). Finally, in a society in which baby-boomer parents now have adolescent children, researchers are finding a strong positive relationship between parental use of alcohol and other drugs and use by their children (Department of Health and Human Services, 1991a; Newcomb, Huba, & Bentler, 1983).

The Biological Connection

In many of these studies, at least one parent of the alcohol-dependent adolescent was also alcohol dependent. Whether there is a genetic predisposition to dependency is difficult to assess. Certainly, the family conditions we have described provide one convincing explanation for an adolescent's drinking. Nevertheless, the results of several studies support a genetic explanation. For example, Bohman (1978) found that adopted sons whose biological fathers were alcoholic were three times as likely to become alcoholic as were the adopted sons of nonalcoholic fathers. Adopted sons whose mothers were alcoholic were twice as likely to become alcoholic as were the adopted sons of nonalcoholic mothers. Additional research tends to support a general finding that children of alcoholic parents stand a greater chance of becoming alcoholics than children whose parents are not (Cadoret, Cain, & Grove, 1980; Cotton, 1979; McCaul, Srikis, Turkkan, Bigelow, & Cromwell, 1990). Indeed in a study that has been likened to the Manhattan Project, National Institute on Alcohol Abuse and Alcoholism

Table 15–4   Trends in Thirty-Day Prevalence of Daily Use of Twenty Types of Drugs

	Percentage who used daily in last 30 days							
	Class of 1975	Class of 1976	Class of 1977	Class of 1978	Class of 1979	Class of 1980	Class of 1981	Class of 1982
Approx. N =	9400	15400	17100	17800	15500	15900	17500	17700
Marijuana/Hashish	6.0	8.2	9.1	10.7	10.3	9.1	7.0	6.3
Inhalants[a]	NA	0.0	0.0	0.1	0.0	0.1	0.1	0.1
Inhalants Adjusted[b]	*NA*	*NA*	*NA*	*NA*	*0.1*	*0.2*	*0.2*	*0.2*
Amyl & Butyl Nitrites[c,d]	NA	NA	NA	NA	0.0	0.1	0.1	0.0
Hallucinogens	0.1	0.1	0.1	0.1	0.1	0.1	0.1	0.1
Hallucinogens Adjusted[e]	*NA*	*NA*	*NA*	*NA*	*0.2*	*0.2*	*0.1*	*0.2*
LSD	0.0	0.0	0.0	0.0	0.0	0.0	0.1	0.0
PCP[c,d]	NA	NA	NA	NA	0.1	0.1	0.1	0.1
Cocaine	0.1	0.1	0.1	0.1	0.2	0.2	0.3	0.2
"Crack"[f]	NA	NA	NA	NA	NA	NA	NA	NA
Other cocaine[g]	NA	NA	NA	NA	NA	NA	NA	NA
Heroin	0.1	0.0	0.0	0.0	0.0	0.0	0.0	0.0
Other opiates[h]	0.1	0.1	0.2	0.1	0.0	0.1	0.1	0.1
Stimulants[h]	0.5	0.4	0.5	0.5	0.6	0.7	1.2	1.1
Stimulants Adjusted[h,i]	*NA*	*NA*	*NA*	*NA*	*NA*	*NA*	*NA*	*0.7*
Crystal Methamphetamine[j]	NA	NA	NA	NA	NA	NA	NA	NA
Sedatives[h,k]	0.3	0.2	0.2	0.2	0.1	0.2	0.2	0.2
Barbiturates[h]	0.1	0.1	0.2	0.1	0.0	0.1	0.1	0.1
Methaqualone[h,k]	0.0	0.0	0.0	0.0	0.0	0.1	0.1	0.1
Tranquilizers[h]	0.1	0.2	0.3	0.1	0.1	0.1	0.1	0.1
Alcohol								
Daily	5.7	5.6	6.1	5.7	6.9	6.0	6.0	5.7
5+ drinks in a row/ last 2 weeks	36.8	37.1	39.4	40.3	41.2	41.2	41.4	40.5
Cigarettes								
Daily	26.9	28.8	28.8	27.5	25.4	21.3	20.3	21.1
Half-pack or more per day	17.9	19.2	19.4	18.8	16.5	14.3	13.5	14.2
Steroids[c]	NA	NA	NA	NA	NA	NA	NA	NA

Notes: Level of significance of difference between the two most recent classes: s = .05, ss = .01, sss = .001. NA indicates data not available. Any apparent inconsistency between the change estimate and the prevalence estimates for the two most recent classes is due to rounding error.

[a]Data based on four questionnaire forms in 1976–1988; N is four-fifths of N indicated. Data based on five questionnaire forms in 1989–1990; N is five-sixths of N indicated.

[b]Adjusted for underreporting of amyl and butyl nitrites. See text for details.

[c]Data based on a single questionnaire form; N is one-fifth of N indicated in 1979–1988 and one-sixth of N indicated in 1989 and 1990.

[d]Question text changed slightly in 1987.

[e]Adjusted for underreporting of PCP. See test for details.

[f]Data based on two questionnaire forms in 1987–1989; N is two-fifths of N indicated in 1987–1988 and two-sixths of N indicated in 1989. Data based on six questionnaire forms in 1990.

Table 15–4 Trends in Thirty-Day Prevalence of Daily Use of Twenty Types of Drugs *(continued)*

Class of 1983	Class of 1984	Class of 1985	Class of 1986	Class of 1987	Class of 1988	Class of 1989	Class of 1990	'89–'90 change
Percentage who used daily in last 30 days								
16300	15900	16000	15200	16300	16300	16700	15200	
5.5	5.0	4.9	4.0	3.3	2.7	2.9	2.2	– 0.7s
0.1	0.1	0.2	0.2	0.1	0.2	0.2	0.3	0.0
0.2	*0.2*	*0.4*	*0.4*	*0.4*	*0.3*	*0.3*	*0.3*	*0.0*
0.2	0.1	0.3	0.5	0.3	0.1	0.3	0.1	– 0.2
0.1	0.1	0.1	0.1	0.1	0.0	0.1	0.1	0.0
0.2	*0.2*	*0.3*	*0.3*	*0.2*	*0.0*	*0.3*	*0.3*	*0.0*
0.1	0.1	0.1	0.0	0.1	0.0	0.0	0.1	0.0
0.1	0.1	0.3	0.2	0.3	0.1	0.2	0.1	– 0.1
0.2	0.2	0.4	0.4	0.3	0.2	0.3	0.1	– 0.2s
NA	NA	NA	NA	0.1	0.1	0.2	0.1	– 0.2s
NA	NA	NA	NA	0.2	0.2	0.1	0.1	0.0
0.1	0.0	0.0	0.0	0.0	0.0	0.1	0.0	0.0
0.1	0.1	0.1	0.1	0.1	0.1	0.2	0.1	– 0.1
1.1	NA	NA	NA	NA	NA	NA	NA	NA
0.8	*0.6*	*0.4*	*0.3*	*0.3*	*0.3*	*0.3*	*0.2*	*– 0.1*
NA	NA	NA	NA	NA	NA	NA	0.1	NA
0.2	0.1	0.1	0.1	0.1	0.1	0.1	0.0	– 0.1
0.1	0.0	0.1	0.1	0.1	0.0	0.1	0.1	0.0
0.0	0.0	0.0	0.0	0.0	0.1	0.0	0.0	0.0
0.1	0.1	0.0	0.0	0.1	0.0	0.1	0.1	0.0
5.5	4.8	5.0	4.8	4.8	4.2	4.2	3.7	– 0.5
40.8	38.7	36.7	36.8	37.5	34.7	33.0	32.2	– 0.8
21.2	18.7	19.5	18.7	18.7	18.1	18.9	19.1	+ 0.2
13.8	12.3	12.5	11.4	11.4	10.6	11.2	11.3	+ 0.1
NA	NA	NA	NA	NA	NA	0.1	0.2	+ 0.1

[g]Data were based on a single questionnaire form in 1987–1989; N is one-fifth of N indicated in 1987–1988 and one-sixth of N indicated in 1989. Data based on four questionnaire forms in 1990; N is four-sixths of N indicated.
[h]Only drug use which was not under a doctor's orders is included here.
[i]Based on the data from the revised question, which attempts to exclude the inappropriate reporting of non-prescription stimulants.
[j]Data based on two questionnaire forms; N is two-sixths of N indicated.
[k]Data based on five questionnaire forms in 1975–1988, six questionnaire forms in 1989, and on a single questionnaire form in 1990; N is one-sixth of N indicated in 1990.
Source: Research Triangle Institute. (1984). *Economic costs to society of alcohol and drug abuse and mental illness.* Chapel Hill, NC: Author.

currently has under way a "massive" study to "crack the biological riddles of the disease" (Holden, 1991, p. 163).

Whether this study or any study will ever find the holy biological grail of an alcoholism gene is questioned by increasing numbers of critics. Their skepticism is fueled by the failure to establish biological connections (deWit & McCracken, 1990) and occasional reports, the last appearing in the *Journal of the American Medical Association* (Blum & Noble, 1990) announcing the long-awaited discovery of that gene. As in every other previous announcement of a genetic explanation for human behaviors like substance abuse and delinquency, the initial report of the finding has not been upheld (Holden, 1991). As Holden (1991, p. 163) reports, increasingly "scientists are beginning to suspect that there may be no genes for alcoholism per se, but rather for a general susceptibility to compulsive behaviors whose specific expression is shaped by environmental and temperamental factors."

As Peele (1986) points out alcoholism rates vary significantly among ethnic groups, genders, and social classes. Furthermore, methodological problems seriously compromise most studies. These problems lead Peele to conclude that genetic models by themselves are inadequate to explain alcohol abuse. Although the genetic model of alcoholism is tantalizing, Peele's caution seems warranted. The genetic argument remains a possible contributing factor but not the sole answer to explaining alcohol abuse.

To summarize, the family appears to be a major influence on adolescent drinking. Studies suggest that the alcohol-dependent young person comes from a strained home environment, and many researchers find similar drinking habits in parents and children. Finally, researchers continue their attempts to discover an alcoholism gene.

Tobacco, Marijuana, Inhalants, Steroids, Stimulants, Barbiturates, Cocaine, and Heroin

Tobacco

Consider the following:

1. In the senior high school class of 1990, 11.3% smoked at least 1/2 a pack a day (National Institute on Drug Abuse, 1991).
2. On average, smokers weigh seven pounds less than nonsmokers (Department of Health and Human Services, 1991b).
3. In 1988 then Surgeon General C. Everett Koop cautioned that, "the pharmacologic and behavioral processes that determine tobacco addiction are similar to those that determine addiction to drugs such as heroin and cocaine" (Byrne, 1988, p. 1143).
4. Tobacco addiction is killing 300,000 Americans each year (Byrne, 1988).

Tobacco *(Nicotiana tabacum)* was, along with syphilis, one of the many "gifts" from the New World. As with every other substance described in this chapter, tobacco was assumed to have healing powers. In England, for example, from 1573 to 1625 it was believed to be a useful drug for heart pains, snake bites, chills, fatigue, and had the "singular and divine virtue" of reducing individual risk to the Black Plague (Austin, 1979, p. 1). It was popularized in England by Sir Walter Raleigh for recreational use and, despite royal attempts to discourage its use, by 1575 tobacco was literally worth its weight in silver.

In the American colonies, tobacco was embraced by Virginia, which used it as currency until the early 1700s and rejected by the Massachusetts Bay Colony which prohibited smoking in 1632. Interestingly, it was U.S. travelers returning home from England that first introduced America to the cigarette in the 1850s. By 1885, cigarette production in the U.S. had reached one billion cigarettes a year and rapidly grew to 80 billion by the 1920s. The first (dare we say) serious medical evidence (beyond Dr. Pierce's protestations) of the harmful effects of cigarette smoking and lung disease was published in 1939. A quarter of a century later, the 1964 Surgeon General's Report established that relationship permanently. Even so 51 million Americans continue to use tobacco products (Austin, 1979; Gullotta & Blau, 1995; Resnick, 1990; Slade, 1989).

Substance Characteristics

Although it can be chewed, tobacco is generally smoked. The active ingredient in tobacco is nicotine, which is readily absorbed from tobacco smoke into the lungs. It then passes quickly into the blood stream and to receptor sites in the brain. Its psychoactive effects include at low doses increasing attention and vigilance and at higher levels inducing relaxation and lowering perceived stress. Withdrawal from the substance typically causes a decreased heart rate and thyroid functioning, weight gain, increases in anger and anxiety, restlessness, and impatience. Interestingly, nicotine accumulates in the body during the day and lasts overnight. Thus, regular smokers are continually exposed to its mood-altering effects. Nicotine is considered to have a high potential for creating a physical dependence such that the drug has been likened to cocaine and heroin. Tolerance (the need for increasing amounts of a drug to maintain its effect) is quite high (Benowitz, 1990; Cherek, Bennett, Roache, & Grabowski, 1990; Department of Health and Human Services, 1991b; Hughes, 1990; Schelling, 1992; Villanueva, et al., 1990).

User/Abuser Characteristics

Studies of adolescents who begin to use tobacco find that parental smoking behavior strongly correlates with adolescent use of the substance. Adolescents who use tobacco tend to have parents who use tobacco. In addition, studies suggest that adolescents who use tobacco have lower self-esteem and perceive themselves to be under greater stress than do nonsmoking adolescents (Department of Health and Human Services, 1991b; Bauman, Fisher, Bryan, & Chenoweth, 1984; Murphy & Price, 1988; Reppucci, Revenson, Aber, & Reppucci, 1991).

Marijuana

Consider the following:

1. In comparison to the high school class of 1979 when 60.4% admitted to using marijuana at least once in their lifetime, 47.9% of the class of 1990 made this admission (National Institute on Drug Abuse, 1991).

2. Of the graduating class of 1990, 47.9% had used marijuana at some time in their lives, 27% had used it in the last year, and 16.7% had used it in the previous month (Johnston, O'Malley, Bachman, 1991).

3. From the class of 1980 to the class of 1990, marijuana abuse (daily use) declined from 9.1% to 2.2% (Johnston, O'Malley, Bachman, 1991).

4. In 1987 a commercial form of THC was approved for use in controlling nausea and vomiting resulting from cancer chemotherapy (Department of Health and Human Services, 1991b).

5. In 1977 then President Jimmy Carter said that although "we can and should continue to discourage the use of marijuana . . . [I support] legislation amending federal law to eliminate all federal criminal penalties for the possession of up to one ounce of marijuana" (President Carter's Address, 1977, p. 6). Currently, 11 states have decriminalized marijuana by making the possession of small amounts a misdemeanor (*New York Times,* March 7, 1993).

The history of marijuana *(Cannabis sativa)* in North America is a curious one involving a king, an American president, ethnic prejudice, and the Great Depression. To begin at the beginning, the earliest English settlements in America raised marijuana (then called "hemp") as a cash crop. The hemp plant was extremely useful. Its fibers could be turned into sails, linens, blankets, clothing, flags, and, most important of all, rope. So important was this commodity to England that King James I ordered the settlers of Virginia to produce hemp for the mother country (Austin, 1979; Grinspoon, 1971; Sloman, 1979).

Production of marijuana continued after the revolution of 1776 without concern for its intoxicating qualities. In fact, George Washington cultivated the plant. Like many other gentlemen of the time, he raised hemp to be sold for making cloth and rope. At the time of the Civil War, the growing of marijuana as a cash crop declined. Other parts of the world, notably Russia and the Philippines, produced a product superior to that grown here.

Like many now illegal substances, marijuana was used from the 1800s to the 1930s for medicinal purposes. However, it never captured the support other drugs were able to attract. The lack of medical enthusiasm for marijuana was due to the variable quality of the psychoactive substance found in the plant, THC (delta-9-tetrahydrocannabinol).

Several social histories of marijuana published in recent years suggest that the events that moved marijuana from being considered a relatively harmless plant to the status of "killer weed" began with the Great Depression. The circumstances surrounding this redefinition include the migration of Mexicans into the United States and the scarcity of work. It appears that in the late 1920s and early 1930s the largest group of users of marijuana for recreational purposes was Mexican Americans. Ethnic prejudices against this immigrant group fueled by the high unemployment of the Great Depression evidently encouraged federal authorities to label marijuana a narcotic (Austin, 1979; Grinspoon, 1971; Sloman, 1979).

Does marijuana offer "one moment of bliss and a lifetime of regret"? Is it "the new drug menace destroying the youth of America" or "a violent narcotic,

. . . the real Public Enemy Number One"? In the 1938 cult classic *Reefer Madness,* the answer to these film-posed questions is an unqualified "Yes!" The likely response of many people educated in the 1970s through the mid-1980s would be "No!" What is the truth?

Substance Characteristics

Although it can be ingested, marijuana is usually smoked. The effects range from mild euphoria to shifting sensory images to hallucinations. Depending on the potency of the sample, the effects are usually experienced within ten minutes and can last for several hours. The potency of marijuana is dependent on the concentration of THC in the plant. Over the past decade the potency or concentration of THC has increased from 0.5% in 1979 to a present estimated 15%. Hashish and hashish oil, both derived from the marijuana plant, contain far greater amounts of THC, so that the "mind-altering" effects of these two drugs are substantially greater. Marijuana is considered to have a low potential for creating psychologi-

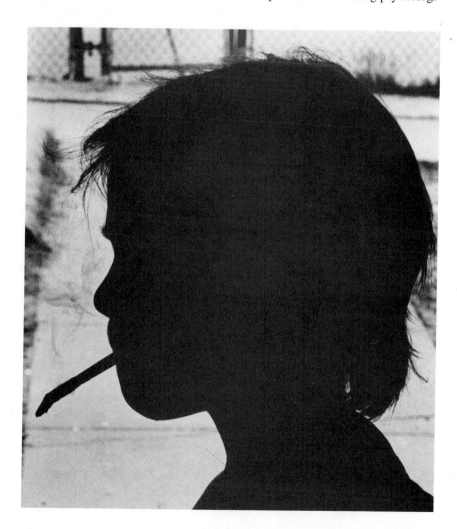

Certain forms of drug abuse are on the decline. Each type of drug seems to have its period of heightened popularity.

cal dependence. Tolerance can occur but is unusual when used infrequently or in small doses (National Institute on Drug Abuse, 1987b; Department of Health and Human Services, 1991b).

User/Abuser Characteristics

Studies of the motivations and personal characteristics of marijuana users and nonusers show no differences. Occasional marijuana users are not seen as maladjusted or psychopathological in their use of this substance (R. Jessor, 1979; Pascale, Hurd, & Primavera, 1980).

In contrast, according to a study funded by the National Institute on Drug Abuse (NIDA), the homes and personal lives of marijuana-*abusing* adolescents are conflict ridden (Hendin, Pollinger, Ulman, & Carr, 1981). The study said the relationships between parents and adolescents were strained to the breaking point. Marijuana-abusing adolescents acted out, often violently, at home and were frequently disruptive in school and other settings.

These young people viewed their parents as insensitive and uncaring toward them. Although all the families participating in this study were intact, each appeared to have a history of marital turmoil dating back to the early childhood of the marijuana-abusing adolescent. Of the 17 young people and their families involved in the study, "several . . . had at least one parent who was alcoholic, a characteristic which has been shown to be significantly correlated with adolescent substance abuse" (p. 71). These young people expressed a "high degree of self-hatred," indicative of low self-esteem (p. 20). Many appeared depressed, and at least one was suicidal.

In the opinion of the researchers, marijuana served several important functions in these young people's lives. The first was public expression of defiance against parental and community authority. Second was the self-destructiveness that seemed to mark the life of each participant. Third was the use of marijuana to numb the intense anger these young people felt toward their parents. Next, it appeared to the authors that these young people used marijuana to compensate for feeling "that they amounted to nothing within the context of their own families" (p. 76). Finally, marijuana permitted these adolescents to escape the competitive academic and peer pressures around them.

We can infer that, in those situations in which marijuana use becomes abuse, it is very difficult to attribute the decrease in personal functioning solely to the drug. The findings of a sense of alienation (R. Jessor et al., 1980), less religiosity (R. Jessor et al., 1980; Perry & Murray, 1985; Thomas & Carver, 1990), lower academic-grade expectations (Kandel, 1981a), and weak parental control, affection, and support (Vicary & Lerner, 1986) for both marijuana-abusing youths and alcohol-dependent adolescents raise a real question of whether it is the drug or the young person's life environment that precipitates increased use. Furthermore, since both alcohol-dependent and marijuana-abusing youths are likely to be abusing other drugs, attributing decreased personal functioning to marijuana alone is highly unrealistic (R. Jessor et al., 1980).

Such a position does not mean that marijuana is without negative effects. Quite the contrary: it has been clearly shown, for instance, that marijuana and driving do not mix (Pace, 1981) and that smoking it is more harmful than cigarette smoking (Kozel & Adams, 1986; Department of Health and Human Services, 1991b). Marijuana has been shown to impair short-term memory and motivation (National Institute on Drug Abuse, 1982), and in persons with a history of emotional illness it may produce an acute toxic psychosis, including delusions, hallucinations, and agitated behavior (R. T. Jones, 1980; National Institute on Drug Abuse, 1987b; Weller & Halikas, 1985).

Inhalants

Consider these facts:

1. Inhalant use decreases with age.
2. Of the graduating high school class of 1990, 18% had used inhalants at some time in their lives, 6.9% had used it in the last year, and 2.7% had used it in the previous month (Johnston, O'Malley, and Bachman, 1991).
3. Inhalant abuse (daily use) by the class of 1990 was almost statistically nonexistent (0.3%) (Johnston, O'Malley, and Bachman, 1991).

The inhaling of model-airplane glue, gasoline, paint thinner, and other substances to achieve an intoxicating effect seems most prevalent among males aged 10 to 14. The young adolescent may turn to solvents because of a lack of access to other substances. Thus, the decline in solvent use as the adolescent grows older is thought to be related to increasing access to other intoxicants (alcohol, sedatives, and so forth). According to one researcher, no other category of substances discussed in this chapter poses such danger to physical health as solvent abuse (S. Cohen, 1979).[*] Disturbingly, the trend in lifetime inhalant use continues to grow. With the exception of the year 1988 when a very modest three-tenths of 1% drop was recorded, lifetime inhalant use has increased from 10.3% in 1976 to 18% in 1990 (National Institute on Drug Abuse, 1991).

Substance Characteristics

Solvent inhalers generally place the substance in a plastic bag, pour it onto a rag, or sniff it directly from the original container. The effects, ranging from alcohol-like intoxication to severe disorientation to unconsciousness, are usually experienced a few minutes after inhaling the solvent. The degree of effect is determined by the nature of the solvent, its strength, and the length of time it is inhaled. Because some solvents, such as tetrachloride and benzene, are poisons, the solvent abuser does run a risk of severe injury or death. Even those chemicals such as toluene that are considered relatively safe have been associated with disorders of the kidneys, nervous system, and bone marrow (Cohen 1979, 1981; National Institute on Drug Abuse, 1987b). Finally, some researchers suggest that long-time solvent abusers run a high risk of brain injury (Cohen, 1979, 1981) although others discount these brain-injury suggestions (G. E. Barnes, 1979). Tolerance varies with the substance inhaled. Although only a minority of young

---

[*]In recent years amyl and butyl nitrates have been included in this category, and as a result the usage of inhalants has statistically increased. The popularity of the nitrates is linked to their over-the-counter availability and their use to facilitate lovemaking in relationships in which anal intercourse is practiced. As we have said, the nitrates are immunosuppressants and thus compound the problems of AIDS sufferers.

people experiment with solvent use and most of those who do experiment do so for only a short time and incur no lasting health damage, solvent use must be considered to have a high potential for physical damage to the user.

User/Abuser Characteristics

Studies report solvent use to be higher among Hispanics and Native Americans than among either Blacks or Whites in the United States (Barnes, 1979; Cohen, 1979; Rodriguez-Andrew, 1985). Barnes attributes the higher incidence of solvent use among the first two groups to the greater stress and alienation they experience within our society. The solvent abuser is pictured as a male, a poor student, and depressed, anxious, and alienated (Barnes, 1979; Cohen, 1979). The influence of the peer group is a major factor in solvent abuse (Cohen, 1979). The family is also a primary contributor. Studies show that poor parent/child relationships, divorce, alcoholism, and other problems are common in families with solvent-abusing adolescents (Barnes, 1979; National Institute on Drug Abuse, 1978a).

Anabolic Steroids

Consider the following:

1. Of the graduating high school class of 1990, 2.9% had used steroids at some time in their lives, 1.7% had used it in the last year, and 1% had used it in the previous month (Johnston, O'Malley, and Bachman, 1991).
2. Steroid abuse (daily use) by the class of 1990 was almost statistically nonexistent (0.2%) (National Institute on Drug Abuse, 1991).
3. Steroids do not increase or enhance athletic ability (Cicero & O'Connor, 1990).

Attempts to improve athletic performance predate the Greek Olympiads. In recent years a group of drugs first developed in Europe in the 1930s has been used and abused by athletes trying to gain an edge on their competition. Those drugs, anabolic steroids, are synthesized derivatives of the male hormone testosterone (Kochakian, 1990). It has been estimated that there are more than 1 million regular steroid users in North America, and that 96% of professional football players may have used the drug, as well as 80 to 99% of bodybuilders (Goldstein, 1990). Among all American adolescent athletes, it is estimated that 7% of the males and 1% of the females may have used the drug (Yesalis, Anderson, Buckley, & Wright, 1990). It has also been estimated that nearly 80% of the steroids produced in the United States are not used for legitimate purposes (Office of Substance Abuse Prevention, 1989) and that black market sales of the drug presently exceed $400 million a year (Goldstein, 1990).

Substance Characteristics

Anabolic steroids are injected into the body in the belief that they will improve muscular development and athletic performance. Users report euphoria, a sense of well-being, increased libido, aggressive and invincible feelings, and tenseness (Cicero & O'Connor, 1990; Katz & Pope, 1990). Interestingly, most studies do not find evidence to support the contention that steroids improve either male muscular development or athletic performance (Cicero & O'Connor, 1990;

Steroid use is all too common in certain types of athletics.

Lamp, 1984; Lombardo, 1990). Steroid use by female athletes has not been as well studied. However, as these drugs are testosterone variants, it is reasonable to believe that they would increase a female's strength. This is, of course, at the cost of creating females who develop many of the secondary sex characteristics of males as a result of their steroid use.

The abuse of steroids by adolescents can result in endocrine disturbances, cardiac and liver problems, stunted growth, testicular atrophy, impotency, and acne (Cicero & O'Connor, 1990; Lamp, 1984).

Steroids do have legitimate medical uses in preventing muscular atrophy in injured individuals, in treating males with testosterone deficiency, and in treating abnormally delayed sexual maturation in adolescent females. There is no evidence that tolerance of the drug develops.

User/Abuser Characteristics

Unlike other substances in this chapter that are taken for their psychoactive effects, users of steroids take the drug to enhance athletic ability. They are achievers, individuals who commit themselves to rigorous training schedules in order to further their athletic ability.

Nevertheless, the drug does have psychoactive side effects. Individuals using steroids may become more aggressive and engage in irrational destructive behavior sometimes referred to as "roid rage" in response to even minor frustrations (Cicero & O'Connor, 1990). Reports suggest users may experience paranoid episodes and depression (Tennant, Black, & Voy, 1988). In one study, for example, Katz and Pope (1990) interviewed 41 male bodybuilders and football players who admitted using steroids. They found that more than 1 in 5 reported experiencing depression after steroid use. Twelve percent (5) reported psychotic symptoms.

Hallucinogens (LSD and PCP)

Consider the following:

1. Of the high school class of 1990, 8.7% at some time in their lives had used LSD (National Institute on Drug Abuse, 1991).
2. Almost 3% of the class of 1990 at some time in their lives used PCP (National Institute on Drug Abuse, 1991).
3. LSD and PCP abuse (daily use) by the class of 1990 was almost statistically nonexistent (0.1%) (Johnston, O'Malley, and Bachman, 1991).
4. PCP can induce a psychotic state in many ways indistinguishable from schizophrenia (Balster, 1990).

The LSD antics of the Doors lead singer Jim Morrison to the Jefferson Airplane's *White Rabbit* and Peter Fonda's "acid dropping" on film in the late 1960s replaced the more innocent antics of the *Beach Blanket Bingo* gang for many adolescents three decades ago. With the high priest of the psychedelic movement, Timothy Leary, urging young people to "turn on, tune in, and drop out," many adolescents—possibly disillusioned with the Vietnam War, and the assassinations of John and Robert Kennedy and Dr. Martin Luther King, Jr.—may have followed Leary's advice. The present-day use of these mind-altering substances remains basically unchanged from 1986.

LSD

Lysergic acid diethylamide is ingested, usually in the form of tablets, small squares of gelatin, or impregnated paper. Similar substances are found naturally in, for example, the ergot fungus, which grows on rye and other cereal grasses, and in morning-glory seeds.* Its effects range from time/distance distortions and hallucinations to psychotic episodes. The drug typically takes effect within 30 minutes, and the effects last 8 to 12 hours in most cases, depending on the dose.

---

*For those interested in swallowing a packet of morning glory seeds or brewing a cup of tea with them, the advice is "don't." For several years most seed companies have been spraying the seeds with chemicals that will cause vomiting and diarrhea in the user.

Flashbacks (the reentry into a hallucinogenic state without taking the substance) are reported in some instances, and for some young people, the psychotic behavior resulting from the ingestion of LSD has continued for much longer than 12 hours. Users do not become physically dependent. Psychological dependence on LSD is considered highly unlikely.

Research on LSD consumers has focused on the abuser of LSD, not the user. With this qualifier in mind, we can describe LSD abusers as often coping poorly with a disorganized and confused personal life and as in search of some meaning to their existence (A. Jones, 1973; Smart & Jones, 1970). Family hardships, such as broken homes, alcoholic parents, and poor parent/adolescent relationships, are frequently present (Welpton, 1968). Abuse of more than one drug is very likely to occur with the LSD user (Seffrin & Seehafer, 1976).

PCP

Phencyclidine can be taken orally, injected, or smoked. First synthesized in 1926, it was considered as an anesthetic for humans in the 1950s but was rejected due to its severe side effects. PCP reappeared in the 1960s as an anesthetic for animals. Since 1978 the drug has not been available on the commercial market. The effects of PCP, as with LSD, vary with regard to the amount and purity of the substance consumed. Reported user experiences range from a sense of detachment, slurred speech, and numbness to hallucinations, image distortions, and a feeling of impending doom to paranoia and violent behavior. PCP's unique and severe behavior toxicity enables it to produce psychoses indistinguishable from schizophrenia in some young people. Tolerance of LSD and PCP can occur, necessitating increasing amounts of the chemicals to achieve the desired effect (Balster, 1990; Fram & Stone, 1986; Wilkins, 1990; Zukin & Javitt, 1990).

The early history of the use of PCP suggests that the adolescents of the hippie counterculture of the 1960s recognized the potency and profound toxicity of this chemical and avoided it. Reports suggest that use of PCP (known then as the PeaCe Pill) was often not intentional but occurred through the purchase of other, impure drugs that contained PCP. Some reports even suggest that many users were "victims of deception" (Pittel & Oppedahl, 1979, p. 251). The concern of current investigators is that PCP is being sought on purpose by many adolescents (National Institute on Drug Abuse, 1978b; Pittel & Oppedahl, 1979). Why is this occurring?

R. C. Petersen and Stillman (1979) suggest that there are several motivating factors encouraging PCP use. For some young people a low dose of PCP produces a "mind-blowing, fantastic" feeling. For other young people the uncertainty of whether the drug experience will be pleasant or unpleasant provides the motivation for use, and for still others, PCP provides an incredible (but mistaken) illusion of strength, power, and invulnerability.

The PCP abuser is likely to use the drug "in runs" lasting two to three days. Weight loss, paranoid ideation, and violent and schizoid behavior in such abusers are not uncommon (Fauman & Fauman, 1979; S. E. Lerner & Burns, 1979; National Institute on Drug Abuse, 1987b; Petersen & Stillman, 1979).

While no one personality type has been linked to this drug (Petersen & Stillman, 1979), PCP abusers are likely to be White and not poor. They are often polydrug users, have arrest records for violent crimes, have school difficulties, and have a record of attempted suicides (Lerner & Burns, 1979; Simonds & Kashani, 1979).

Finally, DeAngelis, Koon, and Goldstein (1980), using a highly restricted sample of PCP users, dispute the findings of researchers who suggest that PCP has disastrous long-term effects on the emotional stability of the adolescent user. Their study of 70 occasional and chronic PCP users does not reveal evidence of the long-term bizarre or violent behavior that has been suggested to be an after-effect of PCP use.

More recent support for this conclusion can also be found in the third triennial report to the U.S. Congress from the Secretary of the Department of Health and Human Services (1991b). It finds less than conclusive evidence that the majority of PCP users become either violent or psychotic. It should be cautioned, however, that these statements do not in any way diminish the unpredictability of this chemical in affecting behavior.

Stimulants

Consider these facts:

1. Lifetime stimulant use by males (17.2%) and females (17.8%) in the high school class of 1990 was virtually identical (Johnston, O'Malley, and Bachman, 1991).
2. Of the graduating class of 1990, 17.5% had used stimulants at some time in their lives, 9.1% had used it in the last year, and 3.7% had used it in the previous month (Johnston, O'Malley, and Bachman, 1991).
3. Stimulant abuse (daily use) by the class of 1990 was almost statistically nonexistent (0.2%) (Johnston, O'Malley, and Bachman, 1991).

Some of the more commonly known stimulants are nicotine, caffeine, cocaine, and methamphetamine or "ice." (See Box 15–1.) Our interest here is in amphetamines, known popularly as "speed."

Substance Characteristics

Amphetamines can be taken orally or injected. Users report effects varying from increased alertness, insomnia, loss of appetite, and euphoria at medically prescribed levels to agitation, depression, confusion, hallucinations, paranoia, and in some situations convulsions at higher levels. The effect of amphetamines increases directly in proportion to the level of usage involved. Unless they are injected into the bloodstream, their effects are felt in about 30 minutes. Although the possibility of physical dependence on amphetamines is low to moderate, the chances of psychological dependence are high. Tolerance can occur very rapidly. For example, abusers have been known to inject 1000 milligrams of amphetamines into their bodies at one time, whereas a prescribed dose is between 2.5 and 15 milligrams per day.

User/Abuser Characteristics

Millions of adolescents and adults have used amphetamines over the years. From the struggling dieter to the student "pulling an all-nighter" and the sleepy truck driver to the professional football player, they have used amphetamines to lose

---

Box 15–1   Ice: The Power of Smoke

For a drug to produce dependence it must be effectively absorbed into the bloodstream. It must rapidly enter the brain and be psychoactive. Smoking is one of the most effective ways to effect the passage of psychoactive drugs to the brain. The inhaled smoke occupies space in the lungs, the sole function of which is to rapidly transfer that air into the bloodstream and then throughout the body. Indeed, the entire blood supply flows through the lungs once every minute (Benowitz, 1990). With the emergence of deadly diseases like AIDS, interest among drug users in smoking rather than in injecting their substances has increased (Cook & Jeffcoat, 1990). With this new interest have come new and more addictive drugs.

One of these is methamphetamine, or "ice." The street name for this synthesized drug comes from its sheetlike transparent crystal appearance. Belonging to the amphetamine family, "ice" when smoked more readily enters the brain than do other amphetamines because it is more soluble in the brain's tissues. The feelings of excitement and euphoria from "ice" may last up to 24 hours, often followed by the need for sleep. The "crash" or depression following the use of the substance has been described as very intense, causing the user to want to use the drug again. Tolerance and dependence to the drug develop very rapidly. As "ice" is a laboratory-made substance, not only could it in theory be produced in limitless amounts, but it also could be made anywhere (Cho, 1990). Thus, the control of this substance is very difficult to enforce.

---

weight, to stay awake, or to stimulate alertness and increase aggression. Their availability in medicine cabinets across the country (thus permitting "closet" drug use) helps to explain their popularity with females (National Institute on Drug Abuse, 1987b).

Amphetamine abusers (these include those same medicine-cabinet borrowers, sleepy students and truck drivers, and athletes) are similar to other drug abusers in many respects. Likely to be multiple-drug abusers, they are described as failures in school and personal relationships (R. Brook, Kaplum, & Whitehead, 1974). The family again emerges as a primary contributing factor, with the home environment described as a cold, unfeeling, and uncaring place (Brook et al., 1974).

Barbiturates

Note the following findings:

1. Approximately 81 million prescriptions for barbiturates are written each year (Department of Health and Human Services, 1991b).
2. Of the high school graduating class of 1990, 6.8% had used barbiturates at some time in their lives, 3.4% had used it in the last year, and 1.3% had used it in the previous month (Johnston, O'Malley, and Bachman, 1991).
3. Barbiturate abuse (daily use) by the class of 1990 was almost statistically nonexistent (0.1%) (Johnston, O'Malley, and Bachman, 1991).
4. Adolescent use of these drugs is about the same for males and females (Johnston, O'Malley, and Bachman, 1991).

Booze and pills have been the death of many a creative artist, from Marilyn Monroe to Elvis Presley. The combination of too much alcohol and too many barbiturates (or just too many barbiturates alone) drastically lowers blood pressure and respiration, resulting in the loss of life for nearly 5,000 people in the United States each year (D. E. Smith, Wesson, & Seymour, 1979).

Substance Characteristics

Barbiturates are most frequently taken orally, but they can be dissolved in water and injected. Injected, they produce the warm, sleepy sensations commonly associated with a "rush." Taken orally, the drug takes effect in about 30 minutes. In low doses, barbiturates produce a mild sedation. As the amount increases, the effects range from a sense of well-being to depression to alcohol-like intoxication marked by slurred speech and impaired motor coordination to unconsciousness, coma, and/or death resulting from an overdose. Tolerance to barbiturates builds rapidly, resulting in the increased danger to the barbiturate abuser of reaching unsafe or lethal doses of the drug in a relatively short time. Barbiturates are regarded as having a moderately high potential for creating a physical and/or psychological dependence (National Institute on Drug Abuse, 1987b; Department of Health and Human Services, 1991b).

We should note before we conclude this section that barbiturate abusers should never attempt to quit the habit without medical supervision. Not all barbiturates are alike in their effect on the individual attempting to quit. The barbiturate abuser runs a real risk of life-threatening convulsions, delirium, and grand mal seizures during withdrawal. To avoid these withdrawal symptoms, the abuser is best advised to find the proper medical care to ensure that a bad experience is not the last experience (National Institute on Drug Abuse, 1987b).

User/Abuser Characteristics

The typical barbiturate user who appears in the emergency room of a hospital is White, female, and between the ages of 20 and 40 (Department of Health and Human Services, 1991b). Although nearly all barbiturate abusers are aware of the dangers of combining alcohol and pills, they do it anyway. This behavior leads some researchers to conclude that barbiturate abusers have suicidal personalities. Anxious, depressed, with low self-esteem, and viewing themselves as failures (Lech, Gary, & Ury, 1975), abusers mirror the alcohol-dependent personality in many aspects of personal, school, and family life.

Cocaine

Here are four important facts:

1. Of the high school graduating class of 1990, 9.4% had used cocaine at some time in their lives, 5.3% had used it in the last year, and 1.9% had used it in the previous month (Johnston, O'Malley, and Bachman, 1991).
2. In the class of 1990, lifetime cocaine use was higher for males (11.5%) than for females (7.2%) (Johnston, O'Malley, and Bachman, 1991).
3. Lifetime prevalence use of this drug was highest among seniors living in the West (13.4%) and lowest in the North Central (7.2%) part of the United States (Johnston, O'Malley, and Bachman, 1991).
4. Cocaine abuse (daily use) by the class of 1990 was almost statistically nonexistent (0.1%) (Johnston, O'Malley, and Bachman, 1991).

With the recent published reports of its abuse by athletes, movie stars, and the very wealthy, cocaine has acquired a degree of notoriety. Its history is particularly fascinating, for its use reaches back hundreds of years, to before the Incan Empire, and involves a pope, a soft-drink company, and the founder of the psychoanalytic movement.

Cocaine is found in the leaves of a South American plant, the coca shrub (*Erythroxylon coca*). Possessing religious significance for the Incan Empire, coca was controlled directly by the Incan emperor, and its use was limited to the privileged nobility of that society. This custom changed with the invasion of the Spanish, who more freely distributed coca among the South American natives because they had discovered that its stimulant effect resulted in higher worker productivity (Inglis, 1975).

Coca did not become popular in Europe until the mid-1850s, when it was introduced into a number of products ranging from patent medicines to wine. The wine, in particular a variety called Mariani's Wine, won a number of high endorsements, including one from Pope Leo XIII. The popularity of coca spread back overseas, this time to North America, where in Atlanta in 1886 a druggist introduced a patent medicine containing coca. Claimed to be a remedy for a number of troublesome ailments, Coca-Cola, as it was called, gained widespread popularity. One additional note on this patent drug is warranted: long before the 1906 Pure Food and Drug Act was passed, the makers of this no-longer-popular patent medicine but now-popular soda-fountain beverage had replaced coca with other substances (Grinspoon & Bakalar, 1976).

The isolation of the "kick" in coca, cocaine, occurred in Germany, where it was used as a stimulant and as an anesthetic in eye surgery. The medical popularity of cocaine as an anesthetic, a reliever of depression, and a substitute for morphine in treating cases of morphine addiction spread quickly. With none other than Dr. Sigmund Freud describing it as a "magical drug," the popularity of cocaine moved from the medical to the public arena (Brecher, 1972).

Portrayed as a quick pick-me-up for the tired of mind or body, more enjoyable than alcohol and without the side effects, cocaine was widely used by the public for several years. Interest in cocaine diminished as reports began to come in that it produced strong psychological dependence, created severe mental disturbances, and in some cases even led to death. Freud's own defense of cocaine abruptly ended with the emotional breakdown of a close friend, Dr. von Fleischl-Marxow. Marxow's use of the drug to treat his morphine addiction had reached outlandish proportions, and he developed a paranoid psychosis marked by formication. (Formication is the belief that insects or snakes are crawling on or under the skin.) This incident had such a profound impact on Freud that he foreswore the use of cocaine from that time forward in his personal life and his medical practice (Grinspoon & Bakalar, 1976).

Substance Characteristics

Cocaine can be injected but is more frequently inhaled ("snorted"). In its free-base form it can be smoked. Its effects on the user range from excitement and increased alertness to, in very large doses or with prolonged use, hallucinations and convulsions. Death can result from an ingested overdose of 1.2 grams or from applying 20 milligrams to the mucous membranes (American Society for Pharmacology, 1987; Gay, Sheppard, Inaba, & Newmeyer, 1973; Jones, 1987; Siegel, 1987).

The powerful addictive ability of cocaine is explained by its effect on the dopaminergic synapse of the brain. Cocaine prolongs the activity of dopamine in the synapse by flooding it with the neurotransmitter. If given unlimited access to the drug, cocaine has the ability to dominate instinctual behaviors like eating, sleeping, and the sexual drive (Gawin, 1991; Holden, 1989; Wise, 1987). This has made the treatment of cocaine addiction particularly difficult. Encouragingly, a recent report in *Science* suggests that a chemical enzyme is under development that may speed the breakdown of cocaine in the bloodstream, thus robbing the drug of its powerful "rush" effect before it reaches the brain (Morell, 1993).

Psychological dependence is very high, and tolerance builds rapidly. Although in the past the high cost of cocaine made it difficult for adolescents to develop a habit (dependence), the appearance of a freebase form of cocaine called "crack" in a 65 to 100 milligram dose for $10 has placed the drug "temporarily" within the price range of young people. The word *temporarily* is used because the cost of maintaining a crack habit will rapidly escalate, forcing the young person into either treatment or illegal activity (Department of Health and Human Services, 1991b). (See Box 15–2.)

User/Abuser Characteristics

It is highly unusual to find a pure cocaine abuser. Rather, research and clinical evidence suggests, the so-called cocaine abuser is in fact a polydrug user (E. H. Adams & Kozel, 1985; Wesson & Smith, 1985). Likely to be fatigued, depressed, and impotent, the cocaine abuser is, not surprisingly, given the cost of supporting a cocaine habit, in serious financial trouble (Clayton, 1985; M. S. Gold, Washton, & Dackis, 1985; Siegel, 1987; Wesson & Smith, 1979, 1985). In turn, the abuser's financial difficulties understandably contribute to strained family relations.

As the availability of cocaine has increased a clearer and sadder picture of the cocaine abuser has developed. Because of cocaine's addictive power, the drug has the ability to dominate an individual's life. For those individuals who are able to contain their use of the substance, evidence suggests that they appear as emotionally healthy as the next person (Grinspoon & Bakalar, 1976; Siegel, 1987).

Heroin

Consider these facts:

1. Only 1.3% of the high school class of 1990 had ever used heroin (National Institute on Drug Abuse, 1991).
2. The use of heroin by adolescents at any time in their lives has declined since 1975, when the figure for the graduating class was 2% (National Institute on Drug Abuse, 1991).
3. Heroin abuse (daily use) by senior classes since 1976 has been statistically nonexistent (Johnston, O'Malley, and Bachman, 1991).

Box 15–2   Crack: Cheap Thrills

Cocaine that has been chemically altered, using baking soda and heat, into a "base" is called crack. The origin of the word can be traced to the tendency of the substance to crackle when it is heated. Processed crack looks like small lumps or soap shavings, with a porcelain-appearing texture.

There is no question but that cocaine can be addictive. The experiences of Dr. von Fleischl-Marxow described earlier in this section certainly confirm that observation. What has controlled the incidence of cocaine dependence for the last four decades has been its high cost. The appearance of crack is deeply disturbing for two reasons. First, its price per "hit" places the substance within the means of nearly everyone. Second, crack is the most potent form of cocaine. Smoking the substance produces an immediate "high" of short duration that is followed by an intense "low" that leaves the user wanting more. Given crack's low cost, that need for more can be satisfied—again and again and again until the individual is addicted. The dependence is so intense that a cocaine-addicted individual will prefer the drug over all else (E. H. Adams & Durell, 1987).*

The powerful addictive ability of the drug and its initial low cost have created an economic job market albeit fraught with danger for many unemployed city youth (Johnson, Williams, Sanabria, & Dei, 1990). These young people either sell the drug on the streets or steer individuals to places where the drug can be purchased and used. These "crack houses" are reminiscent of the opium dens that catered to the addicts of the last century and similar to the "shooting galleries" found in most cities today, where heroin addicts can rent the works to inject themselves with a nickel bag of dope. Whether it be a crack house, opium den, or shooting gallery, its customers have become slaves to a substance (National Institute on Drug Abuse, 1987a).

*Smoking cocaine is not new to our time. At the turn of the century the respected pharmaceutical firm of Parke, Davis & Co. manufactured two such cocaine products—coca cheroots and coca cigarettes—for sale. Each is thought to have contained between 0.5 to 1% cocaine (Jones, 1990).

Heroin has a special meaning in the hearts of most Americans. Through such television shows as *The Naked City, The Streets of San Francisco,* and *Miami Vice* and such films as *The French Connection, The French Connection II, The Deep,* and Andy Warhol's *Trash,* the American public has come to fear the drug.

The opium poppy *(Papaver somniferum)* grows in many areas of the world—from Southeast Asia to India, Turkey, Hungary, Yugoslavia, and Mexico, to name just a few. Its use as a medicine to ease pain and to treat dysentery, malaria, and other ailments dates back to before the birth of Christ. Opium and its chief constituent, morphine (from which heroin is synthesized), were easily obtained in the 19th century throughout North America, as we showed at the beginning of this chapter, and much of the rest of the world as well.* Heroin was first produced in 1898. The availability of all three drugs in the United States was not really limited until the Harrison Narcotic Act of 1914.

Substance Characteristics

Heroin can be sniffed or smoked, but it is most commonly injected. The warm "rush" that comes moments after the injection has been reported to feel like a

---

*China's attempt to stop the British importation of opium into China for use by the populace created the Opium War of 1839–1842. The Chinese government's loss of that war ensured the populace an adequate supply for the next several decades.

whole-body orgasm. This sensation is soon followed in most cases by lethargy and the need to sleep. The potential for physical and psychological dependence is high, and tolerance builds rapidly. Street heroin is sold in "bags" (a single dose) of 100 milligrams. Of this amount, perhaps 5% is heroin. The remainder may be sugar, starch, powdered milk, quinine, or some other substances. Occasionally, heroin users purchase a bag containing a much higher percentage of heroin than they have been accustomed to using. The result of injecting this higher percentage of heroin is an overdose, most often resulting in death.

A second threat to the IV heroin user is the development of AIDS. The use of contaminated needles is rapidly spreading this deadly viral infection among heroin users (Kozel & Adams, 1986). Currently, 25% (and that figure is rapidly escalating) of all AIDS victims are IV drug users (National Institute on Drug Abuse, 1987b; Department of Health and Human Services, 1991b).

User/Abuser Characteristics

Although it is possible to use heroin and not become addicted, the tendency is for users to become abusers and then dependent in a relatively short time (Zinberg, 1979). Part of the reason is the rapid buildup of tolerance to the drug.

Although a heroin-dependent individual can come from any socioeconomic group, the poor are disproportionately represented. Coming from a background of poverty, hopelessness, and conflict, these heroin addicts are viewed as feeling worthless, being manipulative, and unable to handle frustration (Collum & Pike, 1976; Craig, 1986; Kurtines, Hogan, & Weiss, 1975). They are also seen as depressed, aggressive, self-destructive, unable to cope with stress, and escaping reality through denial, rationalization, and drug dependence (Craig, 1986; Woody & Blaine, 1979). The addict is likely to come from a poor home situation marked, again, by family turmoil, parental rejection, and loose supervision. It also appears that (as with the alcohol-dependent individual) the addict is likely to have a parent or parents who abuse alcohol or other drugs (Braucht, Brakarsh, Follinstad, & Berry, 1973; Woody & Blaine, 1979).

Summary

Two substances, solvents and PCP, emerge as the greatest immediate threat for serious physical or psychological damage to the user.* Although a small minority of adolescents become drug abusers or dependent, those who do are most frequently multiple-drug users. The factors contributing to abuse or dependence include personality, family, and community variables.

Most studies show drug-abusing or drug-dependent individuals as having low self-esteem and feelings of helplessness (Reardon & Griffing, 1983). They are anxious, depressed, restless individuals who internalize their anger and depression in self-destructive drug use. Likely to be delinquent (although some researchers take issue with this point; see Farrow & French, 1986; Vingilis,

---

*This statement assumes that the other drugs purchased on the street are in fact the drugs the buyer has asked for and that in the case of injectable substances the user is using "clean works." Since there are no consumer laws protecting the illicit-drug user and since quality control has been known to slip on occasion, wisdom would suggest that one should not experiment. But in wisdom's absence, *caveat emptor* ("let the buyer beware")!

1981), and heavily influenced by their peer group, these young people use delinquency and relationships with their friends as attempts to secure replacements after their rejection of—and rejection by—family, school, and community.

The families of these adolescents are viewed as major contributors to their use of drugs. Loose parental control, poor parent/adolescent relationships, high family discord, and divorce are common. There is also evidence that parental abuse of alcohol and other drugs sets an early and poor example for the child to follow in adolescence.

Alcohol and Drug Use Patterns Among Ethnic and Racial Minority Groups

Varying patterns exist in alcohol and drug use among minorities. Drinking patterns are affected by a host of factors that distinguish ethnic and racial minority groups—poverty and social class, cultural beliefs and practices, prejudice and discrimination, a group's history of usage of substances, relationship patterns, and a group's norms about drinking. In this section we examine substance use and abuse patterns among four ethnic minority groups.

African Americans

There is evidence that alcohol and drug usage is lower among African-American adolescents in contrast to Whites and many other minority groups. Welte and Barnes (1987) find that African Americans, in comparison to five other ethnic minority groups, have the lowest percentage of drinkers among seventh to twelfth grade adolescents (with the exception of Asians). Furthermore, there is a lower percentage of heavy drinkers among African Americans in comparison to Whites, Asians, American Indians, and Hispanics. On the other hand, African-Americans drinkers were found to have the highest number of alcohol-related problems in comparison to the other groups.

Drug use patterns of African Americans are similar to alcohol usage. Newcomb, Maddahian, Skager, and Bentler (1987) report that African Americans' use of drugs is less than that of American Indians and Whites, but not as low as Asians. However, Poulin (1991) notes that differences in drug use between African Americans and Whites are smaller after the age of 20 than in the teenage years.

In preventing alcohol and drug problems in African-American adolescents it is important to build on factors that are related to lower levels of substance use among this group. One factor may be that African-American adolescents appear to have higher resistance to peer and adult role modeling of substance use in comparison to Whites, Hispanics, and Asians (Newcomb & Bentler, 1986). Religious involvement in African-American communities also is thought to be a strong deterrent to adolescent alcohol and drug use (Wallace & Bachman, 1991). Other factors related to lower drinking rates of African-American adolescents, noted by Harper (1988), are that African-American adolescents have less money available than do White youth for drinking purposes and they have decreased access to transportation for drinking purposes. The pattern in adulthood may change, however, with racial discrimination contributing to increased frustration that leads to increased drinking among adult African Americans. In contrast, African-American adolescents are protected from the full impact of racial discrimination by school and parental supervision. Thus, drinking is less likely to be used as a release of frustration among African-American adolescents (Harper, 1988).

Although alcohol and drug use among African-American adolescents appears to be lower than that of Whites and several other minority groups, there is some evidence to suggest that these discrepancies lessen in young adulthood. It is important to take this finding into account when planning prevention and intervention efforts.

Thompson and Simmons-Cooper (1988) suggest four issues that should be considered when planning substance abuse treatment programs for African-American adolescents. First, counselors must become sensitive to the urban African-American language of these youths. Language is reflective of underlying beliefs and values of the African-American youth's community. In this context, the adolescent is sorting through beliefs and values of his or her own subculture and that of the broader U.S. culture. Thus, treatment should involve values clarification in order to recognize and address this very significant component of development among African-American youths.

A second treatment issue given by Thompson and Simmons-Cooper (1988) is a careful examination of the day-to-day behavior of the African-American adolescent. Behavior should be examined vis-à-vis the values of the youth and beliefs. In particular, it is important to recognize and address factors antecedent to substance use and abuse behavior (for instance, racial rejection, shame, abuse, loss of identity, neglect, and so on). Concomitant factors, or factors that emerged after the onset of substance abuse, also should be identified and discussed.

A third treatment issue is to establish behavioral objectives with the youth that are realistic and meaningful.

Finally, treatment requires that emotions be identified and expressed. African-American youths reared in an urban community may use the denial of feelings and the presentation of a tough facade as means to cope. Rather than acting out such emotions as anger, youths should be encouraged to engage in verbal expression of emotions. The expression of positive emotions also should be encouraged.

American Indians

The evidence is overwhelming that alcohol and drug use problems are greater among American Indian adolescents than among non-Indian ethnic and racial minorities and White adolescents (Beauvais & LaBoueff, 1985; Cockerham, Forslund, & Raboin, 1976; Oetting & Beauvais, 1982; Porter, Vieira, Kaplan, Heesch, & Colyar, 1973). For example, Welte and Barnes (1987) found that American Indian students in grades seven to twelve are highest in per capita alcohol consumption, have the highest percentage of heavy drinkers, report the highest number of times being drunk, have the highest number of alcohol-related problems, and are highest on illicit drug use (in contrast to Whites, Orientals, African Americans, West Indians, and Hispanics). Newcomb and associates (1987) also report that use of alcohol and drugs (with the exception of hard drugs) is highest among American Indian students in grades seven, nine and eleven as compared to Whites, Blacks, Hispanics, and Asians.

Among high school females, L. T. Riley, Barenie, Mabe, and Myers (1990) found that American Indians report the highest use of smokeless tobacco in comparison to African American and White adolescents. It also has been reported that younger American Indian adolescents are quite active in their use of inhalants, and that alcohol replaces the use of inhalants by late adolescence for many Indians (Berlin, 1986). Thus, the relation between the use of these two drugs is sequential. Berlin (1986) also notes the high use of marijuana by Indian youths and has observed that this drug and others are readily available on many reservations. Thus, greater accessibility may contribute to marijuana's high use by Indian adolescents.

It has been suggested that issues of biculturalism, cultural identification, and acculturation are related to the high substance use among some American Indian adolescents. Bicultural adolescents report the lowest use of alcohol and drugs, while Indian adolescents who identify only with the non-Indian culture have the highest rates of use of drugs (Oetting & Beauvais, 1982). Indian adolescents who have low identification with the non-Indian culture and high identification with Indian culture report low use of drugs, but elevated use of alcohol. In contrast, Westermeyer and Neider (1985) report that high cultural affiliation is related to lower use of alcohol. Even with the varying findings on this topic, the role of cultural identification in American Indian substance use should be explored further.

Explanations for the high use of substances among American Indians are not easily given due to the complexity of factors to consider. Alcohol use is attributed to many factors, for example, poverty, prejudice, and unemployment (Welte & Barnes, 1987). Edwards and Edwards (1988) recognize the roles of socioeconomic factors, poverty, unemployment, feelings of hopelessness, and despair in substance use among American Indians. Royce (1981) has noted that 42 theories have been proffered on this topic, from cultural, social, economic, biological, psychological, and combination standpoints. In reality, it seems that a combination of intrapsychic and extrapsychic factors are active in this phenomenon. As an intrapsychic factor, Berlin (1986) has identified depression as the most common psychopathology among American Indian adolescents and has tied it to the use of drugs and alcohol. On many Indian reservations depressed Indian males will, perhaps daily, congregate in groups and abuse inhalants and alcohol (Berlin, 1986). Furthermore, alcohol is sometimes used as a symbol of social connection and solidarity between friends and family members (Welte & Barnes, 1987).

Extrapsychic explanations should also be considered in order to understand American Indian substance use and abuse. Indians have a 500-year history of discrimination, including genocide attempts by the dominant culture. Discrimination against and prejudice toward American Indians are still realities. According to Westermeyer (1974), the alarming rate of alcoholism among American Indians is not the biggest problem of Indians nor the cause of other problems. Rather, the social and economic problems are not adequately addressed, and the contributing roles these factors play in alcohol abuse are ignored. Beauvais and LaBoueff (1985) also have recognized this issue stating that the "failure to understand the social, cultural, and geopolitical realities of

American Indian life leads to inappropriate, and thus ineffective, solutions to social problems including alcohol and drug abuse" (p. 139).

It is useful to consider a path model of alcohol use proposed by Oetting, Beauvais, and Edwards (1988) in addressing alcohol and drug prevention and intervention issues. The entry point to this model is family strengths that, in turn, influence religious/cultural identifications, family sanctions, hope for the future, and school adjustment. These factors then influence decision making regarding peer associations. Peer association is the one factor that directly influences involvement with alcohol. Prevention approaches should recognize and address the role of each of these variables in alcohol use and abuse among American Indian adolescents. For example, the role that deviant peer clusters play in adolescent alcohol use cannot be underestimated. Encouraging the development of positive peer structures should be a focus of prevention.

Edwards and Edwards (1988) encourage the use of communitywide approaches in both prevention and intervention efforts with American Indians. Such approaches should incorporate the use of task groups, draw on the expertise of schools, social services, and community organizations, enlist the help of elders from the Indian community, and use peer counselors. By involving as many community facets as possible in prevention and intervention among American Indians, sensitivity to substance abuse issues improves and youths can learn that there are alternatives to the use of alcohol and drugs.

Asian Americans

Of the four groups discussed in this section, Asian Americans have the lowest use of alcohol and drugs. Welte and Barnes (1987) report Asian American seventh- to twelfth-grade students to be lowest in terms of percentage of drinkers and to have the fewest number of alcohol-related problems in comparison to Whites and four other minority groups. However, among those Asians who do drink, their average consumption level is highest. Newcomb and associates (1987) report that Asian students in grades seven, nine, and eleven are lowest on drug use in comparison to American Indians, African Americans, Hispanics, and Whites. Similarly, Newcomb and Bentler (1986) found Asians' use of alcohol and drugs to be lowest in comparison to White, African Americans, and Hispanics.

One factor that may account for Asians' lower levels of substance use might be related to peer relations. Asians appear to spend less time in peer-oriented activities (Wallace & Bachman, 1991). Furthermore, Newcomb and Butler (1986) report that Asian adolescents report the lowest incidence of both peer and adult role modeling of substances (Newcomb & Bentler, 1986). As noted in the discussion on American Indians, Oetting and associates (1988) argue that peer involvement directly impacts alcohol use. Thus, it makes sense that Asian adolescents would have less involvement with substances if their peer involvement is less than other groups.

Other factors that have been linked to lower levels of substance use among Asians include commitment to education and academic success (Wallace & Bachman, 1991).

Although Asians' use of alcohol and drugs is lower than other groups', it is still important not to overlook prevention and intervention needs among this group. In particular, it is important to target in prevention and intervention those Asian adolescents who do drink because, as Welte and Barnes (1987) note, Asian adolescents who do drink consume more than adolescents from other groups.

Hispanics

Alcohol and drug use among Hispanics is not as high as in some groups, but certainly higher than in others. For example, among seventh through twelfth grade students, alcohol and drug usage among Hispanics is reported to be less than that of Whites and American Indians, but higher than that of African Americans and Asians (Welte & Barnes, 1987). Similarly, Newcomb and Bentler (1986) report seventh to ninth grade Hispanics' drinking patterns to be similar to Whites, but more frequent than that of African Americans and Asians. Heavier drinking appears to be more common among Hispanic males and lighter among Hispanic females, in comparison to other groups.

The pattern of tobacco use is similar to that of alcohol and drug usage among Hispanics and other minorities. From data drawn from students in the fourth to the twelfth grades, White adolescents report the greatest tobacco use, followed by Hispanics, then Blacks, and finally Asians (DeMoor, Elder, Young, Wildey, & Molgaard, 1989). There also is evidence that Hispanics have a higher rate of the use of inhalants than many other minority groups (Humm-Delgado & Delgado, 1983). The high usage of alcohol, tobacco, and other drugs among Hispanics is disturbing, particularly because Hispanics are the fastest growing minority group in the United States (Schinke, Moncher, Palleja, Zayas, & Schilling, 1988).

Suggested correlates of substance abuse among Hispanic youth include psychosocial and environmental stress related to highly concentrated urban living (Schinke et al., 1988). These authors suggest that the prevention of substance abuse among this group includes strategies that incorporate the enhancement of coping skills, the promotion of bicultural competence within the Hispanic and the larger American cultures, use of social-learning and cognitive-skill approaches, and the use of the natural strengths of the Hispanic family and community networks. This last point is of particular importance given that drug-using adolescents have been found to report little closeness between themselves and their parents (Jurich, Polson, Jurich, & Bates, 1985). Furthermore, Coombs, Paulson, and Richardson (1991) report that, among both Hispanics and Anglos from ages 9 to 17, substance abusers are more greatly affected by peer influence than are nonusers.

Galan (1988) has suggested several themes of conflict that confront Hispanic youth. These themes or factors should be taken into account when devising prevention programs. These themes include defining ethnic identity according to one's specific Hispanic subgroup, coping with biculturality and the pressures toward acculturation, losses and powerlessness associated with not speaking Spanish, defining masculine and feminine sex roles, insecurity over skin color, family history of alcohol use, and the overall sense of self in relation to the family. The stress and confusion that arise from these issues can interplay with alcohol and drug use and abuse. Certainly awareness of and sensitivity toward these issues can enhance prevention efforts targeted toward Hispanic youths.

In addition to prevention, suggestions for intervention with Hispanic youths can be suggested. Three perspectives on intervention with alcohol and drug-abusing Hispanic adolescents have been suggested by Delgado (1988). First, a continuum of care and services should be provided that incorporate assessment, residential, outpatient, and extended care services. The services must be based on an understanding of the specific needs and issues of Hispanic adolescents and should be staffed by Hispanics. Second, the intake phase of intervention should be culture specific. For example, in the intake, information should be noted on the adolescent's contextual framework of substance usage, language preference, the adolescent's self-perception as a Hispanic, the adolescent's social network, and what kind of prior assistance has been obtained. The third perspective on intervention with Hispanic youths stresses the necessity of making intervention culture specific.

Implications for Treatment and Prevention

Treatment

For nearly all drug-dependent youths, kicking the habit begins with detoxification. Detoxification involves hospitalization to eliminate the acute physical or psychological dependence on the drug.

The primary goal of the detoxification program is to provide the medical care necessary to relieve the physical discomforts that accompany withdrawal. A secondary goal is to assist the drug-dependent individual in finding the most suitable treatment program to help prevent the recurrence of substance dependence.

Therapeutic Communities

Once detoxification has occurred, the drug-dependent individual may decide in favor of a "group home" for treatment. One type of group home is a residence staffed by recovering alcoholics or ex-drug abusers. The therapeutic community uses group pressure and support, remedial education, or employment to help the dependent individual change his or her behavior.

The therapeutic community views the addict's actions as a lifelong destructive pattern of behavior. To change this pattern, the community often demands a complete alteration of the addict's life-style. Drug abstinence, the elimination of criminal behavior, obtaining a job or more education, and the development of such traits as self-reliance and honesty with oneself and others are encouraged in a 24-hour-a-day program that attacks old behaviors.

The intensity of the program is so great that only a small number (10% to 15%) of all those who are admitted to therapeutic communities can complete it. The program is considered effective for those who can. Follow-up studies one to five years later show that most former members are able to hold jobs, stay off drugs, and stay out of trouble with the authorities (DeLeon & Rosenthal, 1979).

Methadone Treatment for Heroin Addiction

For thousands of former heroin addicts in North America today, the treatment program used to prevent the recurrence of heroin addiction is methadone.

Methadone is itself a narcotic that in the proper dose acts to block heroin withdrawal's effect. This blocking action occurs because methadone has a cross-tolerance with heroin; that is, the drug neutralizes the effects of heroin. Additionally, methadone, when taken in regular, prescribed, oral doses, does not produce the "high" commonly associated with narcotics.

Methadone is not an answer in itself to drug rehabilitation, and other services must be provided if the former addict is to achieve a new life without drugs. Most clinics offer job training, remedial education, and counseling.

Whether methadone is an acceptable treatment for drug addiction is subject to heated debate. Proponents of methadone treatment point to its low cost and its success in enabling many former heroin addicts to return to school or work and to live otherwise normal lives. Opponents counter that substituting a legal narcotic for an illegal one accomplishes little or nothing. Abuse of methadone to achieve a "high" is possible, and opponents point out that the life-style of drug use has not been changed. Finally, opponents take a page from history and argue that not long ago heroin was used to combat morphine addiction. Is it not possible, they suggest, that today's cure for heroin dependence will become a problem in itself? (See Box 15–3.)

AA and Other Self-Help Groups

Extending a helping hand to a fellow human being in the same situation is the essence of the self-help group. Founded by former substance abusers, Alcoholics Anonymous (AA) and other programs operate under the belief that the recovering alcoholic or ex-drug abuser is in the best position to understand and help the individual struggling with an alcohol or a drug problem.

In some respects the programs of the therapeutic community and the self-help group are similar. Both rely upon ex-users, not professionals, to provide help. Both focus on completely changing the behavior of the user. Both demand abstinence from alcohol or drugs. Through weekly (or nightly) meetings, group members in both programs attempt to support one another in their goal of abstinence. Should temptation on the street become too great, each program uses a "buddy system"; that is, members are matched to other members to provide extra support for one another outside the meetings.

The success of self-help groups is difficult to determine. Although reports have been enthusiastic, these studies suffer from several problems in design. Nevertheless, given the growing popularity of the self-help movement with the general public, it would seem that the principle of neighbor helping neighbor is, from the public's point of view, effective (N. S. Brown & Ashery, 1979).

Psychotherapy

Individual counseling can happen in many different settings. But whether it occurs in a hospital ward, in a methadone clinic, at a youth-service agency, or in a physician's office, therapy is directed at discussing the abuser's problems and attempting to resolve them.

Psychotherapy can also take many different forms. Therapy styles range from insight-oriented psychoanalysis, which encourages the client to free-associate in the expectation that greater self-knowledge will change behavior, to

---

Box 15–3   Sometimes Drugs Are Medicine

There are many reasons for taking drugs. For many young people, it's the challenge, the risk, the excitement of a new thrill. For others, it's an expression of anger, hatred, protest, or desperation. For still others, it is an attempt to hang on to sanity—an attempt at self-medication to get from today to tomorrow in the only way they know how. The following case study from Thomas Gullotta's files provides an illustration.

Jimmy was a dirty, greasy, unattractive 15-year-old who hung around the center of town watching (nothing more—just watching). My contact with him resulted from a conversation I had with one of his former elementary school teachers. She had begun to suspect Jimmy of being the obscene phone caller whose nightly calls had begun to terrorize her. The suspicion was confirmed a few days later when she confronted him in school.

Jimmy begged her not to tell his parents and promised to do anything in return. She insisted he seek help and referred him to my office. In the days that followed, I saw a young, deeply troubled adolescent whose incestuous desire for his mother had created tremendous inner conflict and guilt. To focus his attentions away from her, he had begun to phone other women, follow them home, and begin to plan to assault them. He recognized the wrongness of his behavior, and, torn between his desire to follow through on his fantasies and his guilt over those fantasies, he had begun to increase his drug usage considerably. Jimmy's unconscious solution to controlling these very frightening feelings was to medicate himself with illicit drugs to the point where he could not act out his desires.

I saw Jimmy for several weeks. I concentrated on helping him recognize and verbalize his need for help. During that time I made no attempt to limit or influence Jimmy's drug use but worked to have him realize why he was medicating himself.

Jimmy eventually admitted his need for help and told his parents about his thoughts, feelings, and fears. Both parents and Jimmy agreed with me that hospital treatment was most appropriate. He checked in several days later, where his illegal self-medication was stopped and replaced with still other medication. Only this time it was prescribed by a physician.

Do you think it was correct to let Jimmy continue his drug abuse? Should Jimmy have been reported to the authorities to protect society? How do you balance the client's right to confidentiality with other people's right to be safe? For that matter, should clients have a right to confidentiality?

---

behavior therapy, which uses a system of rewards and negative reinforcements to attempt to shape behavior into new life-style patterns (Birmingham, 1986).

For each new or existing treatment approach offered, there are dozens of writers praising or damning it. In the absence of any studies evaluating therapy effectiveness, we cannot say which approaches are deserving of damnation. We can state that when used alone, no form of psychotherapy has been very successful in helping the substance-dependent individual abstain from alcohol or drugs. It is when therapy is used in conjunction with other treatment forms (methadone, self-help groups, job training, and so on) that it may be most useful (Wesson & Smith, 1979).

Family Therapy

One reason that individual psychotherapy fails to help the substance-dependent individual may be that these approaches do nothing to change the system from which the individual has come. For the adolescent, this system is the family. We have already noted that parental drinking and drug use seem to have a strong influence on adolescent attitudes toward drugs and alcohol. We have also pointed out that poor parenting practices and poor parent/adolescent relationships seem to contribute to youthful drug abuse and dependence. Proponents of family therapy argue that changing the adolescent's behavior entails changing the family system.

In order to do so, the therapist helps family members solve their problems and achieve more positive and constructive ways of relating to one another. By focusing on the family as a whole and not on the "identified problem" (the drug-using adolescent), the therapist is able to avoid the pitfalls of the family's viewing the problem as only the adolescent's. Instead, this approach encourages the family to examine its own behaviors and the ways in which they contribute to the use of illegal substances by one of its members.

This treatment approach, while promising, is not without its problems. These problems involve the family's motivation for and commitment to changing its behavior. Many adolescents who abuse alcohol or drugs serve very useful functions in the family, such as keeping the parents from divorce or acting out one parent's depression. If disrupting this delicate balance is too threatening, the family will resist and will maintain more familiar and comfortable ways of behaving. The message to the adolescent is then to continue to abuse drugs or alcohol (Stanton, 1979).

Prevention

In a society that bombards its members with promises of instant relief from headaches, common-cold symptoms, dandruff, sleeplessness, and constipation, it is highly unlikely that drug use among the young can be prevented. Similarly, when drinking is considered so "downright upright," and alcohol is associated by advertisers with every social event from family reunions to job promotions, it is highly unrealistic to believe for a moment that drinking among youths can be delayed until they reach adulthood. Prevention in the alcohol and drug arena is directed not toward stopping their use but toward preventing abuse and dependence. The tools available to achieve this goal are education, promotion of social competency, community organization/systems intervention, and natural care giving (Gullotta & Adams, 1982b).

Education

Under the umbrella of education, prevention can take the form of school activities, media announcements, and the distribution of materials. Many states require junior high school students to take at least one course in drug and alcohol education. The courses vary from school to school, but most of these programs combine factual information with social skills training in an attempt to provide the adolescent with the knowledge necessary to make a responsible decision on the use of drugs and alcohol (Engs, 1981; Meyer, 1995).

School-based drug education has been criticized for promoting rather than preventing drug and alcohol use. Some studies (see, for example, Halpin & Whiddon, 1977) show adolescents as having more positive attitudes toward drugs after a drug-education course than before it. School boards and local citizens suggest that drug use has increased among adolescents who have completed drug-education courses. This criticism shows the confusion surrounding responsible decision making. The intention of many school-based drug-education programs is not and should not be to stop alcohol and drug use but rather to "foster responsible choices regarding the consumption of all drugs for all ages. One responsible choice for a particular individual may be not to use any drugs outside of medical prescriptions" (Swisher, 1979, p. 425). For others, the choice may be to use potentially less harmful drugs.

Finally, we caution individuals wanting to prevent drug abuse to recognize that by itself the prevention tool of education is not particularly effective. A recent study by P. Fischer, Richards, Berman, and Krugman (1989) helps underscore this point. These authors were interested in the recall and eye-tracking behaviors of adolescents viewing tobacco advertisements. Their findings suggest that the warnings that appear in every advertisement are rarely, if ever, read.

Promotion of Social Competency

Closely allied with education is the concept of promoting social competency. Social competency can be fostered through educational activities such as clarification of values and the encouragement of self-understanding and self-acceptance. It can be promoted through programs conducted by the YMCA, YWCA, and youth-service agencies, by church programs to improve parent/adolescent relationships through building communication skills, by peer counseling (which is more properly categorized as a tool not of competency promotion but of natural care giving), or by assertiveness training. Social-competency promotion includes involvement in theatre, wilderness courses, boating, boxing, and innumerable other recreational or sports activities that meet the adolescent's social and emotional needs in socially acceptable ways.

The persuasive argument in favor of promoting social competency is that if the adolescent is given opportunities for personal and social growth and if these opportunities provide a feeling of worth, a sense of importance, and a sense of being an asset to society, then drug or alcohol abuse and dependence will diminish (Ellickson & Bell, 1990).

Community Organization/Systems Intervention

More controversial than promoting social competency is using legislation to prevent drug and alcohol abuse. Past attempts to legislate social behavior have proved to be dismal failures. Prohibiting the sale of cigarettes to young people under the age of 18 has not stopped smoking among this age group. Estimates that 70 million Americans have tried marijuana hardly strengthen the case for additional legal constraints, as supporters of the movement to decriminalize it are quick to point out. (See Box 15–4.)

Nevertheless, for some readily available substances—amphetamines, barbiturates, solvents, and alcohol—increased social action in the form of legislation may be an effective tool for decreasing their abuse by adolescents. For amphetamines and barbiturates, society needs to address the following issues. First, is the number of pills manufactured by U.S. firms warranted? Second, are these types of medication overprescribed by physicians? Finally, do the benefits of these drugs outweigh their disadvantages? Answers to these questions might produce enough evidence to warrant increased regulation of these substances. Similarly,

Box 15–4   Should Drugs Be Legalized?

What do Carl Sagan, William F. Buckley, Jr., Nobel laureate economist Milton Friedman, and former Secretary of State George Shultz have in common? All of these noted individuals have spoken recently in favor of the legalization of one or more presently illegal drugs (Nicholson, 1992). Why would these people and others speak in favor of substances that are harmful when abused?

These are several reasons. One reason is the economic cost of the war on drugs. An estimated $8 billion a year are being spent in a seemingly fruitless struggle to keep illegal substances out of this country. Drug-related arrests presently totaling more than 750,000 a year are clogging the courts and overcrowding the prisons such that "real time" is but a small fraction of assigned time (Nadelman, 1992). The profits from the illegal sale of drugs have financed a huge criminal element within this country whose power as a result of those profits can reach into the highest levels of state and federal government.

Next, there are the social costs. The poor and minorities have disproportionately suffered under current drug control policies. It is their homes, their neighborhoods, and their children that are caught in the crossfire for the control of the drug trade (Clifford, 1992).

Third, there is the realization that the overwhelming majority of drug users are not and never will become drug dependent. Their use of substances is for the purpose of enjoyment (Nicholson, 1992). Furthermore, as Duncan (1992) points out, is it not hypocritical to selectively choose some drugs as being permissible like tobacco and alcohol and others like marijuana as being illegal? Reflect for a moment on material in this chapter concerning the "healthy" reasons for drinking alcohol. Are there not "healthy" reasons for using other drugs? And if there are not "healthy" reasons for using alcohol and tobacco, then should they not be made illegal also?

Finally, there is the opportunity to control the quality, access, and profits of illegal substances, if they were

legalized. We note earlier, for example, that drugs like LSD were occasionally laced with substances like PCP ensuring the unknowing user a mind-altering experience that would be frighteningly memorable. Licensed substances with today's quality control methods and layers of packaging materials would be less likely to experience this problem. In addition, licensed substances can be controlled for potency. We noted that the percentage of the psychoactive drug THC in a marijuana cigarette had increased over the last decade. If legalized, this psychoactive agent and the level of others could be controlled. Last but certainly not least, this multibillion-dollar-a-year industry would produce tax revenue that could provide economic opportunities not currently available to inner-city youth and their families.

Opponents of those who would legalize drugs have several powerful counterarguments. Clayton and Leukefeld (1992) and others (Jarvik, 1990) dispute the contention that the war on illegal substances is being lost. They properly point out that drug usage among adolescents has declined significantly and continues to decline. Next, the public opinion polls do not support a lessening of drug control efforts. The general public seems to support the cost of the war on drugs. Third, rather than loosening controls on illegal substances, Clayton and Leukefeld support increasing controls on tobacco and alcohol, agreeing that there are very few "healthy" reasons for drug use.

Other authors (Goldstein, 1990; Wilson, 1990) question whether legalizing drugs would result in savings. With reports that 15% of the nation's health bill is spent on alcohol and alcohol-related problems (Holden, 1987) and sobering information on the low to moderate success of drug treatment programs (Holden, 1987; Tennant, 1990), legalization would worsen an already sad situation. Society, they believe, has not only the right but also the obligation to restrict individuals from potential harm. It is ultimately society and not the wasted individual that incurs the cost of caring for that person.

regulatory control over the chemical content of solvents would provide the means of banning certain poisons and saving lives.

Using the "distribution of consumption" model, which states that the availability of a substance is directly related to its incidence of abuse, Gullotta and Adams (1982b) suggest that alcohol abuse can be reduced. They encourage the use of such approaches as

(a) increasing the price of alcohol; (b) prohibiting the advertising of drugs and alcohol through the media; (c) labeling substances such as alcohol and drugs with warnings of their possible damage to health; (d) increasing taxes on substances; (e) increasing the legal drinking age beyond 21; (f) reducing local tavern hours while stiffening zoning practices and increasing legal holidays when public tavern drinking and purchase of alcohol is prohibited; (g) reducing the alcohol content of beverages; and (h) increasing penalties and instituting mandatory treatment for individuals convicted of drunk driving charges. Activities such as these suggested are unquestionably controversial and likely to stimulate heated opposition from special interest groups. (pp. 418–419)

Furthermore, we grant that legislation in itself is not, nor has it ever been, the answer to drug and alcohol abuse. Used in an enlightened fashion, however, it can provide the necessary motivation for society to reduce its consumption of amphetamines, barbiturates, and alcohol and ensure that solvent manufacturers use the least harmful chemicals whenever possible.

Natural Care Giving

Caring for oneself, for another, for others—that is the essence of natural care giving. For young people a spring of emotional support and strength to avoid substance abuse can flow from several sources.

One form of self-help is found in the numerous peer-leadership, counseling, and cross-age tutoring programs around the United States. These programs recognize that adults are often the last people whom young people consult about sensitive matters such as substance use. Thus, programs that provide youths with factual information and training in the use of that information with peers can be a useful tool in reducing drug usage. Preventionists believe that by extending honest, accurate information through peers, they can increase the probability that adolescents will make informed, responsible decisions (Gullotta & Adams, 1982b). The provision of such information also offers an opportunity for young people to explore with one another the motivations behind substance use and to decide not to be users.

Major Points to Remember

1. Many of the illegal substances discussed in this chapter were commonly used by the public as recently as 80 years ago.
2. Alcohol consumption is associated with a number of serious problems (traffic deaths, fetal alcohol syndrome). Alcohol-related problems cost the U.S. economy many billions of dollars a year.
3. The so-called marijuana stepping-stone theory can really be more accurately applied to alcohol. Alcohol is the entry drug into the use of other substances.
4. Studies show that adolescents who drink are imitating their parents' behavior but that marijuana use is peer influenced.
5. Most young people drink, and many of them drink too much too often. Yet many never develop into alcohol abusers. Those who do appear to have problems with school, with the community, and with their families.

6. In general, the family of the substance-abusing young person is characterized by weak parental control and poor parent/child relationships.

7. There is some evidence that alcoholism has a genetic component. Nevertheless, a social-psychological perspective emphasizing family behavior is at present a more convincing explanation.

8. At least 70 million Americans have tried marijuana at least once. Many users are emotionally "well-adjusted" individuals. Some are not, but it is not possible to establish a causal link between their emotional "maladjustment" and marijuana. Still, we do know that driving under the influence of marijuana is unsafe and that marijuana may well be associated with health problems (cancer and damage to a fetus, for example).

9. Inhalants are most commonly used by younger adolescents. Inhaling solvents poses a serious health risk, since most contain poisons that can cause permanent damage to the user.

10. PCP was called the PeaCe Pill during the 1960s. Peace it does not create. Short-term effects often include very violent behavior. Concern exists over why young people would seek out such a chemical, given its strong behavioral toxicity.

11. Anabolic steroids synthesized from the male hormone testosterone have not been found to increase athletic ability.

12. Female use of stimulants exceeds male use.

13. Barbiturate abusers are at high risk of physical harm. Some researchers believe that the barbiturate abuser has a suicidal personality.

14. Of all the drugs discussed in this chapter, cocaine has the most interesting history. It has been used as a religious drug, a medicine, and a popular pick-me-up and is now the preferred illegal "high" of the wealthy.

15. Daily use of heroin by adolescents is almost nonexistent. Those few who do abuse the drug are described as angry, helpless, manipulating individuals who have turned their anger away from their social condition and their family situation inward against themselves.

16. The treatment of drug-abusing and drug-dependent adolescents often starts with detoxification and can then lead to a number of alternative outpatient treatments. These treatments include (depending on the substance abused) therapeutic communities, methadone treatment, self-help groups, individual psychotherapy, and family therapy.

17. Substance use cannot be prevented. In many respects, minimization of alcohol or drug use is a far better goal than prevention. Drug education with values clarification has been found to be one way to help young people decide for themselves whether to use drugs. Promotion of social competency, community organization/systems intervention, and natural care giving are the other ways for reducing new incidents of substance misuse.

16

Crime and Delinquency

There may be no behavior that more excites the passions of adults than youth misbehaving. Each new generation of parents raises the cry against juvenile mischief through the media, at local school board meetings, and over the evening meal. Their comments range from pronouncements on the need for stricter controls and more discipline to such observations as "I never did that at your age!"

When that mischief crosses some unclear boundary, it is called delinquency. It may very well be that we can define delinquency as knowingly committing acts that are illegal. However, whether that has much bearing on who is considered delinquent is quite another matter. Delinquency has been confused with poverty, urban growth, racism, and sexism, all played against a backdrop of punishment, reform, and more punishment. In this chapter we examine the curious history of the notion of delinquency, the various explanations for the deviant young mind, and the development of the juvenile court and the controversies now surrounding it. Finally, we examine treatment approaches to delinquency and the question of whether delinquency can be prevented.

Historical Overview

The laws governing children in the Massachusetts Bay Colony were straightforward. Disobedient or delinquent children could be severely punished or even put to death by their parents for their misbehavior. Even though rarely enforced, these early codes governing the behavior of the young in New England society were grounded in English common law and the Bible. Gradually, as time passed, the terms *delinquent* and *disobedient,* which had been applied to all children who misbehaved, came to be associated with crime and the conditions of the poor in cities.

In many respects, to understand this change, one needs first to understand the climate in which it originated. The time was the 1820s, and the places were large, new Eastern port cities—New York, Boston, and Philadelphia. Into these cities came waves of new immigrants—the Irish. As immigrants do now in large urban areas, they were met with overcrowding, an insufficient number of jobs, and an established community with a different ethnic background and religion.

The reaction of the established middle-class community (or, as they considered themselves, God's elect) to this incoming flood of humanity was determined by their fear that these immigrants had brought with them the seeds of social revolution. The community's response to this threat was to create a set of new institutions to educate these ruffians in the ways of the New World. In his classic book on the subject, *Thorns and Thistles: Juvenile Delinquency in the United States* (1973), Mennel views this movement to establish "refuge homes" as the best attempt the established community could make to exercise continued influence in the rapidly growing and changing coastal cities.

In pursuing this mission, the early American reformers were not overly particular about whom the refuge houses sheltered. The orphan, the "artful dodger," and the pauper were all equally embraced for assistance in their individual journeys to reformation. In fact, Mennel (1973) suggests, it was not so much crime that was the villain in the middle class as it was pauperism. To the established community, crime, drunkenness, ignorance, or gambling were merely symptoms of the disease of poverty.

With missionary zeal the philanthropists of this time were quick to seize the young immigrant. They did not wish to wait until the child was actually a delinquent but would rather "snatch him as a 'branch from the burning' . . . [and] rescue him from the yawning gulf of poverty, drunkenness, and crime, into which he is about to fall" (Mennel, 1973, p. 12). This missionary fervor was not reserved for male immigrants; it applied equally to females (Brenzel, 1980).

The path to redemption for these young sinners combined large doses of religious teaching with equal amounts of time in what would be considered sweatshops today. Needless to say, discipline was strict, and punishment was liberally applied to those who dared misbehave. Boys spent their days caning chairs or manufacturing simple goods, while the girls perfected their skills doing household chores:

> The chapel bell rings at six, at which time or before, the girls rise, and put themselves and their sleeping rooms in order, and prepare the breakfast; at seven this meal is eaten. Housework is attended to until nine, at which time the chaplain comes in, to take the direction of the morning devotions. Labor holds as many as can be spared from domestic duties in the workroom until dinner; this occurs at twelve. School is held from half-past one until half-past four; supper at five; and sewing, knitting, and reading in the workroom until evening; prayers at eight, after which the girls are dismissed for bed. During the day sufficient time for exercise is allowed in the open air. (Brenzel, 1980, p. 202)

Many young gang members are filled with anger and despair.

To understand the concept of delinquency at this time, it is essential to perceive the city as sinful and religion as needed for salvation. As the recorded sermons of ladies' groups to the young inhabitants of the refuge houses indicate, the established community left no stone unturned in attempting to educate the young in the ways of God. These young "sinners" provided ample evidence, to these reformers' Calvinist way of thinking, of humanity's fallibility and weakness of the flesh. With stories of looseness among girls in their ears and a proper sense of indignation on their tongues, they might—as one did—address "the girls feelingly on the necessity of a preparation for death and mention the sudden decease of a religious child, and . . . her happy close" (Mennel, 1973, p. 17). And if these young people responded by attempting to escape or to burn down the refuge house, was that not more confirmation of their sinfulness and need for salvation?

Increasing urbanization was seen as a major corrupter of the young. In the minds of these social reformers, the city breeds indolence, poverty, and crime. Purifying these youths, and instilling middle-class values in them, called for a return to a simpler life. Thus, it was not unusual for these and later social reformers to separate children permanently from their families and apprentice them to farmers in the hope of changing their lives.

One of the most fervent believers in the practice of "placing out" was Charles Loring Brace. From the 1850s to nearly the close of the 19th century, the agency he helped found, the New York Children's Aid Society, placed hundreds of young children on westbound trains. At each farmtown whistle stop these children climbed down from the train to be inspected by the townsfolk and in some cases "adopted" on the spot. Viewing the solution to delinquency to be in the West's ability to absorb those who did not quite fit into Eastern Establishment ways, Brace was typical of the progressive thinkers of the time. In these reformers' minds the frontier and its rural farming life held the moral, social, and economic solution to the problem Irish, Italians, and those other "worse than heathen Roman Catholics" (Mennel, 1973, p. 63).

Until the late 19th century the word *delinquency* was synonymous with *poverty.* Those who were labeled delinquent were most likely to be orphans, Blacks, immigrants, and male, though less-than-virtuous females were as quickly confined. These young people were viewed as residing in a breeding ground for sin and as too weak to resist it. Their salvation rested not only in strict religious discipline but in a chance to escape from urban life. Once in the countryside, they would purge their bodies and souls of the poisons leading to damnation. Thus, to remedy the problems of crime in the cities, 19th-century social reformers applied liberal doses of religion, discipline, and parent/child separation. As the 19th century closed, this simplistic view of delinquency began to give way to more scientific explanations.

Perspectives on the Causes of Delinquency

Although the link between poverty and crime remains a popular explanation for delinquency, some find physiological sources of criminal behavior, others stress psychological causes, and still others blame society for its failure to provide young people with adequate and acceptable opportunities.

Biological Explanations

Perhaps the most famous of all biological explanations for criminal behavior is Cesare Lombroso's. First described in a pamphlet published in 1876, his theory states that a criminal is physically different from a noncriminal. Criminal types can be identified by such physical traits as a slanting forehead, a jutting jaw, heavy eyebrows, and either excessive hairiness or no body hair at all. Although today most of us would consider Lombroso's theory preposterous, it stimulated countless attempts by other scholars to establish a causal relationship between appearance and criminal behavior.

Earnest Hooton, for instance, a professor of physical anthropology at Harvard University, studied the bodily characteristics of thousands of criminals during the 1920s and 1930s. He concluded that criminals and noncriminals differ significantly on such measurements as chest size, head circumference, ear length, nose size, and forehead height. Hooton did not stop at that point, however. He related physical types to ethnic and racial backgrounds and concluded, for example, that southern Europeans are more likely to commit crimes of violence and force, such as armed robbery, rape, or murder. Northern Europeans were said to be more likely to commit nonphysical crimes, such as fraud or forgery.

Despite the many years separating Lombroso's and Hooton's work, the influence of Charles Darwin's *Origin of Species* is evident in their thinking. Although both Lombroso and Hooton restrained themselves from suggesting, as Thomas Travis did, that reshaping the faces of delinquents would reshape their criminal minds (Mennel, 1973, p. 89), both clearly moved the proposed reasons for criminal behavior out of the realm of environmental conditions and religious infidelity and into the realm of physical characteristics.

The arguments for biological determination are still with us in the 1980s, but in a variety of updated forms. Rather than concentrating on external characteris-

Cesare Lombroso popularized the mistaken belief that criminal personalities could be identified by physical attributes.

tics, researchers have studied possible relationships between chromosomal or neurological abnormalities and antisocial behavior. However, whether the argument is constitutional factors, intelligence, or XYY and XXY chromosomal errors, the evidence that biological factors *alone* explain criminal behavior is both contradictory and inconclusive.

In an exhaustive review of the literature, for example, J. Q. Wilson and Herrnstein (1985) conclude in *Crime and Human Nature* that genetic and familial elements play a primary role in explaining criminal behavior. Using studies of adoptive twins, Wilson and Herrnstein conclude that genetically transmitted biological predispositions are involved in the etiology of most criminal behaviors. Powerful as the argument may seem that children of criminals, even if reared in adoptive homes, are more likely than other children to engage in criminal activity as they grow up, it remains specious. Correlative data can never establish causality. Furthermore, given the retrospective nature of adoptive twin studies, researchers have never been able to control for selective placement, discrimination, or self-fulfilling expectancy effects that may have produced or significantly contributed to the child's behavior.

Similarly, although reports by some scholars may give the impression that low intelligence and criminal behavior go hand in hand (Moffitt, Gabrielli, Mednick, & Schulsinger, 1981; Wilson & Herrnstein, 1985), evidence to support this position is weak. Although it may be appealing to imagine most criminals as bumbling idiots (and those who are caught and thus constitute the available data pool may well be), the available sample is almost devoid of the highly educated, often undetected white-color criminals, who through insider trading, embezzlement, and other financial manipulations bilk the naive public of billions each year.

Finally, are chromosomal malformations and criminal behavior related? For a brief period in the late 1960s and early 1970s researchers excitedly reported findings that XYY and XXY chromosomal errors appeared with regularity in criminals (W. H. Price, Whatmore, & McClemont, 1966; Telfer, Baker, Clark, & Richardson, 1968). Amusingly, as work in this area continued, studies reported the same incidence of chromosomal errors in noncriminal populations and the absence of these chromosomal errors in criminal populations (D. Baker, Telfer, Richardson, & Clark, 1970; Clark, Telfer, Baker, & Rosen, 1970; Ferrier, Ferrier, & Neilson, 1970).

We reject any suggestion that a slanting forehead, ethnic background, genetics, intelligence, chromosomal differences, or any other biological characteristics immediately mark an individual as a criminal. As we review the history of biological explanations for criminal behavior, we are reminded constantly of the use to which proponents would use those explanations against the alleged perpetrator. For example, in the late 1960s at the height of the racial unrest that marked the end of that decade, one group of researchers in a letter to the *Journal of the American Medical Association* suggested that race riots were caused by violent slum dwellers suffering from focal brain lesions. The authors of this letter implied that the solution to correcting these misfiring synapses was psychiatric neurosurgery (Mark, Sweet, & Ervin, 1967). As we noted earlier, psychiatric neurosurgery is the polite phrase used to describe a lobotomy. Interestingly, for at least a while in the early 1970s (an era marked by a high degree of civil and

---

Box 16–1   The Decline of Delinquency in Later Adolescence

What is responsible for the decline in criminal acts as young people grow older? A study published in the *American Journal of Orthopsychiatry* provides some possible explanations (Mulvey & LaRosa, 1986).

The authors interviewed ten males between the ages of 15 and 20 who, in the opinion of youth workers, had "improved markedly within the past two years" (p. 217). The histories of these young men included the commission of serious crimes such as coerced sexual offenses, felonious assaults, and armed robbery. Using a semi-structured interview, the authors obtained the following qualitative data:

- For most young men in this sample a decline in criminal activity accompanied a decline in drug use.
- For most of the sample a decline in criminal activity accompanied a change in social networks away from negative peer influences.
- While job-training activities did not contribute to an initial decision to decrease delinquent activity, most were now involved in obtaining job skills.
- One-half of the sample reported changes in family

relationships. In no case was there an improvement in family functioning. Rather, these young men had either left or been thrown out of their homes. In either situation, the young person saw himself as more in control of his life and living in a less chaotic situation. In each case the decision to stop criminal activity was preceded by a change in understanding. This change was in the direction of viewing one's life in the future and realizing that current behavior could have lasting negative impact.

In the judgment of Mulvey and LaRosa this last observation accounts for the changed behavior in these young men. We concur. In our own experiences working with delinquent youths, we are continually impressed with the behavioral changes that happen as a young person matures. The development of formal-reasoning abilities, the capacity to separate oneself from destructive family and peer relationships, and the capacity to share an intimate identity with another help explain why most delinquent youths do not continue into adulthood as criminals.

Source: E. P. Mulvey & J. F. LaRosa, "Delinquency Cessation and Adolescent Development: Preliminary Data." *American Journal of Orthopsychiatry,* 1986, *56,* pp. 212–224.

social discord) the National Institute of Mental Health underwrote activity in this area. Two decades later the mere suggestion that parts of the brain should be plucked out of the heads of dissidents would itself land the originator of the thought in a residential treatment facility.

Furthermore, criminal activity occurs at higher rates in early and middle adolescence, decreasing rapidly as individuals age. Is there some undiscovered retrovirus that is secretly altering the structure of DNA within most adolescents, thus sparing them from a lifetime of crime? We think not. Rather, the explanations for criminal behavior are found elsewhere in this chapter. (See Box 16–1.)

Psychological Explanations

Psychological explanations focus not on the physical composition of the individual, as biological theories do, but on the internal drives and motivations that influence behavior. One of the most widely accepted psychological explanations for antisocial behavior is based on Sigmund Freud's psychoanalytic theory.

In his work Freud attempted to explain human social development from infancy to adulthood. In his framework early childhood experiences (before the age of 6) leave a lasting impression, for it is in these first years that the child moves from the oral to the genital stage. During this time the child must come to grips with two instinctual urges, the sexual and aggressive drives. Both of these

urges create a constant state of tension in which the body seeks pleasure and satisfaction. Freud conceptualized this tension as resulting from the interaction of
three forces, the id, the ego, and the superego. As we discussed in Chapter 2, the
development of a strong superego is necessary to influence the ego to restrain the
drives of the id. A weak superego will not be able to control the primitive drives
of the young person entering adolescence. In this model these primitive drives
revolve around the sexual desire of the male for his mother or the female for her
father. If this desire (the Oedipus or Electra complex) is not successfully
resolved early in the childhood, it reemerges in adolescence and creates tremendous stress in the individual. To relieve this stress, the adolescent may resort to
delinquency as a defense mechanism (that is, a way in which to relieve emotional stress and maintain emotional stability). Thus, delinquency in a psychoanalytic model becomes an adaptation to intolerable stress. It is the best attempt a
young person can make to balance a weak superego against the demands of the
id for sexual gratification with a parent.

Considered to be in the psychoanalytic tradition, Erik Erikson has expanded
on Freud's model to include the concept of social interaction. His stage theory
(see Chapter 2) suggests that the development of identity is closely related to
antisocial behavior. For Erikson, delinquency occurs in those young people who
are without a strong sense of identity. They experience "role diffusion" and
struggle during their teenage years to resolve the questions "Who am I?" "Why
am I?" and "What am I?" During this process of resolving role diffusion, it is
likely that young people will commit illegal acts or develop severe emotional
problems—neither of which, Erikson notes, need be of a lifelong, crippling
nature if appropriate intervention occurs.

Still considered as belonging to the family of psychological explanations but
emerging out of the laboratory and not "off the couch" is the learning-theory
explanation. Learning theorists disclaim any need for the concepts of the id, the
ego, and the superego. They suggest that a stimulus/response model provides a
clearer explanation of delinquent behavior.

There are two important principles in a learning-theory model. The first,
reinforcement, can be understood to be some behavior or event occurring after a
response that will either increase or decrease the chances of the response's occurring again. In *positive* reinforcement the addition of a positive stimulus is likely
to increase the chances that the response will recur. In *negative* reinforcement the
removal of an unwanted stimulus is likely to increase the chances that the
response will recur. In *punishment* the addition of an unwanted stimulus (for
example, pain) or the removal of a desirable stimulus is likely to decrease the
chances that the response will recur.

The second important learning principle is the concept of modeling. In modeling the young imitate the behavior of other individuals whom they admire or
respect. An example of youthful modeling behavior that immediately comes to
mind is the copying of a Hollywood actress's hair style a few years ago by thousands of young women around the country. Males are not immune to such influences either, as the makers of men's cosmetics and of four-wheel-drive vehicles
well know.

But not all role models are positive, and when a role model's behavior is antisocial, the young person will be tempted to imitate it. When the model is also successful either monetarily or socially, the temptation is extremely strong. If a deviation into criminal activity brings wealth, status, prestige, or peer recognition, the behavior is likely to increase. If the foray into criminal activity is unsuccessful or if the adolescent loses face in the eyes of his or her peer group or in the eyes of significant others (parents, girlfriend/boyfriend), chances are that the behavior will diminish. Next we discuss the other explanations for delinquency and then look at the psychological research on this problem.

Social-Control Explanations

Social-control perspectives are concerned with the individual's degree of belonging to society. The thinking is that the more involved an adolescent is with parents, school, and other socially accepted institutions, such as church, school clubs, or athletic activities, the less likely it is that this individual will become involved in delinquent activity. When these bonds do not exist, the chances are greater that deviant behavior will occur. Each theory attempts to answer why these bonds do not exist or have been broken.

Merton's (1937) *structural-disorganization theory* suggests that lack of equal access to financial, educational, or social resources explains delinquent behavior. Being denied the same economic and social goals that others, because of their status, can attain creates tremendous frustration. Thus, deprived of the legitimate means of obtaining the fruits of the good life because of socioeconomic status, ethnic background, or other factors, the individual resorts to illegal means to obtain them. (See Box 16–2 for an example of how far disenfranchised youths are willing to go to obtain status.)

A. K. Cohen (1955) expands on Merton's ideas by suggesting that adolescents are less concerned with wealth than with status. He notes that the major institution with the power to grant status to young people is the school system. From nursery school on, it provides young people with continual feedback about how their intellectual, physical, and social abilities compare with those of their classmates. The school is the fortress of middle-class values, Cohen would argue. The young person who does not look, dress, speak, or act like the middle-class model is likely to receive less than a fair share of positive recognition in school. Cohen believes that because lower-class youngsters start school with numerous economic and social disadvantages, by the time they have reached adolescence they have been alienated from school and thus alienated from society's greatest socializing mechanism.

In its simplest form social-control theory states that delinquency occurs because a breakdown of the personal and social restraints on the individual permits it to occur. For Hirschi (1969), young people with caring parents, a good school record, positive relationships with their teachers, healthy peer relationships, and educational and vocational opportunities are very unlikely to become delinquents. Hirschi argues that it is these bonds of family, school, peers, and employment that permit socialization to occur. As each of these factors sours, the bonds between conventional morality and the adolescent weaken:

Box 16–2   Violence and Gangs

From the *Blackboard Jungle* to *West Side Story*, to *Colors,* from the large urban communities of Los Angeles, Chicago, and New York to smaller cities like Bridgeport, Salt Lake City, and St. Paul, the scope and seriousness of youth gangs have grown dramatically over the last two decades. Increasingly violent and engaged in illegal money-making activities like street-level drug trafficking, these groups have turned many inner city neighborhoods into battlegrounds pock-marked with seemingly random deadly shootings. For example, in 1990 youth gang killings accounted for 11% of all homicides in Chicago and 34% in Los Angeles. The average age of the killer in these crimes was 20 (Sweet, 1990).

Why do gangs behave so violently over issues so seemingly unimportant as a club's colors? Yablonsky's (1970) typology of three gang types offers some valuable insights. The social gang forms around such activities as sports, cars, motorcycles, or dances. Membership in this group is relatively stable, and friendships can last into adulthood. The delinquent gang basically agrees with the materialistic and status values of society but chooses illegal methods to get what it values. Despite their illegal behavior and occasional violence, Yablonsky believes that members of delinquent gangs are emotionally stable. It is the *violent* gang, however, that best describes the groups emerging from city neighborhoods in recent years to capture the media headlines. This type of gang functions in a psychopathic manner, with members using violence for emotional gratification. According to Yablonsky, "the gang's activity is dominated by sociopathic themes of spontaneous prestige-seeking violence with psychic gratification as the goal." This characterization helps, then, to explain the violent overreaction of gang members to seemingly minor events, such as wandering into another gang's territory or insulting a gang's colors.

Scholars suggest that the young people between 13 and 24 years of age who engage in violent delinquent gang activity abandon their poor family, school, and other community associations for a new identity (Fagan, Piper, & Moore, 1986; Huff, 1990; Spergel & Chance, 1991). The assumption of this identity may be assisted by the problems of depersonalization that occur in aging cities (Laub, 1983; Reiss & Roth, 1993).

Because it provides its members with status, recognition, and a sense of purpose and belonging, the gang can be viewed as a family—although not, in some ways, for females.

The position of women within the male-dominated gang, as least until recently, is anything but equal. They have a low status within the male-dominated group and are excluded from most decision-making sessions. Interestingly, some researchers have found that their presence appears to diminish the gang's violent activity (Bowker, Gross, & Klein, 1980; Mydans, 1989). However, this desire to subjugate women into inferior roles has resulted in the dramatic growth in recent years of independent and more violent female youth gangs (Mydans, 1989). Trapped in the same cycle of poverty and societal and familial rejection, these female youth, like their male counterparts, are drawn together into a communal identity (Bowker & Klein, 1983; Campbell, 1987; A. Campbell, 1990).

However as the essence of the violent gang is violence and not some other communal value, it becomes understandable, too, that to maintain group cohesiveness a constant state of tension must be maintained. Thus, warfare between clubs, internal violence against fellow club members, and other criminal activities serve "to maintain the continuity of the group, to give it structure, and to symbolize the gang's power of life and death over others" (J. Friedman, Mann, & Adelman, 1976, p. 532).

The growing level of violence and the apparent randomness of its application have resulted in community attempts to curb gang activity. Spergel and Chance's (1991) national survey of youth gang problems and programs identified five such strategies. The first and most frequently used was suppression. Forty-four percent of the 254 respondents described increased police activity, arrest and surveillance as a strategy for controlling gang activity. Social intervention services, which included crisis intervention, outreach, and treatment services for youth, was in use by 31.5% of the respondents. The third most widely used strategy (10.9%) was court and police organizational responses like special prosecution and probation units. Community mobilization activities like joint policy and program development work between local community groups ranked fourth (8.9%) in practice. Finally, social

---

Box 16–2   Violence and Gangs (*continued*)

opportunities like basic education, job training, and work incentives was the preferred strategy in 4.8% of the communities. Spergel and Chance (1991, p. 23) conclude from their survey that in communities with serious chronic gang activity that "several variables were found to be strongly associated with effectiveness in dealing with the gang situation: (1) the use of community mobilization and social opportunity as primary strategies, (2) community consensus on the definition

of a gang incident, and (3) the proportion of agencies or organizations that had an external advisory group."

In the meantime, as adolescents in these communities violently struggle for recognition and for purpose, the number of dead youth will grow. Some of them will be gang members, while others will be innocent young people who unknowingly made the mistake of wandering into their path.

[Hirschi's] theory asserts that youngsters who do not develop a bond to the conventional order because of incomplete socialization feel no moral obligation to conform. For [Hirschi], the delinquent is the faulty or unfinished product of socialization. He is an incomplete social being. The social process of making him moral has been interrupted. . . . An unattached, uncommitted, and disbelieving youngster is the product of ineffective social control [socialization]. He is free to engage in delinquent behavior; special delinquent motivation is unnecessary to account for the behavior of a not quite social or not quite moral individual. It is to be expected. (Weis, 1977, p. 35)

Deviance Explanations

There are essentially two schools of thought in the deviance category of explanations for antisocial behavior. The first is Émile Durkheim's (1958) observation that society needs criminal activity. He comments that even in the perfect society, one inhabited by saints, some action will occur that will bring ridicule, scorn, and rejection on the perpetrator: "Imagine a society of saints, a perfect cloister of exemplary individuals. Crimes, properly so called, will there be unknown; but faults which appear venial to the layman will create there the same scandal that the ordinary offense does in ordinary consciousness" (pp. 68–69).

The second school of thought involves the ways in which one comes to acquire and retain a delinquent reputation. Playwrights and sociologists have observed for years that people are often judged unfairly based on factors unrelated to their behavior. In the words of Eliza Doolittle:

You see, really and truly, apart from the things anyone can pick up (the dressing and the proper way of speaking, and so on), the difference between a lady and a flower girl is not how she behaves, but how she's treated. I shall always be a flower girl to Professor Higgins, because he always treats me as a flower girl and always will; but I know I can be a lady to you, because you always treat me as a lady, and always will. (G. B. Shaw, 1957, p. 270)

Crime in Durkheim's (1958) model is a glue holding society together. It is "an integral part of all healthy societies" (p. 67) serving to pull people together in a common sense of indignation and rage over some travesty. In *Wayward Puritans* (1966), an excellent book on the subject. Kai Erikson follows Durkheim in explaining deviance as being conduct which the people of a group consider so dangerous or embarrassing or irritating that they bring special sanctions to bear against the persons who exhibit it. Deviance is not a property inherent in any particular kind of behavior; it is a property conferred upon that behavior by the people who come into direct or indirect contact with it. (P. 6)

This perspective allows us to observe that not all unruly students are sent to the principal and not all pot-smoking teenagers caught by the police are referred to court. We can further observe that the definition of crime changes with the shifting opinions of society. Thus, alcohol may be prohibited in one decade but not in the next. Marijuana users may be described as seriously emotionally disturbed individuals in one decade and in the next decade be described as normal, healthy, but foolish youths. It is possible to call running away an epidemic, pour millions of dollars into attempts to decrease it, and then virtually ignore this behavior a few years later.

The deviance perspective says that crime is a part of life, a necessary thread in the fabric of society without which people could not judge who is good and who is bad. Without the knowledge of who is good and who is bad, society could not function and would begin to disintegrate. The interest of the labeling theorist is in understanding not only society's need for crime but how and why it is that certain groups are likely to be considered deviant rather than others.

Labeling theorists note that those least able to protect themselves are those most frequently labeled deviant. Into this category fall the mentally ill, the poor, minorities, and children. Belonging to more than one of these groups, such as being poor, an ethnic minority, and a child, increases the likelihood of being considered deviant.

Labels can be acquired even in the process of attempting to shed or avoid them. For example, the child who goes to a child-guidance clinic is considered by the family, the school, and the social agency to be receiving help. Help in this context implies weakness and fault. Something is not right with the child. Even if this treatment (the word itself suggests correction) is successful, the labeling theorist would argue, a stigma has been attached to that child. This stigma will reappear whenever the school or family needs it to reappear:

Mother: You must appreciate the fact that Johnny has had problems for years.
Therapist: What do you mean?
Mother: Well, even as a little child he was, you know, difficult to get along with. We had to take him to see a doctor several times. And now that John and I are getting a divorce, he has begun to act up on us again. I just can't understand what's wrong with that child.

This conversation is not atypical of parents' comments. It illustrates that even when Johnny's behavior has at least one good explanation in the environmental changes occurring around him, his parents will choose to ignore that explanation and focus instead on his earlier problems. Similarly, the "Huck Finn" who commits behaviors which [he] considers to be fun and part of play may be considered undesirable and bad by parents, police officers and others, who attempt to suppress them. If the behavior and its negative social reaction continue, the youth may begin to view himself as a bad person rather than [to see] that the problem is just his immediate *behavior*. He may feel set apart from . . . "good children" and seek companions who seem to enjoy the same sort of behavior and who do not act disapprovingly. (Waugh, 1977, p. 136)

Thus, in his own eyes and in the eyes of others, he is a delinquent.

The Delinquent Within the Psychological Model

The literature on delinquency in the fields of psychiatry and psychology is extensive. Although views differ somewhat on the factors responsible for delinquency, certain schools of thought can be discerned. For example, Bloch and Niederhoffer (1958) echo Erik Erikson in viewing delinquency as one of the normal problems of adolescence. Understanding delinquents, they argue, entails examining their identity problems and their attempts to escape from parental authority. In their rejection of parental values and in their experimentation with new roles, it is inevitable that the young will engage in deviant acts at some time.

Other writers adopt a more traditional, Freudian perspective that ties male delinquency to problems of sexual identification. They suggest that the delinquent identifies with his mother. In the attempt to establish a masculine identity, the adolescent turns to delinquency as a way of rejecting the earlier feminine identification and the socially accepted behavior associated with it.

Between these two positions are numerous descriptions of the delinquent as possessing a weak ego, being asocial, having poor peer relations, suffering from social isolation, or being disorderly, nervous, confused, neurotic, or pathological (Jenkins & Hewitt, 1944; Kinch, 1962; A. J. Reiss, 1952). More recent studies do not alter these perceptions. Status offenders are young people who violate laws that apply only to them, such as regulations enforcing school attendance or prohibiting a child from leaving home. Young status offenders have been found to have disturbed socialization patterns and to demonstrate "greater feelings of anger and frustration and a tendency to react more readily with emotion, with accompanying feelings of discomfort due to the presence and control of these feelings" (Stott & Olczak, 1978, p. 82). Delinquents in general appear to have deviant value systems emphasizing short-term goals accompanied by a lack of ambition yet a desire to achieve (Cochrane, 1974). Finally, it appears that the earlier in a child's life that antisocial behavior appears, the more likely the child is to be antisocial later in life (Loeber, 1982).

From descriptions such as these, several typologies of the delinquent have emerged. One of the best is in *The Psychological World of the Juvenile Delinquent* (1979), by Offer, Marohn, and Ostrov. They suggest four delinquent types. The first is the *impulsive* delinquent, who is described as displaying more overt antisocial and violent behavior than the other three types. Although considered "quite disturbed," such young people do possess enough insight into their behavior to recognize their need for help in changing it. *Narcissistic* delinquents are the most passive/aggressive of the four types. Although they may see themselves as emotionally healthy, they are "cunning, manipulative, and superficial." Of all four types, these delinquents are most likely to use others for personal gain. The *empty/borderline* delinquent is quiet and "emotionally empty." With strong dependency needs for love and caring, this young person sees little hope for the future. Offer and his colleagues suggest that for these young people, delinquency is a futile attempt to maintain emotional stability. The fourth type is the *depressed/borderline* delinquent. In many respects these young people have the best prognosis for change. Their family relationships are relatively positive in that they have "strong internalized [parental] value systems," and most show willingness to change their behavior. For many of these young people, delinquency acts to relieve the great guilt and depression they experience.

Offer and his associates (1979) candidly admit that since theirs was a psychological study, they were unable to assess the impact of sex, race, and socioeconomic status on their typology. These factors are discussed later in this chapter.

The Family of the Delinquent

Research suggests that the families of delinquents experience a multitude of problems, including marital strife, transience, unemployment, serious illness, and alcoholism, and that the parents are inconsistent, uncaring, or even hostile in their treatment of their children (Goetting, 1994; Neilson & Gerber, 1979; P. A. Robinson, 1978; Widom, 1989). According to many studies on the families of delinquents:

1. There is a positive relationship between broken homes and delinquency (Farrington, 1990; Glueck & Glueck, 1950; Gove & Crutchfield, 1982; Monahan, 1957; Slocum & Stone, 1963; Toby, 1957; Weeks & Smith, 1939).
2. Discipline is inconsistent in the homes of delinquents (Farrington, 1990; Glueck & Glueck, 1950; McCord & McCord, 1964; Nye, 1958; Patterson & Dishion, 1985; P. A. Robinson, 1978; Slocum & Stone, 1963; Steinberg, 1987a).
3. There has been a lack of affection between delinquents and their parents (D. F. Duncan, 1978; Farrington, 1990; Glueck & Glueck, 1950; McCord & McCord, 1964; Neilson & Gerber, 1979; P. A. Robinson, 1978; Slocum & Stone, 1963; R. M. Smith & Walters, 1978).
4. Marital discord is commonplace in the homes of delinquents (Browning, 1960; Farrington, 1990; Glueck & Glueck, 1950; Gove & Crutchfield, 1982; Nye, 1958; Sorrells, 1977).
5. A father's hostility or absence encourages delinquency (Hirschi, 1969; Nye, 1958; Pine, 1966; R. M. Smith & Walters, 1978).
6. As parental support declines, peer influence and delinquent behavior increase (Poole & Regoli, 1979).
7. Emotional neglect and physical abuse are commonplace in the homes of delinquents (Widom, 1989).

Other researchers have, however, disputed each of these positions. For instance, L. Rosen (1985), in identifying the contribution of familial variables to delinquency, concludes that the absence of father/son interactions in Black families encourages delinquency. For White adolescents, however, the socioeconomic status of the family emerges as a more powerful predictor of delinquent activity. In his study of 734 adolescents, R. E. Johnson (1986) finds little evidence that a broken home per se is a significant factor in the development of delinquency. Rather, it appears that interactional variables (communication patterns between males and stepfathers or discrimination by society against females and their single mothers) account for delinquency.

Finally, in a recent exhaustive literature review on child abuse and increased risk for delinquency, adult criminal behavior, and violent criminal behavior, Widom (1989) notes that although abused children are at risk the majority do not become delinquent, criminal, or violent. She reports that even though a significant number of abused children had later juvenile offenses (26%), nearly three times that number (74%) did not. While a significant number (11%) of abused youth were later arrested for a violent criminal act, almost nine times that many (89%) were not. This is an important observation that deserves attention as it challenges the belief that the intergenerational transmission of violence is inevitable. Rather, other environmental and individual factors can compensate for early negative life experiences, and individuals can succeed.

We suggest that in combination with personal and environmental factors, one or more of these family variables identify adolescents at high risk of delinquency. It is clearly true that not all young people who fail to have a positive relationship with their parents are doomed to delinquency. Nevertheless, when other factors are added to their lives—poverty, uncertainty over who they are, school problems, or deviant peers—the chances of delinquency increase tremendously.

The Juvenile Court

The notion of a juvenile court came from liberal reformers who possessed the same sense of conviction that moved the supporters of refuge homes to action. Before the establishment of the juvenile court in 1899, the judicial system operated under common-law principles that considered a youth's age in determining criminal responsibility. Children under 7 were not held responsible for their behavior. Children between the ages of 7 and 14 could be tried for their misdeeds, but before they could be convicted the prosecutor had to prove that they understood the meaning of their behavior. Youths over the age of 14 were considered responsible for their conduct and treated as adults. Subject to these few considerations, all juveniles over the age of 6 incurred the same penalties as adults for criminal behavior and were incarcerated in the same jails and prisons.

Much of the movement to establish the juvenile-court system was in reaction to the imprisonment of youthful offenders with adults. Or, for the more cynically inclined, consider the argument that convicted young criminals were not imprisoned but allowed to roam the streets. There is evidence that many juries chose to release young criminals rather than imprison them with adults. This ten-

Experience with Juvenile Court is designed to be humane but firm in its intent.

dency to release youths may have been what really moved reformers to establish the separate court system (Gullotta, 1978). Either way, passionate arguments, accompanying moralistic stories of impressionable young children's being schooled in the ways of crime, sin, and degradation, moved legislatures in most states in a very few years to establish a juvenile-court system. The court was to be unlike the adult courts: "The fundamental concern of the court regarding a child is what is he, how has he become what he is, and what had best be done in his interest and in the interest of the state to save him from a downward career" (F. B. McCarthy, 1977, p. 197).

This statement clearly does not imply the adversary relationship that exists in the adult courts. It implies that the judge is a kind, compassionate soul—although a stern parental figure when necessary—whose judgments will always be in the best interests of the child. To accomplish this goal, the court needs more resources than an adult court. Staff members are needed to perform such duties as gathering information on court-referred youths from parents, teachers, and others before these young people appear in court.

Leaning heavily on the legal doctrines of *parens patriae* and *in loco parentis,* the juvenile court attempted to find the best possible disposition for a referred case. Interestingly, the power to make dispositions did not reside with the judge alone. Probation officers funneled out of the system large numbers of court-referred youths for simple judicial supervision. These young people and their parents were advised of what actions the probation officer felt were necessary to prevent the recurrence of criminal activity.

From a historical perspective it is not possible to identify which offenses were diverted away from the court by the probation officer. In some states, shoplifting was a divertable offense; in others it was not. Moreover, in some states some judges considered shoplifting to be a divertable offense, while other judges serving in the same states required all shoplifters to appear before them in court. Thus, "even judges could be inconsistent parents" (Gullotta, 1979, p. 7).

The *Gault* Decision

From its creation in 1899 until 1967, in its zeal to "snatch . . . a 'branch from the burning,' " the juvenile court used case histories, psychological data, and judicial "parental" judgment to act in the best interests of the child. In 1967 the U.S. Supreme Court decided in the *Gault* case that juvenile courts were acting in such a way as to deprive young people of certain constitutional protections. Box 16–3, which contains an excerpt from the Supreme Court's opinion, presents the fascinating story of Gerald Gault's arrest and conviction.

In many respects the handling of the *Gault* case represents the completion of a circle started by reformers in 1899 with the founding of the juvenile-court system. They created the system to protect children from injustice. In 1967 the Supreme Court acted to protect children from that same court system's injustice. Specifically, the Supreme Court decided that young people like Gerald Gault have a right to know the charges against them, to have an attorney represent them, and to have that attorney cross-examine witnesses. Further, young people cannot be deprived of the rights guaranteed by the Fifth Amendment or of the right to appeal a case to a higher court. Essentially the Supreme Court decision declared for the first time that young people are not property but human beings.

Issues in Juvenile-Court Reform

When the Supreme Court decided that Gerald Gault could not be denied the protection of the Constitution, the decision not only freed the boy but triggered juvenile-court reform. It also stimulated a vigorous examination of society's handling of juveniles charged with criminal activity. In the years that followed the *Gault* decision, four issues emerged.

The Ones that Got Away

The first issue challenges our basic understanding of delinquency. The old notion that most adolescents who commit delinquent acts are detected and referred to court has been proved to be largely a myth. Studies indicate that only 3% to 5% of all crime by youths is ever detected (Hindelang, Hirschi, & Weis, 1981; Mannarino & Marsh, 1978) and that adolescent crime levels off after age 16 (Farrington, 1983, 1990) (see Figure 16–1). Furthermore, the overwhelming majority of delinquents are not "mentally ill" (Gibbons, 1986).

These studies indicate that almost all adolescents at one time or another commit acts that, if discovered, would be considered criminal. Indeed, a 1985 U.S. Department of Justice study reports that 26.8% of high school seniors admitted shoplifting an item in the previous 12 months, and 25.2% acknowledged committing an unlawful entry (Rist, 1987). Furthermore, even those who are caught and referred to court stand a better-than-average chance of being

---

Box 16–3   Excerpt from Supreme Court's *Gault* Ruling

On Monday, June 8, 1964, at about 10 A.M., Gerald Francis Gault and a friend Ronald Lewis, were taken into custody by the Sheriff of Gila County [Arizona]. Gerald was then still subject to a six months' probation order which had been entered on February 25, 1964, as a result of his having been in the company of another boy who had stolen a wallet from a lady's purse. The police action on June 8 was taken as the result of a verbal complaint by a neighbor of the boys, Mrs. Cook, about a telephone call made to her in which the caller or callers made lewd or indecent remarks. It will suffice for purposes of this opinion to say that the remarks or questions put to her were of the irritatingly offensive, adolescent, sex variety.

At the time Gerald was picked up, his mother and father were both at work. No notice that Gerald was being taken into custody was left at the home. No other steps were taken to advise them that their son had, in effect, been arrested. Gerald was taken to the Children's Detention Home. When his mother arrived home at about 6 o'clock, Gerald was not there. Gerald's older brother was sent to look for him at the trailer home of the Lewis family. He apparently learned then that Gerald was in custody. He so informed his mother. The two of them went to the Detention Home. The deputy probation officer, Flagg, who was also superintendent of the Detention Home, told Mrs. Gault "why Jerry was there" and said that a hearing would be held in Juvenile Court at 3 o'clock the following day, June 9.

Officer Flagg filed a petition with the Court on the hearing day, June 9, 1964. It was not served on the Gaults. Indeed, none of them saw this petition until the habeas corpus hearing on August 17, 1964. The petition was entirely formal. It made no reference to any factual basis for the judicial action which it initiated. It recited only that "said minor is under the age of 18 years and in need of the protection of this honorable Court [and that] said minor is a delinquent minor." It prayed for a hearing and order regarding "the care and custody of said minor." Officer Flagg executed a formal affidavit in support of the petition.

On June 9, Gerald, his mother, his older brother, and Probation Officers Flagg and Henderson appeared before the Juvenile Judge in chambers. Gerald's father was not there. He was at work out of the city. Mrs. Cook, the complainant, was not there.

No one was sworn at this hearing. No script or recording was made. No memorandum or record of the substance of the proceedings was prepared. Our information about the proceedings, and the subsequent hearings on June 15, derives entirely from the testimony of the Juvenile Court Judge.[1] Mr. and Mrs. Gault and Officer Flagg at the habeas corpus proceeding conducted two months later. From this, it appears that at the July 9 hearing Gerald was questioned by the judge about the telephone call. There was conflict as to what he said. His mother recalled that Gerald said he only dialed Mrs. Cook's number and handed the telephone to his friend, Ronald. Officer Flagg recalled that Gerald had admitted making the lewd remarks. Judge McGhee testified that Gerald "admitted making one of these [lewd] statements." At the conclusion of the hearing, the judge said he would "think about it." Gerald was taken back to the Detention Home. He was not sent to his own home with his parents. On June 11 or 12, after having been detained since June 8, Gerald was released and driven home.[2] There is no explanation in the record as to why he was released. At 5 P.M. on the day of Gerald's release. Mrs. Gault received a note signed by Officer Flagg. It was on plain paper, not letterhead. Its entire text was as follows:

Mrs. Gault:
Judge McGhee has set Monday June 15, 1964 at 11:00 A.M. as the date and time for further Hearings on Gerald's delinquency.

/s/Flagg

At the appointed time on Monday, June 15, Gerald, his father and mother, Ronald Lewis and his father, and Officers Flagg and Henderson were present before

---

[1] Under Arizona law, juvenile hearings are conducted by a judge of the Superior Court, designated by his colleagues on the Superior Court to serve as Juvenile Court Judge. Arizona Const., Art. 6.15; Arizona Revised Statutes (hereinafter ARS) 8-201, 8-202.

[2] There is a conflict between the recollection of Mrs. Gault and that of Officer Flagg. Mrs. Gault testified that Gerald was released on Friday, June 12, Officer Flag stated that it had been on Thursday, June 11. This was from memory; he had no record, and the note was undated.

Box 16–3 Excerpt from Supreme Court's *Gault* Ruling (continued)

Judge McGhee. Witnesses at the habeas corpus proceeding differed in their recollections of Gerald's testimony at the June 15 hearing. Mr. and Mrs. Gault recalled that Gerald again testified that he had only dialed the number and that the other boy had made the remarks. Officer Flagg agreed that at this hearing Gerald did not admit making the lewd remarks.[3] But Judge McGhee recalled that "there was some admission again of some of the lewd statements. He—he didn't admit any of the more serious lewd statements."[4] Again, the complainant, Mrs. Cook, was not present. Mrs. Gault asked that Mrs. Cook be present "so she could see which boy had done the talking, the dirty talking over the phone." The Juvenile Judge said "she didn't have to be present at the hearing." The judge did not speak to Mrs. Cook or communicate with her at any time. Probation Officer Flagg had talked to her once—over the telephone on June 9.

At this June 15 hearing a "referral report" made by the probation officers was filed with the Court, although not disclosed to Gerald or his parents. This listed the charge as "Lewd Phone Calls." At the conclusion of the hearing, the judge committed Gerald as a juvenile delinquent to the State Industrial School "for the period of his minority [that is, until 21], unless sooner discharged by due process of law." An order to that effect was entered. It recited that "after a full hearing and due deliberation the Court finds that said minor is a delinquent child, and that said minor is of the age of 15 years."

No appeal is permitted by Arizona law in juvenile cases. On August 3, 1964, a petition for a writ of habeas corpus was filed with the Supreme Court of Arizona and referred by it to the Superior Court for hearing.

At the habeas corpus hearing on August 17, Judge McGhee was vigorously cross-examined as to the basis for his actions. He testified that he had taken into account the fact that Gerald was on probation. He was asked "under what section of . . . the code you found the boy delinquent?"

His answer is set forth in the margin.[5] In substance, he concluded that Gerald came within ARS 8-201-6(a), which specifies that a "delinquent child" includes one "who has violated a law of the state or an ordinance or regulation of a political subdivision thereof." The law which Gerald was found to have violated is ARS 13-377. This section of the Arizona Criminal Code provides that a person who "in the presence of or hearing of any woman or child . . . uses vulgar, abusive or obscene language, is guilty of a misdemeanor. . . . " The penalty specified in the Criminal Code, which would apply to an adult, is $5 to $50, or imprisonment for not more than two months. The judge also testified that he acted under ARS 8-201-6(d) which includes in the definition of a "delinquent child" one who, as the judge phrased it, is "habitually involved in immoral matters."[6]

Asked about the basis for his conclusion that Gerald was "habitually involved in immoral matters," the judge testified, somewhat vaguely, that two years earlier, on July 2, 1962, a "referral" was made concerning Gerald, "where the boy had stolen a baseball glove from another boy and lied to the Police Department about it." The judge said there was "no hearing," and "no accusation" relating to this incident, "because of lack of material foundation." But it seems to have remained in his mind

---

[3]Officer Flag also testified that Gerald had not, when questioned at the Detention Home, admitted having made many of the lewd statements, but that each boy had sought to put the blame on the other. There was conflicting testimony as to whether Ronald had accused Gerald of making the lewd statements during the June 15 hearing.

[4]Judge McGhee also testified that Gerald had not denied "certain statements" made to him at the hearing by Officer Henderson.

[5]Q. "All right. Now Judge, would you tell me under what section of —of the code you found the boy delinquent?"
A. "Well, there is a —I think it amounts to disturbing the peace. I can't give you the section, but I can tell you the law, that when one person uses lewd language in the presence of another person, that is can amount to—and I consider that when a person makes it over the phone, that it is considered in the presence. I might be wrong, that is one section. The other section upon which I consider the boy delinquent is Section 8-201, Subsection (d), habitually involved in immoral matters."

[6]ARS 8-201-6, the section of the Arizona Juvenile Code which defines a delinquent child, reads: " 'Delinquent child' includes:
"(a) A child who has violated a law of the state or an ordinance or regulation of a political subdivision thereof.
"(b) A child who, by reason of being incorrigible, wayward or habitually disobedient, is uncontrolled by his parent, guardian or custodian.
"(c) A child who is habitually truant from school or home.
"(d) A child who habitually so deports himself as to injure or endanger the morals or health of himself or others."

Box 16–3   Excerpt from Supreme Court's *Gault* Ruling (*continued*)

as a relevant factor. The judge also testified that Gerald had admitted making other nuisance phone calls in the past which, as the judge recalled the boy's testimony, were "silly calls, or funny calls, or something like that."

The Superior Court dismissed the writ, and appellants sought review in the Arizona Supreme Court. That court stated that it considered appellants' assignments of error as urging (1) that the Juvenile Code, ARS 8-201 to 8-239, is unconstitutional because it does not require that parents and children be apprised of the specific charges, does not require proper notice of a hearing, and does not provide for an appeal: and (2) that the proceedings and order relating to Gerald constituted a denial of due process of law because of the absence of adequate notice of the charge and the hearing; failure to notify appellants of certain constitutional rights including the rights to counsel and to confrontation, and the privilege against self-incrimination; the use of unsworn hearsay testimony; and the failure to make a record of the proceedings. Appellants further asserted that it was error for the Juvenile Court to remove Gerald from the custody of his parents without a showing and finding of their unsuitability, and alleged a miscellany of other errors under state law.

The Supreme Court handed down an elaborate and wide-ranging opinion affirming dismissal of the writ

and stating the Court's conclusions as to the issues raised by appellants and other aspects of the juvenile process. In their jurisdictional statement and brief in this Court, appellants do not urge upon us all of the points passed upon by the Supreme Court of Arizona. They urged that we hold the Juvenile Code of Arizona invalid on its face or as applied in this case because contrary to the Due Process Clause of the Fourteenth Amendment, the juvenile is taken from the custody of his parents and committed to a state institution pursuant to proceedings in which the Juvenile Court has virtually unlimited discretion, and in which the following basic rights are denied:

1. Notice of the charges;
2. Right to counsel;
3. Right to confrontation and cross-examination;
4. Privilege against self-incrimination;
5. Right to a transcript of the proceedings; and
6. Right to appellate review.

Do you think that the U.S. Supreme Court acted properly in extending these "adult" rights to adolescents?

Source: In re Gault (Supreme Court of the United States, May 15, 1967). In *Task Force Report: Juvenile Delinquency and Youth Crime*. President's Commission on Law Enforcement and Administration of Justice, U.S. Superintendent of Documents (#0-239-116), 1967.

released to the community. Court records clearly indicate that although thousands of young people are referred to juvenile court, few appear before a judge. Of those who do appear, few are deemed to warrant the close supervision of either probation or detention (National Council on Crime and Delinquency, 1984).

This evidence suggests that perhaps we are approaching the entire issue of delinquency incorrectly. The sheer numbers of young people who commit illegal acts indicate that delinquency is normative behavior. Perhaps society should try to include young people in the community rather than to exclude them (Gibbons, 1986; Lundman, 1984; Spergel & Chance, 1991).

Status Offenders

The second issue is the court's jurisdiction over status offenders. A status offense is an act that, if committed by an adult, would not be considered criminal. Behaviors

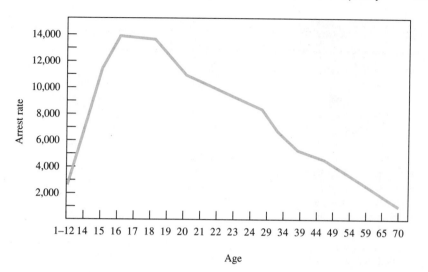

Figure 16–1   Age and arrests per 100,000 in 1975 in the United States. (*Source:* Sykes, G. M. (1980). *The future of crime* (National Institute of Mental Health, DHHS Publication No. ADM 80-912). Washington, DC: U.S. Government Printing Office.)

such as truancy, indecent or immoral conduct, running away, incorrigibility, and school misconduct fall into the status-offense category. (See Box 16–4.)

Critics of the juvenile court argued successfully in the late 1970s and early 1980s that the court's jurisdiction over status offenders perpetuated the refuge-house mentality of imposing middle-class values on children by punishing the ones who challenge those values. They further contended that the court does more harm than good in labeling these young people criminals (Gullotta, 1979). Arguments such as these encouraged the federal government in the 1970s to use the threat of withholding law-enforcement funds to force most states to decriminalize status offenses.

In recent years a rising chorus of criticism against these actions has been heard from court officials and youth workers. Supporters of the court and its jurisdiction over the status offender contend that parents need the court's help in controlling rebellious adolescents' behavior. They suggest that a poorly function-ing family may itself endanger a young person's moral and social development. Proponents also argue that a status offense is often the only means by which a youth suspected of more serious criminal activity can be brought to justice. Without jurisdiction the court could not intervene on the young person's behalf. The issue of the court's jurisdiction over status offenses will continue to be debated heatedly into the 1990s. It involves the complex philosophical questions of what a society's responsibility is for guiding its young and how that responsi-bility compares to a youth's rights under the constitution.

Sexism

The third issue is the differential treatment given female offenders. Evidence suggests that although girls primarily engage in status offenses rather than more serious violations (Steffensmeier & Steffensmeier, 1980), once arrested they are dealt with more harshly by society (R. E. Johnson, 1986).

Box 16–4   Runaway and Throwaway Youth in America

Each year approximately 500,000 young people leave their homes (Sweet, 1990). For some adolescents, running away will be a short-term romantic foray into a Tom Sawyer series of adventures ending when either boredom or an empty wallet dictates a return home. For others, it will be a desperate action to escape from family, school, or community crises with which they cannot cope. For still others, leaving home represents the only option; whether through implicit or explicit messages, these young people have learned that their families no longer want them.

There are several definitions of the term *runaway*. The one we use is, "a youth between the ages of 10 and 17, inclusive, who has been absent from home, at least overnight, without parental or guardian permission" (Opinion Research Center, 1976, p. 3). A *throwaway* or castaway is a young person who did not willingly leave home but was forced to do so by the attitudes or actions of his or her parents or guardian (Gullotta, 1978).

Why do young people leave home? In a classic article on the subject, running away was viewed by Gullotta (1979), "as a conflict between parent and child over a social control issue" (p. 113). The seemingly minor events that result in a young person's desire to leave home suggest that the major difficulty facing the family is a lack of trust and security. Thus, "disobedience over minor issues displaces the really significant issues, allowing for the displacement of intense anger to areas less likely to unsettle an already weak family structure" (p. 113).

In this model a lack of communication between parents and adolescents is the crucial factor in running away. The members of such families are temporarily estranged. Young people see their parents as unwilling to listen and as unable or unwilling to understand them. Parents, on the other hand, see their children as disrespectful, disobedient, and ungrateful. Because both parents and adolescents are uncertain about their roles in the family, each is unwilling to risk sharing. It is fear of rejection, not a lack of caring, "that paralyzes both parent and sibling and leads to subsequent conflict and struggle" and to finally running away.

In keeping with this perspective are the findings of Finkelhor, Hotaling, and Sedlak (1990). Their numbers and characteristics study for the Office of Juvenile Justice and Delinquency Prevention suggests that a family argument about house rules, friends, school, or staying out late preceded a running episode about one third of the time. Interestingly, only 28% of these homes could be described as intact (that is, both parents present) suggesting that parent-child role issues may well be a significant factor. Most runaways (94%) ultimately ran to a friend's or relative's house. Sixty-seven percent of caretakers knew the location of their child at least half the time, and the duration of the run was two days or less for 49% of the youth. As noted elsewhere in this chapter, when the runaway was an adolescent female the chances of referral to court for this status offense were significantly higher (Sickmund, 1990).

In contrast, the throwaway comes from a family in which the parents have cut all ties to the young person. The problem is not simply, "a weakening in a relationship but . . . a breakdown in the fabric of the family, a failure so severe, so emotionally tearing, that the bonds between parent and child are broken" (Gullotta, 1979, p. 113).

Several situations are capable of producing such a strong and complete rejection. One is the discovery of incest between parent and child or between children (Janus, McCormack, Burgess, & Hartman, 1987; Kurtz, Kurts, & Jarvis, 1991). The abuse of drugs, criminal behavior, or promiscuity may result in the termination of the family relationship. Or after a divorce neither parent may want to care for the children. If the children are not simply deserted, life with either of the parents may become so unbearable that the young people leave (Radford, King, & Warren, 1989). In any case the breakdown of the family is complete and irreparable. In some cases it may be the end of repeated attempts, "to stop some parentally perceived undesirable behavior. In other situations, it constitutes a scapegoating or desertion of the child" (Gullotta, 1979, p. 114).

Recent studies underscore this understanding as they describe young people fleeing untenable circumstances (Miller, Eggertson-Tacon, & Quigg, 1990) and of living isolated, depressed, antisocial lives (G. R. Adams, Gullotta, & Clancy, 1985; Hier, Korboot, & Schweitzer, 1990). Finkelhor, Hotaling, and Sedlak (1990) report that 84% of these youth are over the age of 16 with nearly equal numbers of males and females. Only 19% come from intact homes. And in keeping with their earlier statement that family bonds were not merely strained but broken 44% of their population was asked to leave home, 11% ran away and were refused permission to return home, and the remainder ran away and the "caretaker doesn't care" (p. 153).

The problems of throwaway youth are not easily addressed. Hurt, rejected, and filled with rage, they are by no means the easiest of youth with which to deal. The development of runaway shelters is a temporary stopgap measure. Such a shelter provides the youth with a clean bed and hot meal for a few days before that young person hits the road to some new destina-

tion. For youth willing to stay put, the use of independent living programs in which young people are provided with financial aid and social and emotional support is another attempt to bridge the gap in time from dependency to independent adult status. The use of foster homes and residential facilities has generally proven to be unsatisfactory, resulting in young people running away from these settings or needing to be frequently removed and placed in new settings because of unacceptable behavior. Society continues to struggle unsuccessfully in developing alternatives to the family for these youth.

The work of Schwartz, Steketee, and Schneider (1990) continues to document findings that:

1. Girls are more likely than boys to be referred for status offenses involving sexually acting out (Barton, 1976; Conway & Bogdan, 1977; Thornberry, Tolnay, Flanagan, & Glynn, 1991).
2. For the year 1987, girls were ten times more likely to be incarcerated for status offenses than were boys in public training schools and five times more likely to be incarcerated for status offenses than were boys in public detention centers (Schwartz et al., 1990).
3. Girls tend to receive "more severe dispositions" than boys (Barton, 1976; Conway & Bogdan, 1977).

These ongoing circumstances lead Schwartz and associates (1990, p. 13) to conclude that, "we need no longer wonder whether girls and boys are . . . confined . . . for similar offenses. The answer . . . is that they are not." Conway and Bogdan's (1977) observations regarding this disparity made more than a decade ago continue to ring true:

Few incarcerated females are radicals; few are threats to the established order. Most are dupes of males who manipulate them to the point of social embarrassment. If we are not protecting society from these young girls, we must be expressing a Victorian demand that they be protected from their own stupidity. (P. 134)

Why is a boy who loses his virginity held in esteem by friends and viewed indulgently by society, while a girl in the same situation is called loose, free with herself, an easy lay, or other pejorative phrases? It does appear to us that the court tends to view female promiscuity unfairly in comparison with male promiscuity, making the court, in a sense, sexist. Sexism, we would argue, should not intrude on judicial matters. (See Box 16–5 for the case of a young woman counseled by Thomas Gullotta.)

Box 16–5   Doing Nothing Is Sometimes Harder Than Doing Something

Pat was an attractive, sexually active 15-year-old whose arrest by the police motivated her mother to bring Pat to see me. Pat's father, a firm disciplinarian, had died suddenly less than a month before. Her relationship with her mother was positive.

Pat was arrested after a neighbor complained that a group of adolescent males were outside Pat's home. The police found several young males waiting to have sexual intercourse with her. They were sent home with no further action. Pat, however, was arrested and referred to juvenile court.

In speaking with Pat, I saw a depressed, confused young woman searching for love. I believed that her father's death had precipitated much of her recent behavior. I did not see her as emotionally disturbed but as confused and in need of a supportive, caring environment. Pat's sexual activity considerably disturbed the juvenile justice authorities, and they proceeded to adjudicate her as a delinquent.

Not believing that this court action would be in her best interests, I worked out with her lawyer an arrangement with the court—not an ideal arrangement, in our opinion. Pat was placed on probation in a private coeducational school out of state. But Pat failed to last a year in the school. Her dismissal was related to her sexual activity.

The probation officer was eager at this point to commit Pat to state care. But we persuaded the court to return her, as I had initially encouraged, to her mother's care. Over the next several months I was successful in helping mother and daughter deal with their grief over the father's death, but I made little impression on Par's need for sexual gratification. Her sexual activity did not essentially change. Nevertheless, I continued (at times with tremendous reluctance) to advocate her continued freedom in the community.

Pat graduated from high school and a local community college. She has finished her undergraduate education. At 25 she is, by her own account, engaged and working.

Frankly, I admit that my efforts to ease Pat's depression and thus modify her sexual activity can and should be judged mostly a failure. At many times I questioned my own sanity in encouraging Pat's remaining in the community when she made it a point to keep me vividly informed of her latest escapades. Nevertheless, judging by her performance today as a law-abiding citizen, a small dose of maturity and large injections of patience can be successful.

> Was Pat's case handled correctly? How would you have dealt with this situation?

Racism

The last issue is whether racism permeates the juvenile justice system. According to several reports, the juvenile justice system is more likely to pick out Blacks, Hispanics, and other minorities for less-than-equal treatment under the law. The argument is that the police stop and search minority adolescents before they do White adolescents and are quicker to arrest them and refer them to court. Once in court, these young people receive harsher treatment than their White counterparts.

For example, although Black Americans comprise less than 11% of the population of the United States, they constitute 50% of that nation's prison population (Klein, Petersilia, & Turner, 1990; Langan, 1991). As many Black leaders note, presently there are more Black males in prisons than are enrolled in colleges and universities in the United States. Nevertheless, the evidence for these contentions is inconclusive and contradictory. A review of the literature shows that:

1. Some studies indicate that the police refer more Blacks than Whites to court, but by no means does this finding remain constant. Other research suggests that race is not a factor (see, for example, Barton, 1976).

2. Probation officers tend to recommend Blacks more than whites for incarceration. Whites are more likely to be referred for psychiatric examinations (D. O. Lewis, Balla, & Shanok, 1979).
3. The proportion of incarcerated youths who are Black and Hispanic is increasing, while the number of White incarcerated youths is decreasing (National Council on Crime and Delinquency, 1984).

Barton's review of the literature concluded that the available evidence did not support the finding that race was an important element in the juvenile justice process. A decade later B. R. McCarthy and Smith (1986) reached similar conclusions. Their study of 649 juveniles referred to court found that screening and detention decisions were not discriminatory. More recent efforts by Klein, Petersilia, and Turner (1990) continue to support this conclusion.

Their work (Klein et al., 1990) and that of L. E. Cohen and Kluegal (1978) help illuminate what factors do influence courts. The Cohen and Kluegal study of two juvenile courts revealed no evidence that race affected judicial decisions. Instead, they suggest that idleness (that is, lack of a job or of involvement in some other productive activity) and a prior record interact to produce the harshest sentences. The Klein and associates study found that rather than race, a history of previous convictions, being on probation, having been released from prison in the last twelve months, using a weapon, drug/alcohol use, not plea bargaining, failing to be released before the trial, and the lack of a private attorney accounted for 80% of imprisonment decisions in the State of California. Race as a variable in this study did not account for 1% of the decisions. (See Box 16–6 for an excerpt from Gresham Sykes' *The Future of Crime*.)

D. O. Lewis, Balla, and Shanok (1979) have sought to explain why White youths are more frequently referred for psychiatric care than are Black youths. These authors contend that Black adolescents are being deprived of proper psychiatric care. They found numerous situations in which a Black youth's behavior was dismissed as "characteristically impaired" while a White youth displaying the same behavior was diagnosed differently. Lewis and her associates contend that in an attempt to avoid racism, mental-health professionals are failing to diagnose the problems of Black youths accurately:

> Many seriously psychiatrically disturbed, abused, neglected Black children are being channeled to correctional facilities while their White counterparts are more likely to be recognized as in need of help and directed toward therapeutic facilitites. The failure of White mental health professionals to recognize and treat serious psychopathology when it exists in the Black delinquent population accounts in part for the fact that our adult correctional facilities are becoming increasingly filled with members of minority groups. (P. 60)

Gang membership, as a factor that interacts with race, may also affect the processing of youths in the judicial system. In studying Chicanos, Zatz (1985) argues that differential treatment of gang members and nongang members by the legal system occurs in both court processing time of adolescent offenders and the outcome of that process. Although gang membership is not an illegal activity, stereotyping of gang members, along with racial prejudice and discrimination, potentially affects gang members' experiences with the juvenile justice system.

Box 16–6 Crime in the Future

In 1980 the National Institute of Mental Health published a monograph by Gresham Sykes entitled the *Future of Crime*. This box presents the conclusions of that monograph.

Against any encouraging portents of the future of crime, we must set some relatively ominous signs. The failure to solve the problems of the metropolis, we have suggested, points to continuing or increasing frustration and consequent deviance in the form of crime. The flow of migration, both legal and illegal, almost certainly promises an increase in criminal behavior if migrants are forced into ghettos with limited opportunities for social mobility. Chronic unemployment, for those at all levels of the stratification system but particularly for those at the bottom of the social heap, may emerge as a stubborn problem for advanced industrial societies such as the United States. . . . The result is likely to be a growth in crime. . . .

If crimes such as murder, assault, rape, robbery, and larceny become more numerous in the next several decades, a "get-tough" approach to the control of crime is likely to appear still more attractive. The concept of locking up people not to rehabilitate them but simply to prevent them from committing new crimes can be expected to flourish. . . . If offenses of the middle class also increase, perhaps forming a larger part of the total crime problem or gaining a larger share of public concern, reactions to crime could move in new directions. . . . First, there is likely to be a growing emphasis on types of deterrent sanctions thought to be especially suited for members of the middle class, such as heavy fines and much publicity attached to criminal convictions. And second, it can be expected that much effort will be directed to prevention, by means of sophisticated accounting systems, electronic surveillance, computer programs constructed with an eye to security, etc. . . .

Such changes might be seen as an advance, but it must also be pointed out that they create the danger of a bipartite correctional system. Lower-class offenders, convicted of "conventional" crimes, would be subjected increasingly to fixed terms in prison, whereas middle-class offenders who have been convicted of various forms of white-collar crime would be fined or morally censured. It might be claimed, of course, that this is what the United States tends to do now.

Has Sykes vision of crime come true? Do Whites fare better than minority groups? Is white-collar crime more profitable than other types of crime?

Source: G. M. Sykes, *The Future of Crime.* National Institute of Mental Health, DHHS Publication No. ADM 80-912. Washington, D. C.: U.S. Government Printing Office, 1980, pp. 65–66, 68–69.

Zatz (1985) finds that gang membership does not have an independent effect on Chicano gang members' movement through the judicial system to final case disposition. Although there are no direct biasing effects of gang membership, gang members receive differential treatment when other characteristics are present. That is, the label of gang member, alone, does not appear to account for differential processes and outcomes. However, gang membership does affect the authorities' interpretation of cases when other characteristics of the case and of the offense are present. For example, when a complaint for immediate detention of the youth is given, gang members are more frequently placed in detention than are nongang members. In addition, among gang members it was found that the higher their grade in school, the less likely they are to receive severe dispositions. No association between school and disposition for nongang Chicanos is noted. Further, prior referrals increase the chance of a harsher outcome for gang members, but not so for Chicano nongang members.

Just as attitudes of police and juvenile court officials toward minority adolescents are influenced by race and ethnic background of adolescents, attitudes of adolescents toward police also vary according to ethnic group membership. Sullivan, Dunham, and Alpert (1987) investigated the varying attitudes of African-American, Cuban-American, and White teenagers and adults toward police. Factor analysis was used to analyze adolescent and adult responses to 22 attitudinal statements dealing with police. The teenagers from each of these groups appear to conceptualize police differently from their adult counterparts. The strongest factor from the analysis is called a "demeanor factor" that has to do with the subjects' attitudes about police demeanor. Surprisingly, Cuban adolescents perceive police demeanor as mostly positive, describing police as concerned and friendly. However, these adolescents also describe police officers as rude. African-American adolescents perceive police demeanor in more violent terms—that they enjoy kicking people around, are rude, and show no respect for the person. White teenagers describe police in the same terms as African Americans, but also state that the police are courteous, fair, and friendly. African-Americans' attitudes toward police may reflect the kinds of treatment they and those whom they know have experienced at the hands of police. Anglos' and Cubans' attitudes are more mixed and may reflect the kinds of interactions they have had with the police.

Another interesting factor that emerged from the analysis is called an "ethnic factor." This factor is based on three items reading "The police are justified in regarding a (Black, Hispanic, Anglo) as one who needs to be watched more than others." This was not a strong factor for the Cuban adolescents. However, the three ways this item was phrased contributed to the ethnic factor for both the African-American and White teenagers. More specifically, the factor loadings were strong for the Black and Hispanic versions of this item and less for the White version. It appears that African-American and White adolescents are tuned in to some degree of ethnic prejudice in stating that police are justified in their differential treatment of Blacks and Hispanics. The findings of this study point to the complexity of factors in police and minority youths interactions. Attitudes of both the authorities and the youths can influence the kind of interaction between the two.

Summary

Born in 1899 of good intentions, the juvenile court was to be a protective parent, helpful friend, and provider of justice. Over the years some but not all juvenile courts lost sight of these admirable goals. Court excesses were challenged in the landmark 1967 *Gault* case. In the *Gault* decision the U.S. Supreme Court extended to young people the protection of the Constitution.

At the same time revisionist views of the entire juvenile justice system began to appear in greater numbers than ever before and to command greater attention. The concepts of deviancy and labeling emerged. The questions of who is delinquent, how much delinquency exists, whether status offenders should be tried in court, and whether the courts are sexist or racist were addressed, albeit at times inconclusively. The questions of whether crime can be prevented and whether social deviants can be treated are the last questions to be addressed in this chapter.

Can Delinquency Be Treated or Prevented?

The question of whether adolescent criminals can be treated rests on the individual's concept of delinquency. Depending on that conceptual framework, different solutions to the problem of adolescent crime can be recommended. Those who advocate a strict psychological interpretation of delinquency, for instance, argue for treatment approaches that focus on the individual or the individual's family.

The complete range of therapies (individual, group, family, and so on) has been used at one time or another with delinquent populations, but all have failed in varying degrees. Offer and his colleagues (1979) suggest that the failure of therapeutic approaches is partly related to inappropriate psychodynamic assessments. They feel that the impulsive delinquent is best treated in occupational, educational, or other specific settings. Essential to the successful treatment of the impulsive delinquent is the setting of firm limits on behavior and the development of the ability to delay gratification. They suggest that the narcissistic delinquent needs to be able to maintain his or her self-image while in treatment. Use of the surrounding environment to keep the self-concept intact should be allowed. The depressed/borderline delinquent benefits most from an insight-oriented, individual approach. The focus of treatment should be on understanding and on compensating for the loneliness he or she experiences. The empty/borderline delinquent benefits from the same approach but may need medication as well to relieve depression.

Family-therapy proponents emphasize that nearly all psychological theories stress the importance of the family as the primary socializer of the child. Although this influence diminishes as the child grows older, it nevertheless continues throughout adolescence. They argue that when a family experiences dysfunction, its members are likely to become dysfunctional as well. When an adolescent is in a dysfunctional state, the chances of criminal behavior increase. The efforts of family therapists to reestablish cooperative, supportive family units are thus likely to decrease delinquent misbehavior.

There are, however, disturbing reports that psychological interventions may be more destructive than constructive for young people. For example, Joan McCord (1978) examined the life histories of 506 men who had been involved as children in the Cambridge-Somerville Youth Study. This study began in 1935 with several hundred boys described by schools, churches, or other organizations as "average" or "difficult" children. Some of these boys were used as a control group. The other boys and their families received visits from counselors for almost five years. The families were encouraged to call on the counselor for help when problems occurred, and "family problems [became] the focus of attention for nearly one-third of the treatment group" (p. 284). The treatment group received all kinds of services, ranging from tutorial help and medical care to summer-camp scholarships and involvement with scouting. Meanwhile, the control group received no such offers of help and participated only in providing information about themselves.

McCord's (1978) findings are remarkable. Nearly equal numbers of both groups committed crimes as juveniles. Furthermore, treatment for the "difficult" children did not prevent criminal activity; they were just as likely as the "average" children to commit illegal acts. Nor did these findings change with age; the treatment group and the control group showed similar rates of criminal activity in adulthood. Shockingly, it actually appears that the Cambridge-Somerville program did more harm than good. After 30 years the men in the treatment group had committed more crimes, showed more signs of alcoholism and serious mental illness, had a higher incidence of high blood pressure or heart conditions, had jobs with lower prestige, were less satisfied with their jobs, and died younger than the men in the control group. If anything positive can be said about the project, it is that the men in the treatment group fondly remembered their counselors.

There are several possible reasons for the treatment group's experiencing more problems than the control group did. McCord speculates that interacting with adults whose values are different from their parents' values creates later conflicts in children. Perhaps intervention breeds dependence, or perhaps "the program [generated] . . . high expectations that later in life could not be fulfilled." Finally, it may not matter whether children are "average" or "difficult"; if they are given special help, they will eventually believe that they need special help—another example of a self-fulfilling prophecy.

Deviance theorists would support McCord's last observation. They would contend that by visiting these families and offering services, the counselors labeled these children as deviants. This argument is illustrated by the following hypothetical dialogue between a typical mother and son in the control group of the Cambridge-Somerville study:

Son: Mom, why can't I go to camp like Johnny?
Mother: You know we don't have the money. Times are hard, Tim.
Son: How come he gets to go, then?
Mother: Well, now, Tim, you know they got problems. You see that fellow visit them, don't you? He's the one that's got the money for him to go. Now you just wash up and get ready for dinner. Do you hear me, Timothy?
Son: I still want to go—problems or no problems.

Labeling occurs not only in children's acceptance of their condition of helplessness but in their neighbors' attachment of the label to them. Some of the implications of this theory for the treatment and prevention of delinquency are:

1. Benign neglect, or radical nonintervention, should be practiced as far as possible in cases of delinquency. Delinquency is inevitable. Most young people commit illegal acts sometime during adolescence, but few become adult criminals. Many studies indicate that adolescent crime is highest between the ages of 13 and 16 but drops off rapidly after that age, whether or not a young person has been "treated" (Rahav, 1977). The point of the benign neglect, or radical-nonintervention, position is to do as little as possible to treat delinquents differently from their nondelinquent peers.

2. As many young people as possible should be diverted away from the juvenile court system and into the least stigmatizing program available. The position of the deviance theorist is that the juvenile-justice system is the most stigmatizing of the alternatives. Community-based programs are less so and should be used whenever possible.

3. Because juveniles are singled out for special sanctions under the laws governing status offenses, the jurisdiction of the court should be limited. The argument here is that by limiting the court's jurisdiction to criminal cases and referring status offenders to community-based programs, the least amount of damage by labeling is done to the adolescent.

Structural-disorganization theorists would contend that although an adolescent may have personal problems and may be stigmatized by association, it is poverty and inequality that have produced these conditions. Poverty and inequality deprived a young person of the means to achieve the material and social standards that have come to be associated with middle-class life. This deprivation produces the frustration that results in criminal activity. Correcting these social injustices demands direct social-action programs and policies to provide equality of opportunity. Some of the implications of this model for the treatment and prevention of delinquency are:

1. All children should have the same chance at a good education. Educational opportunities can be equalized in a number of ways, some of which are equalization of per-pupil expenditures across communities, busing to achieve socioeconomic integration, federal aid for special remedial programs for all economically disadvantaged children, and affirmative-action enrollment programs for both undergraduate and graduate students at colleges and universities.

2. Housing and job opportunities should be equalized. Examples of programs to accomplish this goal are the current affirmative-action hiring and housing programs.

3. Job-training and skills-improvement programs should be provided. Such programs as CETA (Comprehensive Employment and Training Act) and the provision of federal youth-employment funds are examples of past attempts to achieve equal opportunity in these areas.

Social-control theorists believe that if delinquency is to be controlled, the systems responsible for socializing the young person must be improved. It is their failure to provide adequate supervision and to instill the proper moral values in young people that encourages delinquency. Some implications of this theory for the treatment and prevention of delinquency are:

1. The child rearing practices of the family should be improved in ways that will develop greater self-control in the child.
2. Close identification with school, church, and other socially approved organizations should be encouraged in adolescents, since these organizations have value structures that discourage deviance.
3. The jurisdiction of the juvenile justice authorities should be strengthened. If more power is given to the court and the police, young people will gain greater respect for the law.

In the 1990s the issue of whether crime can be prevented or criminals treated has emerged with new intensity. The public is calling for and getting stiffer penalties and longer sentences against the young who commit criminal acts. Reports of the failure of previous treatment and prevention efforts have to some degree fueled this new get-tough attitude (Gibbons, 1986; Gibbons & Krohn,

1986; Polk, 1984). Thus, Langan's (1991) report that the soaring prison population in the United States could be explained by the greater likelihood of a prison sentence after conviction for nearly every type of crime should come as no surprise. What is intriguing is his finding that with the phenomenal growth in prison beds, currently in excess of 610,000, there has been a corresponding reduction in U.S. crime rates according to crime victimization surveys. Could incarceration be working?

We suspect that the issue is more complicated than any quantitative study will ever be able to determine. The work of William McCord and José Sánchez (1982) impresses us with the complexity of the subject. The authors followed the lives of 340 juvenile offenders from the time of their incarceration to 25 years after their release. The subjects of this study had been sentenced for at least 18 months to one of two correctional institutions. One of these institutions used a therapeutic milieu of treatment and vocational training to rehabilitate. The other practiced punishment. The samples from each institution matched on several social-demographic variables, differing only in race. The institution emphasizing treatment was predominantly Black. The institution emphasizing punishment was predominantly White.

Five years after imprisonment, the graduates from the institution emphasizing treatment had a 9% recidivism rate. The institution emphasizing punishment had a 67% recidivism rate. By middle age, most men from both institutions had stopped their criminal activity, in essence supporting the view that for most individuals criminal activity is short-lived.

Disturbingly, while graduates of the treatment facility experienced lower recidivism five years after incarceration, their rate of recidivism increased after this period. Interestingly, graduates from the punishment facility experienced a lower recidivism rate five years after institutionalization. Does this finding suggest that punishment is preferable to other rehabilitation approaches?

McCord and Sánchez do not believe this to be the case. Rather, the authors focus on the racial composition of the two facilities to explain the difference in later recidivism rates. It is prejudice and discrimination, they suggest, that prevent Black youths from capitalizing on their positive institutional experience and escaping additional criminal acts. White youths, even when subjected to poorer rehabilitation experiences, eventually succeeded in greater numbers because of the color of their skin. Findings such as these that humane treatment can work encouraged Lundman (1984) to recommend:

- That traditional delinquency-prevention efforts be abandoned
- That young people accused of status and minor offenses be diverted from the juvenile justice system
- That juvenile court judges use probation as the most frequent sentencing option
- That "scared-straight" efforts, in which convicts visit schools and frighten young people with tales of prison life, be abandoned
- That community-treatment programs be expanded to include nearly all offenders
- That criminal institutions be reserved for chronic offenders who would be a danger to society

---

Box 16–7   Victimization: A Cross-Cultural Perspective

One of our favorite films is *My Bodyguard*. It tells the simple story of an adolescent in an urban school who, with an outcast friend, stands up to a bully and that bully's gang. The plot is not original. It has appeared in countless other screenplays from *Back to the Future* to *Stand By Me*. In each of these films the young person victimized by others seizes a moment to express his or her outrage in an act of violence that stops the victimization.

Japan also has its bullies. The practice of bullying in Japan is called *ijime*. Although the incidence of this behavior is not as high as it is in the United States—

only 534 incidents were reported in 1984 in Japan's 15,000 middle schools—the behavior concerns the Japanese people. Interestingly, the primary focus of this national concern is not the deviant nature of the bully but the deviant nature of the victim. M. White (1987) reports that from mental-health professional to the common citizen the Japanese view is that the victim provoked the attack. It is the victims' "differentness," their nonconformity, or their weakness that calls attention to them. The attack, from the Japanese perspective, its an attempt to bring the victim back into the fold.

Supporting Lundman's position, authors like Lab (1984) maintain that the juvenile justice system should refrain from intervention in a young person's life until the third or fourth offense. Others like Gullotta and Adams (1982a) and Mulvey and LaRosa (1986), noting that most young people fall out of crime by their late teens, feel that adolescents need to be protected from the negative labeling process that accompanies a criminal conviction.

As we again review these perspectives and the current literature in criminology, we see that different elements of each perspective can be useful with different adolescents in trouble. We most strongly advocate that the least restrictive setting and the least stigmatizing approach be used in juvenile housing, vocational training, and jobs. We believe that the family needs to be strengthened as an institution. We do not agree that police or court jurisdiction over young people should be strengthened. Finally, we believe in the value of counseling, particularly family counseling, despite the disturbing findings of the McCord (1978) study. We believe that, in a time of need, extending a little friendly help that encourages independence and self-determination has value. (See Box 16–7.)

Major Points to Remember

1. Delinquency was redefined during the early 1800s to apply to a more limited number of people. Most often these were immigrants whose ethnic background, customs, and religion differed from those of the established community.

2. As the number of youths considered to be delinquents grew, society responded in a variety of ways. One of the most original was "placing out," or putting young immigrants, often without their parents' knowledge, on westbound trains.

3. Several theories have been proposed to account for criminal behavior. These include biological, psychological, social-control, and deviance explanations of crime.

4. Before the establishment of the juvenile court in 1899, age determined whether a young person was considered responsible for a criminal act.

5. Views differ on whether the juvenile court was established to promote a "parental" system of justice or to ensure that young people were sufficiently disciplined for their misbehavior.

6. The delinquent is often described in studies as having identity problems or as being neurotic or pathological. The delinquent's family is seen as inconsistent, uncaring, or hostile. These findings must be viewed with caution, because research shows that many emotionally healthy young people from stable, caring families engage in delinquency.

7. The enormous popular support for the juvenile court was shattered by the 1967 *Gault* case, in which abuses of the court were revealed and certain constitutional protections were extended by the U.S. Supreme Court to young people charged with a crime.

8. An outcome of the controversy over the juvenile court's handling of young people was a new understanding of juvenile crime. Old notions on who commits crimes and the fairness with which the law is applied, particularly in regard to females and minorities, were reexamined and revised.

9. There are several strategies for treating or preventing delinquency. These include therapy, benign neglect or radical nonintervention, and strengthening of social control. Disturbingly, therapeutic interventions were found, in one famous study, to do more harm than good.

10. The prevention of delinquency involves changing the systems (community, school, and family) that fail to meet the social and emotional needs of young people while at the same time attempting to promote the social competency of youth.

Eating Disorders

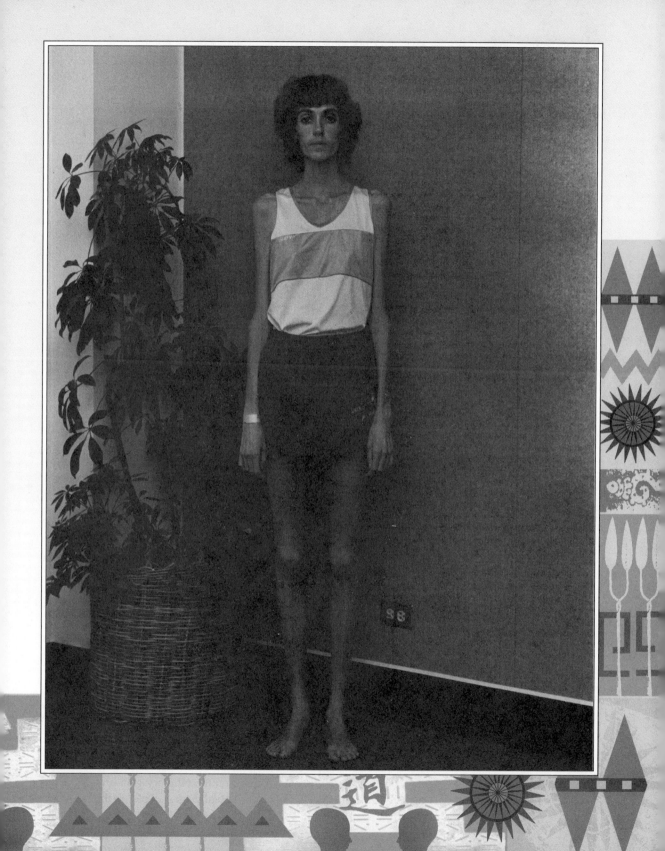

I magine having the willpower to deny the need for food. Imagine being so repulsed after eating that you would have the willpower to induce vomiting. It is difficult for many of us to understand the motives and thought processes that enable a young person to reject the nourishment necessary for life or to choose the discomfort of vomiting. In this chapter we try to make some sense of why a small number of young people willingly endanger their health by starving or purging themselves. To comprehend these behaviors, called *anorexia nervosa* and *bulimia,* we draw from the fields of history, literature, and the social sciences. Then we look at how to help young people experiencing these problems.

Theoretical Perspectives on Eating Disorders

Before examining anorexia nervosa and bulimia more closely, we believe it is useful to place these two disorders within a conceptual framework. There are five theoretical explanations for anorexic and bulimic behaviors, each reflecting its own unique view of the world (see Chapter 2).

Psychoanalytic theory suggests that people with eating disorders equate the act of eating with sexual activity. Thus, the refusal to eat in anorexia becomes a symbolic means by which impregnation can be avoided. Furthermore, the act of self-starvation permits the young person to literally turn back the biological clock from that of a sexually maturing young person to that of a prepubertal youth.

The behaviorist, on the other hand, is not concerned with the historical antecedents or symbolism that might explain this behavior. Rather, the refusal to eat may be a learned behavior, the result of positive environmental reinforcement ("You look much better now that you've lost some weight"). Purging may be a form of avoidance behavior—that is, an intense desire to avoid becoming overweight. Or it may be a form of modeling behavior ("I perceive that to be slim is to be seen as desirable. I want to be desirable. Therefore I will avoid things like food that would make me undesirable.").

In contrast, the family perspective explains eating disorders within the context of interpersonal relationships rather than individual psychopathology. It holds that the young person exhibiting such behavior serves a useful role in enabling a family to avoid potentially destructive internal conflict. In this model the eating disorder focuses attention away from the family as a whole and onto the "disturbed" family member. In this way the family is able to continue an outward appearance of successful functioning.

Although the previous explanations were concerned with the individual's behavior in relationship to self or others, the sociologist examines eating disorders against the backdrop of the larger society. Media images of thin young people enjoying the good life and looking attractive in their clothing reflect a societal standard that all adolescents are expected to achieve. In such a world, beauty is a precious and highly valued commodity, and to be beautiful one must be thin. To deviate from this ideal is to be rejected by society.

The final perspective to consider is biogenic. Suspicions have existed for decades that eating disorders can be explained by biological or genetic factors. At the turn of the century concern focused on the pituitary gland, without success. Currently, attention has shifted to the hypothalamus, a part of the brain, and the role it may play in this behavior. It is known that the hypothalamus controls the endocrine system. It is also known that when the endocrine system detects a shortage of the nutrients needed to survive, it will adjust bodily functions accordingly. As we now proceed to examine anorexia nervosa in detail, consider the usefulness of each of the five theoretical perspectives in making sense of this behavior.

Anorexia Nervosa

A Historical and Literary Perspective

As with so many other behaviors, anorexia nervosa has a rich historical past. For our purposes the story begins in Italy in the mid-1400s with a 15-year-old by the name of Catherine (R. M. Bell, 1985).

Until her 15th year of life, there was nothing particularly extraordinary about this young lady. She appeared to those around her to be an obedient, healthy girl who would soon be ready for marriage. That is until her beloved sister died in childbirth; then a different Catherine emerged. For the next three years she existed on meager portions of bread, raw vegetables, and water. She dressed in extremely uncomfortable woolen garments and added to her suffering by wrapping an iron chain around her hips. During this period she hardly spoke, rarely slept, and routinely beat herself with a chain until her body was covered with wounds. After entering a convent at age 18 and despite the church's pleas that she alter her behavior, she changed little in this daily ritual of self-abuse. At the age of 33, Catherine died.

It is interesting to note that Catherine was canonized as Saint Catherine of Siena by the Roman Catholic Church in part for actions such as these, which were viewed as "holy." More interesting still, over a score of other young Italian women who also achieved sainthood had exhibited similar actions, which by today's standards would be described as examples of anorexic behavior. Rudolph Bell (1985), from whose book *Holy Anorexia* the story of Catherine was taken, notes that these young women strove to exercise their will and independence over a church and a society that paid little attention to women and assigned little value to them. Through their "holy" behavior, Bell contends, these women pursued the goals of spiritual health, fasting, and self-denial.

It would be more than 200 years after the death of Catherine that a young person's denial of the need to eat would appear in the medical literature. In *Phthisiologia: Or a Treatise of Consumptions* Richard Morton (1720) described his unsuccessful attempts in 1686 to save the life of a young woman whose "appetite began to abate" (p. 8). And nearly 200 more years would pass before William Gull (1874) labeled this behavior anorexia nervosa. The word *anorexia* is derived from the Greek meaning lack of appetite.

At roughly the same time, the Russian novelist Leo Tolstoy (1872/1952), in his classic work *War and Peace,* described the disorder, as had many other authors before him. The character "pining away" through self-starvation in Tolstoy's novel was the lovely Natasha:

Box 17–1   Concerns About Weight Among White, Black, and Asian Teenagers

In one investigation of the incidence of bulimic behavior among high school and university students, more White females indicated bulimic behavior than Black, Hispanic, or Asian adolescents (Howat & Saxton, 1988). However, evidence shows that Blacks and Native American teenage females are nonetheless still at risk for potential eating-disordered behavior (for example, see Hiebert, Felice, Wingard, Munoz, & Ferguson, 1988; Holden & Robinson, 1988; Rosen, Shafer, Dummer, Cross, Deuman, & Malmberg, 1988).

Female adolescents express considerable concern about weight and eating (Dornbusch, Carlsmith, Duncan, Gross, Ritter, & Siegel–Gorflick, 1984). Pressures for slimness, dissatisfaction with weight, and high levels of dieting have heightened professional concern. One recent study (Wardle & Marsland, 1990) in London, England, of several hundred children between the ages of 11 and 18 years in multicultural schools with different socioeconomic levels revealed that weight concern was high for all girls—more than 50% reported feeling too fat and needing to lose weight. Weight concern was high for both younger *and* older adolescents. Once again, White girls reported more concerns than did Black or Asian girls. Greater concern was also observed among higher SES neighborhood schools. Overall, these findings suggest different ethnic (and corresponding economic) differences may exist regarding the degree to which teenagers internalize social messages of slimness and body image.

Have you observed any social or cultural factors within White, Black, Asian, or American Indian groups that might explain the observed ethnic differences?

[The disease] was so serious that . . . the consideration of all that had caused her illness, her conduct and the breaking off of her engagement, receded into the background. She was so ill that it was impossible for them to consider in how far she was to blame for what had happened. She could not eat or sleep, grew visibly thinner . . . and, as the doctors made them feel, was in danger. (P. 372)

There are two conclusions that we believe can be drawn from this history. The first is obviously that anorexic behaviors are not recent to our time but clearly existed in the past. Second, these behaviors, while limited, were nevertheless evident enough to capture the attention of novelists. (Also see Box 17–1 for a discussion on concern about weight for girls of different ethnic backgrounds.)

Characteristics and Incidence

To be anorexic involves more than the ability to resist the urge to eat. Indeed, if anorexia were defined only by caloric intake, the 40 million Americans who are daily engaged in a struggle to control their weight (Smead, 1983) would need to be considered anorexic. To apply the term *anorexia nervosa* to describe an individual's behavior, we need to find several of the following characteristics (Feighner et al., 1972):

1. Age: victims are under the age of 25 when they begin to severely limit the intake of food.
2. Weight loss: they lose at least 25% of their ideal body weight.
3. Distorted understanding of behavior: victims, when confronted with their behavior, do not recognize the serious health risks associated with it. They maintain that refusing food brings personal satisfaction. They seek

---

Box 17–2   Anorexia Nervosa: A Cross–Cultural Perspective

Are anorexics in the United Kingdom similar to those in the United States? A study of 21 hospitalized female adolescents provides the following partial answer to the question (Jenkins, 1987).

Socioeconomic data on the young women indicated that they primarily belonged to the "upper social classes." were well educated, and lived in intact families. The diagnostic criteria used to apply the term *anorexia nervosa* to their condition agreed with the criteria used in the United States. Finally, outcome results were as

disappointing as those found in the United States. Many of the women in this small sample continued to experience difficulties after discharge from treatment (Jenkins. 1987).

Although the results of this study would suggest that there are strong similarities between anorexics in the United States and the United Kingdom, the small size and limited scope of the sample limit the conclusions that can be drawn.

---

and find pleasure in maintaining an extremely thin body image. They handle food in unusual or bizarre ways.

4. Physical health: there is no medical explanation for the weight loss.
5. Mental health: there is no known psychiatric condition to explain the weight loss.
6. Appearance and behavior: victims demonstrate at least two of these symptoms—(a) the inability to menstruate, if female; (b) soft, fine hair; (c) a constant resting pulse of 60 or less; (d) occasional periods of hyperactivity; (e) grossly excessive overeating; or (f) induced vomiting. (Incidentally, the last two symptoms are the two principal distinguishing characteristics of bulimia.)

Research studies suggest that, while both males and females can become anorexic, young women widely outnumber young men by factors ranging from 10 to 20:1 (Comerci, 1986). It appears that activities in which low weight is an important element draw higher numbers of young people with eating disorders. For example, young women interested in gymnastics or ballet and young men involved with wrestling or long-distance running are more likely to be diagnosed as anorexic (1986). This problem behavior is also found most often among White young people in upper-middle-income homes (Comerci, 1986). Estimates of the incidence of this behavior range from 1% to 3% of the total adolescent population (Comerci, 1986; D. M. Kagan & Squires, 1984). See Box 17–2 for a cross-cultural look.

Given the severity of the behavior and the potential harm that young people can inflict on themselves, it is disturbing to note that the anorexic does not respond readily to intervention. Reviews of the treatment literature indicate that one- to two-thirds of young people with anorexia continue to have problems after treatment (Agras, Schneider, Arnow, Rawburn, & Telch, 1989; Bemis, 1978; Hsu, 1980; D. M. Schwartz & Thompson, 1981). Estimates of mortality rates range widely from 5% (Comerci, 1986) to 23% (Van Buskirk, 1977), with the most frequent cause of death being cardiac arrest (Muuss, 1985).

Research on Anorexia Nervosa

The current research literature supports aspects of each of the five theoretical perspectives. For example, several researchers note that anorexics have seriously ego-impaired pictures of themselves, reflected in gross misunderstandings of their body image (Bruch, 1981; Kalliopuska, 1982). Many have a morbid fear of fat (Attie & Brooks-Gunn, 1989; Hsu, 1980; Shestowsky, 1983). They tend to be obsessive/compulsive and hysterical individuals (Bemis, 1978) who engage in regressive behaviors (Kalliopuska, 1982). Most are depressed, introverted, stubborn, and perfectionists (Bemis, 1978; Shisslak, Crago, Neal, & Swain, 1987). Some are involved with such impulsive behaviors as substance abuse or self-mutilation (Garfinkel, Moldofsky, & Garner, 1980).

Evidence also supports a finding that the family plays an important role in the behavior of anorexics. Numerous studies report their families as enmeshed, overprotective, and unable to deal openly with conflict. Family members are described as striving for perfection in behavior, appearance, relationships, and careers. In this tightly regimented environment, anorexic individuals use their behavior to declare control over their own lives as well as to maintain homeostasis in the family (A. E. Carroll, 1986; Gilbert & DeBlassie, 1984; Lucas, 1986; Muuss, 1985; Strober, 1981; Strober & Humphrey, 1987; Wonderlich & Swift, 1990).

Sociologists such as Orbach (cited in Bell, 1985) and psychologists like Smead (1983) note that Western society places a high value on attractiveness for women. Whether it is diet soda commercials, Hollywood films, or *The New York Times* Sunday magazine's models, thinness is the desired body state. As a society we have attached particular stereotypes to certain body types. While the thin are our heroes and our romantic stars, those who are more ample portray comics, buffoons, and sidekicks with names like Pancho, Sancho, and Marcellus.* You will remember from Chapter 6 that research strongly supported the position that physical attractiveness dictated adolescent women's social status within the group. To be attractive in our society is to be thin.

Finally, it is clearly evident that significant changes in body chemistry occur when a person engages in anorexic behavior (Attie & Brooks-Gunn, 1989; Casper, 1984; Lucas, 1986; Yager, 1982). What remains unclear is whether these changes existed before the condition or are the result of the behavior. Altshuler and Weiner (1985) appropriately caution that all of the physical and emotional changes observed in anorexics also are seen in people suffering from starvation due to other causes. The person dying from starvation in a famine will experience the same depression an anorexic will experience. That person's hypothalamus will react in the same manner. Thus, although no one will deny that physical changes are occurring, we cannot state with any certainty whether those changes contribute to the disorder.

---

*Pancho was the sidekick of the Cisco Kid. Sancho was the trusted ally of Don Quixote, and Marcellus Washburn was the friend of the infamous Harold Hill of *The Music Man*.

Bulimia

Whereas anorexics deny themselves nourishment, bulimics engage in unrestrained eating sprees only to purge themselves after their indulgence. Indeed, the word *bulimia* is derived from Greek words meaning hungry ox. Interestingly, examples of this type of behavior can be traced back to the mid-15th century and to several of the "holy" anorexics mentioned earlier in this chapter (Bell, 1985). Of concern to us in the next section are the characteristics and incidence of a behavior that is very closely related to anorexia nervosa.

Characteristics and Incidence

Bulimics are uncontrolled binge eaters. They consume enormous amounts of food at a single seating. This gorging is followed by intense feelings of self-repulsion for having grossly overeaten and by actions to purge oneself of the food. Purging most often occurs by self-induced vomiting, but bulimics may also use laxatives, diuretics, or enemas. Sharing the same concern for body image as anorexics, bulimics are considered separately by mental-health professionals because of the way in which they maintain their appearance—that is, their use of

Eating disorders are a major problem of our time. Some adolescents actually binge and purge or starve themselves to death.

purging behaviors rather than self-starvation. Bulimia is diagnosed when a repeated pattern of this behavior occurs (Garfinkel, 1981).

Although bulimia can affect both males and females, young women, again, are afflicted more often. Like anorexia, it appears to be a problem of White, middle-class, late adolescents. Those males most likely to be stricken are athletes with rigid weight requirements that must be met in order to enable them to participate. An estimated 1% of adolescent females and two-tenths of 1% of adolescent males are troubled with this problem (Drewnowski, Hopkins, & Kessler, 1988; Fairburn & Beglin, 1990).

Repeated episodes of bulimic behavior can have serious consequences for physical health. For instance, frequent vomiting can erode the enamel of teeth, inflame the esophagus, and contribute to irregular heartbeat. The abuse of laxatives, enemas, and diuretics can damage the colon, impair the functioning of the kidneys, and contribute to urinary infections.

Research on Bulimia

For each of the theoretical causes of bulimia described earlier, there are supporting research data. For example, studies focusing on personality factors note a high incidence of depression in bulimics (C. Johnson & Maddi, 1986; Schlesier-Carter, Hamilton, O'Neil, Lydiard, & Malcolm, 1989; Smith, Hillard, & Roll, 1991; Williamson, Kelley, Davis, Ruggiero, & Blouin, 1985). A poor sense of self-esteem appears to be coupled with shame and guilt, low-frustration tolerance, high anxiety, and substance abuse (Frank, 1991; Johnson & Maddi, 1986; Lehman & Rodin, 1989; Mitchell, Hatsukami, Eckert, & Pyle, 1985). Johnson and Maddi (1986, p. 17) suggest that bulimic patients can eroticize binge eating episodes, thus offering an alternative response to sexual feelings if they are conflicted about masturbation or heterosexual activity. Similarly, binge eating and subsequent purging behavior can become an effective mechanism for expressing aggressive feelings that research indicates these individuals have difficulty expressing interpersonally.

One possible reason for conflicted sexual feelings may be the sexual abuse some women experienced before developing an eating disorder. Using three clinical case histories as examples, Goldfarb (1987) suggests that prior abusive experiences are an unrecognized factor in many young women suffering from bulimia.

Data on family characteristics echo earlier observations made on the family life of anorexics. For example, C. Johnson and Flach (1985) report that the overwhelming majority of the 105 patients they have treated for bulimia had family structures that were enmeshed and overprotective. Assertive, independent behaviors on the young person's part were discouraged by the parents. Other studies note that bulimics' families are disengaged, are under considerable stress, and have contradictory communication patterns (Attie & Brooks-Gunn, 1989; Williamson et al., 1985; Johnson & Flach, 1985; C. Johnson, Lewis, Love, Lewis, & Stuckey, 1984).

Researchers examining the sociocultural factors contributing to bulimia focus their attention on the numerous and often contradictory changes that have occurred for women in Western society over the past 25 years. Opportunities for careers and life-styles exist today that did not exist in the past. And yet for all of this change, society retains a clear, identifiable prejudice against the physically unattractive woman (Brumberg, 1988).

For example, Wooley and Wooley (1979), in an exhaustive review of the obesity literature, note that overweight young people are viewed as being responsible for their condition. Studies find that young people describe those who are overweight as stupid, sloppy, and ugly. The social scientist observes that if thinness is the cultural ideal, it is no surprise that its pursuit would lead some to either anorexia or bulimia (Johnson et al., 1984).

Finally, as with anorexia, the connection between bulimia and biogenic factors has been suggested. Some researchers are looking at whether bulimia and affective disorders are linked genetically. Johnson and Maddi (1986) caution that given the pattern of this behavior, it is highly unlikely that a biogenic relationship will be discovered. Their point is well taken, for it is hard to imagine that the population with the highest incidence of bulimia (White middle- and upper-income college women) are somehow genetically different from other women. In the final sections of this chapter we examine the approaches used to treat young people with these dysfunctional behaviors and consider how the incidence of these behaviors might be reduced.

Implications for Treatment and Prevention

Treatment

Using the five theoretical views of disorders, it is possible to design therapeutic interventions to help young people demonstrating anorexic or bulimic behavior. For example, several treatment approaches have been formulated from psychodynamic theory. Some of these therapeutic techniques use free association, dream interpretation, and possibly hypnosis to help the young person confront unresolved conflicts. Within a framework of ego psychology, others use a warm, nurturing, supportive counseling relationship to focus attention on what is believed to be a dysfunctional mother/child relationship. And still others use a nondirective, client-centered approach to help young people redefine a flawed image of self and improve painful interpersonal relationships. The effectiveness of these approaches is not clear. Published clinical studies do report modest success. Since these case studies often involve only small numbers of clients and lack follow-up mechanisms, however, they must be treated cautiously (Bayer, 1984; Bemis, 1978; Carroll, 1986; Pettinatti & Wade, 1986).

From a behavioral perspective, the treatment literature contains numerous reports of the use of operant techniques to treat these dysfunctional behaviors. The typical treatment protocol takes place in a hospital and involves the removal of all the rights and privileges of the young person. Behavior that increases the young person's weight—that is, eating—may be rewarded by the return of rights such as increased staff attention, visiting privileges, and access to radio, television, or records. The failure to increase or maintain weight results in the removal of rights and privileges. Although this technique is successful in the short term in restoring weight to the young person experiencing an eating disorder, the literature suggests that a large number of young people fall back into the condition after a few years. Additionally, there are the obvious ethical questions involving forced treatment and the deprivation of human rights. Consideration must also be given to the confounding effects of the inpatient setting and the use of medications on reported success (Bemis, 1978; Kreipe, 1986; Ohlrich & Stephenson, 1986).

Recently, Agras and associates (1989) described the use of an outpatient cognitive behavioral program to reduce bulimic behaviors. Their study used a control group and three treatment approaches to reduce bulimic behaviors in 77 women. They reported the most successful treatment approach used individual therapy with cognitive restructuring exercises directed toward altering food and body images of the subjects. Of the 22 women receiving this treatment approach 56% were able to stop their bulimic behaviors.

A third treatment approach, family therapy, is receiving considerable attention. If this theoretical perspective is correct, the eating-disordered individual is playing a role in a dysfunctional family system that can be changed. If the role is changed and if the family's functioning can be improved, the young person's eating disorder should diminish. The family therapist works to improve the family's communication patterns and to help the family learn how to openly express its anger. The therapist helps the family members let go of their need for perfection, let go of their need for control, and let the young person with the eating disorder achieve independence without resorting to starvation. Initial reports of the results of using this treatment are encouraging. But again these reports involve case studies and lack follow-up components (Bemis, 1978; Carroll, 1986).

The other two theoretical approaches do not offer significant treatment alternatives. The sociocultural perspective is more suited to efforts at preventing eating disorders. The biogenic approach, since it postulates a genetic cause for these problems, implies that very little can be done to treat them.

In summary, there are several interventions for working with the young person with an eating disorder. However, none of these approaches has proven completely successful. Given this reality, most treatment teams working with victims of eating disorders use a combination of approaches. (See Box 17–3 for a case from the files of Thomas Gullotta.)

Prevention

How might the incidence of eating disorders be reduced? Let's consider how each of the tools of prevention could be used.

Education

The use of information to alert, inform, and sensitize each of us to an issue of importance is the function of prevention's first tool. In reviewing the material in this chapter, one must realize that societal forces contribute to the problem. Using public-service announcements and family-life education programs, one can begin the exceedingly slow process of helping men and women understand that women should be judged by the same multiple standards that are used to judge men.

Box 17–3   Cindy: The Perfect Daughter

"Cindy was the perfect daughter."

"You mean she *is,* don't you, Jim?"

"I don't know what I mean anymore about anything. Why is she doing this thing, this crazy thing, to us?"

Jim and his wife, Sally, were in my office to discuss their daughter's behavior. In the previous few months a healthy, physically active, "perfect" child who had never been a problem to anyone had gone on an incredibly regimented diet. Cindy, who at 5 feet 5 inches had weighed 120 pounds, now weighed less than 90 pounds. Her once long, dark, thick hair was now thin. Her menses had stopped, and she had developed health problems. Her condition had so deteriorated that she had been hospitalized for a while and had been tube-fed.

"I just don't understand it," Jim said. "I mean she never ever caused any trouble. She tried to please us in everything she did. It didn't matter what it was. She did everything we asked."

"I remember when she was ten and wanted to take trumpet lessons," Sally said. "Remember, Jim? We thought that wasn't appropriate for a young lady, you know, so Jim and I suggested the piano. There was no argument on her part, no pouting, no temper tantrums. She agreed. I just can't understand why she won't listen to us now. Why is she being disobedient?"

In the weeks that followed, during which I met with Cindy and her parents, the theme of control continually emerged. I was struck with the way in which Cindy had triumphed over her dominating parents. For no matter how they pleaded, threatened, cried, or bribed, their dominance had, in an indirect but very effective way, been broken forever. The image of Cindy in my office remains vivid to this day: a young woman sitting opposite her parents, showing little emotion save for an occasional slight smile, and controlling, by her silence, the events before her. Our sessions over those eight months focused on separation, power, and role issues in the family, and Cindy's parents were somewhat successful in altering their behavior. I am uncertain whether my efforts helped Cindy. Although she did regain some of her lost weight, she remains an extremely thin young woman. She has enrolled in a local college and is studying to become a teacher.

Competency Promotion

It is clear from the research and clinical data presented in this chapter that young people with a poor self-image are at risk for this dysfunctional behavior. Given the role that parents play in the formation of self-esteem and in the development of this problem behavior, the focus for our use of this tool might be on them. Improving parents' skills in family communication and in enabling young people to achieve independence could significantly contribute to a reduction in eating disorders.

Community Organization/Systems Intervention

As we mention earlier, we suspect that Western society plays a role in the incidence of anorexia and bulimia. CO/SI efforts are directed at structural changes within an organization, a community, or a society. If one considers the problem to be a failure to recognize young women for their talents and intelligence rather than for their body, a plan for a possible intervention emerges. Again, change will not come quickly, but we are impressed with the sensitivity that groups such as the National Organization for Women, Mothers Against Drunk Drivers, and the gay movement have already had on changing societal values.

Natural Care Giving

To care, to love another, and to be able to give help as well as to receive help are the essence of this final tool. If care giving can be done within the context of the

Overweight adolescent boys and girls are commonly treated with scorn and ridicule by thin peers.

family, the research in this chapter would predict a reduction in this problem. If it cannot occur within that context, the development of self-help groups can help fill an existing void. Such groups are testimony to the need all humans have for emotional support and caring.

Major Points to Remember

1. Five theoretical perspectives that try to explain eating disorders are the psychoanalytic, behavioral, family, sociological, and biogenic explanations.
2. As with many other behaviors, there is historical evidence that eating disorders existed before modern times.

3. To apply the term *anorexia nervosa* to an individual's behavior, practitioners must find some of the following characteristics: (a) age under 25; (b) weight loss equal to 25% of ideal body weight; (c) a distorted understanding of that weight loss; and (d) no known physical or mental-health reason for the weight loss.

4. More women than men suffer from eating disorders.

5. Research suggests that several factors contribute to eating disorders. These include individual, family, and societal factors.

6. Unlike anorexics, who simply deny themselves nourishment, bulimics engage in unrestrained eating sprees only to purge themselves in guilt.

7. A wide range of treatment modalities have been tried with eating disorders, with modest success.

8. Prevention approaches for this problem focus on improving individual self-esteem as well as working to change society's image of thinness.

"To be or not to be" is a question that most of us struggle to comprehend. And yet the question is so simple. The thought is so clear. Why, then, can we not understand adolescent suicide? Is it because we have forgotten some of the unique aspects of youth itself? In this chapter we examine the clinical meaning of the term *depression* and then, drawing on material from history, the arts, and the behavioral sciences, we attempt to make sense of suicide in adolescence.

Depression: Definition and History

Who among us has not at some time in his or her life felt sad, unhappy, or discouraged? Who among us has not shed a tear over disappointment, in frustration, or the loss of a dream unfilled? What, then, separates these normal behaviors associated with depression from being "clinically" depressed? The answer to that question is essentially time. And time is a subjective factor. Thus, mental health professionals approach this subject cautiously—and with good reason. For while most clinical training would understand depressed mood and associated symptoms (insomnia, tearfulness, lack of appetite) lasting for more than two weeks that interfered with ordinary activities as "clinical" depression, there are instances, as in the loss of a loved one, when this diagnosis would be inappropriate.

Interestingly, these definitional issues troubled scholars less in the past. In ancient times, clinical depression was called melancholia. For the Greeks, who believed the body produced four "humors," fluids that influenced temperament and behavior, it was an excess of black bile that caused depression. Indeed, the word *melancholia* means black bile in Greek. During the Middle ages, depression, still called melancholia, was considered a problem of demonic possession solved by aggressive and often invasive religious intervention (an understanding we suspect that is still shared by much of Hollywood's film-making community). In the 19th century, it was suggested by the psychiatrist Kraepelin that recurrent depression was hereditary (Jackson, 1987) (See Box 18–1). At the present time, most scholars consider "clinical" depression to be caused by a combination of environmental, social, and intrapsychic factors. Biological chemical imbalances are also believed to be a factor in many cases.

Among biological researchers, it is believed that depression can be the result of either stressful events or appear for no reason at all. Many researchers suspect that a deficiency of serotonin may be the culprit (Asberg, 1989). But here, too, as elsewhere in this book, the findings of one group of researchers have not been confirmed by another, and Holden (1991, p. 1451) cautions that depression may be "caused by a maladaptive response to stress, with concomitant disruption of many mechanisms, including serotonin and norepinephrine transmission."

Types

Among mental health professionals "clinical" depression is synonymous with the phrase *affective disorders*. The most common affective disorders are major depression, unipolar depressive disorder, dysthymic disorder, manic episode, bipolar disorder, and cyclothymic disorder. *Major depression* is characterized by a depressed mood. The individual often appears tense, nervous, and miserable. Feeling helpless and hopeless, apathy and thoughts of suicide are not uncom-

---

Box 18–1   The Cure for Love Melancholy

In this otherwise serious chapter, it might be good for all of us to take a breather and look again at the past—in this case at Robert Burton's *The Anatomy of Melancholy*, which was first published in the 17th century. In this monumental work such things as bad air, apples, beef, devils, kissing, pork, and witches are identified as causing melancholy. One serious form of melancholy affecting young people in particular is love melancholy. Burton offers the following advice for the cure and prevention of this illness:

1. The first rule to be observed in this stubborn and unbridled passion, is exercise and diet (p. 526).
2. Guianerius [an ancient medicine man, Burton reports, suggests that the sufferer of love melancholy] go with haircloth [wool] next [to] his skin, to go barefooted, and barelegged in the cold weather, to whip himself now and then, as monks do, but above all to fast (p. 526)
3. [Some sages suggest] bloodletting . . . as a principal remedy (p. 528).

4. [Of course, one should] avoid . . . kissing, dalliance, all speeches, tokens, love letters, and the like (p. 529).
5. As there be divers of this burning lust, or heroical love, as there be many good remedies to case and help: amongst which, good counsel and persuasion [are best] (p. 534).
6. [In what unquestionably was a period of high male chauvinism, to end his lovesickness, the male was urged to] see her undressed, see her, if it be possible, out of her attires . . . it may be she is like Aesop's Jay, or Pliny's Cartharides, she will be loathsome, ridiculous, thou wilt not endure her sight . . . As a posy she smells sweet, is most fresh and fair one day, but dried up, withered, and stinks another (p. 536).
7. The last and best cure of love-melancholy [Burton believes] is to let them have their desire. The last refuge and surest remedy, to be put in practice in the utmost place, when no other means will take effect, is to let them go together, and enjoy one another (p. 547).

Source: R. Burton (1851). *The Anatomy of Melancholy* (4th ed.). Philadelphia, PA: J.W. Moore Publishers.

---

mon. These episodes may last from several weeks to a year. The term *unipolar disorder* is used when major depressive episodes reoccur. *Dysthymic disorder* or depressive neurosis is used when the severity and duration of the depression is shorter than in the previously described conditions and psychotic symptoms like delusions or hallucinations are not present.

In contrast, *manic episodes* describe mood behavior that is excited and euphoric. Nervousness and irritability may also be present. Manic individuals display hyperactive behaviors, such as the need for little rest, and often grandiose and delusional thinking. In a manic phase, it is not unusual that the manic individual will make rash and unwise decisions. These behavioral episodes may last from several days to a few months. The phrase *bipolar disorder* is used when an individual alternates between periods of mania and depression. *Cyclothymic disorder* is applied when an individual displays a repeating pattern of numerous depressions with mild manic symptoms.

Feelings of hopelessness and helplessness (depression) are commonly associated with suicidal behavior (Rangell, 1988). Yet, as one Canadian study found, depression is not uncommon in adolescence (Ehrenberg, Cox, & Koopman, 1990). Surveying 366 Canadian high school students, their study reported that 31.4% of the sample were mildly to clinically depressed. Thus, other factors must be at work also, as we subsequently see in this chapter.

Depression can be so severe that an adolescent can have uncontrollable crying spells.

Attitudes About Suicide Through History

Depending on the time and circumstances, suicide, a "conscious, deliberate attempt to take one's life quickly" (M. L. Farber, 1968, p. 4), was embraced or rejected by the Greeks, Romans, Jews, Christians, and others. For instance, in early Greek society the taking of one's own life was punished by mutilating the dead body. The hand responsible for the action was severed from the corpse. It and the rest of the corpse were then buried away from the graves of the other citizens of that city-state. This punishment was not so much the result of a rejection of suicide per se as it was a determination that the individual had shown disrespect for the gods. "Heroic" actions or careful measures to ensure the gods' understanding made suicide more acceptable to the Greeks. Thus, the self-destruction of the sole surviving Spartan soldier of the battle at Thermopylae was cheered by the populace of Sparta, and citizens of Athens. Massilia, or Keos could, on receiving the approval of the authorities, end their lives using hemlock (Alvarez, 1972).

The Roman Empire showed the same understanding of the role suicide played in society. For Roman citizens, suicide was considered a right and carried no penalties. Only those individuals who chose suicide "without cause" were punished, by denying them proper burial rights and thus condemning their souls to exile from the afterlife. Falling into this class were soldiers, slaves, and criminals. In each of these situations, suicide was punished because Roman society had been insulted or damaged. By committing suicide "without cause," the individual had cheapened the significance of the act for other Romans. The slave and the soldier were punished for depriving the empire of its assets. The slave was the property of the owner. The soldier was the property of the state. The loss of the slave was a financial burden for the master. The loss of the soldier weakened the empire. The criminal was punished for suicide for depriving the state of its right to extract its punishment from the individual (Alvarez, 1972).

The Greeks and Romans did not stand alone in accepting suicide as an acceptable alternative to life. Incidences of self-destruction have been celebrated in many societies. The mass suicide of the Jews defending Masada to prevent their capture by Roman soldiers is just one example. The Japanese ritual of hara-kiri is another.

The history of early Christianity, too, is filled with examples of individuals' embracing suicide as a means of salvation. To the early Christians, life on earth was "at best unimportant" and filled with temptations to sin. Their kingdom was not of this world but of the next. Thus, given the opportunity to sever the tie with this world for eternal happiness in the next, it is understandable that many chose to do so. Alvarez, in *The Savage God* (1972), writes that self-destruction, which was seen as the last option by the Roman citizen, was seized as the first by many of the early Christians. In a sense, then, the Romans' attempts to stamp out Christianity by putting its followers to death encouraged its growth. In their rush to salvation, the Christians must have seen the Roman lions as ensuring martyrdom. Alvarez argues that the early church's elevation of its dead to martyrdom actually encouraged thousands upon thousands of early Christians to put themselves in clearly dangerous situations for no other reason than to have their lives ended. It would not be until 533 A.D. that the writings of Augustine against suicide would sway the church at the Council of Orléans to begin to consider suicide a sin. By 562 A.D., at the Council of Braga, the Fifth Commandment, "Thou shalt not kill," had been reinterpreted on the basis of Augustine's work to apply to the taking of one's own life as well (Alvarez, 1972).

The influence of this change on Western society was remarkable. From one European society to another, the bodies of people who had committed suicide were horribly mistreated. In France the body of an individual suspected of having committed suicide was dragged through the streets, burned, and then thrown on the village garbage heap. In areas where fear of the supernatural ran high, special but no less horrid precautions were taken with the body. These might include such special disposal methods as placing the body in a barrel and setting it adrift on a river or severing the hand responsible for the deed. Some sense of the cruelty of these people to their fellow human beings can be found in this account by a Russian exile in England who wrote to his mistress about the execution of a man for attempting suicide:

> A man was hanged who had cut his throat, but who had been brought back to life. They hanged him for suicide. The doctor had warned them it was impossible to hang him as the throat would burst open and he would breathe through the aperture. They did not listen to his advice and hanged their man. The wound in the neck immediate-

ly opened and the man came back to life again although he was hanged. It took time to convoke the aldermen to decide the question of what was to be done. At length the aldermen assembled and bound up the neck below the wound until he died. (Alvarez, 1972, p. 45)

The fate of this poor creature's remains was no less gruesome. He was taken to a crossroads and there buried with a stake driven through his body. If this sounds like a sensible precaution against having a vampire haunt the living, understand that this procedure was practiced as late as the early 1800s, long after vampires ceased to exist in the imaginations of most people (Alvarez, 1972).

Thus, before the Council of Orléans, suicide was not considered inherently evil. For the Greeks, the Romans, and others with sufficient cause, suicide was an acceptable way out of an intolerable situation. With the Council of Orléans and subsequent councils, suicide came to be redefined as a sin against God and humanity.

Today, there are indications that this attitude may again be changing. Is this change a turning back to the Roman notion expressed by one Indian "that man's ability to destroy himself is his sole birthright" (Beaver, 1972, p. 17)? To answer this question, we must first recognize that self-destruction has been only selectively outlawed. History is full of examples of individuals or groups who committed suicide and have been revered as heroes for their behavior. Refusing to surrender to the enemy despite overwhelming odds, surrendering a safe existence for missionary service in disease-ridden parts of the world, or rushing into a burning building or leaping into a river to save another are all potentially suicidal. War itself is the pitting of one nation against another in a mass suicidal dance of destruction. Yet we have glorified in song and story, on stage and film, the defenders of Masada and the Alamo, and we celebrate their so-called noble destruction. No epic story is without its hero's or heroine's making a conscious decision to risk destruction for some altruistic purpose. It is this seemingly altruistic purpose that lifts these people above their self-destructive action and legitimizes their behavior.

Recently, society has begun to debate whether suicide can extend to other segments of the population without their being held in contempt and disgrace. For example, one Canadian study found adolescents more accepting of the act of suicide than their parents (Boldt, 1982). Rather than attributing responsibility for the act to the individual, as their parents did, the adolescents in this study viewed suicidal individuals as victims existing in a flawed society.

Contributing to this attitudinal change has been the public debate over signers of a "living will." They ask that no extraordinary medical means be used to keep them alive should they become terminally ill. The living will is considered by its opponents to be the first step toward euthanasia. Stating that no individual has the right to take away what God has given, they attack the concept on moral and religious grounds. Supporters of the living will argue that the technology of medicine has outpaced our capacity to handle the implications of *life without life*. It is possible to maintain a mechanical life—a beating heart, a breathing being—when there is no life. It is possible to lengthen terminal cancer victims' existence by weeks, months, even years, but at what emotional and financial expense to the patients and their families? According to proponents of the living will, it returns the power of choice to the individual stricken with a terminal illness.

We have defined suicide to be the "conscious, deliberate attempt to take one's life quickly." We argue that the "altruistic" suicide and the living will are both conscious decisions to destroy oneself. We do not know whether such an act is morally justifiable, but one cannot help observing that discussion about seeking to reclaim control over one's own body and existence is increasing in contemporary society. Suicide, once accepted and then rejected as a means to an end, is being reexamined. In this heated debate the adolescent is never mentioned. It remains inconceivable that a young person just coming into being would ever consider self-destruction. But adolescents are no less capable of committing suicide than are other people. In the next section we examine the demographics of suicide among the young.

Adolescent Suicide: Thoughts and Facts

Thoughts of death and dying are not strange or foreign to adolescents of this or past generations. In fact, teenagers confront death daily in the songs they listen to, the stories they read, and the movies they watch. We discuss throughout this book Erikson's concept of adolescence as a time of searching and exploring the unknown. Death is one such unknown. From our experience as adolescents, we remember trying unsuccessfully to conceptualize nonbeing. We were unsuccessful, for our minds, our bodies, and our energy spoke more to immortality than mortality. Those feelings of immortality create a kind of time distortion in young people. The distance from Monday to Friday is forever. Only when immortality passes (in our own cases in the early 20s or so) does time achieve its fatally excessive speed. As death is unreal in adolescence, so were our perceptions of death. We were part of the generation that grooved (yes, grooved) to such 45s as *Teen Angel, Dead Man's Curve,* and the classic *Leader of the Pack.* We identified with James Dean in *Rebel Without a Cause.* We imagined ourselves in *Bridge over the River Kwai* and how we would behave in that last moment before death.

In examining our experiences, we recognize a sort of death wish in ourselves and our friends. This death wish was not to die so much as it was to experience the sensation of death, and then—as immortal beings—reverse time and situation. Thus, such ridiculous ballads as *Teen Angel,* in which a girl returns to a car stalled on the railroad tracks to search for her boyfriend's school ring only to be crushed by an oncoming locomotive, or *Dead Man's Curve,* in which a drag race on a wet, winding road ends in disaster, sent shivers up and down our spines. Maybe we identified with the survivors of these tragedies, who came so close to the experience themselves but returned to share their adventure in a two-minute song, with sound effects included. Certainly, the excessive speed with which we drove our cars and the other life chances we took then were not the actions of individuals with a correct sense of their mortality.

Our experiences are supported by others' observations that young people have "a very incomplete, distorted concept of death" (R. E. Gould, 1965, pp. 228–229). Death is seen as "not final but rather a reversible process" (McKenry, Tishler, & Christman, 1980, p. 130). In Gould's classic paper three factors influ-

Sometimes depressed youths write a suicide note as a means of calling out for help. Such notes should always be taken seriously.

ence this view of death. The first is that early in adolescence most young people have not yet reached the cognitive stage of formal operations and still deal with very complex issues in concrete terms (see Chapter 7). Unable to look beyond their immediate behavior or to understand the implications of their actions, young people can entertain thoughts of suicide. These thoughts are further stimulated by the cultural attitude that death is a taboo subject. Second, hearing euphemisms such as that a pet has been "put to sleep" or that someone has "passed away" encourages, Gould feels, the viewing of death as something other than "harsh and unpleasant." Finally, television bombards young people with death and violence in a remarkably antiseptic fashion. The coyote in *Road Runner* cartoons suffers repeated physical catastrophes only to return moments later pursuing his dinner. Adolescents' favorite TV stars are clubbed, shot, stabbed, and beaten on an almost weekly basis. These individuals never experience the massive swelling that results from a beating about the head, they never seem immobilized by the soreness in their muscles, and they never seem paralyzed by the pain of a puncture wound. These three factors of immature intellectual development, cultural taboos against talking about death, and television's excessive and unrealistic portrayal of violence interact to encourage the attitude that death is trivial.

These factors have come together on more than one occasion to result in the deaths of young people. (See Box 18–2.) Recently, Judas Priest was cleared of prompting two fans to commit suicide by the use of subliminal messages on the band's "Stained Class" album. They join Ozzy Osbourne who was unsuccessfully sued by a California couple whose son had killed himself after listening to Osbourne's song *Suicide Solution*. Osbourne, who once bit off a bat's head during a concert and like Alice Cooper has simulated onstage hangings, was

Box 18–2   Of Suicide, Rock Music, and Copy Cats

Music and images of death are not new, nor is the theme of suicide in that music. To some of our previously mentioned favorite hits, we would share a number-one hit of 1961 *Moody River* sung by Mr. Wholesome himself, Pat Boone. In this song Pat sings about his girlfriend throwing herself into a river and perishing. This is a theme repeated in Jody Reynolds's 1958 classic *Endless Sleep,* only he arrived in time. Undoubtedly, the greatest death song singer of all time has to be Dickey Lee. From *Patches* to *Laura*, his dates never made it through the song, let alone the night.

In contrast to today's slurred lyrics and subliminal suggestions that adolescents "do it" in Judas Priest's *Better by You, Better Than Me* or the alleged urging "to end your life" in Osbourne's *Suicide Solution,* singers of the past were quite clear in their lyrical intentions. For example, in *Patches* Dickey Lee wails, "Patches, oh what can I do/I swear I'll always love you/It may not be right, but I'll join you tonight."

Why, then, the concern over music lyrics? The issue is contagion. Contagion is the phenomenon in which an individual exposed to a suggestion will act on it. Several authors have documented that attention given to adolescent suicides increases the frequency of suicidal attemps by that age group using the same means (Davidson & Gould, 1989; Phillips & Carstensen, 1988; Range, Goggin, & Steede, 1988). To discourage these so-called copy-cat deaths, Phillips and Carstensen recommend that (1) the media not dwell on the death of the adolescent; (2) the news article not appear on the front page; (3) the victim not be glorified; (4) the negative consequences of the action be shared; and (5) alternatives to suicide be stressed (available counseling services, crisis phonelines, and so on). These steps, it is hoped, will discourage adolescents from copying the actions of Running Bear and Little White Dove or Billy Jo McCallister from romping through the "happy hunting grounds" to jumping off the Tallahatchee Bridge.

accused of causing the boy's death with an alleged lyric urging young people "to end your life." Other young people have died trying to leap cars with motorcycles, jumping from high places into water, or driving at breakneck speeds. To cries that greater restraint must be exercised by entertainers and the media to avoid stimulating young people to end their lives, we must comment that times have certainly changed. The generation after ours had the opportunity to catch death "live" on the 6 o'clock news as our generation died in Vietnam—this time for real. And the current generation in "living" color can catch more of the same in places with names like Lebanon and Croatia. The music of the 1950s and early 1960s turned from the silly and frivolous (like *Itsy-Bitsy, Teeny-Weeny, Yellow Polka-Dot Bikini*) to the quietly satirical *Suicide is Painless* or the heavy metal sound of *The End.*

Interestingly, although the U.S. suicide rate climbed an astonishing 200% from 1955 to 1978 (Macdonald, 1987), it has since declined (Adams, Bennion, Openshaw, & Bingham, 1990; Holinger & Offer, 1989). More interesting still is that adolescent suicide is uncommon. For the year 1985, the nubmer of suicides committed by young people between the ages of 15 and 19 was 1,849, or 10 per 100,000. For 10 to 14-year-olds, it was 275, or 1.6 per 100,000. Clearly, these are not statistically significant numbers, when the population of U.S. youth between the ages of 0 and 19 is considered. Furthermore, although these figures comprise 6.3% of all suicides for all ages for 1985, this age group comprised 8% of the total population for that year. From a statistical perspective, it could be concluded that adolescent suicides were actually *underrepresented* in the overall population for that year.

What protective factors might be at work to reduce the risk of suicide for this age group? Fischer and Shaffer (1990) suggest three possible factors. The first is that the affective disorders, particularly major depression, most commonly appear in adult life. The next is that American youth have many opportunities to receive and benefit from social support systems. These systems may be found formally in churches, schools, and youth groups, and informally in peer and adult friendships. Finally, a degree of cognitive maturity is necessary, these authors believe, before psychological constructs like hopelessness and depression can occur.

Still, from another numerical standpoint, these figures are significant in that U.S. youth do not die in great numbers. Thus, even these small numbers of deaths elevate suicide to be the second leading cause of death among adolescents in the United States. Finally, numbers are not people. Figures cannot express the suffering these youths experienced that led them to conclude that life was not worth the trouble. Statistics cannot convey the anguish their premature deaths leave behind for their parents, their siblings, and their friends. Even though the facts of adolescent suicide may be clear, the reasons for overstepping the boundary between life and death remain clouded.

Sex Differences

Females attempt suicide more frequently than do males but are less successful in actually dying. Much of the explanation for this lies in the means the sexes use to end their lives. In 1986, for example, to commit suicide males used firearms 64% of the time, hanging (16%), and poisoning (14%), while females used firearms 40% of the time, poisoning (38%), and hanging (13%). Firearms tend to be more lethal than other means, and their increased use by males resulted in a death rate for all ages almost six times higher than for females. Of concern should be the fact that over the past two decades the means by which females attempt to end their lives has changed. In contrast to 1986, in 1970 most females' suicides were by poisoning (U.S. Bureau of the Census, 1991).

Racial Differences

In the United States, Native Americans are two and one-half times more likely than Blacks to commit suicide. With a suicide rate half again as high as that for Whites, some American Indian tribes have the highest suicide rate of all racial groups. Although general suicide rates among American Indian adolescents appear to be the highest, it is important to note, however, that this is not the case for all American Indian tribes (LaFromboise & Bigfoot, 1988). Among American Indians, several factors have been associated with greater risk for adolescent suicide: (1) American Indians who are adopted by White families have a suicide rate twice as high as that of American Indian adolescents on reservations (Berlin, 1985); (2) those tribes exhibiting weak linkages to tribal and religious traditions and characterized by high unemployment have higher rates of suicides (Berlin, 1986); (3) suicide among American Indians is linked to depression and boarding school experiences (Berlin, 1986); (4) it is more common among

American Indian teenagers who are part of the same group that is characterized by drinking and feelings of anger, hopelessness, and helplessness (Berlin, 1986); (5) anniversaries are susceptible periods of time, especially for adolescent males whose male sibling committed suicide (Berlin, 1986); and (6) higher suicide rates are found among some American Indians who feel they have brought shame to their family through perceived failure or wrongdoing (Berlin, 1986).

Adams, Bennion, Openshaw, and Bingham (1990) examined data on adolescent suicide and other classifications of violent death from the National Center for Health Statistics. In comparing statistics from 1979 and 1984, they report that death by suicide decreases for Whites and Blacks, but increases for an "other" category (consisting of American Indians, Pacific Islanders, Asians, Hispanics, and other small minority groups). Furthermore, Whites and "others" are at greater risk for death from suicide and motor vehicle accidents, while Blacks are at greater risk for death from homicides. Consistent with these findings, Bingham, Bennion, Openshaw, and Adams (in press) report rates of suicide higher for White and "other" (minority) adolescents than for Blacks.

Adcock, Nagy, and Simpson (1991) examined attempted susicides and depressive symptoms in Black and White adolescents. Sixteen percent of the Whites and 14% of the Blacks report attempting suicide, but this difference is not statistically significant. In relation to depressive symptoms, Blacks are significantly more likely to report feeling sad and hopeless, although Whites are significantly more likely to report feelings of having nothing to look forward to. For both Blacks and Whites, those who report abstinence in sexual intercourse and alcohol consumptions are significantly less likely to report attempted suicde.

Also in relation to depression, Garrison, Jackson, Marsteller, McKeown, and Addy (1990) administered a depression measure to White and Black males and females over a three-year period beginning at grade seven. From their longitudinal findings they report that White males are generally lowest on depression scores. Black females are consistently the highest in depression. In two out of the three years of data collection, Black males are lower than White females in their depression scores.

In examining the relation between suicidal behavior and aggression, Cairns, Peterson, and Neckerman (1988) found that White adolescents classified as violent or assaultive are more likely to demonstrate suicidal behavior in contrast to their Black counterparts. Among 16- to 17-year-olds, Black males have considerably fewer attempted suicides, in contrast to Black females and White males and females of that age group.

A seeming anomaly arises when we examine these findings and compare suicide rates of Whites 15 to 19-years-old (11 per 100,000) and Blacks 15 to 19-years-old (4.6 per 100,000). What factors cause Blacks to have a suicide rate less than half that for Whites (May, 1987; U.S. Bureau of the Census, 1991)?

Fischer and Shaffer (1990) suggest that a history of oppression and racism against Black people has created an extended social support system that assists them. Furthermore, this history of external oppression pulls Blacks together as a people. Finally, anger not expressed inward tends to be expressed outward. And in this sense the issue of Black suicide rates may be one of interpretation (Braucht, Loya, & Jamieson, 1980). If we considser violent deaths, particularly homicide, to be equivalent to suicide, the figures change radically. For example, Black men are five times more likely than White men to be murdered, and Black women are four times more likely than White women to be murdered (Hacker, 1983). Given these data, many researchers are suggesting that the Black suicide rate does not accurately reflect their suicidal feelings. Evidence in support of this position can be found in an increasing number of studies finding a link between assaultive or violent behavior and suicide (Inamdar, Lewis, Siomopoulos, Shanok, & Lamela, 1982; Pfeffer, Plutchik, & Mizruchi, 1983; Shafii, 1985).

We suggest that adolescent-suicide rates for Blacks are low estimates because their suicidal tendencies are reflected in violent behavior. In addition, society's taboo against this behavior has encouraged many family doctors to report a suicide as an accident in order to protect the memory of the young person.

Are all adolescent suicides foolish adventures that tragically fail? Or are there other factors that work in combination with adolescent curiosity to encourage this behavior? In the next section we examine some of the most prominent theories on suicide.

Theoretical Perspectives on Suicide

Two groups of theories—one founded on psychoanalytic thought, the other on sociological observations—have been proposed as explanations for suicide. The first set of explanations focuses on internal variables, while the second views external social forces as influencing the decision to take one's own life.

The Psychiatric Perspective

Although psychoanalytic theorists differ on the exact motivations of the individual who commits suicide, an essential element in each of their arguments is the concept of punishment. Stekel (1967), a psychoanalyst writing in the latter half of the 19th century, expressed this concept when he observed that "the punishment the child imposes upon himself is simultaneously the punishment he imposes on the instigators of his sufferings" (p. 89). For Stekel, the punishment was an act of revulsion against oneself for masturbating. Stekel believed that suicidal individuals cannot live without masturbation and yet are "disgusted" by it. Their disgust with themselves over their continued masturbation or their thoughts about it or their fears over renewing this habit generalize to a disgust with life and a rejection of the world in general. Stekel wrote of one of his cases:

> The patient of whom I am now speaking, the wife of a doctor, had masturbated from her earliest years; after marriage she found herself sexually frigid. Only the continued masturbation provided sufficient libidinal gratification to keep her in good health. One day she read an article in an encyclopedia about masturbation which frightened her so deeply that she began to abstain. This abstinence caused a severe neurosis that nearly developed into a psychosis with suicidal impulses. The analysis made it clear that the threatened suicide actually represented the ultimate autoerotic act (pp. 95–96).

Alfred Adler (1967), a contemporary of Stekel, agreed that sexual issues are of major importance in pushing a young person to suicide but introduced the

Box 18–3   A Case Study of Suicide

John was a 15-year-old honor student who had attempted for nearly all his life to match his father's expectation of him as a student and as an athlete. In his sophomore year John fell in love for the first time. She was a classmate named Susan. Although his grades remained high, John was no longer interested in participating in spring training for baseball: he wanted to be with Sue. John's father was not receptive to this idea, and as a result the relationship between the two deteriorated rapidly. Their arguments almost always ended with John's father saying "You care for her more than you care for me." Feeling tremendous pressure to break off the relationship, John did stop seeing Sue. Two days after breaking it off, John shot himself. John's dilemma was a painful one. He loved and cared for both his father and Sue. He had tried to meet the standards his father had set for him, but at 15 he experienced his first love and a desire no longer to please his father. In the resulting family arguments John was torn between his father and his girlfriend. By ending his relationship with her, he lost an important person who could not be recovered. Furthermore, John now had strongly ambivalent feelings about his father, whom he held responsible for the breakup. John detested his father for making his life so miserable but loved him because he was his father. Torn between these conflicting emotions and feeling tremendous guilt, John decided to end his life.

argument that other forces may be at work as well. For Adler, feelings of inferiority, revenge, and aggression interacted in such a way as to bring a wish for illness or death in order to punish loved ones for their real or imagined slights. This position was elaborated on by Karl Menninger (1938), who proposed that suicide is actually a displaced desire to kill or to be killed.

It is, however, Sigmund Freud's (1957) conceptualization of suicide as resulting from the loss of a love object that is the most widely accepted of the psychoanalytic theories. In this explanation the suicidal person is seen as loving and then hating some object who has become lost or unavailable. Alternating between the desires to destroy and to cherish the object, the individual recognizes these hostile feelings and feels guilty about having them. This guilt turns the anger away from the object inward, and the anger against oneself is expressed by the act of suicide. (See Box 18–3.)

More recent theories provide other perspectives on suicide. M. L. Farber (1968) wrote that suicide results from a sense of hopelessness. The individual does not see any acceptable way out of an impossible situation and so chooses "a quick self-induced death . . . in preference to the certain prospect of an unbearable life" (p. 26). The trigger can be found in some life incident "that renders life more difficult to cope with and closes off any possibility of improvement in the situation" (p. 41) (see also Crumley, 1982; Tooley, 1980). In the case study described in Box 18–3, this life blow occurred with the ending of John's relationship with Susan. Unable to see an acceptable way out of his troubles, he selected the ultimate solution—suicide.

Shneidman (1976) describes suicide as a plea for help. The suicidal individual has come to the end of his or her emotional resources and through this act attempts to mobilize the support of others. Shneidman's view is supported by the fact that most suicide attempts do fail, thus providing the opportunity for assistance to emerge out of an attempt at self-destruction.

Such theories have provided the basis for categorizations of suicidal-personality types. For example, a typology proposed by C. V. Leonard (1967) describes three suicidal personalities: *dependent/dissatisfied; satisfied/symbiotic,* and *unaccepting/suicidal.* Leonard describes the first type as exasperating, manipulative, unreasonable individuals who demand attention but reject close personal relationships. Unable to get along with relatives and having few friends because of their use of techniques that border on "emotional blackmail," these people become suicidal when they have exhausted their friendships. Immediate attention, Leonard suggests, should be given to establishing a support system for such individuals, with long-term treatment goals of resolving dependency and control issues.

The satisfied/symbiotic type is an overly dependent individual with excessively close ties to one person. Unable to express anger toward this loved one, such individuals have a poorly developed sense of identity, which allows the other person to make most of their life decisions for them. These individuals (John, in the case study, is one example), unable to direct anger against anyone except themselves, attempt suicide when their relationship with their loved one is significantly disturbed. Of all three types, this one is thought to be the most amenable to treatment, which should be directed toward establishing independence.

The third type, unaccepting/suicidal, Leonard views as the individual in control who is threatened by the loss of control. Such individuals are driven by the need to succeed. With a rigid outlook on life in which everything is either black or white, they are most likely to be suicidal when their life environment is disturbed. The absence of power or a lack of control over events of importance to them can, Leonard feels, trigger a successful suicide. This type has the most difficulty admitting to a need for help. Treatment, if it can occur, should focus on diminishing the need for feeling omnipotent.

The Sociological Perspective

The other major group of explanations for suicidal behavior is in the sociological literature. Much of the work in this field is by Émile Durkheim, whose *Suicide: A Sociological Study* (1951, first published in 1897) is credited by Alvarez (1972) with stripping away much of the horror and fear that surrounded suicide until the late 1800s. Durkheim's conceptualization of suicide rests on the individual's integration into society. The individual who is poorly integrated into society commits an *egotistic* suicide, while the individual who chooses a group identity over an individual identity in death commits an *altruistic* suicide (the Jews at Masada are one example). Finally, the individual caught in sudden societal or personal change that creates significant alienation or confusion in the individual commits an *anomic* suicide (DenHouter, 1981; Huffine, 1989).

Central to all three forms of suicide is Durkheim's (1897/1951) concept of anomie. The term *anomie* describes a society that is rootless, that is disintegrating because of some upheaval. As this society frays as a result of economic problems, revolution, value conflicts, or the like, individuals within that society experience increasing emotional difficulties, and as the cultural instability increases, the suicide rate increases. However, whether a suicide is egotistic, altruistic, or anomic, each represents a changing relationship with the environment. In the next section we examine the psychiatric and sociological theories in light of the research findings.

Psychological and Sociological Research on Suicide

What events come together to convince a young person to pursue so rash a course as suicide? A number of studies and clinical observations suggest that seemingly trivial events provoke the decision to attempt suicide. Several studies show, for instance, that fights with parents and the ending of a relationship with a boyfriend or girlfriend are the most frequent triggers. Certainly, these disputes with parents or breakups with friends are painful situations, but since they are near-universal adolescent experiences, much more must be going on (Grueling & De Blassie, 1980; Rubenstein, Heeren, Housman, Rubin, & Stechler, 1989; J. L. Rotheram, 1987).

Several studies show that young people who attempt suicide have extremely strained relationships with their parents. Pfeffer (1981a) finds the following characteristics in many of these families. First, there is an absence of generational boundaries between the parents or these young people and their own parents. Next, spousal relationships are marked by dependency conflicts. These conflicts spill over onto the children as parental anger is inappropriately displaced onto them. Finally, maintaining the same symbiotic ties to their children as their parents maintain to them, the parents of these children discourage attempts at independence and, not surprisingly, live in a closed family system. Such a family environment, while smothering in one respect, is often emotionally detached from its children. This detachment results in most young people's feeling greatly unloved and unwanted. This theme emerges in almost every other study conducted on the subject.

This parental neglect can occur in one of two ways. Many authors note that young people are dependent on their parents for love and support. Parental refusal to provide these essential elements for proper emotional growth places young people at risk (American Academy of Pediatrics, 1980; Fish & Waldhart-Letzel, 1981; M. L. Miller, Chiles, & Barnes, 1982; Pfeffer, 1981b). It is not surprising, then, that many studies report high marital discord or divorce in families with adolescents who attempt suicide (Allen, 1987; Gispert, Wheeler, Marsh, & Davis, 1985; McKenry, et al., 1980; Paluszny, Davenport, & Kim, 1991; Strang & Orlofsky, 1990; Tischler, McKenry, & Morgan, 1981). This conflict between the parents keeps the home in a constant state of tension and may carry over into their relationship with their children (Cohen-Sandler, Berman, & King, 1982; I. Orbach, Gross, & Glaubman, 1981; Paykel, 1989; Pfeffer, 1981a, 1989). In a few cases the depth of parental rejection is such that researchers have gone so far as to suggest that one or both parents encouraged the young person to commit suicide (Molin, 1986; Pfeffer, 1981b; Rosenkrantz, 1978). In the "expendable-child syndrome" (Sabbath, 1969) parents communicate to the adolescent that he or she is unwanted, is a burden to the family, and should never have been born.

The second kind of parental neglect is the result of the death of a parent. Research suggests that the earlier a child loses a parent, the more severe the effects will be (K. Glasser, 1978; Stanley & Barter, 1970). Stanley and Barter, who examined 38 hospitalized suicidal adolescents, report that they differed from a control group in having lost a parent before the age of 12. These authors speculate that the death of a parent at such an early age disrupts the proper resolution of dependency issues. Whether these findings continue to apply later in life is uncertain. For example, G. E. Barnes and Prosen (1985) found in a sample of 1250 outpatients seeking medical assistance from a general practitioner that the loss of the male parent contributed to depression in adulthood. However, they caution that this finding contributed only 2% to explaining the variance in the depression scores of adults (see Crook & Eliot, 1980; Paykel, 1989 for critical reviews of this literature).

These studies suggest that the emotional needs of suicidal adolescents have not been met at home. Thus, it should not be surprising that these young people have been found to have poor self-esteem, poor social support, and problems with authority (Allen, 1987; Block, Block, & Gjerde, 1991; Daniels & Moos, 1990; Farberow, 1989; Shafii, 1985). They also experience higher levels of stress (Daniels & Moos, 1990; Paykel, 1989; Rich, Sherman, & Fowler, 1990; Schotte & Clum, 1982; Slater & Depue, 1981) and school difficulties (Farberow, 1989; Gispert et al., 1985). In addition, they have been described as angry, disagreeable, and impulsive (Gjerde, Block, & Block, 1988; 1991), ego-brittle (Gjerde et al., 1988), and lacking insight (Paluszny, Davenport, & Kim, 1991). Finally, the abuse of alcohol and other substances is not uncommon (Crumley, 1990; Fischer & Schaffer, 1990; Klitzer & Blasinsky, 1990; Schuckit & Schuckit, 1989). (See Table 18–1.)

Interestingly, depression in the suicidal adolescent remains a disputed issue. Although numerous studies report depression as the principal contributing factor to attempted suicides (Cole, 1989; Daniels & Moos, 1990; Pfeffer, Klerman,

Table 18–1   Risk Factors for Increased, and Protective Factors for Decreased, Youth Suicidal Risk

Increased Suicidal Risk	◄—Risk Factors For:	Youth Suicidal Risk	Protective Factors For: —►	Decreased Suicidal Risk

	1. Loss of Social Support
	  a. Death
	  b. Parental Separation/Divorce
	  c. School Changes
	  d. Peer Problems
			1. Presence of Social Support
			  a. Empathy
			  b. Constant Availability
			  c. Limit Setting
			  d. Environmental Structure	

	2. Variability in Parental Functioning
	  a. Affective Disorders
	  b. Suicidal Tendencies
	  c. Alcohol Abuse
			2. Individual Adaptive Skills
			  a. Appraisal of Stress
			  b. Seek Alternative Solutions
			  c. High Furstration Tolerance
			  d. Self-esteem
			  e. Good Impulse Control	

	3. Violence
	  a. Sexual Abuse
	  b. Physical Abuse			

Source: C. R. Pfeffer (1989). Family characteristics and support systems as risk factors for youth suicidal behavior. In ADAMHA *Report of the secretary's task force on youth suicide:* Vol. 2: Risk factors for youth suicide. Department of Health and Human Services, publication #ADM 89–1622. Washington, DC: U.S. Government Printing Office.

Hurt, Lessor, Peskin, & Siefker, 1991), other studies report that depression may not be the primary factor (Glasser, 1981; Peck, 1987). Part of the explanation for this disagreement may be gender differences as Gjerde and associates (1988, 1991) have reported. Adolescent females in their studies have appeared and reported depression, while males typically appeared aggressive, undercontrolled, and impulsive. Furthermore, it is also important to recognize, we believe, that depression can often be hidden in disagreeable and antagonistic behaviors like temper tantrums, rebelliousness, and defiance.

Nonetheless, the suicidal adolescent appears to have a poor family life and to experience considerable emotional deprivation. As Teicher and Jacobs (1966) and others (Davidson, Rosenberg, Mercy, Franklin, & Simmons, 1989) describe it, the long-standing problems of the adolescent accelerate during a period in which parent and adolescent enter into a "squirrel cage" series of arguments ending with a complete "breakdown in communications." Desperate at this point to find meaning in life, the adolescent seeks close companionship. "The adolescent, already alienated to a great extent from the parents, seeks love, understanding, acceptance, reason, predictability—in short, a meaningful social relationship in one of the few remaining forms which allows for the intimacy implicit in such a relationship, i.e., a boyfriend or girlfriend" (p. 1255). In their attempt to gain this measure of satisfaction, young people invest all their remaining resources in this relationship, typically alienating themselves from school and other friends. When this relationship goes sour, they confront their loneliness and decide in desperation to attempt suicide.

Growing evidence suggests that this problem is more acute for some young people than for others. Young people with either an alcoholic parent or a depressed suicidal parent appear to be at significantly higher risk for suicide than their peers (Klitzner & Blasinsky, 1990; McKenry et al., 1980; Orbach et al., 1981; Pfeffer, 1981b; Tishler & McKenry, 1982; Tishler et al., 1981). Robins (1989) and Roy (1989) suggest this risk to be between four and five times the risk to their age cohort. This risk might be understood from either a role-model or a stress perspective. In the first instance the young person is copying the parents' behavior. In the second instance, these parental behaviors place additional emotional stress on the adolescent's ability to cope with life.

From his experience as a clinician, J. M. Toolan (1962) has categorized suicide attempts as possibly falling into five motivational categories. In Toolan's model, adolescents may be trying to:

1. Express anger toward another but instead internalize this anger, resulting in guilt and depression, which trigger a suicide attempt
2. Control another by using suicide as a manipulative act to gain attention or as a punishment
3. Call for help in a "dramatic . . . last ditch effort" to attract attention to their emotional needs
4. Protect themselves from feelings of falling apart or obey hallucinatory voices telling them to commit suicide
5. Join a deceased relative

Toolan (1962) believes, as do many of the writers we have cited, that the young person in each of these situations is attempting to reclaim the loss of a love object. The findings of nearly all the studies reporting high levels of family discord, poor parent/child relationships, and emotional and physical child abuse lend themselves to this explanation. The young person attempting suicide is trying to recapture the emotional security that he or she so desperately wants.

Convincing as this argument may sound, sociologists say that committing suicide is far more complex than "simple" psychological constructs may suggest. For instance, as we have already noted, some Native American tribes have a suicide rate far higher than either Whites or Blacks do.* Can this high suicide rate be explained by assuming that their culture is marked by more family problems than others? Or are there other possible explanations?

Remembering Durkheim's conceptualization that suicide rests on the individual's integration into society, Holinger and Offer (1982) present data suggesting a significant relationship between increases in adolescent suicide rates and the adolescent population. The authors suggest that as the relative number of young people in society increases, competition also increases. As opportunities are finite (the number of desirable jobs, scholarships, varsity positions), the chance for failure increases. Holinger and Offer speculate that such failures contribute to a lower sense of self-worth and a gradual withdrawal of the individual from significant others, so that eventually some will commit suicide.

From a cultural perspective, Huffine (1989) and others (Lester, 1991; McAnarney, 1979; Stack, 1988) note that in societies in which family bonds are close (low anomie), suicide rates are low (see Table 18–2). In those societies experiencing changing family patterns (high anomie), suicide rates are higher. Religious beliefs also have an effect on reported suicide rates, with strongly religious nations reporting lower suicide rates than less religious nations. (See Hoelter, 1979, for an expanded discussion on the influence of religion on reducing suicide rates.) Further, the issue of transition in general affects the suicide rates of different nations. It appears that the more a nation experiences disruption and mobility, the higher the suicide rate is for that nation. For young people, the value a particular society places on achievement affects the suicide rate. Highly industrialized nations that place great importance on education, such as Japan and the United States, have significantly higher suicide rates than nations that do not. (See Box 18–4.) Finally, McAnarney notes that nations that encourage the suppression of aggression have higher rates of reported suicides than do nations that encourage the expression of feelings.

Support for these statements on family anomie and its relationship to suicide can be found in an article by Wenz (1979). His study of 55 families from different socioeconomic backgrounds shows that degree of family anomie is related to adolescents' attempting suicide. As anomie rose in the families in Wenz's study, income dropped and suicide attempts increased. Wenz concludes:

---

*For example, the Apache nation has a very high suicide rate in contrast to the Pueblo nation.

Table 18–2 Suicide Rates for Selected Countries by Sex and Age
(15- to 24-years-old) per 100,000

Male	
Canada	26.9
Italy	5.2
Japan	11.6
United Kingdom	9.3
United States	21.7
Female	
Canada	5.3
Italy	1.3
Japan	6.5
United Kingdom	2.1
United States	4.4
Total Average	
Canada	16.1
Italy	3.3
Japan	9.0
United Kingdom	5.7
United States	13.0

Source: U.S. Census Bureau (1991). *Statistical Abstract of the United States*: 1992 (112th edition). Washington, DC: U.S. Government Printing Office.

Adolescent suicide behavior may be seen as an extreme form of reaction to family anomie; and the adolescent suicide attempt is merely a symptom of a process that involves the entire family. For the adolescent, the only escape from such a family environment is to adopt some form of retreatist behavior (p. 396).

In applying these findings to Native Americans, we must recognize that some tribal life-styles have been systematically attacked by the U.S. government and society in general for more than 300 years. Opportunities have been pervasively denied to Native Americans. Hollywood's movie makers for decades portrayed some Native Americans as *once* noble and dignified savages. This same medium also portrays them as butchering heathens. Images and practices such as these have an insidious effect, conditioning these people to believe that they are little more than excess baggage in the 20th century. It is not surprising, then, to see a once so powerful people, who are now reduced in media portrayals and government handling to powerless positions, choose suicide as an acceptable alternative to an unacceptable life.

But not all Native Americans attempt suicide, and more exceptions to Durkheim's rules of suicide have been found than affirmations, proving that complex behavior defies simplistic answers (McIntosh & Santos, 1980–1981). We suggest that both personality and social conditions interact in such a way as to select some young people for self-destruction. In the next section we look at what efforts can be made to treat or prevent suicidal behavior in young people.

Box 18–4   A Cross–Cultural Perspective: Adolescent Suicide in Japan

Many Americans believe that there is an epidemic of suicide among Japanese young people. Is that assumption correct, and are there differences between North American youths and Japanese youths in their motivations to commit suicide? A study by Mamoru Iga (1981) suggests that there are some cultural similarities and also some important differences.

Earlier in this chapter we examine the family conditions that contribute to North American youths, decision to end their lives. In Iga's study the same difficulties in communication patterns, intimacy, and understanding also existed. The competition factor noted among North American youths (Holinger & Offer, 1982) is even more evident in Japan. The value that the Japanese people place on education is extremely high. Furthermore the structure of their educational system is such that openings for higher educational opportunities are limited. The result is "examination hell." Japanese adolescents live in a world in which they are faced with the pressure of testing situations that will determine their chance for higher education. Failure to pass is failing not only oneself but also one's family (Iga, 1981). Although there are similarities,

important cultural differences also contribute to the suicide rate among Japanese youths. The first is the lack of outlets for displaying emotional behavior in Japanese society. The politeness and restraint that we have come to associate with the Japanese provide few opportunities for adolescents to release the emotional tension that accompanies this life stage. The second factor is the view the Japanese have of death and of suicide itself. Neither death nor suicide is feared or held in revulsion. Both may be noble and beautiful events. Thus, as it once was for Western civilization, suicide is held as a birthright (Iga, 1981).

This evidence certainly would lead us to expect a higher youth suicide rate in Japan than in the United States. In fact, surprising as this may be, Japan has a *lower* suicide rate (9 per 100,000) for youths between the ages of 15 and 24 than either the United States (13 per 100,000) or Canada (16.1 per 100,000).

> Using the theories in this chapter, how might we explain the fact that the United States and Canada have a higher youth suicide rate than Japan?

Implications for Treatment and Prevention

Treatment

The treatment of suicidal behavior in young people demands that attention be paid to both the immediate crisis situation and the underlying problems that precipitated the attempt. Since the suicide attempt is a statement of the adolescent's abandonment of this world, friends and relatives must be mobilized to establish a lifeline of support, guidance, and friendship (Rosenbaum & Beebe, 1975). Schrut (1968) and others (Getz, Allen, Myers, & Lindner, 1983) emphasize that this alliance is critical for the therapist. They also suggest that if therapy is to be successful, the therapist must establish a relationship with the adolescent in which the young person can obtain "understanding, concern, and support." (See Box 18–5).

One of the first issues that must be addressed after a young person has attempted to take his or her life is whether hospitalization is advisable. Trautman (1989) and others (Blumenthal & Kupfer, 1989; Schrut, 1968) offer several guidelines for determining the answer to this question. Young people at lower risk of repeating the attempt are those whose precipitating circumstances suggest an impulsive action, who express a desire to continue to live, who do not show long-standing or presently severe depression, and who have a lifeline of family support available to them. At a higher risk of repeating the attempt to commit

Box 18–5   Psychological First Aid

The following are . . . steps for the mature adult dealing with the suicidal young person:

Step 1: *Listen.* The first thing a person in a mental crisis needs is someone who will listen and really hear what he is saying. Every effort should be made to understand the feelings behind the words.

Step 2: *Evaluate the seriousness of the youngster's thoughts and feelings.* If the person has made clear self–destructive plans, however, the problem is apt to be more acute than when his thinking is less definite.

Step 3: *Evaluate the intensity or severity of the emotional disturbance.* It is possible that the youngster may be extremely upset but not suicidal. If a person has been depressed and then becomes agitated and moves about restlessly, it is usually cause for alarm.

Step 4: *Take every complaint and feeling the patient expresses seriously:* Do not dismiss or undervalue what the person is saying. In some instances, the person may express his difficulty in a low key, but beneath his seeming calm may be profoundly distressed feelings. *All* suicidal talk should be taken seriously.

Step 5: *Do not be afraid to ask directly if the individual has entertained thoughts of suicide.* Suicide may be suggested but not openly mentioned in the crisis period. Experience shows that harm is rarely done by inquiring directly into such thoughts at an appropriate time. As a matter of fact, the individual frequently welcomes the query and is glad to have the opportunity to open up and bring it out.

Step 6: *Do not be misled by the youngster's comments that he is past his emotional crisis.* Often the youth will feel initial relief after talking of suicide, but the same thinking will recur later. Follow–up is crucial to insure a good treatment effort.

Step 7: *Be affirmative but supportive.* Strong, stable guideposts are essential in the life of a distressed individual. Provide emotional strength by giving the impression that you know what you are doing, and that everything possible will be done to prevent the young person from taking his life.

Step 8: *Evaluate the resources available.* The individual may have both inner psychological resources, including various mechanisms for rationalization and intellectualization which can be strengthened and supported, and outer resources in the environment, such as ministers, relatives, and friends whom one can contact. If these are absent, the problem is much more serious. Continuing observation and support are vital.

Step 9: *Act specifically:* Do something tangible; that is, give the youngster something definite to hang onto, such as arranging to see him later or subsequently contacting another person. Nothing is more frustrating to the person that to feel as though he has received nothing from the meeting.

Step 10: *Do not avoid asking for assistance and consultation.* Call upon whoever is needed, depending upon the severity of the case. Do not try to handle everything alone. Convey an attitude of firmness and composure to the person so that he will feel something realistic and appropriate is being done to help him.

Additional . . . techniques for dealing with persons in a suicide crisis may require the following:

- Arrange for a receptive individual to stay with the youth during the acute crisis.
- Do not treat the youngster with horror or deny his thinking.
- Make the environment as safe and provocation-free as possible.
- Never challenge the individual in an attempt to shock him out of his ideas.
- Do not try to win arguments about suicide. They cannot be won.
- Offer and supply emotional support for life.
- Give reassurances that depressed feelings are temporary and will pass.
- Mention that if the choice is to die, the decision can never be reversed.
- Point out that, while life exists, there is always a chance for help and resolution of the problems, but that death is final.
- Focus upon survivors by reminding the youngster about the rights of others. He will leave a stigma on his siblings and other family members. He will predispose his friends and family to emotional problems or suicide.
- Call in family and friends to help establish a lifeline.

Box 18–5   Psychological First Aid (*continued*)

- Allow the youngster to ventilate his feelings.
- Do not leave the individual isolated or unobserved for any appreciable time if he is acutely distressed.

These procedures can help restore feelings of personal worth and dignity, which are equally as important to the young person as to the adult. In so doing, the adult helping agent can make the difference between

life and death. A future potentially productive young citizen will survive.

Why do you think the phrase "mature adult" was used in the first paragraph?

Source: National Institute of Mental Health. (1977). *Trends in mental health: Self-destructive behavior among younger age groups* (DHEW Publication No. ADM 77–365). Washington, DC: U.S. Government Printing Office.

suicide are young people whose precipitating circumstances were "ordinary" life events (a family argument, for example), who are ambivalent about living after the attempt, who show present signs of severe depression or have a history of depression, and who, in the therapist's judgment, do not have the support of family and friends. Other factors such as the means used to attempt suicide (firearms representing the most dangerous) and the young person's age and sex, must also be considered in determining whether the client is an acceptable risk for outpatient treatment.

From this and other epidemiological studies Robins (1989) has developed a table of correlates to suicide attempts. (See Table 18–3.) And Curran (1979) has developed two scales to assist clinicians. (See Tables 18–4 and 18–5.) The first, a distress scale, provides the mental-health worker with a gauge of the adolescent's ability to communicate and relate to feelings as a rough diagnostic measure of the severity of depression. The second, a lethality scale, enables the clinician to make a crude assessment of the seriousness of the attempt. The information drawn from these measures, Curran cautions, is not the sole determinant of the seriousness of an attempt. Rather, this information is combined with other personal, family, and medical data to reach a clinical assessment of the situation.

Rotheram (1987), building on the works cited earlier, has proposed a screening procedure using two assessment interviews. The first, focusing on factors such as suicidal thoughts, history of past attempts, family history, evidence of clinical depression, and substance use, is used to determine potential risk. If risk is assessed to be high, the second diagnostic interview commences. In that interview the skilled clinician determines whether the adolescent is able to marshal enough coping resources to survive without being committed. For example, the clinician asks the adolescent to sign a written contract agreeing not to attempt suicide for a specified period of time. Depending on the adolescent's ability to agree and his or her answers to several other questions, the need for hospitalization is determined.

Whether the adolescent is treated as an outpatient or an inpatient, family therapy in conjunction with individual or group therapy is recommended by

Table 18–3   Predictors of Suicide Attempts in Adolescent Clinic Patients

5 + x Population rate	Used barbs, PCP, hallucinogens, T's & blues, glue Wanted to die Thought of suicide
4–5 x Population rate	Depressed two years or more Attempt before this year Hopelessness Four or more family diagnoses Runaway Alcohol problems this year Incarcerated this year Not living with relatives Psychiatric chief complaint

3–4 x Population rate	Relative attempted
	Specific depressive symptoms ever
	   loss of enjoyment
	   felt slowed down
	   felt worthless
	   irritable
	Five or more depressive symptoms
	Ever incarcerated
	Three or more somatic symptoms not medically explained
	Four or more behavior problems
	Fighting at home involving patient this year
	Has been drunk at least three times in the last year
	Hurt or threatened this year
	Arrested this year

2–3 x Population rate	White female aged 15 to 18 Has thought often about death Any depressive symptom ever Ever in trouble with the law Severe poverty Five or more posttraumatic symptoms

Source: L. N. Robins, (1989). Suicide attempts in teenaged medical patients. In ADAMHA *Report of the secretary's task force on youth suicide:* Vol. 4: Strategies for the prevention of youth suicide. Department of Health and Human Services publication #ADM 89–1622. Washington, DC: U.S. Government Printing Office.

most professionals. The psychological/psychiatric literature described earlier in this chapter presents a clear and convincing argument for the family's contribution to the life problems of the suicidal adolescent. If that young person is to stay with or return to the family, the therapist must help the family grow into a healthier and more enriching environment for the young person (B. A. Walker & Mehr, 1983).

Table 18–4   Distress Scale

Degree	Description
1	Mildly anxious but reasonable and able to accept intervention.
2	Mildly to moderately depressed, with sad face: may have loss of sleep and appetite disturbance. Still functioning in most daily routines: able to accept intervention.
3	Agitated and anxious, unable to communicate well, but one senses in a few hours the patient will be calmer and able to accept intervention and to communicate.
4	Moderately depressed with some disturbance in daily functions including sleep and appetite. Has a feeling of hopelessness and worthlessness, but is able to accept intervention.
5	Moderately depressed with some disturbance in daily functions; has marked feelings of hopelessness and worthlessness, and is unable to accept intervention.
6	An unusual personality disturbance not easily understood in context of how the patient presents himself (for example, hallucinations or delusions or both in an otherwise intact person, or an unexplained obsession with suicide).
7	Severely depressed, withdrawn, unable to function, has retarded thoughts and movements, feels hopeless and worthless.
8	Severe personality disorganization, difficulty with reality testing, illogical thinking, possible delusions and hallucinations, unable to function.

Source: From "Suicide," by B. E. Curran, *Pediatric Clinics of North America,* 1979, 26(4), 737–746. Reprinted by permission.

Prevention

The suicide-prevention centers that started in England and were transplanted to North America in the 1960s represent a form of secondary prevention. Manned by trained professionals and volunteers, their hot lines provide a link between society and the individual contemplating suicide. The key to this form of crisis intervention is the caller's willingness to talk and share his or her feelings. The counselor encourages the ventilation of these emotions and tries to have the caller consider various alternatives to the present dilemma. Once a rapport has been established, the worker will volunteer to make arrangements for the caller to receive professional help. Some callers accept this invitation for help, while others do not.

The effectiveness of suicide-prevention centers is somewhat uncertain. Unquestionably, for the individuals who call looking for help, these organizations provide that critical lifeline of support. However, some authors argue that those at greatest risk of suicide do not use such services. Lester (1972) suggests that the existence of such services may even encourage rather than discourage suicidal behavior.

Primary prevention of suicidal behavior must be aimed at the root causes of suicide. The theories examined earlier in this chapter provide suggestions for diminishing the prevalence of suicide.

Table 18–5   Lethality scale

Degree	Description
1	Threatening to commit suicide in an attempt to control other persons. Example: "If you don't let me go out tonight. I will kill myself."
2	Threatening to commit suicide because of feeling depressed and worthless. Example: "I feel so down I am thinking about taking some pills to end it all."
3	Threatening to commit suicide with a clear plan (patient may not be depressed or manipulative). Example: "I heard a voice telling me to jump out the window."
4	Taking a nonlethal action in an attempt to control other persons. Example: "I cut my wrist with a pin because I had a fight with my boyfriend."
5	Taking a nonlethal action because of depression, then asking for help. Example: "I felt so down that I took a few sleeping pills and then called for help."
6	Taking a nonlethal or questionably lethal action in a planned or impulsive manner and being accidentally discovered. Example: ingesting a bottle of aspirin after a long series of disappointments.
7	Taking clearly lethal action in an impulsive manner. Example: "I had a fight with my mother and I jumped off the roof."
8	Taking clearly lethal action after some thought and planning and being accidentally discovered. Example: a young boy who after several months of depression failed to get into the college of his choice and was found with a shotgun wound in his abdomen.

Source: From "Suicide," by B. E. Curran, *Pediatric Clinics of North America,* 1979, 26(4), 737–746. Reprinted by permission.

Education

Arguments that suicide results from emotional deprivation and family neglect suggest that educational programs need to be developed to strengthen the family unit. We have urged repeatedly in this text that family-life education be made an integral and important part of the young person's entire academic training. Such training could avert the ill-advised but growing popularity of pushing children at ever-earlier ages to achieve (Elkind, 1981).

Education can occur elsewhere than in the classroom. Popular films like *Ordinary People* and *The Heart Is a Lonely Hunter* sensitively portray the anguish that accompanies the decision to end one's life. And printed material like the National Institute of Mental Health's (1984) *Adolescence and Depression* help all of us better understand the pressures young people face and how to provide them with the support necessary to cope with those stresses.

Competency Promotion

In this chapter, as in every other chapter devoted to discussing dysfunctional behavior in adolescence, we have observed a recurring pattern of personality development. Terms such as *low self-esteem* and *helplessness* continually appear.

In fact, one might reasonably argue that given the similarity in family and personality types in all adolescent behavioral dysfunctions, chance as much as any other factor dictates which problems in living such adolescents will experience. The issue that must be grappled with is how to promote social competency. Education for expectant parents, stressing the crucial role they play in developing self-esteem and an internal locus of control in their children, is one approach. Another is providing opportunities through group activities such as scouting, Outward Bound, and sports that develop a sense of power and accomplishment for young people. Perpahs most important is the need for *us* to remember that we should not by our individual interactions with others contribute to their sense of failure and inadequacy.

Community Organization/Systems Intervention

Is it possible to build a utopia in which all individuals can feel worthwhile? Probably not. On the other hand, it certainly is possible to communicate a message through our schools and social programs that all individuals are valued. In other chapters we have argued for humane and sensitive educational environments for our children. We urge that services such as universal day care, adequate medical care, and food programs for young children either be developed or expanded. Our arguments are based on the belief that young children are too valuable a resource to risk neglect and abuse by any one segment of the population, whether that be the state or the parent. The programs and services we are talking about act as a check on the deprivation that may be occurring in a young person's life. They offer a statement of society's commitment to ensuring young people the opportunity to grow into healthy, contributing members of society.

Natural Care Giving

How does a society care for itself? Durkheim's view that suicide is a function of the cohesiveness of society at any one time suggests two interventions. The first, focusing on relationships within the individual's family to promote membership and belonging, is more easily achieved than the second. That is, it is within our power to create and encourage a family environment or friendship environment in which individuals are valued and loved. The second intervention, focusing on external relationships, is far more complex. For instance, do we encourage war or create the perception of an external threat to maintain social cohesiveness? Can we provide meaningful, worthwhile work to everyone who wants to work? Is it possible to bind together a nation in a single purpose without resorting (as Freud might argue) to instinctual Rambolike aggression? Keeping a society healthy without destroying others is a challenge exceeding the authors' capacities. We encourage you to think how it might be done.

Prevention and Intervention Strategies: American Indian Adolescents

From the literature on incidence of suicide among various ethnic and racial groups, it appears that American Indian adolescents are at greatest risk for suicide. Therefore, it is useful to discuss issues of prevention and intervention among this group. LaFramboise and Bigfoot (1988) draw on Bandura's (1978) model of reciprocal determinism (person, behavior, and environment interaction) in suggesting prevention and intervention efforts among American Indians. One application of this approach involves identifying the thoughts, images, and inner conversations used as coping strategies to counteract difficult conditions. Four categories of coping statements that are identified include (a) task-confidence statements, (b) perspective-keeping statements, (c) decatastrophizing statements, and (d) personal strength and determination statements. Statements illustrative of these four categories are used in teaching coping strategies in an American Indian suicide prevention program. Additional materials included are information on suicide, the roles substance abuse and stress play in suicide, cognitive and social skills, and anger management.

Several suicide intervention programs for American Indians are reviewed by Berlin (1985). Strategies thought to be effective in suicide prevention and intervention include developing suicide prevention centers that include holding facilities, providing education about suicide in school, engaging tribal healers and elders in prevention and intervention efforts, addressing issues related to suicide in programs designed for pregnant adolescents and new adolescent mothers and their infants, and incorporating suicide prevention and intervention strategies in alcohol and drug treatment programs.

Levy and Kunitz (1987) have provided a thorough assessment of the topic of suicide prevalence and prevention among Hopi youth. They conclude that suicide and alcohol abuse are linked for this population. Furthermore, individuals identified at most risk for suicide and alcohol abuse are those whose parents did not adhere to endogamous marital norms. A label of deviant is applied to these individuals and their children that places them at risk for alcohol abuse and suicide. Levy and Kunitz (1987) suggest several factors that should be incorporated in suicide prevention programs among Hopis. Community strengths, rather than weaknesses, should be identified. Prevention efforts should target younger adolescents, as well as older youths. In order to identify suicide risk factors, suicide prevention efforts and corresponding research should include individuals thought not currently to be at risk for suicide. In evaluating the effectiveness of suicide prevention programs, also examine the impact of the program on related social problems. To avoid labeling those already defined as deviant, do not identify the program as suicide prevention. Finally, Levy and Kunitz argue that a suicide prevention program among Hopi can be carried out with minimal cost and personnel, and argue for the use of volunteers from the community.

Major Points to Remember

1. Suicide is a "conscious, deliberate attempt to take one's life quickly."
2. Taking one's own life was not punished per se in earlier societies. Rather, the circumstances surrounding the suicide determined whether it was accepted or punished.
3. It was not until 533 A.D. at the Council of Orléans that the Christian church began to view the taking of one's own life as sinful, and it was not until the

Council of Braga in 562 A.D. that the Fifth Commandment, "Thou shalt not kill," was reinterpreted to apply to the taking of one's own life.

4. The "living will" asks that no special medical means be used to keep an individual alive should that person become terminally ill.

5. Many authors find that adolescents view death in a distorted and incomplete way. Death in many young people's eyes is not final but reversible. The factors contributing to this condition are the adolescent's immature intellectual development, cultural taboos against talking about death, and television's unrealistic portrayal of violence.

6. Females attempt suicide more frequently than males, but males are more successful.

7. If suicide rates are closely examined, the highest are found in some minority populations.

8. In very early psychoanalytic thought sexual repression was the cause of taking one's own life. This position has been considerably modified.

9. According to Menninger, suicide is a repressed desire to kill or to be killed.

10. Freud understood suicide to result from the loss of a love object.

11. Others see the taking of one's own life as the reflection of a sense of hopelessness or as a plea for help.

12. Leonard identifies three suicidal types. Dependent/dissatisfied individuals are rejected by friends and family because of their negative personalities. Without support, they attempt to end their lives. Satisfied/symbiotic individuals are overly dependent. Unable to achieve independence, they are capable of suicidal behavior when the security of their dependent relationship is significantly disturbed. Unaccepting/suicidal individuals are highly controlled. They may commit suicide when faced with loss of control over their destinies.

13. One of the most important conceptualizations of suicide is Durkheim's theory that the taking of one's life depends on the individual's integration into society.

14. In Durkheim's model, individuals who are loners, who have not integrated themselves into society, and who end their lives are said to have committed an egotistic suicide. Individuals who choose a group identity over their individual identities and end their lives are seen as committing an altruistic suicide. The last form of suicide in this model is anomic suicide. In this situation sudden societal or personal change so overwhelms the coping abilities of individuals that they end their lives.

15. Central to Durkheim's model is the concept of anomie. Anomie speaks of rootlessness, normlessness. As anomie increases in society, Durkheim suggests, suicide rates increase.

16. Studies show that many young people who attempt suicide feel unloved and unwanted. Family relationships are described as poor.

17. Impulsiveness more than depression is seen by many researchers as the critical variable in an attempt to take one's own life. But this point is heatedly disputed by many.

18. Toolan believes that adolescents attempt suicide to express anger, to control another, to call for help, to protect themselves, or to join a deceased relative.

19. Researchers exploring Durkheim's model have found cross-cultural evidence that where family bonds are close, belief in religion high, and societal disruption low (low anomie), suicide rates are low.

20. The first therapeutic effort that needs to be made to assist an individual who has attempted suicide is to extend a lifeline of support, guidance, and friendship.

21. Preventing the continuing increase of suicide among young people calls for strengthening the family unit while at the same time building a sense of social cohesiveness.

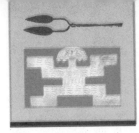

GLOSSARY

Abortion—induced termination of a fetus.

Achievement Motivation—the internal drive to produce and achieve status.

Acute Identity Diffusion—a major abnormality in identity formation.

Adoption—to take a child into the family through a legal process and to raise as one's own.

Age of Majority—a point when one attains adult freedom and responsibilities.

Agency and Communion—individualistic versus interpersonal characteristics, for example, self-assertion versus compliance.

Androgen—hormone secretion from the testes that develops and maintains masculine characteristics.

Androgynous—a blend of masculinity and femininity.

Anomie—a state of alienation, hopelessness, and a feeling of not belonging.

Anorexia Nervosa—a disorder associated with loss of appetite, a focus on thinness, and varying states of psychological self-denial.

Antinormative Behavior—behaviors that are atypical for a person's age that are usually asocial or antisocial.

Authoritarian—favoring absolute obedience to rules.

Autonomy—independent and self-governing.

Barbiturates—sedating medications.

Behaviorism—a school of thought in learning theory focused on stimulus-response associations.

Bisexual—a sexual orientation that includes attraction to both males and females.

Body Image—one's perception of one's body.

Bulimia—a disorder associated with an insatiable appetite, purging, and distorted body image.

Character—a basic personality type.

Chronological Definition of Adolescence—adolescence is defined as the second decade of life.

Cliques—an exclusive group of associates who maintain a close relationship.

Cocaine—a white crystalline extracted from coca leaves that has anesthetic effects.

Cognitive Definition of Adolescence—adolescence begins with the acquisition of the ability to use symbols, abstractions, and complex problem solving in thinking. This definition does not clearly indicate the ending of adolescence, however.

Coital Behavior—sexual intercourse.

Concrete Operations—mental operations in which a person's understanding of specific logical ideas is based on concrete problems.

Condom—a rubber that fits over an erect penis that collects sperm on ejaculation.

Congruence—agreement or conformity of things.

Connectedness—the degree to which a person is close to and affiliated with others.

Contraception—the prevention of conception.

Courtship Violence—undesirable and unnecessary violence between partners during courtship.

Crisis and Commitment—crisis refers to pressure to search for alternatives, commitment refers to the choice or selection made.

Crowd—a group of people who affiliate with one another through identifying with a common leader.

Cultural Rituals—ceremonies that signify a group's awareness of a developmental milestone or stage in life.

Dating Expectations—the process of coming together and judging one another regarding expectations about dating.

Defense Mechanisms—a way of protecting oneself from a perceived threat.

Delinquency—an offense or misdeed by a juvenile.

Dependent Variable—a behavior that is thought to change due to the effects of an independent variable.

Depression—feelings of sadness, dejection, flatness in affect.

Dialectic—arriving at the truth through contradictions or opposites.

Diaphragm—a contraceptive consisting of a flexible disk that covers the uterine cervix.

Discontinuity in Cultural Conditioning—a radical change in societal expectations regarding social behaviors, rights, and privileges.

Displacement—the projection of feelings for one thing onto another.

Dominance Behavior—behaviors that place one in a higher status due to dominance over others.

Double Standards—norms demanding virginity for females but not for males before marriage.

Dualism—consisting of two parts, such as mind and body.

Dysfunctional Identity Types—various forms in which identity diffusion represents psychopathology.

Eclectic—the use of multiple practical definitions of adolescence.

Egalitarianism—the doctrine of equal political, economic, or legal rights regardless of gender, race, etc.

Ego Stage—one of six stages that represent a developmental continuum in character styles.

Egocentrism—thinking or acting as if one's view is the center of experience.

Endocrine Glands—glands that secrete hormones into the body which create physiological changes.

Epidemiologist—a person who studies the incidence, distribution, and control of disease.

Estrogen—hormone secretion from the ovaries that is responsible for the promotion of estrus and the development of female sex characteristics.

Ethnography—the descriptive anthropology of technologically primitive societies through the use of observational methodologies.

Ethology—the science concerned with the behavior of animals.

Expectancy—an anticipatory belief or desire.

Expressive Function—an integrative emotional capacity to experience feelings.

Extended Family—members beyond the nuclear family that includes aunts, uncles, cousins, grandparents, etc.

Family Configuration—the number and order of siblings in a family.

Femininity—individual characteristics associated with a female identity, for example, dependent, compliant, emotional.

Formal Operations—mental operations characterized by hypothetical, logical, and abstract thought.

Functions of Identity—the purposes of an identity: structure, meaning, free will, integration, and potential.

Functions of the Family—cohesion or emotional bonding, adaptability for change, and communication.

Gender Differences—biological or genetic distinctions between boys and girls.

Gender Intensification—widening gender differences that emerge during adolescence.

Genetic Endowment—one's overall inherited potential.

Global Status of Youth—the correlation of the ratio of youth to adults with indicators of national development.

Hallucinogens—drugs, such as mescaline, that induce altered mental states.

Heroin—a derivative from morphine that is highly addictive.

Hierarchy of Power—an ordering of superordinate and subordinate influences.

Homosexuality—sexual orientation toward one's own sex.

Hostile Behavior—behavior with an underpinning of rage or anger.

Hypersensitivity—excessive responsiveness to others' critical or negative comments.

Hypopituitarism—a hormonal disorder that causes shortness.

Hypothalamus—a brain structure that instructs the pituitary gland on optimum level of hormone secretion.

Hypothesis—a proposed association between two or more constructs; a conjecture about the relationship between things.

Hypothyroidism—a hormonal deficiency that is associated with limited brain-cell development.

Identity Conflict—a legitimate crisis.

Identity Crisis—a psychological state of self-consciousness, searching, and exploration.

Identity Deficit—a motivation crisis.

Identity Development—the progressive stages in answering the question "Who am I?"

Identity Statuses—four types of identity self-conceptions based on degree of exploration and of commitment.

Imaginary Audience—the perception that one is being constantly scrutinized by everyone.

Independent Variable—a construct, event, or behavior that is thought to cause some change.

Individuality—qualities that distinguish one person from another; unique characteristics.

Influenceability—the degree to which others influence one's behaviors and viewpoints.

Information Processing—the basic functions of thinking, for instance, attention, memory, and processing capacity.

Inhalants—substances used for inhaling to induce a euphoric state.

Instrumental Function—task- and goal-directed actions.

Intellectualization—the analysis of problems from a purely intellectual perspective while denying feelings associated with the problem.

Intelligence—the general capacity to acquire and apply knowledge through thought and reason.

Intoxication—ingestion of alcohol that induces changes ranging from exhilaration to stupefaction.

Intrauterine Device—a stainless steel or plastic loop, ring, or spiral inserted into the uterus as a means of contraception.

Juvenile Court—a court system constructed for children and adolescents to protect their welfare.

Klinefelter's Syndrome—a chromosome disorder which results in a male body with small genitalia.

Labeling Theory—the assumption that certain social groups (for instance, minorities, the poor, mentally ill) are labeled deviant with perceived membership increasing the likelihood of being labeled as a deviant.

Lancaster System of Education—a system of education based on humiliation as a technique of discipline.

Learner's Permit Theory—notion that adolescence is a period of experimentation that allows increased responsibility and freedom at different ages.

Learning Theory—a theory that maintains most human behavior is learned or conditioned.

Legitimate Crisis—pressure to resolve multiple aspects of self and the incompatible commitments that need reconciliation.

Lesbian—a female with sexual interests in other females.

Life Stage—a period in life where specific developmental tasks are completed.

Locus of Control—a sense that one controls his or her destiny through individual action.

Marijuana—the dried flower clusters and leaves of hemp that are smoked to induce euphoria.

Masculinity—individual characteristics associated with a male identity, for example, aggressiveness, competitiveness, logical thinking.

Masturbation—self-manipulation of sexual body parts.

Mattering—the degree to which a person feels he or she counts to others.

Menarche—the first occurrence of menstruation.

Mental Age—the relative relationship between one's knowledge, verbal ability, perceptual problem solving, and so on and the typical abilities for a person of a given age.

Metaphor—a figure of speech where a phrase is applied to something to which it literally does not apply to suggest a resemblance.

Moral Development—a series of stages based on cognitive reasoning about moral judgments.

Moral Education—education that focuses on value clarification and moral reasoning.

Moral Reasoning—moral rationales for particular moral actions.

Moratorium—a period for exploration and discovery.

Motivation Crisis—an inadequately denied self that lacks commitments, goals, or values from which to make personal choices.

Negative Identity—identification of self with a socially deviant image.

Negative Reinforcement—the removal of unpleasant stimuli in response to a behavior that increases the likelihood of the behavior occurring again.

Negative Stigma—an undesirable social image due to personal characteristics that are not thought to be socially desirable.

Normative Crisis—turning points where crisis and stress may be resolved through growth or decline.

Observational Learning—acquisition of knowledge or behavior through watching the conduct or actions of others.

Ontogeny—the course of development of a person.

Operationalization—definitions of theoretical constructs that are specific enough to be testable.

Pair Relatedness—degree of intimate relationship between two persons.

Parental Discipline Styles—varying ways in which parents interact and communicate with their children.

Parental Identification—an individual's recognizing and valuing of a parent through psychological identification.

Passionate Love—intense emotional feelings that are exciting, amorous, and lustful.

Peer Influence—positive or negative effects caused by one's immediate age-mates.

Personal Fable—the perception that one is special and destined for great accomplishments.

Perspective Taking—the degree to which one takes the viewpoint(s) of others.

Phylogeny—the evolutionary development of a species.

Physiological Definition of Adolescence—adolescence begins when the reproductive organs and secondary sexual characteristics change in late childhood and ends with the full maturation of the reproductive system.

Pill, The—an oral contraceptive device.

Pituitary Gland—the master gland, under the control of the hypothalamus, that secretes neurohormones that influence metabolism, growth, and maturation.

Plane Coordination—the degree of harmony among what the adolescent really is as a person in the eyes of others, how accurately the adolescent sees his or her own characteristics, and the consistency with which the self is presented.

Polygamy—the practice of having more than one spouse or mate at a time.

Positive Reinforcement—a reward that is given in response to a behavior that increases the likelihood that the behavior will occur again in the future.

Precocious Puberty—development of sexually mature gonads before the age of 8 or 9 years.

Project 2000—a government project that has educational goals for children and adolescents to be accomplished by the end of the century.

Promiscuity—indiscriminate sexual behavior.

Prostitution—the act of accepting payment for sexual favors.

Psychoanalytic Theory—a theory by Sigmund Freud regarding the personality development of the id, ego, and superego.

Psychological Well-being—the sum total of a sense of worth, self-confidence, perceived competence, self-efficacy, psychological comfort, and feelings about self.

Psychometric—the standards of reliability and validity of measurement.

Psychopathology—mental disorders.

Psychosocial Moratorium—a period of time allotted to experimentation, exploration, and discovery.

Pubertal Delay—failure of testicles to enlarge by age 14 or breasts by age 13.

Puberty—stage of maturation at which the individual is capable of sexual reproduction.

Quality of Family Life—the nature and quality of family well-being.

Reaction Formation—establishment of trait or behavior that is opposite to an unconscious desire or impulse.

Recapitulation—the apparent repetition of an evolutionary stage.

Rehabilitation—inpatient treatment at a service center such as a hospital.

Relationship Reasoning—moral reasoning of relationships: egotistic, dyadic, interactive.

Risk-taking Behavior—behavior that places a youth into a context where constructive growth or destructive outcomes associated with unhealthy consequences can occur.

Role Ambiguity—uncertain boundaries and definition in a person's role.

Role Confusion—the inability to make a clear statement about the self that is accompanied by shame, doubt, lack of pride, and alienation.

Role Models—individuals who exemplify a behavior, action, or status.

Runaway—a child who leaves home without consent.

Schema—a mental construction of the way one interacts with ideas and objects in the environment.

Secondary Sex Characteristics—genetically transmitted anatomical or physiological characteristics; for example, breasts, facial hair, quality of voice.

Segregation—the separation or isolation of a social or racial group for purposes of education.

Self-consciousness—the degree of anxiety associated with behavior in public through preoccupation with the self.

Self-efficacy—a sense of being effective in influencing one's environment and destiny.

Self-esteem—pride in oneself.

Self-fulfilling Prophecy—confirmation of hypothesis about the self through behavioral actions.

Self-image Disparity—the difference between an individual's assessment of the real versus the ideal self.

Self-perception Orientation—the argument that behaviors determine self-esteem.

Sex-role Development—the degree to which male and female adolescents internalize corresponding societal characteristics thought to be associated with being male and female.

Sex-role Identity—the process of identifying and accepting sex-typed behaviors from societal models and standards.

Situationism/Interactionism—an assumption that personality types are more productive in certain environments.

Sleeper Effect—an effect that occurs long after the original cause.

Social-adaptation Perspective—the argument that self-esteem shapes behavior.

Social Fabric—the social infrastructure of an institution.

Socialization—to convert or adapt to the needs of society.

Sociobiology—human ethology focusing on genetically based evaluative factors that predict individual differences.

Sociological Definition of Adolescence—adolescence begins with the onset of sexual maturation and ends with social criteria such as ritual ceremony.

Spermicide—a contraceptive that destroys sperm on contact.

Stages of Dating—stages across adolescence beginning with sexual awakening, followed by practicing, acceptance of sex roles, and concluding with the development of a permanent object choice.

Stages of Faith—a series of sequential phases or steps in the development of religious beliefs.

Steroids—synthesized derivatives of the male hormone testosterone.

Stimulants—drugs that cause accelerating effects.

Structural-disorganization Theory—Merton's theory that the denial of access to financial, educational, or social resources predicts delinquency.

Substance Abuse—the use of illicit chemicals or substances for purposes of altering one's mood, physiology, or feelings.

Suicide—the taking of one's own life.

Symbolic Interactionism—a theoretical perspective that reality is provided through socially accepted meanings and perceptions of reality that are intertwined with self-perceptions and the anticipated reactions of others.

Synchrony—moving or operating at the same time.

Technology of Prevention—four basic tools that are used to fashion a healthier environment: education, systems intervention, competency promotion, and natural care giving.

Theory—the systematic organization of a set of propositions to explain and describe the nature of behavior.

Therapy—the diagnosis of a health problem and the provision of service to help the individual cope.

Throwaway—a child who is abandoned or forced to leave home.

Traditional Standards—norms that forbid sexual intimacy until marriage.

Trajectories in Development—differing patterns of regressive or progressive change and/or stability.

Truancy—absence from school without permission.

Turner's Syndrome—a chromosome disorder which results in a female body without ovaries.

Venereal Disease—infection that is transmitted by sexual intercourse.

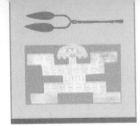

REFERENCES

Abernethy, V., & Abernethy, G. L. (1974). Risk for unwanted pregnancy among mentally ill adolescent girls. *American Journal of Orthopsychiatry, 44,* 442–450.

Abi-Nader, J. (1990). "A house for my mother": Motivating Hispanic high school students. *Anthropology & Education Quarterly, 21,* 41–58.

Abraham, K. G. (1983). The relation between identity status and locus of control among rural high school students. *Journal of Early Adolescence, 3,* 257, 264.

Abraham, K. G. (1986). Ego-identity differences among Anglo-American and Mexican-American adolescents. *Journal of Adolescence, 9,* 151–166.

Abrahams, B., Feldman, S. S., & Nash, S. C. (1978). Sex role self-concept and sex role attitudes: Enduring personality characteristics or adaptations to changing life situations? *Developmental Psychology, 14,* 393–401.

Achenbach, T., & Zigler, E. (1963). Social competence and self-image disparity in psychiatric and non psychiatric patients. *Journal of Abnormal and Social Psychology, 67,* 197–205.

Adams, C. M. (1988). *The effects of social perspective-taking and ideological perspective-taking training on ego-identity formation in late adolescence.* Unpublished doctoral dissertation, Utah State University, Logan.

Adams, E. H., & Durell, J. (1987). Cocaine: A growing public health problem. In J. Grabowski (ed.) *Cocaine: Pharmacology, effects, and treatment of abuse.* DHHS publication # ADM 87-1326.

Adams, E. H., & Kozel, N. J. (1985). Cocaine use in America: Introduction and overview. In N. J. Kozel & E. H. Adams (Eds.), *Cocaine use in America: Epidemiological and clinical perspectives 1–7.* (NIDA research monograph No. 61, # ADM 85-1414). Washington, DC: U.S. Government Printing Office.

Adams, G. R. (1977a). Physical attractiveness, personality and social reactions to peer pressure. *Journal of Psychology, 96,* 287–296.

Adams, G. R. (1977b). Physical attractiveness: Toward a developmental social psychology of beauty. *Human Development, 20,* 217–239.

Adams, G. R. (1980). The effects of physical attractiveness on the socialization process. In G. W. Lucker, K. A. Ribbens, & J. A. McNamara (Eds.), *Psychological aspects of facial form* (Monograph 11, Craniofacial Growth Series). Ann Arbor: Center for Human Growth and Development, University of Michigan.

Adams, G. R. (1982). The physical attractiveness stereotype. In A. G. Miller (Ed.), *In the eye of the beholder: Contemporary issues in stereotyping.* New York: Praeger.

Adams, G. R. (1983). Social competence during adolescence: Social sensitivity, locus of control, empathy, and peer popularity. *Journal of Youth and Adolescence, 12,* 203–211.

Adams, G. R. (1985). Family correlates of female adolescents' ego-identity development. *Journal of Adolescence, 8,* 69–82.

Adams, G. R., Abraham, K., & Markstrom, C. (1987). The association between identity development, self-consciousness, and self-focusing during middle and late adolescence. *Developmental Psychology, 23,* 292–297.

Adams, G. R., Bennion, L., & Huh, K. (1989). Objective measure of ego identity status: A reference manual. (Available from Gerald Adams, Dept. of Family Studies, University of Guelph, Guelph, Ontario, Canada.)

Adams, G. R., Bennion, L., & Openshaw, D. K. (1988). *Windows of vulnerability: Identity, age, gender, and racial differences predictive of risk for violent deaths in childhood and adolescence.* Unpublished research report. Laboratory for Research in Adolescence, Utah State University, Logan.

Adams, G. R., Bennion, L. D., Openshaw, D. K., & Bingham, C. R. (1990). Windows of vulnerability: Identifying critical age, gender, and racial differences predictive of risk for violent deaths in childhood and adolescence. *Journal of Primary Prevention, 10,* 223–240.

Adams, G. R., & Crossman, S. M. (1978). *Physical attractiveness: A cultural imperative,* Roslyn Heights, NY: Libra.

Adams, G. R., & Davis, L. L. (1987). *A dialectic-interactional perspective to the social psychology of physical appearance.* Unpublished manuscript, Utah State University, Logan.

Adams, G. R., Day, T., Dyk, P. H., Frede, E., & Rogers, D. R. (1992). On the dialectics of pubescence and psychosocial development. *Journal of Early Adolescence, 12,* 348–365.

Adams, G. R., Dyk, P., & Bennion, L. D. (1988). Parent-adolescent relationships and identity formation. *Family Perspectives, 21,* 249–260.

Adams, G. R., & Fitch, S. A. (1981). Ego stage and identity status development: A cross-lagged investigation. *Journal of Adolescence, 4,* 163–171.

Adams, G. R., & Fitch, S. A. (1982). Ego state and identity status development: A cross-sequential analysis. *Journal of Personality and Social Psychology, 43,* 574–583.

Adams, G. R., & Fitch, S. A. (1983). Psychological environments of university departments: Effects on college students' identity status and ego state development. *Journal of Personality and Social Psychology, 44,* 1266–1275.

Adams, G. R., & Gullotta, T. P. (1983). *Adolescent life experiences* (1st ed.). Monterey, CA: Brooks/Cole.

Adams, G. R., Gullotta, T. P., & Clancy, M. A. (1985). Homeless adolescents: A descriptive study of similarities and differences between runaways and throwaways. *Adolescence, 79,* 715–724.

Adams, G. R., Higgins-Trenk, A., & Svoboda, C. (1975). *Toward a history of life-span developmental psychology.* Unpublished manuscript. Pennsylvania State University, State College, PA.

Adams, G. R., & Jones, R. M. (1981a). Female adolescents' ego development: Age comparisons and child-rearing perceptions. *Journal of Early Adolescence, 1,* 423–426.

Adams, G. R., & Jones, R. M. (1981b). Imaginary audience behavior: A validation study. *Journal of Early Adolescence, 1,* 1–10.

Adams, G. R., & Jones, R. M. (1983). Female adolescence identity development: Age comparison and perceived child-rearing experience. *Developmental Psychology, 19,* 249–256.

Adams, G. R., Jones, R. M., Schvaneveldt, J. D., & Jensen, G. O. (1982). Antecedents of affective role-taking behaviour: Adolescent perceptions of parental socialization styles. *Journal of Adolescence, 5,* 1–7.

Adams, G. R., & Markstrom, C. M. (in press). Developmental issues in adolescent psychiatry. In G. Hsu & M. Hersen (Eds.), *Recent developments in adolescent psychiatry.* New York: Wiley.

Adams, G. R., & Montemayor, R. (1986, March). *Patterns of growth and identity development: Contributions of the family to ego-identity development during middle and late adolescence.* Paper presented in a poster session of the conference of the Society for Research on Adolescence, Madison, WI.

Adams, G. R., & Montemayor, R. (1988). Patterns of identity development during late adolescence: A descriptive study of stability, progression, and regression. Manuscript submitted for publication.

Adams, G. R., Montemayor, R., & Gullotta, T. P. (Eds.). (1989). *Biology of adolescent behavior and development, Vol. 1: Advances in adolescent development.* Newbury Park, CA: Sage.

Adams, G. R., Ryan, B. A., Corville-Smith, J., Normore, A., & Turner, B. (1992). Dialectics, organicism, and contextualism: A rejoinder to Lerner. *Journal of Early Adolescence, 12,* 389–395.

Adams, G. R., Ryan, J. H., Hoffman, J. J., Dobson, W. R., & Nielsen, E. C. (1985). Ego identity status, conformity behavior and personality in late adolescence. *Journal of Personality and Social Psychology, 47,* 1091–1104.

Adams, G. R., & Schvaneveldt, J. D. (1985). *Understanding research methods.* New York: Longman.

Adams, G. R., Schvaneveldt, J. D., & Jensen, G. O. (1979). Sex, age and perceived competency as correlates of empathic ability in adolescence. *Adolescence, 14,* 811–818.

Adams, G. R., & Shea, J. (1979). The relationship between identity status, locus of control, and ego development. *Journal of Youth and Adolescence, 8,* 81–89.

Adams, G. R., & Shea, J. (1981). Talking and loving: A cross-lagged panel investigation. *Basic and Applied Social Psychology, 2,* 81–88.

Adams, G. R., Shea, J. A., & Fitch, S. A. (1979). Toward the development of an objective assessment of ego-identity status. *Journal of Youth and Adolescence, 8,* 223–237.

Adcock, A. G., Nagy, S., & Simpson, J. A. (1991). Selected risk factors in adolescent suicide attempts. *Adolescence, 26,* 817–828.

Adelson, J. (1986). *Inventing adolescence.* New Brunswick, NJ: Transaction Books.

Adler, A. (1967) [Untitled comments.] In P. Friedman (Ed.), *On suicide: With particular reference to suicide among young students.* New York: International Universities Press.

Adler, N. E., David, H. P., Major, B. N., Roth, S. H., Russo, N. F., & Wyatt, G. E. (1990). Psychological responses after abortion. *Science, 248,* 41–44.

Affleck, M., Morgan, C. S., & Hayes, M. P. (1989). The influence of gender role attitudes on life expectations of college students. *Youth & Society, 20,* 320–341.

Agras, W. S., Schneider, J. A., Arnow, B., Rawburn, S. D., & Telch, C. F. (1989). Cognitive behavioral response prevention treatments for bulimia nervosa. *Journal of Consulting and Clinical Psychology, 57,* 215–221.

Ahrons, C. R. (1981). The continuing coparental relationship between divorced spouses. *American Journal of Orthopsychiatry, 51,* 415–428.

AIDS Information Bulletin. (1983, November 22). Washington, DC: U.S. Public Health Service.

Akhtar, S. (1984). The syndrome of identity diffusion. *American Journal of Psychiatry, 141,* 1381–1385.

Albee, G. (1980). A competency model must replace the defect model. In L. A. Bond & J. C. Rosen (Eds.), *Competence and coping during adulthood.* Hanover, NH: University of New England Press.

Albee, G. W. (1985a, February). The answer is prevention. *Psychology Today,* 60–64.

Albee, G. W (1985b). The argument for primary prevention. *Journal of Primary Prevention, 5* (4), 213–219.

Albee, G. W., & Gullotta, T. P. (1986). Facts and fallacies about primary prevention. *Journal of Primary Prevention, 6*(4) 207–218.

Albrecht, S. L., Bahr, H., & Chadwick, B. (1979). Changing Family and Sex Roles: An assessment of age differences. *Journal of Marriage and the Family, 41,* 41–50.

Alisho, K. C., & Schilling, K. M. (1984). Sex differences in intellectual and ego development in late adolescence. *Journal of Youth and Adolescence, 13,* 213–224.

Allen, B. P. (1987). Youth suicide. *Adolescence, 22,* 271–290.

Allgeier, E. R., & Allgeier, A. R. (1984). *Sexual interactions.* Lexington, MA: D. C. Heath.

Allport, G. (1964). Crises in normal personality development. *Teachers College Record, 66,* 235–241.

Almeida, D. M., & Galambos, N. L. (1991). Examining father involvement and quality of father-adolescent relations. *Journal of Research on Adolescence, 1,* 155–172.

Altshuler, K. Z., & Weiner, M. F. (1985). Anorexia nervosa and depression: A dissenting view. *American Journal of Psychiatry, 142,* 328–332.

Alvarez, A. (1972). *The savage god.* New York: Random House.

Amato, P. R., & Keith, B. (1991). Parental divorce and adult well-being: A meta-analysis. *Journal of Marriage and the Family, 53,* 43–58.

American Academy of Pediatrics Committee on Adolescence. (1980). Teenage suicide. *Pediatrics, 66,* 144–146.

American Society for Pharmacology (1987). Scientific perspectives on cocaine abuse. *The Pharmacologist, 29,* 20–27.

Ammer, C. (1983). *The A to Z of women's health.* New York: Everest House.

Anderson, S. M., & Williams, M. (1985). Cognitive/affective reaction in the improvement of self-esteem: When thoughts and feelings make a difference. *Journal of Personality and Social Psychology, 49,* 1086–1097.

Aneshensel, C. S., Fielder, S., & Becerra, R. M. (1989). Fertility and fertility-related behavior among Mexican-American and non-Hispanic White Female adolescents. *Journal of Health and Social Behavior, 30,* 56–76.

Anthony, K. H. (1985). The shopping mall: A teenage hangout. *Adolescence, 20,* 307–312.

Aral, S. O., Cates, W., & Jenkins, W. C. (1985). Genital herpes: Does knowledge lead to action? *American Journal of Public Health, 75,* 69–71.

Archer, S., & Waterman, A. (1983). Identity in early adolescence: A developmental perspective. *Journal of Early Adolescence, 3,* 203–214.

Archer, S. L. (1989). Gender differences in identity development: Issues of process, domain and timing. *Journal of Adolescence, 12,* 117–138.

Archer, S. L. (1992). A feminist approach to identity research. In G. R. Adams, T. P. Gullotta, R. Montemayor (Eds.), *Identity formation during adolescence. Advances in adolescent development,* Vol. 4. Newbury Park, CA: Sage.

Archer, S. L., & Waterman, A. S. (1990). Varieties of identity diffusions and foreclosures: An exploration of subcategories of the identity statuses. *Journal of Adolescent Research, 5,* 96–111.

Armistead, L., Wierson, M., & Forehand, R. (1990). Adolescents and maternal employment: Is it harmful for a young adolescent to have an employed mother? *Journal of Early Adolescence, 10,* 260–278.

Arnold, J. (1982, March). Rhetoric and reform in middle schools. *Phi Delta Kappan,* 453–456.

Arredondo, P. M. (1984). Identity themes for immigrant young adults. *Adolescence, 19,* 977–993.

Asberg, M. (1989). Neurotransmitter monoamine metabolites in the cerebrospinal fluid as risk factors for suicidal behavior. In ADAMHA. *Report of the secretary's task force on youth suicide: Vol. 2: Risk factors for youth suicide.* U.S. Department of Health and Human Services publication # ADM 89-1622. Washington, DC: U.S. Government Printing Office.

Ashby, M. R., Gilchrist, L. D., & Miramontez, A. (1987). Group treatment for sexually abused American Indian adolescents. *Social Work with Groups, 10,* 21–32.

Asmussen, L. & Larson, R. (1991). The quality of family time among young adolescents in single-parent and married-parent families. *Journal of Marriage and the Family, 53,* 1021–1030.

Attie, I., & Brooks-Gunn, J. (1989). Development of eating problems in adolescent girls: A longitudinal study. *Developmental Psychology, 25,* 70–79.

Austin, G. A. (1979). *Research Issues 24: Perspectives on the history of psychoactive substance use* (DHHS Publication No. ADM 79-810). Washington, DC: U.S. Government Printing Office.

Ausubel, D., & Ausubel, P. (1966). Cognitive development in adolescence. *Review of Educational Research, 36,* 403–413.

Ausubel, D. P., & Sullivan, E. V. (1970). *Theory and problems of child development* (2nd ed.). New York: Grune & Stratton.

Babikian, H. M., & Goldman, A. A. (1971). A study of teenage pregnancy. *American Journal of Psychiatry, 128,* 755–760.

Bachman, J. G., & O'Malley, P. M. (1977). Self-esteem in young men: A longitudinal analysis of the impact of educational and occupational attainment. *Journal of Personality and Social Psychology, 35,* 365–380.

Bailey, J. M., & Prager, K. J. (1984, April). *Androgyny, ego development and psychosocial crisis resolution.* Paper presented at the meeting of the American Education Research Association, New Orleans.

Baizerman, M., Thompson, J., & Stafford-White, K. (1979). Adolescent prostitution. *Children Today, 8*(5), 20–24.

Baker, D., Telfer, M. A., Richardson, G. R., & Clark, G. R. (1970). Chromosome error in men with antisocial behavior. *Journal of the American Medical Association, 214,* 869–878.

Baker, K. (1985). Research evidence of a school discipline problem. *Phi Delta Kappan, 66,* 482–488.

Balster, R. L. (1990). Behavioral pharmacology of PCP, NMDA and sigma receptors. In L. S. Harris (Ed.), *Problems of drug dependence: 1989,* (U.S. Department of Health and Human Services publication # ADM 90-1663.) Washington, DC: U.S. Government Printing Office.

Bandura, A. (1960). *Relationship of family patterns to child behavior disorders: A progress report.* Stanford, CA: Stanford University Press.

Bandura, A. (1965). Vicarious processes: A case of no trial learning. In L. Berkowitz (Ed.), *Advances in experimental social psychology* (Vol. 2). New York: Academic Press.

Bandura, A. (1969). *Principles of behavior modification.* New York: Holt, Rinehart & Winston.

Bandura, A. (1977). Self-efficacy: Toward a unifying theory of behavioral change. *Psychological Review, 84,* 191–215.

Bandura, A. (1978). The self-esteem in reciprocal determinism. *American Psychologist, 33,* 344–358.

Bandura, A. (1982). Self-efficacy mechanism in human agency. *American Psychologist, 37,* 122–147.

Bane, M. J. (1976). *Here to stay: American families in the 20th century.* New York: Basic Books.

Banks, J. A. (1988). Ethnicity, class, cognitive, and motivational styles: Research and teaching implications. *Journal of Negro Education, 57,* 452–466.

Baranowski, M. D. (1982). Grandparent-adolescent relations: Beyond the nuclear family. *Adolescence, 17,* 575–584.

Bardwick, J. M. (1971). *Psychology of women: A study of biocultural conflict.* New York: Harper & Row.

Barker R. G. (1953). *Adjustment to physical handicap and illness: A survey of the social psychology of physique and disability* (Bulletin No. 55). New York: Social Science Research Council.

Barnes, D. M. (1986a). AIDS research in new phase. *Science, 233*(4761), 282–283.

Barnes, D. M. (1986b). Grim projections for AIDS epidemic. *Science, 232*(4758), 1589–1590.

Barnes, D. M. (1987). AIDS: Statistics but few answers. *Science, 236,* 1423–1426.

Barnes, G. E. (1979). Solvent abuse: A review. *International Journal of the Addictions, 14,* 1–26.

Barnes, G. E., & Prosen, H. (1985). Parental death and depression. *Journal of Abnormal Psychology, 94*(1), 64–69.

Barnes, G. M. (1977). The development of adolescent drinking behavior: An evaluative review of the impact of the socialization process within the family. *Adolescence, 12,* 571–591.

Barnes, G. M., & Welte (1986). Patterns and predictors of alcohol use among 7-12th grade students in New York State. *Journal of Studies on Alcohol, 47*(1), 53–62.

Barnett, J. K., Papini, D. R., & Gbur, E. (1991). Familial correlates of sexually active pregnant and non-pregnant adolescents. *Adolescence, 26,* 457–472.

Barretl, R. L., & Robinson, B. E. (1982). Teenage fathers: Neglected too long. *Social Work, 27,* 484–488.

Bartle, S. E., Anderson, S. A., & Sabatelli, R. M. (1989). A model of parenting style, adolescent individuation and adolescent self-esteem: Preliminary findings. *Journal of Adolescent Research, 4,* 283–298.

Barton, W. H. (1976). Discretionary decision making in juvenile justice. *Crime and Delinquency, 22,* 470–480.

Bastian, L. D., & Taylor, B. M. (1991). *School crime.* U.S. Department of Justice. (NCJ-131645): Washington, DC: U.S. Government Printing Office.

Baucom, D. H. (1983). Sex role identity and the decision to regain control among women: A learned helplessness investigation. *Journal of Personality and Social Psychology, 44,* 334–343.

Baucom, D. H., Besch, P. K., & Callahan, S. (1985). Relation between testosterone concentration, sex role identity, and personality among females. *Journal of Personality and Social Psychology, 48,* 1218–1226.

Bauer, G. L. (1985). Restoring order to the public schools. *Phi Delta Kappan, 66,* 488–491.

Bauman, K. E., Fisher, L. A., Bryan, E. S., & Chenoweth, R. L. (1984). Antecedents, subjective expected utility, and behavior: A panel study of adolescent cigarette smoking. *Addictive Behaviors, 9,* 121–136.

Baumeister, R. (1986). *Identity: Cultural change and the struggle for self.* New York: Oxford University Press.

Baumeister, R., Shapiro, J. P., & Tice, D. M. (1985). Two kinds of identity crises. *Journal of Personality, 53,* 407–423.

Baumrind, D. (1978). Parental disciplinary patterns and social competence in children. *Youth & Society, 9,* 239–276.

Baumrind, D. (1982). Are androgynous individuals more effective persons and parents? *Child Development, 53,* 44–75.

Bayer, A. E. (1984). Anorexia and bulimia in adolescents. *Children Today, 13,* 7–11.

Bayley, N. (1970). Development of mental abilities. In P. H. Mussen (Ed.), *Carmichael's "Manual of Child Psychology"* (Vol. 1) (3rd ed.). New York: Wiley.

Beauvais, F., & LaBoueff, S. (1985). Drug and alcohol abuse intervention in American Indian communities. *International Journal of the Addictions, 20,* 139–171.

Beaver, C. W. (1972). Hope and suicide in the concentration camp. In E. S. Schneidman (Ed.), *Death and the college student.* New York: Human Sciences Press.

Becerra, R., & Felder, E. (1985). Adolescent attitudes and behavior. *ISSR Quarterly, 1,* 4–7.

Beck, L., & Muia, J. A. (1980). A portrait of a tragedy: Research findings on the dropout. *High School Journal, 64,* 65–72.

Becker, T. (1976). Self, family, and community: A cross-cultural comparison of American and Israeli youth. *Youth & Society, 8,* 45–66.

Becker, W. C. (1964). Consequences of different kinds of parental discipline. In M. L. Hoffman & L. W. Hoffman (Eds.), *Review of child development research* (Vol. 1). New York: Russell Sage Foundation.

Beech, R. P., & Schoeppe, A. (1974). Development of value systems in adolescents. *Developmental Psychology, 10,* 644–656.

Beilin, H. (1992). Piaget's enduring contribution to developmental psychology. *Developmental Psychology, 28,* 191–204.

Beisser, A. (1980). The American seasonal masculinity rites. In D. F. Sabo & R. Runfola (Eds.), *Jock: Sports and Male Identity.* Englewood Cliffs, NJ: Prentice-Hall.

Beiswinger, G. L. (1979). The High Court, privacy, and teenage sexuality. *Family Coordinator, 28,* 191–198.

Belenky, M. F., Clinchy, B. M., Goldberger, N. R., & Tarule, J. M. (1986). *Women's ways of knowing: The development of self, voice, and mind.* New York: Basic Books.

Bell, L. G., & Bell, D. C. (1982). Family climate and the role of the female adolescent: Determinants of adolescent functioning. *Family Relations, 31,* 519–527.

Bell, L. G., & Erickson, L. (1976, September). *Family process and child development: Some preliminary findings.* Paper presented at the meeting of the American Psychological Association, Washington, DC.

Bell, R. (1987). *Changing bodies, changing lives.* New York: Random House.

Bell, R. M. (1985). *Holy anorexia.* Chicago: University of Chicago Press.

Bem, S. L. (1974). The measurement of psychological androgyny. *Journal of Consulting and Clinical Psychology, 42,* 155–162.

Bem, S. L. (1975). Sex role adaptability: One consequence of psychological androgyny. *Journal of Personality and Social Psychology, 31,* 634–643.

Bem, S. L. (1977). On the utility of alternative procedures for assessing psychological androgyny. *Journal of Consulting. and Clinical Psychology, 45,* 196–205.

Bem, S. L. (1981). Gender schema theory: A cognitive account of sex typing. *Psychological Review, 88,* 354–364.

Bem, S. L., Martyna, W., & Watson, C. (1976). Sex typing and androgyny: Further explorations of the expressive domain. *Journal of Personality and Social Psychology, 34,* 1016–1023.

Bemis, K. M. (1978). Current approaches to the etiology and treatment of anorexia nervosa. *Psychological Bulletin, 85,* 593–617.

Benbow, C. P., & Stanley, J. C. (1980). Sex differences in mathematical ability: Fact or artifact? *Science, 210,* 1262–1264.

Benbow, C. P., & Stanley, J. C. (1983). Sex differences in mathematical ability: More facts. *Science, 222,* 1029–1031.

Bender, L., & Schilder, P. (1937). Suicidal preoccupation and attempts in children. *American Journal of Orthopsychiatry, 7,* 225–234.

Benedict, R. (1938). Continuities and discontinuities in cultural conditioning. *Psychiatry, 1,* 161–167.

Bennion, L. D., & Adams, G. R. (1986). A revision of the extended version of the objective measure of ego identity status: An identity instrument for use with late adolescents. *Journal of Adolescent Research, 1,* 183–198.

Benowitz, N. L. (1990). Clinical pharmacology of inhaled drugs of abuse: Implications in understanding nicotine dependence. In C. N. Chiang & R. L. Hawks (Eds.), *Research findings on smoking abused substances.* (U.S. Department of Health and Human Services publication # ADM 90-1690.) Washington, DC: U.S. Government Printing Office.

Benson, P., Williams, D., & Johnson, A. (1987). *The quicksilver years: The hopes and fears of early adolescence.* New York: Harper & Row.

Benz, C. R., Pfeiffer, I., & Newman, I. (1981). Sex role expectations of classroom teachers, grades 1–12. *American Educational Research Journal, 18,* 289–302.

Berdie, R. R., & Hood, A. B. (1965). *Decisions for tomorrow.* Minneapolis: University of Minnesota Press.

Bereiter, C., Hidi, S., & Dimitroff, G. (1979). Qualitative changes in verbal reasoning during middle and late childhood. *Child Development, 50,* 142–151.

Berg-Cross, L., Kidd, F., & Carr, P. (1990). Cohesion, affect, and self-disclosure in African-American adolescent families. *Journal of Family Psychology, 4,* 235–250.

Bergman, A. B. (1980). Condoms for sexually active adolescents. *American Journal of Diseases in Children, 134,* 247–249.

Berkowitz, L. (1962). *Aggression: A social psychological analysis.* New York: McGraw-Hill.

Berkowitz, L. (1964). The effects of observing violence. *Scientific American, 210*(2), 35–41.

Berlin, I. N. (1985). Prevention of adolescent suicide among some Native American tribes. *Adolescent Psychiatry, 12,* 77–93.

Berlin, I. N. (1986). Psychopathology and its antecedents among American Indian adolescents. In B. B. Lakey & A. E. Kazdin (Eds.), *Advances in clinical child psychology,* Vol. 9. New York: Plenum.

Bernard, J. (1974). The housewife: Between two worlds. In P. L. Stewart & M. G. Cantor (Eds.), *Varieties of work experience.* Cambridge, MA: Schenkman.

Berndt, T. J. (1979). Developmental changes in conformity to peers and parents. *Developmental Psychology, 15,* 608–616.

Berndt, T. J., Miller, K. E., & Park, K. (1989). Adolescents' perceptions of friends' and parents' influence on aspects of their school adjustment, *Journal of Early Adolescence, 9,* 419–435.

Berscheid, E., & Walster, E. (1974). A little bit about love. In T. Houston (Ed.), *Foundations of interpersonal attraction.* New York: Academic Press.

Berzonsky, M. D. (1978). Formal reasoning in adolescence: An alternative view. *Adolescence, 13,* 279–290.

Berzonsky, M. D. (1986). A rejoiner to Waterman: Identity formation, metaphors, and values. *Journal of Early Adolescence, 6,* 123, 126.

Berzonsky, M. D. (1992). A process perspective on identity and stress management. In G. R. Adams, T. P. Gullotta, and R. Montemayor (Eds.), *Identity formation during adolescence, Advances in adolescent development,* Vol. 4. Newbury Park, CA: Sage.

Berzonsky, W. M., Weiner, A. S., & Raphael, D. (1975). Interdependence of formal reasoning. *Developmental Psychology, 11,* 258.

Betancourt, E. F. (1988, February 11). Cuba's callous war on AIDS. *New York Times,* 20.

Bettoli, E. J. (1982). Herpes: Facts and fallacies. *Journal of Practical Nursing, 32*(8), 17–21, 42.

Biddle, B. J., Bank, B., & Marim, M. M. (1980). Social determinants of adolescent drinking. *Journal of Studies on Alcohol, 41,* 215–241.

Billingham, R. E. (1987). Courtship violence: The patterns of conflict resolution strategies across seven levels of emotional commitment. *Family Relations, 36,* 283–289.

Billy, J. O., Rodgers, J. L., & Udry, J. R. (1984). Adolescent sexual behavior and friendship choice. *Social Forces, 62,* 653–678.

Binder, A., & Geis, G. (1984). Ad populum argumentation in criminology: Juvenile diversion as rhetoric. *Crime and Delinquency, 30,* 624–647.

Bingham, C. R., Bennion, L. D., Openshaw, D. K., & Adams, G. R. (in press). An analysis of age, gender and racial differences in recent national trends of youth suicide. *Journal of Adolescence.*

Bird, G. W., & Kemerait, L. N. (1990). Stress among early adolescents in two-earner families. *Journal of Early Adolescence, 10,* 344–365.

Birmingham, M. S. (1986). An out-patient treatment programme for adolescent substance abusers. *Journal of Adolescence, 9*(2), 123–133.

Black, C., & DeBlassie, R. R. (1985). Adolescent pregnancy: Contributing factors, consequences, treatment, and plausible solutions. *Adolescence, 20,* 281–290.

Blau, G. R., & Gullotta, T. P. (1993). Promoting sexual responsibility in adolescence. In T. P. Gullotta, G. R. Adams, & R. Montemayor (Eds.), *Adolescent sexuality.* Newbury Park, CA: Sage.

Bloch, H. A., & Niederhoffer, A. (1958). *The gang.* New York: Philosophical Library.

Block, J. H. (1973). Conceptions of sex roles: Some cross-cultural and longitudinal perspectives. *American Psychologist, 28,* 513–526.

Block, J. H., Block, J. H., & Gjerde, P. F. (1991). Personality antecedents of depressive tendencies in 18 year-olds: A prospective study. *Journal of Personality and Social Psychology, 60,* 725–738.

Block, J. R., Von der Lippe, A., & Block, J. H. (1973). Sex role and socialization patterns: Some personality concomitants and environmental antecedents. *Journal of Consulting and Clinical Psychology, 41,* 321–341.

Block, R. W., & Block, S. A. (1980). Outreach education: A possible preventer of teenage pregnancy. *Adolescence, 15,* 657–666.

Blood, R. O. (1955). A test of Waller's rating-dating complex. *Marriage and Family Living, 17,* 41–47.

Bloom, B. S. (1993, April). *The development of exceptional talent.* Paper presented at the biennial meeting of the Society for Research in Child Development, Detroit.

Bloom, D. E., & Glied, S. (1991). Benefits and costs of HIV testing. *Science, 252,* 1798–1804.

Bloom, M. (1990). The psychosocial constructs of social competency. In T. P. Gullotta, G. R. Adams, & R. Montemayor (Eds.), *Developing social competency in adolescence.* Newbury Park, CA: Sage.

Blos, P. (1962). *On adolescence.* New York: Free Press.

Blos, P. (1967). The second individuation process of adolescence. *Psychoanalytic Study of the Child, 22,* 162–186.

Blos, P. (1979). *The adolescent passage.* New York: International Universities Press.

Blos, P. (1985). *Son and father: Before and beyond the Oedipus complex.* New York: Free Press.

Blum, K., & Nobel, E. P. (1990). Allelic association of human dopamine D2 receptor gene in alcoholism. *Journal of the American Medical Association, 263,* 2055–2060.

Blumenkrantz, D. G., & Gavazzi, S. M. (1993). Guiding transitional events for children and adolescents through a modern day rite of passage. *Journal of Primary Prevention, 13,* 199–212.

Blumenthal, S. J., & Kupfer, D. J. (1989). Overview of early detection and treatment strategies for suicidal behavior in young people. In ADAMHA. *Report of the secretary's task force on youth suicide: Vol. 3: Prevention and interventions in youth suicide.* (U.S. Department of Health and Human Services publication # ADM 89-1622.) Washington, DC: U.S. Government Printing Office.

Blyth, D. A., Hill, J. P., & Smyth, C. K. (1981). The influence of older adolescents on younger adolescents: Do grade-level arrangements make a difference in behaviors, attitudes, and experiences? *Journal of Early Adolescence, 1,* 85–110.

Blyth, D. A., Simmons, R. G., Bulcroft, R., Felt, D., Van Cleave, E. F., & Bush, D. M. (1980). The effects of physical development on self-image and satisfaction with body image for early adolescent males. In R. G. Simmons (Ed.), *Handbook of community and mental health* (Vol. 2). Greenwich, CT: JAI Press.

Blyth, D. A., Simmons, R. G., & Bush, D. (1978). The transition into early adolescence: A longitudinal comparison of youth in two educational contexts. *Sociology of Education, 51,* 149–162.

Blyth, D. A., Simmons, R. G., & Zakin, D. F. (1985). Satisfaction with body image for early adolescent females: The impact of pubertal timing within different school environments. *Journal of Youth and Adolescence, 14,* 207–226.

Bobo, J. K., Cvetkovich, G. T., Gilchrist, L. D., Trimble, J. E., & Schinke, S. P. (1988). Cross-cultural service delivery to minority communities. *Journal of Community Psychology, 16,* 263–272.

Bock, R. D., & Moore, E. G. (1986). *Advantage and disadvantage: A profile of American youth.* Hillsdale, NJ: Erlbaum.

Bodmer, W. F., & Cavalli-Sforza, L. L. (1970). Intelligence and race. *Scientific American, 223*(4), 19–29.

Boeringer, S. B., Shehan, C. L., & Akers, R. L. (1991). Social contexts and social learning in sexual coercion and aggression: Assessing the contribution of fraternity membership. *Family Relations, 40,* 58–64.

Bohman, M. (1978). Some genetic aspects of alcoholism and criminality: A population of adopters. *Archives of General Psychiatry, 35,* 269–276.

Boldt, M. (1982). Normative evaluations of suicide and death: A cross-generational study. *Omega, 13*(2), 145–157.

Bolton, F. G., Laner, R. H., & Kane, S. P. (1980). Child maltreatment risk among adolescent mothers. *American Journal of Orthopsychiatry, 50*(3), 489–504.

Bond, L. A., & Compas, B. E. (Eds.). (1989). *Primary prevention and promotion in the schools.* Newbury Park, CA: Sage.

Booth, W. (1988a). CDC paints a picture of HIV infection in U.S. *Science, 15,* 253.

Booth, W. (1988b). The long, lost survey on sex. *Science, 239* (4844), 1084–1085.

Bosma, H. A. (1992). Identity in adolescence: Managing commitments. In G. R. Adams, T. P. Gullotta, & R. Montemayor (Eds.), *Identity formation during adolescence, Advances in adolescent development.* Vol. 4. Newbury Park, CA: Sage.

Bosma, H. A., & Gerrits, R. S. (1985). Family functioning and identity status in adolescence. *Journal of Early Adolescence, 5,* 69–80.

Bossard, J. H. S. (1954). *The Sociology of Child Development,* New York: Harper & Row.

Bourne, E. (1978a). The state of research on ego identity: A review and appraisal. Part 1. *Journal of Youth and Adolescence, 7,* 223–252.

Bourne, E. (1978b). The state of research on ego identity: A review and appraisal. Part 2. *Journal of Youth and Adolescence, 7,* 371–392.

Bowerman, C. E., & Irish, D. P. (1962). Some relationships of stepchildren to their parents. *Marriage and Family Living, 24,* 113–121.

Bowers, K. S. (1973). Situationism in psychology: An analysis and a critique. *Psychological Review, 80,* 307–336.

Bowker, L. H., Gross, H. S., & Klein, M. W. (1980). Female participation in delinquent gang activities. *Adolescence, 15,* 509–519.

Bowman, P. J. (1990). The adolescent-to-adult transition: Discouragement among jobless Black youth. *New Directions for Child Development, 46,* 87–105.

Boxill, N. A. (1987). How would you feel?: Clinical interviews with Black adolescent mothers. *Child & Youth Services, 9,* 41–51.

Boyce, J., & Benoit, C. (1975). Adolescent pregnancy. *New York State Journal of Medicine, 75,* 872–874.

Boyd, R. D., & Koskela, R. N. (1970). A test of Erikson's theory of ego-state development by means of a self-report instrument. *Journal of Experimental Education, 38,* 1–14.

Bracey, G. W. (1986). Pandora and Pollyanna: Some comments on the wish to mandate. *Phi Delta Kappan, 67,* 452–455.

Bracey, G. W. (1991). Time outside of school. *Phi Delta Kappan, 73,* 88.

Bracey, G. W. (1992). Achievement and employment. *Phi Delta Kappan, 73,* 492–493.

Bracey, G. W. (1993). No magic bullets. *Phi Delta Kappan, 74,* 495–496.

Brandt, A. M. (1988). The syphilis epidemic and its relation to AIDS. *Science, 239,* 315–380.

Braucht, G. N. (1982). Problem drinking among adolescents: A review and analysis of psychosocial research. In NIAAA alcohol and health monograph No. 4 (DHHS Publication # ADM 82-1193) (142–164). Washington, DC: U.S. Government Printing Office.

Braucht, G. N., Brakarsh, D., Follinstad, D., & Berry, K. L. (1973). Deviant drug use in adolescence: A review of psychosocial correlates. *Psychological Bulletin, 79,* 92–106.

Braucht, G. N., Loya, F., & Jamieson, K. J. (1980). Victims of violent death: A critical review. *Psychological Bulletin, 87,* 309–333.

Braungart, R. G., & Braungart, M. M. (1989). Youth status and national development: A global assessment in the 1980s. *Journal of Youth and Adolescence, 18,* 107–130.

Brecher, E. (1972). *Licit and illicit drugs.* Boston: Little, Brown.

Bremner, R. H. (1970). *Children and youth in America* (Vol. 1). Cambridge, MA: Harvard University Press.

Brennan, A. (1985). Participation and self-esteem: A test of six alternative explanations. *Adolescence, 20,* 445–466.

Brenner, M. H. (1980). Estimating the social costs of youth employment problems. In *A review of youth employment problems, programs, and policies: The Vice President's Task Force on Youth Employment* (Vol. 1). Washington, DC: U.S. Department of Labor.

Brenzel, B. M. (1980). Domestication as reform: A study of the socialization of wayward girls, 1856–1905. *Harvard Educational Review, 50,* 196–213.

Brigham, J. C. (1986). *Social psychology.* Boston: Little, Brown.

Brock, B. V., Selke, S., Benedetti, J., Douglas, J. M., & Corey, L. (1990). Frequency of asymptomatic shedding of herpes simplex virus in women with genital herpes. *Journal of the American Medical Association, 263,* 418–420.

Bronfenbrenner, U. (1970). *Two worlds of childhood: U.S. and U.S.S.R.* New York: Russell Sage Foundation.

Bronfenbrenner, U. (1974). The origins of alienation. *Scientific American, 231,* 53–61.

Bronfenbrenner, U. (1986). Alienation. *Phi Delta Kappan, 67,* 430–436.

Brook, J. S., Gordon, A. S., & Brook, D. W. (1980). Perceived paternal relationships, adolescent personality, and female marijuana use. *Journal of Psychology, 105,* 277–285.

Brook, R., Kaplum, J., & Whitehead, P. C. (1974). Personality characteristics of adolescent amphetamine users as measured by the MMPI. *British Journal of the Addictions, 69,* 61–66.

Brookmeyer, R. (1991). Reconstruction and future trends of the AIDS epidemic in the United States. *Science, 253,* 37–42.

Brooks-Gunn, J. (1986). Pubertal processes and girls' psychological adaptation. In R. M. Lerner and T. T. Foch (Eds.), *Biological psychosocial interactions in early adolescence: A lifespan perspective.* Hillsdale, NJ: Erlbaum.

Brooks-Gunn, J., & Furstenberg, F. F. (1991). Adolescent sexual behavior. *American Psychologist, 44,* 249–257.

Brooks-Gunn, J., & Petersen, A. C. (Eds.). (1983). *Girls at puberty: Biological and psychosocial perspectives.* New York: Plenum.

Brooks-Gunn, J., & Ruble, D. N. (1983). The experience of menarche from a developmental perspective. In J. Brooks-Gunn & A. C. Peterson (Eds.), *Girls at puberty.* New York: Plenum.

Brooks-Gunn, J., & Warren, M. P. (1985). The effects of delayed menarche in different contexts: Dance and nondance students. *Journal of Youth and Adolescence, 14,* 285–300.

Brooks-Gunn, J., Warren, M. P., Samuelson, M., & Fox, R. (1986). Physical similarity of and disclosure of menarcheal status to friends: Effects of grade and pubertal status. *Journal of Early Adolescence, 6,* 3–14.

Broudy, H. S. (1972). *The real world of the public schools.* New York: Harcourt Brace Jovanovich.

Broverman, I. K., Broverman, D. M., Clarkson, F. E., Rosenkrantz, P. S., & Vogel, S. R. (1970). Sex role stereotypes and clinical judgments of mental health. *Journal of Consulting and Clinical Psychology, 34,* 1–7.

Brown, B. B., Eicher, S. A., & Petrie, S. (1986). The importance of peer ("crowd") affiliation in adolescence. *Journal of Adolescence, 9,* 73–96.

Brown, E. F., & Hendee, W. R. (1989). Adolescents and their music: Insights into the health of adolescents. *Journal of the American Medical Association, 262,* 1659–1663.

Brown, F. (1980). *Transition of youth to adulthood: A bridge too far.* Boulder, CO: Westview Press.

Brown, J. D., Childers, K. W., Bauman, K. E., & Koch, G. G. (1990). The influence of new media and family structure on young adolescents' television and radio use. *Communication Research, 17,* 65–82.

Brown, M E. (1979). Teenage prostitution. *Adolescence, 14,* 665–680.

Brown, N. S., & Ashery, R. S. (1979). Aftercare in drug abuse programming. In R. Dupont, A. Goldstein, & J. O'Donnell (Eds.), *Handbook on drug abuse.* Washington, DC: U.S. Government Printing Office.

Brown, S. (1970). *Christian answers to teenage sex questions.* Atlanta: Hallux.

Browning, C. J. (1960). Differential impact of family disorganization on male adolescents. *Social Problems, 8,* 37–44.

Browning, D. L. (1983). Aspects of authoritarian attitudes in ego development. *Journal of Personality and Social Psychology, 45,* 137–144.

Bruch, H. (1981). Development considerations of anorexia nervosa and obesity. *Canadian Journal of Psychiatry, 26,* 212–217.

Bruer, H. (1973). *Ego identity status in late-adolescent college males, as measured by a group administered incomplete sentences blank and related to inferred stance toward authority.* Unpublished doctoral dissertation, New York University.

Brumberg, J. J. (1988). *Fasting girls.* Cambridge, MA: Harvard University Press.

Bryant, F. B., & Veroff, J. (1982). The structure of psychological well-being: A socio-historical analysis. *Journal of Personality and Social Psychology, 43,* 653–673.

Buchingham, S. L., & Van Gorp, W. G. (1988). Essential knowledge about AIDS dementia. *Social Work, 33,* 112–115.

Buhrmester, D. (1990). Intimacy of friendship, interpersonal competence, and adjustment during preadolescence and adolescence. *Child Development, 61,* 1101–1111.

Bullough, V. L. (1981). Age at menarche: A misunderstanding. *Science, 213,* 365–366.

Bumpass, L. (1984). Children and marital disruption: A replication and update. *Demography, 21,* 71–82.

Burchard, J. D. (1979). Competitive youth sports and social competence. In N. W. Kent & J. E. Rolf (Eds.), *Primary prevention of psychopathology: Vol. 3. Social competence in children.* Hanover, NH: University of New England Press.

Burchinal, L. G. (1964). Characteristics of adolescents from unbroken, broken, and reconstituted families. *Journal of Marriage and the Family, 26,* 44–51.

Burgess, B. J. (1980). Parenting in the Native-American community. In M. D. Fantini & R. Cardenas (Eds.), *Parenting in a multicultural society.* New York: Longman.

Buriel, R. (1987). Ethnic labeling and identity among Mexican Americans. In J. S. Phinney & M. J. Rotheram (Eds.), *Children's ethnic socialization: Pluralism and development.* Newbury Park, CA: Sage.

Burke, R. S., & Grinder, R. E. (1966). Personality-oriented themes and listening patterns in teen-age music and their relation to certain academic and peer variables. *School Review, 74,* 196–211.

Burkett, S. R. (1980). Religiosity, beliefs, normative standards and adolescent drinking. *Journal of Studies on Alcohol, 41,* 662–671.

Burkholder, S., Ryan, K., & Blanke, V. E. (1981). Values, the key to a community. *Phi Beta Kappan, 62,* 483–485.

Buss, A. H. (1985). Self-consciousness and appearance. In J. A. Graham & A. M. Kligman (Eds.), *The psychology of cosmetic treatments.* New York: Praeger.

Byrne, G. (1988). Nicotine likened to cocaine, heroin. *Science, 240,* 1143.

Cadoret, R. J., Cain, C. A., & Grove, W. M. (1980). Development of alcoholism in adoptees raised apart from alcoholic biologic relatives. *Archives of General Psychiatry, 37,* 561–563.

Cairns, R. B., Peterson, G., & Neckerman, H. J. (1988). Suicidal behavior in aggressive adolescents. *Journal of Clinical Child Psychology, 17,* 298–309.

Camarena, P. M., Sarigiani, P. A. & Petersen, A. C. (1990). Gender-specific pathways to intimacy in early adolescence. *Journal of Youth and Adolescence, 19,* 19–32.

Campbell, A. (1990). Female participation in gangs. In C. R. Huff (Ed.), *Gangs in America*. Newbury Park, CA: Sage.

Campbell, E., Adams, G. R., & Dobson, W. R. (1984). Familial correlates of identity formation in late adolescence: A study of the predictive utility of connectedness and individuality in family relations. *Journal of Youth and Adolescence, 13*, 509–525.

Candee, D. (1974). Ego developmental aspects of New Left ideology. *Journal of Personality and Social Psychology, 30*, 620–630.

Cannon-Bonaventure, K., & Kahn, J. (1979). Interviews with adolescent parents. *Children Today, 8*(5), 17–19.

Caplan, G. (Ed.). (1961). *Prevention of mental disorders in children: Initial explorations*. New York: Basic Books.

Caplan, G. (1964). *Principles of preventive psychiatry*. New York: Basic Books.

Caplan, G. (1974). *Support systems and community mental health*. New York: Behavioral Publications.

Caplan, G. M. (1984). The facts of life about teenage prostitution. *Crime and Delinquency, 30*, 68–74.

Cardoza, D. (1991). College attendance and persistence among Hispanic women: An examination of some contributing factors. *Sex Roles, 24*, 133–147.

Carroll, A. E. (1986). Individual and family therapy eating disorder patients. *Seminar in Adolescent Medicine, 2*, 57–64.

Carroll, J. C. (1980). A cultural-consistency theory of family violence in Mexican American and Jewish ethnic groups. In *The Social Causes of Husband-Wife Violence*. M. A. Straus, & E. T. Hotaling (Eds.). Minneapolis, MN: University of Minnesota Press.

Carruth, B. R., Goldberg, D. L., & Skinner, J. D. (1991). Do parents and peers mediate the influence of television advertising on food-related purchase? *Journal of Adolescent Research, 6*, 253–271.

Carter, D. B., & Patterson, C. J. (1982). Sex roles as social conventions: The development of children's conceptions of sex-role stereotypes. *Developmental Psychology, 18*, 812–824.

Cartwright, J. (1980, February 10). The teenager's view of sexuality. *Seattle Times*, A1, B7.

Cash, T. F., Winstead, B. A., & Janda, L. H. (1986, April). The great American shape-up. *Psychology Today*, 30–37.

Casper, R. C. (1982). Treatment principles in anorexia nervosa. *Adolescent psychiatry*, Chicago: University of Chicago Press.

Casper, R. C. (1984). Hypothalmic dysfunction and symptoms of anorexia nervosa. *Psychiatric Clinics of North America, 7*, 201–213.

Catania, J. A., Coates, T. J., Stall, R., Turner, H., Peterson, J., Hearst, N., Dokini, M. M., Hudes, E., Gagon, J., Wiley, J., & Groves, R. (1992). Prevalence of AIDS-related risk factors and condom use in the United States. *Science, 258*, 1101–1106.

Cate, R. M., Henton, J. M., Koval, J., Christopher, F. S., & Lloyd, S. (1982). Premarital abuse. *Journal of Family Issues, 3*, 79–90.

Cates, W. (1982). Legal abortion: The public record. *Science, 215*, 1586–1590.

Cattell, R. B. (1979). Adolescent age trends in primary personality factors measured in T-data: A contribution to use of standardized measures in practice. *Journal of Adolescence, 2*, 1–16.

Cauble, M. A. (1976). Formal operations, ego identity, and principled morality: Are they related? *Developmental Psychology, 12*, 363–364.

Cavallin, B. J. (1987). Treatment of sexually abused adolescents: Views of a psychologist. *Seminars in Adolescent Medicine, 3*, 39–46.

Centers for Disease Control. (1983a). Acquired immune deficiency syndrome (AIDS) update: U.S. *Journal of American Medical Association, 250*(3), 335–336.

Centers for Disease Control. (1983b). Prevention of acquired immune deficiency syndrome (AIDS): Report of interagency recommendations. *Journal of the American Medical Association, 249*(12), 1544–1545.

Chaiken, S. (1979). Communicator physical attractiveness and persuasion. *Journal of Personality and Social Psychology, 37*, 1387–1397.

Chandler, T. A., Sawicki, R. F., & Stryfeler, J. M. (1981). Relationship between adolescent sexual stereotypes and working mothers. *Journal of Early Adolescence, 1*, 72–83.

Chase, A. W. (1866). *Dr. Chase's recipes; or information for everybody: an invaluable collection of about eight hundred practical recipes*. Ann Arbor, MI: Author.

Chase-Lansdale, P. L., Brooks-Gunn, J., & Palkoff, R. L. (1991). Research and programs for adolescent mothers: Missing links and future promises. *Family Relations, 40*, 396–403.

Chassin, L., & Stager, S. F. (1984). Determinants of self-esteem among incarcerated delinquents. *Social Psychology Quarterly, 47*, 382–390.

Chavey, J. M., & Roney, C. E. (1990). Psychocultural factors affecting the mental health status of Mexican American adolescents. In A. R. Stiffman & L. E. Davis (Eds.), *Ethnic issues in adolescent mental health*. Newbury Park, CA: Sage.

Cherek, D. R., Bennett, R. H., Roache, J. D., & Grabowski, J. (1990). Human aggressive and non-aggressive responding during acute tobacco abstinence. In L. S. Harris (Ed.), *Problems of drug dependence: 1989*. (U.S. Department of Health and Human Services publication # ADM 90-1663.) Washington, DC: U.S. Government Printing Office.

Cherlin, A. J., Furstenberg, F. F., Chase-Lansdale, P. L., Kiernan, K. K., Robins, P. K., Morrison, D. R., & Teitler, J. O. (1991). Longitudinal studies of effects of divorce on children in Great Britain and the United States. *Science, 252*, 1386–1389.

Cheung, P. C., & Lau, S. (1985). Self-esteem: Its relationship to the family and school social environment among Chinese adolescents. *Youth and Society, 14*, 373–387.

Chilman, C. (1973). Why do unmarried women fail to use contraception? *Medical Aspects of Human Sexuality, 7*, 167–168.

Chilman, C. S. (1980). *Adolescent sexuality in a changing American society* (NIH Publication No. 80-1426). Washington, DC: U.S. Government Printing Office.

Chilman, C. S. (1983). Social and psychological research concerning adolescent childbearing: 1970–1980. *Journal of Marriage and the Family, 43*(4), 793–805.

Chilman, C. S. (1990). Promoting healthy adolescent sexuality. *Family Relations, 39*, 123–131.

Cho, A. K. (1990). Ice: A new dosage form for an old drug. *Science, 249*, 631–634.

Chodorow, N. (1978). *The reproduction of mothering*. Berkeley: University of California Press.

Christopher, F. S., & Roosa, M. W. (1990). An evaluation of an adolescent pregnancy prevention program: Is "just say no" enough? *Family Relations, 39*, 68–72.

Cicero, T. J., O'Connor, L. H. (1990). Abuse liability of anabolic steroids and their possible role in abuse of alcohol, morphine, and other substances. In G. C. Lin & L. Erinoff (Eds.), *Anabolic steroid abuse.* (U.S. Department of Health and Human Services publication # ADM 91-1720.) Washington, DC: U.S. Government Printing Office.

Cicourel, A. V., & Kitsuse, J. I. (1963). *The educational decision makers.* Indianapolis: Bobbs-Merrill.

Clark, G. R., Telfer, M. A., Baker, D., & Rosen, M. (1970). Sex chromosomes, crime, and psychosis. *American Journal of Psychiatry, 126*, 1659–1663.

Clark, M. L., & Ayers, M. (1988). The role of reciprocity and proximity in junior high school friendships. *Journal of Youth and Adolescence, 17*, 403–407.

Clausen, J. A. (1975). The social meaning of differential physical and sexual maturation. In S. E. Dragastin & G. H. Elder (Eds.), *Adolescence in the life cycle.* New York: Halsted.

Clayton, R. R. (1985). Cocaine use in the United States: In a blizzard or just snowed? In N. J. Kozel & E. H. Adams (Eds.), Cocaine use in America: *Epidemiological and clinical perspectives* (NIDA research monograph 61, No. ADM 85-1414). Washington, DC: U.S. Government Printing Office.

Clayton, R. R., & Leukefeld, C. G. (1992). The prevention of drug use among youth: Implications of "legalization." *Journal of Primary Prevention, 12*, 289–302.

Clifford, P. R. (1992). Drug use, drug prohibition, and minority communities. *Journal of Primary Prevention, 12*, 303–316.

Clinton, W. (1992). The Clinton plan for excellence in education. *Phi Delta Kappan, 74*, 131, 134–138.

Clothier, F. (1943). Psychological implications of unmarried parenthood. *American Journal of Orthopsychiatry, 13*, 531–549.

Coates, D. L. (1987). Gender differences in the structure and support characteristics of black adolescents' social networks. *Sex Roles, 17*, 667–687.

Cobliner, W. G. (1974). Pregnancy in the single adolescent girl: The role of cognitive functioning. *Journal of Youth and Adolescence, 3*, 17–29.

Cochrane, R. (1974). Values as correlates of deviancy. *British Journal of Social and Clinical Psychology, 13*, 257–267.

Cockerham, W. C., Forslund, M. A., & Raboin, R. M. (1976). Drug use among white and American Indian high school youth. *International Journal of the Addictions, 11*, 209–220.

Cogan, S. F., Becker, R. D., & Hoffman, A. D. (1974). Adolescent males with urogenital anomalies: Their body image and psychosexual development. *Journal of Youth and Adolescence, 4*, 359–373.

Cohen, A. K. (1955). *Delinquent boys: The culture of the gang.* New York: Free Press.

Cohen, L. D. (1991). Sex differences in the course of personality development: A meta-analysis. *Psychological Bulletin, 109*, 252–266.

Cohen, L. E., & Kluegal, J. R. (1978). Determinants of juvenile court dispositions: Ascriptive and achieved factors in two metropolitan courts. *American Sociological Review, 43*, 162–176.

Cohen, R. A. (1969). Conceptual styles, cultural conflict, and nonverbal tests of intelligence. *American Anthropologist, 71*, 828–856.

Cohen, S. (1979). Inhalants. In R. Dupont, A. Goldstein, & J. O'Donnell (Eds.), *Handbook on drug abuse.* Washington, DC: U.S. Government Printing Office.

Cohen, S. (1981). Adolescence and drug abuse: Biomedical consequences. In D. J. Lettieri & J. P. Ludford (Eds.), *Drug abuse and the American adolescent* (NIDA research monograph No. 38, # ADM 81-1166). Washington, DC: U.S. Government Printing Office.

Cohen-Sandler, R., Berman, A. L., & King, R. A. (1982). A follow-up study of hospitalized suicidal children. *Journal of the American Academy of Child Psychiatry, 21*(4), 398–403.

Cole, D. A. (1989). Psychopathology of adolescent suicide: Hopelessness, coping beliefs, and depression. *Journal of Abnormal Psychology, 98*, 248–255.

Coleman, E. (1978). Toward a new model of treatment of homosexuality. *Journal of Homosexuality, 3*, 345–359.

Coleman, J. C. (1978). Current contradictions in adolescent theory. *Journal of Youth and Adolescence, 7*, 1–11.

Coleman, J. S. (1961). *The adolescent society.* New York: Free Press.

Coleman, J. S., & Hoffer, T. (1987). *Public and private high schools: The impact of communities.* New York: Basic Books.

Coleman, J. S., Kilgore, S. B., & Hoffer, T. (1982). Public and private schools. *Society, 19*(2), 4–9.

Coleman, M., Ganong, L. H., & Ellis, P. (1985). Family structure and dating behavior of adolescents. *Adolescence, 20*, 537–543.

Collins, J., Kennedy, J., & Francis, R. (1976). Insights into a dating partner's expectations of how behavior should ensue during the courting process. *Journal of Marriage and the Family, 38*, 373–378.

Collins, J. K., & Harper, J. (1974). The effect of physical maturation on popular traits of the Australian adolescent girl. *Adolescence, 9*, 529–536.

Collum, J., & Pike, G. (1976). The borderline and the addict lifestyle. *Drug Forum, 5*, 39–44.

Comas-Diaz, L. (1992). The future of psychotherapy with ethnic minorities. *Psychotherapy, 29*, 88–94.

Comerci, G. D. (1986). Preface. *Seminars in Adolescent Medicine, 1*, i–ii.

Cometa, M. S., & Eson, M. E. (1978). Logical operations and metaphor interpretation: A Piagetian model. *Child Development, 49*, 649–659.

Conant, J. B. (1967). *The comprehensive high school.* New York: McGraw-Hill.

Congressional Budget Office. (1980). *Improving youth employment prospects.* Washington, DC: U.S. Superintendent of Documents.

Connally, L. (1978). Boy fathers. *Human Behavior, 7*, 40–43.

Connell, P. (1977). Drug taking in Great Britain: A growing problem. In *Research Issues 15: Cocaine—Summaries of psychosocial research.* Washington, DC: U.S. Government Printing Office.

Conway, A., & Bogdan, C. (1977). Sexual delinquency: The persistence of a double standard. *Crime and Delinquency, 23*, 131–135.

Conye, R. K. (1991). Gains in primary prevention: Implications for the counseling profession. *Journal of Counseling and Development, 69*, 277–279.

Cook, C. E., & Jeffcoat, A. R. (1990). Pyrolytic degradation of heroin, phencyclidine, and cocaine: Identification of products and some observations on their metabolism. In C. N. Chiang & R. L. Hawks (Eds.), *Research findings on smoking abused substances.* (U.S. Department of Health and Human Services publication # ADM 90-1690.) Washington, DC: U.S. Government Printing Office.

Coombs, R. H., Paulson, M. J., & Richardson, M. A. (1991). Peer vs. parental influence in substance use among Hispanic and Anglo children and adolescents. *Journal of Youth and Adolescence, 20,* 73–88.

Cooney, T. M., Smyer, M. A., Hagestad, G. O., & Klock, R. (1986). Parental divorce in young adulthood: Some preliminary findings. *American Journal of Orthopsychiatry, 56*(3), 470–477.

Cooper, C. R., Grotevant, H. D., & Condon, S. M. (1983). Individuality and connectedness in the family as a context for adolescent identity formation and role-taking skill. In H. D. Grotevant and C. R. Cooper (Eds.), *Adolescent development in the family* (New Directions in Child Development, No. 22). San Francisco: Jossey-Bass.

Cooper, J., & Mackie, D. (1986). Video games and aggression in children. *Journal of Applied Social Psychology, 16,* 726–744.

Corder, J., & Stephan, C. W. (1984). Females' combination of work and family roles: Adolescents' aspirations. *Journal of Marriage and the Family,* 391–401.

Corey, L., & Holmes, K. K. (1983). Genital herpes virus infections: Current concepts in diagnosis, therapy, and prevention. *Annals of Internal Medicine, 98,* 973–983.

Cost of teenage pregnancies. (1987, February 19). *New York Times.*

Costa, M. E., & Campos, B. P. (1990). Socio-educational contexts and beginning university students' identity development. In C. Vandenplas-Holper & B. P. Campos (Eds.), *Interpersonal and identity development: New directions.* Louvain-La-Neuve, Belgium: Academia.

Costos, D. (1986). Sex role identity in young adults: Its parental antecedents and relation to ego development. *Journal of Personality and Social Psychology, 48,* 373–380.

Cottle, T. (1971). *Time's children.* Boston: Little, Brown.

Cotton, N. S. (1979). The familial incidence of alcoholism. *Journal of Studies on Alcohol, 40,* 89–116.

Cowen, E. L. (1982a). Help is where you find it: Four informal helping groups. *American Psychologist, 37,* 385–395.

Cowen, E. L. (1982b). Primary prevention research: Barriers, needs and opportunities. *Journal of Primary Prevention, 2,* 131–137.

Craig, R. J. (1986). The personality structure of heroin addicts. In S. I. Szara (Ed.), *Neurobiology of behavioral control in drug abuse* (NIDA Research Monograph No. 74, # ADM 85-1506). Washington, DC: U.S. Government Printing Office.

Craig-Bray, L., & Adams, G. R. (1986). Measuring social intimacy in same-sex and opposite-sex contexts. *Journal of Adolescent Research, 1,* 95–102.

Craig-Bray, L., Adams, G. R., & Dobson, W. R. (1988). Identity formation and social relations during late adolescence. *Journal of Youth and Adolescence, 17,* 173–187.

Cremin, L. (1980). *American education: The national experience, 1783–1876.* New York: Harper & Row.

Crener, K. J., MacKett, M., Wohlenberg, C., Notkins, H. C., & Moss, B. (1985). Vaccinia virus recombinant expressing herpes simplex virus type 1 glycoprotein D prevents latest herpes in mice. *Science, 228,* 737–739.

Crockett, L., Losoff, M., & Petersen, A. C. (1984). Perceptions of the peer group and friendship in early adolescence. *Journal of Early Adolescence, 4*(2), 155–181.

Crockett, L. J., Petersen, A. C., Graber, J. A., Schulenberg, J. E., & Ebata, A. (1989). School transitions and adjustments during early adolescence. *Journal of Early Adolescence, 9,* 181–210.

Crook, T., & Eliot, J. (1980). Parental death during childhood and adult depression: A critical review of the literature. *Psychological Bulletin, 87*(2), 252–259.

Cross, J. H., & Allen, J. G. (1970). Ego identity status, adjustment, and academic achievement. *Journal of Consulting and Clinical Psychology, 34,* 288.

Crossman, S. M., Shea, J. A., & Adams, G. R. (1980). Effects of parental divorce during early childhood on ego development and identity formation of college students. *Journal of Divorce, 3,* 263–272.

Crouter, A. C., & Crowley, M. S. (1990). School-age children's time alone with fathers in single- and dual-earner families: Implications for the father-child relationship. *Journal of Early Adolescence, 10,* 296–312.

Crumley, F. E. (1982). The adolescent suicide attempt: A cardinal symptom of a serious psychiatric disorder. *American Journal of Psychotherapy, 36*(2), 158–165.

Crumley, F. E. (1990). Substance abuse and adolescent suicide. *Journal of the American Medical Association, 263,* 3051–3056.

Csikszentmihaly, M., & McCormack, J. (1986). The influence of teachers. *Phi Delta Kappan, 67,* 415–419.

Cubberly, E. P. (1934). *Public education in the United States* (2nd ed.). Boston: Houghton Mifflin.

Culliton, B. J. (1984). Crash development of AIDS test near goal. *Science, 225,* 1128, 1130–1131.

Cunningham, M. R. (1986). Measuring the physical in physical attractiveness: Quasi-experiments on the sociobiology of female facial beauty. *Journal of Personality and Social Psychology, 50,* 925–935.

Curran, B. E. (1979). Understanding suicide. *Pediatric Clinics of North America, 26,* 737–746.

Curran, J. W., Morgan, W. M., Hardy, A. M., Jaffe, H. W., Darrow, W. W., & Dowdle, W. R. (1985). The epidemiology of AIDS: Current status and future prospects. *Science, 229,* 1352–1357.

Curtis, R. L. (1975). Adolescent orientations toward parents and peers: Variations by sex, age, and socioeconomic status. *Adolescence, 10,* 483–494.

Curtis, T. (1992). Possible origin of AIDS. *Science, 256,* 1260.

Cvetkovich, G. (1975). On the psychology of adolescent use of contraception. *Journal of Sex Research, 11,* 256–270.

Damon, W. (1983). *Social and personality development: Infancy through adolescence.* New York: Norton.

Damon, W., & Hart, D. (1982). The development of self-understanding from infancy through adolescence. *Child Development, 53,* 831–857.

Daniel, W. A. (1983). Pubertal changes in adolescence. In J. Brooks-Gunn & A. C. Petersen (Eds.), *Girls at puberty.* New York: Plenum.

Daniels, D., & Moos, R. H. (1990). Assessing life stressors and social resources among adolescents: Applictions to depressed youth. *Journal of Adolescent Research, 5,* 268–289.

Danish, S. J., Petitpas, A. J., & Hale, B. D. (1990). Sport as a context for developing competence. In T. P. Gullotta, G. R. Adams, & R. Montemayor (Eds.), *Developing social competency in adolescence.* Newbury Park, CA: Sage.

Danner, F. W., & Day, M. C. (1977). Eliciting formal operations. *Child Development, 48,* 1600–1606.

Darling, C. A., Kallen, D. J., & Van-Dusen, J. E. (1984). Sex in transition, 1900–1980. *Journal of Youth and Adolescence, 13,* 385–399.

Darling-Hammond, L. (1990). Achieving our goals: Superficial or structural reforms? *Phi Delta Kappan, 72,* 286–295.

D'Augelli, A. R. (1993). Preventing mental health problems among lesbian and gay college students. *Journal of Primary Prevention, 13,* 245–262.

D'Augelli, J., & D'Augelli, A. (1977). Moral reasoning and premarital sexual behavior: Toward reasoning about relationships. *Journal of Social Issues, 33*(2), 46–67.

Davidson, J., & Grant, C. (1988). Growing up hard in the AIDS area. *Maternal Child Care Nursing, 13,* 352–356.

Davidson, L., & Gould, M. S. (1989). Contagion as a risk factor for youth suicide. In ADAMHA. *Report of the secretary's task force on youth suicide: Vol. 2: Risk factors for youth suicide.* (U.S. Department of Health and Human Services publication # ADM 89-1622.) Washington, DC: U.S. Government Printing Office.

Davidson, L. E., Rosenberg, M. L., Mercy, J. A., Franklin, J., & Simmons, J. T. (1989). An epidemiologic study of risk factors in two teenage suicide clusters. *Journal of the American Medical Association, 262,* 2687–2692.

Davis, A. (1944). Socialization and adolescent personality. In *Adolescence: Yearbook of the National Society for the Study of Education* (Part 1). Chicago: University of Chicago Press.

Davis, G. E., & Leitenberg, H. (1987). Adolescent sex offenders. *Psychological Bulletin, 101,* 417–427.

Davis, K. (1940). The sociology of parent-youth conflict. *American Sociological Review, 5,* 523–525.

Davis, L. L. (1984). Clothing and human behavior: A review. *Home Economics Research Journal, 12,* 325–339.

Dawkins, R. L., & Dawkins, M. P. (1983). Alcohol use and delinquency among Black, White, & Hispanic adolescent offenders. *Adolescence, 28*(72), 799–809.

Dawley, H. H., Winstead, D. K., Baxter, A. S., & Gay, J. R. (1979). An attitude survey of the effects of marijuana on sexual enjoyment. *Journal of Clinical Psychology, 35,* 212–217.

DeAmicis, L. A., Klorman, R., Hess, I. W., & McAnarney, E. R. (1981). A comparison of unwed pregnant teenagers and sexually active adolescents seeking contraceptives. *Adolescence, 16*(61), 11–19.

de Anda, D., Becerra, R. M., & Fielder, E. (1990). In their own words: The life experiences of Mexican-American and White pregnant adolescents and adolescent mothers. *Child and Adolescent Social Work, 7,* 301–318.

DeAngelis, G. G., Koon, M., & Goldstein, E. (1980). Treatment of adolescent phencyclidine (PCP) abusers. *Journal of Psychedelic Drugs, 12,* 279–286.

de Baca, M. R. C., Rinaldi, C., Billig, S. H., & Kinnison, B. M. (1991). Santo Domingo school: A rural schoolwide project success. *Educational Evaluation and Policy Analysis, 13,* 363–368.

deCharm, R. (1968). *Personal causation.* New York: Academic Press.

Deisher, R. W., & Bidwell, R. J. (1987). Sexual abuse of male adolescents. *Seminars in Adolescent Medicine, 3,* 47–54.

Deitch, H. L., & Jones, J. A. (1983). The relationships between stages of ego development and personal constructs. *Journal of Clinical Psychology, 39,* 235–239.

Delaney, J., Lupton, J. G., & Toth, E. (1976). *The curse: A cultural history of menstruation.* New York: Dutton.

DeLeon, G., & Rosenthal, M. S. (1979). Therapeutic communities. In R. Dupont, A. Goldstein, & J. O'Donnell (Eds.), *Handbook on drug abuse.* Washington, DC: U.S. Government Printing Office.

Delgado-Gaitan, C. (1988). The value of conformity: Learning to stay in school. *Anthropology & Education Quarterly, 19,* 355–381.

De Lissovoy, V. (1973). High school marriages: A longitudinal study. *Journal of Marriage and the Family, 35,* 245–255.

DeLuca, J. R. (1981). *Fourth special report to the U.S. Congress on alcohol and health* (U.S. Public Health Service, DHHS Publication # ADM 81-1080). Washington, DC: U.S. Government Printing Office.

Dembo, M. H., & Lundell, B. (1979). Factors affecting adolescent contraceptive practices: Implications for sex education. *Adolescence, 14,* 657–665.

DeMoor, C., Elder, J. P., Young, R. L., Wildey, M. B., & Molgaard. (1989). Generic tobacco use among four ethnic groups in a school age population. *Journal of Drug Education, 19,* 257–270.

DenHouter, K. V. (1981). To silence one's self: A brief analysis of the literature on adolescent suicide. *Child Welfare, 60,* 2–9.

Dermer, M., & Pyszczynski, T. (1978). Effects of erotica upon men's loving and liking responses for women they love. *Journal of Personality and Social Psychology, 24,* 1–10.

DeSantis, J. P., Ketterlinus, R. D., & Youniss, J. (1990). Black adolescents' concerns that they are academically able. *Merrill-Palmer Quarterly, 36,* 287–299.

Despert, J. (1952). Suicide and depression in children. *Nervous Child, 9,* 378–384.

Deutsch, M., Katz, I., & Jensen, A. R. (1968). *Social class, race, and psychological development.* New York: Holt, Rinehart & Winston.

DeVall, E., Stoneman, Z., & Brody, G. (1986). The impacts of divorce and maternal employment on pre-adolescent children. *Family Relations, 35,* 153–159.

deWit, H., & McCracken, S. G. (1990). Preference for ethanol in males with or without an alcoholic first degree relative. In L. S. Harris (Ed.), *Problems of drug dependence: 1989.* (U.S. Department of Health and Human Services publication # ADM 90-1663.) Washington, DC: U.S. Government Printing Office.

Deyhle, D. (1986). Break dancing and breakout: Anglos, Utes, and Navajos in a border reservation high school. *Anthropology and Educational Quarterly, 17,* 111–127.

Diaz-Guerrero, R. (1987). Historical sociocultural premises and ethnic socialization. In J. S. Phinney & M. J. Rotheram (Eds.), *Children's ethnic socialization: Pluralism and development.* Newbury Park, CA: Sage.

Dickinson, G. (1978). Adolescent sex information sources: 1964–1974. *Adolescence, 13,* 653–658.

DiClemente, R. J., Zorn, J., & Temoshok, L. (1986). Adolescents and AIDS: A survey of knowledge, attitudes, and beliefs about AIDS in San Francisco. *American Journal of Public Health, 76,* 1443–1445.

Dillard, K. D., & Pol, L. G. (1982). The individual economic costs of teenage childbearing. *Family Relations, 31,* 249–259.

Dilley, J. W., Ochitill, H. N., Peel, M., & Volberding, P. A. (1985). Findings in psychiatric consultations with patients with acquired immune deficiency syndrome. *American Journal of Psychiatrics, 142,* 82–86.

Dion, K. K., & Stein, S. (1978). Physical attractiveness and interpersonal influence. *Journal of Experimental Social Psychology, 14,* 97–108.

Donovan, J. M. (1975a). Identity status and interpersonal style. *Journal of Youth and Adolescence, 4,* 37–56.

Donovan, J. M. (1975b). Identity status: Its relationship to Rorschach performance and to daily life patterns. *Adolescence, 10,* 29–44.

Dornbusch, S. M., Carlsmith, J. M., Duncan, P. D., Gross, R. T., Martin, J. A., Ritter, P. L., Seigel-Goreflick, B. (1984). Sexual maturation, social class, and the desire to be thin among adolescent females. *Developmental Behavioral Pediatrics, 5,* 308–313.

Dornbusch, S. M., Carlsmith, J. M., Gross, R. T., Martin, J. A., Jennings, D., Rosenberg, A., & Duke, P. (1981). Sexual development, age, and dating: A comparison of biological and social influences upon one set of behaviors. *Child Development, 52,* 179–185.

Dornbusch, S. M., Ritter, P. L., Leiderman, P. H., Roberts, D. F., & Fraleigh, M. J. (1987). The relation of parenting style to adolescent school performance. *Child Development, 58,* 1244–1257.

Dornbusch, S. M., Ritter, P. L., Mont-Reynaud, R., & Chen, Z. (1990). Family decision making and academic performance in a diverse high school population. *Journal of Adolescent Research, 5,* 143–160.

Douglass, J. D., & Wong, A. C. (1977). Formal operations: Age and sex differences in Chinese and American children. *Child Development, 48,* 689–692.

Douvan, E. (1963). Employment and the adolescent. In F. Nye & L. Hoffman (Eds.), *The employed mother in America.* Chicago: Rand McNally.

Douvan, E., & Adelson, J. (1966). *The adolescent experience.* New York: Wiley.

Douvan, E., & Gold, M. (1966). Model patterns in American adolescence. In L. M. Hoffman (Ed.), *Review of child development research* (Vol. 2). New York: Russell Sage Foundation.

Dowell, L. J. (1970). Environmental factors of childhood competitive athletics. *Physical Educator, 27,* 17–21.

Dowling, C. G. (1987). *Teenage mothers: Seventeen years later.* New York: The Commonwealth Fund.

Downs, A. C. (1990). The social biological constructs of social competency. In T. P. Gullotta, G. R. Adams, & R. Montemayor (Eds.), *Developing social competency in adolescence.* Newbury Park, CA: Sage.

Downs, A. C., & Hillje, L. S. (1993). Historical and theoretical perspectives on adolescent sexuality: An overview. In T. P. Gullotta, G. R. Adams, & R. Montemayor (Eds.), *Advances in adolescent development, Vol. 5: Adolescent sexuality.* Newbury Park, CA: Sage.

Dressler, W. W. (1987). The stress process in a southern Black community: Implications for prevention research. *Human Organization, 46,* 211–220.

Drewnowski, A., Hopkins, S. A., & Kessler, R. C. (1988). The prevalence of bulimia nervosa in the U.S. college student population. *American Journal of Public Health, 78,* 1322–1325.

Driscoll, R., Davis, K. E., & Lipetz, M. E. (1977). Parental interference and romantic love: The Romeo and Juliet effect. *Journal of Personality and Social Psychology, 35,* 381–391.

Drotman, P. D. (1987). Now is the time to prevent AIDS. *American Journal of Public Health, 77,* 143.

Dryfoos, J. G. (1990). *Adolescents at risk.* New York: Oxford University Press.

DuBois, D. L., & Hirsch, B. J. (1990). School and neighborhood friendship patterns of Blacks and Whites in early adolescence. *Child Development, 61,* 524–536.

Duncan, D. F. (1978). Attitudes toward parents and delinquency in suburban adolescent males. *Adolescence, 13,* 365–369.

Duncan, D. F. (1992). Drug abuse prevention in postlegalization America: What could it be like? *Journal of Primary Prevention, 12,* 317–322.

Duncan, P. D., Ritter, P. L., Dornbusch, S. M., Gross, R. T., & Carlsmith, J. M. (1985). *Journal of Youth and Adolescence, 14,* 227–236.

Dunphy, D. C. (1963). The social structure of urban adolescent peer groups. *Sociometry, 26,* 230–246.

Dupold, J., & Young, D. (1979). Empirical studies of adolescent sexual behavior: A critical review. *Adolescence, 14,* 45–63.

Durkheim, E. (1951). *Suicide: A sociological study.* New York: Free Press. (Original work published 1897.)

Durkheim, E. (1958). *The rules of sociological method* (S. A. Solovay & J. H. Mueller, Trans.). New York: Free Press.

Dusek, J. B. (1978, July). *The development of the self-concept in adolescence* (Final Report on Grant No. R01-HD 9094). Washington, DC: U.S. Department of Health, Education and Welfare, National Institute on Child Health and Human Development.

Duval, S., & Wicklund, R. A. (1972). *A theory of objective self-awareness.* New York: Academic Press.

Dyemade, U. J., & Washington, V. (1990). The role of family factors in the primary prevention of substance abuse among high risk Black youth. In A. R. Stiffman & L. E. Davis (Eds.), *Ethnic issues in adolescent mental health.* Newbury Park, CA: Sage.

Dyk, P. A., & Adams, G. R. (1988). *Identity and intimacy: A test of four theoretical models using cross-lag panel correlations.* Manuscript submitted for publication.

Eagly, A. H. (1987). *Sex differences in social behavior: A social role interpretation.* Hillsdale, NJ: Erlbaum.

Eagly, A. H., Ashmore, R. D., Makhijani, M. G., & Longo, L. C. (1991). What is beautiful is good, but . . . :A meta-analytic review of research on the physical attractiveness stereotype. *Psychological Bulletin, 110,* 109–128.

Eagly, A. H., & Carli, L. L. (1981). Sex of researchers and sex-typed communications as determinants of sex differences in influenceability. *Psychological Bulletin, 90,* 1–20.

Earls, C. M., & David, H. (1990). Early family and sexual experiences of male and female prostitutes. *Canada's Mental Health, 38,* 7–11.

Earls, F., & Siegel, B. (1980). Precocious fathers. *American Journal of Orthopsychiatry, 50,* 469–488.

East, P. L. (1989). Early adolescents' perceived interpersonal risks and benefits: Relations to social support and psychological functioning. *Journal of Early Adolescence, 9,* 374–395.

Eberly, D. J. (1991). *National youth service.* Washington, DC: National Service Secretariat.

Education cost put at $308 billion in 1987–88. (1987, August 23). *New York Times,* 18.

Edwards, E. D., & Edwards, M. E. (1988). Alcoholism prevention/treatment and Native American youth: A community approach. *Journal of Drug Issues, 18,* 103–114.

Edwards, E. D., & Egbert-Edwards, M. (1990). American Indian adolescents:

Combating problems of substance use and abuse through a community model. In A. R. Stiffman & L. E. Davis (Eds.), *Ethnic issues in adolescent mental health*. Newbury Park, CA: Sage.

Egeland, J. A., Gerhard, D. S., Pauls, D. L., Sussex, J. N., Kidd, K. K., Allen, C. R., Hostetter, A. M., & Housman, D. E. (1987). Bipolar affective disorders linked to DNA markers on chromosome II. *Nature, 325*(26), 783–787.

Ehrenberg, M. F., Cox, D. N., & Koopman, R. F. (1990). The prevalence of depression in high school students. *Adolescence, 25*, 905–912.

Ehrmann, W. (1959). *Premarital dating behavior*. New York: Holt, Rinehart & Winston.

Eicher, J. B., Baizerman, S., & Michelman, J. (1991). Adolescent dress, Part II: A qualitative study of suburban high school students. *Adolescence, 26*, 679–686.

Eiser, J. R. (1980). *Cognitive social psychology*. New York: McGraw-Hill.

Eisikovts, Z., & Sagi, A. (1982). Moral development and discipline encounter in delinquent and nondelinquent adolescents. *Journal of Youth and Adolescence, 11*, 217–230.

Ekehammar, B. (1974). Interactionism in personality from a historical perspective. *Psychological Bulletin, 81*, 1026–1048.

Elkind, D. (1967). Egocentrism in adolescence. *Child Development, 38*, 1025–1034.

Elkind, D. (1981). *The hurried child: Growing up too fast too soon*. Reading, MA: Addison/Wesley.

Elkind, D. (1985). Egocentrism redux. *Developmental Review, 5*, 218–226.

Elkind, D., & Bowen, R. (1979). Imaginary audience behavior in children and adolescents. *Developmental Psychology, 15*, 38–44.

Elliot, D. S., Voss, H. L., & Wendling, A. (1966). Capable dropouts and the social milieu of the high school. *Journal of Educational Research, 60*, 181–185.

Elliott, G. R., & Eisdorfer, C. (Eds.). (1982). *Stress and human health: Analysis and implications of research*. New York: Springer.

Ellis, L., & Ames, A. (1987). Neurohormonal functioning and sexual orientation: A theory of homosexuality-heterosexuality. *Psychological Bulletin, 101*, 233–258.

Elster, A. B., Ketterlinus, R., & Lamb, M. E. (1990). Association between parent-hood and problem behavior in a national sample of adolescents. *Pediatrics, 85*, 1044–1049.

Elster, A. B., & McAnarney, E. R. (1980). Medical and psychosocial risks of pregnancy and childbearing during adolescence. *Pediatric Annals, 9*(3), 11–20.

Emery, R. E. (1982). Interparental conflict and the children of discord and divorce. *Psychological Bulletin, 92*, 310–330.

Emler, N., Renwick, S., & Malone, B. (1983). The relationship between moral reasoning and political orientation. *Journal of Personality and Social Psychology, 45*, 1073–1080.

Engel, M. (1959). The stability of the self-concept in adolescence. *Journal of Abnormal and Social Psychology, 58*, 211–215.

Engs, R. C. (1981). Responsibility and alcohol. *Health Education, 12*, 20–22.

Enright, R. D., Ganiere, D. M., Buss, R., Lapsley, D. K., & Olson, L. M. (1983). Promoting identity development in adolescents. *Journal of Early Adolescence, 3*, 247–255.

Enright, R. D., Lapsley, D. K., Drivas, A. E., & Fehr, L. A. (1980). Parental influences on the development of adolescent autonomy and identity. *Journal of Youth and Adolescence, 9*, 529–546.

Enright, R. D., Lapsley, D. K., & Shukla, D. G. (1979). Adolescent egocentrism in early and late adolescence. *Adolescence, 14*, 687–696,

Enright, R. D., Olson, L. M., Ganiere, D., Lapsley, D. K., & Buss, R. (1984). A clinical model for enhancing adolescent ego identity. *Journal of Adolescence, 7*, 119–130.

Enright, R. D., Shukla, D. G., & Lapsley, D. K. (1980). Adolescent egocentrism-sociocentrism and self-consciousness. *Journal of Youth and Adolescence, 9*, 101–116.

Erikson, E. H. (1950). *Childhood and society*. New York: Norton.

Erikson, E. H. (1954). Eight stages of man. In W. E. Martin & C. B. Standler (Eds.), *Readings in child development*. New York: Harcourt Brace Jovanovich.

Erikson, E. H. (1959). *Identity and life styles: Selected papers* (Psychological Issues Monograph Series I, No. 1). New York: International Universities Press.

Erikson, E. H. (1968). *Identity: Youth and crisis*. New York: Norton.

Erikson, K. (1966). *Wayward Puritans*. New York: Wiley.

Eron, L., Walder, L. O., & Lefkowitz, M. M. (1971). *Learning of aggression in children*. Boston: Little, Brown.

Eskilson, A., Wiley, G., Muehlbauer, G., & Doder, L. (1986). Parental pressure, self-esteem and adolescent reported deviance: Bending the twig too far. *Adolescence, 21*, 501–515.

Facts about AIDS. (1983, December). Washington, DC: U.S. Public Health Service.

Fagan, J., Piper, E., & Moore, M. (1986). Violent delinquents and urban youths. *Criminology, 24*, 439–468.

Fairburn, C. G., & Beglin, S. J. (1990). Studies of the epidemiology of bulimia nervosa. *American Journal of Psychiatry, 147*, 401–408.

Falbo, T., & Peplau, L. A. (1979, September). *Sex-role self-concept and power in intimate relationships*. Paper presented at the meeting of the American Psychological Association, New York.

Farber, B. A. (1980). Adolescence. In K. S. Pope (Ed.), *On love and loving*, 44–60. San Francisco: Jossey-Bass.

Farber, M. L. (1968). *Theory of suicide*. New York: Funk & Wagnalls.

Farber, N. B. (1991). The process of pregnant resolution among adolescent mothers. *Adolescence, 26*, 697–716.

Farberow, N. L. (1989). Preparatory and prior suicidal behavior factors. In ADAMHA. *Report of the secretary's task force on youth suicide: Vol. 2: Risk factors for youth suicide*. (U.S. Department of Health and Human Services publication # ADM 89-1622.) Washington, DC: U.S. Government Printing Office.

Farrington, D. (1983). Offending from 10 to 25 years of age. In K Van Dvaen & S Mednick (Eds.), *Prospective studies of crime and delinquency*. Boston: Kluwer-Nighoff.

Farrington, D. P. (1990). Implications of criminal career research for the prevention of offending. *Journal of Adolescence, 13*, 93–113.

Farrow, J. A., & French, J. (1986). The drug abuse-delinquency connection revisited. *Adolescence, 21*(84), 887–900.

Fast, I., & Cain, A. C. (1966). The stepparent role: Potential for disturbances in family functioning. *American Journal of Orthopsychiatry, 36*, 485–491.

Fasteau, M. F. (1980). Sports: The training ground. In D. F. Sabo & R. Runfola (Eds.), *Jock: Sports and male identity*. Englewood Cliffs, NJ: Prentice-Hall.

Fauman, M. A., & Fauman, B. J. (1979). The psychiatric aspects of chronic phencyclidine use: A study of chronic PCP users. In R. C. Petersen & R. C. Stillman (Eds.), *Phencyclidine abuse: An appraisal* (NIDA research monograph 21, # ADM 79-728). Washington, DC: U.S. Government Printing Office.

Faunce, R. C. & Munshaw, C. L. (1964). *Teaching and learning in secondary schools.* Belmont, CA: Wadsworth, 1964.

Faunce, W. A. (1984). School achievements, social status and self-esteem. *Social Psychology Quarterly, 47,* 3–14.

Faust, D., & Arbuthnot, J. (1978). Relationship between moral and Piagetian reasoning and the effectiveness of moral education. *Developmental Psychology, 14,* 435–436.

Faust, M. S. (1977). Somatic development of adolescent girls. *Monographs of the Society for Research in Child Development, 42*(1, Serial No. 169).

Faust, M. S. (1983). Alternative constructions of adolescent growth. In J. Brooks-Gunn and A. C. Petersen (Eds.), *Girls at puberty.* New York: Plenum.

Fay, R. E., Turner, C. F., Klassen, A. D., & Gagnon, J. H. (1989). Prevalence and patterns of same-gender sexual contact among men. *Science, 243,* 338–348.

Feighner, J. P., Robius, E., Gaze, S. B., Woodruff, R. A., Winokur, G., & Munoz, R. (1972). Diagnostic criteria for use in psychiatric research. *Archives of General Psychiatry, 26,* 57–63.

Feinman, J. A. (1979, September). *Growth disorders.* Paper presented at the meeting of the American Psychological Association, New York.

Feinstein, S., & Ardon, M. (1973). Trends in dating patterns and adolescent development. *Journal of Youth and Adolescence, 2,* 157–166.

Feldman, S. S., & Quatman, T. (1988). Factors influencing age expectations for adolescent autonomy: A study of early adolescents and parents. *Journal of Early Adolescence, 8,* 325–343.

Felice, L. G. (1981). Black student dropout behavior: Disengagement from school rejection and racial discrimination. *Journal of Negro Education, 50,* 415–424.

Fendrich, J. M. (1974). Activists ten years later: A test of generational unit continuity. *Journal of Social Issues, 30*(2), 95–118.

Ferrier, P. E., Ferrier, S. A., & Neilson, J. (1970). Chromosome study of a group of male juvenile delinquents. *Pediatric Research, 4,* 205.

Field, T., Widmayer, S., Adler, S., & de Cubas, M. (1990). Teenage parenting in different cultures, family constellations, and caregiving environments: Effects on infant development. *Infant Mental Health Journal, 11,* 158–174.

Fillmore, K. M. (1974). Drinking and problem drinking in early adulthood and middle age: An exploratory 20-year follow-up study. *Quarterly Journal of Studies on Alcohol, 35,* 819–840.

Fine, M. A., Donnelly, B. W., & Voydanoff, P. (1991). The relation between adolescents' perceptions of their family lives and their adjustment in stepfather families. *Journal of Adolescent Research, 6,* 423–436.

Finkel, M. L., & Finkel, J. J. (1978). Male adolescent contraceptive utilization. *Adolescence, 13,* 443–451.

Finkelhor, D., Hotaling, G., & Sedlak, A. (1990). *Missing, abducted, runaway, and throwaway children in America.* U.S. Department of Justice. Washington, DC: U.S. Government Printing Office.

Finn, P. (1979). Teenage drunkenness: Warning signal, transient boisterousness, or symptom of social change? *Adolescence, 14,* 819–834.

Fischer, J. L. (1981). Transitions in relationship style from adolescence to young adulthood. *Journal of Youth and Adolescence, 10,* 11–24.

Fischer, P., Richards, J. W., Berman, E. J., & Krugman, D. M. (1989). Recall and eye tracking study of adolescents viewing tobacco advertisements. *Journal of the American Medical Association, 261,* 84–89.

Fischer, P., & Shaffer, D. (1990). Facts about adolescent suicide: A review of national mortality statistics and recent research. In M. J. Rotherham-Borus, J. Bradley, & N. Obolensky (Eds.), *Planning to live.* Tulsa, OK: National Resource Center for Youth Services.

Fisher, T. D. (1989). An extension of the findings of Moore, Peterson, and Furstenberg (1986) regarding family sexual communication and adolescent sexual behavior. *Journal of Marriage and the Family, 51,* 637–639.

Fitch, S. A., & Adams, G. R. (1981, April). *The identity-intimacy process revisited.* Paper presented at the meeting of the Society for Research in Child Development, Boston.

Fitch, S. A., & Adams, G. R. (1983). Ego-identity and intimacy status: Replication and extension. *Developmental Psychology, 19,* 839–845.

Flavell, J. H. (1963). *The developmental psychology of Jean Piaget.* New York: Van Nostrand.

Flavell, J. H. (1977). *Cognitive development.* Englewood Cliffs, NJ: Prentice-Hall.

Flavell, J. H. (1983). *Cognitive development.* New York: Wiley.

Flewelling, R. L., & Bauman, K. E. (1990). Family structure as a predictor of initial substance use and sexual intercourse in early adolescence. *Journal of Marriage and the Family, 52,* 171–181.

Flygare, T. J. (1978). The Supreme Court approves corporal punishment. *Phi Delta Kappan, 59,* 347–348.

Flynn, J. R. (1987). Massive IQ gains in 14 nations: What IQ tests really measure. *Psychological Bulletin, 101,* 171–191.

Ford, D. Y. (1992). Self-perceptions of underachievement and support for the achievement ideology among early adolescent African-Americans. *Journal of Early Adolescence, 12,* 228–252.

Ford, M. E. (1981). *Androgyny as self-assertion and integration: Implications for psychological and social competence.* Unpublished paper. Stanford University.

Forehand, R., McCombs, A., Long, N., Brody, G., & Fauber, R. (1988). Early adolescent adjustment to recent parental divorce: The role of interparental conflict and adolescent sex as mediating variables. *Journal of Consulting and Clinical Psychology, 56,* 624–627.

Fowler, J. (1981). *Stages of faith.* New York: Harper & Row.

Fox, C. H. (1992). Possible origin of AIDS. *Science, 256,* 1259–1260.

Fox, R. A., Baisch, M. J., Goldberg, B. D., & Hockmuth, M. C. (1987). Parenting attitudes of pregnant adolescents. *Psychology Reports, 61,* 403–406.

Fram, D. H., & Stone, N. (1986). Clinical observations in the treatment of adolescent and young adult PCP abusers in D. H. Cloyex (Ed.), *Phencyclidine: An update* (NIDA Research Monograph No. 64, # ADM 86-1443). Washington, DC: U.S. Government Printing Office.

Francis, L. J. (1987). The decline in attitudes toward religion among 8–15 year olds. *Educational Studies, 13,* 125–134.

Frank, E. S. (1991). Shame and guilt in eating disorders. *American Journal of Orthopsychiatry, 61,* 303–306.

Frank, S. J., McLaughlin, A. M., & Crusco, A. (1984). Sex role attributes, symptom distress, and defensive style among college men and women. *Journal of Personality and Social Psychology, 47,* 182–192.

Franklin, D. (1988). Race, class, and adolescent pregnancy: An ecological analysis. *American Journal of Psychotherapy, 58,* 339–354.

Frederick, C. J. (1978). Current trends in suicidal behavior in the United States. *American Journal of Psychotherapy, 32,* 172–200.

Freeman, E. W., Rickels, K., Huggins, G. R., Mudd, E. H., Garcia, C. R., & Dickens, H. O. (1980). Adolescent contraceptive use: Comparisons of male and female attitudes and information. *American Journal of Public Health, 70,* 790–796.

Freilino, M. K., & Hummel, R. (1985). Achievement and identity in college-age U.S. adult women students. *Journal of Youth and Adolescence, 14,* 1–10.

Freischlag, J., & Schmidke, C. (1979). Violence in sports: Its causes and some solutions. *Physical Educator, 36,* 182–185.

Freud, A. (1958). Adolescence. In *The psychoanalytic study of the child.* New York: International Universities Press.

Freud, K., & Blanchard, R. (1986). The concept of courtship disorder. *Journal of Sex and Marital Therapy, 12,* 79–92.

Freud, S. (1926). *Inhibitions, symptoms and anxiety.* London: Hogarth Press.

Freud, S. (1933). *New introductory lectures on psychoanalysis.* London: Hogarth Press.

Freud, S. (1947). *The ego and the id.* London: Hogarth Press.

Freud, S. (1948). *Beyond the pleasure principle.* London: Hogarth Press.

Freud, S. (1953). *A general introduction to psychoanalysis.* New York: Permabooks.

Freud, S. (1957). Mourning and melancholia. In J. Strachey (Ed. and Trans.), *The standard edition of the complete psychological works of Sigmund Freud* (Vol. 14). London: Hogarth Press.

Freud, S. (1969). Some early unpublished letters to Freud. *International Journal of Psychoanalysis, 50,* 419–427.

Friede, A., Hogue, J. R. C., Doyle, L. L., Hammerslough, C. R., Sniezek, J. E., Arrighi, H. (1986). Do the sisters of childbearing teenagers have increased rates of childbearing? *American Journal of Public Health, 76,* 1221–1224.

Friedman, H. J. (1980). The father's parenting experience in divorce. *American Journal of Psychiatry, 137,* 1177–1181.

Friedman, J., Mann, F., & Adelman, H. (1976). Juvenile street gangs: The victimization of youth. *Adolescence, 11,* 527–533.

Frisch, R. E. (1983). Fatness, puberty, and fertility. The effects of nutrition and physical training on menarche and ovulation. In J. Brooks-Gunn and A. C. Petersen (Eds.), *Girls at puberty.* New York: Plenum.

Frisch, R. E., & Revelle, R. (1971). Height and weight at menarche and a hypothesis of menarche. *Archive of Disease in Childhood, 46,* 695.

Furnham, A. (1985). Youth unemployment: A review of the literature. *Journal of Adolescence, 8,* 109–124.

Furstenberg, F. F., Jr. (1970). Premarital pregnancy among black teenagers. *Transaction, 7,* 52–55.

Furstenberg, F. F., Jr. (1971). Birth control experiences among pregnant adolescents. *Social Problems, 19,* 192–203.

Furstenberg, F. F., Jr., (1976). The social consequences of teenage parenthood. *Family Planning Perspectives, 8,* 148–164.

Furstenberg, F. F., Jr., (1980). Recycling the family: Perspectives for a new family form. *Marriage and Family Review, 2*(3), 1–22.

Furstenberg, F. F., Allison, P. D., & Morgan, S. P. (1987). Paternal participation and children's well-being after marital dissolution. *American Sociological Reveiw, 52,* 695–701.

Furstenberg, F. F., Jr., Brooks-Gunn, J., & Chase-Lansdale, L. (1989). Teenaged pregnancy and childbearing. *American Psychologist, 44,* 313–320.

Furstenberg, F. F., Jr., Brooks-Gunn, J., & Morgan, S. P. (1987). Adolescent mothers and their children in later life. *Family Planning Perspectives, 19,* 142–152.

Furstenberg, F. F., Jr., Moore, K. A., & Peterson, J. L. (1986). Sex education and sexual experience among adolescents. *American Journal of Public Health, 75,* 1221–1222.

Furstenberg, F. F., Jr., Morgan, S. P., Moore, K. A., & Peterson, J. L. (1987). Race differences in timing of first intercourse. *American Sociological Review, 52,* 511–518.

Furth, H. G. (1970). *Piaget for Teachers.* Englewood Cliffs, NJ: Prentice-Hall.

Futterman, E. H. (1980). Child psychiatry perspectives: After the civilized divorce. *Journal of the American Academy of Child Psychiatry, 19,* 525–530.

Gage, N. L. (1990). Dealing with the dropout problem. *Phi Delta Kappan, 72,* 280–285.

Galambos, N. L., Almeida, D. M., & Petersen, A. C. (1990). Masculinity, femininity, and sex role attitudes in early adolescence: Exploring gender intensification. *Child Development, 61,* 1905–1914.

Galan, F. J. (1988). Alcoholism prevention and Hispanic youth. *The Journal of Drug Issues, 18,* 49–58.

Ganiere, D. M., & Enright, R. D. (1989). Exploring three approaches to identity development. *Journal of Youth and Adolescence, 18,* 283–296.

Gantman, C. A. (1978). Family interaction patterns among families with normal, disturbed, and drug-abusing adolescents. *Journal of Youth and Adolescence, 7,* 429–440.

Garbarino, J., Sebes, J., & Schellenbach, C. (1984). Families at risk for destructive parent-child relations in adolescence. *Child Development, 55,* 174–183.

Garcia, M. O., & Rodriguez, P. F. (1989). Psychological effects of political repression in Argentina and El Salvador. In D. R. Koslow & E. Salett (Eds.), *Crossing cultures in mental health.* Washington, DC: Society for International Education Training and Research.

Garfinkel, P. E. (1981). Some recent observations on the pathogenesis of anorexia nervosa. *Canadian Journal of Psychiatry, 26,* 218–223.

Garfinkel, P. E., Moldofsky, H., & Garner, D. M. (1980). The heterogeneity of anorexia nervosa. *Archives of General Psychiatry, 37,* 1036–1040.

Garrison, C. Z., Jackson, K. L., Marsteller, F., McKeown, R., & Addy, C. (1990). A longitudinal study of depressive symptomatology in young adolescents. *Journal of the American Academy of Child and Adolescent Psychiatry, 29,* 581–585.

Garver, L. (1990). No, you can't have nintendo. *Newsweek,* (June 11), 8.

Garwood, S. G., & Allen, L. (1979). Self-concept and identified problem differences between pre- and post-menarcheal adolescents. *Journal of Clinical Psychology, 35,* 8–14.

Gattuso, J. (Ed.). (1991). *Native America.* Singapore: APA Publications.

Gawin, F. H. (1991). Cocaine addiction: Psychology and neurophysiology. *Science, 251,* 1580–1586.

Gay, G., Sheppard, C., Inaba, D., & Newmeyer, J. (1973). Cocaine in perspective: "Gift from the gods" to the rich man's drug. *Drug Forum, 2,* 409–430.

Gecas, V. (1982). The self-concept. *Annual Review of Sociology, 8,* 1–33.

General Accounting Office. (1989). *Effective school programs.* (No. GAO/HRD-89-132BR.) Washington, DC: U.S. Government Printing Office.

Gerbner, G., Gross, L., Morgan, M., & Signorielli, N. (1984). Facts, fantasies, and schools. *Society, 21*(6), 9–13.

Gersick, K. E., Grady, K., Sexton, E., & Lyons, M. (1981). Personality and sociodemographic factors in adolescent drug use. In D. J. Lettieri & J. P. Ludford (Eds.), *Drug abuse and the American adolescent* (NIDA research monograph 38, # ADM 81-1166). Washington, DC: U.S. Government Printing Office.

Gesell, A. (1946). The ontogenesis of infant behavior. In L. Carmichael (Ed.), *Manual of child psychology.* New York: Wiley.

Gesell, A., & Ilg, F. L. (1946). *The child from five to ten.* New York: Harper & Row.

Gesell, A., Ilg, F. L., & Ames, L. B. (1956). *Youth: The years from ten to sixteen.* New York: Harper & Row.

Getz, W. L., Allen, D. B., Myers, R. N., & Linder, K. C. (1983). *Brief counseling of suicidal persons.* Lexington, MA: Lexington Books.

Gfellner, B. M. (1986a). Changes in ego and moral development in adolescents: A longitudinal study. *Journal of Adolescence, 9,* 281–302.

Gfellner, B. M. (1986b). Ego development and moral development in relation to age and grade level during adolescence. *Journal of Youth and Adolescence, 15,* 147–163.

Gibbons, D. C. (1986). Juvenile Delinquency: Can social science find a cure? *Crime and Delinquency, 32,* 186–204.

Gibbons, D. C., & Krohn, M. D. (1986). *Delinquent behavior.* Englewood Cliffs, NJ: Prentice-Hall.

Gibbs, J. T. (1984). Black adolescents and youth: An endangered species. *American Journal of Orthopsychiatry, 54,* 6–21.

Gibbs, J. T. (1987). Identity and marginality: Issues in the treatment of biracial adolescents. *American Journal of Orthopsychiatry, 57,* 17–26.

Gibbs, J. T. (1989). Black American adolescents. In J. T. Gibbs & L. N. Huang (Eds.), *Children of color.* San Francisco: Jossey-Bass.

Gibbs, J. T. (1990). Mental health issues of Black adolescents: Implications for policy and practice. In A. R. Stiffman & L. E. Davis (Eds.), *Ethnic issues in adolescent mental health.* Newbury Park, CA: Sage.

Gibbs, J. T., & Huang, N. (Eds.). (1989). *Children of color: Psychological interventions with minority youth.* San Francisco: Jossey-Bass.

Gilbert, E. H ., & DeBlassie, R. R. (1984). Anorexia nervosa: Adolescent starvation by choice. *Adolescence, 19,* 839–846.

Gilligan, C. (1982). *In a different voice.* Cambridge, MA: Harvard University Press.

Gilligan, C., Ward, J. V., & Taylor, J. M. (Eds.). (1988). *Mapping the moral domain.* Cambridge, MA: Harvard University Press.

Ginsburg, S. D., & Orlofsky, J. L. (1981). Ego-identity status, ego-development and locus of control in college women. *Journal of Youth and Adolescence, 10,* 297–307.

Gispert, M., Wheeler, K., Marsh, L., & Davis, M. S. (1985). Suicidal adolescents: Factors in evaluation. *Adolescence, 20,* 753–762.

Gjerde, P. F., Block, J., & Block, J. H. (1991). The preschool family context of 18 year olds with depressive symptoms: A prospective study. *Journal of Research on Adolescence, 1,* 63–91.

Glasser, K. (1978). The treatment of depressed and suicidal adolescents. *American Journal of Psychotherapy, 32,* 252–269.

Glasser, K. (1981). Psychopathologic patterns in depressed adolescents. *American Journal of Psychotherapy, 35*(3), 368–382.

Glasser, M. (1977). Homosexuality in adolescence. *British Journal of Medical Psychology, 50*(3), 217–225.

Glick, M., & Zigler, E. (1985). Self-image: A cognitive developmental approach. In R. L. Leahy (Ed.), *The development of the self.* New York: Academic Press.

Glueck, S., & Glueck, E. T. (1950). *Unraveling juvenile delinquency.* New York: Commonwealth Fund.

Glueck, S., & Glueck, E. T. (1957). Working mothers and delinquency. *Mental Hygiene, 41,* 327–352.

Goetting, A. (1994). The parenting-crime connection. *Journal of Primary Prevention, 14,* in press.

Goffman, E. (1963). Stigma: *Notes on the management of spoiled identity.* Englewood Cliffs, NJ: Prentice-Hall.

Gold, B. D. (1987). Self-image of punk rock and non punk rock juvenile delinquents. *Adolescence, 22,* 535–544.

Gold, M. S. (1984). *800-Cocaine.* New York: Bantam Books.

Gold, M. S., Washton, A. M., & Dackis, C. A. (1985). Cocaine abuse: Neurochemistry, phenomenology, and treatment. In N. J. Kozel & E. H. Adams (Eds.), *Cocaine use in America: Epidemiological and clinical perspectives* (NIDA Research Monograph 61, # ADM 85-1414). Washington, DC: U.S. Government Printing Office.

Gold, S. N. (1980). Relations between level of ego development and adjustment patterns in adolescents. *Journal of Personality Assessment, 44,* 630–638.

Goldberg, C. (1977). School phobia in adolescence. *Adolescence, 12,* 499–509.

Goldfarb, L. A. (1987). Sexual abuse antecedent to anorexia nervosa, bulimia, and compulsive overeating: Three case reports. *International Journal of Eating Disorders, 6,* 675–680.

Goldman, J. A., Rosenzweig, C. M., & Lutter, A. D. (1980). Effect of simularity of ego identity status on interpersonal attraction. *Journal of Youth and Adolescence, 9,* 153–163.

Goldman, W., & Lewis, P. (1977). Beautiful is good: Evidence that the physically attractive are more socially skillful. *Journal of Experimental Social Psychology, 13,* 125–130.

Goldsmith, S., Gabrielson, M., Gabrielson, I., Matthews, V., & Potts, L. (1972). Teenagers, sex, and contraception. *Family Planning Perspectives, 4,* 32–38.

Goldstein, A., & Kalant, H. (1990). Drug policy: Striking the right balance. *Science, 249,* 1513–1521.

Goldstein, H. S. (1974). Reconstituted families: The second marriage and its children. *Psychiatric Quarterly, 48,* 433–440.

Goldstein, P. J. (1990). Anabolic steroids: An ethnographic approach. In G. C. Lin & L. Erinoff (Eds.), *Anabolic steroid abuse.* (U.S. Department of Health and Human Services publication # ADM 91-1720.) Washington, DC: U.S. Government Printing Office.

Golombek, H., & Marton, P. (1992). Adolescent over time: A longitudinal study of personality development. In S. C. Feinstein (Ed.), *Adolescent psychiatry:*

Developmental and clinical studies. Chicago: University of Chicago Press.

Goodlad, J. I. (1984). *A place called School.* New York: McGraw-Hill.

Goodlad, J. I. (1985). The great American schooling experiment. *Phi Delta Kappan, 67,* 266–271.

Goodman, E., & Cohall, A. T. (1989). Acquired immunodeficiency syndrome and adolescents: Knowledge, attitudes, and behaviors in a New York City adolescent minority population. *Pediatrics, 84,* 36–42.

Goossens, L. (1984). Imaginary audience behavior as a function of age, sex, and formal operational thinking. *International Journal of Behavioral Development, 7,* 77–93.

Goranson, R. E. (1975). The impact of TV violence. *Contemporary Psychology, 20,* 291–293.

Gordon, M. (1981). Was Waller ever right? The rating and dating complex reconsidered. *Journal of Marriage and the Family, 43,* 67–76.

Gordon, S. (1978). *You would if you loved me.* New York: Bantam Books.

Gottfried, A. E., & Gottfried, A. W. (1988). *Maternal employment and children's development.* New York: Plenum.

Gottlieb, D., & Ramsey, C. (1964). *The American adolescent.* Homewood, IL: Dorsey Press.

Gould, J. L., & Grant, C. (1981, May). The instinct to learn. *Science '81,* 44–50.

Gould, R. E. (1965). Suicide problems in children and adolescents. *American Journal of Psychotherapy, 19,* 228–246.

Gove, W. R., & Crutchfield, R. D. (1982). The family and juvenile delinquency. *Sociological Quarterly, 23,* 301–319.

Gray, W., & Hudson, L. (1984). Formal operations and the imaginary audience. *Developmental Psychology, 20,* 619–627.

Gray-Little, B., & Applebaum, M. I. (1979). Instrumentality effects in the assessment of racial differences in self-esteem. *Journal of Personality and Social Psychology, 37,* 1221–1229.

Greenberger, E., Josselson, R., Knerr, C., & Knerr, B. (1975). The measurement and structure of psychosocial maturity. *Journal of Youth and Adolescence, 4,* 127–144.

Greenberger, E., & Sorenson, A. B. (1974). Toward a concept of psychosocial maturity. *Journal of Youth and Adolescence, 3,* 329–358.

Greenberger, E., & Steinberg, L. D. (1981). The workplace as a context for the socialization of youth. *Journal of Youth and Adolescence, 10*(3), 185–210.

Greenberger, E., & Steinberg, L. (1986). *When teenagers work: The psychological and social costs of adolescent employment.* New York: Basic Books.

Greenberger, E., Steinberg, L. D., Vaux, A., & McAuliffe, S. (1980). Adolescents who work: Effects of part-time employment on family and peer relations. *Journal of Youth and Adolescence, 9*(3), 189–202.

Greene, A. L., & Grimsley, M. D. (1990). Age and gender differences in adolescents' preferences for parental advice. *Journal of Adolescent Research, 5,* 396–413.

Greenfield, P. M., Bruzzone, L., Koyamatsu, K., Satuloff, W., Nixon, K., Brodie, M., & Kingsdale, D. (1987). What is rock music doing to the minds of our youth? A first experimental look at the effects of rock music lyrics and music videos. *Journal of Early Adolescence, 7,* 315–329.

Gregg, C. T. (1983). *A virus of love and other tales of medical detection.* New York: Scribner's.

Gregory, T. B., & Smith, G. R. (1987). *High schools as communities.* Bloomington, IN: Phi Delta Kappan.

Greif, E. B., & Ulman, K. J. (1982). The psychological impact of menarche on early adolescent females: A review. *Child Development, 53,* 1413–1430.

Greydanus, D. E. (1980). Contraception in adolescence: An overview for the pediatrician. *Pediatric Annals, 9*(3), 52–63.

Griffiths, M. D. (1991). Amusement machine playing in childhood and adolescence: A comparative analysis of video games and fruit machines. *Journal of Adolescence, 14,* 53–74.

Grinder, R. E. (1967). *A history of genetic psychology.* New York: Wiley.

Grinspoon, L. (1971). *Marijuana reconsidered.* Cambridge, MA: Harvard University Press.

Grinspoon, L., & Bakalar, J. B. (1976). *Cocaine: A drug and its social evolution.* New York: Basic Books.

Grossman, B., Wirt, R., & Davids, A. (1985). Self-esteem, ethnic identity, and behavioral adjustment among Anglo and Chicano adolescents in West Texas. *Journal of Adolescence, 8,* 57–68.

Grotevant, H. D. (1983). The contribution of the family to the facilitation of identity formation in early adolescence. *Journal of Early Adolescence, 3,* 225–237.

Grotevant, H. D. (1992). Assigned and chosen identity components: A process perspective on their integration. In G. R. Adams, T. P. Gullotta, and R. Montemayor (Eds.), *Identity formation during adolescence, Vol. 4: Advances in adolescent development.* Newbury Park, CA: Sage.

Grotevant, H. D., & Adams, G. R. (1984). Development of an object measure to assess ego identity in adolescence: Validation and replication. *Journal of Youth and Adolescence, 13,* 419–438.

Grotevant, H. D., & Thorbecke, W. L. (1980, March). *Sex differences in vocational identity: Getting to the same place by different paths.* Paper presented at the meeting of the Southwestern Society for Research in Human Development, Lawrence, KS.

Grueling, J. W., & De Blassie, R. B. (1980). Adolescent suicide. *Adolescence, 15,* 589–601.

Guilford, J. P. (1967). *The nature of human intelligence.* New York: McGraw-Hill.

Guilian, D., Vaca, K., & Noonan, C. A. (1990). Secretion of neurotoxins by mononuclear phagocytes infected with HIV-1. *Science, 250,* 1593–1596.

Gull, W. W. (1874). Anorexia nervosa. *Transcript of Clinical Sociology, 7,* 22–28.

Gullotta, T. P. (1978, November). *The juvenile offender: The police, the courts, and the social agency.* Paper presented at the meeting of the American Association of Psychiatric Services for Children, Atlanta.

Gullotta, T. P. (1979, November). *Should the juvenile court be continued, altered, or abolished?* Paper presented at the meeting of the National Association of Social Workers, San Antonio.

Gullotta, T. P. (1981). Can prevention survive its popularity? *Journal of Primary Prevention, 1*(3), 145–146.

Gullotta, T. P. (1987). Prevention's technology. *Journal of Primary Prevention, 7*(4), 176–196.

Gullotta, T. P. (1990). Preface. In T. P. Gullotta, G. R. Adams, & R. Montemayor (Eds.), *Developing social competency in adolescence.* Newbury Park, CA: Sage.

Gullotta, T. P. (1992, July). *Effective primary prevention programs.* Paper presented at the meeting of the Psychiatric World Congress, Brussels, Belgium.

Gullotta, T. P. (1994). Understanding adolescent behavior. In G. Blau & T. P.

Gullotta (Eds.), Dysfunctional behavior in adolescence: Causes, treatment, and prevention. Newburg Park, CA: Sage.

Gullotta, T. P., & Letarte, L. (1994). School based health centers. *Adolescence,* in press.

Gullotta, T. P., & Adams, G. R. (1982a). Minimizing juvenile deliquency: Implications for prevention programs. *Journal of Early Adolescence, 2,* 105–117.

Gullotta, T. P., & Adams, G. R. (1982b). Substance abuse minimization: Conceptualizing prevention in adolescent youth programs. *Journal of Youth and Adolescence, 11*(5), 409–424.

Gullotta, T. P., Adams, G. R., & Alexander, S. J. (1986). *Today's marriages and families: A wellness approach.* Pacific Grove, CA: Brooks/Cole.

Gullotta, T. P., Adams, G. R., & Montemayor, R. (Eds.). (1993). *Adolescent sexuality.* Newbury Park, CA: Sage.

Gullotta, T. P., & Blau, G. (1995). A social history of selected drug misuse in the United States. In T. P. Gullotta, G. R. Adams, & R. Montemayor (Eds.), *Adolescent substance misuse.* Newbury Park, CA: Sage.

Gullotta, T. P., Whewell, M. C., Blau, G., & Bloom, M. (1995). The prevention and treatment of child abuse in households of substance abusers. *Child Welfare,* in press.

Gwartney-Gibbs, P. A., Stockard, J., & Bohmer, S. (1987). Learning courtship aggression: The influence of parents, peers, and personal experience. *Family Relations, 36,* 276–282.

Haan, N., Langer, J., & Kohlberg, L. (1976). Family patterns of moral reasoning. *Child Development, 47,* 1204–1206.

Hafner, A., Ingels, S., Schneider, B., & Stevenson, D. (1990). *A profile of the American 8th grader.* Washington, DC: U.S. Department of Education NCES 90–458.

Hahn, A. (1987). America's dropouts. *Phi Delta Kappan, 69,* 184–189.

Hall, C. S. (1954). *A primer of Freudian psychology.* New York: New American Library.

Hall, C. S., & Lindzey, G. (1967). *Theories of personality.* New York: Wiley.

Hall, G. S. (1904). *Adolescence: Its psychology, and its relations to physiology, anthropology, sociology, sex, crime, religion, and education* (2 vols.). New York: Appleton-Century-Crofts.

Hall, G. S. (1916). *Adolescence.* New York: Appleton-Century-Crofts.

Hallinan, M. T., & Smith, S. S. (1985). The effects of classroom racial composition on students' interracial friendliness. *Social Psychology Quarterly, 48,* 3–16.

Halpin, G., & Whiddon, T. (1977). Drug education: Solution or problem? *Psychological Reports, 40,* 372–374.

Halt, R. E. (1979). The relationship between ego identity status and moral reasoning in university women. *Journal of Psychology, 103,* 203–207.

Hamilton, S. F. (1982). Working toward employment. *Society, 19*(6), 19–29.

Hampton, R., & Gullotta, T. P. (Eds.). (1995). *Preventing community violence.* Newbury Park, CA: Sage.

Handelsman, C. D., Cabral, R. J., & Weisfeld, G. E. (1987). Sources of information and adolescent sexual knowledge and behavior. *Journal of Adolescent Research, 2,* 455–463.

Haney, B., & Gold, M. (1977). The juvenile delinquent nobody knows. In D. Rogers (Ed.), *Issues in adolescent psychology.* Englewood Cliffs, NJ: Prentice-Hall.

Hanson, S. L., & Ooms, T. (1991). The economic costs and rewards of two-earner, two-parent families. *Journal of Marriage and the Family, 53,* 622–634.

Hanson, W B., & Flay, B. R. (1990). Relative effectiveness of comprehensive community programming for drug abuse prevention with high-risk and low-risk adolescents. *Journal of Consulting and Clinical Psychology, 58,* 447–456.

Hardy, J. B., & Duggan, A. K. (1988). Teenage fathers and the fathers of infants of urban teenage mothers. *American Journal of Public Health, 78,* 919–922.

Harmoni, R., Mann, L., & Power, C. (1987). *Adolescent decision making: The development of competence.* Unpublished manuscript, the Flinders University of South Australia.

Harper, F. D. (1988). Alcohol and Black youth: An overview. *The Journal of Drug Issues, 18,* 7–14.

Harrington, D., & Dubowitz, H. (1993). What can be done to prevent child maltreatment? In R. Hampton, T. P. Gullotta, G. R. Adams, E. Potter, & R. Weissberg (Eds.), *Preventing family violence.* Newbury Park, CA: Sage.

Harris, K. M., & Morgan, S. P. (1991). Fathers, sons, and daughters: Differential paternal involvement in parenting. *Journal of Marriage and the Family, 53,* 531–544.

Harris, L., & Associates (1986). *American teens speak: Sex, myths, TV and birth control.* New York: Planned Parenthood.

Hart, B., & Hilton, I. (1988). Dimensions of personality organization as predictors of teenage pregnancy risk. *Journal of Personality Assessment, 52,* 116–132.

Hart, M. (1971, October). Sports: Women sit in the back of the bus. *Psychology Today,* 64–66.

Hartford, T. C., Willis, C. H., & Deabler, H. L. (1967). Personality correlates of masculinity-femininity. *Psychological Reports, 21,* 881–884.

Hartley, G. (1990). *American youth and sports participation.* North Palm Beach, FL: Athletic Footwear Association.

Hatfield, E., & Sprechner, S. (1986). *Measuring passionate love in intimate relationships. Journal of Adolescence, 9,* 383–410.

Hauck, W. E., Martens, M., & Wetzel, M. (1986). Shyness, group dependence and self-concept: Attributes of the imaginary audience. *Adolescence, 21,* 529_534.

Hauser, S. T. (1972a). Black and white identity development: Aspects and perspectives. *Journal of Youth and Adolescence, 1,* 113–130.

Hauser, S. T. (1972b). Adolescent self-image development. *Archives of General Psychiatry, 27,* 537–541.

Hauser, S. T. (1976). Loevinger's model and measure of ego development: A critical review. *Psychological Bulletin, 83,* 928–955.

Hauser, S. T., (1978). Ego development and interpersonal styles in adolescence. *Journal of Youth and Adolescence, 7,* 333–352.

Hauser, S. T., Liebman, W., Houlihan, J., Powers, S. I., Jacobson, A. M., Noam, G. G., Weiss, B., & Follansbee, D. (1985). Family contexts of pubertal timing. *Journal of Youth and Adolescence, 14,* 317–338.

Hauser, S. T., Powers, S. I., & Noam, G. G. (1991). Adolescents and their families: Paths of ego development. New York: Free Press.

Hauser, S. T., Powers, S. I., Noam, G. G., Jacobson, A. M., Weiss, B., & Follansbee, D. J. (1984). Familiar contexts of adolescent ego development. *Child Development, 55,* 195–213.

Havighurst, R. J. (1972). *Developmental tasks and education* (2nd ed.). New York: Longmans, Green.

Hawby, R. A. (1990). The bumpy road to drug-free schools. *Phi Delta Kappan, 72*, 310–314.

Hayes, C. D. (Ed.). (1987). *Risking the future: Vol. 1. Adolescent sexuality, pregnancy, and childbearing.* Washington, DC: National Academy Press.

Hayes, L. (1992). The cost of dropping out. *Phi Delta Kappan, 73*, 413.

Hechinger, F. M. (1992). Fateful choices. New York: Carnegie Corporation of New York.

Hechinger, F. M., & Hechinger, G. (1975). *Growing up in America.* New York: McGraw-Hill.

Hecht, I. H., & Jurkovic, G. J. (1978). The performance-verbal IQ discrepancy in differentiated subgroups of delinquent adolescent boys. *Journal of Youth and Adolescence, 7*, 197–202.

Heino, F. L., Meyer-Bahlburg, L., Ehrhardt, A. A., Bell, J. J., Cohen, S. F., Healey, J. M., Feldman, J. F., Morishima, A., Baker, S. W., & New, M. I. (1985). Idiopathic precocious puberty in girls: Psychosexual development. *Journal of Youth and Adolescence, 14*, 339–354.

Henderson, G. H. (1980). Consequences of school age pregnancy and motherhood. *Family Relations, 29*, 185–190.

Henderson, V. L., & Dweck, C. S. (1990). Motivation and achievement. In S. S. Feldman and G. R. Elliott (Eds.), *At the threshold: The developing adolescent.* Cambridge, MA: Harvard University Press.

Hendin, H., Pollinger, A., Ulman, R., & Carr, A. C. (1981). *Research 40: Adolescent marijuana abusers and their families* (DHHS Publication # ADM 81-1168). Washington, DC: U.S. Government Printing Office.

Hendricks, L. E., Howard, C. S., & Caesar, P. P. (1983). Help-seeking behavior among select populations of black unmarried adolescent fathers: Implications for social service agencies. *American Journal of Public Health, 71*(7), 733–735.

Henry, W. A. (1990). Beyond the melting pot. *Time, 135*, 28–31.

Henton, J. M., Cate, R., Koval, J., Lloyd, S., & Christopher, S. (1983). Romance and violence in dating relationships. *Journal of Family Issues, 4*, 467–482.

Herman, C. P., Zanna, M. P., & Higgins, E. T. (Eds.). (1986). *Physical appearance, stigma, and social behavior: The Ontario Symposium* (Vol. 3). Hillsdale, NJ: Erlbaum.

Herold, E. (1974). Stages of date selection: A reconciliation of divergent findings on campus values on dating. *Adolescence, 9*, 113–120.

Herzog, A., & Bachman, J. G. (1982). *Sex role attitudes among high school seniors: Views about work and family roles.* Ann Arbor: Survey Research Center, Institute for Social Research, University of Michigan.

Hetherington, E. M., & Furstenberg, F. F. (1989). Sounding the alarm. *Readings, 4*, 4–8.

Hiebert, K. A., Felice, M. E., Wingard, D. L., Munoz, R., & Ferguson, J. M. (1988). *International Journal of Eating Disorders, 7*, 693–696.

Hier, S. J., Korboot, P. J., & Schweitzer, R. D. (1990). Social adjustment and symptomatology in two types of homeless adolescents and throwaways. *Adolescence, 25*, 761–772.

Higham, E. (1980). Variations in adolescent psychonormal development. In J. Adelson (Ed.), *Handbook of adolescent psychology.* New York: Wiley.

Highlights. (1984, March). *Science '84*, 14.

Hill, C. (1986). A developmental perspective on adolescent "rebellion" in the church. *Journal of Psychology and Theology, 14*, 306–318.

Hill, J., Holmbeck, G., Marlow, L., Green, T., & Lynch, M. (1985a). Menarcheal status and parental-child relations in families of seventh grade girls. *Journal of Youth and Adolescence, 14*, 301–316.

Hill, J., Holmbeck, G., Marlow, L., Green, T., & Lynch, M. (1985b). Pubertal status and parental-child relations in families of seventh grade boys. *Journal of Early Adolescence, 5*, 31–44.

Hill, J. P., & Lynch, M. E. (1983). The intensification of gender-related role expectations during early adolescence. In J. Brooks-Gunn and A. C. Petersen (Eds.), *Girls at puberty: Biological and psychosocial perspectives.* New York: Plenum.

Hill, S. M., Shaw, L. B., & Sproat, K. (1980). Teenagers: What are their choices about work? In *A review of youth employment problems, programs and policies: The Vice President's Task Force on Youth Employment* (Vol. 1). Washington, DC: U.S. Department of Labor.

Hiller, D. V., & Philliber, W. W. (1985). Internal consistency and correlates of the Bem Sex Role Inventory. *Social Psychology Quarterly, 5*, 215–227.

Hillman, S. B., & Sawilowsky, S. S. (1991). Maternal employment and early adolescent substance use. *Adolescence, 26*, 829–837.

Hindelang, M., Hirschi, T., & Weis, J. (1981). *Measuring delinquency.* Beverly Hills, CA: Sage.

Hinkle, S., & Brown, R. (1990). Intergroup comparisons and social identity: Some links and lacunae. In D. Abrams & M. A. Hogg (Eds.), *Social identity theory.* New York: Springer-Verlag.

Hinton, K., & Margerum, B. J. (1984). Adolescent attitudes and values concerning used clothing. *Adolescence, 19*, 397–402.

Hirschi, T. (1969). *Causes of delinquency.* Berkeley: University of California Press.

Hispanic Policy Development Project. (1987). *The Research Bulletin, 1*, 1–12.

Hispanics least educated, lowest paid of all major U.S. population groups. (1986). *Phi Delta Kappan, 67*, 474–475.

Hoch, P. (1980). School for sexism. In D. F. Sabo & R. Runfola (Eds.), *Jock: Sports and male identity.* Englewood Cliffs, NJ: Prentice-Hall.

Hodgkinson, H. (1979). What's right with education. *Phi Delta Kappan, 61*, 159–162.

Hodgkinson, H. L. (1989). *The same client.* Washington, DC: Institute for Educational Policy.

Hodgson, J. W., & Fischer, J. L. (1979). Sex differences in identity and intimacy development in college youth. *Journal of Youth and Adolescence, 8*, 37–50.

Hoelter, J. W. (1979). Religiosity, fear of death, and suicide acceptability. *Suicide and Life-threatening Behavior, 9*,(3), 163–171.

Hoffman, M. A., Ushpiz, V., & Levy-Shiff, R. (1988). Social support and self-esteem in adolescence. *Journal of Youth and Adolescence, 17*, 307–316.

Hogan, R. (1973). Moral conduct and moral character: A psychological perspective. *Psychological Bulletin, 79*, 217–232.

Hoge, D. R., Petrills, G. H., & Smith, E. (1982). Transmission of religious and social values from parents to teenage children. *Journal of Marriage and the Family, 43*, 569–579.

Holden, C. (1987). Is alcoholism treatment effective? *Science, 236*, 20–22.

Holden, C. (1989). Flipping the main switch in the central reward system. *Science, 248*, 246–247.

Holden, C. (1991). Depression: The news isn't depressing. *Science, 254,* 1450–1452.

Holden, C. (1992). Twin studies link genes to homosexuality. *Science, 225,* 33.

Holden, N. L., & Robinson, P. H. (1988). Anorexia nervosa and bulimia nervosa in British Blacks. *British Journal of Psychiatry, 152,* 544–549.

Holinger, P. C. (1978). Adolescent suicide: An epidemiological study of recent trends. *American Journal of Psychiatry, 135,* 754–756.

Holinger, P. C. (1979). Violent deaths among the young: Recent trends in suicide, homicide, and accidents. *American Journal of Psychiatry, 136,* 1144–1147.

Holinger, P. C., & Offer, D. (1982). Prediction of adolescent suicide: A population model. *American Journal of Psychiatry, 139*(3): 302–307.

Holinger, P. C., & Offer, D. (1989). Sociodemographic, epidemiologic, and individual attributes. In ADAMHA. *Report of the secretary's task force on youth suicide: Vol. 2: Risk factors for youth suicide.* U.S. Department of Health and Human Services publication # ADM 89-1622. Washington, DC: U.S. Government Printing Office.

Hollinger, C. L., & Fleming, C. S. (1985). Social orientation and the social self-esteem of gifted and talented female adolescents. *Journal of Youth and Adolescence, 14,* 389–399.

Hollister, W. G. (1977). The management of primary prevention programs. In D. C. Klein & S. E. Goldston (Eds.), *Primary prevention: An idea whose time has come* (National Institute of Mental Health, DHEW Publication # ADM 77-447), Washington, DC: U.S. Government Printing Office.

Holstein, C. B. (1976). Irreversible stepwise sequence in the development of moral judgment: A longitudinal study of males and females. *Child Developent, 47,* 51–61.

Holt, J. (1976). *Instead of Education.* New York: Dutton.

Holt, R. R. (1980). Loevinger's measure of ego development: Reliability and national norms for male and female short forms. *Journal of Personality and Social Psychology, 39,* 909–920.

Hopkins, R. (1977). Sexual behavior in adolescence. *Journal of Social Issues, 33*(2), 67–84.

Hornick, J. P., Doran, L., & Crawford, S. H. (1979). Premarital contraceptives usage among male and female adolescents. *Family Coordinator, 28,* 181–190.

Horwitz, S. M., Klerman, L. V., & Jekel, J. F. (1991). School-age mothers: Predictors of long-term educational and economic outcomes. *Pediatrics, 87,* 862–868.

Howard, M. P., & Anderson, R. J. (1978). Early identification of potential school dropouts: A literature review. *Child Welfare, 57,* 221–231.

Howat, P. A., Rubinson, L. G., & O'Rourke, T. W. (1979). Trends in sexual attitudes and behavior among selected college students. *Journal of Sex Education and Theory, 1*(6), 78–83.

Howat, P. M., & Saxton, A. M. (1988). The incidence of bulimic behavior in a secondary and university school population. *Journal of Youth and Adolescence, 17,* 221–232.

Hsu, J., Tseng, W. S., Ashton, G., McDermott, J. F., & Char, W. (1985). Adolescent development and minority perspectives. *American Journal of Psychiatry, 142,* 577–581.

Hsu, L. K. G. (1980). Outcome of anorexia nervosa. *Archives of General Psychiatry, 37,* 1041–1046.

Huang, L. N., & Ying Y. (1989). Chinese American children and adolescents. In J. T. Gibbs & L. N. Huang (Eds.), *Children of color.* San Francisco: Jossey-Bass.

Hudgins, W., & Prentice, N. M. (1973). Moral judgment in delinquent and non-delinquent adolescents and their mothers. *Journal of Abnormal Psychology, 82,* 145–151.

Huff, C. R. (Ed.). (1990). *Gangs in America.* Newbury Park, CA: Sage.

Huffine, C. L. (1989). Social and cultural risk factors for youth suicide. In ADAMHA. *Report of the secretary's task force on youth suicide: Vol. 2: Risk factors for youth suicide.* (U.S. Department of Health and Human Services publication # ADM 89-1622.) Washington, DC: U.S. Government Printing Office.

Hughes, J. R. (1990). Nicotine abstinence effects. In L. S. Harris (Ed.), *Problems of drug dependence: 1989.* (U.S. Department of Health and Human Services publication # ADM 90-1663.) Washington, DC: U.S. Government Printing Office.

Hultkrantz, A. (1980). *The religions of the American Indians.* Berkeley: University of California Press.

Humm-Delgado, D., & Delgado, M. (1983). Hispanic adolescents and substance abuse: Issues for the 1980s. In R. Isralowitz & M. Singer (Eds.), *Adolescent substance abuse.* New York: Haworth Press.

Hundleby, J. D., & Mercer, G. W. (1987). Family and friends as social environments and their relationship to young adolescents' use of alcohol, tobacco, and marijuana. *Journal of Marriage and the Family, 49,* 151–164.

Hunter, F. T. (1985). Individual adolescents' perceptions of interactions with friends and parents. *Journal of Early Adolescence, 5*(3), 295–305.

Huston, A. C. (1983). Sex-typing. In E. M. Hetherington (Ed.), *Handbook of child psychology.* New York: Wiley.

Huston, A. C., & Alvarez, M. (1990). The socialization context of gender role development in early adolescence. In R. Montemayor, G. R. Adams, & T. P. Gullotta (Eds.), *From childhood to adolescence: A transitional period? Vol. 2: Advances in Adolescent Development.* Newbury Park, CA: Sage.

Hutchison, R. (1987). Ethnicity and urban recreation: Whites, Blacks, and Hispanics in Chicago's public parks. *Journal of Leisure Research, 19,* 205–222.

Hyde, J. S., Krajnik, M., & Skuldt-Niederberger, K. (1991). Androgyny across the life span: A replication and longitudinal follow-up. *Developmental Psychology, 27,* 516–519.

Hyde, J. S., & Phillis, D. E. (1979). Androgyny across the life span. *Development Psychology, 15,* 334–336.

Hyman, H., Wright, E., & Reed, J. S. (1975). *The enduring effects of education.* Chicago: University of Chicago Press.

Iacovetta, R. G. (1975). Adolescent-adult interaction and peer group involvement. *Adolescence, 10,* 325–336.

Ianni, F. A., & Reuss-Ianni, E. (1980). School violence. *Today's Education, 4,* 20G–23G.

Ickes, W., & Barnes, R. D. (1979). Boys and girls together—and alienated: On enacting stereotyped sex roles in mixed-sex dyads. *Journal of Personality and Social Psychology, 36,* 669–683.

Iga, M. (1981). Suicide of Japanese youth. *Suicide and Life-Threatening Behavior, 11*(1), 17–30.

Iheanacho, S. O. (1988). Minority self-concept: A research review. *Journal of Instructional Psychology, 15,* 3–11.

Ihle, R. (1981). This Pulitzer Prize winner moves beyond the scope of traditional education history. *Phi Delta Kappan, 62,* 749–750.

Illich, I. (1970). *Deschooling society.* New York: Harper & Row.

Inamdar, S. C., Lewis, D. O., Siomopoulos, G., Shanok, S. S., & Lamela, M. (1982). Violent and suicidal behavior in psychotic adolescents. *American Journal of Psychiatry, 139*(7), 932–935.

Inglis, B. (1975). *The forbidden game: A social history of drugs.* New York: Scribner's.

Inhelder, B., & Piaget J. (1958). *The growth of logical thinking from childhood to adolescence.* New York: Basic Books.

Inselberg, R. M. (1961). Marital problems and satisfaction in high school marriages. *Marriage and Family Living, 53,* 766–772.

Institute for Social Research. (1992). *Monitoring the future.* Ann Arbor, MI: Author.

Irwin, C. E., Jr. (1987). *Adolescent social behavior and health.* In W. Damon (Ed.), *New Directions for Child Development* (Vol. 37), 1–12. San Francisco: Jossey-Bass.

Isberg, R. S., Houser, S. T., Jacobson, A. M., Powers, S. I., Noam, G., Weiss-Perry, B., & Follansbee, D. (1989). Parental contexts of adolescent self-esteem; a developmental perspective. *Journal of Youth and Adolescence, 18,* 1–23.

Iso-Aloha, S., & Hatfield, B. (1986). *Psychology of sports: A social psychology approach.* Dubuque, IA: William C. Brown.

Jackson, D. (1975). The meaning of dating from the role perspective of nondating pre-adolescents. *Adolescence, 10,* 123–125.

Jackson, D., & Huston, T. L. (1975). Physical attractiveness and assertiveness. *Journal of Social Psychology, 96,* 79–84.

Jackson, S. W. (1987). *Melancholia and depression: From hippocratic times to modern times.* New Haven, CT: Yale University Press.

Jacobson, A. M., Hauser, S. T., Powers, S., & Noam, G. (1984). The influences of chronic illness and ego development on self-esteem in diabetic and psychiatric adolescent patients. *Journal of Youth and Adolescence, 13,* 489–507.

Jaffe, J. H. (1979). The swinging pendulum: The treatment of drug users in America. In R. Dupont, A. Goldstein, & J. O'Donnell (Eds.), *Handbook on drug abuse.* Washington, DC: U.S. Government Printing Office.

Janis, I. L., & Mann, L. (1977). *Decision making: A psychological analysis of conflict, choice and commitment.* New York: Free Press.

Janus, M. D., McCormack, A., Burgess, A. W., & Hartman, C. (1987). *Adolescent runaways: Causes and consequences.* Lexington, MA: Lexington Books.

Jarvik, M. E. (1990). The drug dilemma: Manipulating the demand. *Science, 250,* 387–392.

Jason, L. A., Kurasaki, K. S., Neuson, L., & Garcia, C. (1993). Training parents in a preventive intervention for transfer children. *Journal of Primary Prevention, 13,* 213–227.

Jencks, C. S., & Brown, M. D. (1975). Effects of high schools on their students. *Harvard Educational Review, 45,* 273–324.

Jencks, C. S., Smith, M., Acland, H., Bane, M. J., Cohen, D., Gintis, H., Heyns, B., & Michelson, S. (1972). *Inequality: A reassessment of the effect of family and schooling in America.* New York: Basic Books.

Jenkins, R. L., & Hewitt, L. (1944). Types of personality structure encountered in child guidance clinics. *American Journal of Orthopsychiatry, 14,* 84–94.

Jensen, A. R. (1969). How much can we boost IQ and scholastic achievement? *Harvard Educational Review, 39,* 1–123.

Jessop, D. J. (1981). Family relationships as viewed by parents and adolescents: A specification. *Journal of Marriage and the Family, 43,* 95–108.

Jessor, R. (1979). Marijuana: A review of recent psychosocial research. In R. Dupont, A. Goldstein, & J. O'Donnell (Eds.), *Handbook on drug abuse.* Washington, DC: U.S. Government Printing Office.

Jessor, R. (1993). Successful adolescent development among youth in high-risk settings. *American Psychologist, 48,* 117–126.

Jessor, R., Chase, J. A., & Donovan, J. E. (1980). Psychosocial correlates of marijuana use and perhaps drinking in a national sample of adolescents. *American Journal of Public Health, 70,* 604–612.

Jessor, R., Costa, F., Jessor, L., & Donovan, J. E. (1983). Time of first intercourse: A prospective study. *Journal of Personality and Social Psychology, 44,* 608–626.

Jessor, S. L., & Jessor, R. (1975). Transition from virginity to non-virginity among youth: A social-psychological study over time. *Developmental Psychology, 11,* 473–484.

Johnson, B. D., Williams, T., Sanabria, H., Dci, K. (1990). Social impact of crack dealing in the inner city. In L. S. Harris (Ed.), *Problems of drug dependence: 1989,* DHHS publication # ADM 90-1663.

Johnson, C., & Flach, A. (1985). Family characteristics of 105 patients with bulimia. *American Journal of Psychiatry, 142,* 1321–1324.

Johnson, C., Lewis, C., & Hagman, J. (1984). The syndrome of bulimia. *Psychiatric Clinics of North America, 7,* 247–273.

Johnson, C., Lewis, C., Love., S., Lewis, L., & Stuckey, M. (1984). Incidence and correlates of bulimic behavior in a female high school population. *Journal of Youth and Adolescence, 13,* 15–26.

Johnson, C., & Maddi, K. L. (1986). Factors that affect the onset of bulimia. *Seminars in Adolescent Medicine, 2,* 11–19.

Johnson, C. A., Pentz, M. A., Weber, M. D., Dwyer, J. H., Baer, N., Mackinnon, D. P., Hanson, W. B., & Flay, B. R. (1990). Relative effectiveness of comprehensive community programming for drug abuse prevention with high-risk and low-risk adolescents. *Journal of Consulting and Clinical Psychology, 58,* 447–456.

Johnson, G. M., Shontz, F. C., & Locue, T. P. (1984). Relationship between adolescent drug use and parental drug behaviors. *Adolescence, 19*(74), 295–299.

Johnson, R. (1972). *Aggression in man and animals.* Philadelphia: Saunders.

Johnson, R. E. (1986). Family structure and delinquency: General patterns and gender differences. *Criminology, 24,* 65–80.

Johnston, L. D., O'Malley, P. M., & Bachman, J. G. (1987). *National trends in drug use and related factors among American high school students and young adults, 1975–1986* (DHHS Publication # ADM 87-1535). Washington, DC: U.S. Government Printing Office.

Johnston, L. D., O'Malley, P. M., & Bachman, J. G. (1988, January 13). University of Michigan national news conference, Washington, DC.

Johnston, L. D., O'Malley, P. M., & Bachman, J. G. (1991). *Drug use among American high school seniors, college students and young adults, 1975–1990.* National Institute on Drug Abuse, (U.S. Department of Health and Human Services publication # ADM 91-1813.) Washington, DC: U.S. Government Printing Office.

Jones, A. (1973). Personality and value differences related to the use of LSD-25. *International Journal of the Addictions, 8,* 549–557.

Jones, H. (1949). Adolescence in our society. In *The family in a democratic society.* New York: Columbia University Press.

Jones, M. C. (1965). Psychological correlates of somatic development. *Child Development, 36,* 899–911.

Jones, M. C. (1968). Personality correlates and antecedents in drinking patterns in males. *Journal of Clinical and Consulting Psychology, 32,* 2–12.

Jones, M. C., & Bayley, N. (1950). Physical maturing among boys as related to behavior. *Journal of Educational Psychology, 41,* 129–148.

Jones, R. M. (1992). Ego identity and adolescent problem behavior. In G. R. Adams, T. P. Gullotta, & R. Montemayor (Eds.), *Identity formation during adolescence, Vol. 4: Advances in adolescent development.* Newbury Park, CA: Sage.

Jones, R. T. (1980). Human effects: An overview. In R. C. Petersen (Ed.), *Research 31: Marijuana Research Findings* (NIDA, DHHS Publication # ADM 80-1001). Washington, DC: U.S. Government Printing Office.

Jones, R. T. (1987). The pharmacology of cocaine. In J. Grabowski (Ed.), *Cocaine: Pharmacology, effects, and treatment of abuse.* (U.S. Department of Health and Human Services publication # ADM 87-1326.) Washington, DC: U.S. Government Printing Office.

Jones, R. T. (1990). The pharmacology of cocaine smoking in humans. In C. N. Chiang, & R. L. Hawks (Eds.), *Research findings on smoking abused substances.* (DHHS publication # ADM 90–1690.) Washington, DC: U.S. Government Printing Office.

Jorgensen, S. R. (1993). Adolescent pregnancy and parenting. In T. P. Gullotta, G. R. Adams, & R. Montemayor (Eds.), *Adolescent sexuality.* Newbury Park, CA: Sage.

Jorgensen, S. R., & Alexander, S. (1981). Reducing the risk of adolescent pregnancy: Toward certification of family life education. *High School Journal, 64*(6), 257–268.

Jorgensen, S. R., King, S. L., & Torrey, R. A. (1980). Dyadic and social network influences on adolescent exposure to pregnancy risk. *Journal of Marriage and the Family, 42*(1), 141–155.

Josselson, R. (1982). Personality structure and identity status in women as viewed through early memories. *Journal of Youth and Adolescence, 11,* 293–299.

Joselson, R. (1987). *Finding herself: Pathways to identity development in women.* San Francisco: Jossey-Bass.

Jurich, A., & Jurich, J. (1974). The effect of cognitive moral development upon the selection of premarital sexual standards. *Journal of Marriage and the Family, 36,* 736–741.

Jurich, A. P., Polson, C. J., Jurich, J. A., & Bates, R. A. (1985). Family factors in the lives of drug users and abusers. *Adolescence, 20,* 143–160.

Jurkovic, G. J., & Prentice, N. M (1977). The relation of moral and cognitive development to dimensions of juvenile delinquency. *Journal of Abnormal Psychology, 26,* 414–420.

Kacergius, M. A., & Adams, G. R. (1980). Erikson stage resolution: The relationship between identity and intimacy. *Journal of Youth and Adolescence, 9,* 117–126.

Kagan, D. M., & Squires, R. L. (1984). Eating disorders among adolescents: Patterns and prevalence. *Adolescence, 19,* 15–29.

Kagan, J. S. (1969). Inadequate evidence and illogical conclusions. *Harvard Educational Review, 39,* 274–277.

Kahle, L. R., Kulka, R. A., & Klingel, D. M. (1980). Low adolescent self-esteem leads to multiple interpersonal problems: A test of social adaptation theory. *Journal of Personality and Social Psychology, 39,* 496–502.

Kahn, J. H., & Nursten, J. P. (1962). School refusal: A comprehensive view of school phobia and other failures of school attendance. *American Journal of Orthopsychiatry, 32,* 707–718.

Kahn, S., Zimmerman, G., Csikszentmihali, M. K., & Getzels, J. W. (1985). Relations between identity in young adulthood and intimacy at midlife. *Journal of Personality and Social Psychology, 49,* 1316–1322.

Kalliopuska, M. (1982). Body-image disturbances in patients with anorexia nervosa. *Psychological Reports, 51,* 715–722.

Kalter, N. (1977). Children of divorce in an outpatient psychiatric population. *American Journal of Orthopsychiatry, 47,* 40–51.

Kamptner, N. L. (1988). Identity development in late adolescence: Casual modelling of social and familial influences. *Journal of Youth and Adolescence, 17,* 493–514.

Kandel, D. B. (1973). Adolescent marijuana use: Role of parents and peers. *Science, 181,* 1067–1070.

Kandel, D. B. (1974). Inter- and intra-generational influences on adolescent marijuana use. *Journal of Social Issues, 50,* 107–135.

Kandel, D. B. (1981a). Drug use by youth: An overview. In D. J. Lettieri & J. P. Lundford (Eds.), *Drug abuse and the American adolescent* (NIDA Research Monograph No. 38, # ADM 81-1166), 1–24. Washington, DC: U.S. Government Printing Office.

Kandel, D. B. (1981b, April). *Peer influences in Adolescence.* Paper presented at the meeting of the Society for Research in Child Development, Boston.

Kandel, D. B. (1990). Parenting styles, drug use, and children's adjustment in families of young adults. *Journal of Marriage and the Family, 52,* 183–196.

Kandel, D. B., & Faust, R. (1975). Sequence and stages in patterns of adolescent drug use. *Archives of General Psychiatry, 32,* 923–932.

Kandel, D. B., Kessler, R., & Margulies, R. (1978). Adolescent initiation into stages of drug use: A developmental analysis. In D. B. Kandel (Ed.), *Longitudinal research on drug use: Empirical findings and methodological issues.* Washington, DC: Hemisphere-Wiley.

Kandel, D. B., Treiman, D., Faust, R., & Single, E. (1986). Adolescent involvement in legal and illegal drug use: A multiple classification analysis. *Social Forces, 55,* 438–458.

Kane, F. J., Moan, C. A., & Bolling, B. (1974). Motivational factors in pregnant adolescents. *Diseases of the Nervous System, 34*(3), 131–134.

Kanki, P. J., Alroy, J., Essex, M. (1985). Isolation of T-lymphotropic retrovirus related to HtLV-III/LAV from wild-caught African green monkeys. *Science, 230,* 951–954.

Kanter, J. F., & Zelnick, M. (1972). Sexual experience of young unmarried women in the United States. *Family Planning Perspectives, 4,* 9–18.

Kanter, J. F., & Zelnick, M. (1973). Contraception and pregnancy: Experience of young unmarried women in the United States. *Family Planning Perspectives, 5,* 21–35.

Karplus, R. (1981). Education and formal thought—a modest proposal. In I. Siegel, D. Brodzinsky, & R. Golinkoff (Eds.), *Piagetian theory and research: New directions and applications.* Hillsdale, NJ: Erlbaum.

Katz, D. L., & Pope, H. G. (1990). Anabolic-androgenic steroid-induced mental status changes. In G. C. Lin & L. Erinoff (Eds.), *Anabolic steroid abuse.* (U.S. Department of Health and Human Services publication # ADM 91-1720.) Washington, DC: U.S. Government Printing Office.

Katz, M. B. (1973). *Education in American history.* New York: Praeger.

Katz, M. B. (1975). *Class, bureaucrocacy, and schools: The illusion of educational change in America.* New York: Praeger.

Kaufman, J. E., & Rosenbaum, J. E. (1992). The education and employment of low-income Black youth in White suburbs. *Educational Evaluation and Policy Analysis, 14,* 229–240.

Kazdin, A. E. (1987). Treatment of antisocial behavior in children: Current status and future directions. *Psychological Bulletin, 102,* 187–203.

Keating, C. F. (1985). Gender and the physiognomy of dominance and attractiveness. *Social Psychology Quarterly, 48,* 61–70.

Keating, D. (1990). Adolescent thinking. In S. S. Feldman & G. R. Elliott (Eds.), *At the threshold: The developing adolescent.* Cambridge, MA: Harvard University Press.

Keating, D. P. (1980). Thinking processes in adolescence. In J. Adelson (Ed.), *Handbook of adolescent psychology.* New York: Wiley.

Keating, D. P. (1975). Precocious cognitive development at the level of formal operations. *Child Development, 46,* 276–280.

Kendrick, D. T., & Cialdini, R. B. (1977). Romantic attraction: Misattribution versus reinforcement explanations. *Journal of Personality and Social Psychology, 35,* 381–391.

Kensiton, K. (1970). *Youth and dissent.* New York: Harcourt Brace Jovanovich.

Keniston, K. (1977). *All our children.* New York: Harcourt Brace Jovanovich.

Kenkel, N., & Gage, B. A. (1983). The restricted and gender-typed occupational aspirations of young women: Can they be modified? *Family Relations, 32,* 129–138.

Kenney, A. M. (1987). Teen pregnancy: An issue for schools. *Phi Delta Kappan, 68,* 728–736.

Kent, M. O. (1980). Remarriage: A family system perspective. *Social Caseworks, 61,* 146–153.

Kerfoot, M. (1980). The family context of adolescent suicidal behavior. *Journal of Adolescence, 3,* 335–346.

Kessler, M., & Albee, G. W. (1977). An overview of the literature of primary prevention. In G. W. Albee & J. M. Jaffe (Eds.), *Primary prevention of psychopathology: Vol. 1. The issues.* Hanover, NH: University Press of New England.

Kessler, R. C., & McRae, J. A. (1982). The effect of wives' employment on the mental health of married men and women. *American Sociological Review, 47,* 216–227.

Kett, J. F. (1977). *Rites of passage: Adolescence in America 1790 to the present.* New York: Basic Books.

Ketterlinus, R. D., Lamb, M. E., & Nitz, K. (1991). Developmental and ecological sources of stress among adolescent parents. *Family Relations, 40,* 435–441.

Kinch, J. W. (1962). Self-conceptions of types of delinquents. *Sociological Inquiry, 32,* 228–234.

King, P. (1988). Heavy metal music and drug abuse in adolescence. *Postgraduate Medicine, 83,* 295–301, 304.

Kinsey, A., Pomeroy, W., & Martin, C. (1948). *Sexual behavior of the human male.* Philadelphia: Saunders.

Kinsey, A., Pomeroy, W., Martin, C., & Gebhard, P. (1953). *Sexual behavior of the human female.* Philadelphia: Saunders.

Kirst, M. W. (1991). The need to broaden our perspective concerning American educational attainment. *Phi Delta Kappan, 73,* 118–120.

Kishton, J., Starrett, R. H., & Lucas, J. L. (1984). Polar versus milestone variables in adolescent ego development. *Journal of Early Adolescence, 4,* 53–64.

Kitchener, K. S., King, P. M., Davison, M. L., Parker, C. A., & Wood, P. K. (1984). A longitudinal study of moral and ego development in young adults. *Journal of Youth and Adolescence, 13* 197–211.

Kleck, R. E. (1975). Issues in social effectiveness: The case of the mentally retarded. In M. J. Begab & S. A. Richardson (Eds.), *The mentally retarded and society.* Baltimore: University Park Press.

Klein, D. C., & Goldston, S. E. (Eds.). (1977). *Primary prevention: An idea whose time has come* (National Institute of Mental Health, DHEW Publication # ADM 77-447). Washington, DC: U.S. Government Printing Office.

Klein, M. M., & Shulman, S. (1981). Adolescent masculinity-femininity in relation to parental models of masculinity-femininity and marital adjustment. *Adolescence, 16,* 45–48.

Klein, S., Petersilia, J., & Turner, S. (1990). Race and imprisonment decisions in California. *Science, 247,* 812–816.

Klitzner, M., & Blasinsky, M. (1990). Substance abuse and suicide. In M. J. Rotherham-Borus, J. Bradley, & N. Obolensky (Eds.), *Planning to live.* Tulsa, OK: National Resource Center for Youth Services.

Knees, D. (1983). Clothing deprivation feelings of three adolescent ethnic groups. *Adolescence, 28,* 659–674.

Knox, D., & Wilson, K. (1981). Dating behaviors of university students. *Family Relations, 30,* 255–258.

Kochakian, C. D. (1990). History of anabolic steroids. In G. C. Lin & L. Erinoff (Eds.), *Anabolic steroid abuse.* (U.S. Department of Health and Human Services publication # ADM 91-1720.) Washington, DC: U.S. Government Printng Office.

Koester, A. W., & May, J. K. (1985). Profiles of adolescents' clothing practices: Purchase, daily selection, and care. *Adolescence, 20*(77), 97–113.

Koff, E., Rierdan, J., & Jacobson, S. (1981). The personal and interpersonal significance of menarche. *Journal of the American Academy of Child Psychiatry, 20,* 148–158.

Koff, E., Rierdan, J., & Silverstone, E. (1978). Changes in representation of body image as a function of menarcheal status. *Developmental Psychology, 14,* 635–642.

Kohlberg, L. (1969). Stage and sequence: The cognitive-developmental approach to socialization. In D. A. Goslin (Ed.), *Handbook of socialization theory and research.* Chicago: Rand McNally.

Kolata, G. (1986). New drug counters alcohol intoxication. *Science, 234,* 1198–1199.

Kolata, G. (1987a). Clinical trials planned for new AIDS drug. *Science, 235,* 1138–1139.

Kolata, G. (1987b). Manic depressive gene tied to chromosome 11. *Science, 235,* 1139–1140.

Kompara, D. R. (1980). Difficulties in the socialization process of stepparenting. *Family Relations, 29,* 69–73.

Koop, C. E. (1987). Surgeon general's report on acquired immune deficiency syndrome. *Public Health Reports, 102,* 1–2.

Kozel, N. J., & Adams, E. H. (1986). Epidemiology of drug abuse: An overview. *Science, 234,* 970–974.

Kraine, M., Cannon, D., & Bagford, J. (1977). Rating-dating of simple prestige homogamy? Data on dating in the Greek system on a Midwestern campus. *Journal of Marriage and the Family, 39,* 663–674.

Kramer, L. R. (1991). The social construction of ability perceptions: An ethnographic study of gifted adolescent girls. *Journal of Early Adolescence, 11,* 340–362.

Kreidberg, G., Butcher, A. L., & White, K. M. (1978). Vocational role choice in second and sixth grade children. *Sex Roles, 4,* 175–181.

Kreipe, R. E. (1986). Inpatient management of anorexia nervosa and bulimia. *Seminars in Adolescent Medicine, 2,* 27–36.

Kretschmer, E. (1951). *Koperbau und Charakter.* Berlin: Springer.

Kroger, J. (1985). Separation-individuation and ego-identity status in New Zealand University students. *Journal of Youth and Adolescence, 14,* 133–147.

Kroger, J. (1989). *Identity in adolescence.* London: Routledge.

Kroger, J., & Haslett, S. J. (1988). Separation-individual and ego identity status in late adolescence: A two-year longitudinal study. *Journal of Youth and Adolescence, 17,* 59–80.

Kroh, O. (1951). Psychologie der Entwicklung. In *Lexikon der Padagogik* (Vol. 2). Bern: Francke.

Kronholm, W. (1986, May 22). Funds sought to combat venereal disease. *The Day* (New London, CT), A9.

Kuhn, D. (1976a). Relation of two Piagetian stage transitions to IQ. *Developmental Psychology, 12,* 157–161.

Kuhn, D. (1976b). Short-term longitudinal evidence for the sequentiality of Kohlberg's early stages of moral judgment. *Developmental Psychology, 12,* 162–166.

Kuhn, D., & Angelev, J. (1976). An experimental study of the development of formal operational thought. *Child Development, 47,* 696–706.

Kuhn, D., Ho, V., & Adams, C. (1979). Formal reasoning among pre- and late adolescents. *Child Development, 50,* 1128–1135.

Kulin, H. E., & Reiter, E. O (1973). Gonadotropins during childhood and adolescence. A review. *Pediatrics, 51,* 260–271.

Kulka, R. A., & Weingarten, H. (1979). The long-term effects of parental divorce in childhood on adult adjustment. *Journal of Social Issues, 33*(4), 50–78.

Kurdek, L. A. (1981). An integrative perspective on children's divorce adjustment. *American Psychologist, 36,* 856–866.

Kurdek, L. A., Blisk, D., & Siesky, A. E. (1981). Correlates of children's long-term adjustment to their parent's divorce. *Developmental Psychology, 17,* 565–579.

Kurdek, L. A., & Siesky, A. E. (1980a). Effects of divorce on children: The relationship between parent and child perspectives. *Journal of Divorce, 4,* 85–90.

Kurdek, L. A., & Siesky, A. E. (1980b). Sex role self-concepts of single divorced parents and their children. *Journal of Divorce, 3,* 249–261.

Kurtines, W., Hogan, R., & Weiss, D. (1975). Personality dynamics of heroin use. *Journal of Abnormal Psychology, 84,* 87–89.

Kurtz, P. D., Kurtz, G. L., & Jarvis, S. V. (1991). Problems of maltreated runaway youth. *Adolescence, 26,* 543–556.

L. A. has estimated 600 gangs, report says (New York, UPI) (1988, March 13). Reported in *Herald Journal,* Logan, UT, 6.

Lab, S. P. (1984). Patterns in juvenile misbehavior. *Crime and Delinquency, 30,* 293–308.

LaBarre, M. (1968). Pregnancy experiences among married adolescents. *American Journal of Orthopsychiatry, 38,* 47–55.

LaFromboise, T. D., & Bigfoot, D. S. (1988). Cultural and cognitive considerations in the prevention of American Indian adolescent suicide. *Journal of Adolescence, 11* 139–153.

LaFromboise, T. D., & Low, K. G. (1989). American Indian children and adoles-

cents. In J. T. Gibbs & L. N. Huang (Eds.), *Children of color.* San Francisco: Jossey-Bass.

Lamanna, M. A., & Reidmann, A. (1991). *Marriages and families: Making choices and facing change* (4th ed.). Belmont, CA: Wadsworth.

Lamb, R., & Zusman, J. (1979). Drs. Lamb and Zusman reply. *American Journal of Psychiatry, 136,* 1949.

Lambe, L. K. (1982). The impact of sex-role orientation on self-esteem in early adolescence. *Child Development, 53,* 1530–1535.

Lambert, B. G., Rothschild, B. F., Atland, R., & Green, L. B. (1978). *Adolescence: Transition from childhood to maturity.* Monterey, CA: Brooks/Cole.

Lamke, L. K., & Abraham, K. G. (1984, October). *Adolescent identity formation and sex-role development: Critical linkages.* Paper presented at the annual meeting of the National Council on Family Relations, San Francisco.

Lamke, L. K., & Filsinger, E. E. (1983). Parental antecedents of sex role orientation. *Adolescence, 18,* 429–432.

Landers, A. (1980, February 28). Ann Landers says she's changed her mind about premarital sex. *Hartford Courant,* 27.

Landers, S. (1993). Family leave ushers in new era. *NASW News, 3,* 1, 8.

Landis, P. H. (1950). Sequential marriage. *Journal of Home Economics, 42,* 625–628.

Langan, P. A. (1991). America's soaring prison population. *Science, 251,* 1568–1573.

Langner, T., & Michael, S. (1963). *Life stress and mental health.* New York: Free Press.

Langston, D. P. (1983). *Living with herpes.* Garden City, NY: Dolphin Books.

Lapsley, D. K. (1985). Elkind on egocentrism. *Developmental Review, 5,* 227–236.

Lapsley, D. K. (1990). Continuity and discontinuity in adolescent social cognitive development. In R. Montemayor, G. R. Adams, & T. P. Gullotta (Eds.), *From childhood to adolescence: A transitional period?* Newbury Park, CA: Sage.

Lapsley, D. K., Harwell, M. R., Olson, L. M., Flannery, D., & Quintana, S. M. (1984). Moral judgment, personality, and attitude to authority in early and late adolescence. *Journal of Youth and Adolescence, 13,* 527–542.

Lapsley, D., & Murphy, M. (1985). Another look at the theoretical assumptions of adolescent egocentrism. *Developmental Review, 5,* 201–217.

Larrick, N. (1987). Illiteracy starts too soon. *Phi Delta Kappan, 69,* 184–189.

Laub, J. H. (1983). Urbanism, race, and crime. *Journal of Research in Crime and Delinquency, 20,* 183–198.

LaVoie, J. C. (1973). *Some perspectives of adolescence.* Unpublished manuscript, available from the University of Nebraska, Department of Psychology, Omaha, NE 68101.

LaVoie, J. C. (1976). Ego identity formation in middle adolescence. *Journal of Youth and Adolescence, 5,* 371–385.

LaVoie, J. C., & Collins, B. R. (1975). Effect of youth culture music on high school students' academic performance. *Journal of Youth and Adolescence, 4,* 57–65.

Lawrence, F. C., Tasker, G. E., Daly, C. T., Orthiel, A. L., & Wozniak, P. H. (1986). Adolescents' time spent viewing television. *Adolescence, 21,* 431–436.

Laws, J. L., & Schwartz, P. (1977). *Sexual scripts: The social construction of female sexuality.* Hinsdale, IL: Dryden Press.

Leadbeater, B. J., & Dionne, J. (1981). The adolescent's use of formal operational thinking in solving problems related to identity resolution. *Adolescence, 16,* 111–121.

Leahy, R. L., & Eiter, M. (1980). Moral judgment and the development of real and ideal androgynous self-image during adolescence and young adulthood. *Developmental Psychology, 16,* 362–370.

Leahy, R., & Shirk, S. R. (1985). Social cognition and the development of the self. In R. L. Leahy (Ed.), *The development of the self.* New York: Academic Press.

Lech, S., Gary, D., & Ury, H. (1975). Characteristics of heavy users of outpatient prescription drugs. *Clinical Toxology, 8,* 599–610.

Lee, C. C. (1990). Psychology and African Americans: New perspectives for the 1990s. *The Journal of Training & Practice in Professional Psychology, 4,* 36–44.

Lee, J. A. (1977). A typology of styles of loving. *Personality and Social Psychology Bulletin, 3,* 173–182.

Lehman, A. K., & Rodin, J. (1989). Styles of self-nurturance and disordered eating. *Journal of Consulting and Clinical Psychology, 57,* 117–122.

Leibert, R. M., & Sprafkin, J. (1988). *The early window effect of television on children and youth.* (3rd ed.) New York: Pergamon.

Leigh, G. K. (1986). Adolescent involvement in family systems. In G. K. Leigh & G. W. Peterson (Eds.), *Adolescents in families.* Cincinnati: South-Western Publishing Co.

Leigh, G. K., & Peterson, G. W. (Eds.). (1986). *Adolescents in families.* Cincinnati: South-Western Publishing Co.

Lenard, L. (1982, November). The battle to wipe out herpes. *Science Digest,* 36–38.

Lennon, S. J. (1986). Adolescent attitudes toward designer jeans: Further evidence. *Adolescence, 21,* 475–482.

Leonard, C. V. (1967). *Understanding and preventing suicide.* Springfield, IL: Charles C. Thomas.

Leonard, G. B. (1971). *The transformation: A guide to the inevitable changes in humankind.* New York: Delacorte Press.

Leong, F. T. (1986). Counseling and psychotherapy with Asian-Americans: Review of the literature. *Journal of Counseling Psychology, 33,* 196–206.

Lerner, R. M. (1976). *Concepts and theories of human development.* Reading, MA: Addison-Wesley.

Lerner, R. M. (1978). Nature, nurture, and dynamic interactionism. *Human Development, 21,* 1–20.

Lerner, R. M. (1979). A dynamic interaction concept of individual and social relationship development. In R. L. Burgess & T. L. Huston (Eds.), *Social exchange in developing relationships,* New York: Academic Press.

Lerner, R. M. (1985). Adolescent maturational changes and psychosocial development: A dynamic interactional perspective. *Journal of Youth and Adolescence, 14* 355–372.

Lerner, R. M. (1992). Dialectics, developmental contextualism, and the further enhancement of theory about puberty and psychosocial development. *Journal of Early Adolescence, 12,* 366–388.

Lerner, R. M. (1993). Early adolescence: Toward an agenda for the integration of research, policy, and intervention. In R. M. Lerner (Ed.), *Early adolescence: Perspectives on research policy and integration.* Hillsdale, NJ: Erlbaum.

Lerner, R. M., Jovanovic, J., Delaney, M., Hess, L. E., & Von Eye, A. (1988). *Early adolescent physical attractiveness and academic competence.* Unpublished manuscript, Pennsylvania State University, State College, PA.

Lerner, R. M., & Lerner, J. V. (1977). Effects of age, sex, and physical attractiveness on child-peer relations, academic performance, and elementary school adjustment. *Developmental Psychology, 13,* 585–590.

Lerner, R. M., Lerner, J. V., & Tubman, J (1989). Organismic and contextual bases of development in adolescence: A developmental contextual view. In G. R. Adams, R. Montemayor, & T. P. Gullotta (Eds.), *Biology of adolescent behavior and development,* Vol. 1. Newbury Park, CA: Sage.

Lerner, R. M., Orlos, J. B., & Knapp, J. R. (1976). Physical attractiveness, physical effectiveness and self-concept in late adolescence. *Adolescence, 11,* 313–326.

Lerner, S. E., & Burns, R. S. (1979). Phencyclidine use among youth: History, epidemiology, and acute and chronic intoxication. In R. C. Petersen & R. C. Stillman (Eds.), *Phencyclidine abuse: An appraisal* (NIDA research monograph 21, # ADM 79-728). Washington, DC: U.S. Government Printing Office.

Lester, D. (1972). The myth of suicide prevention. *Comparative Psychiatry, 13,* 555–560.

Lester, D. (1991). Social correlates of youth suicide rates in the United States. *Adolescence, 26,* 55–58.

Leukefeld, C. G., & Fimbres, M. (1987). *Responding to AIDS.* Silver Spring, MD: National Association of Social Workers. (1974).

Leukenfeld, C. G., & Haverkos, H. W. (1993). Sexually transmitted diseases. In T. P. Gullotta, G. R. Adams, & R. Montemayor (Eds.), *Advances in adolescent development Vol. 5: Adolescent sexuality.* Newbury Park, CA: Sage.

LeVay, S. (1991). A difference in hypothalamic structure between heterosexual and homosexual men. *Science, 254,* 1034–1037.

Levine, E. S., & Padilla, A. M. (1980). *Cross cultures in therapy: Pluralistic counseling for the Hispanic.* Monterey, CA: Brooks/Cole.

Levinger, G. (1974). A three-level approach to attraction: Toward an understanding of pair relatedness. In T. Huston (Ed.), *Foundations of interpersonal attraction.* New York: Academic Press.

Levinger, G., & Snoek, J. D. (1972). *Attraction in relationships: A new look at interpersonal attraction.* New York: General Learning Press.

Levy, J. E., & Kunitz, S. J. (1987). A suicide prevention program for Hopi youth. *Social Science and Medicine, 25,* 931–940.

Lewin, K. (1935). *A dynamic theory of personality.* New York: McGraw-Hill.

Lewin, K. (1939). Field theory and experiments in social psychology: Concepts and methods. *American Journal of Sociology, 44,* 868–897.

Lewin, K. (1948). *Resolving social conflict.* New York: Harper & Row.

Lewis, A. C. (1986a). Affecting disaffected youths. *Phi Delta Kappan, 67,* 555–556.

Lewis, A. C. (1986b). The search continues for effective schools. *Phi Delta Kappan, 68,* 187–188.

Lewis, D. O., Balla, D. A., & Shanok, S. S. (1979). Some evidence of race bias in the diagnosis and treatment of the juvenile offender. *American Journal of Orthopsychiatry, 49,* 53–61.

Lewis, G. L. (1978). Changes in women's role participation. In I. H. Frieze, J. E. Parsons, P. B. Johnson, D. Ruble, & G. Zellmen (Eds.), *Women and sex roles.* New York: Norton.

Lidz, T. (1963). *The family and human adaptation.* New York: International Universities Press.

Lips, H. M., & Colwill, N. L. (1978). *The psychology of sex differences.* Englewood Cliffs, NJ: Prentice-Hall.

Litovsky, V. G., & Dusek, J. B. (1985). Perceptions of child rearing and self-concept development during the early years of adolescence. *Journal of Youth and Adolescence, 14,* 373–387.

Littrell, M. A., Damhorst, M. L., & Littrell, J. M. (1990). Clothing interests, body satisfaction, and eating behavior of adolescent females: Related or independent dimensions? *Adolescence, 25,* 77–96.

Litwack, L. (1973). Education: Separate and unequal. In M. B. Katz (Ed.), *Education in American History: Reading on the Social Issues.* New York: Praeger.

Lloyd, S. A. (1991). The dark side of courtship: Violence and sexual exploitation. *Family Relations, 40,* 14–20.

Locke, D. (1983). Doing what comes morally: The relation between behavior and stages of moral reasoning. *Human Development, 26,* 11–25.

Loeb, R. (1973). Adolescent groups. *Sociology and Social Research, 58,* 13–22.

Loeber, R. (1982). The stability of antisocial and delinquent child behavior: A review. *Child Development, 53,* 1431–1446.

Loevinger, J. (1976). *Ego development.* San Francisco: Jossey-Bass.

Logan, D. D. (1980). The menarche experience in twenty-three foreign countries. *Adolescence, 15,* 247–256.

Logan, D. D., Calder, J. A., & Cohen, B. L. (1980). Toward a contemporary tradition for menarche. *Journal of Youth and Adolescence, 9,* 263–269.

Logan, R. D. (1978). Identity diffusion and psychosocial defense mechanisms. *Adolescence, 13,* 503–508.

Lombardo, J. A. (1990). Anabolic-androgenic studies. In G. C. Lin & L. Erinoff (Eds.), *Anabolic steroid abuse.* (U.S. Department of Health and Human Services publication # ADM 91-1720.) Washington, DC: U.S. Government Printing Office.

Long, B. H. (1986). Parental discord vs. family structure: Effects of divorce on the self-esteem of daughters. *Journal of Youth and Adolescence, 15,* 19–27.

Long, N., Forehand, R., Fauber, R., & Brody, G. H. (1987). Self-perceived and independently observed competence of young adolescents as a function of parental marital conflict and recent divorce. *Journal of Abnormal Child Psychology, 15,* 15–27.

Looft, W. R., Adams, G. R., Higgins-Trenk, A., & Svoboda, C. P. (1975). *Toward a history of life span developmental psychology.* Unpublished manuscript available from G. Adams, Department of Family and Human Development, Utah State University, Logan, UT 84322.

Lorenzi, M. E., Klerman, L. V., & Jekel, J. F. (1972). School-age parents: How permanent a relationship? *Adolescence, 12,* 13–22.

Lorr, M., & Manning, T. T. (1978). Measurement of ego development by sentence completion and personality test. *Journal of Clinical Psychology, 34,* 354–360.

Louden, D. M. (1980). A comparative study of self-esteem among minority group adolescents in Britain. *Journal of Adolescence, 3,* 17–34.

Lowe, C S., & Radius, S. M. (1987). Young adults' contraceptive practices: An investigation of influences. *Adolescence, 22,* 291–304.

Lucas, A. R. (1986). Anorexia nervosa: Historical background and biopsychosocial determinants. *Seminars in Adolescent Medicine, 2,* 1–9.

Luepnitz, D. A. (1979). Which aspects of divorce affect children? *Family Coordinator, 28,* 79–85.

Lueptow, L. B. (1981). Sex-typing and change in the occupational choices of high school seniors: 1964–1976. *Sociology of Education, 54,* 16–24.

Lui, K., Darrow, W. W., & Rutherford, G. W. (1988). A model-based estimate of the mean incubation period for AIDS in homosexual men. *Science, 240,* 1333–1335.

Lumiere, R., & Cook, S. (1983). *Healthy sex.* New York: Simon & Schuster.

Lundman, R. J. (1984). *Prevention and control of juvenile delinquency.* New York: Oxford University Press.

Lundy, J. R. (1972). Some personality correlates of contraceptive use among unmarried female college students. *Journal of Psychology, 80,* 9–14.

Luthar, S. A., & Zigler, E. (1991). Vulnerability and competence: A review of research on resilience in childhood. *American Journal of Orthopsychiatry, 61,* 6–22.

Lutz, P. (1983). The stepfamily: An adolescent perspective. *Family Relations, 32,* 367–375.

Lyman, H. M., Fenger, C., Jones, H. W., & Belfield, W. T. (1887). *The practical home physician.* Albany, NY: Shelleck, Ross.

Maccoby, E., & Jacklin, C. N. (1974). *The psychology of sex differences.* Stanford, CA: Stanford University Press.

Maccoby, E. E. (1990). Gender and relationships: A developmental account. *American Psychologist, 45,* 513–520.

Macdonald, D. I. (1987, fall). Suicide among youth (ages 15–24). *ADMHA Update* (mimeograph). Washington, DC: U.S. Government, Alcohol, Drugs Abuse and Mental Health Administration.

Maddi, S. R. (1968). *Personality theories: A comparative analysis.* Homewood, IL: Dorsey Press.

Magnusson, D., & Allen, V. L. (1983). *Human development: An interactional perspective.* New York: Academic Press.

Magnusson, D., Stattin, H., & Allen, V. L. (1985). Biological maturation and social development: A longitudinal study of some adjustment processes from mid-adolescence to adulthood.

Journal of Youth and Adolescence, 14, 267–284.

Maier, H. W. (1965). *Three theories of child development.* New York: Harper & Row.

Mallory, M. E. (1989). Q-sort definition of ego identity status. *Journal of Youth and Adolescence, 18,* 399–412.

Manaster, G. J., Saddler, C. D., & Wukasch, L. (1977). The ideal self and cognitive development in adolescence. *Adolescence, 12,* 547–558.

Mann, B. J., & Bourduin, C. M. (1991). A critical review of psychotherapy outcome studies with adolescents: 1978–1988. *Adolescence, 26,* 505–541.

Mann, L. (1985). Decision making. In N. T. Feather (Ed.), *Australian psychology: Review of research.* Sydney: Allen & Unwin.

Mannarino, A. P., & Marsh, M. E. (1978). The relationship between sex role identification and juvenile delinquency in adolescent girls. *Adolescence, 13,* 643–651.

Marcia, J. (1966). Development and validation of ego-identity status. *Journal of Personality and Social Psychology, 3,* 551–558.

Marcia, J. (1976). Identity six years after: A follow-up study. *Journal of Youth and Adolescence, 5,* 145–160.

Marcia, J. E. (1980). Identity in adolescence. In J. Adelson (Ed.), *Handbook of adolescent psychology.* New York: Wiley.

Marcy, P. T. (1981). Factors affecting the fecundity and fertility of historical populations: A review. *Journal of Family History, 6,* 329–336.

Maresh, C. M. (1992). Parents' behavior disgraces school sports events. *Hartford Courant* (January 19), C3.

Margolin, L., Blyth, D. A., & Carbone, D. (1988). The family as a looking glass: Interpreting family influences on adolescent self-esteem from a symbolic interaction perspective. *Journal of Early Adolescence, 8,* 211–224.

Mark, V. H., Sweet, W. H., & Ervin, F. R. (1967). The role of brain disease in riots and urban violence. *Journal of the American Medical Association, 201,* 895.

Markstrom-Adams, C. (1989). Androgyny and its relation to adolescent psychosocial well-being: A review of the literature. *Sex Roles, 21,* 325–340.

Markstrom-Adams, C. (1991). Attitudes on dating, courtship and marriage: Perspectives on in-group versus out-group

relationships by religious minority and majority adolescents. *Family Relations, 40,* 91–96.

Markstrom-Adams, C. (1991, April). Issues related to the design of research, data collection, and data interpretation among North American Indians. In C. Markstrom-Adams, *Methodological considerations in conducting research among ethnic minority children and adolescents.* Symposium conducted at the biennial meetings of the Society for Research in Child Development, Seattle.

Markstrom-Adams, C. (1992). A consideration of intervening factors in adolescent identity formation. In G. R. Adams, T. P. Gullotta, & R. Montemayor (Eds.), *Identity formation during adolescence, Vol. 4: Advances in adolescent development.* Newbury Park, CA: Sage.

Markstrom-Adams, C., & Adams, G. R. *Ethnic group, maturational rate differences, and gender in passive-active psychosocial functioning during middle adolescence.* Unpublished manuscript. University of Guelph, Guelph, Canada.

Markus, H., & Kunda, Z. (1986). Stability and malleability of the self-concept. *Journal of Personality and Social Psychology, 51,* 858–866.

Marotz-Baden, R., Adams, G. R., Bueche, N., Munro, B., & Munro, G. (1979). Family form or family process? Reconsidering the deficit family model approach. *Family Coordinator, 28,* 5–14.

Marquand, R. (1985, December 8). New subculture of youths causes alarm among educators. *Hartford Courant,* 44.

Marshall, W. A., & Tanner, J. M. (1969). Variations in the pattern of pubertal changes in girls. *Archive of Disease in Childhood, 44,* 130.

Marshall, W. A., & Tanner, J. M. (1970). Variations in the pattern of pubertal changes in boys. *Archive of Disease in Childhood, 45,* 13.

Martin, C. L., & Halverson, C. F. (1981). A schematic processing model of sex typing and stereotyping in children. *Child Development, 52,* 1119–1134.

Martinez, R., & Dukes, R. L. (1991). Ethnic and gender differences in self-esteem. *Youth & Society, 22,* 318–338.

Martorano, S. C. (1977). A developmental analysis of performance on Piaget's formal operations tasks. *Developmental Psychology, 13,* 666–672.

Marx, J. L. (1986). The slow, insidious nature of the HTLV's. *Science, 231,* 450–451.

Marx, J. L. (1989). Do sperm spread the AIDS virus? *Science, 245,* 30.

Marziali, E., & Alexander, L. (1991). The power of the therapeutic relationship. *American Journal of Orthopsychiatry, 61,* 383–391.

Mathes, E. (1975). Effects of physical attractiveness and anxiety on heterosexual attraction over a series of five encounters. *Journal of Marriage and the Family, 37,* 769–773.

Mathes, E., Adams, H. E., Davies, R. M. (1985). Jealousy: Loss of relationship rewards, loss of self-esteem, depression, anxiety, and anger. *Journal of Personality and Social Psychology, 48,* 1552–1561.

Matteson, D. R. (1975). *Adolescence today: Sex roles and the search for identity.* Homewood, IL: Dorsey Press.

Matteson, D. R. (1977). Exploration and commitment: Sex differences and methodological problems in the use of identity status categories. *Journal of Youth and Adolescence, 6,* 353–374.

May, P. A. (1987). Suicide among American Indian youth. *Children Today, 16,* 22–25.

McAnarney, E. R. (1979). Adolescent and young adult suicide in the United States: A reflection of social unrest. *Adolescence, 14,* 765–774.

McCabe, M. P., & Collins, J. K. (1984). Measurement of depth of desired and experienced sexual involvement at different stages of dating. *Journal of Sex Research, 20,* 377–390.

McCall, R. B., Appelbaum, M. J., & Hogarty, P. S. (1973). Developmental changes in mental performance. *Monographs of the Society for Research in Child Development, 38*(3, Serial No. 150).

McCall, R. B., & Stocking, S. H. (1980). *Divorce: A summary of research about the effects of divorce on families.* Boys Town, NE: Boys Town Center for the Study of Youth Development.

McCammon, E. P. (1981). Comparison of oral and written forms of the Sentence Completion Test for ego development. *Developmental Psychology, 17,* 233–235.

McCandless, B. R. (1970). *Adolescents: Behavior and development.* Hinsdale, IL: Dryden Press.

McCarthy, B. R., & Smith, B. L. (1986). The conceptualization of discrimination in the juvenile justice process: The impact of administrative factors and screening decisions on juvenile court dispositions. *Criminology, 24,* 41–64.

McCarthy, F. B. (1977). Should juvenile delinquency be abolished? *Crime and Delinquency, 23,* 196–203.

McCarthy, J. (1978). Sports violence: Caveat vendor. *Journal of Physical Education and Recreation, 49*(9), 34, 58.

McCaul, M. E., Svikis, D. S., Turkkan, J. S., Bigelow, G. E., & Cromwell, C. C. (1990). Degree of familial alcoholism: Effects on substance use by college males. In L. S. Harris (Ed.), *Problems of drug dependence: 1989.* U.S. Department of Health and Human Services publication # ADM 90-1663. Washington, DC: U.S. Government Printing Office.

McClellan, M. C. (1987). Teenage pregnancy. *Phi Delta Kappan, 68,* 789–792.

McCord, J. (1978). A thirty-year follow-up of treatment effects. *American Psychologist, 33,* 284–289.

McCord, J., & McCord, W. (1964). The effects of parental role model on criminality. In R. Cavan (Ed.), *Readings in juvenile delinquency.* Philadelphia: Lippincott.

McCord, W., & Sanchez, J. (1982). Curing criminal negligence. *Psychology Today, 16,* 79–82.

McCullough, M., & Scherman, A. (1991). Adolescent pregnancy: Contributing factors and strategies for prevention. *Adolescence, 26,* 809–816.

McDermott, D. (1984). The relationship of parental drug use and parents' attitudes concerning adolescent drug use to adolescent drug use. *Adolescence, 19*(73), 89–97.

McDonald, G. W. (1977). Parental identification by the adolescent: A social power approach. *Journal of Marriage and the Family, 39,* 705–720.

McDonald, G. W. (1980). Parental power and adolescents' parental identification: A reexamination. *Journal of Marriage and the Family 42,* 289–296.

McEwin, C. K. (1981). Interscholastic sports and the early adolescent. *Journal of Early Adolescence, 1*(2), 123–133.

McGowan, B. G., & Kohn, A. (1990). Social support and teen pregnancy in the inner city. In A. R. Stiffman & L. E. Davis (Eds.), *Ethnic issues in adolescent mental health.* Newbury Park, CA: Sage.

McIntosh, J. L., & Santos, J. F. (1980–1981). Suicide among Native Americans: A compilation of findings. *Omega, 11,* 303–316.

McKenry, P. C., Tishler, C. L., & Christman, K. L. (1980). Adolescent suicide and the classroom teacher. *Journal of School Health, 50,* 130–132.

McKenry, P. C., Walters, L. H., & Johnson, C. (1979). Adolescent pregnancy: A review of the literature. *Family Coordinator, 28,* 16–28.

McLaughlin, V. (1973). Patterns of work and family organization: Buffalo's Italians. In M. Gordon (Ed.), *The American family in social-historical perspective.* New York: St. Martin's Press.

McNamara, V., King, L. A., & Green, M. F. (1979). Adolescent perspectives on sexuality, contraception, and pregnancy. *Journal of MAG, 68,* 811–814.

McShane, D., & Adams, G. R. (1988). Mental health research and service issues for minority youth. *Journal of Adolescence, 11,* 85–86.

Mead, G. H. (1934). *Mind, self, and society.* Chicago: University of Chicago Press.

Mead, M. (1928a). *Coming of age in Samoa.* New York: Morrow.

Mead, M. (1928b). *Growing up in New Guinea.* New York: Morrow.

Mead, M. (1949). *Male and female.* New York: Morrow.

Mecklenburger, J. A. (1993). The braking of the "break-the-mold" express. *Phi Delta Kappan, 74,* 280–289.

Meilman, P. W. (1979). Cross-sectional age changes in ego identity status during adolescence. *Developmental Psychology, 15,* 230–231.

Meltzer, F. (1987). Editor's introduction: Partitive plays, pipe dreams. *Critical Inquiry, 13,* 215–221.

Mennel, R. (1973). *Thorns and thistles: Juvenile delinquency in the United States.* Hanover, NH: University of New England Press.

Menninger, K. A. (1938). *Man against himself.* New York: Harcourt Brace Jovanovich.

Menninger, K. A. (1965). *The human mind.* New York: Knopf.

Merritt, T. A., Lawrence, R. A., & Naeye, R. L. (1980). The infants of adolescent mothers. *Pediatric Annals, 9*(3), 32–49.

Merton, R. K. (1937). Social structure and anomie. *American Sociological Review, 3,* 672–682.

Messinger, L., & Walker, K. N (1981). From marriage breakdown to remarriage: Parental talks and therapeutic guidelines. *American Journal of Orthopsychiatry, 51,* 429–438.

Meuller, D. P., & Cooper, P. W. (1986). Children of single parent families: How they fare as young adults. *Family Relations, 35,* 169–176.

Meyer, A. (1995). Primary prevention approaches to reducing substance misuse. In T. P. Gullotta, G. R. Adams, & R. Montemayor (Eds.), *Adolescent substance misuse.* Newbury Park, CA: Sage.

Meyer, V. F. (1991). A critique of adolescent pregnancy prevention research. The invisible white male. *Adolescence, 26,* 217–222.

Mikulecky, L. (1990). National adult literacy and lifelong learning goals. *Phi Delta Kappan, 72,* 304–309.

Miller, A. T., Eggertson-Tacon, C., & Quigg, B. (1990). Patterns of runaway behavior within a larger systems context: The road to empowerment. *Adolescence, 25,* 271–290.

Miller, B. C. (1987, February 28). *Adolescent sexuality, contraception, and pregnancy.* Paper presented at the fourth Biennial Conference on Adolescent Research. Tucson, AZ.

Miller, B. C., & Bingham, C. R. (1989). Family configuration in relation to the sexual behaviour of female adolescents. *Journal of Marriage and the Family, 51,* 499–506.

Miller, B. C., Christensen, R., & Olson, T. D. (1987). Self-esteem in relation to adolescent sexual attitudes and behavior. *Youth and Society, 18,* 16–32.

Miller, B. C., Christopherson, C. R., & King, P. K. (1993). Sexual behavior in adolescence. In T. P. Gullotta, G. R. Adams, & R. Montemayor (Eds.), *Adolescent sexuality.* Newbury Park, CA: Sage.

Miller, B. C., & Fox, G. L. (1987). Theories of adolescent heterosexual behavior. *Journal of Adolescent Research, 2,* 269–282.

Miller, B. C., & Heaton, T. B. (1991). Age at first sexual intercourse and the timing of marriage and childbirth. *Journal of Marriage and the Family, 53,* 719–732.

Miller, B. C., McCoy, J. K., & Olson, T. D. (1986). Dating age and stage as correlates of adolescent sexual attitudes and behavior. *Journal of Adolescent Research, 1,* 361–371.

Miller, B. C., McCoy, J. K., & Olson, T. D. (1987). Sexual attitudes and behavior of high school students in relation to background and contextual factors. Manuscript submitted for publication.

Miller, B. C., McCoy, J. K., Olson, T. D., & Wallace, C. M. (1986). Parental discipline and control attempts in relation to adolescent sexual attitudes and behavior. *Journal of Marriage and the Family, 48,* 503–512.

Miller, B. C., & Moore, K. A. (1990). Adolescent sexual behavior, pregnancy, and parenting: Research through the 1980s. *Journal of Marriage and the Family, 52,* 1025–1044.

Miller, B. C., Norton, M. C., Dyk, P., McCoy, J. K., & Olson, T. D. (1988). *Parent-teen communication and closeness as correlates of adolescent sexual behavior.* Utah State University, Logan, UT. Manuscript submitted for publication.

Miller, M. L., Chiles, J. A., & Barnes, V. E. (1982). Suicide attempters within a delinquent population. *Journal of Consulting and Clinical Psychology, 50*(4), 491–498.

Miller, P., & Simon, W. (1974). Adolescent sexual behavior: Context and change. *Social Problems, 22,* 58–75.

Miller, R. L. (1989). Desegregation experiences of minority students: Adolescent coping strategies in five Connecticut high schools. *Journal of Adolescent Research, 4,* 173–189.

Miller, R. L. (1990). Beyond contact theory: The impact of community affluence of integration efforts in five suburban high schools. *Youth & Society, 22,* 12–34.

Miller, R. L., & Miller, B. (1990). Mothering the biracial child: Bridging the gaps between African-American and White parenting styles. *Women in Therapy, 10,* 169–179.

Miller, W. (1982). Youth gangs. *Children Today, 11,* 10–11.

Mills, C. J. (1981). Sex roles, personality, and intellectual abilities in adolescents. *Journal of Youth and Adolescence, 10,* 85–112.

Mills, C. J., & Noyes, H. L. (1984). Patterns and correlates of initial and subsequent drug use among adolescents. *Journal of Consulting and Clinical Psychology, 52,* 231–243.

Mirandé, A. (1977). The Chicano family: A reanalysis of conflicting views. *Journal of Marriage and the Family, 39,* 745–756.

Mirandé, A. (1986). Adolescence and Chicano families. In G. K. Leigh & G. W. Peterson (Eds.), *Adolescents in Families.* Cincinnati: South-Western Publishing Co.

Mischel, W. (1973). Toward a cognitive social learning reconceptualization of personality. *Psychological Review, 80,* 252–283.

Mischel, W. (1979). On the interface of cognition and personality: Beyond the person-situation debate. *American Psychologist, 34,* 740–754.

Mitchell, J. E. (1975). Moral dilemmas of early adolescence. *Adolescence, 10,* 442–446.

Mitchell, J. E. (1976). Adolescent intimacy. *Adolescence, 11,* 275–280.

Mitchell, J. E., Hatsukami, D., Eckert, E. D., & Pyle, R. L. (1985). Characteristics of 275 patients with bulimia. *American Journal of Psychiatry, 142,* 482–485.

Moelvey, E. P., & LaRosa, J. F. (1986). Delinquency cessation and adolescent development: Preliminary data. *American Journal of Orthopsychiatry, 56,* 212–224.

Moffitt, T. E., Gabrielli, W. F., Mednick, S. A., & Schulsinger, F. (1981). Socioeconomic status, IQ, and delinquency. *Journal of Abnormal Psychology, 90,* 152–156.

Molin, R. S. (1986). Covert suicide and families of adolescents. *Adolescence, 21*(81), 177–184.

Monahan, T. P. (1957). Family status and the delinquent child: A reappraisal and some new findings. *Social Forces, 35,* 250–258.

Money, J. (1975). Intellectual functioning in childhood endocrinopathies and related cytogenetic disorders. In L. Gardner (Ed.), *Endocrine and genetic diseases of childhood and adolescence* (2nd ed.). Philadelphia: Saunders.

Money, J., & Clopper, R. (1974). Psychosocial and psychosexual aspects of errors of pubertal onset and development. *Human Biology, 46,* 173–181.

Money, J., & Walker, P. (1971). Psychosexual development, maternalism, nonpromiscuity and body image in 15 females with precocious puberty. *Archives of Sexual Behavior, 1,* 45–60.

Monroe, P. (1940). *Founding of the American public school system.* New York: Macmillan.

Montemayor, R. (1981, April). *Correlates of parent-adolescent conflict.* Paper presented at the meeting of the Utah Council on Family Relations, Provo, UT.

Montemayor, R. (1990). Continuity and change in the behavior of nonhuman primates during the transition of adolescence. In R. Montemayor, G. R. Adams, & T. P. Gullotta (Eds.), *From childhood to adolescence: A transitional period? Vol. 2: Advances in adolescent development.* Newbury Park, CA: Sage.

Montemayor, R., & Hanson, E. (1985). A naturalistic view of conflict between adolescents and their parents and siblings. *Journal of Early Adolescence, 5*(1), 23–30.

Montemayor, R., & Van Komen, R. (1980). Age segregation of adolescents in and out of school. *Journal of Youth and Adolescence, 9,* 371–381.

Montemayor, R., & Van Komen, R. (1985). The development of sex differences in friendships and peer group structure during adolescence. *Journal of Early Adolescence, 5*(3), 285–294.

Moore, S., & Rosenthal, D. (1991). Adolescent invulnerability and perceptions of AIDS risk. *Journal of Adolescence Research, 6,* 164–180.

Moran, P. B., & Eckenrode, J. (1991). Gender differences in the costs and benefits of peer relationships during adolescence. *Journal of Adolescent Research, 6,* 396–409.

Morell, V. (1993). Enzyme may blunt cocaine's action. *Science, 259,* 1828.

Morgan, M. (1987). Television, sex role attitudes, and sex role behavior. *Journal of Early Adolescence, 7,* 269–282.

Morris, N. M., & Udry, J. R. (1980). Validation of a self-administered instrument to assess stage of adolescent development. *Journal of Youth and Adolescence, 9,* 271–280.

Mortimer, J. T., Finch, M., Shanahan, M., & Rhu, S. (1992). Work experience, mental health, and behavioral adjustment in adolescence. *Journal of Research on Adolescence, 2,* 25–57.

Morton, R. (1720). *Phthisiologia: Or a treatise of consumptions, wherein the differences, nature, causes, signs, and cure of all sorts of consumptions are explained.* London: Sam, Smith, & Beny.

Mosher, D. L., & Tomkins, S. S. (1987). Scripting the macho man: Hypermasculine socialization and enculturation. *The Journal of Sex Research, 26,* 60–84.

Moshman, D. (1979). Development of formal hypothesis-testing ability. *Developmental Psychology, 15,* 104–112.

Mosteller, F., & Moynihan, D. P. (1972). *On equality of educational opportunity.* New York: Vintage.

Mueller, D. P., & Cooper, P. W. (1986). Children of single-parent families: How they fare as young adults. *Family Relations, 35,* 169–176.

Muensterberger, W. (1975). The adolescent in society. In A. H. Esman (Ed.)., *The psychology of adolescence.* New York: International Universities Press.

Mulcahey, G. A. (1973). Sex differences in patterns of self-disclosure among adolescents: A developmental perspective. *Journal of Youth and Adolescence, 2,* 343–356.

Mullis, R. L., & McKinley, K. (1989). Gender-role orientation of adolescent females: Effects on self-esteem and locus of control. *Journal of Adolescent Research, 4,* 506–516.

Mulvey, E. P., & LaRosa, J. F. (1986). Delinquency cessation and adolescent development: Preliminary data. *American Journal of Orthopsychiatry, 56,* 212–224.

Munro, G., & Adams, G. R. (1977a). Adolescent values: Measuring instrumental and expressive orientations. *Adolescence, 12,* 321–328.

Munro, G., & Adams, G. R. (1977b). Ego-identity formation in college students and working youth. *Developmental Psychology, 13,* 523–524.

Murphy, N. T., & Price, C. J. (1988). The influence of self-esteem, parental smoking, and living in a tobacco production region on adolescent smoking behaviors. *Journal of School Health, 58,* 401–404.

Murray, J. P. (1980). *Television and youth: 25 years of research and controversy.* Boys Town, NE: Boys Town Center for the Study of Youth Development.

Mussen, P. H., & Jones, M. C. (1957). Self-conceptions, motivations, and interpersonal attitudes of late and early maturing boys. *Child Development, 28,* 243–256.

Muuss, R. E. (1975). *Theories of adolescence.* New York: Random House.

Muuss, R. E. (1985). Adolescent eating disorder: Anorexia nervosa. *Adolescence, 20,* 525–536.

Muuss, R. E. (1986). Adolescent eating disorder: Bulimia. *Adolescence, 21,* 257–267.

Mydans, S. (1988, April 17). In Bangladesh, women can't go home again. *New York Times,* 8.

Nadelman, E. A. (1989). Drug prohibition in the United States: Costs, consequences, and alternatives. *Science, 245,* 939–947.

Nadelson, C. C., Notman, M. T., & Gillon, J. W. (1980). Sexual knowledge and attitudes of adolescents: Relationship to contraceptive use. *Obstetrics and Gynecology, 55,* 340–345.

Nagata, D. K. (1989). Japanese American children and adolescents. In J. T. Gibbs & L. N. Huang (Eds.), *Children of color.* San Francisco: Jossey-Bass.

Nasaw, D. (1979). *Schooled to order: A social history of public schooling in the United States.* New York: Oxford University Press.

National Advisory Mental Health Council. (1990). *National plan for research on child and adolescent mental disorders.* Washington, DC: National Institute of Mental Health.

National Commission on Children. (1991). *Speaking of kids.* Washington, DC: Author.

National Council on Crime and Delinquency. (1984). *Rethinking juvenile justice: National statistical trends.* Minneapolis: University of Minnesota Press.

National Institute of Alcohol Abuse and Alcoholism. (1981). *Preventing fetal alcohol effects: A practical guide for OB/GYN physicians and nurses* (Public Health Service, DHHS Publication # ADM 81-1163). Washington, DC: U.S. Government Printing Office.

National Institute of Alcohol Abuse and Alcoholism. (1984). *Alcohol and Health* (DHHS Publication # ADM 84-1291). Washington, DC: U.S. Government Printing Office.

National Institute of Mental Health. (1977). *Trends in mental health: Self-destructive behavior among younger age groups* (DHEW Publication # ADM 77-365). Washington, DC: U.S. Government Printing Office.

National Institute of Mental Health. (1978). *Yours, mine and ours: Tips for stepparents* (DHEW Publication # ADM 78-676). Washington, DC: U.S. Government Printing Office.

National Institute of Mental Health. (1980). *Definitions for use in mental health information systems* (DHHS Publication # ADM 80-833). Washington, DC: U.S. Government Printing Office.

National Institute of Mental Health. (1982). *Television and behavior: Ten years of scientific progress and implications for the eighties* (DHHS Publication # ADM 82-1195). Washington, DC: U.S. Government Printing Office.

National Institute of Mental Health. (1984). *Adolescence and depression* (DHHS Publication # ADM 84-1337). Washington, DC: U.S. Government Printing Office.

National Institute on Drug Abuse. (1978a). *Inhalants* (DHHS Publication # ADM 79-742). Washington, DC: U.S. Government Printing Office.

National Institute on Drug Abuse. (1978b). Phencyclidine—PCP. *Report Series 14, No. 2* (DHEW Publication # ADM 79-672). Washington, DC: U.S. Government Printing Office.

National Institute on Drug Abuse. (1982). *Marijuana and youth: Clinical Observations on motivation and learning* (DHHS Publication # ADM 82-1186). Washington, DC: U.S. Government Printing Office.

National Institute on Drug Abuse. (1987a). *Cocaine/crack* (DHHS Publication # ADM 87-1427). Washington, DC: U.S. Government Printing Office.

National Institute on Drug Abuse. (1987b). *Drug abuse and drug abuse research: The second triennial report to Congress* (DHHS Publication # ADM 87-1486). Washington, DC: U.S. Government Printing Office.

Needle, R. H., Su, S. S., & Doherty, W. J. (1990). Divorce, remarriage, and adolescent substance use: A prospective longitudinal study. *Journal of Marriage and the Family, 52,* 157–169.

Neighbors, H. W. (1990). The prevention of psychopathology in African Americans: An epidemiologic perspective. *Community Mental Health Journal, 26,* 167–179.

Neilson, A., & Gerber, D. (1979). Psychosocial aspects of truancy in early adolescence. *Adolescence, 14,* 313–326.

Neimark, E. D. (1982). Adolescent thought: Transition to formal operations. In B. B. Wolman (Ed.), *Handbook of developmental psychology.* Englewood Cliffs, NJ: Prentice-Hall.

Nelson, G. (1982). Coping with the loss of father. *Journal of Family Issues, 3,* 41–60.

Nelson, M., & Nelson, G. K. (1982). Problems of equity in the reconstituted family: A social exchange analysis. *Family Relations, 31,* 223–231.

Nesselroade, J. R., & Baltes, P. B. (1974). Adolescent personality development and historical change: 1970–1972. *Monographs of the Society for Research in Child Development, 39*(1, Serial No. 154)

Nettina, S. L. (1990). Syphilis. *American Journal of Nursing, 43,* 68–70.

Nevid, J. S. (1984). Sex differences in factors of romantic attraction. *Sex Roles, 11,* 401–411.

Newcomb, M. D. (1984). Sexual behavior, responsiveness, and attitudes among women: A test of two theories. *Journal of Sex and Marital Therapy, 10,* 272–286.

Newcomb, M. D., & Bentler, P. M. (1986). Substance use and ethnicity: Differential impact of peer and adult models. *The Journal of Psychology, 120,* 83–95.

Newcomb, M. D., Huba, G. J., & Bentler, P. M. (1983). Mothers' influence on the drug use of their children: Confirmatory tests of direct modeling and mediational theories. *Developmental Psychology, 19,* 714–726.

Newcomb, M. D., Huba, G. J., & Bentler, P. M. (1986). Determinants of sexual and dating behaviors among adolescents. *Journal of Personality and Social Psychology, 50,* 428–438.

Newcomb, M. D., Maddahian, E., Skager, R., & Bentler, P. M. (1987). Substance abuse and psychosocial risk factors among teenagers: Associations with sex, age, ethnicity, and type of school. *American Journal of Drug and Alcohol Abuse, 13,* 413–433.

Newcomb, T. (1937). Recent changes in attitude toward sex and marriage. *American Sociological Review, 2,* 659–667.

Newcomer, S., & Udry, J. R. (1987). Parental marital status effects on adolescent sexual behavior. *Journal of Marriage and the Family, 49,* 235–240.

Newman, B. M. (1976). The study of interpersonal behavior in adolescence. *Adolescence, 11,* 127–142.

Newman, P. R., & Newman, B. M. (1976). Early adolescence and its conflict: Group identity versus alienation. *Adolescence, 11,* 261–274.

Newton-Ruddy, L., & Handelsman, M. M. (1986). Jungian feminine psychology and adolescent prostitutes. *Adolescence, 21,* 815–825.

New York Times (1993). Repotted, 7 March, 1, 9.

New York Times News Service. (1990). AIDS discovered in tissue from 1959. *New London Day,* July 24, A3.

Nicholson, T. (1992). The primary prevention of illicit drug problems: An argument for decriminalization and legalization. *Journal of Primary Prevention, 12,* 275–288.

Nicholson, T. (1995). Social policy and adolescent drug consumption: The legalization option. In T. P. Gullotta, G. R. Adams, & R. Montemayor (Eds.), *Adolescent substance misuse.* Newbury Park, CA: Sage.

Niles, F. S. (1981). The youth culture controversy: An evaluation. *Journal of Early Adolescence, 1*(3), 265–271.

Noam, G., Hauser, S. T., Santostefano, S., Garrison, W., Jacobson, A. M., Powers, S. I., & Mead, M. (1984). Ego development and psychopathology: A study of hospitalized adolescents. *Child Development, 55,* 184–194.

Norman, C. (1985). Africa and the origins of AIDS. *Science, 230,* 1141.

Notar, M., & McDaniel, S. A. (1986). Feminist attitudes and mother-daughter relationships in adolescence. *Adolescence, 21,* 11–21.

Nottelmann, E. D., & Welsh, C. J. (1986). The long and the short of physical stature in early adolescence. *Journal of Early Adolescence, 6,* 15–27.

Nye, I. F. (1957). Child adjustment in broken and in unhappy broken homes. *Marriage & Family Living, 19,* 356–361.

Nye, I. F. (1958). *Family relationships and delinquent behavior.* New York: Wiley.

Nye, I. F., & Lamberts, M. B. (1980). *School-age parenthood.* Pullman: Washington State University Cooperative Extension.

Nystrom, C. L. (1983, March). What television teaches about sex. *Educational Leadership,* 19–24.

O'Donnell, W. J. (1976). Adolescent self-esteem related to feelings toward parents and friends. *Journal of Youth and Adolescence, 5,* 179–186.

Oetting, E. R., & Beauvais, F. (1982). *Drug use among American youth: Summary of findings (1975–1981).* Fort Collins, CO: Western Behavioral Studies.

Oetting, E. R., Beauvais, F., & Edwards, R. (1988). Alcohol and Indian youth: Social and psychological correlates and prevention. *The Journal of Drug Issues, 18,* 87–101.

Offer, D., Marohn, R., & Ostrov, E. (1979). *The psychological world of the juvenile delinquent.* New York: Basic Books.

Offer, D., Ostrov, E., & Howard, K. I. (1977). The self-image of adolescents: A study of four cultures. *Journal of Youth and Adolescence, 6,* 265–280.

Offer, D., Ostrov, E., & Howard, K. I. (1981). *The adolescent: A psychological self-portrait.* New York: Basic Books.

Offer, D., Ostrov, E., Howard, K. I., & Atkinson, R. (1988). *The teenage world: Adolescents' self-image in ten countries.* New York: Plenum Medical Books.

Office of Technology Assessment. (1991). *Adolescent health, Vol. II.* No. OTA-H-466. Washington, DC: U.S. Government Printing Office.

Offord, D. R., Abrams, N., Allen, N., & Poushinsky, M. (1979). Broken homes, parental psychiatric illness, and female delinquency. *American Journal of Orthopsychiatry, 49,* 252–263.

Ogbu, J. U. (1987). Variability in minority school performance: A problem in search of an explanation. *Anthropology & Education Quarterly, 18,* 312–334.

Ogilvie, B. C., & Tutko, T. A. (1971, October). Sport: If you want to build character, try something else. *Psychology Today,* 60–63.

O'Gorman, P. A., Stringfield, S., & Smith, I. (Eds.). (1976). *Defining adolescent alcohol use: Implications toward and definition of adolescent alcoholism.* Washington, DC: National Council on Alcoholism.

Ohlrich, E. S., & Stephenson, J. N. (1986). Pitfalls in the care of patients with anorexia nervosa & bulimia. *Seminars in Adolescent Medicine, 2,* 81–88.

Olowu, A. A. (1983). A cross-culture study of adolescent self-image concept. *Journal of Adolescence, 6,* 263–274.

Olson, D. H., Russell, C. S., & Sprenkle, D. H. (1980). Marital and family therapy: A decade review. *Journal of Marriage and the Family, 42,* 973–994.

O'Neill, W. (1973). Divorce in the progressive era. In M. Gordon, (Ed.), *The American family in social-historical perspective.* New York: St. Martin's Press.

Oommen, A. J., Johnson, P. C., & Ray, G. (1982). Herpes simplex type 2 virus encephalitis presenting as psychosis. *American Journal of Medicine, 73,* 445–448.

Openshaw, D. K., Rollins, B. C., & Thomas, D. L. (1984). Parental influences on adolescent self-esteem. *Journal of Early Adolescence, 4,* 259–274.

Openshaw, D. K., Thomas, D. L., & Rollins, B. C. (1981). Adolescent self-esteem: A multidimensional perspective. *Journal of Early Adolescence, 1,* 273–282.

Openshaw, D. K., Thomas, D. L., & Rollins, B. C. (1983). Socialization and adolescent self-esteem: Symbolic interaction and social learning explanations. *Adolescence, 28,* 317–329.

Opinion Research Corporation. (1976). *National statistical survey on runaway youth (Part 1).* Princeton, NJ: Author.

Orbach, I., Gross, Y., & Glaubman, H. (1981). Some common characteristics of latency-age suicidal children: A tentative model based on case study analysis. *Suicide and Life-Threatening Behavior, 11*(3), 180–190.

Orbach, S. (1984). The construction of femininity: Some critical issues in the psychology of women. Cited in R. M. Bell (1985), *Holy anorexia.* Chicago: University of Chicago Press.

Orlick, T. D. (1972). *A socio-psychological analysis of early sports participation.* Unpublished doctoral dissertation, University of Alberta.

Orlofsky, J. L., & O'Heron, C. A. (1987). Stereotypic and nonstereotypic sex role trait and behavior orientations: Implications for personal adjustment. *Journal of Personality and Social Psychology, 52,* 1034–1042.

Orlofsky, J., & Frank M. (1986). Personality structure as viewed through early memories and identity status in college men and women. *Journal of Personality and Social Psychology, 50,* 580–586.

Orlofsky, J. L. (1978). Identity formation, achievement, and fear of success in college men and women. *Journal of Youth and Adolescence, 7,* 49–62.

Orlofsky, J., Aslin, A., Ginsburg, S. D. (1977). Differential effectivenss of two classification procedures on the Bem Sex Role Inventory. *Journal of Personality Assessment, 41,* 414–416.

Orlofsky, J., Marcia, J., & Lesser, I. (1973). Ego identity status and the intimacy vs. isolation crisis in young adulthood. *Journal of Personality and Social Psychology, 27,* 211–219.

Orthner, D. K. (1990). Parental work and early adolescence. *Journal of Early Adolescence, 10,* 246–259.

Otto, L. B., & Alwin, D. F. (1977). Athletics, aspirations, and attainments. *Sociology of Education, 50*(2), 102–113.

Overmier, K. (1990). Biracial adolescents: Areas of conflict in identity formation. *The Journal of Applied Social Sciences, 14,* 157–176.

Pace, N. A. (1981). Driving on pot. In L. H. Gross (Ed.), *The parent's guide to teenagers.* New York: Macmillan.

Paikoff, R. L., & Brooks-Gunn, J. (1991). Do parent-child relationships change during puberty? *Psychological Bulletin, 110,* 47–66.

Paikoff, R. L., Brooks-Gunn, J., & Warren, M. P. (1991). Effects of girls' hormonal status on affective expression over the course of one year. *Journal of Youth and Adolescence, 20,* 191–214.

Palca, J. (1991). HIV risk higher for infants born twins. *Science, 254,* 1729.

Palca, J. (1992). Human SIV infections suspected. *Science, 257,* 606.

Palermo, E. (1980). Remarriage: Parental perceptions of step relations with children and adolescents. *Journal of Psychiatric Nursing, 18*(4), 9–13.

Pallas, A. M., & Alexander, K. L. (1983). Sex differences in quantitative SAT performance: New evidence on the differential coursework hypothesis. *American Educational Research Journal, 20,* 165–182.

Paluszny, M., Davenport, C., & Kim, W. J. (1991). Suicide attempts and ideation: Adolescents evaluated on a pediatric ward. *Adolescence, 26,* 208–215.

Papini, D. R., Micka, J. C., & Barnett, J. K. (1989). Perceptions of intrapsychic and extrapsychic functioning as bases of adolescent ego identity statuses. *Journal of Adolescent Research, 4,* 462–482.

Parikh, B. (1980). Development of moral judgment and its relation to family environmental factors in Indian and American families. *Child Development, 51,* 1030–1039.

Parish, T. S. (1987). Family and environment. In V. B. Van Hasselt & M. Hersen (Eds.), *The handbook of adolescent psychology.* New York: Pergamon Press.

Parish, T. S. (1981). The impact of divorce on the family. *Adolescence, 16,* 577–580.

Parish, T., & Dostal, J. W. (1980). Evaluations of self and parent figures by children from intact, divorced, and reconstituted families. *Journal of Youth and Adolescence, 9,* 347–351.

Parish, T., & Taylor, J. (1979). The impact of divorce and subsequent father absence on children's and adolescents' self-concepts. *Journal of Youth and Adolescence, 8,* 427–432.

Parkhouse, B. (1979). To win what do you have to lose? *Journal of Physical Education and Recreation, 50*(6), 15–17.

Parks, S. (1986). *The critical years: Young adults and the search for meaning, faith and commitment.* San Francisco: Harper.

Parloff, M. B. (1977). *Shopping for the right therapy* (National Institute of Mental Health, DHEW Publication # ADM 77-426). Washington, DC: U.S. Government Printing Office.

Parson, R. J. (1988). Empowerment for role alternatives for low income minority girls: A group work approach. *Social Work with Groups, 11,* 27–45.

Parsons, T. (1959). The school class as a social system. *Harvard Educational Review, 29,* 297–318.

Parsons, T., & Bales, R. F. (Eds.). (1955). *Family socialization and interaction process.* New York: Free Press.

Pascale, R., Hurd, M., & Primavera, L. H. (1980). The effects of chronic marijuana use. *Journal of Social Psychology, 110,* 273–283.

Pate-Bain, H., Achilles, C. M., Boyd-Zaharias, T., & McKenna, B. (1992). Class size does make a difference. *Phi Delta Kappan, 74,* 253–256.

Patterson, G. R., & Dishion, T. J. (1985). Contributions of families and peers to delinquency. *Criminology, 23,* 63–79.

Patton, W., & Nolles, P. (1991). The family and the unemployed adolescent. *Journal of Adolescence, 14,* 343–362.

Paul, M. J., & Fischer, J. L. (1980). Correlates of self-concept among Black early adolescents. *Journal of Youth and Adolescence, 9,* 163–174.

Paulhus, D. L., & Martin, C. L. (1986). Predicting adult temperament from minor physical anomalies. *Journal of Personality and Social Psychology, 50,* 1235–1239.

Paulson, J. E., Koman, J. J., & Hill, J. P. (1990). Maternal employment and parent-child relations in families of seventh graders. *Journal of Early Adolescence, 10,* 279–295.

Paykel, E. S. (1989). Stress and life events. In ADAMHA. *Report of the secretary's task force on youth suicide: Vol. 2: Risk factors for youth suicide.* (U.S. Department of Health and Human Services publication # ADM 89-1622.) Washington, DC: U.S. Government Printing Office.

Peck, D. L. (1987). Social-psychological correlates of adolescent and youthful suicide. *Adolescence, 22,* 863–878.

Peele, S. (1986). The implications and limitations of genetic models of alcoholism and other addictions. *Journal of Studies on Alcohol, 47*(1), 63–73.

Pela, O. A. (1984). Psychosocial aspects of drug dependence: The Nigerian experience. *Adolescence, 19*(76), 971–975.

Perry, C. L., & Murray, D. M. (1985). The prevention of adolescent drug abuse: Implications from etiological, developmental, behavioral, and environmental models. *Journal of Primary Prevention, 6*(1), 31–52.

Perry, W. G. (1970). *Forms of intellectual and ethical development in college students.* New York: Holt, Rinehart & Winston.

Peskin, H. (1973). Influence of the developmental schedule of puberty on learning and ego development. *Journal of Youth and Adolescence, 2,* 273–290.

Pestrak, V. A., & Martin, P. (1985). Cognitive development and aspects of adolescent sexuality. *Adolescence, 20,* 981–987.

Petersen, A. C., & Crockett, L. (1985). Pubertal timing and grade effects on adjustment. *Journal of Youth and Adolescence, 14,* 191–206.

Petersen, A. C., & Taylor, B. (1980). The biological approach to adolescence. In J. Adelson (Ed.), *The handbook of adolescent psychology.* New York: Wiley.

Petersen, A. C. (1979a, February). Can puberty come any earlier? *Psychology Today,* 45–46.

Petersen, A. C. (1979b, March). *The psychological significance of pubertal changes to adolescent girls.* Paper presented at the meeting of the Society for Research in Child Development, San Francisco.

Petersen, R. C., & Stillman, R. C. (1979). Phencyclidine: An overview. In R. C. Petersen & R. C. Stillman, *Phencyclidine (PCP) Abuse: An Appraisal.* (NIDA Research Monograph 21, # ADM 79-728), 1–17. Washington, DC: U.S. Government Printing Office.

Peterson, G. B. & Hey, R. N. (1976). *Family power, support and moral development: An empirical investigation of the interface between stage psychology and family development.* Unpublished manuscript.

Peterson, G. W., Rollins, B. C., Thomas, D. L., & Heaps, L. K. (1982). Social placement of adolescents: Sex-role influences on family decisions regarding the careers of youth. *Journal of Marriage and the Family, 44,* 647–658.

Pettinatti, H. M., & Wade, J. H. (1986). Hypnosis in the treatment of anorexia and bulimia patients. *Seminars in Adolescent Medicine, 2,* 75–80.

Pfeffer, C. R. (1981a). The family system of suicidal children. *American Journal of Psychotherapy, 35*(3), 330–341.

Pfeffer, C. R. (1981b). Suicidal behavior of children: A review in the implications for research and practice. *American Journal of Psychiatry, 138*(2), 154–159.

Pfeffer, C. R. (1989). Family characteristics and support systems as risk factors for youth suicidal behavior. In ADAMHA. *Report of the secretary's task force on youth suicide: Vol. 2: Risk factors for youth suicide.* U.S. Department of Health and Human Services publication # ADM 89-1622. Washington, DC: U.S. Government Printing Office.

Pfeffer, C. R., Klerman, G. L., Hurt, S. W., Lessor, M., Peskin, J. R. & Siefker, C. A. (1991). Suicidal children grow up: Demographic and clinical risk factors for adolescent suicide attempts. *Journal American Academy of Child Adolescent Psychiatry, 30,* 609–616.

Pfeffer, C. R., Plutchik, R., & Mizruchi, M. S. (1983). Suicidal and assaultive behavior in children: Classification, measurement, and interrelations. *American Journal of Psychiatry, 140*(2), 154–157.

Phillips, D. P., & Carstensen, L. L. (1988). The effect of suicide stories on various demographic groups 1968–1985. *Suicide and Life-Threatening behaviors, 18,* 100–114.

Phinney, J. S. (1989). Stages of ethnic identity development in minority group adolescents. *Journal of Early Adolescence, 9,* 34–49.

Phinney, J. S. (1990a). *The Multigroup Ethnic Identity Measure: A new scale for use with adolescents and adults from diverse groups.* Unpublished manuscript, California State University, Los Angeles, CA.

Phinney, J. S. (1990b). Ethnic identity in adolescents and adults: Review of research. *Psychological Bulletin, 108,* 499–514.

Phinney, J. S., Alipuria, L. (1990). Ethnic identity in older adolescents from four ethnic groups. *Journal of Adolescence, 13,* 171–184.

Phinney, J. S., & Rosenthal, D. A. (1992). Ethnic identity in adolescence: Process, context, and outcome. In G. R. Adams, T. P. Gullotta, & R. Montemayor (Eds.), *Identity formation during adolescence, Vol. 4: Advances in adolescent development.* Newbury Park, CA: Sage.

Phinney, J. S., & Tarver, S. (1988). Ethnic identity search and commitment in black and white eighth graders. *Journal of Early Adolescence, 8,* 265–277.

Phipps-Yonas, S. (1980). Teenage pregnancy and motherhood. *American Journal of Orthopsychiatry, 50,* 403–441.

Pierce, R. V. (1895). *The People's Common Sense Medical Advisor.* Buffalo, NY: World's Dispensary Printing Office and Bindery.

Pine, G. J. (1966). The affluent delinquent. *Phi Delta Kappan, 48,* 138–143.

Piot, P., Plummer, F. A., Nhalu, F. S., Lamboray, J., Chin, J., & Mann, J. M. (1988). AIDS: An international perspective. *Science, 239* 573–579.

Pittel, S. M., & Oppedahl, M. C. (1979). The enigma of PCP. In R. Dupont, A. Goldstein, & J. O'Donnell (Eds.), *Handbook on drug abuse.* Washington, DC: U.S. Government Printing Office.

Pleck, J. H. (1979). Men's family work: Three perspectives and some new data. *Family Coordinator, 28,* 481–495.

Pleck, J. H., Sonenstein, F. L., & Kie, L. C. (1991). Adolescent males' condom use: Relationships between perceived cost-benefits and consistency. *Journal of Marriage and the Family, 53,* 733–745.

Plomin, R. (1990). The role of inheritance in behavior. *Science, 248,* 183–188.

Plotnick, R. D., & Butler, S. S. (1991). Attitudes and adolescent nonmarital childbearing. *Journal of Adolescent Research, 6,* 470–492.

Podd, M. H. (1972). Ego identity status and morality: The relationship between two developmental constructs. *Developmental Psychology, 6,* 499–507.

Polit-O'Hara, D., & Kahn, J. R. (1985). Communication and contraceptive practices in adolescent couples. *Adolescence, 20,* 23–43.

Polk, V. (1984). Juvenile diversion: A look at the record. *Crime and Delinquency, 30,* 648–659.

Poole, E. D., & Regoli, R. M. (1979). Parental support, delinquent friends, and delinquency. A test of interaction effects. *Journal of Criminal Law and Criminology, 70* (2), 188–193.

Porter, M. R., Vieira, T. A., Kaplan, G. J., Heesch, J. R., & Colyar, A. B. (1973). Drug use in Anchorage, Alaska: A survey of 15,634 students in grades 6 through 12—1971. *Journal of the American Medical Association, 223,* 657–664.

Portes, P. R., Dunham, R. M., & Williams, S. (1986). Assessing child-rearing style in ecological settings: Its relation to culture, social class, early age intervention, and scholastic achievement. *Adolescence, 21,* 723–735.

Poulin, J. E. (1991). Racial differences in the use of drugs and alcohol among low income youth and young adults. *Journal of Sociology & Social Welfare,* 159–166.

Powell, A. G. (1985). Being unspecial in the shopping mall high school. *Phi Delta Kappan, 67,* 255–261.

Powell, G. J. (1984a). Coping with adversity: The psychologic development of Afro-American children. In G. J. Powell, J. Yamamoto, A. Morales, & A. Romero (Eds.), *The psychosocial development of minority group children.* New York: Brunner/Mazel.

Powell, G. J. (1984b). School desegregation: The psychological, social, and educational implications. In G. J. Powell, J. Yamamoto, A. Morales, & A. Romero (Eds.), *The psychosocial development of minority group children.* New York: Brunner/Mazel.

Powell, G. J. (1985). Self-concepts among Afro-American students in racially isolated minority schools: Some regional differences. *Journal of the American Academy of Child Psychiatry, 24,* 142–149.

Powers, S. I., Hauser, S. T., Schwartz, J M., Noam, G. G., & Jacobson, A. M. (1983). Adolescent ego development and family interaction: A structural-developmental perspective. In H. D. Grotevant and C. R. Cooper (Eds.), *Adolescent Development in the Family.* New Directions in Child Development, No. 22. San Francisco: Jossey-Bass.

Prager, K. J. (1982). Identity development and self-esteem in young women. *Journal of Genetic Psychology, 141,* 177–182.

Prager, K. J. (1983). Identity status, sex-role orientations, and self-esteem in late adolescent females. *Journal of Genetic Psychology, 143,* 159–167.

Pratt, M. W., Golding, G., & Hunter, W. J. (1983). Aging as ripening: Character and consistency of moral judgment in young, mature, and older adults. *Human Development, 26,* 277–288.

President Carter's Address to the U.S. Congress on Drug Use. (1977, September–October). *Drug Survival News, 6.*

Price, R., Cowen, E., Lorion, R., & Ramos-McKay, J. (Eds.). (1988). *14 ounces of prevention: A casebook for practitioners.* Washington, DC: American Psychological Association.

Price, R. W., Bres, B., Sidtis, J., Rosenblum, M., Scheck, A. C., & Cleary, P. (1988). The brain in AIDS: Central nervous system HIV-1 infection and AIDS dementia complex. *Science, 239,* 586–592.

Price, W. H., Whatmore, P. B., & McClemont, W. F. (1966). Criminal patients with XYY sex chromosome complement. *Lancet, 1,* 565–566.

Prosen, S. S., & Farmer, J. H. (1982). Understanding stepfamiles: Issues and implications for counselors. *Personnel and Guidance Journal, 60,* 393–397.

Protinsky, H., & Wilkerson, J. (1986). Ego identity, egocentrism, and formal operations. *Adolescence, 21,* 461–466.

Protter, B. S. (1973). *Ego identity status: Construct validity and temporal orientation.* Unpublished doctoral dissertation, Purdue University.

Quality Education for Minorities Project. (1990). *Education that works: An action plan for the education of minorities.* Cambridge, MA: Massachusetts Institute of Technology.

Radford, J. L., King, A. J. C., & Warren, W. K. (1989). *Street youth and AIDS.* Ottawa, Ontario.

Rahav, G. (1977). Juvenile delinquency as minority crime. *Adolescence, 12,* 471–475.

Rains, P. (1971). *Becoming an unwed mother.* Chicago: Aldine-Atherton.

Ramirez, O. (1989). Mexican American children and adolescents. In J. T. Gibbs & L. N. Hung (Eds.), *Children of color: Psychological intervention with minority youth.* San Francisco: Jossey-Bass.

Ramsey, C. E. (1967). *Problems of youth.* Belmont, CA: Dickinson.

Ramsey, G. (1943). The sexual development of boys. *American Journal of Psychiatry, 56,* 217–234.

Range, L. M., Goggin, W. C., & Steede, K. K. (1988). Perception of behavioral contagion of adolescent suicide. *Suicide and Life-Threatening Behavior, 18,* 334–341.

Rangell, L. (1988). The decision to terminate one's life: Psychoanalytic thoughts on suicide. *Suicide and Life-Threatening Behavior, 18,* 28–36.

Rankin, R. P., & Maneker, J. S. (1985). The duration of marriage in a divorcing population: The impact of children. *Journal of Marriage and the Family, 47,* 43–52.

Ransom, J. W., Schlesinger, S., & Derdeyn, A. P. (1979). A stepfamily in formation. *American Journal of Orthopsychiatry, 49,* 36–43.

Rappaport, H., Enrich, K., & Wilson, A. (1985). Relation between ego identity and temporal perspective. *Journal of Personality and Social Psychology, 48,* 1609–1630.

Rasmussen, J. E. (1964). Relationship of ego identity to psychosocial effectiveness. *Psychological Reports, 15,* 815–825.

Ravitch, D. (1977). *The revisionists revisited: A critique of the radical attack on the schools.* New York: Basic Books.

Read, D., Adams, G. R., & Dobson, W. R. (1984). Ego-identity status, personality, and social influence style. *Journal of Personality and Social Psychology, 46,* 169–177.

Reardon, B., & Griffing, P. (1983). Factors related to the self-concept of institutionalized, White, male adolescent drug dealers. *Adolescence, 28(69),* 29–41.

Records. (1986, May 12). *New York Times,* 27, 30.

Redmond, M. A. (1985). Attitudes of adolescent males toward adolescent pregnancy and fatherhood. *Family Relations, 34,* 337–342.

Redmore, C. D., & Loevinger, J. (1979). Ego development in adolescence: Longitudinal studies. *Journal of Youth and Adolescence, 8,* 1–20.

Reed, S. (1988). Children with AIDS. *Phi Delta Kappan, 69,* K1–K12.

Rees, J. M., & Trahms, C. M. (1989). Nutritional influences on physical growth and behavior in adolescence. In G. R. Adams, R. Montemayor, & T. P. Gullotta (Eds.), *Biology of adolescent behavior and development, Vol. 1: Advances in adolescent development.* Newbury Park, CA: Sage.

Rehlberg, R. A. (1969). Behavioral and attitudinal consequences of high school interscholastic sports: A speculative consideration. *Adolescence, 4,* 69–88.

Reigel, K. F. (1976). The dialectics of human development. *American Psychologist, 31,* 398–400.

Reigel, K. F. (1977). The dialectics of time. In N. Datan & H. W. Reese (Eds.), *Life-span developmental psychology: Dialectical perspective on experimental research.* New York: Academic Press.

Reigel, K. F., & Mecham, J. A. (1976). *The developing individual in a changing world: Vol. 1. Historical and cultural issues.* Chicago: Aldine.

Reinhard, D. W. (1977). The reaction of adolescent boys and girls to the divorce of their parents. *Journal of Clinical Child Psychology, 6*(2), 21–23.

Reisman, J. M. (1985). Friendship and its implications for mental health or social competence. *Journal of Early Adolescence, 5*(3), 383–391.

Reiss, A. J. (1952). Social correlates of psychological types of delinquency. *American Sociological Review, 17,* 710–718.

Reiss, I. (1967). *The social context of premarital sexual permissiveness.* New York: Holt, Rinehart & Winston.

Reiss, I. L., Banwart, A., & Foreman, H. (1975). Premarital contraceptive usage: A study and some theoretical explorations. *Journal of Marriage and the Family, 37,* 619–630.

Remplein, H. (1956). *Die seelische Entwicklung in der Kindheit und Reifezeit.* Munich: Reinhard.

Reppucci, J. D., Revenson, T. A., Aber, M., & Reppucci, N. D. (1991). Unrealistic optimism among adolescent smokers and non-smokers. *Journal of Primary Prevention, 11,* 227–236.

Research Triangle Institute. (1984). *Economic costs to society of alcohol and drug abuse and mental illness.* Chapel Hill, NC: Author.

Resnick, H. (Ed.). (1990). *Youth and drugs: Society's mixed messages.* # ADM 90-1689. Washington, DC: Public Health Service.

Rest, J. R. (1975). Longitudinal study of the defining issues test of moral judgment: A strategy for analyzing developmental change. *Developmental Psychology, 11,* 738–748.

Rich, C. L., Sherman, M., & Fowler, R. C. (1990). San Diego suicide study: The adolescents. *Adolescence, 25,* 855–865.

Richardson, R. L., & Gerlach, S. C. (1980). Black dropouts. *Urban Education, 14,* 489–494.

Rickel, A. U., & Hendren, M. C. (1993). Abberant sexual experiences in adolescence. In T. P. Gullotta, G. R. Adams, & R. Montemayor (Eds.), *Adolescent sexuality.* Newbury Park, CA: Sage.

Riegel, K. F. (1976). The dialectics of human development. *American Psychologist, 31,* 398–400.

Riegel, K. F. (1977). The dialectics of time. In N. Datan & H. W. Reese (Eds.), *Life-span developmental psychology: Dialectical perspective on*

experimental research. New York: Academic Press.

Riegel, K. F., & Meacham, J. A. (1976). *The developing individual in a changing world: Vol. 1 Historical and cultural issues.* Chicago: Aldine.

Rierdan, J., & Koff, E. (1980). The psychological impact of menarche: Integrative versus disruptive change. *Journal of Youth and Adolescence, 9,* 49–58.

Rierdan, J., & Koff, E. (1991). Depressive symptomatology among very early maturing girls. *Journal of Youth and Adolescence, 20,* 415–426.

Riley, T., Adams, G. R., & Nielsen, E. (1984). Adolescent egocentrism: The association among imaginary audience behavior, cognitive development, and parental support and rejection. *Journal of Youth and Adolescence, 13,* 401–417.

Riley, W. T., Barenie, J. T., Mabe, P. A., & Myers, D. R. (1990). Smokeless tobacco use in adolescent females: Prevalence and psychosocial factors among racial/ethnic groups. *Journal of Behavioral Medicine, 13,* 207–220.

Rinsley, D. B., & Rinsley, C. (1987). Incest: Its development and familiar context. *Seminars in Adolescent Medicine, 3,* 9–16.

Riot, P., Plymmer, F. A., Mhalu, F. S., Lamboray, J., Chin, J., & Mann, J. M. (1988). AIDS: An international perspective. *Science, 239,* 573–579.

Rist, M. C. (1981). Students at risk. *The American School Board Journal, 174,* A9, A13.

Rist, R. (1970). Student social class and teacher expectations: The self-fulfilling prophecy in ghetto education. *Harvard Educational Review, 40,* 411–451.

Rist, R. C. (1982). Playing on the margin. *Society, 19*(6), 15–18.

Rivara, F. P., Sweeney, P. J., Henderson, B. F. (1987). Risk of fatherhood among Black teenage males. *American Journal of Public Health, 77,* 203–205.

Rivenbark, W. J. (1956). *Self-disclosure and sociometric choice in the adolescent period.* Unpublished doctoral dissertation, University of Florida.

Robbins, C., Kaplan, H. B., & Martin, S. S. (1985). Antecedents of pregnancy among unmarried adolescents. *Journal of Marriage and the Family, 47,* 567–584.

Roberge, J. J. (1976). Developmental analyses of two formal operational structures: Combinatorial thinking and conditional reasoning. *Developmental Psychology, 12,* 563–564.

Roberts, L. R., Sarigiani, P. A., Petersen, A. C., & Newman, J. L. (1990). Gender differences in the relationship between achievement and self-image during early adolescence. *Journal of Early Adolescence, 10,* 159–175.

Robins, L. N. (1989). Suicide attempts in teen-aged medical patients. In ADAMHA. *Report of the secretary's task force on youth suicide: Vol. 4: Strategies for the prevention of youth suicide.* (U.S. Department of Health and Human Services publication # ADM 89-1622.) Washington, DC: U.S. Government Printing Office.

Robinson, B. E. (1988). Teenage pregnancy from the father's perspective. *American Journal of Orthopsychiatry, 58,* 46–51.

Robinson, I., Ziss, K., Ganza, B., Katz, S., & Robinson, E. (1991). Twenty years of the sexual revolution, 1965–1985: An update. *Journal of Marriage and the Family, 53,* 216–220.

Robinson, J., & Godbey, G. (1978). Work and leisure in America: How we spend out time. *Journal of Physical Education and Recreation, 49*(8), 38–39.

Robinson, P. A. (1978). Parents of beyond control adolescents. *Adolescence, 13,* 109–118.

Robinson, T., & Ward, J. V. (1991). "A belief in self far greater than anyone's disbelief": Cultivating resistance among African American female adolescents. *Women and Therapy, 11,* 87–103.

Rodriguez, J. F. (1980). Youth employment: A needs assessment. In *A review of youth employment problems, programs, and policies: The Vice President's Task Force on Youth Employment* (Vol. 1). Washington, DC: U.S. Department of Labor.

Rodriguez, O., & Zayas, L. H. (1990). Hispanic adolescents and antisocial behavior: Sociocultural factors and treatment implications. In A. R. Stiffman & L. E. Davis (Eds.), *Ethnic issues in adolescent mental health.* Newbury Park, CA: Sage.

Rodriguez-Andrew, S. (1985). Inhalant abuse. *Children Today, 14,* 23–25.

Roessner, B. (1981). Remedies sought as teenage suicide rates soar. *Hartfort Courant,* 34.

Rogers, C., & Dymond, R. (1954). *Psychotherapy and personality change.* Chicago: University of Chicago Press.

Rogers, C. R. (1965). The therapeutic relationship: Recent theory and research. *Australian Journal of Psychology, 17,* 95–108.

Roosa, M. W. (1986). Adolescent mothers school drop-outs and school based intervention programs. *Family Relations, 35,* 313–317.

Roosa, M. W. (1991). Adolescent pregnancy programs collection: An introduction. *Family Relations, 40,* 370–372.

Roper, B. C., & LaBeff, E. (1977). Sex roles and feminism revisited: An intergenerational attitude comparison. *Journal of Marriage and the Family, 39,* 113–120.

Rosen, L. (1985). Family and delinnquency: Structure or function? *Criminology, 23,* 553–573.

Rosen, L. W., Shafer, C. L., Dummer, G. M., Cross, L. K., Deuman, G. W., & Malmberg, S. R. (1988). Prevalence of pathogenic weight-control behaviors among Native American women and girls. *International Journal of Eating Disorders, 7,* 807–811.

Rosen, R. H. (1980). Adolescent pregnancy decision-making: Are parents important? *Adolescence, 15*(57), 43.

Rosenbaum, C. P., & Beebe, J. E. (1975). *Psychiatric treatment.* New York: McGraw-Hill.

Rosenbaum, E., & Kandel, D B. (1990). Early onset of adolescent sexual behavior and drug involvement. *Journal of Marriage and the Family, 52,* 783–798.

Rosenberg, F. R., & Rosenberg, M. (1978). Self-esteem and delinquency. *Journal of Youth and Adolescence, 7,* 279–294.

Rosenberg, M. (1962). The dissonant religious context and emotional disturbance. *American Journal of Sociology, 68,* 1–10.

Rosenberg, M. (1963). Parental interest and children's self-conception. *Sociometry, 26,* 35–49.

Rosenberg, M. (1965). *Society and the adolescent self-image.* Prnceton, NJ: Princeton University Press.

Rosenberg, M. (1975). The dissonant context and the adolescent self-concept. In S. E. Dragastin & G. H. Elder (Eds.), *Adolescence in the life cycle.* New York: Wiley.

Rosenberg, M. (1979). *Conceiving the self.* New York: Basic Books.

Rosenberg, M. (1985). Self-concept and psychological well-being in adolescence. In R. L. Leaky (Ed.), *The development of the self,* 205–242. New York: Academic Press.

Rosenberg, M., & Kaplan, H. B. (Eds.). (1982). *Social psychology of the self-concept.* Arlington Heights, IL: Harlan Davidson.

Rosenkrantz, A. L. (1978). A note on adolescent suicide: Incidence, dynamics, and some suggestions for treatment. *Adolescence, 13,* 209–213.

Rosenthal, D. A., Moore, S. M., & Taylor, M. J. (1983). Ethnicity and adjustment: A study of the self-image of Anglo, Greek- and Italian-Australian working class adolescents. *Journal of Youth and Adolescence, 12,* 117–135.

Rosenthal, R., & Jacobson, L. (1968). *Pygmalion in the classroom.* New York: Holt, Rinehart & Winston.

Ross, L. (1990). Canada's youth: 1986 census of Canada. Ottawa: Canadian Government Publishing Centre.

Rotberg, I. C. (1990). I never promised you first place. *Phi Delta Kappan, 72,* 296–303.

Rothbaum, F. (1977). Developmental and gender differences in the sex stereotyping of nurturance and dominance. *Developmental Psychology, 13,* 531–532.

Rotheram, M. J. (1987). Evaluation of imminent danger for suicide among youth. *American Journal of Orthopsychiatry, 57*(1), 102–110.

Rotheram, M. J., & Phinney, J. S. (1987). Ethnic behavior patterns as an aspect of identity. In J. S. Phinney & M. J. Rotheram (Eds.), *Children's ethnic socialization: Pluralism and development.* Newbury Park, CA: Sage.

Rotheram-Borus, M. J. (1989). Ethnic differences in adolescents' identity status and associated behavior problems. *Journal of Adolescence, 12,* 361–374.

Rotheram-Borus, M. J. (1990). Adolescents' reference-group choices self-esteem, and adjustment. *Journal of Personality and Social Psychology, 59,* 1075–1081.

Rothman, E. K. (1987). *Hands and hearts: A social history of courtship in America.* Cambridge, MA: Harvard University Press.

Rotnem, D., Genel, M., Hintz, R., & Cohen, D. (1977). Personality development in children with growth hormone deficiency. *Journal of the American Academy of Child Psychiatry, 16,* 412–426.

Rowe, D. C. (1986). Genetic and environmental components of antisocial behavior: A study of 265 twin pairs. *Criminology, 24,* 513–532.

Rowe, I., & Marcia, J. E. (1980). Ego identity status, formal operations, and moral development. *Journal of Youth and Adolescence, 9,* 87–100.

Rowley, S. (1987). Psychological effects of intensive training in young athletes. *Journal of Child Psychology and Psychiatry, 28,* 371–377.

Roy, A. (1989). Genetics and suicidal behavior. In ADAMHA. *Report of the secretary's task force on youth suicide: Vol. 2: Risk factors for youth suicide.* (U.S. Department of Health and Human Services publication # ADM 89-1622.) Washington, DC: U.S. Government Printing Office.

Royce, J. E. (1981). *Alcohol problems and alcoholism.* New York: Free Press.

Rozee, P., & Van Boemel, G. (1989). The psychological effects of war trauma and abuse on older Cambodian refugee women. *Women & Therapy, 8,* 23–49.

Rua, J. (1990). *Treatment works.* Washington, DC: U.S. Government Printing Office.

Rubenstein, J., Watson, F., Drolette, M., & Rubenstein, H. (1976). Young adolescents' sexual interests. *Adolescence, 11,* 487–496.

Rubenstein, J., Watson, F., & Rubentein, H. (1977). An analysis of sex education books for adolescents by means of adolescents' sexual interests. *Adolescence, 12,* 54–71.

Rubenstein, J. L., Heeren, T., Housman, D., Rubin, C., & Stechler, G. (1989). Suicidal behavior in "normal" adolescents. *American Journal of Orthopsychiatry, 59,* 59–71.

Rubin, L. D., & Price, J. H. (1979). Divorce and its effects on children. *Journal of School Health, 49,* 552–556.

Ruble, D. N., & Brooks-Gunn, J. (1982). The experience of menarche. *Child Development, 53,* 1557–1566.

Runck, B. (1986). *Coping with AIDS* (DHHS Publication No. ADM 85-1432). Washington, DC: U.S. Government Printing Office.

Russ-Eft, S., Sprenger, M., & Beever, A. (1979). Antecedents of adolescent parenthood and consequences at age 30. *Family Coordinator, 18,* 173–178.

Rust, J. O., & McGraw, A. (1984). Influence of masculinity-feminity on adolescent self-esteem and peer acceptance. *Adolescence, 19,* 359–366.

Sabbath, J. C. (1969). The suicidal adolescent: The expendable child. *Journal of the American Academy of Child Psychiatry, 8,* 272–289.

Sabo, D. F., & Runfola, R. (Eds.). (1980). *Jock: Sports and the male identity.* Englewood Cliffs, NJ: Prentice-Hall.

Sage, G. H . (1978). American values and sport: Formation of a bureaucratic personality. *Journal of Physical Education and Recreation, 49*(8), 42–44.

Sahler, O. J. Z. (1980). Adolescent parenting: Potential for child abuse and neglect. *Pediatric Annals, 9*(3), 67–75.

St. Pierre, R., & Miller, D. N. (1986). Future directions for school-based alcohol education. *Health Education* Dec./Jan., 11–13.

Santrock, J. W. (1987). The effects of divorce on adolescents: Needed research perspectives. *Family Therapy, 14,* 47–157.

Santrock, J. W., Warshak, R., Lindbergh, C., & Meadows, L. (1982). Children's and parents' observed social behavior in stepfather families. *Child Development, 53,* 472–480.

Sarigiani, P. A., Wilson, J. L., Petersen, A. C., & Vicary, J. R. (1990). Self-image and educational plans of adolescents from two contrasting communities. *Journal of Early Adolescence, 10,* 37–55.

Sato, N., & McLaughlin, M. W. (1992). Context matters: Teaching in Japan and in the U.S. *Phi Delta Kappan, 73,* 359–366.

Savin-Williams, R. C. (1979). Dominance hierarchies in groups of early adolescents. *Child Development, 50,* 923–935.

Savin-Williams, R. C. (1987). *Adolescence: An ethological perspective.* New York: Springer.

Savin-Williams, R. C., & Demo, D. H. (1983). Conceiving or misconceiving the self: Issues in adolescent self-esteem. *Journal of Early Adolescence, 3,* 121–140.

Savin-Williams, R. C., & Rodriguez, R. G. (1993). A developmental, clinical perspective on lesbian, gay male, and bisexual youths. In T. P. Gullotta, G. R. Adams, & R. Montemayor (Eds.), *Adolescent sexuality.* Newbury Park, CA: Sage.

Scanzoni, J. (1976). Sex role change and influences on birth intentions. *Journal of Marriage and the Family, 38,* 43–60.

Scanzoni, J., & Fox, G. L. (1980). Sex roles, family and society: The seventies and beyond. *Journal of Marriage and the Family, 42,* 743–758.

Scarr, S., & Weinberg, R. A. (1976). I.Q. test performance of black children adopted by white families. *American Psychologist, 31,* 726–730.

Scarr, S., Weinberg, R. A., & Levine, A. (1986). *Understanding development.* New York: Harcourt Brace Jovanovich.

Schachter, S. (1964). The interaction of cognitive and psychological determinants of emotional state. In L. Berkowitz (Ed.), *Advances in experimental social psychology* (Vol. 1). New York: Academic Press.

Schaefer, E. S. (1959). A circumplex model for maternal behavior. *Journal of Abnormal and Social Psychology, 59,* 226–235.

Scheck, D. C., Emerick, R., & El-Assal, M. M. (1973). Adolescents' perceptions of parent-child relations and the development of internal-external control orientation. *Journal of Marriage and the Family, 35,* 643–645.

Schelling, T. C. (1992). Addictive drugs: The cigarette experience. *Science, 255,* 430– 433.

Schenkel, S. (1975). Relationship among ego identity status, field-independence, and traditional femininity. *Journal of Youth and Adolescence, 4,* 73–82.

Schiedel, D. G., & Marcia, J. E. (1985). Ego identity, intimacy, sex role orientation, and gender. *Developmental Psychology, 21,* 149–160.

Schilder, P., & Wechsler, D. (1934). The attitudes of children toward death. *Journal of Genetic Psychology, 45,* 406– 418.

Schinke, S. P., Blythe, B. J., & Gilchrist, L. D. (1981). Cognitive-behavioral prevention of adolescent pregnancy. *Journal of Counseling Psychology, 28*(5), 451– 454.

Schinke, S. P., McAlister, A. L., Orlandi, M. A., & Botvin, G. J. (1990). The social environmental constructs of social competency. In T. P. Gullotta, G. R. Adams, & R. Montemayor (Eds.), *Developing social competency in adolescence.* Newbury Park, CA: Sage.

Schinke, S. P., Moncher, M. S., Palleja, J., Zayas, L. H., Schilling, R. F. (1988). Hispanic youth, substance abuse, and stress: Implications for prevention research. *The International Journal of the Addictions, 23,* 809–826.

Schlaefli, A., Rest, J. R., & Thoms, S. J. (1985). Does moral education improve moral judgment? A meta-analysis of intervention studies using the Defining Issues Test. *Review of Educational Research, 55,* 319–352.

Schlegel, A., & Barry, H. (1991). *Adolescence: An anthropological inquiry.* New York: Free Press.

Schlesier-Carter, B., Hamilton, S. A., O'Neil, P. M., Lydiard, R. B., & Malcolm, R. (1989). Depression and bulimia: The link between depression and bulimic cognitions. *Journal of Abnormal Psychology, 98,* 322–325.

Schneider, B., & Lee, Y. (1990). A model for academic success: The school and home environment of East Asian students. *Anthropology & Education Quarterly, 21,* 358–377.

Schneider, S. (1982). Helping adolescents deal with pregnancy: A psychiatric approach. *Adolescence, 17*(66), 285–292.

Schotte, D. E., & Clum, G. A. (1982). Suicide ideation in a college population: A test of a model. *Journal of Consulting and Clinical Psychology, 50*(5), 690–696.

Schrut, A. (1968). Some typical patterns in the behavior and background of adolescent girls who attempt suicide. *American Journal of Psychiatry, 125,* 69–74.

Schuckit, M. A., & Schuckit, J. J. (1989). Substance use and abuse: A risk factor in youth suicide. In ADAMHA. *Report of the secretary's task force on youth suicide: Vol. 2: Risk factors for youth suicide.* (U.S. Department of Health and Human Services publication # ADM 89-1622.) Washington, DC: U.S. Government Printing Office.

Schulman, G. L. (1972). Myths that intrude on the adaptation of the stepfamily. *Social Caseworks, 52,* 131–139.

Schutte, N. S., Malouff, J. M., Post-Gorden, J. C., & Rodasta, A. L. (1988). Effects of playing video games on children's aggressive and other behaviors. *Journal of Applied Psychology, 18,* 454–460.

Schvaneveldt, J. D., & Adams, G. R. (1983). Adolescents and the decision making process. *Theory into Practice, 22,* 98–104.

Schwartz, D. B. (1980). Perspectives on adolescent pregnancy. *Wisconsin Medical Journal, 79,* 35–36.

Schwartz, D. M., & Thompson, M. G. (1981). Do anorectics get well? Current research and future needs. *American Journal of Psychiatry, 138,* 319–323.

Schwartz, I. M., Steketee, M. W., & Schneider, V. W. (1990). Federal juvenile justice policy and the incarceration of girls. Unpublished manuscript,

Science. (1989). AIDS tests fail. *Science, 246,* 1564.

Science. (1991a). Children who want to bear children. *Science, 254,* 1215.

Science. (1991b). Tracking the AIDS drugs. *Science, 254,* 1113.

Scitovsky, A. A., & Rice, D. P. (1987). Estimates of the direct and indirect costs of acquired immune deficiency syndrome in the United States, 1985, 1986, 1991. *Public Health Reports, 102,* 15–17.

Schwartz, D. M., Thompson, M. G., & Johnson, C. L. (1985). Anorexia nervosa and bulimia: The sociocultural context. In S. W. Emmett (Ed.), *Theory and treatment of anorexia nervosa and bulimia.* New York: Brunner/Mazel.

Sears, R. R., Maccoby, E., & Levin, H. (1957). *Patterns of child rearing.* New York: Harper & Row.

Sebald, H. (1968). *Adolescence: A sociological analysis.* New York: Appleton-Century Crofts.

Sebald, H. (1984). *Adolescence: A social psychological analysis.* Englewood Cliffs, NJ: Prentice-Hall.

Sebald, H. (1989). Adolescent peer orientation: Changes in the support system during the last three decades. *Adolescence, 24,* 937–945.

Secretary of Health and Human Services. (1990). Alcohol and health: Seventh special report to U.S. Congress. # ADM 90-1656. Washington, DC: U.S. Government Printing Office.

Seevers, M. (1977). Drug addiction problems. In *Research Issues 15: Cocaine—Summaries of Psychosocial Research.* Washington, DC: U.S. Government Printing Office. (Original work published 1939).

Seffrin, J. R., & Seehafer, R. W. (1976). Multiple drug use patterns among a group of high school students: Regular users vs. nonusers of specific drug types. *Journal of School Health, 46,* 413–416.

Segest, E., Mygind, O., Harris, C. N., & Bay, H. (1991). The correlation between general disease prevention and prevention of HIV-contagion among adolescents. *Journal of Adolescence, 14,* 389–396.

Seiden, A. M. (1976). Overview: Research on the psychology of women: Gender differences and sexual and reproductive life. *American Journal of Psychiatry, 133,* 995–1007.

Select Committee on Children, Youth, and Families (1992, Dec. 22). *A decade of denial: Teens and AIDS in America.*

Washington, DC: U.S. Government Printing Office.

Seligman, P. (1986). A brief family intervention with an adolescent referred for drug taking. *Journal of Adolescence, 9*(3), 123–133.

Selman, R. (1980). *The growth of interpersonal understanding.* New York: Academic Press.

Selman, R. L. (1976a). Social-cognitive understanding: A guide to educational and clinical practice. In T. Lickona (Ed.), *Moral development and behavior.* New York: Holt, Rinehart & Winston.

Selman, R. L. (1976b). Toward a structural-developmental analysis of interpersonal relationship concepts: Research with normal and disturbed preadolescent boys. In A. Pick (Ed.), *Tenth Annual Minnesota Symposium on Child Psychology.* Minneapolis: University of Minnesota Press.

Selman, R. L. (1980). *The growth of interpersonal understanding: Developmental and clinical analysis.* New York: Academic Press.

Selnow, G. W., & Crano, W. D. (1986). Formal vs. informal group affiliations: Implications for alcohol and drug use among adolescents. *Journal of Studies on Alcohol, 47*(1), 48–52.

Selva, P. C. D., & Dusek, J. B. (1984). Sex-role orientation and resolution of Eriksonian crisis during the late adolescent years. *Journal of Personality and Social Psychology, 47,* 204–212.

Sessa, F. M., & Steinberg, L. (1991). Family structure and the development of autonomy during adolescence. *Journal of Early Adolescence, 11,* 38–55.

Seymour, E. W. (1956). Comparative study of certain behavior characteristics of participant and non-participant boys in Little League baseball. *Research Quarterly, 27,* 338–346.

Shaffer, D., Pettigrew, A., Wolkind, S., & Zajicek, E. (1978). Psychiatric aspects of pregnancy in school girls: A review. *Psychological Medicine, 8,* 119–130.

Shafii, M. (1985). Psychological autopsy of completed suicide in children and adolescents. *American Journal of Psychiatry, 142,* 1061.

Shapiro, C. H . (1980). Sexual learning: The short-changed adolescent male. *Social Work, 25,* 489–493.

Shatin, L. (1981). Psychopathogenic abuses of music in hospitals. *Interaction, 4,* 61–68.

Shaw, G. B. (1957). *Pygmalion.* New York: Dodd, Mead.

Shaw, J. S. (1982). Psychology, androgyny and stressful life events. *Journal of Personality and Social Psychology, 43,* 145–153.

Sheldon, S. (1987, August 15). High illiteracy is fact, not fiction. *The Day,* (New London, CT).

Sherer, M. (1985). Effects of group intervention on moral development of distressed youths in Israel. *Journal of Youth and Adolescence, 14,* 513–526.

Sherry, M. (1993). Searching for new American schools. *Phi Delta Kappan, 74,* 299–302.

Shestowsky, B. J. (1983). Ego identity development and obesity in adolescent girls. *Adolescence, 18,* 551–559.

Shimahara, N. K. (1985). Japanese education and its implications for U.S. education. *Phi Delta Kappan, 67,* 418–421.

Shipman, G. (1968). The psychodynamics of sex education. *Family Coordinator, 17,* 3–12.

Shisslak, C. M., Crago, M., Neal, M. E., & Swain, B. (1987). Primary prevention of eating disorders. *Journal of Consulting and Clinical Psychology, 55,* 660–667.

Shneidman, E. S. (Ed.). (1976). *Suicidology: Contemporary developments.* New York: Grune & Stratton.

Sickmund, M. (1990). *Runaways in juvenile courts.* U.S. Department of Justice No. NCJ 124881. Washington, DC: U.S. Government Printing Office.

Siegel, R. K. (1987). Changing patterns of cocaine use: Longitudinal observations, consequences, and treatment. In J. Grabowski (Ed.), *Cocaine: Pharmacology, effects, and treatment of abuse.* (U.S. Department of Health and Human Services publication # ADM 87-1326.) Washington, DC: U.S. Government Printing Office.

Silber, T. (1981). Gonorrhea in adolescence: Its impact and consequences. *Adolescence, 16*(63), 537–541.

Silberman, C. (1970). *Crisis in the classroom.* New York: Random House.

Simmons, A. B. (1990). "New" wave immigrants: Origins and characteristics. In S. S. Halli, F. Trovato, & L. Driedger (Eds.), *Ethnic demography: Canadian immigrant, racial and cultural variations.* Ottawa: Carleton University Press.

Simmons, D. D. (1970). Development of an objective measure of identity achievement status. *Journal of Projective Techniques and Personality Assessment, 34,* 241–244.

Simmons, R. G., & Blyth, D. A. (1987). *Moving into adolescence: The impact of pubertal change and school context.* New York: Aldine.

Simmons, R. G., Blyth, D. G., & McKinney, K. L. (1983). The social and psychological effects of puberty on white females. In J. Brooks-Gunn and A. C. Peterson (Eds.), *Girls in puberty: Biological and psychosocial perspectives* (pp. 229–272). New York: Plenum Press.

Simmons, R. G., Blyth, D. A., Van Cleave, E. F., & Bush, D. M. (1979). Entry into early adolescence: The impact of school structure, puberty, and early dating on self-esteem. *American Sociological Review, 44,* 948–967.

Simmons, R. G., Bulcroft, R., Blyth, D. A., & Bush, D. M. (1979, March). *The vulnerable adolescent: School context and self-esteem.* Paper presented at the meeting of the Society for Research in Child Development, Washington, DC.

Simmons, R. G., & Rosenberg, F. (1975). Sex, sex-roles and self-images. *Journal of Youth and Adolescence, 4,* 229–258.

Simmons, R. G., Rosenberg, F., & Rosenberg, M. (1973). Disturbances in the self-image at adolescence. *American Sociological Review, 38,* 553–568.

Simon, J. A. (1979). America's attitudes toward youth sports. *Physical Educator, 36,* 186–190.

Simonds, J. F., & Kashani, J. (1979). Phenycyclidine use in delinquent males committed to a training school. *Adolescence, 14,* 721–725.

Sizer, T. R. (1983). High school reform: The need for engineering. *Phi Delta Kappan,* June, 679–683.

Skubic, E. (1956). Studies of Little League and Middle League baseball. *Research Quarterly, 27,* 97–110.

Slade, J. (1989). The tobacco epidemic: Lessons from history. *Journal of Psychoactive Drugs, 21,* 281–291.

Slaughter, D. T. (Ed.). (1988). Black children and poverty: A developmental perspective. *New Directions for Child Development,* No. 42. San Francisco: Jossey-Bass.

Slocum, W., & Stone, C. K. (1963). Family culture patterns and delinquent-type behavior. *Marriage and Family Living, 25,* 202–208.

Sloman, L. (1979). *The history of marijuana in America: Reefer madness.* New York: Bobbs-Merrill.

Slugoski, B. R., Marcia, J. E., & Koopman, R. J. (1984). Cognitive and social interactional characteristics of ego identity statuses in college males. *Journal of Personality and Social Psychology, 47,* 646–661.

Smart, R., & Jones, D. (1970). Illicit LSD users: Their personality characteristics and psychotherapy. *Journal of Abnormal Psychology, 75,* 286–292.

Smead, V. S. (1983). Anorexia nervosa, buliminarexia, and bulimia: Labeled pathology and the western female. *Women and Therapy, 2,* 19–35.

Smetana, J. G., Yau, J., & Hanson, S. (1991). Conflict resolution in families with adolescents. *Journal of Research on Adolescence, 1,* 189–206.

Smith, A., Goodwin, R., Gullotta, C. F., & Gullotta, T. P. (1979). Community mental health and the arts: The experiences of a small New England community. *Children Today, 8*(1), 17–20.

Smith, D. E., Wesson, D. R., & Seymour, E. B. (1979). The abuse of barbiturates and other sedative-hypnotics. In R. Dupont, A. Goldstein, & J. O'Donnell (Eds.), *Handbook on drug abuse.* Washington, DC: U.S. Government Printing Office.

Smith, E. A., & Udry, J. R. (1985). Coital and non-coital sexual behavior of white and black adolescents. *American Journal of Public Health, 75,* 1200–1203.

Smith, E. W. (1975). The role of the grandmother in adolescent pregnancy and parenting. *Journal of School Health, 45,* 278–283.

Smith, J. E., Hillard, M. C., & Roll, S. (1991). Rorschach evaluation of adolescent bulimics. *Adolescence, 26,* 687–696.

Smith, M. D., & Self, G. D. (1980). The congruence between mothers' and daughters' sex-role attitudes: A research note. *Journal of Marriage and the Family, 42,* 105–109.

Smith, P. B., Munford, D. M., & Hammer, E. (1979). Childrearing attitudes of single teenage mothers. *American Journal of Nursing, 79,* 2115–2116.

Smith, R. M., & Walters, J. (1978). Delinquent and non-delinquent males' perceptions of their fathers. *Adolescence, 13,* 21–28.

Smith, T. E. (1976). Push versus pull: Intra-family versus peer-group variables on possible determinants of adolescent orientations toward parents. *Youth and Society, 8,* 5–26.

Smith, W. M. (1952). Rating and dating: A restudy. *Marriage and Family Living, 14,* 312–317.

Smollar, J., & Ooms, T. (1987). *Young unwed fathers.* Rockville, MD: Shared Resource Center.

Snyder, E. E. (1969). Socioeconomic variations, values, and social participation among high school students. In D. Rogers (Ed.), *Issues in adolescent psychology.* New York: Appleton-Century-Crofts.

Snyder, M., Tanke, E. D., & Berscheid, E. (1977). Social perception and interpersonal behavior: On the self-fulfilling nature of social stereotypes. *Journal of Personality and Social Psychology, 35,* 656–666.

Solomon, M. R. (1986, April). Dress for effect. *Psychology Today, 20*–26.

Sommer, B., & Nagel, S. (1991). Ecological and typological characteristics in early adolescent truancy. *Journal of Early Adolescence, 11,* 379–392.

Sorensen, R. (1973). *Adolescent sexuality in contemporary America.* New York: World.

Sorrels, J. M. (1977). Kids who kill. *Crime and delinquency, 23,* 312–320.

Sowell, T. (1981). Historical data show Black/White IQ gap neither unique nor related to segregation. *Phi Delta Kappan, 62,* 753.

Sowell, T. (1986). *Education: Assumptions versus history.* Stanford, CA: Hoover Institution Press.

Spady, W. G. (1971). Status, achievement, and motivation in the American high school. *School Review, 79,* 379–403.

Spanier, G. (1976). Perceived sex knowledge, exposure to eroticism, and premarital sex behavior. *Sociological Quarterly, 17,* 247–261.

Spanier, G. (1978). Sex education and premarital sexual behavior among American college students. *Adolescence, 13,* 659–675.

Spanier, G. B., & Glick, P. C. (1981). Marital instability in the United States: Some correlates and recent changes. *Family Relztion, 31,* 329–338.

Spence, J. T., & Helmreich, R. L. (1979). Comparison of masculine and feminine personality attributes and sex-role attitudes across age groups. *Developmental Psychology, 15,* 583–590.

Spencer, M. B. (1985). Cultural cognition and social cognition as identity factors in Black children's personal-social growth. In M. B. Spencer, G. K. Brookins, & W. R. Allen (Eds.), *Beginnings: The social and affective development of Black children.* Hillsdale, NJ: Erlbaum.

Spencer, M. B. (1987). Black children's ethnic identity formation: Risk and resilience of castelike minorities. In J. S. Phinney & M. J. Rotheram (Eds.), *Children's ethnic socialization: Pluralism and development.* Newbury Park, CA: Sage.

Spencer, M. B., & Markstrom-Adams, C. (1990). Identity processes among racial and ethnic minority children in America. *Child Development, 61,* 290–310.

Spergel, I. A., & Chance, R. L. (1991). National youth gang suppression and intervention program. *National Institute of Justice Reports, #224,* 21–24.

Sperling, M. (1967). School-phobia classification, dyamics, and treatment. *Psychoanalytic Study of the Child, 22,* 375–401.

Spranger, E. (1955). *Psychologie des Jungendalters,* Heidelberg: Quelle & Meyer.

Stack, S. (1988). Suicide: Media impacts in war and peace, 1910–1920. *Suicide and Life-Threatening Behavior, 18,* 342–357.

Stager, S. F., Chassin, L., & Young, R. D. (1983). Determinants of self-esteem among labeled adolescents. *Social Psychology Quarterly, 46,* 3–10.

Stake, J. E., DeVille, C. J., & Pennell, C. L. (1983). The effects of assertiveness training on the performance self-esteem of adolescent girls. *Journal of Youth and Adolescence, 12,* 435–442.

Stanley, E. J., & Barter, J. T. (1970). Adolescent suicidal behavior. *American Journal of Orthopsychiatry, 40,* 87–96.

Stanton, D. M. (1979). Family treatment of drug problems: A review. In R. Dupont, A. Goldstein, & J. O'Donnell (Eds.), *Handbook on drug abuse.* Washington, DC: U.S. Government Printing Office.

Starrett, R. H. (1983). The conceptual commonality between impulsiveness as a personality trait and as an ego development stage. *Personality and Individual Differences, 4,* 265–274.

Steffensmeier, D. J., & Steffensmeier, R. H. (1980). Trends in female delinquency. *Criminology, 18,* 62–85.

Stein, J. A., Newcomb, M. D., & Bentler, P. M (1987). An 8-year study of multiple influences on drug use and drug use consequences. *Journal of Personality and Social Psychology, 53,* 1094–1105.

Steinberg, L. (1987a). Familial factors in delinquency: The developmental perspective. *Journal of Adolescent Research, 2,* 235–268.

Steinberg, L. (1987b). The impact of puberty on family relations: Effects of pubertal status and pubertal timing. *Developmental Psychology, 23,* 451–460.

Steinberg, L. (1989). Pubertal maturation and parent-adolescent distance: An evolutionary perspective. In G. R. Adams, R. Montemayor, & T. P. Gullotta (Eds.), *Biology of adolescent behavior and development, Vol. 1: Advances in adolescent development.* Newbury Park, CA: Sage.

Steinberg, L., Greenberger, E., Jacobi, M, & Garduque, L. (1981). Early work experience: A partial antidote for adolescent egocentrism. *Journal of Youth and Adolescence, 10,* 141–158.

Steinberg, L. D. (1979, March). *Changes in family relations at puberty.* Paper presented at the meeting of the Society for Research in Child Development, San Francisco.

Steinberg, L. D. (1981). Transformation in family relations at puberty. *Developmental Psychology, 17,* 833–840.

Steinberg, L. D., & Hill, J. P. (1978). Patterns of family interaction as a function of age, the onset of puberty, and formal thinking. *Developmental Psychology, 14,* 683–684.

Steinkamp, M., & Maehr, M. (1984). Gender differences in motivational orientations toward achievement in school science: A quantitative synthesis. *American Educational Research Journal, 21,* 39–59.

Steinhausen, H. (1977). Psychoendocrinological studies of dwarfism in childhood and adolescence. *Zeitschrift fur Kinder- und Jugendpsychiatrie, 5,* 346–359.

Steinman, S. (1981). The experience of children in a joint-custody arrangement: A report of a study. *American Journal of Orthopsychiatry, 51,* 403–414.

Stekel, W. (1967). [Untitled comments.] In P. Friedman (Ed.), *On suicide: With particular reference to suicide among young students.* New York: International Universities Press.

Sternberg, R. (1977). *Intelligence, information processing, and analogical reasoning: The componential analysis of human abilities.* Hillsdale, NJ: Erlbaum.

Sternberg, R. J. (1980). Sketch of a componential sub-theory of human intelligence. *Behavioral and Brain Sciences, 3,* 573–584.

Sternberg, R. J., & Powell, J. S. (1983). The development of intelligence. In J.

H. Flavell & E. M. Markman (Eds.), *Handbook of child psychology: Vol. 1. Cognitive development.* New York: Wiley.

Stets, F. E., & Henderson, D. A. (1991). Contextual factors surrounding conflict resolution while dating: Results from a national study. *Family Relations, 40,* 29–36.

Stevens, S. (1980). *Infant caregiving: The role of the father.* Unpublished manuscript, available from Scott Stevens, United Social and Mental Health Services, 51 Westcott Road, Danielson, CT.

Stierlin, H. (1974). *Separating: Parents and adolescents.* New York: Quadrangle.

Stone, C. A., & Day, M. C. (1978). Levels of availability of a formal operational strategy. *Child Development, 49,* 1054–1065.

Stott, M. W., & Olczak, P. V. (1978). Relating personality characteristics to juvenile offense categories: Differences between status offenders and juvenile delinquents. *Journal of Clinical Psychology, 34,* 80–84.

Strang, S. P., & Orlofsky, J. L. (1990). Factors underlying suicidal ideation among college students: A test of Teicher and Jacobs' model. *Journal of Adolescence, 13,* 39–52.

Streitmatter, J. L. (1988). Ethnicity as a mediating variable of early adolescent identity development. *Journal of Adolescence, 11,* 335–346.

Streitmatter, J. L. (1989). Identity development and academic achievement in early adolescence. *Journal of Early Adolescence, 9,* 99–111.

Streitmatter, J. L., & Pate, G. S. (1989). Identity status development and cognitive prejudice in early adolescents. *Journal of Early Adolescence, 9,* 142–152.

Strober, M. (1981). A comparative analysis of personality organization in juvenile anorexia nervosa. *Journal of Youth and Adolescence, 10,* 285–295.

Strober, M., & Humphrey, L. L. (1987). Familial contributions to the etiology and course of anorexia nervosa and bulimia. *Journal of Consulting and Clinical Psychology, 55,* 654–659.

Stroman, C. A. (1991). Television's role in the socialization of African American children and adolescents. *Journal of Negro Education, 60,* 314–327.

Strother, D. B. (1986). Dropping out. *Phi Delta Kappan, 68,* 325–328.

Stuart, C., & Gokiert, M. L. (1990). Child and youth care education for the culturally different student: a Native people's example. *Child & Youth Services, 13,* 253–261.

Studer, M., & Thornton, A. (1987). Adolescent religiosity and contraceptive usage. *Journal of Marriage and the Family, 49,* 117–128.

Stumphauzer, J. S. (1980). Learning to drink: Adolescents and alcohol. *Addictive Behaviors, 5,* 277–283.

Sullivan, K., & Sullivan, A. (1980). Adolescent-parent separation. *Developmental Psychology, 16,* 93–99.

Sullivan, P. S., Dunham, R. G., & Alpert, G. P. (1987). Attitude structures of different ethnic and age groups concerning police. *The Journal of Criminal Law & Criminology, 78,* 177–196.

Sun, S. W., & Lull, J. (1986). The adolescent audience for music videos and why they watch. *Journal of Communications, 36,* 115–125.

Surra, C. A. (1990). Research and theory on mate selection and premarital relationships in the 1980s. *Journal of Marriage and the Family, 52,* 844–865.

Susman, E. J., Inoff-Germain, G., Nottelmann, E. D., Loriaux, D. L., & Cutler, G. B. (1987). Hormones, emotional dispositions, and aggressive attributes in early adolescence. *Child Development, 58,* 1114–1134.

Susman, E. J., Nottlemann, E. O., Inoff-Germain, E. G., Dorn, L. D., Cutler, G. B., Loriaux, D. L., & Chrousos, G. P. (1985). The relation of relative hormonal levels and physical development and social emotional behavior in young adolescents. *Journal of Youth and Adolescence, 14,* 245–264.

Swaim, R. C., Oetting, E. R., Edwards, R. W., & Beauvais, F. (1989). Links from emotional distress to adolescent drug abuse: A path model. *Journal of Consulting and Clinical Psychology, 57,* 227–231.

Swartz, D. M., Thompson, M. G., & Johnson, C. L. (1985). Anorexia nervosa and bulimia: The sociocultural context. In S. W. Emmett (Ed.), *Theory and treatment of anorexia nervosa and bulimia.* New York: Brunner/Mazel.

Sweet, R. W. (1990). *Missing children: Found facts.* U.S. Department of Justice No. NCJ 130916. Washington, DC: U.S. Government Printing Office.

Swinton, D. H. (1980). Towards defining the universe of need for youth employment policy. In *A review of youth employment problems, programs, and policies: The Vice President's Task Force on Youth Employment* (Vol. 1). Washington, DC: U.S. Department of Labor.

Swisher, J. D. (1979). Prevention issues. In R. Dupont, A. Goldstein, & J. O'Donnell (Eds.), *Handbook on drug abuse.* Washington, DC: U.S. Government Printing Office.

Sykes, G. M. (1980). *The future of crime* (National Institute of Mental Health, DHHS Publication No. ADM 80-912). Washington, DC: U.S. Government Printing Office.

Tanner, J. M. (1962). *Growth at adolescence.* Springfield, IL: Charles C Thomas.

Tanner, J. M. (1975). Growth and endocrinology of the adolescent. In L. I. Gardner (Ed.), *Endocrine and genetic diseases of childhood* (2nd ed.). Philadelphia: Saunders.

Taylor, R. J. (1986). Receipt of support from family among Black Americans: Demographic and familial differences. *Journal of Marriage and the Family, 48,* 67–77.

Teenage suicides escalate; toll is 6 deaths per day. (1982, January 29). *Adamha News,* p. 5.

Teicher, J. D., & Jacobs, J. (1966). Adolescents who attempt suicide: Preliminary findings. *American Journal of Psychiatry, 122,* 1248–1257.

Telfer, M. A., Baker, D., Clark, F. R., & Richardson, C. E. (1968). Incidence of gross chromosomal errors among tall criminal American males. *Science, 185,* 1249–1250.

TenHouten, W. D. (1989). Application of dual brain theory to cross-cultural studies of cognitive development and education. *Sociological Perspectives, 32,* 153–167.

Tennant, F., Black, D. L., & Voy, R. O. (1988). Anabolic steroid dependence with opioid-type features. *New England Journal of Medicine, 84,* 578.

Tesch, S. A., & Whitbourne, S. K., (1980, September). *Intimacy status, identity status, and sex-role orientation in adulthood.* Paper presented at the meeting of the American Psychological Association, Montreal.

Tesch, S. A., & Whitbourne, S. K. (1982). Intimacy and identity status in young adults. *Journal of Personality and Social Psychology, 43,* 1041–1051.

Tesser, A., & Paulhus, D. L. (1976). Toward a casual model love. *Journal of Personality and Social Psychology, 34,* 1095–1105.

Teti, D. M., Lamb, M. E., Elster, A. B. (1987). Socio-economic and marital consequences of adolescent marriage in 3 cohorts of adult males. *Journal of Marriage and the Family, 49,* 499–506.

Thomas, D. L., & Carver, C. (1990). Religion and adolescent social competence. In T. P. Gullotta, G. R. Adams, & R. Montemayor (Eds.), *Developing social competency in adolescence.* Newbury Park, CA: Sage.

Thompson, K. P. (1993). Media, music, and adolescents. In R. M. Lerner (Ed.), *Early adolescents: Perspectives on research, policy, and intervention.* Hillsdale, NJ: Erlbaum.

Thompson, T., & Simmons, Cooper, C. (1988). Chemical dependency treatment and Black adolescents. *The Journal of Drug Issues, 18,* 21–31.

Thompson, W. E. (1987). Courtship violence: Toward a conceptual understanding. *Youth & Society, 18,* 162–176.

Thornberry, T. P., Moore, M., & Christenson, R. L. (1985). The effect of dropping out of high school on subsequent criminal behavior. *Criminology, 23,* 3–18.

Thornberry, T. P., Tolnay, S. E., Flanagan, T. J., & Glynn, P. (1991). *Children in custody.* U.S. Department of Justice No. NCJ 127675. Washington, DC: U.S. Government Printing Office.

Thornburg, H. D. (1981). The amount of sex information learning obtained during early adolescence. *Journal of Early Adolescence, 1,* 171–183.

Thornton, A. (1990). The courtship process of adolescent sexuality. *Journal of Family Issues, 11,* 239–273.

Thornton, A., Alwin, D. E., & Camburn, D. (1983). Causes and consequences of sex-role attitudes and attitude change. *American Sociological Review, 48,* 211–227.

Thornton, A., & Camburn, D. (1989). Religious participation and adolescent sexual behavior and attitudes. *Journal of Marriage and the Family, 51,* 641–653.

Thornton, A. D., & Camburn, D. (1987). The influence of the family on premarital sexual attitudes and behavior. *Demography, 24,* 323–340.

Tiedeman, D. V. (1961). Decision and vocational development: A paradigm and its implication. *Personnel and Guidance Journal, 40,* 15–21.

Tishler, C. L., & McKenry, P. C. (1982). Parental negative self and adolescent suicide attempts. *Journal of American Academy of Child Psychiatry, 21*(4), 404–408.

Tishler, C. L., McKenry, P. C., & Morgan, K. C. (1981). Adolescent suicide attempt: Some significant factors. *Suicide and Life-Threatening Behavior, 11*(2), 86–92.

Tobin-Richards, M. H., Boxer, A. M., & Petersen, A. C. (1983). The psychological significance of pubertal change: Sex differences in perceptions of self during early adolescence. In J. Brooks-Gunn and A. C. Petersen (Eds.), *Girls at puberty.* New York: Plenum.

Toby, J. (1957). The differential impact of family disorganization. *American Sociological Review, 22,* 505–512.

Toder, N., & Marcia, J. (1973). Ego identity status and response to conformity pressure in college women. *Journal of Personality and Social Psychology, 26,* 287–294.

Tolstoy, L. (1952). *War and Peace.* Chicago: Encyclopaedia Brittanica. (Original work published 1872)

Tomeh, A. K. (1978). Sex role orientation: An analysis of structural and attitudinal predictors. *Journal of Marriage and the Family, 40,* 341–354.

Toolan, J. M. (1962). Suicide and suicide attempts in children and adolescents. *American Journal of Psychiatry, 118,* 719–724.

Toolan, M. D. (1981). Depression and suicide in children: An overview. *American Journal of Psychotherapy, 35*(3), 311–322.

Tooley, K. M. (1980). The remembrance of things past. *American Journal of Orthopsychiatry, 48*(1), 174–182.

Townsend, J. K., & Worobey, J. (1987). Mother and daughter perception of their relationship: The influence of adolescent pregnancy status. *Adolescence, 22,* 487–496.

Trautman, P. D. (1989). Specific treatment modalities for adolescent attempters. In ADAMHA. *Report of the Secretary's task force on youth suicide: Vol. 3: Prevention and interventions in youth suicide.* (U.S. Department of Health and Human Services publication # ADM 89-1622.) Washington, DC: U.S. Government Printing Office.

Tremper, C., & Feshback, N. (1982). *Attitudes of parents and adolescents toward decision making by minors.* Unpublished research paper, University of California, Los Angeles.

Trimble, J. E., & LaFromboise, T. (1985). American Indians and the counseling process: Culture, adaptation, and style. In P. Pedersen (Ed.), *Handbook of cross-cultural counseling and therapy.* Westport, CT: Greenwood.

Trueba, H. T. (1988). Culturally based explanations of minority students' academic achievement. *Anthropology & Education Quarterly, 19,* 270–287.

Tsui, A. M., & Sammons, M. T. (1988). Group intervention with adolescent Vietnamese refugees. *Journal of Specialists in Group Work, 13,* 90–95.

Tucker, L. A. (1986). The relationship of television viewing to physical fitness and obesity. *Adolescence, 21*(84), 797–806.

Tudor, C. G., Petersen, D. M., & Elifson, K. W. (1980). An examination of the relationship between peer and parental influences and adolescent drug use. *Adolescence, 15,* 783–797.

Turner, R., Shehab, Z., Osborne, K., & Hendley, J. O. (1982). Shedding and survival of herpes simplex virus from "fever blisters." *Pediatrics, 70*(4), 547–549.

Turner, S. M., & Mo, L. (1984). Chinese adolescence self-concept as measured by the Offer Self-Image Questionnaire. *Journal of Youth and Adolescence, 13,* 131–143.

Tzuriel, D. (1981, August). *Sex role typing and ego identity in Israeli, Oriental and Western adolescents.* Paper presented at the 89th annual convention of the American Psychological Association, Los Angeles.

Uddenberg, N. (1976). Mother-father and daughter-male relationships: A comparison. *Archives of Sexual Behavior, 5*(1), 69–78.

Umpierre, S. A., Hill, J. A., & Anderson, D. J. (1985). Effect of "Coke" on sperm motility. *New England Journal of Medicine, 313*(21), 1351.

Urberg, K. A. (1979). Sex role conceptualizations in adolescents and adults. *Developmental Psychology, 15,* 90–92.

Urdy, R. J. (1988). Biological predispositions and social control in adolescent sexual behavior. *American Sociological Review, 53,* 709–722.

U.S. Advisory Board on Child Abuse and Neglect. (1991). *Creating caring communities.* (U.S. Department of Health and Human Services # 017-092-00104-5.) Washington, DC: U.S. Government Printing Office.

U.S. Bureau of the Census. (1975). *Historical statistics of the United States family: Colonial times to 1970.* Stock No. 003-024-001209. Washington, DC: U.S. Government Printing Office.

U.S. Bureau of the Census. (1985). *Statistical Abstract of the United States: 1986* (106th ed.). Washington, DC: U.S. Government Printing Office.

U.S. Bureau of the Census. (1987). What it's worth: Educational background and economic status (U.S. Department of Commerce Series P-70, No. 11). Washington, DC: U.S. Government Printing Office.

U.S. Bureau of the Census. (1990). Almost 7 million stepchildren in married-couple families. *Census and You, 25,* 6. Washington, DC: U.S. Government Printing Office.

U.S. Bureau of the Census. (1991a). Average college student older than before. *Census and You, 26,* 5. Washington, DC: U.S. Government Printing Office.

U.S. Bureau of the Census. (1991b). Does education really pay off? *Census and You, 26,* 8–9. Washington, DC: U.S. Government Printing Office.

U.S. Bureau of the Census. (1991c). The economics of family disruption. *Census and You, 26,* 5. Washington, DC: U.S. Government Printing Office.

U.S. Bureau of the Census. (1991d). Number of two-parent family households still decreasing. *Census and You, 26,* 3. Washington, DC: U.S. Government Printing Office.

U.S. Bureau of the Census. (1991e). *Statistical abstract of the United States: 1991* (111th ed.). Washington, DC: U.S. Government Printing Office.

U.S. Bureau of the Census. (1992a). Divorces and annulments—median duration of marriage, median age at divorce, and children involved: 1970 to 1988. *Statistical Abstract of the United States* (112th ed.). Washington, DC: U.S. Government Printing Office.

U.S. Bureau of the Census. (1992b). Marriages and divorces—number and rate, by state: 1980 to 1990. *Statistical Abstract of the United States* (112th ed.). Washington, DC: U.S. Government Printing Office.

U.S. Bureau of the Census. (1992c). *Statistical Abstract of the United States: 1992* (112th ed.). Washington, DC: U.S. Government Printing Office.

U.S. Bureau of the Census. (1993). Nation's population projected to grow by 50 percent over next 50 years. *Census and You, 28,* 1. Washington, DC: U.S. Government Printing Office.

U.S. Department of Education. (1989). *An international assessment of mathematics and science*. Washington, DC: U.S. Government Printing Office.

U.S. Department of Health and Human Services. (1985). *Vital statistics in the U.S. 1980: Vol. 2. Mortality* (Part A). Washington, DC: U.S. Government Printing Office.

U.S. Department of Health and Human Services. (1991a). *Facts and information resources: Underage drinking*. Healthy Difference Program. Washington, DC: U.S. Government Printing Office.

U.S. Department of Health and Human Services. (1991b). *Drug abuse and drug abuse research*. (DHHS publication # ADM 91-1704.) Washington, DC: U.S. Government Printing Office.

U.S. Department of Labor. (1987). *Count me in: Youth 2000*. Washington, DC: U.S. Government Printing Office.

U.S. Public Health Service. (1978). *Family planning methods of contraception* (DHEW Publication No. HSA 78-5646). Washington, DC: U.S. Government Printing Office.

Utech, D. A., & Hoving, K. L. (1969). Parents and peers as competing influences in the decisions of children of differing ages. *Journal of Social Psychology, 78*, 267–274.

Vaillant, G. E. (1977). *Adaptation to life*. Boston: Little, Brown.

Valenstein, E. S. (1986). *Great and desperate cures*. New York: Basic Books.

Van Buskirk, S. S. (1977). A two phase perspective on the treatment of anorexia nervosa. *Psychological Bulletin, 84*, 529–538.

Vandenplas-Holper, C., & Campos, B. P. (Eds.). (1990). *Interpersonal and identity development: New directons*. Louvain-LaNeuve, Belgium: Academia.

Vanek, J. (1980). Work, leisure, and family roles on U.S. farms. *Journal of Family History, 5*, 422–431.

Van Emde Boas, C. (1980). 10 commandments for parents providing sex education. *Journal of Sex Education and Therapy, 6*(1), 19.

Vener, A., & Stewart, C. (1974). Adolescent sexual behavior in Middle America revisited: 1970–1973. *Journal of Marriage and the Family, 36*, 728–735.

Vener, A., Stewart, C., & Hager, D. (1972). The sexual behavior of adolescents in Middle America: Generational and American-British comparison. *Journal of Marriage and the Family, 34*, 696–705.

Veroff, J., Depner, C., Kulka, R., & Douvan, E. (1980). Comparison of American motives: 1957 versus 1976. *Journal of Personality and Social Psychology, 39*, 1249–1262.

Vicary, J. R., & Lerner, J. V. (1986). Parental attributes and adolescent drug use. *Journal of Adolescence, 9*(2), 115–122.

Viernstein, M. C., McGinn, P. V., & Hogan, R. (1977). The personality correlates of differential verbal and mathematical ability in talented adolescents. *Journal of Youth and Adolescence, 6*, 169–178.

Villanueva, H. F., James, J. R., & Rosecrans, J. A. (1990). Evidence of pharmacological tolerance to nicotine. In L. S. Harris (Ed.), *Problems of drug dependence: 1989*. U.S. Department of Health and Human Services publication # ADM 90-1663. Washington, DC: U.S. Government Printing Office.

Vincent, R. C., Davis, D. K., & Bronszkowski, L. A. (1987). Sexism in MTV: The portrayal of women in rock videos. *Journalism Quarterly, 64*, 750–755, 941.

Vingilis, E. (1981). A literature review of the young drinking offender: Is he a problem drinker? *British Journal of the Addictions, 76*, 27–46.

Vinovskis, M. A. (1981). An 'epidemic' of adolescent pregnancy? Some historical considerations. *Journal of Family History, 6*(2), 205–230.

Violent schools–safe schools: The Safe School Study report to the Congress—Executive Summary. (1979). In R. Rubel (Ed.), *Crime and disruption in schools* (Stock No. 027-000-0863-3). Washington, DC: U.S. Department of Justice, National Institute of Law Enforcement and Criminal Justice.

Viscarello, R. R. (1990). Human immunodeficiency virus infection and pregnancy. *Resident and Staff Physician, 37*, 35–42.

Visher, E. B., & Visher, J. S. (1978). Common problems of stepparents and their spouses. *American Journal of Orthopsychiatry, 48*, 252–262.

Visher, E. B., & Visher, J. S. (1983). Stepparenting: Blending families. In H. I. McCubbin & C. R. Figley (Eds.), *Stress and the family: Copng with normative transitions* (Vol. 1). New York: Brunner/Mazel.

Vitaliano, P. P., Boyer, D., & James J. (1981). Perceptions of juvenile experience: Females involved in prostitution

versus property offenses. *Criminal Justice and Behavior, 8*(3), 325–342.

Wadsworth, B. J. (1971). *Piaget's theory of cognitive development*. New York: McKay.

Wagner, C. A. (1980). Sexuality of American adolescents. *Adolescence, 15*, 567–579.

Wagner, J. (1976). *A study of the relationship between formal operations and ego identity in adolescence*. Unpublished doctoral dissertation, State University of New York at Buffalo.

Walker, B A., & Mehr, M. (1983). Adolescent suicide—a family crisis: A model for addictive intervention by family therapists. *Adolescence, 28*(70), 285–292.

Walker, K. N., & Messinger, L.(1979). Remarriage after divorce: Dissolution and reconstruction of family boundaries. *Family Process, 18*, 185–192.

Walker, L. J. (1986). Experiential and cognitive sources of moral development in adulthood. *Human Development, 29*, 113–124.

Walker, L. S., & Greene, J. W. (1986). The social context of adolescent self-esteem. *Journal of Youth and Adolescence, 15*, 315–322.

Wallace, J. M., & Bachman, J. G. (1991). Explaining racial/ethnic differences in adolescent drug use: The impact of background and lifestyle. *Social Problems, 38*, 333–357.

Wallerstein, J. S. (1983). Children of divorce: The psychological tasks of the child. *American Journal of Orthopsychiatry, 53*, 230–243.

Wallerstein, J. S. (1985). Children of divorce: Preliminary reports of a 10-year follow-up of older children and adolescents. *Journal of American Academy of Child Psychiatry, 24*, 545–553.

Wallerstein, J. S. (1987). Children of divorce: Report of a ten-year follow up of early latency-age children. *American Journal of Orthopsychiatry, 57*(2), 199–211.

Wallerstein, J. S. (1989). Children after divorce: Wounds that don't heal. *New York Times Magazine*, (January 22, 1989), 19–21, 41–44.

Wallerstein, J. S., & Blakeslee, S. (1989). *Second chance: Men, women, and children a decade after divorce*. New York: Tricknor & Fields.

Wallerstein, J. S., & Kelley, J. B. (1980a). Effects of divorce on the visiting father-child relationship. *American Journal of Psychiatry, 137*, 1534–1539.

Wallerstein, J. S., & Kelley, J. B. (1980b). *Surviving the breakup: How children and parents cope with divorce.* New York: Basic Books.

Wallston, B. (1973). The effects of maternal employment on children. *Journal of Child Psychology and Psychiatrist, 14,* 81–95.

Walters, J., McKenry, P. C., & Walters, L. H. (1979). Adolescents' knowledge of child bearing. *Family Coordinator, 28,* 163–171.

Walters, J., & Walters, L. H. (1980). Trends affecting adolescent views of sexuality, employment, marriage, and child rearing. *Family Relations, 29,* 191–198.

Wanamaker, C. E., & Reznikoff, M. (1989). Effects of aggressive and nonaggressive rock songs on projective and structured tests. *The Journal of Psychology, 123,* 561–570.

Wardle, J., & Marsland, L. (1990). Adolescent concerns about weight and eating: A social-development perspective. *Journal of Psychosomatic Research, 14,* 377–391.

Warren, M. P. (1983). Physical and biological aspects of puberty. In J. Brooks-Gunn & A. C. Petersen (Eds.), *Girls at puberty.* New York: Plenum.

Watanabe, H. K. (1985). A survey of adolescent military family members' self-image. *Journal of Youth and Adolescence, 14,* 99–107.

Waterman, A. S. (1982). Identity development from adolescence to adulthood: An extension of theory and a review of research. *Development Psychology, 18,* 341–358.

Waterman, A. S. (1984). *The psychology of individualism.* New York: Praeger.

Waterman, A. S. (1986). A rejoinder to Berzonsky: Identity formation, metaphors, and values. *Journal of Early Adolescence, 6,* 119–121.

Waterman, A. S. (1990). Personal expressiveness as defining dimension of psychosocial identity. In C. Vandenplas-Holper & B. P. Campos (Eds.), *Interpersonal and identity development: New directions.* Louvain-LaNeuve; Belgium: Academia.

Waterman, A. S. (1992). Identity as an aspect of Optimal Psychological Functioning. In G. R. Adams, T. P. Gullotta, & R. Montemayor (Eds.), *Identity formation during adolescence, Vol. 4: Advances in adolescent development.* Newbury Park, CA: Sage.

Waterman, A. S., & Archer, S. (1979). Ego identity status and expressive writing among high school and college students. *Journal of Youth and Adolescence, 8,* 327–342.

Waterman, A. S., Geary, P. S., & Waterman, C. K. (1974). A longitudinal study of changes in ego identity status from the freshman to the senior at college. *Developmental Psychology, 10,* 387–392.

Waterman, A. S., & Goldman, J. A. (1976). A longitudinal study of ego identity development at a liberal arts college. *Journal of Youth and Adolescence, 5,* 361–370.

Waterman, A. S., & Waterman, C. K. (1970). The relationship between ego identity status and satisfaction with college. *Journal of Educational Research, 64,* 165–168.

Waterman, C. K., Beubel, M. E., & Waterman, A. S. (1970). Relationship between resolution of the identity crisis and outcomes of previous psychosocial crises. *Proceedings of the 78th annual convention of the American Psychological Association, 5,* 467–468. (Summary)

Waterman, C. K., & Waterman, A. S. (1974). Ego identity status and decision styles. *Journal of Youth and Adolescence, 3,* 1–6.

Watson, J. B., (1914). *Behavior: An introduction to comparative psychology.* New York: Holt, Rinehart & Winston.

Wattenberg, B. J. (1987). *The birth dearth.* New York: Pharos Books.

Waugh, I. (1977). Labeling theory. In *Preventing delinquency* (Vol. 1) (LEAA Publication No. 0-241-090/26). Washington, DC: U.S. Government Printing Office.

Wayson, W. W. (1985). The politics of violence in school: Doublespeak and disruptions in public confidence. *Phi Delta Kappan, 67,* 418–421.

Wechsler, D. (1955). *Manual of the Wechsler Adult Intelligence Scale.* New York: Psychological Corp.

Weeks, A. H., & Smith, M. G. (1939). Juvenile delinquency and broken homes in Spokane, Washington. *Social Forces, 18,* 48–59.

Weideger, P. (1976). *Menstruation and menopause.* New York: Knopf.

Weis, J. (1977). Comparative analysis of social control theories of delinquency. In *Preventing delinquency* (Vol. 1) (LEAA Publication No. 0-241-090/26). Washington, DC: U.S. Government Printing Office.

Weissberg, R. P., Caplan, M., & Harwood, R. L. (1991). Promoting competent young people in competence-enhancing environments: A systems-based perspective on primary prevention. *Journal of Consulting and Clinical Psychology, 59,* 830–841.

Weiss, J. R., Weiss, B., Alicke, M. D., & Klotz, M. L. (1987). Effectiveness of psychotherapy with children and adolescents: A meta-analysis for clinicians. *Journal of Consulting and Clinical Psychology, 55,* 542–549.

Weitz, S. (1977). *Sex roles.* New York: Oxford University Press.

Weller, R. A., & Halikas, J. A. (1985). Marijuana use and psychiatric illness: A follow-up study. *American Journal of Psychiatry, 142,* 848–850.

Wellesley College Center for Research on Women. (1992). *How schools short-change girls.* Washington, DC: National Education Association.

Wells, K. (1980). Gender-role identity and psychological adjustment in adolescence. *Journal of Youth and Adolescence, 9,* 59–74.

Wells, L. E., & Marwell, G. (1976). *Self-esteem: Its conceptualization and measurement.* Beverly Hills, CA: Sage.

Welpton, D. (1968). Psychodynamics of chronic lysergic acid diethylamide use. *Journal of Nervous and Mental Diseases, 147,* 377–385.

Welsh, R. S. (1978). Delinquency, corporal punishment, and the schools. *Crime and Delinquency, 24,* 336–354.

Welte, J. W., & Barnes, G. M. (1987). Alcohol use among adolescent minority groups. *Journal of Studies on Alcohol, 48,* 329–336.

Wentzel, K. R., Feldman, S. S., & Weinberger, D. A. (1991). Parental child rearing and academic achievement in boys. *Journal of Early Adolescence, 11,* 321–339.

Wenz, F. V. (1979). Self-injury behavior, economic status and the family anomie among adolescents. *Adolescence, 14,* 387–397.

Wesson, D. R., & Smith, D. E. (1979). Treatment of the polydrug abuser. In R. Dupont, A. Goldstein, & J. O'Donnell (Eds.), *Handbook on drug abuse,* Washington, DC: U.S. Government Printing Office.

Wesson, D. R., & Smith, D. E. (1985). Cocaine: Treatment perspectives. In N. J. Kozel & E. H. Adams (Eds.), *Cocaine use in America: Epidemiological and clinical perspectives* (NIDA research monograph 61, # ADM 85-1414). Washington, DC: U.S. Government Printing Office.

West, S. (1983). One step behind a killer. *Science '83, 4*(2), 36–45.

Westermeyer, J. (1974). "The drunken Indian": Myths and realities. *Psychiatric Annals, 4,* 29–36.

Westermeyer, J., & Neider, J. (1985). Cultural affiliation among American Indian alcoholics: Correlations and change over a ten-year period. *Journal of Operational Psychiatry, 16,* 17–23.

Westney, D. E., Jenkins, R., & Benjamin, C. A. (1983). Sociosexual development of preadolescents. In J. Brooks-Gunn and A. C. Peterson (Eds.), *Girls in puberty.* New York: Plenum.

Westney, O. E., Cole, O. J., & Mumford, T. L. (1986). Adolescent unwed prospective fathers: Readiness for fatherhood and behavior toward the mother and the expected infant. *Adolescence, 21,* 901–911.

Wetzel, J. R. (1987). *American youth: A statistical snapshot.* Washington, DC: William T. Grant Foundation Commission on Youth and America's Future (Suite 301, 1001 Connecticut Ave., N.W., 20036-5541.)

Wheeler, L., Reis, H., & Nezlek, J. (1983). Loneliness, social interaction, and sex roles. *Journal of Personality and Social Psychology, 45,* 943–953.

Whisnant, L., & Zegan, S. L. (1975). A study of attitudes toward menarche in White middle class American adolescent girls. *American Journal of Psychiatry, 132,* 809–814.

Whitaker, C. J., & Bastian, L. D. (1991). *Teenage victims.* U.S. Department of Justice. NCJ-128129. Washington, DC: U.S. Government Printing Office.

Whitbeck, L. B., Simons, R. L., Conger, R. D., & Lorenz, F. O. (1989). Value socialization and peer group affiliation among early adolescents. *Journal of Early Adolescence, 9,* 436–453.

Whitbourne, S. K., & Tesch, S. A. (1985). A comparison of identity and intimacy statuses in college students and alumni. *Developmental Psychology, 21,* 1039–1044.

White, M. (1987). *The Japanese educational challenge.* New York: Free Press.

White, R. W. (1960). Competence and the psychosexual stages of development. In M. Jones (Ed.), *Nebraska symposium on motivation* (Vol. 8). Lincoln: University of Nebraska Press.

Whiteside, M. F. (1982). Remarriage: A family development process. *Journal of Marital and Family Therapy, 8,*(2), 59–68.

Whittaker, S., & Bry, B. H. (1991). Overt and covert parental conflict and adolescent problems: Observed marital interaction in clinic and nonclinic families. *Adolescence, 26,* 865–877.

Widom, C. S. (1989). The cycle of violence. *Science, 244,* 160–166.

Wigfeld, A., Eccles, J. S., MacIver, D., Reuman, D. A., & Midgley, C. (1991). Transitions during early adolescence: Changes in children's domain-specific self-perceptions and general self-esteem across the transition to junior high school. *Developmental Psychology, 27,* 552–565.

Wilen, J. B., & Petersen, A. C. (1980, June). *Young adolescents' responses to the timing of pubertal changes.* Paper presented at the conference The Psychology of Adolescents, Chicago.

Wilkins, J. (1990). Clinical implications of PCP, NMDA and opiate receptors. In L. S. Harris (Ed.), *Problems of drug dependence: 1989.* U.S. Department of Health and Human Services publication # ADM 90-1663. Washington, DC: U.S. Government Printing Office.

Williams, C. L., & Berry, J. W. (1991). Primary prevention of acculturative stress among refugees. *American Psychologist, 46,* 632–641.

Williamson, D. A., Kelley, M. L., Davis, C. J., Ruggiero, L., & Blouin, D. C. (1985). Psychopathology of eating disorders: A controlled comparison of bulimia, obese, and normal subjects. *Journal of Consulting and Clinical Psychology, 53,* 161–166.

Wilson, E. O. (1975). *Sociobiology: The new synthesis.* Cambridge, MA: Harvard University Press.

Wilson, J. Q. (1990). Against the legalization of drugs. *Commentary, 89,* 21–28.

Wilson, J. Q., & Herrnstein, R. J. (1985). *Crime and human nature.* New York: Simon & Schuster.

Wilson, K. L., Zurcher, L. A., McAdams, D. C., & Curtis, R. L. (1975). An exploratory analysis from two national samples. *Journal of Marriage and the Family, 37,* 526–536.

Wilson, W. J. (1978). *The declining significance of race: Blacks and changing American institutions.* Chicago: University of Chicago Press.

Winch, R. F. (1943). The relationship between courtship behavior and atti-tudes toward parents among college men. *American Sociological Review, 8,* 164–174.

Wise, R. A. (1987). Neural mechanisms of the reinforcing action of cocaine. In J. Grabowski (Ed.), *Cocaine: Pharmacology, effects, and treatment of abuse.* (U.S. Department of Health and Human Services publication # ADM 87-1326.) Washington, DC: U.S. Government Printing Office.

Wise, S., & Grossman, F. K. (1980). Adolescent mothers and their infants: Psychological factors in early attachment and interaction. *American Journal of Orthopsychiatry, 50*(3), 454–468.

Witt, S. J., & Cunningham, W. R. (1980). Family configuration and fluid/crystallized intelligence. *Adolescence, 15,* 105–121.

Wonderlich, S. A., & Swift, W. J. (1990). Perceptions of parental relationships in the eating disorders: The relevance of depressed mood. *Journal of Abnormal Psychology, 99,* 353–360.

Woodring, P. (1989). A new approach to the dropout problem. *Phi Delta Kappan, 70,* 468–469.

Woody, G. E., & Blaine, J. (1979). Depression in narcotics addicts. In R. Dupont, A. Goldstein, & J. O'Donnell (Eds.), *Handbook on drug abuse.* Washington, DC: U.S. Government Printing Office.

Wooley, S., & Wooley, O. (1979). Obesity and women: A closer look at the facts. *Women's Studies International, 2,* 69–79.

Worell, J., & Danner, F. (1989). *The adolescent as decision-maker: Applications to development and education.* New York: Academic Press.

Work, W. C., Cowen, E. L., Parker, G. R., & Wyman, P. A. (1990). Stress resilient children in an urban setting. *Journal of Primary Prevention, 11,* 3–17.

Workman, B. (1986). Dear professor: This is what I want you to know. *Phi Delta Kappan, 68,* 668–671.

Wright, C. H. (1980). The prevention of teenage pregnancy: The only answer. *Journal of the National Medical Association, 72*(1), 11–13.

Wright, L. S. (1985). High school polydrug users and abusers. *Adolescence, 20*(80), 853–861.

W. T. Grant Foundation. (1988). *The forgotten half: Pathways to success for America's youth and young families.* Washington, DC: Author.

Wyatt, G. E. (1989). Reexamining factors predicting Afro-American and White

American women's age at first coitus. *Archives of Sexual Behavior, 18,* 271–298.

Wyatt, G. E. (1990). Changing influences on adolescent sexuality over the past forty years. In J. Bancroft & J. M. Reinisch (Eds.), *Adolescence and puberty.* New York: Oxford University Press.

Yablonsky, L. (1970). *The violent gang.* Baltimore: Penguin.

Yaffe, E. (1982). High school athletics: A Colorado study. *Phi Delta Kappan, 64,* 177–181.

Yager, J. (1982). Family issues in the pathogenesis of anorexia nervosa. *Psychosomatic Medicine, 44,* 43–60.

Yamaguchi, K., & Kandel, D. (1984). Patterns of drug use from adolescence to young adulthood III: Predictors of progression. *American Journal of Public Health, 74,* 673–681.

Yesalis, C. E., Anderson, W. A., Buckley, W. E., & Wright, J. E. (1990). Incidence of the nonmedical use of anabolic-androgenic steroids. In G. C. Lin & L. Erinoff (Eds.), *Anabolic steroid abuse.* U.S. Department of Health and Human Services. Washington, DC: U.S. Government Printing Office.

Young, E., & Parish, T. (1977). Impact of father absence during childhood on the psychological adjustment of college females. *Sex Roles, 3,* 217–227.

Young, J. W., & Ferguson, L. R. (1979). Developmental changes through adolescence in the spontaneous nomination of reference groups as a function of decision content. *Journal of Youth and Adolescence, 8,* 239–252.

Youniss, J. U., & Smollar, J. (1985). *Adolescent relations with mothers, fathers, and friends.* Chicago: University of Chicago Press.

Zajonc, R. B. (1976). Family configuration and intelligence. *Science, 192,* 227–236.

Zajonc, R. B., & Markus, G. B. (1975). Birth order and intellectual development. *Psychological Review, 82,* 74–88.

Zakin, D. F., Blyth, D. A., & Simmons, R. G. (1984). Physical attractiveness as a mediator of the impact of early pubertal changes for girls. *Journal of Youth and Adolescence, 13,* 439–450.

Zaslow, M. J., & Takanishi, R. (1993). Priorities for research on adolescent development. *American Psychologist, 48,* 185–192.

Zatz, M. S. (1985). Los Cholos: Legal processing of Chicano gang members. *Social Problems, 33,* 13–20.

Zayas, L. H., Schinke, S. P., & Casareno, D. (1987). Hispanic adolescent fathers: At risk and underresearched. *Children and Youth Services Review, 9,* 235–248.

Zellman, G., Johnson, P. B., Giarrusso, R., & Goodchilds, J. D. (1979, September). *Adolescent expectations for dating relationships: Consensus and conflict between the sexes.* Paper presented at the meeting of the American Psychological Association, New York.

Zelnick, M. (1979). Sex education and knowledge of pregnancy risk among U.S. teenage women. *Family Planning Perspectives, 11,* 355–357.

Zelnick, M., & Kantner, J. F. (1980). Sexual activity, contraceptive use and pregnancy among metropolitan-area teenagers: 1971–1979. *Family Planning Perspectives, 12,* 230–237.

Ziegler, C., & Dusek, J. B. (1985). Perceptions of child rearing and adolescent sex role development. *Journal of Early Adolescence, 5,* 215–227.

Ziegler, C. B., Dusek, J. B., & Carter, D. B. (1984). Self-concept and sex-role orientation: An investigation of multidimensional aspects of personality development in adolescence. *Journal of Early Adolescence, 4,* 25–39.

Zimring, F. E. (1982). *The changing legal world of adolescence.* New York: Free Press.

Zinberg, N. E. (1979). Nonaddictive opiate use. In R. Dupont, A. Goldstein, & J. O'Donnell (Eds.), *Handbook on drug abuse.* Washington, DC: U.S. Government Printing Office.

Zongker, C. E. (1980). Self-concept differences between single and married school-age mothers. *Journal of Youth and Adolescence, 9*(2), 175–184.

Zukin, S. R., & Javitt, D. C. (1990). Mechanisms of phencyclidine (PCP)-n-methyl-d-aspartate (NMDA) receptor interaction: Implications for drug abuse research. In L. S. Harris (Ed.), *Problems of drug dependence: 1989.* (U.S. Department of Health and Human Services publication # ADM 90-1663.) Washington, DC: U.S. Government Printing Office.

CREDITS

Chapter 1

1, Rosanne Olson/ALLSTOCK. **7, left,** Michael Dwyer/Stock, Boston. **7, right,** Jeffry Myers/Stock, Boston. **10, left,** Rob Lang/FPG International. **10, center,** Paul Barton/The Stock Market. **10, right,** Lionel J-M. Delevingne/Stock, Boston. **13,** Christopher Brown/Stock, Boston. **19,** Lawrence Migdale/Tony Stone Images.

Chapter 2

29, Duedric Hill/Gary Brown/FPG International. **31,** THE BETTMANN ARCHIVE. **35, left,** THE BETTMANN ARCHIVE. **35, right,** Courtesy of Dr. Elaine Hatfield. **38,** CULVER PICTURES. **39,** THE BETTMANN ARCHIVE. **41,** THE BETTMANN ARCHIVE. **45,** Courtesy of Joseph M. Lerner. **47,** Courtesy of Albert Bandura. **48,** Courtesy of Robert Selman. **50,** AP/Wide World Photos.

Chapter 3

61, Laima Druskis/Stock, Boston. **67,** Michael Weisbrot/Stock, Boston. **78,** Jim Whitmer/FPG International.

Chapter 4

93, Bob Daemmrich/Stock, Boston. **98,** Spencer Grant/Stock, Boston. **99,** Jim Whitmer/FPG International. **110,** Frances M. Cox/Stock, Boston. **118,** Olive R. Pierce/Stock, Boston.

Chapter 5

123, James P. Dwyer/Stock, Boston. **133,** Freelance Photographer's Guild/FPG International. **141, left,** THE BETTMANN ARCHIVE. **141, right,** THE BETTMANN ARCHIVE.

Chapter 6

161, Barbara Alper/Stock, Boston. **165, top,** Arthur Tilley/FPG International. **165, left,** Don Smetzer/Tony Stone Images. **165, right,** Navaswan/FPG International. **169,** Jean-Claude Lejeune/Stock, Boston.

Chapter 7

187, Spencer Grant/Stock, Boston. **193,** Diane Graham-Henry/Tony Stone Images. **205,** Jeffry Myers/FPG International. **217,** Jim Whitmer/FPG International.

Chapter 8

221, John Running/Stock, Boston. **226,** Jean-Claude Lejeune/Stock, Boston. **236,** *The Boston Globe.*

Chapter 9

247, Michael Grecco/Stock, Boston. **251,** Charles Gatewood/Stock, Boston. **255,** Gale Zucker/Stock, Boston

Chapter 10

267, Peter Menzel/Stock, Boston. **270,** Carolyn A. McKeone/FPG International. **273,** Courtesy of James Marcia. **286,** Spencer Grant/FPG International. **288,** Marleen Ferguson/Tony Stone Images.

Chapter 11

293, Bob Daemmrich/Stock, Boston. **298,** Judy Gelles/Stock, Boston. **307, right,** Fredrik D. Bodin/Stock, Boston. **307, left,** Frank Siteman/Stock, Boston.

Chapter 12

317, Spencer Grant/Stock, Boston. **324,** Gabe Palmer/The Stock Market. **333,** Michael Weisbrot/Stock, Boston. **340,** Charles Gupton/Tony Stone Images.

Chapter 13

345, Gale Zucker/Stock, Boston. **355,** Courtesy of George Albee (photo by Sally McCay). **358,** Jim Cronk/Photographic Illustrations. **359,** David M. Grossman.

Chapter 14

366, J. Bernot/Stock, Boston. **369,** Stock, Boston. **387,** Gabe Palmer/The Stock Market. **403,** Michael Weisbrot/Stock, Boston.

Chapter 15

407, Roy Morsch/The Stock Market. **425,** Anestis Diakopolous/Stock, Boston. **429,** Tom Cheek/Stock, Boston.

Chapter 16

453, Gale Zucker/Stock, Boston. **455,** © Emilio A. Mercado/Jeroboam, Inc. **457,** Chiolini Photo Agency. **468,** Mary Ellen Mark/-Archive.

Chapter 17

487, Wm. Thompson/THE PICTURE CUBE. **493,** Gale Zucker/Stock, Boston. **498,** Robert E. Daemmrich/Tony Stone Images.

Chapter 18

501, Frances M. Cox/Stock, Boston. **504,** Steven Gottlieb/FPG International. **508,** Akos Szilvasi/Stock, Boston.

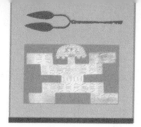

INDEX